Fifth Edition

Essentials of Human Communication

Joseph A. DeVito

*Hunter College of the
City University of New York*

PEARSON

Boston   New York   San Francisco
Mexico City   Montreal   Toronto   London   Madrid   Munich   Paris
Hong Kong   Singapore   Tokyo   Cape Town   Sydney

Executive Editor: Karon Bowers
Series Editor: Brian Wheel
Series Editorial Assistant: Jennifer Trebby
Senior Development Editors: Ellen Darion, Sharon Geary
Marketing Manager: Mandee Eckersley
Associate Editor: Andrea Christie
Senior Producion Editor: Annette Pagliaro
Editorial Production: Nesbitt Graphics, Inc.
Composition Buyer: Linda Cox
Manufacturing Buyer: Megan Cochran
Cover Administrator: Joel Gendron
Text Design: Nesbitt Graphics, Inc.
Photo Research: Julie Tesser
Text Composition: Nesbitt Graphics, Inc.

For related titles and support materials, visit our online catalog at www.ablongman.com.

Between the time Website information is gathered and then published, it is not unusual for some sites to have closed. Also, the transcription of URLs can result in unintended typographical errors. The publisher would appreciate notification where these errors occur so that they may be corrected in subsequent editions.

Library of Congress Cataloging-in-Publication Data

DeVito, Joseph A.
    Essentials of human communication / Joseph A. DeVito.—5th ed.
        p. cm.
    Includes bibliographical references and index.
    ISBN 0-205-41488-5 (pbk.)
        1. Communication. I. Title.

P90.D483 2005
302.2—dc22

                                                                2004043697

Printed in the United States of America

10 9 8 7 6 5 4 3 2   VHP 08 07 06 04

Brief Contents

CD-ROM Units

These sections are included on the CD-ROM with bonus units, which is available to be packaged with this book. Some restrictions apply.

The Mass Media

Emotional Communication

Criticism in the Public Speaking Classroom

Developing Special Occasion Speeches

Contents

CD-ROM Units

These sections are included on the CD-ROM with bonus units, which is available to be packaged with this book. Some restrictions apply.

The Mass Media

The Functional and Dysfunctional Media
To Help
To Play
To Relate, to Create Ties of Union
To Inform
To Influence

Becoming a Critical Consumer of Media
Learn How the Media Work
Make Use of a Wide Variety of Media
Question the Credibility of the Media
Exercise Critical Thinking
Talk Back to the Media

Emotional Communication

Emotions and Emotional Messages
The Body, Mind, and Culture in Emotions
Emotions, Arousal, and Expression
Emotions, Culture, and Gender
Principles of Emotional Communication

Obstacles in Communicating Emotions
Societal Rules and Customs
Fear
Inadequate Interpersonal Skills

Guidelines for Communicating Emotions
Describe Your Feelings
Identify the Reasons for Your Feelings
Anchor Your Feelings to the Present
Own Your Own Feelings

Criticism in the Public Speaking Classroom

The Nature and Values of Criticism

Cultural Differences in Approaches to Criticism

Standards and Principles of Criticism
Standards of Criticism
Principles of Expressing Criticism

Developing Special Occasion Speeches

The Speech of Introduction
Guidelines for Speeches of Introduction
Sample Speeches of Introduction

The Speech of Presentation and Acceptance
Guidelines for Speeches of Presentation
A Sample Speech of Presentation
Guidelines for Speeches of Acceptance
Sample Speeches of Acceptance

The Speech to Secure Goodwill
Guidelines for Speeches Aimed at Securing
Goodwill
Sample Speeches to Secure Goodwill

The Speech of Tribute
Guidelines for Speeches of Tribute
A Sample Speech of Tribute

Additional Special Occasion Speeches
Dedication Speeches
Commencement Speeches
Eulogies
Farewell Speeches
Toasts

The Special Occasion Speech in Cultural Perspective

A Sample Special Occasion Speech

Specialized Contents

Communicating Ethically

These features examine ethical issues and dilemmas to illustrate the close connection between ethics and communication, to encourage you to think about the ethical implications of your messages, and to stimulate you to formulate your own code of ethical communication.

Communicating with Power

These features present principles of power and suggestions for making your own messages more powerful and more influential.

Listen to This

These discussions provide suggestions for listening more effectively in a wide variety of communication situations.

Self-Tests

These self-assessment tests help you analyze and improve your own communication patterns and strategies.

Skill Development Experiences

These exercises will enable you to work actively with the skills discussed in the text; they will help you internalize the skills and make them a part of your everyday communication behavior.

Welcome to

Essentials of Human Communication

The previous editions of *Essentials of Human Communication* were all great successes, largely because the book answered the need for a brief, interesting, but serious text that emphasized the *essential* skills of human communication, including interpersonal communication, small group communication, and public speaking. I continue to try my best to follow Einstein's directive that "things should be made as simple as possible, but not simpler." This new fifth edition remains true to that central purpose but improves on the fourth edition in several important ways.

Essentials of Human Communication is divided into two parts. Part One, "Foundations of Human Communication," includes six chapters that cover the concepts and principles of human communication: the communication process, the self, perception, listening, verbal messages, and nonverbal messages. These chapters explain the basic principles and skills underlying all forms of communication—the way communication works, the key principles of effective self-disclosure, the strategies for achieving more accurate perception, ways to listen more effectively, and guidelines for using language and the numerous nonverbal channels to best convey your meaning.

Part Two, "The Contexts of Human Communication," includes eight chapters that cover the concepts and skills of interpersonal communication (Chapters 7 and 8), small group interaction (Chapters 9 and 10), and public speaking (Chapters 11 through 14). These chapters explain the nature of these communication forms and emphasize the skills that make possible more effective interpersonal conversation and relationships, small group participation and leadership, and public speaking (particularly informative and persuasive speaking). A separate pamphlet, *Interviewing and Human Communication,* is available with this text and covers the important skills of interviewing for information and for employment.

Major Themes

Integrated throughout the book are several major themes that will personalize the material and make it more relevant to your everyday communication encounters. With a focus on the knowledge and abilities you need to develop to become a competent communicator, these themes include communication skills, workplace communication, expressing power, listening skills, critical thinking skills, cultural sensitivity, and ethical principles.

Communication Skills

Essentials of Human Communication and its companion guide, *Interviewing and Human Communication,* provide you with the skills you need to communicate successfully in your personal, social, and workplace interactions. These skills are integrated throughout the text and the **Skill Development Experiences** provide opportunities to practice these skills. These skills include:

Check Your Perceptions

Perception checking is another way to reduce uncertainty and to make your perceptions more accurate. The goal of perception checking is not to prove that your initial perception is correct but to explore further the thoughts and feelings of the other person. With this simple technique, you lessen your chances of misinterpreting another's feelings. At the same time, you give the other person an opportunity to elaborate on his or her thoughts and feelings. In its most basic form, perception checking involves two components.

- Describe what you see or hear, recognizing that even descriptions are not really objective but are heavily influenced by who you are, your emotional state, and so on. At the same time, you may wish to describe what you think is happening. Again, try to do this as descriptively (not evaluatively) as you can. Sometimes you may wish to offer several possibilities:
  - You've called me from work a lot this week. You seem concerned about how things are at home.
  - You've not wanted to talk with me all week. You say that my work is fine, but you don't seem to want to give me the same responsibilities that other editorial assistants have.
- Avoid mind reading; avoid trying to read the thoughts and feelings of another person just from observing their behaviors. A person's motives are not open to outside inspection; you can only make assumptions based on overt behaviors. And regardless of how many behaviors you observe and how carefully you examine them, you can only guess what is going on in someone's mind. So seek confirmation. Ask the other person if your perception is accurate. But be careful that your request for confirmation does not sound as though you already know the answer. Avoid phrasing your questions defensively; avoid saying, for example, "You really don't want to go out, do you? I knew you didn't when you turned on that lousy television." Instead, ask for confirmation in as supportive a way as possible:
  - Would you rather watch TV?

- perceptual and listening effectiveness—how to make more accurate judgments of people and how to really hear what people say and mean
- verbal and nonverbal message construction and reception—and how to use words and all the nonverbal elements to best achieve your purposes
- interpersonal communication—how to manage conversation, interpersonal conflicts, and interpersonal relationships with friends, romantic partners, family, and colleagues
- interviewing—how to interview someone for information and how to make the right impression in an employment interview so as to get the job you want
- small group communication—how to participate in and lead small groups for generating ideas, sharing information, and solving problems
- public speaking—how to effectively inform and persuade a wide variety of different audiences

Communication in the Workplace

Because communication is an eminently practical subject, with applications in all aspects of life, this book makes a special effort to illustrate the uses of communication skills in the real world, particularly in the world of work. Among the specifically work-related topics are mentoring relationships, networking, office romance, and workplace groups. In addition, numerous examples of workplace situations that call for the application of communication skills appear throughout the text.

As you work through this text and the course, you'll find it useful to ask, "How can I apply this material to the workplace?" "How can I use this material to function more effectively on the job?"

Mentoring

Another function of leadership that extends well beyond the small group situation is that of mentoring. A **mentoring** relationship occurs when an experienced individual helps to train a less experienced person. An accomplished teacher, for example, might mentor a younger teacher who is newly arrived or who has never taught before. The mentor guides the new person through the ropes, teaches the strategies and techniques for success, and otherwise communicates his or her accumulated knowledge and experience to the "mentee."

The mentoring relationship provides an ideal learning environment. It's usually a one-on-one relationship between expert and novice, a relationship that is supportive and trusting. There's a mutual and open sharing of information and thoughts about the job. The relationship enables the novice to try out new skills under the guidance of an expert, to ask questions, and to obtain the feedback so necessary to learning complex skills. It's a relationship that's perhaps best characterized as one in which the experienced and powerful mentor empowers the novice, giving the novice the tools and techniques needed for gaining the same power the mentor now holds.

One study found the mentoring relationship to be one of the three primary paths for career achievement among African American men and women (Bridges, 1996). And another study (of middle-level managers) demonstrated that those who had mentors and participated in mentoring relationships got more promotions and higher salaries than those who didn't have mentors (Scandura, 1992).

? VIEWPOINT
Using the traits approach, the functional approach, the transformational approach, or the situational approach, how would you describe yourself as a leader? What do you think is the single most important principle for a group leader to follow?

Power

Because all communication messages and relationships have a power dimension, **Communicating with Power** boxes appear in each chapter. These boxes (1) explain the nature and principles of power and (2) identify the skills of power, the ways in which power is exercised, and the ways to manage power in your own communication. Ranging from explanations of types of power (expert, reward, and legitimate, for example) to skills such as dealing with power plays, expressing confidence, using compliance-gaining strategies, expressing power in speech and gesture, and empowering others, these features link the concepts of power and empowerment to those of human communication.

Each of these boxes ends with a section called "Enhancing Your Communication Power," which asks you to explain how you might increase your own power in interpersonal, group, and public communication situations. A list of these Communicating with Power boxes appears in the Specialized Contents on page x.

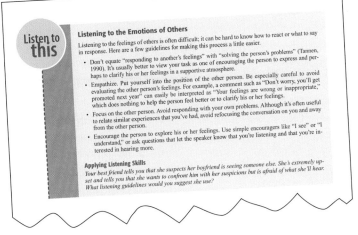

Communicating with power

Power through Self-Presentation

One way to exert power and influence is to use self-presentation strategies: to present yourself in ways that will encourage others to like you and to do as you wish (Jones & Pittman, 1982; Jones, 1990). Here are some examples:

- Use *ingratiation*. Express agreement, pay compliments, or do favors for the other person. But be aware that you run the risk of being seen as a sycophant, as someone who will stop at nothing to be liked.
- Use *self-promotion*. Present yourself as competent so that the other person will respect you. But be careful that you aren't perceived as incompetent because of the widespread belief that competent people *demonstrate* competence rather than talking about it.
- Use *exemplification*. Present yourself as worthy, moral, and virtuous. But beware of appearing sanctimonious or "holier than thou," a quality that most people dislike.
- Use *supplication*. Present yourself as helpless and in need of assistance: "Can you type my paper? I'm such a bad typist." But use caution: As a supplicant you risk being seen as incompetent or perhaps lazy.

Enhancing Your Communication Power
Which self-presentation strategy do you think would prove most helpful in an employment interview situation? How might it play out?

Listening

Effective listening is crucial to all forms of human communication. Some textbooks give this critical topic only a minor role, but *Essentials* brings listening into prominence in two ways. First, Chapter 4 is entirely devoted to listening: the stages of listening, the styles of effective listening, and the influences of culture and gender on listening.

In addition, each chapter contains a **Listen to This** box that highlights the role of listening in relation to the topics discussed in the chapter. Listen to This boxes discuss, for example, listening to yourself, listening to other perspectives, listening to empower, and listening to complaints, as well as a wide variety of other issues. Each Listen to This box ends with a case that asks you to develop listening suggestions to help resolve a specific problem. That is, you're asked to interact with the principles of listening instead of just reading about them; this interactive process will help you internalize these important concepts. A list of these Listen to This boxes appears in the Specialized Contents on page xi.

Listen to this

Listening to the Emotions of Others

Listening to the feelings of others is often difficult; it can be hard to know how to react or what to say in response. Here are a few guidelines for making this process a little easier.

- Don't equate "responding to another's feelings" with "solving the person's problems" (Tannen, 1990). It's usually better to view your task as one of encouraging the person to express and perhaps to clarify his or her feelings in a supportive atmosphere.
- Empathize. Put yourself into the position of the other person. Be especially careful to avoid evaluating the other person's feelings. For example, a comment such as "Don't worry, you'll get promoted next year" can easily be interpreted as "Your feelings are wrong or inappropriate," which does nothing to help the person feel better or to clarify his or her feelings.
- Focus on the other person. Avoid responding with your own problems. Although it's often useful to relate similar experiences that you've had, avoid refocusing the conversation on you and away from the other person.
- Encourage the person to explore his or her feelings. Use simple encouragers like "I see" or "I understand," or ask questions that let the speaker know that you're listening and that you're interested in hearing more.

Applying Listening Skills
Your best friend tells you that she suspects her boyfriend is seeing someone else. She's extremely upset and tells you that she wants to confront him with her suspicions but is afraid of what she'll hear. What listening guidelines would you suggest she use?

Critical Thinking

Critical thinking enriches all human communication experiences, so this book gives special prominence to this subject. In the fourth edition of *Essentials,* a summary section on critical thinking appeared in each chapter. This new edition approaches

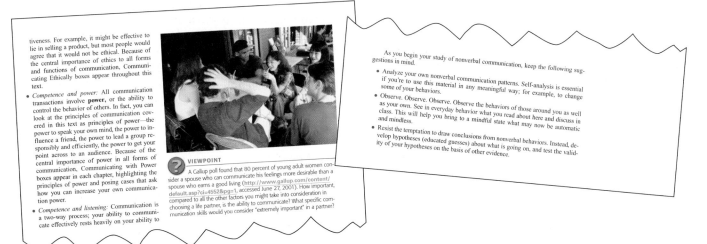

tiveness. For example, it might be effective to lie in selling a product, but most people would agree that it would not be ethical. Because of the central importance of ethics to all forms and functions of communication, Communicating Ethically boxes appear throughout this text.

- *Competence and power:* All communication transactions involve **power,** or the ability to control the behavior of others. In fact, you can look at the principles of communication covered in this text as principles of power—the power to speak your own mind, the power to influence a friend, the power to lead a group responsibly and efficiently, the power to get your point across to an audience. Because of the central importance of power in all forms of communication, Communicating with Power boxes appear in each chapter, highlighting the principles of power and posing cases that ask how you can increase your own communication power.
- *Competence and listening:* Communication is a two-way process; your ability to communicate effectively rests heavily on your ability to

VIEWPOINT
A Gallup poll found that 80 percent of young adult women consider a spouse who can communicate his feelings more desirable than a spouse who earns a good living (http://www.gallup.com/content/default.asp?ci=4552&pg=1, accessed June 27, 2001). How important, compared to all the other factors you might take into consideration in choosing a life partner, is the ability to communicate? What specific communication skills would you consider "extremely important" in a partner?

As you begin your study of nonverbal communication, keep the following suggestions in mind.

- Analyze your own nonverbal communication patterns. Self-analysis is essential if you're to use this material in any meaningful way; for example, to change some of your behaviors.
- Observe. Observe. Observe the behaviors of those around you as well as your own. See in everyday behavior what you read about here and discuss in class. This will help you bring to a mindful state what may now be automatic and mindless.
- Resist the temptation to draw conclusions from nonverbal behaviors. Instead, develop hypotheses (educated guesses) about what is going on, and test the validity of your hypotheses on the basis of other evidence.

critical thinking differently, using a simple two-pronged approach. First, the text integrates principles of critical thinking at the points at which they are most relevant. Second, the marginal items, self-tests, scenarios presented in each of the boxed items, and photo ViewPoints ask you to *apply* the principles of critical thinking and communication effectiveness to specific situations.

Culture and Colors

Colors vary greatly in their meanings from one culture to another. Table 6.4 presents some of these cultural differences—but before looking at the table, think about the meanings given to colors such as red, green, black, white, blue, yellow, and purple in your own culture(s).

| TABLE 6.4 | Some Cultural Meanings of Color |

This table, constructed from research reported by Henry Dreyfuss (1971), Nancy Hoft (1995), and Norine Dresser (1996), summarizes some of the different meanings that colors may communicate and how colors are viewed in different cultures. As you read this table, consider the meanings you give to these colors and where your meanings came from.

COLOR	CULTURAL MEANINGS AND COMMENTS
Red	Red signifies prosperity and rebirth in China and is used for festive and joyous occasions. It signifies masculinity in France and the United Kingdom, blasphemy or death in many African countries, and anger and danger in Japan. Red ink is used by Korean Buddhists only to write a person's name at the time of death or on the anniversary of the person's death; it therefore creates problems when American teachers use red ink to mark Korean students' homework.
Green	Green signifies capitalism, "go ahead," and envy in the United States; patriotism in Ireland; femininity among some Native Americans; fertility and strength in Egypt; and youth and energy in Japan.
Black	Black signifies old age in Thailand, courage in parts of Malaysia, and death in much of Europe and North America.
White	White signifies purity in Thailand, purity and peace in many Muslim and Hindu cultures, and death and mourning in Japan and other Asian countries.
Blue	Blue signifies something negative in Iran, virtue and truth in Egypt, joy in Ghana, and defeat among the Cherokee.
Yellow	Yellow signifies wealth and authority in China, caution and cowardice in the United States, happiness and prosperity in Egypt; and femininity in many countries throughout the world.
Purple	Purple signifies death in Latin America, royalty in Europe, virtue and faith in Egypt, grace and nobility in Japan, and barbarism in China.

Cultural Awareness and Sensitivity

You're living in a world defined by cultural diversity, a world where you interact and become friends and romantic partners, join together in families, chat online, and work together with people differing in gender, age, affectional orientation, socioeconomic position, race, religion, and nationality. Culture and cultural differences are always influential in communication. Even intrapersonal communication, in which you talk to yourself, is heavily influenced by your culture's values and beliefs. For this reason, this text fully integrates culture into the discussions of all forms of communication. Thus, for example, the section on self-disclosure explores how different ethnic groups and genders view this form of communication. Similarly, the discussion of criticism examines how members of different cultural groups deal with criticism.

Every chapter of *Essentials of Human Communication* contains discussions of culture and its relationship to the chapter topic:

- **Chapter 1** discusses culture and competence, the relevance of culture, the aim of a cultural perspective, and ethnocentrism; the chapter also provides a self-test on cultural beliefs and values and an exercise to examine cultural beliefs.

- **Chapter 2** considers cultural teachings in self-concept formation, intercultural openness, culture and gender in self-disclosure, and masculine and feminine cultures.

- **Chapter 3** explores the influence of culture on perceptual judgments, personality theory and culture, the role of stereotypes in perception, cultural influences on uncertainty and its avoidance, and cultural sensitivity in perceptual accuracy.

- **Chapter 4** discusses the influences of culture and gender on listening.

- **Chapter 5** covers gender and cultural differences in directness and politeness; cultural rules in verbal communication; sexism, heterosexism, racism, and ageism; and cultural identifiers.

- **Chapter 6** considers cultural differences in nonverbal communication throughout the text discussions; several areas, however, receive more extended consideration: facial expressions, colors, touch, silence, and time (including differences between monochronism and polychronism and the role of the social clock).

- **Chapter 7** investigates cultural context and conflict, face-enhancing and face-detracting strategies, and the relevance of cultural sensitivity (including differences between high- and low-context cultures) in conversation and conflict.

- **Chapter 8** takes a detailed look at the role of culture and gender in interpersonal relationships, and particularly in friendship and love relationships.

- **Chapter 9** addresses the nature and importance of cultural norms in small group communication.

- **Chapter 10** puts membership and leadership into cultural perspective and discusses differences between individual and collective orientations and high and low power distances.

- **Chapter 11** offers guidelines to help public speakers avoid taboo topics when addressing culturally varied audiences as well as guidance for analyzing multicultural audiences.
- **Chapter 12** considers cultural considerations in the language of public speaking, culture shock, and cultural sensitivity in speech criticism.
- **Chapter 13** examines cultural variations in language usage.
- **Chapter 14** covers cultural differences in approaches to the use of logical, motivational, and credibility appeals.

Ethics

Essentials of Human Communication follows the example set by Aristotle, Cicero, and Quintilian—the three great theorists of the ancient world—who viewed ethics as an integral part of communication instruction. This text, too, regards ethics as central; and **Communicating Ethically** boxes highlight ethical issues as they relate to concepts and skills presented throughout the book. These boxes cover such issues as lying, revealing secrets, and plagiarism and are positioned near the content to which they most clearly relate.

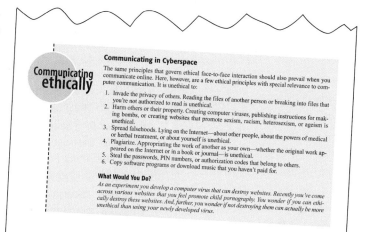

Each Communicating Ethically box contains an ethical dilemma—a case that asks, "What would you do?" in the situation described. As with the other boxed features, these cases are designed to stimulate you to interact with the material on a more personal level. A list of these Communicating Ethically boxes appears in the Specialized Contents on page x.

What's New in the Fifth Edition?

Introduced in this edition are both a new margin feature and a series of chapter-by-chapter improvements.

New Feature: What Do You Say?

The new **What Do You Say?** feature presents situational dilemmas—points at which you have to make a communication choice. The objective of these brief marginal items, approximately six per chapter, is to let you apply the principles and skills to real-world scenarios. For example, after reading about ambiguity, you're asked how you would reduce ambiguity by finding out how your dating partner views your relationship. After reading about group leadership, you're asked how you'd deal with a group in which a few members monopolize the discussion. After reading about the principles of persuasive speaking, you're asked how you'd establish your own credibility with a specific audience.

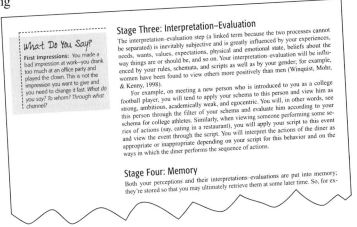

There is no one right answer to any of these scenarios; also, what will work in one situation may not work in another. Your objective in responding to these items is to think of as many communication options as you can and, based on your understanding of how communication works, to try to estimate which options are likely to be most effective for you.

Chapter-by-Chapter Improvements

For those who have used the previous editions of *Essentials,* here, in brief, is a chapter-by-chapter explanation of some of the major improvements made in this fifth edition.

Chapter 1. New to this chapter are a revised and expanded discussion of the benefits of communication training; a consideration of communication between blind and sighted people; a greatly expanded discussion of ethnocentrism, including a new self-test; a discussion of message overload and suggestions for dealing with it; and a section on message and relationship ambiguity.

Chapter 2. A new section presents guidelines for self-disclosing, for facilitating and responding to the disclosures of others, and for resisting the pressure to self-disclose.

Chapter 3. The section on increasing accuracy in perception now emphasizes practical ways to improve perception.

Chapter 4. A new discussion of communication between deaf and hearing people has been added. Also, the section on effective listening, now called "Styles of Effective Listening," has been totally recast to emphasize selecting the listening styles most appropriate to each given situation.

Chapter 5. The introductory material is now organized around the basic principles of verbal messages; the discussion of cultural rules and maxims has been restructured; and there are new discussions of ageism and ethical online communication.

Chapter 6. The section on the functions of nonverbal communication discussion now incorporates new research. Tattoos and body piercings are now included as nonverbal messages, and the discussions of cultural influences on nonverbal communication have been brought together and expanded.

Chapter 7. This chapter includes new discussions of communication between people with and without speech and language disorders, dialogue and monologue, closing conversations in e-mail, conflict styles, and assertiveness as a conflict strategy. The totally restructured section on effective conversation now emphasizes specific suggestions for using the conversational skills.

Chapter 8. This chapter has been totally rewritten and now includes an introductory section on the characteristics of interpersonal relationships, a self-test on the advantages and disadvantages of relationships, and sections on relationships and technology and relationships in the workplace.

Chapter 9. New here is a discussion exploring the distinction between relationship and task groups; the focus group explanation has been reworked. Interviewing, formerly the topic of Chapter 9, is now covered in a separate companion guide, *Interviewing and Human Communication.*

Chapter 10. Several new discussions appear here: an expanded treatment of the situational approach to leadership that covers the telling, selling, participating, and delegating styles; a new self-test on the four approaches to leadership (traits, functional, transformational, and situational); and a new exercise on dealing with dysfunctional roles.

Chapter 11. Significantly revised sections include dealing with communication apprehension and analyzing the sociology of the audience. New sections include adapting to the audience during the speech, evaluating research findings, and integrating research into the speech. Also added is a poorly constructed informative speech for analysis.

Chapter 12. The section on common faults of introductions and conclusions now incorporates suggestions on what to do before and after the speech.

Chapter 13. A new informative speech with annotations has been added.

Chapter 14. There is a new persuasive speech with annotations. The section on motivational appeals has been rewritten to coordinate with Maslow's hierarchy of needs model, and the sections on strategies for persuasive speaking have been revised.

Glossary. Replacing the combined glossary of concepts and skills are two separate glossaries—one on concepts and one on skills. The 174 entries in the new skills glossary briefly summarize the major skills considered throughout the text.

Additional Units. An accompanying CD-ROM, available on request with a new textbook, offers four complete units not available in the printed text: Mass Media, Emotional Communication, Criticism in the Public Speaking Classroom, and Developing Special Occasion Speeches.

The Pedagogy

As in previous editions of *Essentials,* the pedagogy here is highly interactive. Here are some of the more important pedagogical features.

What Do You Say? Scenarios

As already noted, the new **What Do You Say?** margin feature presents you with situations calling for communication decisions. Each of these items gives you an opportunity to apply the skills you're reading about.

Chapter Openers (Concepts and Skills)

Each chapter-opening grid highlights the chapter topics and their corresponding skills. This feature links the main concepts covered in the chapter to the skills you should master after reading each of the major sections in the chapter. This opening grid also offers a brief preview of the chapter that helps to focus attention on the major issues covered.

Listening, Ethics, and Power Boxes

The **Listen to This, Communicating Ethically,** and **Communicating with Power** boxes not only connect the crucial topics of listening, ethics, and power to the chapter topics but also present interactive cases to stimulate discussion and to encourage you to apply the material to your own communication interactions and experiences.

Self-Tests

Fifteen **self-tests** appear in this edition. Some include standard research instruments, such as tests for measuring apprehension, love, time orientation, and argumentativeness. Other self-tests are more pedagogical and are designed to involve you in concepts discussed in the chapter. These self-tests focus on your willingness to self-disclose, the kind of leader you are, and how credible you are, among other personal traits. Each self-test ends with two questions: (1) "How did you do?" gives you the scoring instructions so you can score your own test and (2) "What will you do?" asks you to think about any action you may want to take in light of how you performed on the self-test. Many of the self-tests have been rewritten, and some have been reduced in length for greater clarity.

In Web Explorations marginal notes, you'll find references to additional exercises and self-tests relevant to the chapter material that you can do online or download; visit the website at www.ablongman.com/devito.

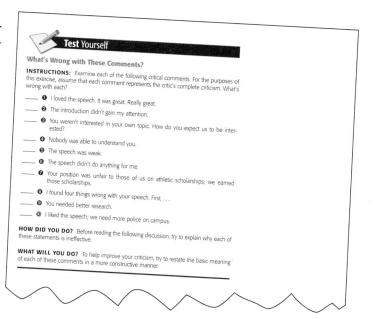

Test Yourself

What's Wrong with These Comments?

INSTRUCTIONS: Examine each of the following critical comments. For the purposes of this exercise, assume that each comment represents the critic's complete criticism. What's wrong with each?

___ ❶ I loved the speech. It was great. Really great.

___ ❷ The introduction didn't gain my attention.

___ ❸ You weren't interested in your own topic. How do you expect us to be interested?

___ ❹ Nobody was able to understand you.

___ ❺ The speech was weak.

___ ❻ The speech didn't do anything for me.

___ ❼ Your position was unfair to those of us on athletic scholarships; we earned those scholarships.

___ ❽ I found four things wrong with your speech. First, . . .

___ ❾ You needed better research.

___ ❿ I liked the speech; we need more police on campus.

HOW DID YOU DO? Before reading the following discussion, try to explain why each of these statements is ineffective.

WHAT WILL YOU DO? To help improve your criticism, try to restate the basic meaning of each of these comments in a more constructive manner.

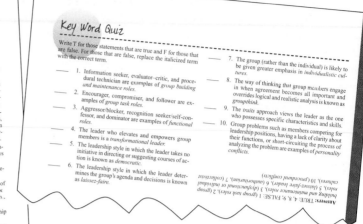

Summary of Concepts and Skills

In this chapter we explored interpersonal relationships—their nature, development, deterioration, and repair. We also examined several theories that explain what happens in interpersonal relationships, and we considered the effects of culture, gender, technology, and the workplace on relationships.

1. Both face-to-face and online relationships have advantages (for example, they lessen loneliness and enhance your self-esteem) and disadvantages (for example, they involve increased obligations and may increase isolation).
2. Relationships typically have six stages: contact, involvement, intimacy, deterioration, repair, and dissolution. Each of these stages can be further broken down into an early and a later phase.
3. Love is perhaps the most important form of intimacy. Several types of love are eros, ludus, storge, pragma, mania, and agape.
4. Among the major causes of relationship deterioration are a lessening of the reasons for establishing the relationship, changes in the people involved, sexual difficulties, and work and financial problems.
5. Relationships of all kinds and in all their aspects are heavily influenced by culture, as are the theories that explain relationships and the topics research focuses on.
6. Gender differences in both friendship and love are often considerable and influence the ways in which these relationships are viewed and the communication that takes place within them.
7. All aspects of relationships—from development through maintenance, and sometimes to dissolution—are greatly influenced by the Internet and the opportunities it affords for communication.
8. Workplace relationships can create both opportunities and problems, both of which need to be assessed by anyone contemplating such relationships.

Check your competence in using the skills of effective relationship development, using the following rating scale:
1 = almost always; 2 = often; 3 = sometimes; 4 = rarely; and
5 = hardly ever.

___ 1. I understand that relationships involve both advantages and disadvantages.
___ 2. I adjust my communication patterns on the basis of the relationship's intimacy.
___ 3. I can identify changes in communication patterns that may signal deterioration.
___ 4. I can use the accepted repair strategies to heal an ailing relationship—for example, reversing negative communication patterns, using cherishing behaviors, and adopting a positive action program.
___ 5. I can apply to my own relationships communication skills such as identifying relational messages, exchanging perspectives due to differences in punctuation, empathic and supportive understanding, and eliminating unfair fight strategies.
___ 6. I can effectively manage physical proximity, reinforcement, and emphasizing similarities as ways to increase interpersonal attractiveness.
___ 7. I can identify and to some extent control the rewards and costs of my relationships.
___ 8. I can appreciate the other person's perception of relationship equity and can modify my own behavior to make the relationship more productive and satisfying.
___ 9. I increase the breadth and depth of a relationship gradually.
___ 10. I understand relationships as cultural institutions.
___ 11. I take gender differences into consideration in trying to understand friendship and love.

Key Word Quiz

Write T for those statements that are true and F for those that are false. For those that are false, replace the italicized term with the correct term.

___ 1. Information seeker, evaluator–critic, and procedural technician are examples of *group building and maintenance roles.*
___ 2. Encourager, compromiser, and follower are examples of *group task roles.*
___ 3. Aggressor/blocker, recognition seeker/self-confessor, and dominator are examples of *functional roles.*
___ 4. The leader who elevates and empowers group members is a *transformational leader.*
___ 5. The leadership style in which the leader takes no initiative in directing or suggesting courses of action is known as *democratic.*
___ 6. The leadership style in which the leader determines the group's agenda and decisions is known as *laissez-faire.*

___ 7. The group (rather than the individual) is likely to be given greater emphasis in *individualistic cultures.*
___ 8. The way of thinking that group members engage in when agreement becomes all important and overrides logical and realistic analysis is known as *groupthink.*
___ 9. The *traits* approach views the leader as the one who possesses specific characteristics and skills.
___ 10. Group problems such as members competing for leadership positions, having a lack of clarity about their functions, or short-circuiting the process of analyzing the problem are examples of *personality conflicts.*

Answers: TRUE: 4, 8, 9. FALSE: 1 (*group task roles*), 2 (*group building and maintenance roles*), 3 (*dysfunctional or individual roles*), 5 (*laissez-faire leader*), 6 (*authoritarian*), 7 (*collectivist cultures*), 10 (*procedural conflicts*).

Summaries of Concepts and Skills

Each chapter-end summary includes both a conceptual summary and a skills summary. The *conceptual summary* provides a brief paragraph summarizing the chapter's focus and a list of statements that summarize the essential content of the chapter. The *skills summary* presents the major skills covered in the chapter in a checklist format to allow you to determine your own current level of mastery and to identify skills requiring further practice.

Key Word Quiz

A brief 10-item **Key Word Quiz** at the end of each chapter will help you review the significant vocabulary terms introduced in the chapter. The answers to these quizzes appear upside down immediately after the exercises.

Skill Development Experiences

This edition contains 48 Skill Development Experiences integrated into the text. Many are new to this edition, and all have been rewritten to emphasize practical communication skills. These exercises promote the mastery of specific communication skills in an enjoyable way and in a supportive atmosphere.

Messages Express Both Facts and Inferences

A second key principle is the importance of avoiding **fact–inference confusion.** Often, when we listen or speak, we don't distinguish between statements of fact and those of inference. Yet there are great differences between the two. Barriers to clear thinking can develop if we treat inferences as facts.

For example, you can say, "She is wearing a blue jacket" as well as "He is harboring an illogical hatred." Although the sentences have similar structures, they are different. You can observe the jacket and the blue color, but how do you observe "illogical hatred"? Obviously, this is not a descriptive but an **inferential statement.** In contrast, a **factual statement** must be made by the observer after observation and must be limited to what is observed (Weinberg, 1959).

There is nothing wrong with making inferential statements. You must make them to talk about much that is meaningful to you. The problem arises when you act as if those inferential statements are factual. Consider the following anecdote (Maynard, 1963): A woman went for a walk one day and met a friend whom she had not seen, heard from, or heard of in 10 years. After an exchange of greetings, the woman said: "Is this your little boy?" and her friend replied, "Yes, I got married about six years ago." The woman then asked the child, "What is your name?" and the little boy replied, "Same as my father's." "Oh," said the woman, "then it must be Peter."

How did the woman know the boy's father's name was Peter? The answer is obvious, but only after we recognize that in reading this short passage we have made an unconscious inference. Specifically, we have inferred that the woman's friend is a woman. Actually, the friend is a man named Peter.

You may test your ability to distinguish facts from inferences by taking the following self-test, "Can you distinguish facts from inferences?" (based on the tests constructed by William Haney [1973]).

Web Explorations
A variety of experiences on verbal messages will help you practice and extend some of the skills identified here (www.ablongman.com/devito): (1) Using the Abstraction Ladder as a Critical Thinking Tool, (2) "Must Lie" Situations, (3) Rephrasing Clichés, (4) Identifying the Barriers to Communication, (5) How Do You Talk about the Middle? (6) Recognizing Gender Differences, (7) How Direct Are You? (8) Is Lying Unethical? and (9) How Do You Feel about Communicating Feelings?

The Website

Included on the book's website at www.ablongman.com/devito and prepared by the author of the text, are more than 100 exercises, self-tests, and detailed explanations of concepts discussed more briefly in the text. These items are organized by chapter and are all referred to in the Web Explorations marginal notes in the text.

Research Navigator

Allyn & Bacon's Research Navigator website is a powerful and extensive online database of popular and academic articles in communication and related areas of interest. Providing credible and reliable source material from, among others, the EBSCO Academic Journal and Abstract Database, *New York Times* Search by Subject Archive, and *Financial Times* Article Archive and Company Financials, Research Navigator helps students quickly and efficiently make the most of their research time. Research Navigator marginal notes throughout the text prompt you to go to www.researchnavigator.com to read an article, investigate key terms, and find answers related to topics, terms, and questions based on the chapter content.

Increase Your Cultural Awareness

Recognizing and being mindful of cultural differences will help increase your accuracy in perception. For example, Russian or Chinese performers such as ballet dancers will often applaud their audience by clapping. Americans seeing this may easily interpret this as egotistical. Similarly, a German man will enter a restaurant before the woman in order to see if the place is respectable enough for the woman. This simple custom may appear rude to people from cultures in which it's considered courteous to allow the woman to enter first (Axtell, 1991).

Cultural awareness will help counteract the difficulty most people have in understanding the nonverbal messages of people from other cultures. For example, be aware that it's easier to decode emotions communicated facially by members of your own culture than to read emotions shown by members of other cultures (Weathers, Frank, & Spell, 2002). This "in-group advantage" will assist your perceptional accuracy for members of your own culture but will often hinder your accuracy for members of other cultures (Elfenbein & Ambady, 2002).

Within every cultural group, too, there are wide and important differences. Not all Americans are alike, and neither are all Indonesians, Greeks, Mexicans, and so on. When you make assumptions that all people of a certain culture are alike, you're thinking in stereotypes. In addition to recognizing differences between another culture and your own, recognizing differences among members of any given culture will help you perceive situations more accurately.

Research Navigator.c⊕m
www.researchnavigator.com

Find Answers: Try finding answers to one of the following questions, or design a research study to answer it: Are people who attribute controllability to the situation of homeless people more negative in their evaluation of homelessness than those who attribute an absence of controllability? Do different cultures hold different implicit personality theories? Do men and women hold different theories?

Supplementary Materials

Instructor's Resources

Print Supplements

Instructor's Manual and Test Bank with Transparency Masters, by Christina Standerfer, University of Central Arkansas. This detailed Instructor's Manual and Test Bank contains learning objectives for each chapter, chapter outlines, discussion questions, and skill development activities to illustrate the concepts, principles, and skill of human communication. The Instructor's Manual includes "Asides" created by Joseph A. DeVito. In addition, the Test Bank portion of the manual contains numerous multiple choice, true/false, fill-in-the-blank, and essay questions. The manual also includes transparency masters that frame key concepts and skills.

A Guide for New Teachers of Introduction to Communication, **Second Edition,** by Susanna G. Porter, Kennesaw State University. This instructor's guide is designed to help new teachers effectively teach the introductory communication course.

A Guide for New Public Speaking Teachers: Building Toward Success, **Third Edition,** by Calvin L. Troup, Duquesne University. The guide is designed to help new teachers prepare their introductory public speaking course effectively by covering such topics as preparation for the term, planning and structuring the course, evaluating speeches, utilizing the textbook, and integrating technology into the classroom. The third edition includes a brief guide on teaching students for whom English is not a first language.

The Blockbuster Approach: A Guide to Teaching Interpersonal Communication with Video, **Third Edition,** by Thomas E. Jewell, Bergen Community College. The guide provides lists and descriptions of commercial videos that can be used in the classroom to illustrate interpersonal concepts and complex interpersonal relationships. Sample activities are available.

ESL Guide for Public Speaking, by Debra Gonsher Vinik, Bronx Community College of the City University of New York. This guide provides strategies and resources for instructors teaching in a bilingual or multi-lingual classroom. It also includes suggestions for further reading and a listing of related websites.

Allyn & Bacon Public Speaking Transparency Package includes 100 full-color transparencies created with PowerPoint software provide visual support for classroom lectures and discussions.

Great Ideas for Teaching Speech (GIFTS), **Thirteenth Edition,** by Raymond Zeuschner, California Polytechnic State University. GIFTS includes descriptions and guidelines for assignments successfully used by experienced public speaking instructors in their classrooms.

Electronic Supplements

VideoWorkshop for Introduction to Communication, **Version 2.0,** by Kathryn Dindia, University of Wisconsin. VideoWorkshop is a way to bring video into your course for maximized learning. This total teaching and learning system includes quality video footage on an easy-to-use CD-ROM plus a Student Learning Guide and an Instructor's Teaching Guide—both with textbook-specific Correlation Grids. The result? A program that brings textbook concepts to life with ease and that helps your students understand, analyze, and apply the objectives of the course. Visit www.ablongman.com/videoworkshop for more information.

TestGen EQ: Computerized Test Bank The user-friendly interface enables instructors to view, edit, and add questions, transfer questions to tests, and print tests in a variety of fonts. Search and sort features allow instructors to locate questions quickly and arrange them in preferred order.

PowerPoint Presentation Package, by Matthew N. Drumheller, McMurry University. This text-specific package consists of a collection of lecture outlines and graphic images keyed to every chapter in the text. Available on the web at http://suppscentral.ablongman.com/.

Allyn & Bacon Digital Media Archive CD-ROM for Communication, **Version 2.0** This CD-ROM contains electronic images of charts, graphs, maps, tables, and figures, along with media elements such as video, audio clips, and related web links. These media assets are fully customizable to use with our pre-formatted Power-Point outlines or to import into instructor's own lectures (Windows and Mac).

Allyn & Bacon Interpersonal Communication Videos Allyn & Bacon offers three Interpersonal Videos ranging from 30 to 50 minutes that contain scenarios illustrating key concepts in interpersonal communication. Accompanying user guides feature transcripts, teaching activities, and class discussion questions for each episode. Contact your Allyn & Bacon representative for ordering information. Some restrictions apply.

Interpersonal Movie Library This collection contains popular feature films dealing with a range of interpersonal topics. Contact your Allyn & Bacon representative for ordering information. Some restrictions apply.

The Allyn & Bacon Public Speaking Video This video includes excerpts of classic and contemporary speeches as well as student speeches to illustrate the public speaking process. One speech is delivered two times under different circumstances by the same person to illustrate the difference between effective and noneffective delivery based on appearance, nonverbal, and verbal style. Contact your Allyn & Bacon representative for ordering information. Some restrictions apply.

The Allyn & Bacon Student Speeches Video Library A video collection of student speeches that include three 2-hour American Forensic Association videos of award-winning student speeches and four videos with a range of student speeches delivered in the classroom. Contact your Allyn & Bacon representative for ordering information. Some restrictions apply.

The Allyn & Bacon Public Speaking Key Topics Video Library This library contains three videos that address core topics covered in the classroom: Critiquing Student Speeches, Speaker Apprehension, and Addressing Your Audience. Contact your Allyn & Bacon representative for ordering information. Some restrictions apply.

The Allyn & Bacon Communication Video Library A collection of communication videos produced by Film for the Humanities and Sciences. Topics include, but are not limited to: Business Presentations, Great American Speeches, and Conflict Resolution. Contact your local Allyn & Bacon sales representative for ordering information. Some restrictions apply.

Allyn & Bacon Classic and Contemporary Speeches DVD presents a collection of over 120 minutes of video footage in an easy-to-use DVD format. Each speech is accompanied by a biographical and historical summary that helps students to understand the context and motivation behind each speech. Contact your Allyn & Bacon sales representative for additional details and ordering information.

CourseCompass for Introduction to Communication, powered by Blackboard and hosted nationally, is the most flexible online course management system on the market today. By using this powerful suite of online tools in conjunction with Allyn & Bacon's preloaded textbook and testing content, you can create an online presence for your course in under thirty minutes. The Introduction to Communication course features preloaded content such as quiz questions, video clips, instructor's manuals, PowerPoint presentations, still images, course preparation and instruction materials, VideoWorkshop for Introduction to Communication, weblinks, and much more! Log on to www.coursecompass.com to access this dynamic teaching resource. The content is also compatible with Blackboard and WebCT.

Student Resources

Print Supplements

Interviewing and Human Communication, by Joseph A. Devito. This booklet introduces students to the process of interviewing, including the job résumé and the letters that are an essential part of the entire interview process. It also provides work sheets for preparing for both the information-gathering interview and the employment interview.

Listening, ethical, and power issues as they relate to interviewing are included in boxes as are skill development exercises to help you work actively with the concepts discussed here. Skills topics include practicing interviewing skills, displaying communication confidence in the employment interview, and responding to unlawful questions. Scenarios asking you to apply your interviewing skills in different situations, quotations to highlight different perspectives, ideas for exploring online materials, and invitations to use our online Research Navigator tool to learn more about interviewing are included in the margins. In addition, to make it easier for you to use the interviewing preparation guides in the booklet, these guides are also available on the website at www.ablongman.com/devito and may be downloaded for you to complete and submit to your instructor, or to keep in your personal records. This product is available FREE when packaged with this text. Contact your Allyn & Bacon representative for ordering information. Some restrictions apply.

Research Navigator Guide for Speech Communication, by Terrence Doyle, Northern Virginia Community College, and Linda R. Barr, University of the Virgin Islands. This resource guide is designed to teach students how to conduct high-quality online research and document it properly. The guide provides access to Research Navigator (www.researchnavigator.com), which contains exclusive databases of credible and reliable source material, including EBSCO's ContentSelect Academic Journal Database and the New York Times Search by Subject Archive. This product is available FREE when packaged with this text. Contact your Allyn & Bacon representative for ordering information. Some restrictions apply.

Preparing Visual Aids for Presentations, **Third Edition,** by Dan Cavanaugh. This brief booklet provides a host of ideas for using today's multimedia tools to improve presentations and includes suggestions for planning a presentation, guidelines for designing visual aids and storyboarding, and a PowerPoint presentation walk-through. This product is available FREE when packaged with this text. Contact your Allyn & Bacon representative for ordering information. Some restrictions apply.

Outlining Workbook, by Reeze L. Hanson and Sharon Condon, Haskell Indian Nations University. This workbook includes activities, exercises, and answers to help students develop and master the critical skill of outlining. This product is available FREE when packaged with this text. Contact your Allyn & Bacon representative for ordering information. Some restrictions apply.

Speech Preparation Workbook, by Jennifer Dreyer and Gregory H. Patton, San Diego State University. This workbook takes students through the various stages of speech creation—from audience analysis to writing the speech—and provides supplementary assignments and tear-out forms. This product is available FREE when packaged with this text. Contact your Allyn & Bacon representative for ordering information. Some restrictions apply.

Brainstorms, by Joseph A. DeVito. A guide to thinking more creatively about communication or anything else, this is a perfect complement to the text's unique emphasis on critical thinking. Students find 19 practical, easy-to-use creative thinking techniques, along with insights into the creative thinking process. This product is available FREE when packaged with this text. Contact your Allyn & Bacon representative for ordering information. Some restrictions apply.

Public Speaking in the Multicultural Environment, **Second Edition,** by Devorah A. Lieberman, Portland State University. This booklet includes activities in a two-chapter essay that encourages students to analyze cultural diversity within their audiences and adapt their presentations accordingly. This product is available FREE when packaged with this text. Contact your Allyn & Bacon representative for ordering information. Some restrictions apply.

Electronic Supplements

Additional Units. An accompanying CD-ROM offers four complete units, not included in the printed text:

- **Mass Media.** Discusses the functional and dysfunctional effects of the mass media and how you can become a more critical (and active) media consumer.
- **Emotional Communication.** Provides a concentrated focus on this one form of interpersonal communication. It covers emotions and emotional messages, obstacles in communicating emotions, and guidelines for communicating emotions effectively.
- **Criticism in the Public Speaking Classroom.** Addresses ways and means to criticize classroom speeches effectively and covers the nature and values of criticism, cultural differences, and standards and principles of criticism.
- **Developing Special Occasion Speeches.** Provides thorough coverage of a variety of special occasion speeches: speeches of introduction, presentation, and acceptance; speeches aimed at securing goodwill; and speeches of tribute. In addition, some cultural influences on the special occasion speech are considered.

Available on request in a special package with a new textbook. Ask your local representative for details.

VideoWorkshop for Introduction to Communication, **Version 2.0,** by Kathryn Dindia, University of Wisconsin. VideoWorkshop includes quality video footage on an easy-to-use CD-ROM plus a Student Learning Guide with textbook-specific Correlation Grids. The result? A program that brings textbook concepts to life with ease and that helps students understand, analyze, and apply the objectives of the course. Visit www.ablongman.com/videoworkshop for more information.

Companion Website with Online Practice Tests, by Joseph A. DeVito and Diana Murphy. Accessed at www.ablongman.com/devito, this site provides an assortment of activities and web links to enrich the course. The site also contains self-tests and skill development exercises designed exclusively for this website.

Allyn & Bacon Communication Studies Website, by Terrence Doyle, Northern Virginia Community College, and Tim Borchers, Minnesota State University at Moorhead, and ***Allyn & Bacon Public Speaking Website,*** by Nan Peck, Northern Virginia Community College. These websites contain modules built with enrichment materials, web links, and interactive activities designed to enhance students' understanding of key concepts. The Communication Studies Website includes interpersonal, small group communication, and public speaking topics. Access this site at www .ablongman.com/commstudies. The Public Speaking Website, updated for 2004, helps students build, organize, and research speeches while learning about the process of public speaking. Access this website at www.ablongman.com/pubspeak.

The Speech Writer's Workshop CD-ROM, **Version 2.0** This CD-ROM assists students with speech preparation by supplying a Speech Handbook that includes tips for researching and preparing speeches; a Speech Workshop that guides students step-by-step through the speech writing process; a Topics Dictionary that provides hundreds of ideas for speeches; and the Documentor citation database that helps students to format bibliographic entries in either MLA or APA style. Available FREE when packaged with this text. Contact your Allyn & Bacon representative for ordering information. Some restrictions apply.

Interactive Speechwriter Software, **Version 1.1,** by Martin R. Cox. This software contains sample speeches, tutorials, self-test questions on key concepts, and templates for writing formative, persuasive, and motivated sequence speeches to enhance students' understanding of key concepts discussed in the text. This product is available for student purchase or FREE when value packed with this text. Contact your Allyn & Bacon representative for ordering information. Some restrictions apply.

Communication Tutor Center (access code required), www.aw.com/tutorcenter. The Tutor Center provides students with free, one-on-one interactive tutoring from qualified public speaking instructors on all material in the text. The Tutor Center offers students help with understanding major communication principles as well as methods for study. In addition, students have the option of submitting self-taped speeches for review and critique by Tutor Center instructors to help prepare for and improve their speech assignments. Tutoring assistance is offered by phone, fax, Internet, and e-mail during Tutor Center hours. For more details and ordering information, contact your Allyn & Bacon representative.

Allyn & Bacon Classic and Contemporary Speeches DVD presents a collection of over 120 minutes of video footage in an easy-to-use DVD format. Each speech is accompanied by a biographical and historical summary that helps students to understand the context and motivation behind each speech. Contact your Allyn & Bacon sales representative for additional details and ordering information.

Acknowledgments

I would like to thank the many reviewers who critically analyzed the previous edition. They gave graciously of their time and expertise and offered a variety of useful and insightful suggestions for this new edition. I thank you all; your comments have resulted in many improvements. Thank you to Carole Barbato, Kent State University; Thomas Bovino, Suffolk Community College; Kathleen Perri, Valencia Community College; Joseph Ortiz, Scottsdale Community College; Roxanne Davidson, Montgomery College; Bill Starosta, Howard University; Charles Findley, Northeastern University; and Judi Brownell, Cornell University.

I also owe a great debt to the people at Allyn and Bacon who took such excellent care of this manuscript. I especially wish to thank editors Karon Bowers and Brian Wheel; senior developmental editors Ellen Darion and Sharon Geary; senior production editor Annette Pagliaro; project manager Susan McIntyre, of Nesbitt Graphics; copy editor Jay Howland; and photo researcher Julie Tesser.

Joseph A. DeVito
jdevito@hunter.cuny.edu

Credits

Text Credits

Page 15: Figure 1.6, From "A World of Students: US Schools face growing role as melting pot" from USA TODAY. Copyright September 24, 1997. Reprinted with permission.

Page 24: From "Ethnic identity and close friendship in Chinese-American college students" by Stella Ting Toomey in INTERNATIONAL JOURNAL OF INTERCULTURAL RELATIONS 5, 1981, pp. 383–406. Reprinted with permission from Elsevier.

Pages 24–25: This test is taken from James W. Neuliep, Michelle Chaudoir, and James C. McCroskey (2001). A cross-cultural comparison of ethnocentrism among Japanese and United States college students. *Communication Research Reports 18* (Spring): 137–146. Used by permission of Eastern Communication Association.

Page 32: Figure 2.2, From Joseph Luft, *Group Process: An Introduction to Group Dynamics*, 3rd ed. Copyright © 1984. New York: McGraw-Hill. Reprinted with permission.

Pages 123–124: From "Time in Perspective" by Alexander Gonzalez and Philip G. Zimbardo in PSYCHOLOGY TODAY, March 1985. Reprinted with permission from Psychology Today Magazine, Copyright © 1985 Sussex Publishers Inc.

Page 151: Figure 7.2, From THE MANAGERIAL GRID III, 3rd Edition by Blake & Mouton (Authors), Grid International Inc., copyright owners. Reprinted by permission.

Pages 158–159: This scale was developed by Dominic Infante and Andrew Rancer and appears in Dominic Infante and Andrew Rancer, "A Conceptualization and Measure of Argumentatitiveness" in *Journal of Personality Assessment 46* (1982), pp. 72–80. Reprinted by permission of Lawrence Erlbaum Associates and the author.

Pages 170–171: From "A Relationship-Specific Version of the Love Attitudes Scale" by C. Hendrick and S. Hendrick. Copyright © 1990 Select Press, *Journal of Social Behavior and Personality 5, 1990.* Reprinted by permission.

Page 193: From *An Introduction to Rhetorical Communication*, 7th ed., by James C. McCroskey. Copyright © 1997 by Allyn and Bacon. Reprinted by permission.

Page 211: Figure 10.1, "Model of Situational Leadership" by Paul Hersey and Kenneth Blanchard in *Management of Organizational Behavior,* p. 277. © Copyrighted material. Reprinted with permission of Center for Leadership Studies, Escondido, CA 92025. All Rights Reserved.

Page 225: From *An Introduction to Rhetorical Communication*, 7th ed., by James C. McCroskey. Copyright © 1997 by Allyn and Bacon. Reprinted by permission.

Pages 283–284: This test was adapted for public speaking on the basis of the conversational satisfaction test developed by Michael Hecht, "The Conceptualization and Measurement of Interpersonal Communication Satisfaction," *Human Communication Research 4* (1978): 253–264 and is used by permission of the author and International Communication Association.

Pages 304–307: "The Electric Heart" by Steve Zammit. Reprinted by permission of the author.

Page 320: Fgure 14.1, "Maslow's Hierarchy of Needs" from Abraham Maslow, *Motivation and Personality*. Copyright © 1970. Reprinted by permission of Prentice-Hall, Inc., Upper Saddle River, NJ.

Pages 326–329: Gunasekera, U. (1999). "The Perils of Philanthropy" in L. G. Schnoor (Ed.), *Winning Orations of the Interstate Oratorical Association*, 1999, pp. 98–100. Reprinted with permission from Interstate Oratorical Association, Mankato, MN, Larry Schnoor, Executive Secretary.

Page 333: "A Word Is Dead" reprinted by permission of the publishers and the Trustees of Amherst College from THE POEMS OF EMILY DICKINSON, Thomas H. Johnson, ed., Cambridge, Mass.: The Belknap Press of Harvard University Press, Copyright © 1951, 1955, 1979 by the President and Fellows of Harvard College.

Photo Credits

Page 1: Penny Tweedie/Stone/Getty Images; Page 8: Bill Bachman/The Image Works; Page 13: David Harry Steward/Stone/Getty Images; Page 16: AP/Wide World Photos; Page 28: Gary Conner/ PhotoEdit; Page 33: AP/Wide World; Page 36: Bob Daemmrich/ The Image Works; Page 40: Mark Antman/The Image Works; Page 45: Ben Mangor/Superstock; Page 50: Masterfile/Masterfile; Page 58: Steven Rubin/The Image Works; Page 60: Neil Farrin/Stone/Getty Images; Page 64: Stuart Cohen/Getty Images; Page 69: Everett Collection; Page 73: Gary A. Conner/PhotoEdit; Page 77: Myrleen Ferguson Cate/PhotoEdit; Page 81: Doug Menuez/Getty Images; Page 85: Will Hart; Page 96: Lara Jo Regan/Getty Images; Page 100: Lucienne Pashley/Getty Images; Page 104: Jonathan Kirn/Stone/Getty Images; Page 110: Kevin Radford/Superstock; Page 125: Davie Simson/Stock Boston; Page 129: Lucienne Pashley/Superstock; Page 133: Esbin-Anderson/The Image Works; Page 147: Bruce Ayers/Stone/Getty Images; Page 154: Zefa/Masterfile; Page 158: Christopher Bissel/Stone/Getty Images; Page 162: CBS Photo Archive; Page 166: Myrleen Ferguson Cate/PhotoEdit; Page 172: Richard Lord/The Image Works; Page 178: Everett Collection; Page 186: Spencer Grant/PhotoEdit; Page 191: Michael Newman/PhotoEdit; Page 196: Mark Richards/PhotoEdit; Page 200: Gary D. Landsman/Corbis; Page 204: Charles Gupton/Stone/Getty Images; Page 207: Bob Daemmrich; Page 212: Jerry Howard/Stock Boston; Page 217: Dan Bosler/Stone/Getty Images; Page 222: Michael Newman/PhotoEdit; Page 225: AP/Wide World Photos; Page 241: Ryan McVay/Getty Images; Page 247: Spencer Grant/PhotoEdit; Page 253: Dana White/PhotoEdit; Page 257: Bob Daemmrich/Stock Boston; Page 272: Jonathan Nourok/PhotoEdit; Page 279: Gary Conner/PhotoEdit; Page 282: David Young-Wolff/PhotoEdit; Page 285: Joseph Nettis/Stock Boston; Page 291: Colin Young-Wolff/PhotoEdit; Page 294: David Young-Wolff/PhotoEdit; Page 309: Jacob Silberberg/Getty Images; Page 312: Bill E. Barnes/Stock Boston; Page 322: Chris Hondros/Getty Images; Page 325: Gary Conner/PhotoEdit.

1 Introduction to the Essentials of Human Communication

Chapter Concepts	Chapter Skills
This chapter explains the nature of communication and its essential concepts and principles.	After completing this chapter, you should be able to:
Communication Models and Concepts	communicate as speaker/listener with an awareness of the varied components involved in the communication act.
Principles of Communication	communicate as speaker/listener with a recognition of the principles of human communication.
Culture and Human Communication	communicate with an understanding of cultural influences and differences.

> **"** Communication is power. Those who have mastered its effective use can change their own experience of the world and the world's experience of them. **"**
>
> —Anthony Robbins

Of all the knowledge and skills you have, those concerning communication are among your most important and useful. Whether in your personal life, in social contexts, or in your work life, your communication ability is your most vital asset. Here, in brief, are just a few of the skills you'll learn through this text and this course.

- *Self-presentation skills* enable you to present yourself as (and just for starters) a confident, likable, approachable, and credible person. It is also largely through your communication skills that you display negative qualities as well.

- *Relationship skills* help you build friendships, enter into love relationships, work together with colleagues, and interact with family members. These are the skills for initiating, maintaining, repairing, and sometimes dissolving relationships of all kinds. These are the skills that make you or break you as a relationship partner.

- *Interviewing skills* enable you to interact to gain information, to successfully present yourself to get the job you want, and to participate effectively in a wide variety of other interview types. (This topic is covered in a separate supplement, *Interviewing and Human Communication*.)

- *Group interaction and leadership skills* help you participate effectively in relationship and task groups—informative, problem-solving, and brainstorming groups, at home or at work—as a member and as a leader.

- *Presentation skills* enable you to communicate information to and influence the attitudes and behaviors of small and large audiences.

You'll accomplish these objectives and acquire these skills as you engage in and master a variety of communication forms. **Intrapersonal communication** is the communication you have with yourself. Through intrapersonal communication you talk with, learn about, and judge yourself. You persuade yourself of this or that, reason about possible decisions to make, and rehearse messages that you plan to send to others. **Interpersonal communication** occurs when you interact with a person with whom you have some kind of relationship; it can take place face-to-face as well as through electronic channels (as in e-mail or instant messaging, for example) or even in traditional letter writing. Through interpersonal communication you interact with others, learn about them and yourself, and reveal yourself to others. Whether with new acquaintances, old friends, lovers, family members, or colleagues at work, it's through interpersonal communication that you establish, maintain, sometimes destroy, and sometimes repair personal relationships.

Interviewing is communication that proceeds by question and answer. Through interviewing you learn about others and what they know, counsel or get counseling from others, and get or don't get the job you want. Today much interviewing (especially initial interviews) takes place through e-mail and (video) phone conferencing.

Small group communication is communication among groups of say 5 to 10 people and serves both relationship and task needs. Through small group communication you interact with others, solve problems, develop new ideas, and share knowledge and experiences. You live your work and social life largely in groups, from school orientation meetings to executive board meetings, from informal social groups to formal meetings discussing issues of international concern. Increasingly, you may also live your life in chat rooms, where you may interact with people from different cultures living thousands of miles away. Chat rooms seem to exist for just about every topic or interest you can imagine; and if you can't find one you want, you can always form your own.

Public communication is communication between a speaker and an audience. Audiences range in size from several people to hundreds, thousands, and even millions. Through public communication others inform and persuade you. And you, in turn, inform and persuade others—to act, to buy, or to think in a particular way. Much as you can address large audiences face-to-face, you also can address such audiences electronically. Through newsgroups, for example, you can post your "speech" for anyone to read and then read their reactions to your message. And with the help of the more traditional mass media of radio and television (both network and cable), you can address audiences in the hundreds of millions as they sit alone or in small groups scattered throughout the world.

Mediated communication occurs when you send a message through some electronic device to a receiver. Forms of mediated communication include both mass communication (newspapers, television, and film, for example) and computer communication (e-mail, chat groups, and newsgroups, for example). The audiences here may be scattered throughout the world and may number in the millions. (This area of communication is presented on the CD-ROM available with this text.)

This book, then, focuses on all these forms of communication—and on you as both message sender and message receiver. It has three major purposes:

- It aims to explain the *concepts and principles,* the theory and research in human communication, so that you'll have a firm foundation of understanding of what communication is and how it works.

- It seeks to provide you with *skills* in human communication that will help you increase your own communication competence and effectiveness in the real world. Lots of social interaction and workplace examples throughout the book present useful and practical techniques that you'll take with you when you leave the college classroom. Unlike the children in the cartoon here, you will have no doubt about the usefulness of what you'll learn in this course.

- It endeavors to help you increase your *critical thinking* ability, both in general and about communication in particular—so as to know what your communication options are and to have the knowledge to select the right ones.

In approaching the study of human communication, keep the following in mind. First, human communication involves both theory and research *and* practical skills for increasing communication effectiveness. Seek to understand the theories and research *and* to improve your communication skills. Each will assist you in mastering the other: A knowledge of theory and research will help you better understand the skills, and a knowledge of skills will help you better understand theory.

"Finger painting is fun, but will we ever use it in real life?"

Second, as mentioned, human communication is not limited to face-to-face interaction but includes the broad array of computer communication experiences—and the lines between these modes are blurring with each technological advance. For example, although most of us communicate via simple text in e-mail and chat, both Microsoft and Apple recently incorporated audio and video capabilities into their chat programs, with Messenger 6 and iChat AV respectively (*New York Times,* June 26, 2003, pp. G1, G7). Although these currently require high-speed connections and the latest hardware and software on both ends, it's clear that the use of combined text, audio, and video messages will become more and more widespread. And further advances are sure to come. For example, at present you can save or forward your text messages, but you can't do that (yet) with your audio and video messages. Similarly, with text chat you can communicate with lots of people at the same time, but with audio–video, you're limited (currently) to one person.

Third, effective human communication requires that you analyze yourself as a critical thinker and communicator. Self-understanding is essential if you're to use this material to change some of your own behaviors. Be open to new ideas, even those that may contradict your existing beliefs. Be willing to change your ways of communicating and even your ways of thinking.

Fourth, many of the skills of human communication extend over a wide range of communication types. Throughout this text, skills for improving interpersonal, small group, and public speaking are presented. But don't limit these skills to the context in which they're introduced; extend them to other areas as well. For example, the skills of interpersonal communication will in many cases also prove useful in small groups and in public speaking. Similarly, you'll find the skills of group and public interaction useful in interpersonal settings as well.

A good way to begin your study of human communication is to examine your own beliefs about communication. Compare some common beliefs and the research and theory that bear on these beliefs:

> ▭ **Belief:** *The more you communicate, the better your communication will be.*
>
> *Research–Theory Finds: If you practice bad habits, you're more likely to grow less effective than to become more effective. Consequently, it's important to learn and practice the principles of effectiveness.*

> ▭ **Belief:** *When two people are in a close relationship, neither person should have to explicitly communicate needs and wants; the other person should know what these are.*
>
> *Research–Theory Finds: This assumption is at the heart of many interpersonal difficulties—people aren't mind readers, and to assume that they are merely sets up barriers to open and honest communication.*

> ▭ **Belief:** *Interpersonal or group conflict is a reliable sign that the relationship or group is in trouble.*
>
> *Research–Theory Finds: Conflict is inevitable in relationships and in groups. In fact, if the conflict is approached effectively, it may actually benefit everyone.*

> ▭ **Belief:** *Like good communicators, leaders are born, not made.*
>
> *Research–Theory Finds: Leadership, like communication and listening, is a learned skill. You'll develop leadership abilities as you learn the principles of human communication and those unique to group leadership.*

> ▭ **Belief:** *Fear of speaking in public is detrimental and must be eliminated.*
>
> *Research–Theory Finds: Most speakers are nervous; managing, not eliminating, the fear will enable you to become effective regardless of your current level of anxiety.*

Communication Models and Concepts

In early **models** (representations) or theories, the communication process was seen as linear. According to this *linear* view of communication, the speaker spoke and the listener listened. Communication was seen as proceeding in a relatively straight line. Speaking and listening were seen as taking place at different times; when you spoke, you didn't listen, and when you listened, you didn't speak (Figure 1.1).

The linear view was soon replaced with an *interactional* view, in which the speaker and listener were seen as exchanging turns at speaking and listening. For example, A spoke while B listened; then B spoke in response while A listened (Figure 1.2). The interactional model still viewed speaking and listening as separate acts that did not overlap and that were not performed at the same time by the same person.

A more satisfying view, the one held currently, sees communication as a *transactional* process in which each person serves simultaneously as speaker and listener. At the same time that you send messages, you're also receiving messages from your own communications and from the reactions of the other person (see Figure 1.3 on page 6).

The transactional viewpoint sees each person as both speaker and listener, as simultaneously communicating and receiving messages (Watzlawick, Beavin, & Jackson, 1967; Watzlawick, 1977, 1978; Barnlund, 1970). Also, the transactional view sees the elements of communication as interdependent (never independent). Each exists in relation to the others. A change in any one element of the process produces changes in the other elements. For example, if you're having a meeting with a group of your coworkers and your boss enters the room, this change in "audience" will lead to other changes. Perhaps you'll change what you're saying or how you're saying it. Regardless of what change is introduced, other changes will occur as a result.

In communication people act and react on the basis of the present situation as well as on the basis of their histories, past experiences, attitudes, cultural beliefs, and a host of related factors. One implication of this is that actions and reactions in communication are determined not only by what is said, but also by the way the person interprets what is said. Your responses to a movie, for example, don't depend solely on the words and pictures in the movies; they also depend on your previous experiences, present emotions, knowledge, physical well-being, and lots more. Another implication is that two people listening to the same message will often derive two very different meanings. Although the words and symbols are the same, each person interprets them differently.

Communication occurs when you send or receive messages and when you assign meaning to another person's signals. All human communication is distorted by noise, occurs within a context, has some effect, and involves some opportunity for feedback. We can expand the basic transactional model of communication by adding these essential elements, as shown in Figure 1.4 on page 6.

Communication Context

Communication exists in a context, and that context to a large extent determines the meaning of any verbal or nonverbal message. The same words or behaviors may have totally different meanings when they occur in different contexts. For example, the greeting "How are you?" means "Hello" to someone you pass regularly on the street

> **If** your lips would keep from slips
> Five things observe with care;
> To whom you speak, of whom you speak,
> And how, and when, and where. **"**
>
> —W. E. Norris

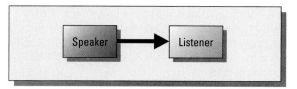

Figure 1.1

The Linear View of Human Communication
Communication researchers Paul Nelson and Judy Pearson (1996) suggest that you think of the speaker as passing a ball to the listener, who either catches it or fumbles it. Can you think of another analogy or metaphor for this linear view of communication?

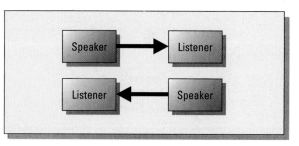

Figure 1.2

The Interactional View of Human Communication
In the interactional view, continuing with the ball-passing analogy, the speaker passes the ball to the listener, who then either passes the ball back or fumbles it (Nelson & Pearson, 1996). What other analogy would work here?

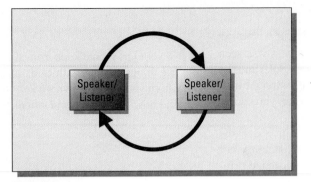

Figure 1.3

The Transactional View of Human Communication

In the transactional view, a complex ball game is under way. Each player can send and receive any number of balls at any time. Players are able to throw and catch balls at the same time (Nelson & Pearson, 1996). Can you think of other analogies for this view?

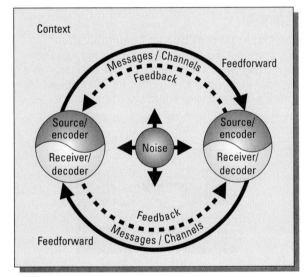

Figure 1.4

The Essentials of Human Communication

This is a general model of communication between two people and most accurately depicts interpersonal communication. It puts into visual form the various elements of the communication process. How would you revise this model to depict small group interaction? To depict public speaking?

but "Is your health improving?" to a friend in the hospital. A wink to an attractive person on a bus means something completely different from a wink that signifies a put-on or a lie. Divorced from the context, its impossible to tell what meaning was intended from just examining the signals.

The context will also influence what you say and how you say it. You communicate differently depending on the specific context you're in.

Contexts have at least four aspects: physical, cultural, social–psychological, and temporal on time.

- The *physical context* is the tangible or concrete environment, the room, park, or auditorium; you don't talk the same way at a noisy football game as you do at a quiet funeral.

- The *cultural context* involves the lifestyles, beliefs, values, behavior, and communication of a group; it is the rules of a group of people for considering something right or wrong.

- The *social–psychological context* has to do with the status relationships among speakers, the formality of the situation, the norms of a group or organization; you don't talk the same way in the cafeteria as you would at a formal dinner at your boss's house.

- The *temporal context* is a message's position within a sequence of events; you don't talk the same way after someone tells of the death of a close relative as you do after someone tells of winning the lottery.

These four contexts interact—each influences and is influenced by the others. For example, arriving late for a date (temporal context) may lead to changes in the degree of friendliness (social–psychological context), which would depend on the cultures of you and your date (cultural context) and may lead to changes in where you go on the date (physical context).

Sources–Receivers

Each person involved in communication is both a source (speaker) and a receiver (listener), hence the term *sources–receivers*. You send messages when you speak, write, gesture, or smile. You receive messages in listening, reading, seeing, smelling, and so on. At the same time that you send messages, you're also receiving messages: You're receiving your own messages (you hear yourself, you feel your own movements, you see many of your own gestures), and, at least in face-to-face communication, you're receiving the messages of the other person—visually, auditorily, or even through touch or smell. As you speak, you look at the person for responses—for approval, understanding, sympathy, agreement, and so on. As you decipher these nonverbal signals, you're performing receiver functions.

When you put your ideas into speech, you're putting them into a code, hence **encoding.** When you translate the sound waves (the speech signals) that impinge on your ears into ideas, you take them out of the code they're in, hence **decoding.** Thus, speakers or writers are referred to as *encoders* and listeners or readers as *decoders.* The linked term *encoding–decoding* emphasizes the fact that you perform these functions simultaneously.

Usually, you encode an idea into a code that the other person understands—for example, English, Spanish, or Indonesian, depending on the shared knowledge that you and your listener possess. At times, however, you may want to exclude others by speaking in a language that only one of your listeners knows or using jargon. Adults, when speaking of things they don't want children to understand, may spell out key words—a code that the young children don't yet understand. Computer communication enables you to do a similar thing. For example, when sending your credit card number to a vendor, you might send it in encrypted form, coded into a symbol system that others will not be able to understand (decode). Similarly, in chat groups you might write in a language that only certain of your readers will understand.

Messages

Communication **messages** take many forms and are transmitted or received through one or a combination of sensory organs. You communicate verbally (with words) and nonverbally (without words). Your meanings or intentions are conveyed with words (Chapter 5) and with the clothes you wear, the way you walk, and the way you smile (Chapter 6). Everything about you communicates a message.

Metamessages   A **metamessage** is a message that refers to another message; it is communication about communication. For example, remarks such as "This statement is false" or "Do you understand what I am trying to tell you?" refer to communication and are therefore "metacommunicational."

Nonverbal behavior may also be metacommunicational. Obvious examples include crossing your fingers behind your back or winking when telling a lie. On a less obvious level, consider the blind date. As you say, "I had a really nice time," your nonverbal messages—the lack of a smile, the failure to maintain eye contact, the extra long pauses—metacommunicate and contradict the verbal "really nice time," suggesting that you did not enjoy the evening. Nonverbal messages may also metacommunicate about other nonverbal messages. The individual who, on meeting a stranger, both smiles and extends a totally lifeless hand shows how one nonverbal behavior may contradict another.

Feedback Messages   When you send a message—say, in speaking to another person—you also hear yourself. That is, you get **feedback** from your own messages; you hear what you say, you feel the way you move, you see what you write. In addition to this self-feedback, you also get feedback from others. This feedback can take many forms. A frown or a smile, a yea or a nay, a pat on the back or a punch in the mouth are all types of feedback.

Feedback tells the speaker what effect he or she is having on listeners. On the basis of feedback—for example, boos or wild applause in public speaking—the speaker may adjust, modify, strengthen, deemphasize, or change the content or form of the messages. We'll return to this concept in the discussion of conversation (Chapter 7). Similarly, the message you get back from a robot-administered mailing list (Chapter 9) informing you that it doesn't understand your "plain English" is feedback. When the robot answers your "Please enter my subscription to the communication and gender mailing list" with "Command 'please' not recognized," it is giving you negative feedback—information that tells you something is wrong. Sometimes negative feedback comes with advice on how to correct the problem. A good example of this is the robot's "Commands must be in message BODY, not in HEADER."

Feedforward Messages   **Feedforward** is information you provide before sending your primary messages (Richards, 1951). Feedforward reveals something about the messages to come and includes, for example, the preface or table of contents of a book, the opening paragraph of a chapter, movie previews, magazine covers, and introductions in public speeches.

Giving Effective Feedback

Here are three situations in which you might want to give feedback. For each situation *(a)* indicate the kind of feedback that you would consider appropriate (positive or negative? person-focused or message-focused? immediate or delayed? low self-censorship or high self-censorship? supportive or critical?); then *(b)* write one or two sentences in which you express feedback that has the qualities you identified in *(a)*.

1. A colleague persists in talking explicitly about sex despite your previous and frequent objections.
2. A telemarketer—the fifth this evening—asks you to change your long-distance carrier.
3. A homeless person smiles at you on the street and asks for some change.

Feedforward may be verbal ("Wait until you hear this one") or nonverbal (a prolonged pause or hands motioning for silence to signal that an important message is about to be spoken). Or, as is most often the case, it is some combination of verbal and nonverbal. Feedforward may refer to the content of the message to follow (I'll tell you exactly what they said to each other") or to the form ("I won't spare you the gory details"). In e-mail, feedforward is given in the header, where the name of the sender, the date, and the subject of the message are identified. Caller ID is another good example of feedforward. As with feedback, feedforward is also considered in the discussion of conversation (Chapter 7).

Message Overload   Message overload, often called **information overload,** is one of the greatest obstacles to communication efficiency and has even been linked to health problems in corporate managers (Lee, 2000). The ease with which people can

 VIEWPOINT

How effective do you find the "feedback theory of relationships," which holds that in satisfying relationships feedback is positive, person focused, immediate, low in self-censorship, and supportive and that in unsatisfying relationships feedback is negative, self-focused, non-immediate, high in self-censorship, and critical? How well do you think this theory explains relationships with which you're familiar?

copy or forward e-mail and Internet messages to large numbers of recipients with a few taps of the keyboard has obviously contributed to message overload, as have the junk mail and spam that seem to multiply every day. Invariably, you must select certain messages to attend to and other messages to ignore. Today, for example, the American worker is exposed to more messages in one year than a person living in 1900 was in an entire lifetime. Today the average employee receives more than 50 e-mails daily. In one day the average manager sends and receives more than 100 documents.

One of the reasons message overload is a problem is that it absorbs an enormous amount of time. The more messages you have to deal with, the less time you have for the messages or tasks that are central to your purposes. Similarly, under conditions of message overload, errors are more likely—simply because you cannot devote the needed time to any one item. The more rushed you are, the more likely you are to make mistakes. Another problem is that message overload makes it difficult for you to determine efficiently which messages need immediate attention and which don't, which messages may be discarded and which must be retained.

Consider your own ways of dealing with message overload (Uris, 1986). Do you

- think before passing on messages, realizing that not all messages must be passed on, that not everyone needs to know everything?
- use the messages as they come to you and then throw them out? For example, do you write the date for a meeting on your calendar and then throw out the announcement or delete the e-mail?
- organize your messages? Have you created folders to help you store and retrieve the information you need quickly?
- get rid of extra copies? When you receive multiple copies, do you get rid of all but the one you need?
- distinguish between messages you should save and messages that are only cluttering up your space?

What Do You Say?

Message Overload: Several relatives have developed chain e-mail lists and send you virtually everything they come across as they surf the Internet. You need to stop this e-mail overload. *What do you say? To whom? Through what channel?*

Channel

The communication **channel** is the vehicle or medium through which messages pass. Communication rarely takes place over only one channel. Rather, two, three, or four channels may be used simultaneously. In face-to-face conversations, for example, you speak and listen (vocal channel), but you also gesture and receive signals visually (visual channel). You also emit and smell odors (olfactory channel) and often touch one another; this, too, is communication (tactile channel).

Another way to classify channels is by the means of communication. Thus, face-to-face contact, telephones, e-mail, movies, television, smoke signals, and telegraph all are types of channels.

At times one or more channels may be damaged. For example, in individuals who are blind, the visual channel is impaired and adjustments have to be made. Table 1.1 on page 10 gives you an idea of how such adjustments between blind and sighted persons can make communication more effective.

Noise

Noise interferes with your receiving a message someone is sending or with their receiving your message. Noise may be physical (others talking loudly, cars honking, illegible handwriting, "garbage" on your computer screen); physiological (hearing or visual impairment, articulation disorders); psychological (preconceived ideas, wandering thoughts); or semantic (misunderstood meanings). Technically, noise is anything that distorts the message, anything that prevents the receiver from receiving the message.

TABLE 1.1 *Interpersonal Communication Tips*

BETWEEN BLIND AND SIGHTED PEOPLE

People vary greatly in their visual abilities. Some people have unimpaired vision, some are partially sighted, and some are totally blind. Ninety percent of people who are "legally blind" have some vision. Everyone, however, has the same need for communication and information. Here are some tips for making communication between blind and sighted people more effective.

If you're the sighted person and are talking with a blind person:

1. Identify yourself; don't assume the blind person will recognize your voice.
2. Face the blind person; you'll be easier to hear. At the same time, don't shout. People who are visually impaired are not necessarily hearing impaired. Speak at your normal volume.
3. Because your gestures, eye movements, and facial expressions cannot be seen, encode into speech all the meanings you wish to communicate.
4. Use audible turn-taking cues. When you pass the role of speaker to a person who's visually impaired, don't rely on nonverbal cues; instead, say something like "Do you agree with that, Joe?"
5. Use normal vocabulary and discuss topics that you'd discuss with sighted people. Don't avoid words like see or look or even blind. Don't avoid discussing a television show or a painting or the way your new car looks; these are normal conversational topics for all people.
6. In guiding a person who is blind, follow these simple suggestions:
   a. If you want to offer assistance, ask first. Say, "Would you like me to hold your arm as we go upstairs?" instead of just grabbing the person.
   b. Identify obstacles before reaching them: "There are three steps coming up."
   c. When you have to leave, make sure the blind person is comfortable where he or she is. For example, ask the person if he or she would like to sit while you get the coffee.

If you're the blind person and are interacting with a sighted person:

1. Help the sighted person meet your special communication needs. If you want your surroundings described, ask. If you want the person to read the road signs, ask.
2. Be patient with the sighted person. Many people are nervous talking with people who are blind, feeling anxious about offending. Put them at ease in a way that also makes you more comfortable.

Sources: These suggestions were drawn from The Cincinnati Association for the Blind, http://www.cincyblind.org, and The Royal National Institute of the Blind, http://www.rnib.org, both acessed April 5, 2002.

A useful concept in understanding noise and its importance in communication is **signal-to-noise ratio.** In this term the word *signal* refers to information that you'd find useful, and *noise* refers to information that is useless (to you). So, for example, a mailing list or newsgroup that contains lots of useful information is high on signal and low on noise; one that contains lots of useless information is high on noise and low on signal.

Because messages may be visual as well as spoken, noise, too, may be visual. For example, sunglasses that prevent someone from seeing the nonverbal messages sent by your eyes can be considered noise, as can blurred type on a printed page. Table 1.2 identifies the four types of noise in more detail.

All communications contain noise. Noise can't be totally eliminated, but its effects can be reduced. Making your language more precise, sharpening your skills for sending and receiving nonverbal messages, and improving your listening and feedback skills are some ways to combat the influence of noise.

Effects

Communication always has some **effect** on those involved in the communication act. For every communication act, there is some consequence. For example, you may

TABLE 1.2 Four Types of Noise

One of the most important skills in communication is recognizing the types of noise and developing ways to combat them. Consider, for example, what kinds of noise occur in the classroom. What kinds of noise occur in your family communications? What kinds occur at work? What can you do to combat these kinds of noise?

TYPE OF NOISE	DEFINITION	EXAMPLES
Physical	Interference that is external to both speaker and listener and interferes with the physical transmission of the signal or message	Screeching of passing cars, hum of computer, sunglasses
Physiological	Physical barriers within the speaker or listener	Visual impairments, hearing loss, articulation problems, memory loss
Psychological	Cognitive or mental interference, biases, and stereotypes	Biases and prejudices in senders and receivers, closed-mindedness, inaccurate expectations, extreme emotionalism (anger, hate, love, grief)
Semantic	Assignment of different meanings by speaker and listener	Use of different languages, use of jargon or overly complex terms not understood by listener, dialectical differences in meaning

gain knowledge or learn how to analyze, synthesize, or evaluate something. These are intellectual or cognitive effects. You may acquire new feelings, attitudes, or beliefs or change existing ones (affective effects). You may learn new bodily movements, such as how to throw a curve ball, paint a picture, give a compliment, or express surprise (psychomotor effects).

Communication Competence

The term **communication competence** refers to your knowledge of how communication works and your ability to use communication effectively (Spitzberg & Cupach, 1989, 2002). Communication competence includes, for example, the knowledge that in certain contexts and with certain listeners, some messages and some ways of communicating are appropriate and effective and others are not.

What Do You Say?

Negative Communication Effects: An e-mail that you wrote to your instructor in anger (but never intended to send) was sent. You want to reduce the negative effects. *What do you say?*

Communicating ethically

Approaching Ethics

In making ethical decisions, you can take the position that ethics is objective or that it's subjective. An *objective view* claims that the morality of an act of communication is absolute and exists apart from the values or beliefs of any individual or culture; there are standards that apply to all people in all situations at all times. If lying, false advertising, using illegally obtained evidence, or revealing secrets you've promised to keep are unethical, then, according to the objective view, such behaviors are always unethical, regardless of the circumstances surrounding them or of the values and beliefs of the culture.

A *subjective view* claims that the ethics of communication depends on the particular culture's values and beliefs as well as on the particular circumstances. Thus, in a subjective view you might claim that lying to win votes or sell cigarettes is wrong, but that lying is ethical if the end result is positive—as when we try to make people feel better by telling them that they look great or that they will get well soon.

What Would You Do?

A colleague at work repeatedly takes home office supplies. He argues that because he is underpaid and was recently denied a well-deserved promotion, he's justified in taking additional compensation. You agree that he is underpaid and that he did deserve the promotion. He asks you if you think his behavior is unethical. What would someone say who took an objective view of ethics? What would someone say who took a subjective view? What would you say?

The more you know about communication, the more choices you'll have available for your day-to-day interactions. It's like learning vocabulary. The more vocabulary you know, the more ways you have for expressing yourself. In a similar way, the aim of this book is to increase your communicative competence and thus to give you a broad range of options to use in your own communications.

This text both presents information about communication theory and research and explains the skills and techniques for more effective communication. In addition, the other themes of this book will help you sharpen and increase your competence in a variety of ways. These themes, in addition to communication skills, are culture, critical thinking, ethics, power, and listening (see Figure 1.5).

- *Competence and culture:* Communication competence is culture specific; that is, the principles of effective communication vary from one culture to another, and what proves effective in one culture may prove ineffective in another. For example, in American culture you would call a person you wished to date three or four days in advance. In certain Asian cultures, you might call the person's parents weeks or even months in advance. Thus, discussions of cultural implications accompany all of the major topics considered in this text.

- *Competence and critical thinking:* The ability to think critically about the communication situations you face and the options for communicating that you have

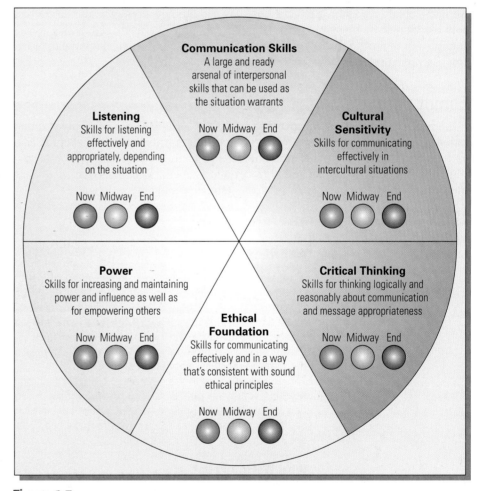

Figure 1.5

The Competent Communicator

Indicate how competent you feel you are in each of these six areas right now: Give yourself scores from 1 (little competence) to 100 (a great deal of competence). Return to this midway through the course and at the end of the course and record your scores on the diagram. Your scores should improve significantly.

Increasing and Decreasing Power

The power you wield is not static; it can be increased or decreased depending on what you do and don't do. For example, you can increase your physical power by lifting weights, your power in groups by learning the techniques of negotiation, and your persuasive power by mastering the principles of public speaking.

You can also decrease or lose power. Probably the most common way to lose power is by trying unsuccessfully to control another's behavior. For example, if you threaten someone with punishment and then fail to carry out your threat, you'll most likely lose power. Another way to lose power is to allow others to control you or to take unfair advantage of you. When you don't confront these power tactics in others, you lose power.

Enhancing Your Communication Power

Your dating partner has been making unreasonable demands on your time, asking that you do things that the partner could just as easily do. You want to put a stop to this, but you don't want to seem unwilling to do your share of the relationship work. What can you do that will eliminate this problem and increase your communication power? What would decrease your power?

available is crucial to your success and effectiveness. Consequently, opportunities for critical thinking and suggestions for thinking more critically in all communication situations are offered throughout this text.

- *Competence and ethics:* **Ethics** has been part of communication training for more than 2,000 years; *Essentials of Human Communication* follows in that tradition. There is a right-versus-wrong aspect to any and all communication acts, and this aspect is separate from that of effectiveness. For example, it might be effective to lie in selling a product, but most people would agree that it would not be ethical. Because of the central importance of ethics to all forms and functions of communication, Communicating Ethically boxes appear throughout this text.

- *Competence and power:* All communication transactions involve **power,** or the ability to control the behavior of others. In fact, you can look at the principles of communication covered in this text as principles of power—the power to speak your own mind, the power to influence a friend, the power to lead a group responsibly and efficiently, the power to get your point across to an audience. Because of the central importance of power in all forms of communication, Communicating with Power boxes appear in each chapter, highlighting the principles of power and posing cases that ask how you can increase your own communication power.

- *Competence and listening:* Communication is a two-way process; your ability to communicate effectively rests heavily on your ability to listen. An entire chapter, Chapter 4, is devoted to the principles and techniques of listening. In addition, each chapter contains a Listen to This box that connects listening with the content of the chapter and asks you to consider how you might apply listening skills to specific communication situations.

VIEWPOINT

A Gallup poll found that 80 percent of young adult women consider a spouse who can communicate his feelings more desirable than a spouse who earns a good living (http://www.gallup.com/content/default.asp?ci=4552&pg=1, accessed June 27, 2001). How important, compared to all the other factors you might take into consideration in choosing a life partner, is the ability to communicate? What specific communication skills would you consider "extremely important" in a partner?

Listening to Communicate

Listening is integral to all communication; it's a process that is coordinate with speaking. If you measured the importance of communication activities by the time you spent on them, then—according to the research studies available—listening would be your most important activity. Studies conducted from 1929 to 1980 showed that listening was the most often used form of communication. In a study conducted in 1929 (Rankin), listening occupied 45 percent of people's communication time. In a study of college students conducted in 1980 (Barker, Edwards, Gaines, Gladney, & Holley), listening also occupied the most time: 53 percent, compared to reading (17 percent), speaking (16 percent), and writing (14 percent). But in light of the widespread use of the Internet, these studies are now dated and their findings of limited value. Your communication patterns are very different from those of someone who grew up before home computers became common. However, anecdotal evidence (though certainly not conclusive in any way) suggests that listening still occupies a considerable portion of your communication time.

Applying Listening Skills

In what situations do you listen most effectively? In what situations do you listen less effectively? How might you improve your listening in situations in which your listening is not as effective as it might be?

Principles of Communication

Several principles are essential to an understanding of human communication in all its forms. These principles, as you'll see throughout the text, also have numerous practical implications for your own communication effectiveness. Let's look at each in detail.

Communication Is a Process of Adjustment

Communication can take place only to the extent that the communicators use the same system of signals (Pittenger, Hockett, & Danehy, 1960). You will be unable to communicate with another person to the extent that your language systems differ. In reality, however, no two people use identical signal systems, so this principle is relevant to all forms of communication. Parents and children, for example, not only have largely different vocabularies, but also may assign different meanings to the terms they do share. Different cultures, even when they use a common language, often have greatly different nonverbal communication systems. To the extent that these systems differ, meaningful and effective communication will not take place.

Part of the art of communication is identifying the other person's signals, learning how they're used, and understanding what they mean. Those in close relationships will realize that learning the other person's signals takes a great deal of time and often a great deal of patience. If you want to understand what another person means (by smiling, by saying "I love you," by arguing about trivia, by making self-deprecating comments) rather than just acknowledging what the other person says or does, you have to learn that person's system of signals.

This principle is especially important in intercultural communication. People from different cultures often use different signals—and sometimes use similar signals to mean quite different things. Focused eye contact means honesty and openness in much of the United States. But that same behavior may signify arrogance or disrespect in Japan and in many Hispanic cultures, particularly if engaged in by a youngster with someone significantly older. Figure 1.6 illustrates how the same signals can mean quite different things in other cultures.

> **" Important principles may and must be flexible. "**
>
> —Abraham Lincoln

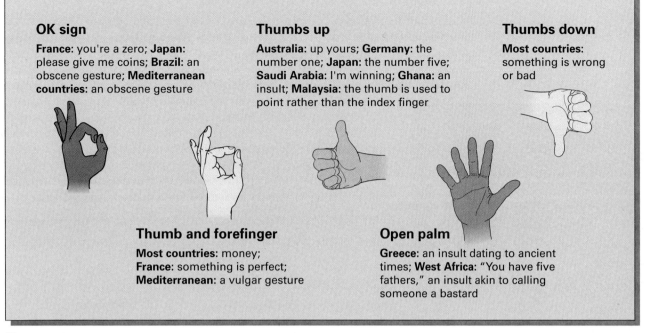

Figure **1.6**

Cultural Meanings of Gestures

Cultural differences in the meanings of nonverbal gestures are often significant. The over-the-head clasped hands that signify victory to an American may signify friendship to a Russian. To an American, holding up two fingers to make a V signifies victory or peace. To certain South Americans, however, it is an obscene gesture that corresponds to the American's extended middle finger. This figure highlights some additional nonverbal differences. Can you identify others?

Communication Accommodation An interesting theory revolving largely around adjustment is **communication accommodation theory.** This theory holds that speakers adjust to, or accommodate to, the speaking style of their listeners in order to gain, for example, social approval and greater communication efficiency (Giles, Mulac, Bradac, & Johnson, 1987). For example, when two people have a similar speech rate, they seem to be attracted more to each other than to those with dissimilar rates (Buller, LePoire, Aune, & Eloy, 1992). Speech rate similarity has also been associated with greater sociability and intimacy between communicators (Buller & Aune, 1992).

Similarly, the speaker who uses language intensity similar to that of his or her listeners is judged to have greater credibility than the speaker who uses different intensity (Aune & Kikuchi, 1993). Still another study found that roommates who had similar communication attitudes (both roommates were high in communication competence and willingness to communicate and low in verbal aggressiveness) were highest in roommate liking and satisfaction (Martin & Anderson, 1995). And in interethnic interactions, people who saw themselves as similar in communication styles were attracted to each other more than to those they perceived as having different communication styles (Lee & Gudykunst, 2001). Although accommodation theory has not been tested on computer communication, it would predict that styles of written communication in e-mail or chat groups would also evidence accommodation.

As you'll see throughout this text, communication characteristics are influenced greatly by culture (Albert & Nelson, 1993). Thus, the communication similarities that lead to attraction and more positive perceptions are more likely to be present in *intra*cultural communication than in *inter*cultural encounters. This may present an important (but not insurmountable) obstacle to intercultural communication.

Communication Is a Package of Messages

Communication normally occurs in "packages" of verbal and nonverbal behaviors or messages (Pittenger, Hockett, & Danehy, 1960). Usually, verbal and nonverbal behaviors reinforce or support each other. You don't usually express fear with words while the rest of your body relaxes. You don't normally express anger with your bodily posture while your face smiles. Your entire being works as a whole—verbally and nonverbally—to express your thoughts and feelings.

Usually, we pay little attention to the packaged nature of communication. But when the messages contradict each other—when the weak handshake belies the confident verbal greeting, when the nervous posture belies the focused stare—we notice. Invariably, we begin to question the communicator's sincerity and honesty. Consider, for example, how you would react to **mixed messages** such as these:

- "Even if I do fail the course, so what? I don't need it for graduation."
- "I haven't had a date in the last three years. People are jerks."

Communication Is Ambiguous

Some degree of **ambiguity** is present in all communication; in other words, to some degree all messages can be interpreted as having more than one possible meaning. When you express an idea, you never communicate your meaning exactly and totally; rather, you communicate your meaning with *some* accuracy—enough to give the other person a reasonably clear idea of what you mean. Sometimes, of course, you're less accurate than you anticipated, and your listener gets the wrong idea or gets offended. To reduce this inevitable uncertainty, you may qualify what you're saying, give an example, or ask, "Do you know what I mean?"

Like messages, relationships also contain elements of ambiguity or uncertainty. Consider your own close relationships and ask yourself the following questions. Answer using a six-point scale on which 1 = completely or almost completely *uncertain* and 6 = completely or almost completely *certain*. How certain are you about

1. what you can or cannot say to each other in this relationship?
2. whether or not you and your partner feel the same way about each other?
3. how you and your partner would describe this relationship?
4. the future of the relationship?

Very likely you were not able to respond with 6s for all four questions. These questions—taken from a relationship uncertainty scale (Knobloch & Solomon, 1999)—and similar others illustrate that you probably experience some degree of uncertainty about the norms that govern your relationship communication (question 1), the degree to which you each see the relationship in similar ways (question 2), the definition of the relationship (question 3), and the relationship's future (question 4).

You can look at the skills of communication presented throughout this text as techniques and strategies for reducing ambiguity: for making your meaning as clear as possible.

Communication Involves Content and Relationship Dimensions

Communication exists on at least two levels. A single message can refer to something external to both speaker and listener (for example, the weather) as well as to

VIEWPOINT

How would you describe your own ethnocentrism (the tendency to see your own culture as superior to others, cf. pp. 24–26) immediately after the events of September 11, 2001, and over the next several months? For example, did you become more ethnocentric after those events? Less ethnocentric? How would you describe your current level of ethnocentrism? How do political and social events influence your level of ethnocentrism?

What Do You Say?

Relationship Ambiguity: You've dated someone three times, and you'd like to invite your date to meet your parents. But you aren't sure how your date will interpret this invitation. *What do you say? In what context?*

the relationship between speaker and listener (for example, who is in charge). These two aspects are referred to as **content and relationship dimensions** of communication (Watzlawick, Beavin, & Jackson, 1967).

For example, let's say that a marketing manager at a Web design firm asks a worker to see him or her after the meeting. The content aspect of this request relates to what the manager wants the worker to do; namely, to see him or her after the meeting. The relationship aspect, however, has to do with the relationship between the manager and the worker; it states how the communication is to be dealt with. For example, the request indicates a status difference between the two parties: The manager can command the worker. If the worker commanded the manager, it would appear awkward and out of place—it would violate the normal relationship between manager and worker.

"It's not about the story. It's about Daddy taking time out of his busy day to read you the story."

Some research shows that women send more **relationship messages** than men; they talk more about relationships in general and about the present relationship in particular. Men engage in more content talk; they talk more about things external to the relationship (Wood, 1994; Pearson, West, & Turner, 1995).

Problems often result from failure to distinguish between the content and the relationship levels of communication. Consider a couple, Pat and Chris. Pat made plans to attend a rally with friends during the weekend without first asking Chris, and an argument has ensued. Both would probably have agreed that attending the rally was the right choice to make. Thus, the argument is not centered on the content level. The argument, instead, centers on the relationship level. Chris expected to be consulted about plans for the weekend. Pat, in not doing this, rejected this definition of the relationship.

Examine the following interchange and note how relationship considerations are ignored.

> **Pat:** I'm going to the rally tomorrow. The people at the health center are all going to voice their protest, and I'm going with them. [Pat focuses on the content and ignores any relational implications of the message.]
>
> **Chris:** Why can't we ever do anything together? [Chris responds primarily on a relational level and ignores the content implications of the message, expressing displeasure at being ignored in this decision.]
>
> **Pat:** We can do something together anytime; tomorrow's the day of the rally. [Again, Pat focuses almost exclusively on the content.]

Here is essentially the same situation, but with something added: sensitivity to relationship messages.

> **Pat:** The people at the center are going to the rally tomorrow and I'd like to go with them. Would that be all right with you? [Although Pat focuses on content, there is always an awareness of the relational dimensions by asking if this would be a problem. Pat also shows this in expressing a desire rather than a decision to attend this rally.]
>
> **Chris:** That sounds great, but I'd really like to do something together tomorrow. [Chris focuses on the relational dimension but also acknowledges Pat's content orientation. Note, too, that Chris does not respond defensively.]
>
> **Pat:** How about meeting me at Luigi's for dinner after the rally? [Pat responds to the relational aspect—without abandoning the desire to attend the rally. Pat tries to negotiate a solution that will meet the needs of both parties.]
>
> **Chris:** That sounds great. I'm dying for spaghetti and meatballs. [Chris responds to both messages, approving of both Pat's attending the rally and of their dinner date.]

What Do You Say?

Content and Relationship Messages: One of your friends frequently belittles you, though always in a playful way. Playful or not, it's embarrassing, and you're determined to stop the behavior—but you don't want to lose the friendship. *What do you say? Through what channel?*

Communication Is Punctuated

Communication events are continuous transactions that have no clear-cut beginning or ending. As a participant in or an observer of communication, you divide this continuous, circular process into causes and effects, or stimuli and responses. The **punctuation of communication** is the segmenting of the continuous stream of communication into smaller pieces (Watzlawick, Beavin, & Jackson, 1967). Some of these pieces you label causes (or stimuli) and others effects (or responses).

Consider this example: The manager of a local supermarket lacks interest in the employees, seldom offering any suggestions for improvement or any praise for jobs well done. The employees are apathetic and morale is low. Each action (the manager's lack of involvement and the employees' low morale) stimulates the other. Each serves as the stimulus for the other but there is no identifiable initial stimulus. Each event may be seen as a stimulus or as a response.

To understand what the other person in an interaction means from his or her point of view, see the sequence of events as punctuated by the other person. Further, recognize that punctuation does not reflect what exists in reality. Rather, it reflects the unique, subjective, and fallible perception of each individual (the other person as well as yourself).

Communication Is Purposeful

You communicate for a purpose; some motivation leads you to communicate. When you speak or write, you're trying to send some message and trying to accomplish some goal. Although different cultures emphasize different purposes and motives (Rubin, Fernandez-Collado, & Hernandez-Sampieri, 1992), five general purposes seem relatively common to most if not all forms of communication:

- to learn: to acquire knowledge of others, the world, and yourself
- to relate: to form relationships with others, to interact with others as individuals
- to help: to assist others by listening, offering solutions
- to influence: to strengthen or change the attitudes or behaviors of others
- to play: to enjoy the experience of the moment

Popular belief and recent research both agree that men and women use communication for different purposes. Generally, as mentioned earlier, men seem to communicate more for information and women more for relationship purposes (Gamble & Gamble, 2003; Stewart, Cooper, Stewart, with Friedley, 2003). Gender differences also occur in computer communication. For example, women users of ICQs (Internet search and chat tools—ICQ stands for "I seek you") chat more for relationship reasons; men chat more to play and to relax (Leung, 2001).

You can gain a different perspective on communication purposes by looking at Figure 1.7, which integrates the five general purposes with the motives that energize your communication and the results you hope to achieve when you communicate.

Communication Is Inevitable, Irreversible, and Unrepeatable

Communication is inevitable; that is, in interactional situations it is always taking place, even when a person may not intend or want to communicate. To understand the **inevitability** of communication, think about a student sitting in the back of a classroom with an expressionless face, perhaps staring out the window. Although the student might claim not to be communicating with the instructor, the instructor may derive a variety of messages from this behavior. Perhaps the instructor assumes that the student lacks interest, is bored, or is worried about something. In any event, the

www.researchnavigator.com

Investigate Key Terms: Investigate one of the key terms discussed in this chapter (for example, encoding, decoding, competence, messages, feedback, feedforward, channel, noise, context, purpose, ethics, or mindfulness). What additional insights can you provide?

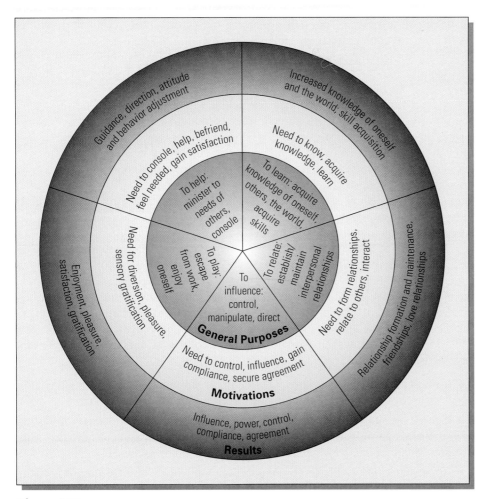

Figure **1.7**

The Multipurpose Nature of Human Communication
The innermost circle contains the general purposes of communication. The middle circle contains the motivations. The outer circle contains the results that you might hope to achieve by engaging in communication. A similar typology of purposes comes from research on motives for communicating. In a series of studies, Rubin and her colleagues (Graham, 1994; Graham, Barbato, & Perse, 1993; Rubin, Fernandez-Collado, & Hernandez-Sampieri, 1992; Rubin & Martin, 1994, 1998; Rubin, Perse, & Barbato, 1988; and Rubin & Rubin, 1992) have identified six primary motives for communication: pleasure, affection, inclusion, escape, relaxation, and control. How do these compare to the five purposes discussed here?

teacher is receiving messages even though the student may not intentionally be sending any (Watzlawick, Beavin, & Jackson, 1967; Motley, 1990a, 1990b; Bavelas, 1990). This does not mean that all behavior is communication. For instance, if the student looked out the window and the teacher didn't notice, no communication would have taken place. The two people must be in an interactional situation and the behavior must be perceived for the principle of inevitability to operate.

Notice, too, that when you're in an interactional situation, you cannot *not* respond to the messages of others. For example, if you notice someone winking at you, you must respond in some way. Even if you don't respond actively or openly, your lack of response is itself a response, and it communicates.

Another all-important attribute of communication is its **irreversibility.** Once you say something or click "send" on your e-mail, you cannot uncommunicate the message. You can, of course, try to reduce its effects. You can say, for example, "I really didn't mean what I said." But regardless of how hard you try to negate or reduce

❝ Never say anything on the phone that you wouldn't want your mother to hear at your trial. ❞

—Sydney Biddle Barrows

the effects of a message, the message itself, once it has been received, cannot be taken back. In a public speaking situation in which the speech is recorded or broadcast, inappropriate messages may have national or even international effects. Here, attempts to reverse what someone has said (for example, efforts to offer clarification) often have the effect of further publicizing the original statement.

In face-to-face communication the actual signals (nonverbal messages and sound waves in the air) are evanescent; they fade almost as they are uttered. Some written messages, especially computer-mediated messages such as those sent through e-mail, are unerasable. E-mails among employees in large corporations or even at colleges are often stored on disk or tape and may not be considered private by managers and administrators (Sethna, Barnes, Brust, & Kaye, 1999). Much litigation is currently proceeding using the evidence of racist or sexist e-mails that senders thought had been erased but hadn't. Currently, e-mails and entire hard drives are finding their way into divorce proceedings.

As a result of the permanency of electronic communication, you may wish to be cautious in these messages. E-mail is probably your most common form of computer communication, but these cautions apply to all forms of electronic communication, including newsgroup postings, instant messages, and website messages. In an organizational context, it's important to find out what the e-mail policy of the company is. According to one survey 75 percent of companies have written e-mail policies, and less than half train their workers in e-mail policies (Coombes, 2003). Several key points to remember:

- E-mails are difficult to destroy. Often e-mails you think you deleted will remain on servers and workstations and may be retrieved by a clever hacker.

- E-mails may easily be made public; the ease of forwarding e-mails or of posting comments on websites make it especially important that you consider that what you intend for one person may actually be received by many.

- E-mails are not privileged communication and can easily be used against you, especially in the workplace. Criticism of others may one day be turned against you. "Jokes" that you pass on to a friend may one day be used as evidence of a hostile working environment and cost your employer millions, as happened at Chevron a few years ago.

- E-mails provide permanent records; they make it impossible for you to say, for example, "That's not exactly what I said"—because it will be exactly what you said, right there in black and white.

- E-mail files may be accessed by others, whether by a nosy colleague at the next desk or by a visiting neighbor, and then sent to others.

In all forms of communication, because of irreversibility (and unerasability), be careful not to say things you may be sorry for later. Especially in conflict situations, when tempers run high, avoid saying things you may later wish to withdraw. Commitment messages—"I love you" messages and their variants—also need to be monitored. Messages that you considered private but that might be interpreted as sexist, racist, or homophobic may later be retrieved by others and create all sorts of problems for you and your organization. In group and public communication situations, when the messages are received by many people, it's especially crucial to recognize the irreversibility of communication.

Finally, communication is *unrepeatable*. A communication act can never be duplicated. The reason is simple: Everyone and everything is constantly changing. As a result, you can never recapture the exact same situation, frame of mind, or relationship dynamics that defined a previous communication act. For example, you can never repeat meeting someone for the first time, comforting a grieving friend, leading a small group for the first time, or giving a public speech. You can never replace an initial impression; you can only try to counteract this initial (and perhaps negative) impression by going through the motions again.

What Do You Say?

Irreversibility: Without thinking, you make some culturally insensitive remarks and immediately notice lots of nonverbal negative feedback. You want to explain that you're really not the kind of person who normally talks this way. *What do you say?*

Culture and Human Communication

Culture consists of the beliefs, ways of behaving, and artifacts of a group. By definition, culture is transmitted through communication and learning rather than through genes.

A walk through any large city, many small towns, or just about any college campus will convince you that the United States is largely a collection of lots of different cultures (Figure 1.8 on page 22). These cultures coexist somewhat separately, but all influence one another. This coexistence has led some researchers to refer to these cultures as cocultures (Shuter, 1990; Samovar & Porter, 1991; Jandt, 2003).

Gender is considered a cultural variable largely because cultures teach boys and girls different attitudes, beliefs, values, and ways of communicating and relating to one another. This means that you act like a man or a woman in part because of what your culture has taught you about how men and women should act. This is not, of course, to deny that biological differences also play a role in the differences between male and female behavior. In fact, research continues to uncover biological roots of behavior we once thought was entirely learned—acting happy or shy, for example (McCroskey, 1997).

Yet we're living in a time of changing gender roles. Many men, for example, are doing a great deal more housekeeping chores and caring for their children. More obvious perhaps is that many women are becoming much more visible in fields once occupied exclusively by men—politics, law enforcement, the military, and the clergy are just some examples. And, of course, women are increasingly entering corporate executive ranks; the glass ceiling may not have disappeared, but it has cracked.

Because your communication is heavily influenced by the culture in which you were raised, culture is highly relevant to communication, and a cultural perspective serves numerous important purposes.

> **"** I am not an Athenian or a Greek, but a citizen of the world. **"**
>
> —Socrates

The Importance of Culture

There are lots of reasons for the cultural emphasis you'll find in this book.

Demographic Changes Most obvious, perhaps, are the vast demographic changes taking place throughout the United States. Whereas at one time the United States was largely a country populated by Europeans, it's now a country greatly influenced by the enormous number of new citizens from Latin and South America,

Web Explorations

A variety of exercises and self-tests will help you better understand the concepts and principles discussed in this chapter (www.ablongman.com/devito): (1) Comparing Communication Channels, (2) How Can You Give Effective Feedforward? (3) Analyzing an Interaction, (4) How Do You Respond to Contradictory Messages? (5) Cultural Beliefs, (6) From Culture to Gender, and (7) Cultural Identities.

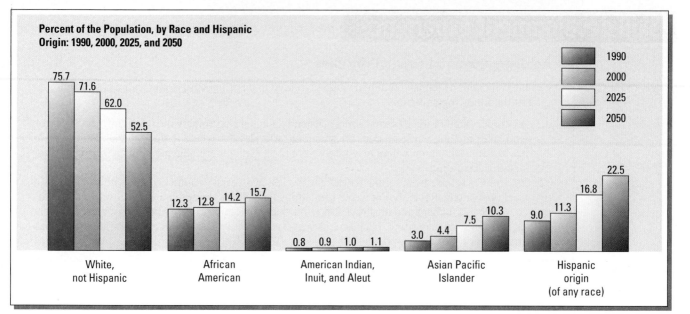

Percent of the Population, by Race and Hispanic Origin: 1990, 2000, 2025, and 2050

Legend:
- 1990
- 2000
- 2025
- 2050

White, not Hispanic: 75.7, 71.6, 62.0, 52.5
African American: 12.3, 12.8, 14.2, 15.7
American Indian, Inuit, and Aleut: 0.8, 0.9, 1.0, 1.1
Asian Pacific Islander: 3.0, 4.4, 7.5, 10.3
Hispanic origin (of any race): 9.0, 11.3, 16.8, 22.5

Figure 1.8

The Faces of the Nation

This figure shows the percentages of the U.S. population made up of various ethnic groups in 1990 and 2000 and the projections for the years 2025 and 2050 (U.S. Bureau of the Census, 2001). It's important to realize that within each group there are also wide cultural variations. Whites from Sweden are culturally quite different from whites from Greece or Russia, and Asians from Japan are culturally quite different from those from China or Korea. To complicate matters even further, not all Japanese or all Chinese or all Koreans are culturally similar. There are wide variations within each country, just as there are cultural differences between whites from, say, Manhattan and rural Tennessee. Visit one of the population websites and examine the cultural makeup of your state or county (www.census.gov). How do the figures for your state or county compare to those presented here for the country as a whole?

Africa, and Asia. This is especially true on college and university campuses. With these changes have come different customs and the need to understand and adapt to new ways of looking at communication. For example, consider health care workers and patients. Each group needs to understand how the other communicates about illness, sees ways to prevent health problems, and views taking medication. Police officers and civilians need to understand each other's views of "disorderly conduct," "the right of assembly," and "free speech."

Sensitivity to Cultural Differences   As a people we've become increasingly sensitive to cultural differences. U.S. society has moved from an assimilationist perspective (the idea that people should leave their native culture behind and adapt to their new culture) to a view that values cultural diversity (people should retain their native cultural ways). And with some notable exceptions—hate speech, racism, sexism, homophobia, and classism come quickly to mind—we're more concerned with saying the right thing and ultimately with developing a society in which all cultures can coexist and enrich each other. At the same time, the ability to interact effectively with members of other cultures often translates into financial gain and increased employment opportunities and advancement prospects.

Economic Interdependence   Today, most countries are economically dependent on one another. Our economic lives depend on our ability to communicate effectively across cultures. Similarly, our political well-being depends in great part on that of other cultures. Political unrest in any part of the world—Africa, Eastern Europe,

Understanding Cultural Beliefs

Here are five topics about which many people have strong cultural beliefs: *the nature of God, the importance of family, the rules of sexual appropriateness, the role of education,* and *the importance of money*. For any one, two, or three of these beliefs, try to answer these questions:

- Who taught you the belief? How did they teach it to you?
- When and where were you taught this?
- Why do you suppose you were taught this? What motives led your "teachers" to pass on this belief to you?

or the Middle East, to take a few examples—affects our own security. Intercultural communication and understanding now seem more crucial than ever.

Communication Technology   The rapid spread of communication technology has brought foreign and sometimes very different cultures right into our living rooms. News from foreign countries is commonplace. You see nightly—in vivid color—what is going on in remote countries. Technology has made intercultural communication easy, practical, and inevitable. Daily, the media bombard you with evidence of racial tensions, religious disagreements, sexual bias, and, in general, the problems caused when intercultural communication fails. And, of course, the Internet has made intercultural communication as easy as writing a note on your computer. You can now communicate by e-mail just as easily with someone in Europe or Asia, for example, as with someone in another city or state.

The Aim of a Cultural Perspective

Because culture permeates all forms of communication, it's necessary to understand its influences if you're to understand how communication works and master its skills. As illustrated throughout this text, culture influences communications of all types (Moon, 1996). It influences what you say to yourself and how you talk with friends, lovers, and family in everyday conversation. It influences how you interact in groups and how much importance you place on the group versus the individual. It influences the topics you talk about and the strategies you use in communicating information or in persuading. And it influences how you use the media and how much credibility you attribute to them.

A cultural emphasis helps you distinguish what is universal (true for all people) from what is relative (true for people in one culture but not for people in other cultures) (Matsumoto, 1991). The principles for communicating information and for changing listeners' attitudes, for example, will vary from one culture to another. If you're to understand communication, you need to know how its principles vary and how they must be qualified and adjusted on the basis of cultural differences. Success in communication—on your job and in your social life—will depend on your ability to communicate effectively with others who are culturally different from yourself.

Cultural differences exist across the communication spectrum—from the way you use eye contact to the way you develop or dissolve a relationship (Chang & Holt, 1996). But these differences should not blind you to the great number of similarities among even the most widely separated cultures. Close interpersonal relationships, for example, are common in all cultures, although they may be entered into for very different reasons by members of different cultures. Further, when reading about cultural differences, remember that they are usually matters of degree. Thus, for example,

> **"** From the moment of his birth the customs into which [a person] is born shape his experience and behavior. By the time he can talk, he is the little creature of his culture. **"**
>
> —Ruth Benedict

most cultures value honesty, but not all value it to the same extent. The advances in media and technology and the widespread use of the Internet, among other factors, are influencing cultures and cultural change and are perhaps homogenizing cultures, lessening intercultural differences and increasing similarities. They're also Americanizing various cultures—because the dominant values and customs evidenced in the media and on the Internet are in large part American, a product of the United States' current dominance in both media and technology.

This book's emphasis on cultural understanding does not imply that you should accept all cultural practices or that all cultural practices are equal (Hatfield & Rapson, 1996). For example, cockfighting, foxhunting, and bullfighting are parts of the cultures of some Latin American countries, England, and Spain, respectively; but you need not find these activities acceptable or equal to cultural practices in which animals are treated kindly. Further, a cultural emphasis does not imply that you have to accept or follow even the practices of your own culture. For example, even if the majority in your culture find cockfighting acceptable, you need not agree with or follow the practice. Similarly, you can reject your culture's values and beliefs; its religion or political system; or its attitudes toward the homeless, the disabled, or the culturally different. Of course, going against your culture's traditions and values is often very difficult. Still, it's important to realize that culture influences but does not determine your values or behavior. Often, for example, personality factors (your degree of assertiveness, extroversion, or optimism, for example) will prove more influential than culture (Hatfield & Rapson, 1996).

Ethnic Identity and Ethnocentrism

As you learn your culture's ways, you develop an **ethnic identity,** a commitment to the beliefs and philosophy of your culture (Chung & Ting-Toomey, 1999). The degree to which you identify with your cultural group can be measured by your responses to measures such as the list below (from Ting-Toomey, 1981). Using a five-point scale from 1 = strongly disagree to 5 = strongly agree, indicate how true of you the following statements are:

- I am increasing my involvement in activities with my ethnic group.
- I involve myself in causes that will help members of my ethnic group.
- It feels natural being part of my ethnic group.
- I have spent time trying to find out more about my own ethnic group.
- I am happy to be a member of my ethnic group.
- I have a strong sense of belonging to my ethnic group.
- I often talk to other members of my group to learn more about my ethnic culture.

High scores (say, 5s and 4s) indicate a strong commitment to your culture's values and beliefs; low numbers (1s and 2s) indicate a relatively weak commitment.

A different type of cultural identification is ethnocentrism. Before reading about this important concept, examine your own cultural thinking by taking the self-test below.

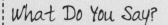

Test Yourself

How Ethnocentric Are You?

INSTRUCTIONS: Here are 18 statements representing your beliefs about your culture. For each statement indicate how much you agree or disagree, using the following scale: Strongly agree = 5; agree = 4; neither agree nor disagree = 3; disagree = 2; and strongly disagree = 1.

What Do You Say?

Ethnocentrism: Your friends are extremely ethnocentric, never acknowledging that other cultures have any value. You want to show them that their ethnocentrism is getting in the way of their learning and profiting from the contributions of other cultures. *What do you say?*

_____ ❶ Most cultures are backward compared to my culture.

_____ ❷ My culture should be the role model for other cultures.

_____ ❸ Lifestyles in other cultures are just as valid as those in my culture.

_____ ❹ Other cultures should try to be like my culture.

_____ ❺ I'm not interested in the values and customs of other cultures.

_____ ❻ People in my culture could learn a lot from people in other cultures.

_____ ❼ Most people from other cultures just don't know what's good for them.

_____ ❽ I have little respect for the values and customs of other cultures.

_____ ❾ Most people would be happier if they lived like people in my culture.

_____ ❿ People in my culture have just about the best lifestyles of anywhere.

_____ ⓫ Lifestyles in other cultures are not as valid as those in my culture.

_____ ⓬ I'm very interested in the values and customs of other cultures.

_____ ⓭ I respect the values and customs of other cultures.

_____ ⓮ I do not cooperate with people who are different.

_____ ⓯ I do not trust people who are different.

_____ ⓰ I dislike interacting with people from different cultures.

_____ ⓱ Other cultures are smart to look up to my culture.

_____ ⓲ People from other cultures act strange and unusual when they come into my culture.

HOW DID YOU DO? This test gave you the opportunity to examine some of your own cultural beliefs—particularly those cultural beliefs that contribute to ethnocentrism. The person low in ethnocentrism would have high scores (4s and 5s) for items 3, 6, 12, and 13 and low scores (1s and 2s) for all the others. The person high in ethnocentrism would have low scores for items 3, 6, 12, and 13 and high scores for all the others.

WHAT WILL YOU DO? Use this test to bring your own cultural beliefs to consciousness so you can examine them logically and objectively. Ask yourself if your beliefs are productive and will help you achieve your professional and social goals, or if they're counterproductive and will actually hinder your achieving your goals.

Source: This test is taken from James W. Neuliep, Michelle Chaudoir, & James C. McCroskey (2001). A cross-cultural comparison of ethnocentrism among Japanese and United States college students. _Communication Research Reports, 18_ (Spring), 137–146.

As you've probably gathered from taking this test, **ethnocentrism** is the tendency to see others and their behaviors through your own cultural filters, often as distortions of your own behaviors. It's the tendency to evaluate the values, beliefs, and behaviors of your own culture as superior and as more positive, logical, and natural than those of other cultures. Although ethnocentrism may give you pride in your own culture and its achievements and encourage you to sacrifice for the culture, it also may lead you to see other cultures as inferior and may make you unwilling to profit from the contributions of other cultures. For example, recent research shows a "substantial relationship" between ethnocentrism and homophobia (Wrench & McCroskey, 2003).

Ethnocentrism exists on a continuum. People are not either ethnocentric or non-ethnocentric; rather, most are somewhere between these polar opposites. And, of

www.researchnavigator.com

Find Answers: Try finding answers to one of the following questions or design a research study to answer it: Are communication skills related to relationship success (as a friend, lover, or parent)? How is communication applicable to your own profession? Do men and women communicate in the same way?

course, your degree of ethnocentrism often varies depending on the group on which you focus. For example, if you're Greek American, you may have a low degree of ethnocentrism when dealing with Italian Americans but a high degree when dealing with Turkish Americans or Japanese Americans. Your degree of ethnocentrism (and we're all ethnocentric to at least some degree) will influence your communication in all its forms, as we'll see throughout this text.

Summary of Concepts and Skills

This chapter considered the nature of communication, its major components, and some major communication principles.

1. Communication is transactional. Communication is a process of interrelated parts.
2. Communication is the act, by one or more persons, of sending and receiving messages that are distorted by noise, occur within a context, have some effect (and some ethical dimension), and provide some opportunity for feedback.
3. The essentials of communication—the elements present in every communication act—are context (physical, cultural, social–psychological, and temporal), source–receiver, message, channel, noise (physical, psychological, and semantic), sending or encoding processes, receiving or decoding processes, feedback and feedforward, effect, and competence, including ethics.
4. Communication messages may vary in form and may be sent and received through any combination of sensory organs. Communication messages may also metacommunicate—communicate about other messages. The communication channel is the medium through which the messages are sent.
5. *Feedback* refers to messages or information that is sent back to the source. It may come from the source itself or from the receiver. *Feedforward* messages are communications that preface other messages.
6. Noise is anything that distorts the message; it is present to some degree in every communication.
7. Communication ethics—the moral rightness or wrongness of a message—is an integral part of every effort to communicate.
8. Communication is a process of adjustment in which each person must adjust his or her signals to the understanding of the other if meaning is to be transmitted. In fact, communication accommodation theory holds that people imitate the speaking style of the other person as a way of gaining social approval.
9. Normally, communication is a package of signals, each reinforcing the other. When signals oppose each other, contradictory messages are sent.
10. Communication and relationships are always—in part—ambiguous.
11. Communication involves both content and relationship dimensions.
12. Communication sequences are punctuated for processing. Individuals divide the communication sequence into stimuli and responses in different ways.
13. Communication is purposeful. Through communication, you learn, relate, help, influence, and play.
14. In any interactional situation, communication is inevitable (you cannot not communicate, nor can you not respond to communication), irreversible (you cannot take back messages), and unrepeatable (you cannot exactly repeat messages).
15. Culture permeates all forms of communication, and intercultural communication is becoming more and more frequent as the United States becomes home to a variety of cultures and does business around the world.
16. Ethnocentrism, existing on a continuum, is the tendency to evaluate the beliefs, attitudes, and values of our own culture positively and those of other cultures negatively.

Several important communication skills emphasized in this chapter are presented here in summary form (as they are in every chapter). These skill checklists don't include all the skills covered in the chapter but rather are representative of the most important skills. Check your ability to apply these skills. You will gain the most from this brief experience if you think carefully about each skill and try to identify instances from your recent communications in which you did or did not act on the basis of the specific skill. Use the following rating scale: 1 = almost always; 2 = often; 3 = sometimes; 4 = rarely; and 5 = hardly ever.

_____ 1. I'm sensitive to contexts of communication. I recognize that changes in physical, cultural, social–psychological, and temporal contexts will alter meaning.

_____ 2. I look for meaning not only in words, but also in nonverbal behaviors.

_____ 3. I am sensitive to the feedback that I give to others and that others give to me.

_____ 4. I combat the effects of the various types of physical, psychological, and semantic noise that distort messages.

_____ 5. Because communication is a package of signals, I use my verbal and nonverbal messages to reinforce rather than to contradict each other; and I respond to contradictory messages by identifying and openly discussing the dual meanings communicated.

_____ 6. I listen to the relational messages that I and others send and respond to the relational messages of others to increase meaningful interaction.

_____ 7. I actively look for the punctuation patterns that I and others use in order to better understand the meanings communicated.

_____ 8. Because communication is transactional, I recognize the mutual influences of all elements and the fact that messages are sent and received simultaneously by each speaker/listener.

_____ 9. Because communication is purposeful, I look carefully at both the speaker's and the listener's purposes.

_____ 10. Because communication is inevitable, irreversible, and unrepeatable, I look carefully for hidden meanings, am cautious in communicating messages that I may later wish to withdraw, and am aware that any communication act occurs but once.

_____ 11. I am sensitive to cultural variation and differences, and I see my own culture's teachings and those of other cultures without undue bias.

Key Word Quiz

Write T for statements that are true and F for those that are false. For statements that are false, replace the italicized term with the correct term.

_____ 1. *Intrapersonal communication* is communication with yourself.

_____ 2. The tendency to see others and their behaviors through your own cultural filters and to evaluate your cultural values and beliefs as more positive than those of other cultures is known as *ethnocentrism*.

_____ 3. The process of putting ideas into a code—for example, thinking of an idea and then describing it in words—is known as *decoding*.

_____ 4. The knowledge of how communication works and the ability to use communication effectively is called *communication competence*.

_____ 5. Messages that refer to other messages are called *metamessages*.

_____ 6. The messages you get back from your own messages and from the responses of others to what you communicate are known as *feedforward*.

_____ 7. The aspect of communication that refers to matters external to both speaker and listener is known as the *relationship dimension* of communication.

_____ 8. The ways in which the sequence of communication is divided up into, say, causes and effects or stimuli and responses is known as *punctuation*.

_____ 9. The view of communication that sees each person as taking both speaker and listener roles simultaneously is an *interactional* one.

_____ 10. Interpersonal communication is *inevitable, reversible,* and *unrepeatable.*

Answers: TRUE: 1, 2, 4, 5, 8; FALSE: 3 (*encoding*), 6 (*feedback*), 7 (*content communication*), 9 (*transactional*), 10 (*irreversible*)

2 The Self in Human Communication

Chapter Concepts	Chapter Skills
This chapter introduces the self and explains how your self-concept, self-awareness, and self-disclosures work in communication.	After completing this chapter, you should be able to:
Self-Concept	communicate with an understanding of your self-concept, your strengths and weaknesses.
Self-Awareness	increase your own self-awareness.
Self-Disclosure	evaluate the costs and rewards of self-disclosure and regulate your disclosures accordingly.

In all communications, the most important part is you. Who you are and how you see yourself influence the way you communicate and how you respond to others. In this chapter we explore the self: the self-concept and how it develops; self-awareness and ways to increase it; and self-disclosure, or communication that reveals who you are. Another aspect of the self is **self-esteem,** or the value you place on yourself. Self-esteem is covered in the "Listening to Yourself" box, the "Power through Affirmation" box, and the ViewPoint on page 33.

❝ No matter what else human beings may be communicating about, or may think they are communicating about, they are always communicating about themselves, about one another, and about the immediate context of the communication. **❞**

—R. Pittinger, Charles Hockett, and John Danehy

Self-Concept

Your self-concept is your image of who you are. It's how you perceive yourself: your feelings and thoughts about your strengths and weaknesses, your abilities and limitations. Self-concept develops from the image that others have of you, comparisons between yourself and others, your cultural experiences, and your evaluation of your own thoughts and behaviors (Figure 2.1 on page 30).

Others' Images of You

If you wished to see how your hair looked, you'd probably look in a mirror. But what would you do if you wanted to see how friendly or how assertive you are? According to the concept of the **looking-glass self** (Cooley, 1922), you'd look at the image of yourself that others reveal to you through the way they communicate with you.

Of course, you would not look to just anyone. Rather, you would look to those who are most significant in your life—to your *significant others,* such as your friends and romantic partners. If these significant others think highly of you, you will see a positive self-image reflected in their behaviors; if they think little of you, you will see a more negative image.

Comparisons with Others

Another way you develop a self-concept is to compare yourself with others: to engage in **social comparison,** most often with your peers (Festinger, 1954). For example, after an exam, you probably want to know how you performed relative to the other students in your class. This gives you a clearer idea of how effectively you performed. If you play on a baseball team, it's important to know your batting average in comparison with the batting average of others on the team. You gain a different perspective when you see yourself in comparison to your peers.

❝ Even when we are quite alone, how often do we think with pleasure or pain of what others think of us—of their imagined approbation or disapprobation. **❞**

—Charles Darwin

Figure 2.1

The Sources of Self-Concept
This diagram depicts the four sources of self-concept, the four contributors to how you see yourself. As you read about self-concept, consider the influence of each factor throughout your life. Which factor influenced you most as a preteen? Which influences you most now? Which will influence you most 25 or 30 years from now?

Others' Images
How do significant others see me?

Your Self-Interpretations and Self-Evaluations
How do I evaluate my own feelings and behaviors?

Self-Concept

Social Comparisons
How do I compare to my peers?

Cultural Teachings
How do I fulfill the teachings of my culture?

Cultural Teachings

Through your parents, your teachers, and the media, your culture instills in you a variety of beliefs, values, and attitudes about such things as success (how you define it and how you should achieve it); the relevance of a person's religion, race, or nationality; and the ethical principles people should follow in business and in their personal lives. These teachings provide benchmarks against which you can measure yourself. Your ability to, for example, achieve what your culture defines as success, will contribute to a positive **self-concept.** Your failure to achieve what your culture teaches will contribute to a negative self-concept.

Skill development experience

Expanding Intercultural Openness

Select a specific culture (national, racial, or religious) that's different from your own, and insert this culture in each of the statements below. Indicate how open you would be to communicating in each scenario. Use the following scale: 5 = very open and willing; 4 = open and willing; 3 = neutral; 2 = closed and unwilling; and 1 = very closed and unwilling. If you wish to increase your openness, what might you do to achieve this?

- Have a "best friendship" with [a culturally different person]. _____
- Have a long romantic relationship with [a culturally different person]. _____
- Adopt a child from [a different culture]. _____
- Participate in a therapy group composed predominantly of people who are [culturally different from you]. _____
- Ascribe a level of credibility to [a culturally different person] identical to that you ascribe to a culturally similar person—all other things being equal. _____

Especially important in self-concept are cultural teachings about gender roles—about how a man or woman should act. In fact, a popular classification of cultures is in terms of their masculinity and femininity (Hofstede, 1997). A highly "masculine" culture endorses an image of men as assertive, oriented to material success, and strong; women, on the other hand, are viewed as modest, focused on the quality of life, and tender. A highly "feminine" culture encourages both men and women to be modest, oriented to maintaining the quality of life, and tender.

Masculine cultures socialize people to be assertive, ambitious, and competitive. For example, members of masculine cultures are more likely to confront conflicts directly and to competitively fight out any differences; they're more likely to emphasize win–lose conflict strategies. Feminine cultures socialize people to be modest and to emphasize close interpersonal relationships. Feminine cultures, for example, are more likely to emphasize compromise and negotiation in resolving conflicts; they're more likely to emphasize win–win solutions.

"It may surprise you to know that, contrary to your experience, you're actually very happily married."

Self-Interpretations and Self-Evaluations

You also react to your own behavior: Your self-interpretations and self-evaluations contribute to your self-concept. For example, let's say you believe that lying is wrong. If you lie, you will probably evaluate this behavior in terms of your internalized beliefs about lying and will react negatively to your own behavior. You may, for

Communicating with power

Power through Affirmation

Self-esteem makes you think more positively about yourself; it makes you feel empowered and competent. To enhance your self-esteem, it's frequently recommended that you remind yourself of your successes—that you focus on your good acts; your good deeds; your positive qualities, strengths, and virtues; and your productive and meaningful relationships with friends, loved ones, and relatives (Aronson, Cohen, & Nail, 1998; Aronson, Wilson, & Akert, 1999). The idea behind this advice is that the way you talk to yourself influences what you think of yourself. For example, if you tell yourself that you're a success, that others like you, and that you'll be welcomed when asking for a date, you'll come to feel better about yourself. Self-affirmations such as the following are often recommended: "I'm a worthy person"; "I'm responsible and can be depended on"; "I'm capable of loving and being loved"; "I deserve good things to happen to me"; "I can forgive myself for mistakes and misjudgments"; "I deserve to be treated with respect."

Some researchers, however, argue that such affirmations—although popular in self-help books—may not be very helpful. These critics suggest that if you have low self-esteem, you're not going to believe your own self-affirmations, not having a very high opinion of yourself to begin with (Paul, 2001). As an alternative to self-affirmation, these researchers recommend securing affirmation from others. For example, you would work toward becoming more interpersonally competent so as to lead people to respond more positively to you. You'd also focus on interacting with positive and affirming people and at the same time avoiding noxious and overly critical people (Rogers, 1970). In this way you'd get more positive feedback from others; and this, some would argue, may be more helpful than self-talk in raising self-esteem.

Enhancing Your Communication Power

How might you go about increasing your self-esteem? Would you try self-affirmations? If so, which ones would you use? With which people would you interact to get positive feedback?

www.researchnavigator.com

Read an Article: Read a popular or scholarly article on the self (for example, on self-concept, self-awareness, or self-esteem), self-disclosure, or communication apprehension. On the basis of this article, what can you add to the discussion presented here?

> **❝** I am an invisible man. . . . I am a man of substance, of flesh and bone, fiber and liquids—and I might even be said to possess a mind. I am invisible, understand, simply because people refuse to see me. **❞**
>
> —Ralph Ellison

example, experience guilt about violating your own beliefs. On the other hand, let's say that you pull someone out of a burning building at great personal risk. You will probably evaluate this behavior positively; you will feel good about this behavior and, as a result, about yourself.

The more you understand why you view yourself as you do, the better you'll understand who you are. You can gain additional insight into yourself by looking more closely at self-awareness and especially at the Johari model of the self.

Self-Awareness

Self-awareness, or self-knowledge, is basic to all communication. To attain self-awareness you need to examine the several aspects of yourself as they might appear to others as well as to yourself. One tool that is commonly used for this examination is called the **Johari window,** a metaphoric division of the self into four areas (Figure 2.2).

Your Four Selves

Divided into four areas or "panes," the Johari window shows different aspects or versions of the self. The four versions are the open self, blind self, hidden self, and unknown self. These areas are not separate from one another but interdependent. As one dominates, the others recede to a greater or lesser degree; or, to stay with our metaphor, as one windowpane becomes larger, one or another becomes smaller.

The Open Self The open self represents all the information, behaviors, attitudes, and feelings about yourself that you know and that others also know. This could include your name, skin color, sex, age, religion, and political beliefs. The "size" of the open self varies according to your personality and the people to whom you're relating. You may be more open with some people than you are with others. You are probably selectively open—open about some things, but not about others.

The Blind Self The blind self represents knowledge about you that others have but you don't. This might include your habit of finishing other people's sentences or your way of rubbing your nose when you become anxious. It may include your tendency to overreact to imagined insults or to compete for attention. A large blind

Figure 2.2

The Johari Window

This diagram is a commonly used tool for examining what we know and don't know about ourselves. It can also help to explain the nature of self-disclosure, covered later in this chapter. The window gets its name from its inventors, *Jo*seph Luft and *Harr*y Ingham.

Source: From Joseph Luft, *Group Process: An Introduction to Group Dynamics,* 3rd ed. Copyright © 1984. New York: McGraw-Hill. Reprinted with permission.

	Known to self	Not known to self
Known to others	**Open Self** Information about yourself that you and others know	**Blind self** Information about yourself that you don't know but that others do know
Not known to others	**Hidden self** Information about yourself that you know but others don't know	**Unknown self** Information about yourself that neither you nor others know

self indicates low self-awareness and interferes with accurate communication. So it's important to reduce your blind self and learn what others know about you.

The Unknown Self The unknown self represents those parts of yourself that neither you nor others know. This is information that is buried in your subconscious. Sometimes this area is revealed through hypnosis, dreams, psychological tests, or psychotherapy. Another way is to explore yourself in an open, honest, and understanding way with those you trust—parents, lovers, and friends.

The Hidden Self The hidden self represents all the knowledge you have of yourself but keep secret from others. This windowpane includes all your successfully kept secrets. It may include your dreams and fantasies; embarrassing experiences; and any attitudes, beliefs, and values of which you may be ashamed. You probably keep secrets from some people and not from others. For example, you might not tell your parents you were dating someone of another race or religion, but you might tell a close friend.

Growing in Self-Awareness

Because self-awareness is so important in communication, try to increase awareness of your own needs, desires, habits, beliefs, and attitudes. Here are a few ways to do this:

Listen to Others Conveniently, others are constantly giving you the very feedback you need to increase self-awareness. In every interpersonal interaction, people comment on you in some way—on what you do, what you say, how you look. Sometimes these comments are explicit: "Loosen up" or "Don't take things so hard." Often they

 VIEWPOINT

In the photo above, whistleblower Sharron Watkins (left) and former CEO, Jeffrey Skillings (middle) prepare to testify to Congress about the Enron company collapse. Based on what you've learned about self-esteem, would you assume that each of the parties involved in the Enron scandal possessed high self-esteem? In recent years self-esteem has come under attack (for example, Bushman & Baumeister, 1998; Baumeister, Bushman, & Campbell, 2000; Bower, 2001; Coover & Murphy, 2000; Hewitt, 1998). Much current thinking holds that high self-esteem is not desirable: It does nothing to improve academic performance and it does not predict success, and in fact it may lead to antisocial (especially aggressive) behavior. On the other hand, it's difficult even to imagine a person functioning successfully without positive self-feelings. What do you think about the benefits or liabilities of self-esteem? Would you have included this topic in this text?

What Do You Say?

Blind Self: You're going to enter a new job—a position that you hope you'll keep for the major part of your professional career—and you really need honest feedback on your total performance at your present job. *What do you say? To whom? Through what channel?*

❝ **We Wear the Mask**
We wear the mask that grins and lies,
It hides our cheeks and shades our
   eyes—
This debt we pay to human guile:
With torn and bleeding hearts we
   smile,
And mouth with myriad subtleties.

Why should the world be otherwise,
In counting all our tears and sighs?
Nay, let them only see us, while
We wear the mask.

We smile, but, O great Christ, our cries
To thee from tortured souls arise.
We sing, but oh the clay is vile
Beneath our feet, and long the mile;
But let the world dream otherwise,
We wear the mask! ❞

—Paul Laurence Dunbar

Listening to Yourself

Not only do you talk about yourself—in, say, self-disclosure—but you also talk to yourself. So listen carefully to what you tell yourself, especially to self-destructive statements.

Self-destructive statements damage your self-esteem and prevent you from building meaningful and productive relationships. They may be about yourself ("I'm not creative"), your world ("Men and women are natural adversaries"), or your relationships ("I know I'm going to be hurt again"). Recognizing that you may have internalized such beliefs is a first step to eliminating them. A second step involves recognizing that these beliefs are self-defeating and replacing them with more realistic ideas (Ellis, 1988).

Applying Listening Skills

Your friend is the classic textbook example of someone who tells himself and believes just about every self-destructive statement you can think of. What suggestions would you offer him?

What Do You Say?

Self-Esteem: Your best friend has hit a new low in self-esteem; a long-term relationship failed, an expected promotion never materialized, and a large investment went sour. You want to help your friend regain self-esteem. *What do you say? To whom? Through what channel?*

---

are "hidden" in the way others look at you or in what they talk about. Pay close attention to this kind of information and use it to increase your own self-awareness.

Increase Your Open Self   Revealing yourself to others will help increase your self-awareness. At the very least, you will bring into focus what you may have buried within. As you discuss yourself, you may see connections that you had previously missed. With feedback from others, you may gain still more insight. Also, by increasing your open self, you increase the chances that others will reveal what they know about you.

Seek Information about Yourself   Seek out information to reduce your blind self. (Of course, you don't want to seek such information from just anyone. People who are overly negative, who have personal agendas, or who know you only slightly are generally poor sources when you are seeking self-insight.) Encourage people to reveal what they know about you. Use situations that arise every day to gain self-information: "Do you think I came down too hard on the kids today?" "Do you think I was assertive enough when asking for the raise?" But seek this self-awareness in moderation. If you do it too often, your friends will soon look for someone else with whom to talk.

Dialogue with Yourself   No one knows you better than you know yourself. Ask yourself self-awareness questions: What motivates me to act as I do? What are my short-term and long-term goals? How do I plan to achieve them? What are my strengths and weaknesses?

Self-Disclosure

Self-disclosure is a type of communication in which you reveal information about yourself (Jourard, 1968, 1971a, 1971b). You can look at self-disclosure as taking information from the hidden self and moving it to the open self. Overt statements about the self as well as slips of the tongue, unconscious nonverbal movements, and public confessions can all be considered forms of self-disclosure. Usually, however, the term *self-disclosure* is used to refer to the conscious revealing of information, as in the statements "I'm

"So, when he says, 'What a good boy am I,' Jack is really reinforcing his self-esteem."

afraid to compete; I guess I'm afraid I'll lose" or "I love you" or "I finally saved enough and I'm buying a car this week."

Self-disclosure is "information"—something previously unknown by the receiver. This information may vary from the relatively commonplace ("I'm really afraid of that French exam") to the extremely significant ("I'm depressed, I feel like committing suicide"). Often, as mentioned, self-disclosure involves revealing information that is in our hidden self, that we actively keep others from learning. For self-disclosure to occur, the communication must involve at least two people. You cannot self-disclose to yourself—the information must be received and understood by another individual.

In addition to disclosing information about yourself, you may also disclose information about those close to you if it has a significant bearing on your life, social status, or professional capabilities. Thus, self-disclosure could refer to your own actions or to the actions of, say, your parents or children, because these have a direct relationship to who you are.

www.researchnavigator.com

Investigate Key Terms:
Investigate one of the key terms discussed in this chapter (for example, self-concept, self-awareness, self-esteem, social comparison, self-awareness, self-disclosure, secret, masculine and feminine cultures, affirmation). What additional insights can you provide?

Factors Influencing Self-Disclosure

Many factors influence whether or not you disclose, what you disclose, and to whom you disclose. Among the most important factors are who you are, your culture, your gender, who your listeners are, and your topic and channel.

Who You Are Highly sociable and extroverted people self-disclose more than those who are less sociable and more introverted. People who are comfortable communicating also self-disclose more than those who are apprehensive about talking in general.

Competent people engage in self-disclosure more than less competent people. Perhaps competent people have greater self-confidence and more positive things to reveal. Similarly, their self-confidence may make them more willing to risk possible negative reactions (McCroskey & Wheeless, 1976).

Communicating ethically

Outing

An interesting variation on self-disclosure occurs when someone else takes information from your hidden self and makes it public. Third-party disclosure can concern any aspect of a person's hidden self—an athlete's prison record or drug habit, a movie star's ill health or alcoholism, or a politician's shady friends or financial dealings. However, the media have made a special case out of revealing a person's affectional orientation in the process called "outing" (Gross, 1991; Signorile, 1993; Johansson & Percy, 1994).

Those against outing argue that people have a right to privacy and that no one should take that right from them. Because the outing of a gay man or a lesbian can lead to severe consequences—for example, the loss of a job, expulsion from the military, or social and physical harassment—no one but the individual himself or herself has the right to reveal such information. Those in favor of outing argue that it's an expedient political and social weapon to silence those gay men and lesbians who—perhaps in an effort to keep their own affectional orientations secret—support or refuse to protest homophobic policies.

What Would You Do?

You are editing the college newspaper, and a debate is brewing on campus over the establishment of a Gay and Lesbian Student Center. You're convinced that the center should be supported. One of its most outspoken opponents is a professor you know to be a closeted lesbian. You know that if you out her she'll lose her influence. Would it be ethical to out this professor so as to strengthen the cause of the student center?

Your Culture   Different cultures view self-disclosure differently. People in the United States, for example, disclose more than do those in Great Britain, Germany, Japan, or Puerto Rico (Gudykunst, 1983). American students disclose more than do students from nine different Middle East countries (Jourard, 1971a). Similarly, American students self-disclose more on a variety of controversial issues and also self-disclose more to different types of people than do Chinese students (Chen, 1992). Singaporean Chinese students consider more topics to be taboo and inappropriate for self-disclosure than their British counterparts (Goodwin & Lee, 1994). Among the Kabre of Togo, secrecy is a major part of everyday interactions (Piot, 1993).

Some cultures (especially those high in masculinity) view the disclosing of inner feelings as a weakness. Among some groups, for example, it would be considered "out of place" for a man to cry at a happy occasion such as a wedding, whereas in some Latin cultures that same display of emotion would go unnoticed. Similarly, it's considered undesirable in Japan for colleagues to reveal personal information, whereas in much of the United States it's expected (Barnlund, 1989; Hall & Hall, 1987).

These differences aside, there are also important similarities across cultures. For example, people from Great Britain, Germany, the United States, and Puerto Rico are all more apt to disclose personal information—hobbies, interests, attitudes, and opinions on politics and religion—than information on finances, sex, personality, and interpersonal relationships (Jourard, 1971a). Similarly, one study showed self-disclosure patterns between American males to be virtually identical to those between Korean males (Won-Doornink, 1991).

 **VIEWPOINT**

You belong to a variety of cultures—and because each of these cultures exerts influence on your attitudes and beliefs, you may find that some cultural influences contradict each other. Thus, for example, you may have been taught to be the best in your field but also to be cooperative and helpful to others, perhaps even to those you find yourself competing against. Such contradictory beliefs may easily cause intrapersonal conflicts. In extreme cases you may decide to reject the attitudes and beliefs of one culture—often the "old-world" culture—in favor of those of the culture with which you feel more comfortable. Have you ever experienced such intrapersonal conflicts? What happened?

Your Gender   The popular stereotype of gender differences in self-disclosure emphasizes males' reluctance to speak about themselves. For the most part, research supports this view; women do disclose more than men. There are exceptions, however. For example, men and women make negative disclosures about equally (Naifeh & Smith, 1984), and boys are more likely than girls to disclose family information on the Internet (www.CNN.com, accessed May 17, 2000). Another notable exception occurs in initial encounters. Here, men will disclose more intimately than women, perhaps "in order to control the relationship's development" (Derlega, Winstead, Wong, & Hunter, 1985).

Specifically, women disclose more than men about their previous romantic relationships, their feelings about their closest same-sex friends, their greatest fears, and what they don't like about their partners (Sprecher, 1987). Women also increase the depth of their disclosures as the relationship becomes more intimate, whereas men seem not to change their self-disclosure levels. Men, for example, have more taboo topics that they will not disclose to their friends than women do (Goodwin & Lee, 1994). Finally, women also self-disclose more to members of their extended families than men (Komarovsky, 1964; Argyle & Henderson, 1985; Moghaddam, Taylor, & Wright, 1993).

Your Listeners   Self-disclosure occurs more readily in small groups than in large groups. Dyads, or groups of two people, are the most hospitable setting for self-disclosure. With one listener, you can attend to the responses carefully. You can monitor your disclosures, continuing if there's support from your listener and stopping if there's not. With more than one listener, such monitoring becomes difficult, because the listeners' responses are sure to vary.

Because you disclose, at least generally, on the basis of support you receive, you probably disclose to people you like (Derlega, Winstead, Wong, & Greenspan, 1987) and to people you trust (Wheeless & Grotz, 1977). You probably also come to like those to whom you disclose (Berg & Archer, 1983). At times, self-disclosure occurs more in temporary than in permanent relationships—for example, between strangers on a train or plane, in a kind of "in-flight intimacy" (McGill, 1985). In this situation, two people set up an intimate, self-disclosing relationship during a brief travel period, but they don't pursue it beyond that point. In a similar way, you might set up a relationship with one or several people on the Internet and engage in significant disclosure. Perhaps knowing that you'll never see these other people, and that they will never know where you live or work or what you look like, makes it easier to open up to them.

You are more likely to disclose when the person you are with discloses. This **dyadic effect** (what one person does, the other person does likewise) probably leads you to feel more secure and reinforces your own self-disclosing behavior. Disclosures are also more intimate when they're made in response to the disclosures of others (Berg & Archer, 1983).

Your Topic and Channel   You also are more likely to disclose about some topics than others. For example, you are probably more likely to self-disclose information about your job or hobbies than about your sex life or financial situation (Jourard, 1968, 1971a). Further, you are more likely to disclose favorable information than unfavorable information. Generally, the more personal and negative the topic, the less likely you are to self-disclose.

The channel through which you disclose can be a factor too. Interestingly enough, research finds that reciprocal self-disclosure occurs more quickly and at higher levels of intimacy online than it does in face-to-face interactions (Levine, 2000; Joinson, 2001).

The self-test "How willing to self-disclose are you?" on page 38 focuses on the influences of four of the factors just discussed: you, your culture, your listeners, and your topic.

Web Explorations

A variety of exercises and self-tests will help you work actively with the concepts discussed in this chapter (www.ablongman.com/devito): (1) I'd Prefer to Be, (2) Time for Self-Disclosure, (3) Disclosing Your Hidden Self, (4) How Assertive Are Your Messages? (5) What Do You Have a Right to Know? and (6) How Open Are You Interculturally?

What Do You Say?

Disclosure Encouragement: Your next-door neighbor is extremely secretive. You want to encourage greater disclosure but don't want to seem pushy or nosy. *What do you say?*

How Willing to Self-Disclose Are You?

INSTRUCTIONS: Respond to each of the following statements by indicating the likelihood that you would disclose such items of information to, say, other members of this class in a one-on-one *interpersonal* situation, In a five- or six-member *small group* situation, and in a *public communication* setting in which you would speak to all members of the class. Use the following scale to fill in all three columns: 1 = would definitely self-disclose; 2 = would probably self-disclose; 3 = don't know; 4 = would probably not self-disclose; and 5 = would definitely not self-disclose.

Information	Interpersonal Communication	Small Group Communication	Public Communication
❶ My attitudes toward other religions, nationalities, and races	_____	_____	___X___
❷ My financial status, how much money I earn, how much I owe, how much I have saved	_____	___X___	_____
❸ My feelings about my parents	___X___	_____	_____
❹ My sexual fantasies	___X___	_____	_____
❺ My physical and mental health	___X___	_____	_____
❻ My ideal romantic partner	_____	_____	___X___
❼ My drinking and/or drug behavior	_____	_____	___X___
❽ My most embarrassing moment	___X___	_____	_____
❾ My unfulfilled desires	_____	___X___	_____
❿ My self-concept	_____	___X___	_____

HOW DID YOU DO? There are, of course, no right or wrong answers to this self-test. Generally, people will self-disclose most in the interpersonal communication situations, least in the public communication situations, and somewhere in between in small group settings.

WHAT WILL YOU DO? This test, and ideally discussing it with others who also complete it, should get you started thinking about your own self-disclosing behavior and especially the factors that influence it. How does your own personality influence your self-disclosure behavior? Are you more likely to disclose interpersonally than in small group or public situations? Are you more likely to disclose in small groups than in public situations? Are there certain people to whom you feel relatively free to disclose and others to whom you feel much less free? What distinguishes these two groups of people? Are there certain topics you are less willing to disclose than others? Are you more likely to disclose positive secrets than negative ones? Are there topics about which you wish you had the opportunity to self-disclose but somehow can't find the right situation? As a listener, are there topics you would rather not hear about from certain people?

> **"** In order to have a conversation with someone you must reveal yourself. **"**
>
> —James Baldwin

The Rewards and Dangers of Self-Disclosure

Self-disclosure often brings rewards, but it can also create problems. Whether or not you self-disclose will depend on your assessment of the possible rewards and dangers. Here are some of the most important.

The Rewards of Self-Disclosure   Self-disclosure contributes to self-knowledge; it helps you gain a new perspective on yourself and a deeper understanding of your own behavior. In therapy, for example, insight often comes while you are disclosing. Through self-disclosure, then, you may come to understand yourself more thoroughly.

Self-disclosure improves your coping abilities; it helps you deal with problems, especially guilt. You may fear that you will not be accepted because of something you have done or because of some feeling or attitude you have. Because you feel these things are a basis for rejection, you may develop guilt. By self-disclosing such a feeling and receiving support rather than rejection, you may be better able to deal with guilt, perhaps reducing or even eliminating it.

Self-disclosure often improves communication. You understand the messages of others largely to the extent that you understand the individuals. You can tell what certain nuances mean, when the person is serious or joking, and when the person is being sarcastic out of fear or out of resentment. You might study a person's behavior or even live together for years, but if that person rarely self-discloses, you are far from understanding that individual as a complete person.

Skill development experience

Revealing Yourself

At what point in a relationship—if any—do you have an obligation to reveal the information listed in the first column below? Record your responses for romantic relationships in the second column and for friendships in the third. To indicate at what point you would feel an obligation to reveal each type of information, use numbers from 1 to 10, with 1 being initial contact and 10 being extreme intimacy. If you feel you would never have an obligation to reveal this information, use 0. After completing these items, try formulating in one sentence the obligation you have as a friend or as a romantic partner to reveal information about yourself.

Information	Romantic Relationship	Friendship Relationship
HIV status	4	8
Past sexual experiences	4	6
Annual salary, net worth	6	4
Affectional orientation		
Race, nationality, and religion	4	4
Social and political beliefs and attitudes	2	2

Self-disclosure helps you establish meaningful relationships. By self-disclosing you tell others that you trust, respect, and care enough about them and your relationship to reveal yourself. This, in turn, leads the other individual to self-disclose and forms at least the start of a relationship that is honest and open and allows for more complete communication. Within a sexual relationship, self-disclosure increases sexual rewards and general relationship satisfaction. These two benefits in turn increase sexual satisfaction (Byers & Demmons, 1999).

The Dangers of Self-Disclosure   Self-disclosure involves risks, however. Realize that the more you reveal about yourself to others, the more areas of your life you expose to possible attack. Especially in the competitive context of work (or even romance), the more that others know about you, the more they'll be able to use against you. This simple fact has prompted power watcher Michael Korda (1975, p. 302) to advise that you "never reveal all of yourself to other people, [but] hold something back in reserve so that people are never quite sure if they really know you." This advice is not necessarily to suggest that you be secretive; rather, Korda is advocating "remaining slightly mysterious, as if [you] were always capable of doing something surprising and unexpected."

When you self-disclose, you risk personal and social rejection. Parents, normally the most supportive people in most individuals' lives, frequently reject children who self-disclose their homosexuality, their plans to marry someone of a different race, or their belief in another faith. Your best friends, your closest intimates, may reject you for similar self-disclosures.

Sometimes self-disclosure may result in material losses. Politicians who disclose that they have been in therapy may lose the support of their own political party and find that voters are unwilling to vote for them. Teachers who disclose disagreement with school administrators may find themselves being denied tenure, teaching undesirable schedules, and becoming victims of "budget cuts." In the business world self-disclosures of alcoholism or drug addiction often result in dismissal, demotion, or social exclusion.

Remember that self-disclosure, like any other communication, is irreversible (see Chapter 1). You cannot self-disclose and then take it back. Nor can you erase the conclusions and inferences listeners make on the basis of your disclosures. Remember, too, to examine the rewards and dangers of self-disclosure in terms of particular cultural rules. As with all cultural rules, following rules about self-disclosure brings approval, and violating them brings disapproval.

Guidelines for Self-Disclosure

Because self-disclosure is so important and so delicate a matter, here are some guidelines for (1) deciding whether and how to self-disclose, (2) responding to the disclosures of others, and (3) resisting the pressure to self-disclose.

Guidelines for Making Self-Disclosures   In addition to weighing the potential rewards and dangers of self-disclosure, consider the following factors as well. These hints will help you raise the right questions before you make what must be *your* decision.

Consider the Motivation for the Self-Disclosure.   Self-disclosure should be motivated by a concern for the relationship, for the others involved, and for yourself. Some people self-disclose out of a desire to hurt the listener. Persons who tell their parents that they never loved them or that the parents hindered their emotional development may be disclosing out of a desire to hurt and perhaps to punish rather than to

What Do You Say?

Corrective Self-Disclosure:
When you met your current partner, with whom you want to spend the rest of your life, you minimized the extent of your romantic past. You now want to come clean and disclose your past. *What do you say? Through what channel?*

VIEWPOINT

What one principle or skill concerning self-disclosure do you find most important? What do you find to be the single most common error people make in self-disclosing or in listening to the disclosures of others?

improve the relationship. Neither, of course, should you self-disclose in order to punish yourself, perhaps because of some guilt feeling or unresolved conflict. Self-disclosure should serve a useful and productive function for all persons involved.

Consider the Appropriateness of the Self-Disclosure. Self-disclosure should be appropriate to the context and to the relationship between you and your listener. Before making any significant self-disclosure, ask whether this is the right time and place. Could a better time and setting be arranged? Ask, too, whether this self-disclosure is appropriate to the relationship. Generally, the more intimate the disclosure, the closer the relationship should be. It's probably best to resist making intimate disclosures (especially negative ones) with nonintimates or with casual acquaintances, or in the early stages of a relationship.

Consider the Disclosures of the Other Person. During your disclosures, give the other person a chance to reciprocate with his or her own disclosures. If the other person does not reciprocate, reassess your own self-disclosures. It may be that for this person at this time and in this context, your disclosures are not welcome or appropriate. So it's generally best to disclose gradually and in small increments. When you disclose too rapidly and all at once, you can't monitor your listener's responses and retreat if they're not positive enough. Further, you prevent the listener from responding with his or her own disclosures and thereby upset the natural balance that is so helpful in this kind of communication exchange.

Consider the Possible Burdens Self-Disclosure Might Entail. Carefully weigh the potential problems that you may incur as a result of your disclosure. Can you afford to lose your job if you disclose your prison record? Are you willing to risk relational difficulties if you disclose your infidelities? Also, ask yourself whether you're making unreasonable demands on the listener. For example, consider the person who swears his or her mother-in-law to secrecy and then discloses having an affair with a neighbor. This disclosure places an unfair burden on the mother-in-law, who is now torn between breaking her promise of secrecy and allowing her child to believe a lie. Parents often place unreasonable burdens on their children by disclosing relationship problems, financial difficulties, or self-doubts, not realizing that the children may be too young or too emotionally involved to deal effectively with this information.

> ❝ Confiding a secret to an unworthy person is like carrying grain in a bag with a hole. ❞
>
> —Ethiopian proverb

Guidelines for Facilitating and Responding to Self-Disclosures When someone discloses to you, it's usually a sign of trust and affection. In serving this most important receiver function, keep the following guidelines in mind. These guidelines will also help you facilitate the disclosures of another person.

Skill development experience

Regulating Self-Disclosure

For each of the following instances of impending self-disclosure, identify the factors that the person should consider or the questions the person should ask before disclosing. Once you've identified the factors, compose a few sentences that you would recommend that each person say in disclosing.

1. Tom is engaged to Cathy, but over the past few months he has been dating another woman and has fallen in love with her. He now wants to break his engagement and disclose his new relationship.
2. Sam has been in a romantic relationship with another man for the past several years. Sam wants to tell his parents and his colleagues at work.
3. Kathy and Kelley, now seniors in college, have been friends since grade school. The problem is that Kathy has been secretly dating Kelley's boyfriend, Hogan. Kathy plans to disclose this affair and to tell Kelley that she and Hogan are getting engaged.

Practice the Skills of Effective and Active Listening. The skills of effective listening (Chapter 4) are especially important when you are listening to self-disclosures: Listen actively, listen for different levels of meaning, listen with empathy, and listen with an open mind. Paraphrase the speaker so as to be sure you understand both the thoughts and the feelings communicated. Express an understanding of the speaker's feelings in order to give the speaker the opportunity to see his or her feelings more objectively and through the eyes of another. Ask questions to ensure your own understanding and to signal your interest and attention.

Support and Reinforce the Discloser. Express support for the person during and after the disclosures. Try refraining from evaluation. Concentrate on understanding and empathizing with the discloser. Allow the discloser to choose the pace; don't rush the discloser with too-frequent "So how did it all end?" responses. Make your supportiveness clear to the discloser through your verbal and nonverbal responses: Maintain eye contact, lean toward the speaker, ask relevant questions, and echo the speaker's thoughts and feelings.

Be Willing to Reciprocate. When you make relevant and appropriate disclosures of your own in response to the other person's disclosures, you're demonstrating your understanding of the other's meanings and at the same time a willingness to communicate on this meaningful level.

Keep the Disclosures Confidential. When someone discloses to you, it's because the person wants you to know about his or her feelings and thoughts. If you reveal these disclosures to others, negative effects are inevitable. Revealing what was said will probably inhibit this individual's future disclosures in general and his or her disclosures to you in particular, and it's likely that your relationship will suffer considerably. But most important, betraying a confidence is unfair; it debases what could be and should be a meaningful interpersonal experience.

It's interesting to note that one of the netiquette rules of e-mail is that you shouldn't forward mail to third parties without the writer's permission. This rule is useful for self-disclosure generally: Maintain confidentiality; don't pass on disclosures made to you to others without the person's permission.

Don't Use the Disclosures against the Person. Many self-disclosures expose some kind of vulnerability or weakness. If you later turn around and use a disclosure against the person, you betray the confidence and trust invested in you. Regardless of how angry you may get, resist the temptation to use the disclosures of others as weapons—the relationship is sure to suffer and may never fully recover.

Guidelines for Resisting Pressure to Self-Disclose You may, on occasion, find yourself in a position in which a friend, colleague, or romantic partner is pressuring you to self-disclose. In such situations you may wish to weigh the pros and cons of self-disclosure and make your own decision as to whether and what you'll disclose. If your decision is to not disclose and you're still being pressured, then you need to say something. Here are a few suggestions.

Don't Be Pushed. Although there may be certain legal or ethical reasons for disclosing, generally you don't have to disclose if you don't want to. Don't be pushed into disclosing because others are doing it or because you're asked to. Realize that you're in control of what you reveal and of when and to whom you reveal it. Remember that self-disclosure has significant consequences. So if you're not sure you want to reveal something, at least not until you've had additional time to think about it, then don't.

Be Indirect and Move to Another Topic. Avoid the question that asks you to disclose, and change the subject. This is often a polite way of saying, "I'm not talking about it," and may be the preferred choice in certain situations and with certain people. Most often people will get the hint and will understand your refusal to disclose. If they don't, then you may have to refuse in a more direct and assertive way.

Be Assertive in Your Refusal to Disclose. If necessary, say, very directly, "I'd rather not talk about that now" or "Now is not the time for this type of discussion."

> **"** I date this girl for two years—and then the nagging starts: 'I wanna know your name.' **"**
>
> —Mike Binder

Summary of Concepts and Skills

In this chapter we looked at the most important part of the communication process: the self. We discussed (1) self-concept and how it develops, (2) self-awareness and how to increase it, and (3) self-disclosure and how to engage in it more effectively.

1. *Self-concept* is the image that you have of yourself and is composed of feelings and thoughts about both your abilities and your limitations. Self-concept develops from the image that others have of you, the comparisons you make between yourself and others, the teachings of your culture, and your own interpretations and evaluations of your thoughts and behaviors.

2. The Johari window model of the self is one way to view self-awareness. In this model there are four major areas: the open self, the blind self, the hidden self, and the unknown self. To increase self-awareness, analyze yourself, listen to others to see yourself as they do, actively seek information from others about yourself, see yourself from different perspectives, and increase your open self.

3. Self-disclosure is a form of communication in which information about the self that is normally kept hidden is communicated to one or more others.

4. Self-disclosure is more likely to occur when the potential discloser (1) feels competent, is sociable and extroverted, and is not apprehensive about communication; (2) comes from a culture that encourages self-disclosure; (3) is a woman; (4) is talking to supportive listeners who also disclose; and (5) talks about impersonal rather than personal topics and reveals positive rather than negative information.

5. The rewards of self-disclosure include increased self-knowledge, the ability to cope with difficult situations and guilt, communication efficiency, and chances for more meaningful relationships. The dangers of self-disclosure include personal and social rejection, material loss, and intrapersonal difficulties.

6. Before self-disclosing, consider the cultural rules operating, the motivation for the self-disclosure, the possible burdens you might impose on your listener or yourself, the appropriateness of the self-disclosure, and the disclosures of the other person.

7. When listening to disclosures, take into consideration the cultural rules governing the communication situation, try to understand what the discloser is feeling, support the discloser, refrain from criticism and evaluation, and keep the disclosures confidential.

8. When you don't want to disclose, try being firm, being indirect and changing the topic, or assertively stating your unwillingness to disclose.

The skills for increasing self-awareness and for effective self-disclosure are critical to effective communication in all its forms. Check your ability to apply these skills, using the following rating scale: 1 = almost always, 2 = often, 3 = sometimes, 4 = rarely, and 5 = hardly ever.

_____ 1. I seek to understand my self-concept and to be realistic about my strengths and my weaknesses.

_____ 2. I actively seek to increase self-awareness by talking with myself, listening to others, reducing my blind self, seeing myself from different perspectives, and increasing my open self.

_____ 3. I regulate my disclosures on the basis of the unique communication situation.

_____ 4. In deciding whether to self-disclose, I take into consideration (1) the cultural rules, (2) my motivation, (3) the possible burdens on my listener, (4) the appropriateness to the other person and the context, (5) the other person's disclosures, and (6) the possible burdens the disclosures may impose on me.

_____ 5. I respond to the disclosures of others by trying to feel what the other person is feeling, using effective and active listening skills, expressing supportiveness, refraining from criticism and evaluation, and keeping the disclosures confidential.

_____ 6. I resist disclosing when I don't want to by being firm, by trying indirectness and changing the topic, and/or by stating assertively my refusal to disclose.

Key Word Quiz

Write T for those statements that are true and F for those that are false. For those that are false replace the italicized term with the correct term.

_____ 1. The process by which you compare yourself with others, most often your peers, is known as *social comparison*.

_____ 2. A way of looking at yourself largely through the image that others reveal to you by their behaviors and especially by the way they treat you and react to you is known as the *looking-glass self*.

_____ 3. Your *self-concept* is your image of who you are.

_____ 4. Your self-evaluation is your *self-esteem*.

_____ 5. All the information that you know about yourself but that others don't know is in your *blind self*.

_____ 6. All the information that others know about you but that you don't know is in your *hidden self*.

_____ 7. Raising your self-esteem by saying and concentrating on the good things about yourself is known as *self-affirmation*.

_____ 8. *Masculine cultures* emphasize success and socialize members to be assertive.

_____ 9. The process of talking to others about yourself, of revealing things that you normally keep hidden, is known as *interpersonal communication*.

_____ 10. The *dyadic effect* describes the tendency of one person in a dyad to do essentially what the other person does.

Answers: TRUE: 1, 2, 3, 7, 8, 10; FALSE: 4 (*self-awareness*), 5 (*hidden self*), 6 (*blind self*), 9 (*self-disclosure*)

3 Perception in Human Communication

Chapter Concepts	Chapter Skills
This chapter covers the way you perceive people and events and how you can make these perceptions more accurate.	After completing this chapter, you should be able to:
The Stages of Perception	perceive others with the knowledge that perceptions are influenced by who you are and by external stimuli.
Perceptual Processes	avoid common perceptual barriers.
Increasing Accuracy in Perception	perceive others more accurately, using a variety of strategies.

The Stages of Perception

Perception is the process by which you become aware of objects, events, and especially people through your senses: sight, smell, taste, touch, and hearing. Perception is an active, not a passive, process. Your perceptions result from what exists in the outside world *and* from your own experiences, desires, needs and wants, loves and hatreds. Among the reasons why perception is so important in interpersonal communication is that it influences your communication choices. The messages you send and listen to will depend on how you see the world, on how you size up specific situations, on what you think of the people with whom you interact.

Interpersonal perception is a continuous series of processes that blend into one another. *For convenience of discussion* we can separate them into five stages: (1) You sense, you pick up some kind of stimulation; (2) you organize the stimuli in some way; (3) you interpret and evaluate what you perceive; (4) you store your perception in memory; and (5) you retrieve it when needed.

Stage One: Stimulation

At the first stage of perception, your sense organs are stimulated—you hear a new CD, you see a friend, you smell someone's perfume, you taste an orange, you feel another's sweaty palm. Naturally, you don't perceive everything; rather, you engage in *selective perception,* which includes selective attention and selective exposure. In *selective attention,* you attend to those things that you anticipate will fulfill your needs or will prove enjoyable. For instance, when daydreaming in class, you don't hear what the instructor is saying until he or she calls your name. Your selective attention mechanism focuses your senses on your name.

The principle of **selective exposure** states that people tend to expose themselves to information that will confirm their existing beliefs, that will contribute to their objectives, or that will prove satisfying in some way. For example, after you buy a car, you're more apt to read and listen to advertisements for the car you just bought, because these messages tell you that you made the right decision. At the same time, you will tend to avoid advertisements for the cars that you considered but eventually rejected, because these messages would tell you that you made the wrong decision.

You're also more likely to perceive stimuli that are greater in intensity than surrounding stimuli and to perceive stimuli that have novelty value. For example, television commercials normally play at a greater intensity than regular programming to ensure that you take special notice. You're also more likely to notice the coworker who dresses in a novel way than you are to notice the one who dresses like everyone else. You will quickly perceive someone who shows up in class wearing a tuxedo or at a formal party in shorts.

Stage Two: Organization

At the second stage, you organize the information your senses pick up. Three interesting ways in which people organize their perceptions are by rules, by schemata, and by scripts. Let's look at each briefly.

Organization by Rules   One frequently used rule is that of **proximity,** or physical closeness. The rule, simply stated, says that things that are physically close together constitute a unit. Thus, using this rule, you would perceive people who are often together, or messages spoken one right after the other, as units, as belonging together. You also assume that the verbal and nonverbal signals sent at about the same time are related and constitute a unified whole: You assume they follow a *temporal rule* that says that things occurring together in time belong together.

Another rule is **similarity:** the idea that things that are physically similar or look alike belong together and form a unit. This principle leads you to see people who dress alike as belonging together. Similarly, you might assume that people who work at the same jobs, who are of the same religion, who live in the same building, or who talk with the same accent belong together.

You use the principle of **contrast** when you conclude that some items (people or messages, for example) don't belong together because they are too different from each other to be part of the same perceptual organization. So, for example, in a conversation or a public speech, listeners will focus their attention on changes in intensity or rate because these contrast with the rest of the message.

Organization by Schemata   Another way you organize material is by creating **schemata**, mental templates or structures that help you organize the millions of items of information you come into contact with every day as well as those you already have in memory. Schemata may thus be viewed as general ideas about people (Pat and Chris, Japanese, Baptists, New Yorkers); about yourself (your qualities, abilities, and even liabilities); or about social roles (the attributes of police officers, professors, or multibillionaire CEOs). The word *schemata,* by the way, is the plural of *schema* and is preferred to the alternative plural *schemas.*

You develop schemata from your own experience—actual experience as well as vicarious experience from television, reading, and hearsay. Thus, for example, you may have a schema that portrays college athletes as strong, ambitious, academically weak, and egocentric. And, of course, you've probably developed schemata for different religious, racial, and national groups; for men and women; and for people of different affectional orientations. Each group that you have some familiarity with will be represented in your mind in some kind of schema. Schemata help you organize your perceptions by allowing you to classify millions of people into a manageable number of categories or classes. As you'll soon see, however, schemata can also create problems—they can influence you to see what is not there or to miss seeing what is there.

Organization by Scripts   A **script** is a type of schema. Like a schema, a script is an organized body of information; but a script focuses on an action, event, or procedure. It's a general idea of how some event should play out or unfold; it's the rules governing events and their sequence. For example, you probably have a script for eating in a restaurant with the actions organized into a pattern something like this: Enter, take a seat, review the menu, order from the menu, eat your food, ask for the bill, leave a tip, pay the bill, exit the restaurant. Similarly, you probably have scripts for how you do laundry, how you behave in an interview, the stages you go through in introducing someone to someone else, and the way you ask for a date.

What Do You Say?

First Impressions: You made a bad impression at work—you drank too much at an office party and played the clown. This is not the impression you want to give and you need to change it fast. *What do you say? To whom? Through what channel?*

Stage Three: Interpretation–Evaluation

The interpretation–evaluation step (a linked term because the two processes cannot be separated) is inevitably subjective and is greatly influenced by your experiences, needs, wants, values, expectations, physical and emotional state, beliefs about the way things are or should be, and so on. Your interpretation–evaluation will be influenced by your rules, schemata, and scripts as well as by your gender; for example, women have been found to view others more positively than men (Winquist, Mohr, & Kenny, 1998).

For example, on meeting a new person who is introduced to you as a college football player, you will tend to apply your schema to this person and view him as strong, ambitious, academically weak, and egocentric. You will, in other words, see this person through the filter of your schema and evaluate him according to your schema for college athletes. Similarly, when viewing someone performing some series of actions (say, eating in a restaurant), you will apply your script to this event and view the event through the script. You will interpret the actions of the diner as appropriate or inappropriate depending on your script for this behavior and on the ways in which the diner performs the sequence of actions.

Stage Four: Memory

Both your perceptions and their interpretations–evaluations are put into memory; they're stored so that you may ultimately retrieve them at some later time. So, for example, you have in memory your schema for college athletes, and you know that Ben Williams is a football player. Ben Williams is then stored in memory with "cognitive tags" that tell you that he's strong, ambitious, academically weak, and egocentric. That is, despite the fact that you've not witnessed Ben's strength or ambitions and have no idea of his academic record or his psychological profile, you still may store your memory of Ben along with the qualities that make up your script for "college athletes."

Now, let's say that at different times you hear that Ben failed Spanish I (normally an A or B course at your school), that Ben got an A in chemistry (normally a tough course), and that Ben is transferring to Harvard as a theoretical physics major. Schemata act as filters or gatekeepers; they allow certain information to be stored in relatively objective form, much as you heard or read it, but may distort or prevent other information from being stored. As a result, these three items of information

Listen to this

Listening to Others' Perceptions

"Galileo and the Ghosts" is a technique for envisioning how a particular group of people would perceive a problem, person, or situation (DeVito, 1996). It involves two steps:

1. Set up a mental "ghostthinking team," much as corporations and research institutes maintain think tanks. Select a team of four to eight "people" you admire; for example, historical figures like Aristotle or Galileo, fictional figures like Wonder Woman or Sherlock Holmes, public figures like Oprah Winfrey or Ralph Nader, or persons from other cultures or of a different gender or affectional orientation.
2. Pose a question or problem and then listen to how this team of ghosts perceive your problem. Of course, you're really listening to yourself—but to yourself acting in the roles of other people. The technique forces you to step outside your normal role and to consider the perceptions of someone totally different from you.

Applying Listening Skills

Set up a ghost team to help you become a more responsive and supportive friend, more popular at work, or a better student. Whom would you select? What specific questions would you ask? What might each member say?

about Ben may get stored very differently in your memory along with your schema for college athletes.

For example, you may readily store the information that Ben failed Spanish, because it's consistent with your schema; it fits neatly into the template that you have of college athletes. Information that's consistent with your schema—as in this example—will strengthen your schema and make it more resistant to change (Aronson, Wilson, & Akert, 2002). Depending on the strength of your schema, you may also store in memory (even though you didn't hear it) the "information" that Ben did poorly in other courses as well. The information that Ben got an A in chemistry, because it contradicts your schema (it just doesn't seem right), may easily be distorted or lost. The information that Ben is transferring to Harvard, however, is a bit different. This information also is inconsistent with your schema; but it is so drastically inconsistent that you may begin to look at this mindfully. Perhaps you'll begin to question your schema for athletes, or perhaps you'll view Ben as an exception to the general rule. In either case, you're going to etch Ben's transferring to Harvard very clearly in your mind.

Stage Five: Recall

At some later date, you may want to recall or access information you have stored in memory. Let's say you want to retrieve your information about Ben because he's the topic of discussion among you and a few friends. As you'll see in the discussion of listening in the next chapter, memory isn't reproductive; you don't simply reproduce what you've heard or seen. Rather, you reconstruct what you've heard or seen into a whole that is meaningful to you—depending in great part on your schemata and scripts—and it's this reconstruction that you store in memory. Now, when you want to retrieve this information from memory, you may recall it with a variety of inaccuracies. You're likely to

- recall information that is consistent with your schema. In fact, you may not even recall the specific information you're looking for (say about Ben) but actually just your schema (which contains the information about college athletes and therefore about Ben).

- fail to recall information that is inconsistent with your schema. You have no place to put that information, so you easily lose it or forget it.

- recall information that drastically contradicts your schema because it forces you to think (and perhaps rethink) about your schema and its accuracy; it may even force you to revise your schema in general.

Reflections on the Model of Perception

Before moving on to the more specific processes involved in interpersonal perception, let's spell out some of the implications of this five-stage model for your own interpersonal perceptions.

1. Everyone relies on shortcuts—rules, schemata, and scripts, for example, are all useful shortcuts to simplify understanding, remembering, and recalling information about people and events. If you didn't have these shortcuts, you'd have to treat each person, role, or action differently from each other person, role, or action. This would make every experience totally new, totally unrelated to anything you already know. If you didn't use these shortcuts, you'd be unable to generalize, draw connections, or otherwise profit from previously acquired knowledge.

2. Shortcuts, however, may mislead you; they may contribute to your remembering things that are consistent with your schemata (even if they didn't occur) and distorting or forgetting information that is inconsistent.

www.researchnavigator.com

Read an Article: Read a scholarly or popular article on perception, how it works, and/or how it can be made more effective. On the basis of this article, what can you add to the discussion presented here?

Taking Another's Perspective

Looking at the world through another's perspective, rather than only through your own, is pivotal in achieving mutual understanding. For each of the situations below, identify specific circumstances that would lead you to form a *positive perception* and specific circumstances that might lead to a *negative perception*. After you've completed these, state the principle of perception that you feel this exercise illustrated.

1. A passerby ignores a homeless person who asks for money.
2. A middle-aged man walks down the street with his arm around a teenage girl.
3. A mother refuses to let her teenage son into her house.

? VIEWPOINT

One research study found that when male interviewers were told that female job applicants were interested in them, they elicited more flirtatious behavior from the women than when they were told that the women applicants were not interested in them. Further, the interviewers reported that they did not perceive any differences in the flirtatious behaviors of the applicants (Ridge & Reber, 2002). Why do you think this happened?

3. What you remember about a person or an event isn't an objective recollection but is more likely heavily influenced by your preconceptions or your schemata about what belongs and what doesn't belong, what fits neatly into the templates in your brain and what doesn't fit. Your reconstruction of an event or person contains a lot of information that was not in the original experience and may omit a lot that was in this experience.

4. Judgments about members of other cultures are often ethnocentric; because you form schemata and scripts on the basis of your own cultural beliefs and experiences, you can easily (but inappropriately) apply these to members of other cultures. It's easy to infer that when members of other cultures do things that conform to your scripts, they're right, and when they do things that contradict your scripts, they're wrong—a classic example of ethnocentric thinking. As you can appreciate, this tendency can easily contribute to intercultural misunderstandings.

5. A similar problem arises when you base your schemata for different cultural groups on stereotypes that you may have derived from television or movies. So, for example, you may have schemata for religious Muslims that you derived from stereotypes presented in the media. If you then apply these schemata to all Muslims, you risk seeing only what conforms to your script and failing to see or distorting what does not conform to your script.

6. Memory is especially unreliable when the information can be interpreted in different ways; that is, when information is ambiguous. For example, suppose you hear that "Ben didn't do as well in his other courses as he would have liked." If your schema for Ben is "brilliant," you may "remember" that Ben got B's. But if, as in our example, your schema is of the academically weak athlete, you may "remember" that Ben got D's. Conveniently, but unreliably, schemata reduce ambiguity.

Perceptual Processes

Before reading about the specific processes that you use in perceiving other people, examine your own perception strategies by taking the self-test, "How accurate are you at people perception?"

How Accurate Are You at People Perception?

INSTRUCTIONS: Respond to each of the following statements with T for true if the statement is usually or generally accurate in describing your behavior or with F for false if the statement is usually or generally inaccurate in describing your behavior.

_____ ❶ When I know some things about another person, I can pretty easily fill in what I don't know.

_____ ❷ I make predictions about people's behaviors that generally prove to be true.

_____ ❸ I base most of my impressions of people on the first few minutes of our meeting.

_____ ❹ I have clear ideas of what people of different national, racial, and religious groups are really like.

_____ ❺ I generally attribute people's attitudes and behaviors to their most obvious physical or psychological characteristic.

_____ ❻ I believe that the world is basically just, that good things happen to good people and bad things happen to bad people.

HOW DID YOU DO? This brief perception test was designed not to provide you with a specific perception score but to raise questions about concepts we'll explore in this chapter. All of the statements refer to perceptual processes that we may use but that often get us into trouble, leading us to form inaccurate impressions. These processes include implicit personality theory (statement 1), self-fulfilling prophecy (2), primacy–recency (3), and stereotyping (4). Statements 5 and 6 typify two kinds of mistakes we often make in attempting to attribute motives to other people's and even our own behaviors: overattribution (5) and the self-serving bias (6), which often involves a belief that the world is fundamentally just. Ideally, you would have responded to all of these statements with "false", indicating that you regularly avoid falling into these potential traps.

WHAT WILL YOU DO? As you read this chapter, think about these perceptual tendencies, and consider how you might avoid them so as to achieve more accurate and reasonable people perception. At the same time, recognize that situations vary widely and that this text's suggestions will prove useful in most but not all cases. In fact, you may want to identify situations in which you shouldn't follow these general suggestions.

Implicit Personality Theory

Consider the following brief statements. Note the word in parentheses that you think best completes each sentence:

Carlo is energetic, eager, and (intelligent, stupid).

Kim is bold, defiant, and (extroverted, introverted).

Joe is bright, lively, and (thin, heavy).

Ava is attractive, intelligent, and (likable, unlikable).

Susan is cheerful, positive, and (outgoing, shy).

Angel is handsome, tall, and (friendly, unfriendly).

What makes some of these choices seem right and others seem wrong is your **implicit personality theory,** the system of rules that tells you which characteristics go with which other characteristics. Your theory may, for example, have told you that a person who is energetic and eager is also likely to be intelligent, not stupid, although there is no logical reason why a stupid person could not be energetic and eager. Similarly, you may find yourself hired for a job on the basis of your demonstrated competitiveness because the personnel director has the implicit personality theory that along with competitiveness comes the willingness to work hard and the determination to succeed.

The widely documented **halo effect** is a function of the implicit personality theory (Dion, Berscheid, & Walster, 1972; Riggio, 1987). That is, if you believe a person has some positive qualities, you're likely to infer that she or he also possesses other positive qualities. There is also a *reverse halo effect:* if you know a person possesses several negative qualities, you're likely to infer that the person also has other negative qualities.

When using implicit personality theories, apply them carefully and critically so as to avoid perceiving qualities that your theory tells you should be present in an individual when they actually are not. For example, you may see "goodwill" in a friend's "charitable" acts when a tax deduction may have been the real motive.

Similarly, be careful of ignoring or distorting qualities that don't conform to your theory but that are actually present in the individual. For example, you may ignore negative qualities in your friends that you would easily perceive in your enemies.

As you might expect, the implicit personality theories that people hold differ from culture to culture, from group to group, and even from person to person. For example, the Chinese have a concept called *shi gu,* which refers to a person who is skillful, devoted to family, worldly, and reserved (Aronson, Wilson, & Akert, 2002). This concept isn't easily encoded in English, as you can tell by trying to find a general concept that covers this type of person. In English, on the other hand, we have a concept of the "artistic type," a generalization that seems absent in the Chinese languages. Thus, although it is easy for speakers of English or Chinese to refer to specific concepts—such as socially skilled or creative—each language creates its own generalized categories. As a result, in Chinese languages, the qualities that make up *shi gu* are more easily seen as going together than they might be for an English speaker; they're part of the implicit personality theory of more Chinese speakers than of, say, English speakers.

Communicating with power

Power through Self-Presentation

One way to exert power and influence is to use self-presentation strategies: to present yourself in ways that will encourage others to like you and to do as you wish (Jones & Pittman, 1982; Jones, 1990). Here are some examples:

- Use *ingratiation.* Express agreement, pay compliments, or do favors for the other person. But be aware that you run the risk of being seen as a sycophant, as someone who will stop at nothing to be liked.

- Use *self-promotion.* Present yourself as competent so that the other person will respect you. But be careful that you aren't perceived as incompetent because of the widespread belief that competent people *demonstrate* competence rather than talking about it.

- Use *exemplification.* Present yourself as worthy, moral, and virtuous. But beware of appearing sanctimonious or "holier than thou," a quality that most people dislike.

- Use *supplication.* Present yourself as helpless and in need of assistance: "Can you type my paper? I'm such a bad typist." But use caution: As a supplicant you risk being seen as incompetent or perhaps lazy.

Enhancing Your Communication Power
Which self-presentation strategy do you think would prove most helpful in an employment interview situation? How might it play out?

The Self-Fulfilling Prophecy

A **self-fulfilling prophecy** occurs when you make a prediction that comes true because you act on it as if it were true (Merton, 1957). Put differently, a self-fulfilling prophecy occurs when you act on your schema as if it were true and in doing so make it true. There are four basic steps in the self-fulfilling prophecy:

1. You make a prediction or formulate a belief about a person or a situation. For example, you expect Pat to be friendly in interpersonal encounters.
2. You act toward the person or situation as if that prediction or belief were true. For example, you act as if Pat were a friendly person.
3. Because you act as if the belief were true, it becomes true. For example, because of the way you act toward Pat, Pat becomes comfortable and friendly.
4. You observe *your* effect on the person or the resulting situation, and what you see strengthens your beliefs. For example, you observe Pat's friendliness, and this reinforces your belief that Pat is in fact friendly.

The self-fulfilling prophecy can also be seen when you make predictions about yourself and fulfill them. For example, suppose you enter a group situation convinced that the other members will dislike you. Almost invariably you'll be proved right; the other members will appear to you to dislike you. What you may be doing is acting in a way that encourages the group to respond to you negatively. In this way, you fulfill your prophecies about yourself.

A widely known example of the self-fulfilling prophecy is the **Pygmalion effect.** In one study, teachers were told that certain pupils were expected to do exceptionally well, that they were late bloomers. The names of these students were actually selected at random by the experimenters. The results, however, were not random. The students whose names were given to the teachers actually performed at a higher level than the others. In fact, these students' IQ scores even improved more than did the other students'. The teachers' expectations probably prompted them to give extra attention to the selected students, thereby positively affecting their performance (Rosenthal & Jacobson, 1968; Insel & Jacobson, 1975).

The same general effect is found in military training and business settings where trainees and workers performed better when their supervisors were given positive information about them (McNatt, 2001). Researchers also have noted the Pygmalion effect in such areas as leadership, athletic coaching, and effective stepfamilies (Eden, 1992; Solomon et al., 1996; Einstein, 1995). Findings such as these have led one researcher to suggest applying the Pygmalion effect as a way to improve worker productivity; the idea would be to promote positive attitudes about employees on the part of supervisors, thereby helping employees to feel that their supervisors and the organization as a whole value them highly (McNatt, 2001).

As you can see from these examples, self-fulfilling prophecies can short-circuit critical thinking and influence behavior in powerful ways. As a result, self-fulfilling prophecies can lead you to see what you predicted rather than what is really there (for example, to perceive yourself as a failure because you have predicted it rather than because of any actual failures).

> 𝟔𝟔 Manage every second of a first meeting. Do not delude yourself that a bad impression can be easily corrected. Putting things right is a lot harder than getting them right the first time. 𝟗𝟗
>
> —David Lewis

Primacy–Recency

Assume for a moment that you're enrolled in a course in which half the classes are extremely dull and half extremely exciting. At the end of the semester, you evaluate the course and the instructor. Would your evaluation be more favorable if the dull classes occurred in the first half of the semester and the exciting classes in the second? Or, would it be more favorable if the order were reversed? If what comes first exerts the most influence, you have a **primacy effect.** If what comes last (or most recently) exerts the most influence, you have a **recency effect.**

What Do You Say?

Primacy–Recency: Your partner forms initial impressions of people and never changes them. You want to show that this is illogical and is preventing you (and your partner) from developing relationships with exciting people who may have given a negative first impression. *What do you say? Through what channel?*

In the classic study on the effects of **primacy–recency** in interpersonal perception, college students perceived a person who was described as "intelligent, industrious, impulsive, critical, stubborn, and envious" more positively than a person described as "envious, stubborn, critical, impulsive, industrious, and intelligent" (Asch, 1946). Clearly, there's a tendency to use early information to get a general idea about a person and to use later information to make this impression more specific. The initial information helps you form a schema for the person. Once that schema is formed, you're likely to resist information that contradicts it.

One interesting practical implication of primacy–recency is that the first impression you make is likely to be the most important. The reason for this is that the schema that others form of you functions as a filter to admit or block additional information about you. If the initial impression or schema is positive, others are likely to remember additional positive information because it confirms their schema and to forget or distort negative information because it contradicts their schema. They are also more likely to interpret as positive information that is actually ambiguous. You win in all three ways—if the initial impression is positive.

The tendency to give greater weight to early information and to interpret later information in light of early impressions can lead you to formulate a total picture of an individual on the basis of initial impressions that may not be typical or accurate. For example, if you judge a job applicant as generally nervous when he or she may simply be showing normal nervousness at being interviewed for a much-needed job, you will have misperceived this individual.

Similarly, this tendency can lead you to discount or distort subsequent perceptions so as not to disrupt your initial impression or upset your original schema. For example, you may fail to see signs of deceit in someone you like because of your early impressions that this person is a good and honest individual.

Stereotyping

One of the most common shortcuts in interpersonal perception is stereotyping. A sociological or psychological **stereotype** is a fixed impression of a group of people; it's a schema. We all have attitudinal stereotypes—of national, religious, sexual, or racial groups, or perhaps of criminals, prostitutes, teachers, or plumbers. If you have these

---

Skill development experience

Perceptual Empathizing

Try empathizing with each of the individuals involved in the following scenarios, indicating how each person might *reasonably* view the situation. After completing both scenarios, try formulating a summary statement of your own empathic strengths and weaknesses.

1. Pat, a single parent, has two small children (ages 7 and 12) who often lack some of the important things children their age should have—such as school supplies, sneakers, and toys—because Pat can't afford them. Yet Pat smokes two packs of cigarettes a day.

   Pat sees . . .
   The 12-year-old daughter sees . . .
   The children's teachers see . . .

2. Chris has extremely high standards and feels that getting all A's is an absolute necessity. In fear of that first B (after three and a half years of college), Chris cheats on an examination and gets caught by the instructor.

   Chris sees . . .
   The instructor sees . . .
   The average B or C student sees . . .

fixed impressions, you will, on meeting a member of a particular group, often see that person primarily as a member of that group and apply to him or her all the characteristics you assign to that group. If you meet someone who is a prostitute, for example, there is a host of characteristics for prostitutes that you may apply to this one person. To complicate matters further, you will often "see" in this person's behavior the manifestation of characteristics that you would not "see" if you didn't know what the person did for a living. Stereotypes can easily distort accurate perception and prevent you from seeing an individual as an individual rather than as a member of a group. Stereotypes can be especially prevalent in online communication; because there are few visual and auditory cues, it's not surprising that people often form impressions of online communication partners with a heavy reliance on stereotypes (Jacobson, 1999).

"It's all according to your point of view. To me, *you're* a monster."

The tendency to group people and to respond to individuals primarily as members of groups can lead you to perceive an individual as possessing those qualities (usually negative) that you believe characterize his or her group (for example, "all Mexicans are . . . ," or "all Baptists are . . ."). As a result, you may fail to appreciate the multifaceted nature of all individuals and groups. Stereotyping also can lead you to ignore each person's unique characteristics so that you fail to benefit from the special contributions each individual can bring to an encounter.

Attribution

Attribution is the process by which we try to explain the reason or motivation for a person's behavior. One way to engage in attribution is to ask if the person was in control of the behavior. For example, suppose you invite your friend Desmond to dinner for 7 p.m. and he arrives at 9. Consider how you would respond to each of these reasons:

> Reason 1: I just couldn't tear myself away from the beach. I really wanted to get a great tan.

> Reason 2: I was driving here when I saw some young kids mugging an old couple. I broke it up and took the couple home. They were so frightened that I had to stay with them until their children arrived. Their phone was out of order, so I had no way of calling to tell you I'd be late.

> Reason 3: I got in a car accident and was taken to the hospital.

Assuming you believed all three explanations, you would attribute very different motives to Desmond's behavior. With reasons 1 and 2, you would conclude that Desmond was in control of his behavior; with reason 3, that he was not. Further, you would probably respond negatively to reason 1 (Desmond was selfish and inconsiderate) and positively to reason 2 (Desmond was a Good Samaritan). Because Desmond was not in control of his behavior in reason 3, you would probably not attribute either positive or negative motivation to his behavior. Instead, you would probably feel sorry that he got into an accident.

You probably make similar judgments based on controllability in numerous situations. Consider, for example, how you would respond to the following situations:

- Doris fails her history midterm exam.
- Sidney's car is repossessed because he failed to keep up the payments.
- Margie is 150 pounds overweight and is complaining that she feels awful.
- Thomas's wife has just filed for divorce and he is feeling depressed.

You would most likely be sympathetic to each of these people if you felt that he or she was not in control of what happened; for example, if the examination was unfair, if Sidney lost his job because of employee discrimination, if Margie had a

Checking Your Perceptions

Select one of the following messages and write perception checks in which you *(a)* describe what you see or hear in the communication and the meaning you're interpreting from these perceptions and *(b)* ask for confirmation.

1. "I called three people. They all have something to do on Saturday night. I guess I'll just curl up with a good book or a good movie. It'll be better than a lousy date, anyway."
2. "My parents are getting divorced after 20 years of marriage. My mother and father are both dating other people now, so I guess everything is okay."
3. "I'm never going to find someone to love me. I can't stand being alone any longer. It's over."

by unknown situations. Examples of such low-anxiety cultures include those of Singapore, Jamaica, Denmark, Sweden, Hong Kong, Ireland, Great Britain, Malaysia, India, Philippines, and the United States. People in other cultures do much to avoid uncertainty and have a great deal of anxiety about not knowing what will happen next; they see uncertainty as a threatening issue that must be counteracted. Examples of such high-anxiety cultures include Greece, Portugal, Guatemala, Uruguay, Belgium, El Salvador, Japan, Yugoslavia, Peru, France, Chile, Spain, and Costa Rica (Hofstede, 1997).

The potential for communication problems can be great when people come from cultures with different attitudes toward uncertainty. For example, managers from cultures with weak uncertainty avoidance (low anxiety) will accept employees who work only when they have to and will not get too upset when workers are late. Managers from cultures with strong uncertainty avoidance (high anxiety) will expect workers to be busy at all times and will have little tolerance for lateness.

Because weak-uncertainty-avoidance cultures have tolerance for ambiguity and uncertainty, members of these cultures minimize the importance of rules governing communication and relationships (Hofstede, 1997; Lustig & Koester, 2002). That is, they readily tolerate people who don't follow the same rules as the cultural majority; they may even encourage different approaches and perspectives. In contrast, strong-uncertainty-avoidance cultures create and enforce very clear-cut rules for communication.

Students from weak-uncertainty-avoidance cultures appreciate freedom in education and prefer vague assignments without specific timetables. These students want to be rewarded for creativity and will even accept an instructor's (occasional) lack of knowledge. Students from strong-uncertainty-avoidance cultures prefer highly structured experiences in which there is little ambiguity; they prefer specific objectives, detailed instructions, and definite timetables. These students expect to be judged on the basis of the right answers and expect the instructor to have all the answers all the time (Hofstede, 1997).

A variety of **uncertainty reduction strategies** can help reduce uncertainty in interpersonal communication (Berger & Bradac, 1982; Gudykunst, 1994).

- Observing another person while he or she is engaged in an active task, preferably interacting with others in relatively informal social situations, often will reveal a great deal about the person: People are less apt to monitor their behaviors and more likely to reveal their true selves in informal situations.
- You can manipulate situations so as to be able to observe a person in more specific and more revealing contexts. Employment interviews, theatrical auditions,

VIEWPOINT

What one suggestion for increasing perceptual accuracy do you find the most important? What perceptual errors do you find are made most often? With what consequences?

and student teaching placements are examples of situations designed to reduce uncertainty by letting observers see how people act and react.

- When you log on to an Internet chat group for the first time and you lurk, reading the exchanges among other group members before saying anything yourself, you're learning about the people in the group and about the group itself and thus reducing uncertainty. When uncertainty is reduced, you're more likely to make contributions that will be appropriate to the group and less likely to violate any of the group's norms; in short, you're more likely to communicate effectively.

- Another way to reduce uncertainty is to collect information about the person by asking others. For example, you might ask a colleague if a third person finds you interesting and might like to have dinner with you.

- And of course you can interact with the individual. For example, you can ask questions: "Do you enjoy sports?" "What did you think of that computer science course?" "What would you do if you got fired?" You also gain knowledge of another by disclosing information about yourself. Your disclosures will help create an environment that encourages disclosures from the person about whom you wish to learn more.

Increase Your Cultural Awareness

Recognizing and being mindful of cultural differences will help increase your accuracy in perception. For example, Russian or Chinese performers such as ballet dancers will often applaud their audience by clapping. Americans seeing this may easily interpret this as egotistical. Similarly, a German man will enter a restaurant before the woman in order to see if the place is respectable enough for the woman. This simple custom may appear rude to people from cultures in which it's considered courteous to allow the woman to enter first (Axtell, 1991).

Cultural awareness will help counteract the difficulty most people have in understanding the nonverbal messages of people from other cultures. For example, be aware that it's easier to decode emotions communicated facially by members of your own culture than to read emotions shown by members of other cultures (Weathers, Frank, & Spell, 2002). This "in-group advantage" will assist your perceptional accuracy for members of your own culture but will often hinder your accuracy for members of other cultures (Elfenbein & Ambady, 2002).

Within every cultural group, too, there are wide and important differences. Not all Americans are alike, and neither are all Indonesians, Greeks, Mexicans, and so on. When you make assumptions that all people of a certain culture are alike, you're thinking in stereotypes. In addition to recognizing differences between another culture and your own, recognizing differences among members of any given culture will help you perceive situations more accurately.

Summary of Concepts and Skills

In this chapter we explored the way we receive messages through perception, how perception works, the processes that influence it, and how to make your perceptions more accurate.

1. Perception is the process by which you become aware of the many stimuli impinging on your senses. It occurs in five stages: Sensory stimulation occurs, sensory stimulation is organized, sensory stimulation is interpreted–evaluated, sensory stimulation is held in memory, and sensory stimulation is recalled.

2. The following processes influence perception: (1) implicit personality theory, (2) self-fulfilling prophecy, (3) primacy–recency, (4) stereotyping, and (5) attribution.

3. *Implicit personality theories* are the private personality theories that we all hold and that influence how we perceive other people.

4. A self-fulfilling prophecy occurs when you make a prediction or formulate a belief that comes true because you have made the prediction and acted as if it were true.

5. The principle of *primacy–recency* has to do with the relative influence of stimuli as a result of their order. If what occurs first exerts greater influence, you have a primacy effect. If what occurs last exerts greater influence, you have a recency effect.

6. *Stereotyping* is the tendency to develop and maintain fixed, unchanging perceptions of groups of people and to use these perceptions to evaluate individual members of these groups, ignoring individuals' unique characteristics.

7. *Attribution* is the process through which you try to understand the behaviors of others (and your own, in self-attribution), particularly the reasons or motivations for these behaviors. One important part of attribution is judging controllability. Errors of attribution include the self-serving bias, overattribution, and the fundamental attribution errors.

8. Several strategies can increase the accuracy of interpersonal perceptions: (1) Perceive critically; for example, recognizing your role in perception, formulating hypotheses rather than conclusions, looking for a variety of cues (especially contradictory ones), avoiding mind reading, and being aware of your own biases. (2) Check perceptions; that is, describe what you see or hear and ask for confirmation. (3) Reduce uncertainty by, for example,

lurking before joining a group, collecting information about the person or situation, and interacting and observing the interaction. And (4) be culturally aware, recognizing the differences between you and others as well as the differences among members of the culturally different group.

Throughout this discussion of perception, a variety of skills were identified. Check your ability to apply these skills, using the following scale: 1 = almost always; 2 = often; 3 = sometimes; 4 = rarely; and 5 = hardly ever.

_____ 1. I think mindfully when I use perceptual shortcuts so that they don't mislead me and result in inaccurate perceptions.

_____ 2. I guard against ethnocentric thinking by viewing the behavior and customs of others from a multicultural view rather than from just my cultural view.

_____ 3. I bring to consciousness my implicit personality theories.

_____ 4. To guard against the self-fulfilling prophecy, I take a second look at my perceptions when they conform too closely to my expectations.

_____ 5. To prevent distortions from perceptual accentuation, I consciously search for information that may contradict what I expect or want to see.

_____ 6. Recognizing how primacy–recency works, I actively guard against first impressions that might prevent accurate perceptions of future events; I formulate hypotheses rather than conclusions.

_____ 7. I recognize stereotyping in the messages of others and avoid it in my own.

_____ 8. I am aware of and am careful to avoid the self-serving bias, overattribution, and the fundamental attribution error when trying to account for another person's behavior.

_____ 9. I think critically about perception, analyzing my perceptions, checking my perceptions for accuracy, using uncertainty reduction strategies, and acting with cultural sensitivity.

Key Word Quiz

Write T for those statements that are true and F for those that are false. For those that are false, replace the italicized term with the correct term.

_____ 1. The mental templates or structures that help you organize new information as well as the information you already have in memory are called *schemata*.

_____ 2. Concluding that a person has positive qualities because you know that he or she has other positive qualities is known as *mind reading*.

_____ 3. The process by which we try to explain the motivation for a person's behavior is known as *attribution*.

_____ 4. A fixed impression of a group of people is known as a *stereotype*.

_____ 5. An organization of information about some action, event, or procedure is called a *script*.

_____ 6. Selective attention and selective exposure are examples of *perceptual organization by rules*.

_____ 7. Taking credit for the positive things you do and attributing your negative actions to external uncontrollable factors is often the result of the *self-serving bias*.

_____ 8. When what comes first exerts the most influence, you have a *recency effect*.

_____ 9. When you make a prediction and it comes true because you made the prediction and acted as if it were true, the process is called the *self-fulfilling prophecy*.

_____ 10. Attributing just about everything a person does to one or two obvious characteristics is known as *personality theory*.

Answers: TRUE: 1, 3, 4, 5, 7, 9; FALSE: 2 (the *halo effect*), 6 (*selective perception*), 8 (*primacy effect*), 10 (*overattribution*)

4 Listening in Human Communication

Chapter Concepts	Chapter Skills	
This chapter introduces listening and offers ways to improve your own listening effectiveness.	After completing this chapter, you should be able to:	**65**
Stages of Listening	listen more effectively during each of the five listening stages.	
Styles of Effective Listening	adjust your listening through your understanding of empathic and objective, nonjudgmental and critical, surface and depth, and active and inactive listening.	
Listening Differences: Culture and Gender	communicate with an awareness of cultural and gender differences in listening.	

Perception and listening are the two major ways in which you receive and make sense of messages. Taken together, the skills of perception and listening will enable you to perceive more accurately, to understand better, and to interpret and evaluate messages more accurately. Perception, as explained in the previous chapter, is the process by which you sense, organize, interpret–evaluate, remember, and recall a wide variety of stimuli. It's the basic process that underlies your receiving any and all stimuli. **Listening** is a more specialized process, a type of perception by which you receive auditory signals.

Effective listening helps you to *learn*—to acquire knowledge of others, the world, and yourself; to avoid problems and difficulties; and to make more reasoned and reasonable decisions. It enables you to profit from the insights of others, to hear and be able to respond to warnings of impending problems, and to acquire more information relevant to decisions you'll be called on to make. For example, listening to workers talk about safety equipment will, research shows, make a difference in the overall safety of your workplace (Preidt, 2000). Listening to Peter talk about his travels to Cuba will help you learn more about Peter and about life in Cuba; listening to student reactions will help the teacher plan more relevant classes; listening to the difficulties your sales staff has may help you offer more pertinent sales training.

Effective listening helps you *relate* to others. Because people come to like those who are attentive and supportive, you're likely to gain social acceptance and popularity through listening. When you communicate genuine concern for others through attentive and supportive listening, their liking for you will increase.

Through listening you can *influence* the attitudes and behaviors of others. People are more likely to respect and follow those they feel have listened to and understood them. For example, employees are more likely to follow your advice as a leader if they feel you listen carefully to their contributions and concerns. The effective listener is also more likely to emerge as group leader and is a more effective adaptive seller and salesperson in general (Johnson & Bechler, 1998; Kramer, 1997; Castleberry & Shepherd, 1993).

Your ability to listen effectively enables you to engage in communication as enjoyment, as *play*. Knowing when to suspend critical and evaluative thinking and when simply to engage in appreciative and accepting listening is crucial to effective communication generally. For example, listening to coworkers' anecdotes will allow you to gain a more comfortable balance between the world of work and the world of play.

> **❝** They [higher management] believe more and more that listening skills are crucial to job performance and are demanding that managers do something about it. Listening can no longer be sloughed off as just one more item in the vocabulary of communication. **❞**
>
> —Warren Reed

Referent and Expert Power

Two related bases of power are referent and expert. You have **referent power** over another person when the person wants to be like you. For example, a successful stockbroker may have referent power over a college intern because the intern wants to be like the broker. The assumption made by the intern is that he or she will be more like the broker if he or she behaves and believes as the broker does. Generally, your referent power over another person increases when you're well liked and well respected, when you're perceived as attractive and prestigious, and when you're of the same sex and have similar attitudes and experiences as the other person.

You have **expert power** if another person regards you as having expertise or knowledge. Expert power increases when you're seen as unbiased, with nothing to gain personally from influencing others.

Enhancing Your Communication Power

In what ways might you enhance your referent or expert power in your interpersonal, small group, and public speaking interactions?

Effective listening enables you to *help* others. You'll hear more, empathize more, and come to understand others more deeply. For example, listening to your child's complaints about her teacher (instead of saying, "Now what did you do wrong?") will increase your ability to help your child cope with school and her teacher.

Stages of Listening

Listening is an active and complex process that occurs in five stages: receiving, understanding, remembering, evaluating, and responding (Figure 4.1). Note that the process is circular: The responses of person A serve as the stimuli for person B, whose responses, in turn, serve as the stimuli for person A, and so on.

Figure **4.1**

A Five-Stage Model of the Listening Process
This model depicts the various stages involved in listening. Note that receiving or hearing is not the same thing as listening, but is in fact only the first step in a five-step process. This model draws on a variety of previous models that listening researchers have developed (for example, Alessandra, 1986; Barker, 1990; Brownell, 1987; Steil, Barker, & Watson, 1983). In what other ways might you visualize the listening process?

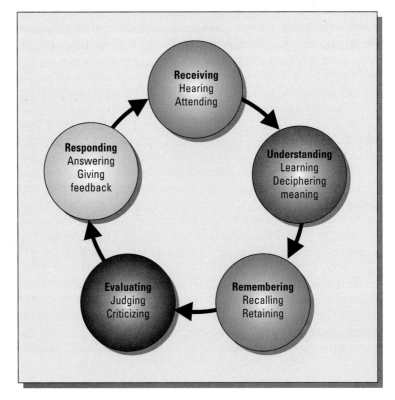

Receiving

Hearing, which is not the same as listening, begins and ends with the first stage of the listening process, receiving. Hearing simply happens when you open your ears or get within range of some auditory stimulus. Listening, on the other hand, is quite different. Listening begins but does not end with receiving (or hearing) messages the speaker sends.

At the receiving stage, you note not only what is said (verbally and nonverbally), but also what is omitted. For example, you receive not only the politician's summary of accomplishments in education, but also the omission of failures in health care or pollution control.

This receiving stage of listening can be made more effective if you

- focus attention on the speaker's verbal and nonverbal messages, on what is said and what is not said;
- avoid distractions in the environment;
- focus attention on the speaker's messages, not on what you will say next;
- maintain your role as listener by not interrupting the speaker; and
- confront mixed messages—messages that communicate different and contradictory meanings.

In this brief discussion of receiving, and in fact throughout this chapter on listening, the unstated assumption is that both individuals can receive auditory signals without difficulty. But for many people who have hearing impairments, listening presents a variety of problems. Table 4.1 on page 68 provides tips for communication between deaf and hearing people.

Understanding

Understanding occurs when you decode the speaker's signals, when you learn what the speaker means. Understanding means grasping both the thoughts that are expressed and the emotional tone that accompanies them—for example, the urgency, joy, or sorrow expressed in the message.

The understanding phase of listening can be made more effective if you

- relate the speaker's new information to what you already know (in what way will this new proposal change our present health care?);
- see the speaker's messages from the speaker's point of view, in part by not judging the message until it's fully understood as the speaker intended it;
- ask questions for clarification or request additional details or examples if needed; and/or
- rephrase (paraphrase) the speaker's ideas, a simple process that's especially important when listening to complicated instructions.

> **"** The opposite of talking isn't listening. The opposite of talking is waiting. **"**
>
> —Fran Lebowitz

> **"** [Listening is] a very dangerous thing. If one listens one may be convinced. **"**
>
> —Oscar Wilde

Blondie

© Reprinted with special permission of King Features Syndicate.

TABLE 4.1 *Interpersonal Communication Tips*

BETWEEN DEAF AND HEARING PEOPLE

People differ greatly in their hearing ability; some are totally deaf and can hear nothing, others have some hearing loss and can hear some sounds, and still others have impaired hearing but can hear most speech. Although many people with profound hearing loss can speak, their speech may seem labored and less clear than the speech of those with unimpaired hearing. Here are some suggestions to help deaf and hearing people communicate more effectively.

If you have unimpaired hearing:

1. Set up a comfortable context. Reduce the distance between yourself and the person with a hearing impairment. Reduce the background noise. Turn off the television and even the air conditioner.

2. Face the person and avoid any interference with the visual cues from your speech; for example, avoid smoking, chewing gum, or holding your hand over your mouth. Make sure the lighting is adequate.

3. Speak with an adequate volume, but avoid shouting which can distort your speech and may insult the person. Be careful to avoid reducing volume at the ends of your sentences.

4. Because some words are easier to lip-read than others, it often helps if you can rephrase your ideas in different ways.

5. In group situations only one person should speak at a time. Similarly, avoid the tendency to talk to a person with hearing loss through a third party. Elementary school teachers, for example, have been found to direct fewer comments to deaf children than to hearing students (Cawthon, 2001). So direct your comments to the person himself or herself.

6. Ask the person if there is anything you can do to make it easier for him or her to understand you.

7. Don't avoid terms like *hear, listen, music,* or *deaf* when they're relevant to the conversation. Trying to avoid these common terms will make your speech sound artificial.

8. Use nonverbal cues to help communicate your meaning; gestures indicating size or location and facial expressions indicating emotions and feelings are often helpful.

If you have impaired hearing:

1. Do your best to eliminate background noise.

2. Move closer to the speaker if this helps. Alert the other person that this closer distance will help you hear better.

3. If you feel the speaker can make adjustments that will make it easier for you to understand, ask. For example, ask the speaker to repeat a message, to speak more slowly or more distinctly, or to increase his or her volume.

4. If you hear better in one ear than another, position yourself accordingly and, if necessary, clue the other person in to this fact.

5. If necessary, ask the person to write down certain information, such as phone numbers or website addresses. Carrying a pad and pencil will prove helpful, both for this purpose and in the event that you wish to write something down for others.

Sources: These suggestions were drawn from a variety of sources: *Tips for Communicating with Deaf People* (Rochester Institute of Technology, National Technical Institute for the Deaf, Division of Public Affairs); http://www.his.com/~lola/deaf.html; http://www.zak.co.il/deaf-info/old/comm_strategies.html; and http://www.agbell.org/information/brochures_communication.cfm. All websites accessed April 5, 2002.

Remembering

Messages that you receive and understand need to be retained for at least some period of time. In some small group and public speaking situations, you can augment your memory by taking notes or by taping the messages. In most interpersonal communication situations, however, such note taking would be considered inappropriate, although you often do write down a phone number or an appointment or directions.

What you remember is not what was actually said but what you think (or remember) was said. You don't simply *reproduce* in your memory what the speaker said; rather, you *reconstruct* the messages you hear into a system that makes sense to you—a concept noted in the discussion of perception in Chapter 3.

You can make this remembering phase of listening more effective if you

- identify the central ideas and the major support advanced;

- summarize the message in an easier-to-retain form, not ignoring crucial details or qualifications;

> ❝ A good memory and a tongue tied in the middle is a combination which gives immortality to conversation. ❞
>
> —Mark Twain

 VIEWPOINT

In the famous McMartin preschool trial—the photo here is a scene from the HBO movie based on that trial—children accused the McMartins of sexual molestation, but the jury found that the children's recollections were false and were implanted in the children's memories by overzealous prosecutors and therapists. This seems quite easy to accomplish. For example, in one study researchers repeatedly asked children about a fictitious event. By the 10th week more than 50 percent of the children reported that the event happened and provided reasonable details about the incident (Porter, Brit, Yuille, & Lehman, 2000; Brody, 2000). In what other, less dramatic ways can "false memory syndrome" occur?

- repeat names and key concepts to yourself or, if appropriate, aloud;
- take notes, if appropriate; and/or
- identify patterns and use them to organize what the speaker is saying (if this is a formal talk with a recognizable organizational structure).

Evaluating

Evaluating consists of judging the messages you hear. At times you may try to evaluate the speaker's underlying intent, often without much conscious awareness. For example, Elaine tells you she is up for a promotion and is really excited about it. You may then try to judge her intention. Does she want you to use your influence with the company president? Is she preoccupied with the possible promotion and therefore telling everyone? Is she looking for a pat on the back? Generally, if you know the person well, you will be able to identify the intention and respond appropriately.

In other situations, your evaluation is more in the nature of critical analysis. For example, in a business meeting on upgrading office equipment, you'd evaluate the office manager's proposals while listening to them. As you're listening, you'd be asking yourself, "Are the proposals practical? Will they increase productivity? What is the evidence? Are there more practical alternatives?"

This evaluation stage of listening can be made more effective if you

- resist evaluating until you fully understand the speaker's point of view;
- assume that the speaker is a person of goodwill and give the speaker the benefit of any doubt by asking for clarification on issues you object to (are there any other reasons for accepting this new proposal?);

www.researchnavigator.com

Read an Article: Read a scholarly or popular article on listening, styles or types of listening, or culture or gender differences in listening. On the basis of this article, what can you add to the discussion presented here?

What Do You Say?

Hate Speech: Your work colleagues frequently use derogatory racial terms. You want to protest this kind of talk but at the same time you don't want to alienate people you're going to have to work closely with for some time to come. *What do you say? To whom? Through what channel?*

- distinguish facts from inferences (see Chapter 5), opinions, and personal interpretations by the speaker; and
- identify any biases, self-interests, or prejudices that might lead the speaker to slant information unfairly.

Responding

Responding occurs in two forms: (1) responses you make while the speaker is talking and (2) responses you make after the speaker has stopped talking. Responses made while the speaker is talking should be supportive and should acknowledge that you're listening. These responses are *backchanneling cues:* messages (words and gestures) that let the speaker know you're paying attention, as when you nod in agreement or say, "I see" or "Uh-huh."

Responses after the speaker has stopped talking are generally more elaborate and might include empathy ("I know how you must feel"); requests for clarification ("Do you mean this new health plan will replace the old one, or will it be just a supplement?"); challenges ("I think your evidence is weak"); and/or agreement ("You're absolutely right, and I'll support your proposal when it comes up for a vote").

You can improve this responding phase of listening if you

- express support for the speaker throughout the talk by using varied backchanneling cues (though using only one—for example, saying, "Uh-huh," throughout—will make it appear that you're not listening but are merely on automatic pilot);
- express support for the speaker in your final responses; and
- take ownership of your responses by stating your thoughts and feelings as your own and using "I" messages (saying, "I think the new proposal will entail greater expense than you outlined" rather than "Everyone will object to the plan's cost").

"I can't get off the phone, he won't stop listening!"

Reprinted by permission of Jerry Marcus.

Communicating ethically

Listening Ethically

Communication is a two-way process; both speaker and listener share in the success or failure of the interaction. And both share in the moral implications of the communication exchange. Two major principles govern the ethics of listening.

First, give the speaker an *honest hearing.* Avoid prejudging. Put aside prejudices and preconceptions and evaluate the speaker's message fairly. At the same time, empathize with the speaker. You don't have to agree, but try to understand emotionally as well as intellectually what the speaker means. Then accept or reject the speaker's ideas on the basis of the information offered, not on the basis of some bias.

Second, give the speaker *honest responses.* Give open and honest feedback to the speaker. In a learning environment such as a communication class, giving ethical feedback means giving honest and constructive criticism to help the speaker improve. It also means reflecting honestly on the questions that the speaker raises.

What Would You Do?

You're teaching a class in communication, and in the public speaking segment, one of your students wants to give a speech on "the values of Nazism." You know that this will cause all sorts of problems, yet you wonder if you should place yourself in the position of censor. What would you do? What would you do if the student wanted to speak on techniques for cheating on income taxes, ways to create computer viruses, or the values of steroids?

Listening to the Emotions of Others

Listening to the feelings of others is often difficult; it can be hard to know how to react or what to say in response. Here are a few guidelines for making this process a little easier.

- Don't equate "responding to another's feelings" with "solving the person's problems" (Tannen, 1990). It's usually better to view your task as one of encouraging the person to express and perhaps to clarify his or her feelings in a supportive atmosphere.

- Empathize. Put yourself into the position of the other person. Be especially careful to avoid evaluating the other person's feelings. For example, a comment such as "Don't worry, you'll get promoted next year" can easily be interpreted as "Your feelings are wrong or inappropriate," which does nothing to help the person feel better or to clarify his or her feelings.

- Focus on the other person. Avoid responding with your own problems. Although it's often useful to relate similar experiences that you've had, avoid refocusing the conversation on you and away from the other person.

- Encourage the person to explore his or her feelings. Use simple encouragers like "I see" or "I understand," or ask questions that let the speaker know that you're listening and that you're interested in hearing more.

Applying Listening Skills

Your best friend tells you that she suspects her boyfriend is seeing someone else. She's extremely upset and tells you that she wants to confront him with her suspicions but is afraid of what she'll hear. What listening guidelines would you suggest she use?

Styles of Effective Listening

Before reading about the principles of effective listening, examine your own listening habits and tendencies by taking the following self-test, "How good a listener are you?" The "desirable" answers are obvious, of course, but try to give responses that are true for you in most of your listening experiences.

Test Yourself

How Good a Listener Are You?

INSTRUCTIONS: Respond to each question using the following scale: 1 = always; 2 = frequently; 3 = sometimes; 4 = seldom; and 5 = never.

_____ ❶ I listen to what the speaker is saying and feeling; I try to feel what the speaker feels.

_____ ❷ I listen objectively; I focus on the logic of the ideas rather than on the emotional meaning of the message.

_____ ❸ I listen without judging the speaker.

_____ ❹ I listen critically; I rarely suspend my critical, evaluative faculties.

_____ ❺ I listen to the literal meaning, to what the speaker says, rather than play psychiatrist and focus on the hidden or deeper meanings.

_____ ❻ I listen for the speaker's hidden meanings, to what the speaker means but isn't verbalizing.

❝ From listening comes wisdom, and from speaking repentance. ❞

—Italian Proverb

> ❝ The first duty of love is to listen. ❞
>
> —Paul Tillich

HOW DID YOU DO? These statements focus on the ways of listening discussed in this chapter. All of these ways are appropriate at some times but not at others: It depends. So the only responses that are really inappropriate are "always" and "never." Effective listening is listening that is tailored to the specific communication situation.

WHAT WILL YOU DO? Consider how you might use your responses on this self-test to begin to improve your listening effectiveness. A good way to begin doing this is to review the statements and try to identify situations in which each statement would be appropriate and situations in which each would be inappropriate.

As stressed throughout this chapter, listening is situational: the type of listening that is appropriate will vary with the situation, each set of circumstances calling for a somewhat different combination of listening styles. The art of effective listening is largely a matter of making appropriate choices along the following four dimensions: empathic and objective listening, nonjudgmental and critical listening, surface and depth listening, and active and inactive listening.

Empathic and Objective Listening

If you're to understand what a person means and what a person is feeling, you need to listen with some degree of empathy (Rogers, 1970; Rogers & Farson, 1981). To empathize with others is to feel with them, to see the world as they see it, to feel what they feel. Only when you achieve this can you fully understand another person's meaning. Empathic listening will also help you enhance your relationships (Barrett & Godfrey, 1988; Snyder, 1992).

Although for most communication situations empathic listening is the preferred mode of responding, there are times when you need to go beyond it and to measure the speaker's meanings and feelings against some objective reality. It's important to listen to Peter tell you how the entire world hates him and to understand how Peter feels and why he feels this way. But then you need to look a bit more objectively at the situation and perhaps see Peter's paranoia or self-hatred. Sometimes you have to put your empathic responses aside and listen with objectivity and detachment.

In adjusting your empathic and objective listening focus, keep the following recommendations in mind.

- Punctuate from the speaker's point of view (Chapter 1). That is, see the sequence of events as the speaker does and try to figure out how this perspective can influence what the speaker says and does.
- Engage in equal, two-way conversation. To encourage openness and empathy, try to eliminate any physical or psychological barriers to equality; for example, step from behind the large desk separating you from your employees. Avoid interrupting the speaker—a sign that what you have to say is more important.
- Seek to understand both thoughts and feelings. Don't consider your listening task finished until you've understood what the speaker is feeling as well as what he or she is thinking.
- Avoid "offensive listening"—the tendency to listen to bits and pieces of information that will enable you to attack the speaker or find fault with something the speaker has said.
- Strive especially to be objective when listening to friends or foes alike. Your attitudes may lead you to distort messages—to block out positive messages about a foe or negative messages about a friend. Guard against "expectancy hearing," in which you fail to hear what the speaker is really saying and instead hear what you expect.

What Do You Say?

Empathic Listening: Your neighbors who've avoided work all their lives and lived off unfairly obtained government disability payments have just won the lottery for $16 million. They want you to share their joy and invite you over for a champagne toast. *What do you say?*

Nonjudgmental and Critical Listening

Effective listening includes both nonjudgmental and critical responses. You need to listen nonjudgmentally—with an open mind and with a view toward understanding. But you also need to listen critically—with a view toward making some kind of evaluation or judgment. Clearly, it's important to listen first for understanding while suspending judgment. Only after you've fully understood the relevant messages should you evaluate or judge.

Supplement open-minded listening with critical listening. Listening with an open mind will help you understand the messages better; listening with a critical mind will help you analyze and evaluate the messages. In adjusting your nonjudgmental and critical listening, focus on the following guidelines:

- Keep an open mind. Avoid prejudging. Delay your judgments until you fully understand both the content and the intention the speaker is communicating. Avoid either positive or negative evaluation until you have a reasonably complete understanding.

- Avoid filtering out or oversimplifying difficult or complex messages. Similarly, avoid filtering out undesirable messages. Clearly, you don't want to hear that something you believe is untrue, that people you care for are unkind, or that ideals you hold are self-destructive. Yet it's important that you reexamine your beliefs by listening to these messages.

- Recognize your own biases. These may interfere with accurate listening and cause you to distort message reception through a process of *assimilation*—the tendency to integrate and interpret what you hear or think you hear in keeping with your own biases, prejudices, and expectations. For example, are your ethnic, national, or religious biases preventing you from appreciating a speaker's point of view?

- Avoid uncritical listening when you need to make evaluations and judgments.

- Recognize and combat the normal tendency to *sharpen*—a process in which we tend to highlight, emphasize, and perhaps embellish one or two aspects of a message. Often the concepts that are sharpened are incidental remarks that somehow get emphasized and now stand out from the rest of the message.

 VIEWPOINT

Empathy may also have a negative side. For example, you are likely most empathic with those who are similar to you—racially and ethnically as well as in appearance and social status. The more empathy you feel toward your own group, however, the less empathy you may feel toward other groups. So although empathy may encourage understanding, it may also create dividing lines or even hostility between "you" and "them" (Angier, 1995). Have you ever witnessed these negative effects of empathy?

Surface and Depth Listening

In Shakespeare's *Julius Caesar*, Marc Antony, in giving the funeral oration for Caesar, says: "I come to bury Caesar, not to praise him. / The evil that men do lives after them; / The good is oft interred with their bones." And later: "For Brutus is an honourable man; / So are they all, all honourable men." But Antony, as we know, did come to praise Caesar and to convince the crowd that Brutus was not an honorable man.

In most messages there's an obvious meaning that you can derive from a literal reading of the words and sentences. But in reality, most messages have more than one level of meaning. Sometimes, as in *Julius Caesar*, the other level is the opposite of the literal meaning; at other times it seems totally unrelated. Consider some frequently heard types of messages. Carol asks you how you like her new haircut. On one level, the meaning is clear: Do you like the haircut? But there's also another and

Regulating Your Listening Perspective

What listening styles would you most likely use in each of these situations? What listening styles would be obviously inappropriate in each situation?

1. Your steady dating partner for the last five years tells you that his/her spells of depression are becoming more frequent and more long-lasting.
2. Your five-year-old daughter says she wants to become a nurse.
3. Your brother tells you he's been accepted into Harvard's MBA program.
4. Your supervisor explains the new computerized mail system.

truthful. As a result, people may respond with positive feedback (say, in commenting on a business colleague's proposal) even though they don't really feel positive. Listen to feedback, as you would to all messages, with a full recognition that various cultures view feedback very differently.

Listening and Gender

Deborah Tannen opens her chapter on listening in her best-selling *You Just Don't Understand: Women and Men in Conversation* with several anecdotes illustrating that when men and women talk, men lecture and women listen. The lecturer assumes the role of the superior or that of the teacher or expert. The listener is then made to assume the role of the inferior, the student, or the nonexpert.

Women, according to Tannen, seek to build rapport and establish relationships and so use listening to achieve these ends. For example, women use more listening cues that let the other person know they are paying attention and are interested. Men not only use fewer listening cues but also interrupt more. Additionally, men will often change the topic to an area they know more about or switch from a subject that is relational or people oriented to a topic that is more factual, such as sports statistics, economic developments, or political problems. Men, research shows, play up their expertise, emphasize it, and use it to dominate the conversation. Women play down their expertise.

Now, you might be tempted to conclude from this that women play fair in conversation and that men don't—for example, you might think that men consistently seek to put themselves in a position superior to women. But this may be too simple an explanation. Research shows that men communicate this way not only with women but with other men as well. Men are not showing disrespect for their female conversational partners; they are simply communicating as they normally do. Women, too, communicate as they do not only with men but also with other women.

Tannen argues that the goal of a man in conversation is to be accorded respect. Therefore, a man seeks to display his knowledge and expertise even if he has to change from a topic he knows little about to something he knows a great deal about. A woman, on the other hand, seeks to be liked; so she expresses agreement, rarely interrupts a man to take her turn as speaker, and gives a lot of verbal and nonverbal cues to show that she is listening.

Men and women also show that they are listening in different ways. A woman is more apt to give lots of listening cues, such as interjecting, "Yeah, uh-uh," nodding in agreement, and smiling. Women also make more eye contact when listening than men do; men are more apt to look around and away from the speaker (Brownell, 2002). A man is more likely to listen quietly, without giving lots of listening cues as feedback. Tannen also argues, however, that men do listen less to women than women listen to men. The reason, says Tannen, is that listening places the person in an inferior position whereas speaking places the person in a superior position.

www.researchnavigator.com

Find Answers: Try finding answers to one of the following questions, or design a research study to answer it: Are women and men equally effective listeners? What kinds of listening make health professional–patient communication more effective? What attitudes do business executives have toward the importance of listening in the workplace?

There is no evidence to show that these differences represent any negative motives on the part of men to prove themselves superior or of women to ingratiate themselves. Rather, these differences in listening are largely the result of the way in which men and women have been socialized. Also, it should be mentioned that not all researchers would agree that there is sufficient evidence to support the claims that Tannen and others make about gender differences (Goldsmith & Fulfs, 1999). In any case, in U.S. society gender differences are undergoing many changes. So it's best to take all generalizations about gender as starting points for investigation and not as airtight conclusions.

Summary of Concepts and Skills

This chapter has discussed the way we listen and how we can listen more effectively.

1. Listening serves a variety of purposes: We listen to learn; to relate to others; to influence the attitudes, beliefs, and behaviors of others; to play; and to help.
2. Listening is a five-step process consisting of receiving, understanding, remembering, evaluating, and responding. Receiving is essentially the hearing process; the messages from another person are received at this stage. Understanding is the stage of comprehension; you make sense out of the messages. In the remembering stage you store messages and your understanding of them in your memory for at least some time. In evaluating you judge the messages and apply your critical thinking skills to them. The final stage, responding, includes both the responses you make while the speaker is speaking and the responses you may make after the speaker has stopped talking.
3. Effective listening involves a process of making adjustments—depending on the situation—along dimensions such as empathic and objective listening, nonjudgmental and critical listening, surface and depth listening, and active and inactive listening.
4. Culture influences listening in a variety of ways. Contributing to listening difficulties are cultural differences in language and speech, nonverbal behaviors, direct and indirect styles, and differences in giving feedback.
5. Men and women listen differently and perhaps for different reasons. For example, women give more listening cues—messages that say, "I'm listening"—than men. According to some theorists, women use listening to show empathy and to build rapport, whereas men minimize listening because it puts them in a subordinate position.

Throughout this discussion of listening, a variety of skills were identified. Check your ability to apply these skills using the following scale: 1 = almost always; 2 = often; 3 = sometimes; 4 = rarely; and 5 = hardly ever.

_____ 1. I recognize that listening serves a variety of purposes, and I adjust my listening on the basis of my purposes; for example, to learn, relate, influence, play, or help.

_____ 2. I realize that listening is a multistage process, and I regulate my listening behavior as appropriate in receiving, understanding, remembering, evaluating, and responding.

_____ 3. In receiving messages I seek to increase my chances of effective listening by, for example, paying attention to the speaker's verbal and nonverbal messages; avoiding distractions; and focusing on what the speaker is saying, not on what I'm going to say next.

_____ 4. I facilitate understanding in listening by relating new information to what I already know and trying to see the messages from the speaker's point of view.

_____ 5. In remembering the speaker's messages, I try to identify the central ideas and the major supporting materials, summarize the main ideas, and repeat important concepts to etch them more firmly in my mind.

_____ 6. In evaluating messages, I first make sure I understand the speaker's point of view and seek to identify any sources of bias or self-interest.

_____ 7. In responding, I am supportive of the speaker and own my own thoughts and feelings.

_____ 8. I am especially careful to adjust my listening on the basis of the immediate situation between empathic and objective, nonjudgmental and critical, and surface and depth listening.

_____ 9. I practice active listening when appropriate by paraphrasing the speaker's meaning, expressing my understanding of the speaker's feelings, and asking questions.

_____ 10. I recognize the influence of culture on listening and the cultural differences in listening and take these into consideration when listening in intercultural situations.

_____ 11. I recognize gender differences in listening and take these into consideration when communicating with members of the opposite sex.

Key Word Quiz

Write T for those statements that are true and F for those that are false. For those that are false, replace the italicized term with the correct term.

_____ 1. The communication activity on which most people spend the most time is *talking*.

_____ 2. Listening is a *passive process*.

_____ 3. The first step in the listening process is *understanding*.

_____ 4. Memory for speech is a *reproductive process*.

_____ 5. Listening to understand and to feel what the other person is feeling is called *empathic listening*.

_____ 6. Research generally supports the finding that women give more *listening cues* than men.

_____ 7. Generally, compared to men, women engage in less conversational *interruption*.

_____ 8. The tendency for a particular item of information to take on increased importance is known as *sharpening*.

_____ 9. The tendency to interpret what you hear or think you hear according to your own biases and expectations is known as *assimilation*.

_____ 10. The process of restating in your own words your understanding of the speaker's thoughts and feelings is known as *paraphrasing*.

Answers: TRUE: 5, 6, 7, 8, 9, 10; FALSE: 1 (*listening*), 2 (*active process*), 3 (*receiving, hearing, or attending*), 4 (*reconstructive process*)

5 Verbal Messages

Chapter Concepts	Chapter Skills
This chapter covers the verbal message system and offers suggestions for making your own verbal messages more effective.	After completing this chapter, you should be able to:
Principles of Verbal Messages	communicate with a recognition of denotation and connotation, abstraction, directness, the rules of language, and frequent differences between people's words and their meanings.
Disconfirmation and Confirmation	regulate your confirmations while avoiding sexist, racist, and heterosexist language that puts down other groups.
Using Verbal Messages Effectively	avoid the major barriers to effective language usage.

When you communicate, you use two major signal systems—verbal and nonverbal. This chapter focuses on the verbal message system—the system's key principles, the concepts of confirmation and disconfirmation, and the ways you can use verbal messages most effectively. The next chapter will examine the nonverbal message system.

Principles of Verbal Messages

As you grew up, you learned the language of the people around you. You learned its phonological or sound system; its semantic system, or system of word meanings; and its syntactic system, which enabled you to put words into meaningful sentence patterns. Our concern in this chapter is not with the grammatical structure of language (that's the linguist's job) but with the verbal messages you speak and hear and sometimes read. These verbal messages, of course, rely on the rules of the grammar; you can't just make up sounds or words or string words together at random and expect to be understood. But following the rules of grammar, as we'll see, is not enough to achieve effective communication. For this we need to understand the principles of verbal messages. We'll look at six principles, beginning with the fact that verbal messages are both denotative and connotative.

Messages Are Denotative and Connotative

You speak both denotatively and connotatively. **Denotation** has to do with the objective meaning of a term, the meaning you would find in a dictionary. It's the meaning that people who share a common language assign to a word. **Connotation** is the subjective or emotional meaning that specific speakers or listeners give to a word. Take as an example the word *death*. To a doctor, this word might mean (or denote) the time when the heart stops. This is an objective description of a particular event. On the other hand, to a mother who is informed of her son's death, the word means (or connotes) much more. It recalls her son's youth, ambition, family, illness, and so on. To her it is a highly emotional, subjective, and personal word. These emotional, subjective, or personal reactions are the word's connotative meaning.

Semanticist S. I. Hayakawa (Hayakawa & Hayakawa, 1989) coined the terms **snarl words** and **purr words** to clarify further the distinction between denotation and connotation. Snarl words are highly negative: "She's an idiot," "He's a pig," "They're a bunch of losers." Purr words are highly positive: "She's a real sweetheart,"

Language exerts hidden power, like a moon on the tides.

—Rita Mae Brown

"He's a dream," "They're the greatest." Snarl and purr words, although they may sometimes seem to have denotative meaning and to refer to the "real world," are actually connotative in meaning. These terms do not describe objective realities but rather the speaker's feelings about people or events.

Messages Vary in Abstraction

Consider the following list of terms:

entertainment

film

American film

Classic American film

Casablanca

At the top is an **abstraction** or general concept—the word *entertainment.* Note that *entertainment* includes all the other items on the list plus various other items— *television, novels, drama, comics,* and so on. *Film* is more specific and concrete. It includes all of the items below it as well as various other items such as *Indian film* or *Russian film.* It excludes, however, all entertainment that is not film. *American film* is again more specific than *film* and excludes all films that are not American. *Classic American film* further limits *American film* to those considered timeless. *Casablanca* specifies concretely the one item to which reference is made.

As this example illustrates, verbal messages vary from general and abstract to specific and concrete. Effective verbal messages include words from a wide range of abstractions. At times, a general term may suit your needs best; at other times, a more specific term may serve better. Generally, however, the specific term will prove the better choice. As you get more specific—less abstract—you more effectively guide the images that come to your listeners' minds.

Messages Vary in Directness

Think about how you would respond to someone saying the following sentences:

1A. I'm so bored; I have nothing to do tonight.

2A. I'd like to go to the movies. Would you like to come?

1B. Would you feel like hamburgers tonight?

2B. I'd like hamburgers tonight. How about you?

Verbal messages may be direct or indirect. In these examples the statements numbered 1 represent **indirect speech:** they are attempts to get the listeners to say or do something without committing the speakers. The statements numbered 2 are more **direct speech**—they more clearly state the speakers' preferences and then ask listeners whether they agree. (Note that many indirect messages are nonverbal, as when you glance at your watch to communicate that it is late and that you had better be going.)

Advantages and Disadvantages of Indirect Messages   Indirect messages have both advantages and disadvantages. Indirect messages allow you to express a desire without insulting or offending anyone; they allow you to observe the rules of polite interaction. So instead of saying, "I'm bored with this conversation," you say, "It's getting late and I have to get up early tomorrow," or you look at your watch and pretend to be surprised by the time. In this way you are stating a preference indirectly so as to avoid offending someone. Not all direct requests, however, should be considered impolite. One study of Spanish and English speakers, for example, found

" One great use of words is to hide our thoughts. **"**

—Voltaire

Climbing the Abstraction Ladder

For each of the terms listed below, indicate at least four possible terms that indicate increasing specificity. The first example is provided as an illustration:

Level 1	Level 2 (More specific than 1)	Level 3 (More specific than 2)	Level 4 (More specific than 3)	Level 5 (More specific than 4)
building	office building	steel-and-glass office building	steel-and-glass office skyscraper	Chicago's Sears Tower
entertainment				
communication medium				
toy				
sports				

no evidence to support the assumption that politeness and directness were incompatible (Mir, 1993).

Sometimes indirect messages allow you to ask for compliments in a socially acceptable manner. For example, if you say, "I was thinking of getting a nose job," you may be hoping to get a response such as "A nose job? You? Your nose is perfect."

Indirect messages, however, can also create problems. They often are overly ambiguous and can easily be misunderstood. Indirect messages may also be seen as manipulative—as attempts to get something without openly asking for it, as in "All my friends have a really big party for their first anniversary."

Gender and Cultural Differences in Directness The popular stereotype in much of the United States holds that women tend to be indirect in making requests and in giving orders. This indirectness communicates a powerlessness and discomfort with their own authority. Men, the stereotype continues, tend to be direct, sometimes to the point of being blunt or rude. This directness communicates power and comfort with their authority.

Deborah Tannen (1994a) provides an interesting perspective on these stereotypes. Women are, it seems, more indirect in giving orders; they are more likely to say, for example, "It would be great if these letters could go out today" than "Have these letters out by 3." But Tannen (1994a, p. 84) argues that "issuing orders indirectly can be the prerogative of those in power" and does not show powerlessness. Power, to Tannen, is the ability to choose your own style of communication.

Men are also indirect, but in different situations. For example, men are more likely to use indirectness when they express weakness, reveal a problem, or admit an error (Rundquist, 1992; Tannen, 1994a, 1994b). Men are more likely to speak indirectly when expressing emotions other than anger. They are also more indirect when they refuse expressions of increased romantic intimacy. Men are thus indirect, the theory goes, when they are saying something that goes against the masculine stereotype.

Many Asian and Latin American cultures stress the value of indirectness, largely because it helps people avoid overt criticism

"I'd like you to head up the new team of the recently let go."

and losing face. A somewhat different kind of indirectness is seen in the greater use of third parties or mediators to resolve conflict among the Chinese than among North Americans (Ma, 1992). In most of the United States, however, directness is the preferred style. "Be up front" and "Tell it like it is" are commonly heard communication guidelines. Contrast these with the following two principles of indirectness found in the Japanese language (Tannen, 1994a):

> *[O]moiyari,* close to empathy, says that listeners need to understand the speaker without the speaker's being specific or direct. This style places a much greater demand on the listener than would a direct speaking style.

> *[S]assuru* advises listeners to anticipate a speaker's meanings and to use subtle cues from the speaker to infer his or her total meaning.

In thinking about direct and indirect messages, it is important to realize how easy it is for misunderstandings to occur. For example, a person from a culture that values an indirect style of speech may be speaking indirectly to be polite. If, however, you are from a culture that values a more direct style of speech, you may assume that the person is using indirectness to be manipulative, because this may be how your culture regards indirectness.

VIEWPOINT

When asked what they would like to change about the communication of the opposite sex, men said they wanted women to be more direct and women said they wanted men to stop interrupting and offering advice (Noble, 1994). What one change would you like to see in the communication system of the opposite sex? Of your own sex?

Messages Are Culturally Influenced

As noted in the introduction to this chapter, verbal messages must follow, in large part, the rules or grammar of the language. Another set of rules is cultural, however. **Cultural rules** focus on the principles that your culture considers important. When you follow these principles in communicating, you're seen as a properly functioning member of the culture. When you violate the principles, you risk being seen as deviant or perhaps as insulting. Let's consider how these cultural principles or maxims work in verbal communication.

The Principle of Cooperation In much of the United States we operate under the principle of **cooperation:** the assumption that in any communication interaction, both parties will make an effort to help each other understand each other. That is, we assume cooperation. This general principle has four subprinciples or maxims. As you read down the list, ask yourself how you follow these maxims in your everyday conversation:

- *The maxim of quality:* Say what you know or assume to be true, and do not say what you know to be false.
- *The maxim of relation:* Talk about what is relevant to the conversation.
- *The maxim of manner:* Be clear, avoid ambiguities (as much as possible), be relatively brief, and organize your thoughts into a meaningful pattern.
- *The maxim of quantity:* Be as informative as necessary to communicate the information.

Note that this last maxim, of quantity, is frequently violated in e-mail communication. Here are three ways in which e-mail often violates the maxim of quantity and some suggestions on how to avoid these violations:

1. Chain e-mails often violate the maxim of quantity by sending people information they don't really need or want. Some people maintain lists of e-mail addresses and send the same information to everyone on their lists. But it's highly unlikely that everyone on every list needs or wants to read the latest joke. Suggestion: Avoid

chain e-mail, at least most of the time. When something comes along that you think someone you know would like to read, then send it on to a specific person or to two or three specific people.

2. Chain e-mails often contain the e-mail addresses of everyone on the chain. These extensive headers clog the system and also reveal e-mail addresses that some people may want to keep private or to share at their own discretion. Suggestion: When you do send chain e-mails (and in some situations, they serve useful purposes), conceal the e-mail addresses of your recipients by using some general description such as "undisclosed recipients."

3. Lengthy attachments take time to download and often create problems when people have incompatible equipment. Not everyone wants to see every single photo from your last vacation. Suggestion: Use attachments in moderation; find out first who would like to receive photos and who would not.

Cultural Conversational Maxims   Of course, not all of the maxims followed in the United States are the same as maxims that prevail in other parts of the world. Here are three maxims that are especially important in other cultures. Do you follow these maxims as well as those belonging to the principle of cooperation?

- *The maxim of peaceful relations:* Keep peace in relationship communication, even to the point of agreeing with someone when you really disagree (Midooka, 1990).

- *The maxim of face-saving:* Never embarrass anyone, especially in public. Always allow people to save face, even if this means avoiding the truth—as when you tell someone he or she did good work although the job was actually poorly executed.

- *The maxim of self-denigration:* Avoid taking credit for accomplishments and minimize your abilities or talents in conversation (Gu, 1997).

What Do You Say?

Cultural Maxims: In introducing yourself to your class, you discuss your high grades, your successes in sports, and your plans to transfer to Harvard. The students following you, however, all appear very modest. You quickly realize that you misunderstood the culture of this classroom. *What do you say?*

Communicating with power

Power Talk

One of the ways you communicate power is by using powerful language. Here are some suggestions for communicating power, based largely on research in the United States (Molloy, 1981; Kleinke, 1986; Johnson, 1987; Ng & Bradac, 1993).

- Avoid hesitations; they make you sound unprepared and uncertain.
- Avoid uncertainty expressions *(maybe, perhaps, could be);* these communicate a lack of commitment, direction, and conviction.
- Avoid overpoliteness; such forms signal subordinate status.
- Avoid disqualifiers *(I didn't read the entire article, but . . .);* they may call into question the validity of your statements.
- Avoid tag questions, or questions that ask for agreement *(That was great, wasn't it?);* these may signal your own uncertainty.
- Avoid slang and vulgar expressions; these usually signal low social class and little power.
- Avoid phrases that weaken your sentences, such as *It seems to me that . . .* or *Perhaps . . .* or *Maybe. . . .*
- Avoid weak verbs. Instead of saying "He walked to the podium," consider *rushed, wandered, flew, ambled,* or *raced.* Consult a thesaurus to replace any verb you suspect might be weak.
- Avoid clichés, overused phrases that have lost their novelty and part of their meaning, such as *in this day and age, tell it like it is, no sooner said than done, it goes without saying,* and *few and far between.*

Enhancing Your Communication Power

Can you identify powerful and powerless forms of speech that you regularly use? What forms of speech might you consider increasing and decreasing to enhance your power?

Communicating ethically

Communicating in Cyberspace

The same principles that govern ethical face-to-face interaction should also prevail when you communicate online. Here, however, are a few ethical principles with special relevance to computer communication. It is unethical to:

1. Invade the privacy of others. Reading the files of another person or breaking into files that you're not authorized to read is unethical.
2. Harm others or their property. Creating computer viruses, publishing instructions for making bombs, or creating websites that promote sexism, racism, heterosexism, or ageism is unethical.
3. Spread falsehoods. Lying on the Internet—about other people, about the powers of medical or herbal treatment, or about yourself is unethical.
4. Plagiarize. Appropriating the work of another as your own—whether the original work appeared on the Internet or in a book or journal—is unethical.
5. Steal the passwords, PIN numbers, or authorization codes that belong to others.
6. Copy software programs or download music that you haven't paid for.

What Would You Do?

As an experiment you develop a computer virus that can destroy websites. Recently you've come across various websites that you feel promote child pornography. You wonder if you can ethically destroy these websites. And, further, you wonder if not destroying them can actually be more unethical than using your newly developed virus.

Messages Vary in Politeness

Before reading about politeness in verbal communication, examine your own level of politeness by taking the self-test that follows.

How Polite Are Your Messages?

The list below represents a kind of message politeness scale, a device for measuring politeness in verbal messages. Indicate how accurately each statement describes your *typical* communication with peers, using a 10-point scale on which 10 means "very accurate description of my typical messages" and 1 means "very inaccurate description of my typical messages." Avoid giving responses that you feel might be considered "socially acceptable"; instead, give responses that genuinely reflect your typical message behavior.

_____ ❶ I say "please" when asking someone to do something.

_____ ❷ I make an effort to make sure that other people are not embarrassed.

_____ ❸ I ask people I call if it's a good time to talk.

_____ ❹ I will raise my voice to take charge of the conversation.

_____ ❺ I give the speaker cues to show that I'm listening and interested.

_____ ❻ I interrupt the speaker when I think I have something important to say.

HOW DID YOU DO? The aim of this scale is to encourage you to consider some of the aspects of verbal politeness and to encourage you to examine your own politeness behaviors. As you can see, high numbers (say, above 45) indicate considerable politeness, whereas low numbers (say, below 30) indicate a lack of politeness.

Are there some statements in this scale that you feel are not indicative of politeness as you see it? Are there other indicators that are more important than those mentioned here and that should be included in a scale measuring politeness? Using this scale, your modification of it, or a totally new measuring instrument, consider how you might increase your own level of politeness.

Politeness is important in all forms of interaction, including online as well as face-to-face interactions. Not surprisingly, researchers find that people view polite e-mail users more positively than impolite users (Jessmer & Anderson, 2001). Politeness is also universal across all cultures (Brown & Levinson, 1988). Cultures differ, however, in how they define politeness and in how much they emphasize politeness compared with, say, openness or honesty. Cultures also differ in their rules for expressing politeness (or impoliteness) and in the punishments they impose for violations of these rules (Mao, 1994; Strecker, 1993). Asian peoples, especially the Chinese and Japanese, are often singled out because they emphasize politeness more and mete out harsher social punishments for violations than would most people in, say, the United States or Western Europe (Fraser, 1990).

In general, politeness seems to vary with the type of relationship. One researcher, for example, has proposed that politeness varies among strangers, friends, and intimates as depicted in Figure 5.1.

There are also large gender differences—as well as some similarities— in the expression of politeness (J. Holmes, 1995). Generally, studies from various different cultures show that women's speech is more polite than men's speech, even on the telephone (Brown, 1980; Wetzel, 1988; J. Holmes, 1995; Smoreda & Licoppe, 2000). Women seek areas of agreement in conversation and in conflict situations more often than men do. Similarly, young girls are more apt to try to modify disagreements, whereas young boys are more apt to express more "bald disagreements" (J. Holmes, 1995). Women also use more polite speech when seeking to gain another person's compliance than men do (Baxter, 1984).

There are also gender similarities. For example, in both the United States and New Zealand, men and women seem to pay compliments in similar ways (Manes & Wolfson, 1981; J. Holmes, 1995), and both men and women use politeness strategies when communicating bad news in an organization (Lee, 1993).

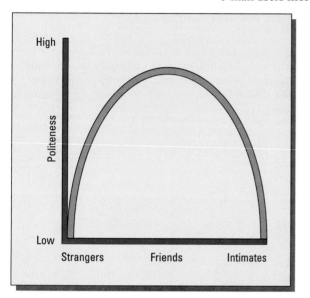

Figure 5.1

Wolfson's Bulge Model of Politeness

This figure depicts a proposed relationship between levels of politeness and degrees of intimacy. Politeness, according to this inverted U model, is greatest with friends and significantly less with strangers and intimates. Can you build a case for an opposite theory—that politeness is especially high with both strangers and intimates and least with friends?

❝ 'When *I* use a word,' Humpty Dumpty said in rather a scornful tone, 'it means just what I choose it to mean; neither more nor less.' **❞**

—Lewis Carroll

Message Meanings Are in People

To discover the meanings people try to communicate, it's necessary to look into the people in addition to the words. An example of the confusion that can result when this relatively simple fact is not taken into consideration was provided by Ronald D. Laing, H. Phillipson, and A. Russell Lee (1966) and analyzed with insight by Paul Watzlawick (1977). A couple on the second night of their honeymoon are sitting at a hotel bar. The woman strikes up a conversation with the couple next to her. The husband refuses to communicate with the couple and becomes antagonistic toward both them and his wife. The wife then grows angry because he has created such an awkward and unpleasant situation. Each becomes increasingly disturbed, and the evening ends in a bitter conflict, with each convinced of the other's lack of consideration. Eight years later, they analyze this argument. Apparently the concept *honeymoon* had meant different things to each. To the husband, their honeymoon would be a "golden opportunity to ignore the rest of the world and simply explore each other." He felt his wife's interaction with the other couple implied there was something lacking in him. To the wife, the honeymoon meant an opportunity to try out her new role as wife. "I had never had a conversation with another couple as a wife before," she said. "Previous to this I had always been a 'girlfriend' or 'fiancée' or 'daughter' or 'sister.'"

Also recognize that as you change, you also change the meanings you created out of past messages. Thus, although the message sent may not have changed, the meanings you created from it yesterday and the meanings you create today may be quite different. Yesterday, when a special someone said, "I love you," you created certain meanings. But today, when you learn that the same "I love you" was said to three other people or when you fall in love with someone else, you drastically change the meanings you perceive from those three words.

What Do You Say?

Politeness: You meet a friend who's with someone you've never met before. You begin swearing and cursing about your college experience—using language even stronger than normal—until your friend breaks in and introduces you to Professor Williams, your new major advisor. *What do you say?*

Disconfirmation and Confirmation

The terms *confirmation* and *disconfirmation* refer to the extent to which you acknowledge another person. Consider this situation. You've been living with someone for the last six months and you arrive home late one night. Your partner, let's say Pat, is angry and complains about your being so late. Which of the following is most likely to be your response?

1. Stop screaming. I'm not interested in what you're babbling about. I'll do what I want, when I want. I'm going to bed.

2. What are you so angry about? Didn't you get in three hours late last Thursday when you went to that office party? So knock it off.

3. You have a right to be angry. I should have called to tell you I was going to be late, but I got involved in an argument at work, and I couldn't leave until it was resolved.

In response 1, you dismiss Pat's anger and even indicate dismissal of Pat as a person. In response 2, you reject the validity of Pat's reasons for being angry but do not dismiss either Pat's feelings of anger or Pat as a person. In response 3, you acknowledge Pat's anger and the reasons for it. In addition, you provide some kind of explanation and, in doing so, show that both Pat's feelings and Pat as a person are important and that Pat has the right to know what happened. The first response is an example of disconfirmation, the second of rejection, and the third of confirmation.

Psychologist William James once observed that "no more fiendish punishment could be devised, even were such a thing physically possible, than that one should be turned loose in society and remain absolutely unnoticed by all the members thereof." In this often-quoted observation, James identifies the essence of disconfirmation (Watzlawick, Beavin, & Jackson, 1967; Veenendall & Feinstein, 1995). **Disconfirmation** is a communication pattern in which we ignore someone's presence as well as that person's communications. We say, in effect, that this person and what this person has to say are not worth serious attention or effort—that this person and this person's contributions are so unimportant or insignificant that there is no reason to concern ourselves with her or him. The Amish community practices an extreme form of disconfirmation called "shunning," in which the community members totally ignore a person who has violated one or more of their rules. The specific aim of shunning is to get the person to repent and to reenter the community of the faithful. But it seems that all cultures practice some form of exclusion for those who violate important cultural rules.

www.researchnavigator.com

Read an Article: Read a scholarly or popular article on language, confirmation or disconfirmation, or the relationship of language and culture. On the basis of this article, what can you add to the discussion presented here?

Communicating ethically

Lying

Lying occurs when "one person intends to mislead another, doing so deliberately, without prior notification of this purpose, and without having been explicitly asked to do so by the target [the person the liar intends to mislead]" (Ekman, 1985, p. 28). As this definition makes clear, a person can lie by omission as well as by commission. If you omit something relevant, and if this omission causes others to be misled, you've lied just as surely as if you had made a false statement (Bok, 1978).

Similarly, although most lies are verbal, some are nonverbal—and most seem to involve at least some nonverbal elements. Common examples of nonverbal lying include the innocent facial expression and focused eye contact despite consciousness of unethical behavior, and the knowing nod despite the inner awareness of ignorance.

What Would You Do?

On the basis of your own ethical beliefs about lying, would you (1) lie in an employment interview in response to an overly personal (and irrelevant) or illegal question? (2) lie to make another person feel good—for example, telling someone that he or she looked great or had a great sense of humor? (3) lie to get out of jury duty? (4) lie to get yourself out of an unwanted date, an extra office chore, or a boring conversation? Given your answers, try formulating in one sentence your ethical position on lying.

Note that disconfirmation is not the same as **rejection.** In rejection, you disagree with the person; you indicate your unwillingness to accept something the other person says or does. In disconfirming someone, however, you deny that person's significance; you claim that what this person says or does simply does not count.

Confirmation is the opposite communication pattern. In confirmation you not only acknowledge the presence of the other person but also indicate your acceptance of this person, of this person's self-definition, and of your relationship as defined or viewed by this other person.

Disconfirmation and confirmation may be communicated in a wide variety of ways. Table 5.1 shows just a few examples.

TABLE 5.1   Confirmation and Disconfirmation

As you review this table, try to imagine a specific illustration for each of the ways of communicating disconfirmation and confirmation (Pearson, 1993; Galvin, Bylund, & Brommel, 2004).

CONFIRMATION	DISCONFIRMATION
1. Acknowledge the presence and the contributions of the other by either supporting or taking issue with what the other says.	1. Ignore the presence and the messages of the other person; ignore or express (nonverbally and verbally) indifference to anything the other says.
2. Make nonverbal contact by maintaining direct eye contact, touching, hugging, kissing, or otherwise demonstrating acknowledgment of the other; engage in dialogue—communication in which both persons are speakers and listeners, both are involved, and both are concerned with each other.	2. Make no nonverbal contact; avoid direct eye contact; avoid touching the other person; engage in monologue—communication in which one person speaks and one person listens, there is no real interaction, and there is no real concern or respect for each other.
3. Demonstrate understanding of what the other says and means and reflect these feelings to demonstrate your understanding.	3. Jump to interpretation or evaluation rather than working at understanding what the other means; express your own feelings, ignore the feelings of the other, or give abstract, intellectualized responses.
4. Ask questions of the other concerning both thoughts and feelings and acknowledge the questions of the other; return phone calls, and answer e-mails and letters.	4. Make statements about yourself; ignore any lack of clarity in the other's remarks; ignore the other's requests; and fail to answer questions, return phone calls, or answer e-mails and letters.
5. Encourage the other to express thoughts and feelings, and respond directly and exclusively to what the other says.	5. Interrupt or otherwise make it difficult for the other to express him- or herself; respond only tangentially or by shifting the focus in another direction.

You can gain insight into a wide variety of offensive language practices by viewing them as types of disconfirmation—as language that alienates and separates and prevents effective communication. Four common practices are sexism, heterosexism, racism, and ageism.

Sexism

Sexist language is language that puts down someone because of her or his gender. Usually, the term refers to language that denigrates women, but it can also legitimately refer to language that denigrates men. Usually sexist language is used by one sex against the other, but it need not be limited to these cases; women can be sexist against women and men can be sexist against men. The National Council of Teachers of English has proposed guidelines for nonsexist (gender-free, gender-neutral, or sex-fair) language. These concern the use of generic *man,* the use of generic *he* and *his,* and sex-role stereotyping (Penfield, 1987).

Generic Man   The word *man* refers most clearly to an adult male. To use the term to refer to both men and women emphasizes "maleness" at the expense of "femaleness." Similarly, the terms *mankind* and *the common man* and even *cavemen* imply a primary focus on adult males. Gender-neutral terms can easily be substituted. Instead of *mankind,* you can say *humanity, people,* or *human beings.* Instead of *the common man,* you can say *the average person* or *ordinary people.* Instead of *cavemen,* you can say *prehistoric people* or *cave dwellers.*

Similarly, the use of terms such as *policeman* and *fireman* and other terms that presume maleness as the norm and femaleness as a deviation from this norm are clear and common examples of sexist language. Using nonsexist alternatives for these and similar terms (for example, *police officer* and *firefighter* instead of *policeman* and *fireman*) and making these alternatives a part of your active vocabulary will include the female sex as "normal" in such professions. Similarly, using "female forms" such as *actress* or *stewardess* is considered sexist; these derivations of *actor* and *steward,* again, emphasize that the male form is the norm and the female is the deviation from the norm.

Generic He and His   The use of the masculine pronoun to refer to any individual regardless of sex is certainly declining. But as recently as 1975 all college textbooks,

Skill development experience

Confirming, Rejecting, and Disconfirming

For each situation *(a)* write three potential responses as indicated; then *(b)* after completing all three situations, indicate what effects each type of response is likely to generate.

1. Enrique receives this semester's grades in the mail; they're a lot better than previous semesters' grades but are still not great. After opening the letter, Enrique says, "I really tried hard to get my grades up this semester." Enrique's parents respond

   With disconfirmation: _____
   With rejection: _____
   With confirmation: _____

2. Sandra's colleague at work comes to her overjoyed and tells her that she has just been promoted to vice president of marketing, skipping three steps in the hierarchy and tripling her salary. Sandra responds

   With disconfirmation: _____
   With rejection: _____
   With confirmation: _____

for example, used the masculine pronoun as generic. There is no legitimate reason why the feminine pronoun can't alternate with the masculine pronoun in referring to hypothetical individuals, or why terms such as *he and she* or *her and him* can't be used instead of just *he* or *him*. Perhaps the best solution is to restructure your sentences to eliminate any reference to gender. Here are a few examples from the NCTE Guidelines (Penfield, 1987):

Sexist	Gender-Free
The average student is worried about his grades.	The average student is worried about grades.
Ask the student to hand in his work as soon as he is finished.	Ask students to hand in their work as soon as they are finished.

Sex-Role Stereotyping   The words we use often reflect a sex-role bias—the assumption that certain roles or professions belong to men and others belong to women. To eliminate sex-role stereotyping, avoid, for example, making the hypothetical elementary school teacher female and the college professor male. Avoid referring to doctors as male and nurses as female. Avoid noting the sex of a professional with terms such as *female doctor* or *male nurse*. When you are referring to a specific doctor or nurse, the person's sex will become clear when you use the appropriate pronoun: "Dr. Smith wrote the prescription for her new patient" or "The nurse recorded the patient's temperature himself."

Heterosexism

A close relative of sexism is heterosexism, a relatively new addition to the list of linguistic prejudices. As the term implies, **heterosexist language** is language used to disparage gay men and lesbians. As with racist language, we see heterosexism in the derogatory terms used for lesbians and gay men as well as in more subtle forms of language usage. For example, when you qualify a profession—as in *gay athlete* or *lesbian doctor*—you are in effect stating that athletes and doctors are not normally gay or lesbian. Further, you are highlighting the affectional orientation of the athlete and the doctor in a context in which it may have no relevance, in the same way that gender or racial distinctions often have no relevance to the issue at hand.

Still another instance of heterosexism—and perhaps the most difficult to deal with—is the presumption of heterosexuality. Usually, people assume that the person they are talking to or about is heterosexual. They are usually correct, because most people are heterosexual. At the same time, however, this assumption denies the lesbian and gay identity a certain legitimacy. The practice is similar to the presumptions of whiteness and maleness that we have made significant inroads in eliminating. Here are a few suggestions for avoiding heterosexist, or what some call homophobic, language.

- Avoid offensive nonverbal mannerisms that parody stereotypes when talking about gays and lesbians.

- Avoid "complimenting" gay men and lesbians by saying that "they don't look it." To gays and lesbians, this is not a compliment. Similarly, expressing disappointment that a person is gay—often thought to be a compliment, as in comments such as "What a waste!"—is not a compliment.

- Avoid the assumption that every gay or lesbian knows what every other gay or lesbian is thinking. It's very similar to asking a Japanese person why Sony is investing heavily in the United States or, as one comic put it, asking an African American, "What do you think Jesse Jackson meant by that last speech?"

- Avoid denying individual differences. Saying things such as "Lesbians are so loyal" or "Gay men are so open with their feelings," which ignore the reality of wide differences within any group, are potentially insulting to all groups.

What Do You Say?

Homophobia: You're bringing your college roommate home for the holidays; she's an outspoken lesbian, and your family is extremely homophobic. You want to prepare both your family and your roommate for their holiday get-together. *What do you say? To whom? Through what channel?*

- Avoid overattribution—the tendency, in this case, to attribute just about everything a person does, says, and believes to his or her being gay or lesbian. This tendency helps to recall and perpetuate stereotypes (see Chapter 3).
- Remember that relationship milestones are important to all people. Ignoring anniversaries or birthdays of, say, a relative's partner is resented by everyone.

Racism

According to Andrea Rich (1974), "any language that, through a conscious or unconscious attempt by the user, places a particular racial or ethnic group in an inferior position is racist." **Racist language** expresses racist attitudes. It also contributes to the development of racist attitudes in those who use or hear the language. This effect, of course, is similar to the way sexist and heterosexist language perpetuate sexist and heterosexist attitudes. Even when racism is subtle, unintentional, or even unconscious, its effects are systematically damaging (Dovidio, Gaertner, Kawakami, & Hodson, 2002).

Members of one culture use racist terms to disparage members of other cultures, their customs, or their accomplishments and to establish and maintain power over other groups. Racist language emphasizes differences rather than similarities and separates rather than unites members of different cultures. The social consequences of racist language in terms of employment, education, housing opportunities, and general community acceptance are well known.

It has often been pointed out (Bosmajian, 1974; Davis, 1973) that there are aspects of language that may be inherently racist. For example, one examination of English found 134 synonyms for *white*. Of these, 44 had positive connotations (for example, *clean, chaste,* and *unblemished*) and only 10 had negative connotations (for example, *whitewash* and *pale*). The remaining terms were relatively neutral. Of the 120 synonyms for *black*, 60 had unfavorable connotations (*unclean, foreboding,* and *deadly*) and none had positive connotations.

Consider the following expressions:

- the Korean doctor
- the Chicano prodigy
- the African American mathematician
- the white nurse
- the old druggist

Often, people use these identifiers to emphasize that the combination of race and occupation (or talent or accomplishment) is rare and unexpected, that this member of a given ethnic group is an exception. Using racial identifiers also implies that racial factors are somehow important in the context. In some cases, of course, a racial identifier is in fact relevant to the conversation. For example, in commenting on changes in Hollywood films, you might say, "This is the first year that both best acting awards were won by African Americans." In the vast majority of cases, however, identifiers of these types are best left unused.

Ageism

Ageism is discrimination based on age. One researcher offers a more comprehensive definition: "any attitude, action, or institutional structure which subordinates a person or group because of age or any assignment of roles in society purely on the basis of age" (Traxler, 1980, p. 14). In the United States and throughout much of the industrialized world, ageism signifies discrimination against the old and against aging in general. But ageism can also involve prejudice against other age groups. For example, if you describe all teenagers as selfish and undependable, you're discriminating against a group purely because of their age and thus are ageist in your statements.

> " Racism is the dogma that one ethnic group is condemned by nature to congenital inferiority and another group is destined to congenital superiority. "
>
> —Ruth Benedict

> " For a black writer in this country to be born into the English language is to realize that the assumptions on which the language operates are his enemy. . . . I was forced to reconsider similes: as black as sin, as black as night, blackhearted. "
>
> —James Baldwin

In some cultures—some Asian and some African cultures, for example—the old are revered and respected. Younger people seek them out for advice on economic, ethical, and relationship issues.

Popular language is replete with examples of ageist phrases; *little old lady, old hag, old-timer, over the hill, old coot,* and *old fogy* are just some examples. As with sexism or racism, qualifying a description of someone in terms of his or her age demonstrates ageism. For example, if you refer to "a quick-witted 75-year -old" or "an agile 65-year-old" or "a responsible teenager," you are implying that these qualities are unusual in people of these ages and thus need special mention. You're saying that "quick-wittedness" and " being 75" do not normally go together, and you imply the same abnormality for "agility" and "being 65" and for "responsibility" and "being a teenager." The problem with this kind of stereotyping is that it's simply wrong. There are many 80-year-olds who are extremely quick witted (and many 30-year-olds who aren't).

You also communicate ageism when you speak to older people in overly simple words or explain things that don't need explaining. Nonverbally, you demonstrate ageist communication when, for example, you avoid touching an older person but touch others, or when you avoid making direct eye contact with the older person but readily do so with others. Also, it's a mistake to speak to an older person at an overly high volume; this suggests that all older people have hearing difficulties, and it tends to draw attention to the fact that you are talking down to the older person.

Of course, the media perpetuate ageist stereotypes by depicting older people as unproductive, complaining, and unromantic. Rarely, for example, do television shows or films show older people working productively, being cooperative and pleasant, and engaging in romantic and sexual relationships.

One useful way to avoid ageism is to recognize and avoid the illogical stereotypes that ageist language is based on.

- Avoid talking down to a person because he or she is older. Older people are not mentally slow; most people remain mentally alert well into old age.

- Don't assume you have to refresh an older person's memory each time you see the person. Older people can and do remember things.

- Avoid implying that relationships are no longer important. Older people continue to be interested in relationships.

- Don't speak at an abnormally high volume or maintain overly close physical distances. Being older does not mean being hard of hearing or being unable to see; most older people hear and see quite well, sometimes with hearing aids or glasses.

- Engage older people in conversation as you would wish to be engaged. Older people are interested in the world around them.

Even though you want to avoid ageist communication, there are times when you may wish to make adjustments when talking with someone who does have language or communication difficulties. The American Speech and Hearing Association offers several useful suggestions (http://www.asha.org/public/speech/development/communicating-better-with-older-people.htm, accessed January 31, 2003):

- Reduce as much background noise as you can.

- Ease into the conversation by beginning with casual topics and then moving into more familiar topics. Stay with each topic for a while; avoid jumping too quickly from one topic to another.

- Speak in relatively short sentences and questions.

" Of all the self-fulfilling prophecies in our culture, the assumption that aging means decline and poor health is probably the deadliest. **"**

—Marilyn Ferguson

- Give the person added time to respond, and resist showing any signs of impatience. Some older people react more slowly and need extra time.
- Listen actively. Practice the skills of active listening discussed in the previous chapter.

Cultural Identifiers

Perhaps the best way to develop nonsexist, nonheterosexist, nonracist, and nonageist language is to examine the preferred cultural identifiers to use in talking to and about members of different groups. Remember, however, that preferred terms frequently change over time, so keep in touch with the most current preferences. The preferences and many of the specific examples identified here are drawn largely from the findings of the Task Force on Bias-Free Language of the Association of American University Presses (Schwartz, 1995).

Generally, the term *girl* should be used only to refer to very young females and is equivalent to *boy*. Neither term should be used for people older than say 13 or 14. *Girl* is never used to refer to a grown woman, nor is *boy* used to refer to people in blue-collar positions, as it once was. *Lady* is negatively evaluated by many because it connotes the stereotype of the prim and proper woman. *Woman* or *young woman* is preferred. *Older person* is preferred to *elder, elderly, senior,* or *senior citizen* (which technically refers to someone older than 65).

Generally, *gay* is the preferred term to refer to a man who has an affectional preference for other men and *lesbian* is the preferred term for a woman who has an affectional preference for other women (Lever, 1995). (*Lesbian* means "homosexual woman," so the term *lesbian woman* is redundant.) *Homosexual* refers to both gays and lesbians, but more often to a sexual orientation to members of one's own sex. *Gay* and *lesbian* refer to a lifestyle and not just to sexual orientation. *Gay* as a noun, although widely used, may prove offensive in some contexts, as in "We have two gays on the team." Because most scientific thinking holds that sexuality is not a matter of choice, the term *sexual orientation,* rather than *sexual preference* or *sexual status* (which is also vague), is preferred.

What Do You Say?

Cultural Identifiers: During a conversation, a group of your classmates all use negative cultural identifiers about themselves. Trying to be one of the group, you too use these terms—but almost immediately realize that the linguistic privilege allowing insiders to use self-derogatory names does not apply to outsiders. *What do you say?*

Listen to this

Listening without Prejudice

Just as racist, sexist, heterosexist, and ageist attitudes will influence your language, they can also influence your listening. In prejudiced listening you hear what the speaker is saying through the stereotypes you hold; you listen differently to a person because of his or her gender, race, affectional orientation, or age, even though these characteristics are irrelevant to the message.

Sexist, racist, heterosexist, and ageist listening occurs in a wide variety of situations. For example, when you dismiss a valid argument or attribute validity to an invalid argument because the speaker is of a particular gender, race, affectional orientation, or age you're listening with prejudice.

To be sure, there are many instances in which these characteristics are relevant and pertinent to your evaluation of the message. For example, the gender of a speaker talking about pregnancy, fathering a child, birth control, or surrogate motherhood is, most would agree, probably relevant to the message. So in these cases it is not sexist listening to take the gender of the speaker into consideration. It is sexist listening, however, to assume that only one gender can be an authority on a particular topic or that one gender's opinions are without value. The same is true when we listen differently in light of a person's race or affectional orientation.

Applying Listening Skills

Your friend Maria refuses to listen to men when they voice their opinions on any "woman's issue"— whether it's abortion, women in religion, the glass ceiling, adoption rights, or divorce settlements. What would you say to Maria?

Many people feel that it's permissible for members of a cultural group to refer to themselves with terms that if used by outsiders would be considered unacceptable—racist or sexist, for example. These terms, however, may actually reinforce negative stereotypes. By using these terms, group members may come to accept the labels and their negative connotations. Others would argue that by using such terms they're making them less negative. What effects, if any, do you think such self-talk has?

> Is it wrong for me to love my own? Is it wicked for me because my skin is red? Because I am a Sioux; because I was born where my father lived; because I would die for my people and my country?
>
> —Sitting Bull

What Do You Say?

Cultural Identifiers: One of your instructors persists in calling the female students "girls", refers to gay men and lesbians as "queers", and uses racial terms that most people consider highly inappropriate. You want to object to this type of talk. *What do you say? To whom? Through what channel?*

Generally, most African Americans prefer *African American* to *black* (Hecht, Collier, & Ribeau, 1993), although *black* is often used with *white,* as well as in a variety of other contexts (for example, Department of Black and Puerto Rican Studies, the *Journal of Black History,* and Black History Month). The American Psychological Association recommends that both terms be capitalized, but the *Chicago Manual of Style* (the manual used by most newspapers and publishing houses) recommends using lowercase. The terms *Negro* and *colored,* although used in the names of some organizations (for example, the United Negro College Fund and the National Association for the Advancement of Colored People), are not used outside these contexts.

White is generally used to refer to those whose roots are in European cultures and usually does not include Hispanics. Analogous to *African American* (which itself is based on a long tradition of terms such as *Irish American* and *Italian American*) is the phrase *European American.* Few European Americans, however, call themselves that; most prefer their national origins emphasized, as in, for example, *German American* or *Greek American.* This preference may well change as Europe moves toward becoming a more cohesive and united entity. *People of color*—a more literary-sounding term appropriate perhaps to public speaking but awkward in most conversations—is preferred to *nonwhite,* which implies that whiteness is the norm and nonwhiteness is a deviation from that norm. The same is true of the term *non-Christian:* It implies that people who have other beliefs deviate from the norm.

Generally, the term *Hispanic* refers to anyone who identifies himself or herself as belonging to a Spanish-speaking culture. *Latina* (female) and *Latino* (male) refer to persons whose roots are in one of the Latin American countries, such as Haiti, the Dominican Republic, Nicaragua, or Guatemala. *Hispanic American* refers to United States residents whose ancestry is in a Spanish culture; the term includes Mexican, Caribbean, and Central and South Americans. In emphasizing a Spanish heritage, however, the term is really inaccurate, because it leaves out the large numbers of people in the Caribbean and in South America whose origins are African, Native American, French, or Portuguese. *Chicana* (female) and *Chicano* (male) refer to persons with roots in Mexico, although it often connotes a nationalist attitude (Jandt, 1995) and is considered offensive by many Mexican Americans. *Mexican American* is generally preferred.

Inuk (plural, *Inuit*), also spelled with two *n*'s (*Innuk* and *Innuit*), is preferred to *Eskimo* (a term the United States Census Bureau uses), which was applied to the indigenous peoples of Alaska and Canada by Europeans and literally means "raw meat eaters."

The word *Indian* technically refers only to someone from India, not to members of other Asian countries or to the indigenous peoples of North America. *American Indian* or *Native American* is preferred, even though many Native Americans do refer to themselves as *Indians* and *Indian people*. In Canada indigenous people are called *first people*. The term *native American* (with a lowercase *n*) is most often used to refer to persons born in the United States. Although technically the term could refer to anyone born in North or South America, people outside the United States generally prefer more specific designations such as *Argentinean, Cuban,* or *Canadian*. The term *native* means an indigenous inhabitant; it is not used to mean "someone having a less developed culture."

Muslim (rather than the older *Moslem*) is the preferred form to refer to a person who adheres to the religious teachings of Islam. *Quran* (rather than *Koran*) is the preferred term for the scriptures of Islam. *Jewish people* is often preferred to *Jews,* and *Jewess* (a Jewish female) is considered derogatory.

When history was being written from a European perspective, Europe was taken as the focal point and the rest of the world was defined in terms of its location relative to that continent. Thus, Asia became the East or the Orient, and Asians became *Orientals*—a term that is today considered inappropriate or "Eurocentric." Thus, people from Asia are *Asians,* just as people from Africa are *Africans* and people from Europe are *Europeans*.

Using Verbal Messages Effectively

Three general principles will help you use verbal messages more effectively and more critically. We'll look at each in turn. As you'll see, these principles all concern the connection between the way you think and the way you talk.

Messages Symbolize Reality (Partially)

Language describes the objects, people, and events in the world with varying degrees of accuracy. But words and sentences are symbols; they're not actual objects, people, or events, even though we sometimes act as if they are. Two ways in which we sometimes act as if words and things were the same are communicating intensionally and communicating with an allness attitude.

Intensional Orientation   Have you ever reacted to the way something was labeled or described rather than to the actual item? Have you ever bought something because of its name rather than because of the actual object? If so, you were probably responding intensionally.

An **intensional orientation** (the *s* in *intensional* is intentional) is a tendency to view people, objects, and events in the way they are talked about—the way they are labeled. For example, if Sally were labeled "uninteresting," if you responded intensionally, you would evaluate her as uninteresting before listening to what she had to say. You would see Sally through a filter imposed by the label "uninteresting." The opposite tendency, **extensional orientation,** is the tendency to look first at the actual people, objects, and events and only afterward at their labels. In this case it would mean looking at Sally without any preconceived labels, guided by what she says and does, not by the words used to label her.

The way to avoid intensional orientation is to extensionalize. You can do this by focusing your attention on the people, things, and events in the world as you see them and not as they are presented in the words of others. For example, when you meet Jack and Jill, observe and interact with them. Then form your impressions.

www.researchnavigator.com

Investigate Key Terms: Investigate one of the key terms discussed in this chapter (for example, intensional orientation, allness, denotation and connotation, polarization, language, symbol, disconfirmation, racism, sexism, heterosexism, or ageism). What additional insights can you provide?

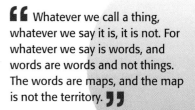
❝ Whatever we call a thing, whatever we say it is, it is not. For whatever we say is words, and words are words and not things. The words are maps, and the map is not the territory. **❞**

—Harry Weinberg

Don't respond to them as "greedy, money-grubbing landlords" because Harry labeled them this way. Don't respond to Carmen as "lazy and inconsiderate" because Elaine told you she was.

Allness   No one can know all or say all about anything. The parable of the six blind men and the elephant is an excellent example of an **allness** orientation and its problems. You may recall the John Saxe poem that tells of six blind men of Indostan who examined an elephant, an animal they had only heard about. The first blind man touched the elephant's side and concluded the elephant was like a wall. The second felt the tusk and said the elephant must be like a spear. The third held the trunk and concluded the elephant was like a snake. The fourth touched the knee and knew the elephant was like a tree. The fifth felt the ear and said the elephant was like a fan. And the sixth grabbed the tail and said the elephant was like a rope.

Each reached his own conclusion; each argued that he was correct and that the others were wrong. Each was correct and, at the same time, wrong. We are all in the position of the six blind men. We never see all of anything. We never experience anything fully. We see a part, then conclude what the whole is like. We have to draw conclusions on the basis of insufficient evidence (and we always have insufficient evidence). We must recognize that when we make judgments based only on a part, we are making inferences that can later prove wrong once we have more complete information.

A useful **extensional device** to encourage a **nonallness** orientation is to end each statement, explicitly or mentally, with **et cetera,** or **etc.**—a reminder that there is more to learn, more to know, and more to say: that every statement is inevitably incomplete. Be careful, however, that you do not use *etc.* as a substitute for being specific.

Messages Express Both Facts and Inferences

A second key principle is the importance of avoiding **fact–inference confusion.** Often, when we listen or speak, we don't distinguish between statements of fact and those of inference. Yet there are great differences between the two. Barriers to clear thinking can develop if we treat inferences as facts.

For example, you can say, "She is wearing a blue jacket" as well as "He is harboring an illogical hatred." Although the sentences have similar structures, they are different. You can observe the jacket and the blue color, but how do you observe "illogical hatred"? Obviously, this is not a descriptive but an **inferential statement.** In contrast, a **factual statement** must be made by the observer after observation and must be limited to what is observed (Weinberg, 1959).

There is nothing wrong with making inferential statements. You must make them to talk about much that is meaningful to you. The problem arises when you act as if those inferential statements are factual. Consider the following anecdote (Maynard, 1963): A woman went for a walk one day and met a friend whom she had not seen, heard from, or heard of in 10 years. After an exchange of greetings, the woman said: "Is this your little boy?" and her friend replied, "Yes, I got married about six years ago." The woman then asked the child, "What is your name?" and the little boy replied, "Same as my father's." "Oh," said the woman, "then it must be Peter."

How did the woman know the boy's father's name when she had had no contact with her friend in the last 10 years? The answer is obvious, but only after we recognize that in reading this short passage we have made an unconscious inference. Specifically, we have inferred that the woman's friend is a woman. Actually, the friend is a man named Peter.

You may test your ability to distinguish facts from inferences by taking the following self-test, "Can you distinguish facts from inferences?" (based on the tests constructed by William Haney [1973]).

Web Explorations

A variety of experiences on verbal messages will help you practice and extend some of the skills identified here (www.ablongman.com/devito): (1) Using the Abstraction Ladder as a Critical Thinking Tool, (2) "Must Lie" Situations, (3) Rephrasing Clichés, (4) Identifying the Barriers to Communication, (5) How Do You Talk about the Middle? (6) Recognizing Gender Differences, (7) How Direct Are You? (8) Is Lying Unethical? and (9) How Do You Feel about Communicating Feelings?

Can You Distinguish Facts from Inferences?

INSTRUCTIONS: Carefully read the following report and the observations based on it. Indicate whether you think the observations are true, false, or doubtful on the basis of the information presented in the report. Write T if the observation is definitely true, F if the observation is definitely false, and ? if the observation may be either true or false. Judge each observation in order. Do not reread the observations after you have indicated your judgment, and do not change any of your answers.

A well-liked college teacher had just completed making up the final examinations and had turned off the lights in the office. Just then a tall, broad figure with dark glasses appeared and demanded the examination. The professor opened the drawer. Everything in the drawer was picked up and the individual ran down the corridor. The dean was notified immediately.

_____ ❶ The thief was tall, broad, and wore dark glasses.

_____ ❷ The professor turned off the lights.

_____ ❸ A tall figure demanded the examination.

_____ ❹ The examination was picked up by someone.

_____ ❺ The examination was picked up by the professor.

_____ ❻ A tall, broad figure appeared after the professor turned off the lights in the office.

_____ ❼ The man who opened the drawer was the professor.

_____ ❽ The professor ran down the corridor.

_____ ❾ The drawer was never actually opened.

_____ ❿ Three persons are referred to in this report.

HOW DID YOU DO? After you respond to all the statements, form small groups of five or six and discuss the answers. Look at each statement from each member's point of view. For each statement, ask yourself, "How can you be absolutely certain that the statement is true or false?" You should find that only one statement can be clearly identified as true and only one as false; eight should be marked ?.

WHAT WILL YOU DO? Think about this exercise and try to formulate specific guidelines that will help you distinguish facts from inferences.

To avoid fact–inference confusion, always make inferential statements tentatively and leave open the possibility of being wrong. If, for example, you treat the statement "Our biology teacher was fired for poor teaching" as factual, you eliminate alternative explanations. When making inferential statements, be psychologically prepared to be proved wrong. In this way, you'll be less hurt if you're shown to be wrong.

Be especially sensitive to this distinction when you're listening. Most talk is inferential. Beware of the speaker (whether in interpersonal, group, or public speaking) who presents everything as fact. Analyze closely and you'll uncover a world of inferences.

? VIEWPOINT

What one principle or skill of verbal messages do you think would most significantly increase your own communication effectiveness? Can you visualize specific interpersonal, small group, and public speaking situations in which this principle or skill might prove especially useful?

Messages Can Obscure Distinctions

Language can obscure distinctions between people or events that are covered by the same label but are really quite different (indiscrimination). Language also can make it easy to focus on extremes rather than on the vast middle ground between opposites (polarization). And it can obscure the fact that change is constant and inevitable (static evaluation).

Indiscrimination **Indiscrimination** is the failure to distinguish between similar but different people, objects, or events. It occurs when we focus on classes of things and fail to see that each thing is unique and needs to be looked at individually.

Although no two things are identical, our language provides us with common nouns, such as *teacher, student, friend, enemy, war, politician,* and *liberal.* These lead us to focus on similarities—to group together all teachers, all students, all politicians, and so on. At the same time, the terms divert attention away from the uniqueness of each person, each object, and each event.

This kind of misevaluation is at the heart of stereotyping on the basis of nationality, race, religion, sex, or affectional orientation. A stereotype, you'll remember from Chapter 3, is a fixed mental picture of a group that is applied to each individual in the group without regard to his or her unique qualities.

Whether stereotypes are positive or negative, they create the same problem. They provide us with shortcuts that are often inappropriate. For instance, when you meet a particular person, your first reaction may be to pigeonhole him or her into some category—perhaps religious, national, or academic. Then you assign to this person all the qualities that are part of your stereotype. Regardless of the category you use or the specific qualities you are ready to assign, you fail to give sufficient attention to the individual's unique characteristics. Two people may both be Christian, Asian, and lesbian, for example, but each will be different from the other. Indiscrimination is a denial of another's uniqueness.

A useful antidote to indiscrimination is an extensional device known as the **index.** This mental subscript identifies each individual as an individual, even though a group of these individuals may be covered by the same label. Thus, politician$_1$ is not politician$_2$; teacher$_1$ is not teacher$_2$. The index helps us to discriminate between without discriminating against.

Polarization **Polarization** is the tendency to look at the world in terms of opposites and to describe it in extremes—good or bad, positive or negative, healthy or sick, intelligent or stupid. Polarization is often referred to as the fallacy of "either/or" or "black-and-white" thinking. In reality most people, objects, and events exist

Research Navigator.com

www.researchnavigator.com

Find Answers: Try finding answers to one of the following questions, or design a research study to answer it: Are confirmation and disconfirmation expressed differently in face-to-face and in Internet communications? What are some common responses to the use of racist, sexist, heterosexist, and ageist language on your campus? Do men and women differ in the way they lie, in what they lie about, or in the frequency with which they lie?

Talking in E-Prime

E-prime (E′) is a form of normal English that omits the verb *to be* (Bourland, 1965–1966; Wilson 1989). The purpose of using e-prime is to avoid suggesting that such-and-such "is" a permanent, built-in attribute of someone or something. For example, in e-prime you would say, not "Sam is lousy at math" but "Sam failed two math tests." To appreciate the difference between statements that use the verb *to be* and those that do not, *(a)* rewrite the following sentences in the second column without using the verb *to be* in any of its forms (*is, are, am, was,* etc.) and *(b)* indicate in the third column the differences in meaning between the original statements and the e-prime rewrites.

Normal English	E-Prime	Meaning Differences
1. I'm not very good at making friends. 2. They're just uninformed. 3. Are you happy? 4. This class is bad.		

somewhere between the extremes. Yet we have a strong tendency to view only the extremes and to categorize things in terms of these polar opposites.

We create problems when we polarize in inappropriate situations. Consider this example: "The politician is either for us or against us." These options do not include all possibilities. The politician may be for us in some things and against us in other things or may be neutral.

To correct this tendency to polarize, beware of implying (and believing) that all individuals and events must fit into one extreme or the other, with no alternatives in between. And when others imply that there are only two sides or alternatives, look for the middle ground.

Static Evaluation   People and things change at a rapid rate, but our messages about them may not keep pace. The statements you make about an event or person need to change as quickly and as dramatically as people and events change. When you retain an evaluation (most often in the form of an internalized message) despite the changes in the person or thing, you're engaging in **static evaluation.**

It's important to act in accordance with the notion of change, not merely to accept it intellectually. If you failed at something once, that docs not necessarily mean that you'll fail again. If you were rejected once, that does not mean you'll be rejected again. You've changed since the first failure and the first rejection. You're a different person now, and you need to make new evaluations and initiate new efforts.

The mental **date** is a useful extensional device for keeping language (and thinking) up to date and for guarding against static evaluation. Date your statements and especially your evaluations; remember that Pat Smith$_{1999}$ is not Pat Smith $_{2005}$, that academic abilities$_{2001}$ are not academic abilities$_{2005}$. In talking and in listening, look carefully at messages that claim that what was true still is. It may or may not be. Look for change; be suspicious of the implication of nonchange.

> **"** What we know of other people is only our memory of the moments during which we knew them. And they have changed since then . . . at every meeting we are meeting a stranger. **"**
>
> —T. S. Eliot

Summary of Concepts and Skills

In this chapter we considered verbal messages. We looked at the nature of language and identified several major ways in which language works. We looked at the concept of disconfirmation, especially as it relates to sexist, heterosexist, and racist language. And we explored ways to make verbal communication more effective.

1. Language is both denotative (objective and generally easily agreed upon) and connotative (subjective and generally highly individual in meaning).
2. Language varies in abstraction; it can range from extremely general to extremely specific.
3. Language varies in directness; it can state exactly what you mean, or it can hedge and state your meaning very indirectly.
4. Language is rule based; grammatical and cultural rules guide performance.
5. Language meanings are in people, not simply in words.
6. *Disconfirmation* is the process of ignoring the presence and the communications of others. *Confirmation* means accepting, supporting, and acknowledging the importance of the other person.
7. Racist, sexist, heterosexist, and ageist language disconfirms, puts down, and negatively evaluates various groups.
8. To make verbal messages more effective, realize that language symbolizes reality and is not the reality itself; that language can express both facts and inferences but doesn't indicate this grammatically; that language can obscure distinctions, as when it provides lots of extreme terms but few terms to describe the middle ground; and that language tends to be static, whereas people and events are forever changing.

The study of verbal messages and of how meaning is communicated from one person to another has important implications for the skills of effective communication. Check your ability to apply these skills, using the following rating scale: 1 = almost always; 2 = often; 3 = sometimes; 4 = rarely; and 5 = hardly ever.

_____ 1. I try to understand not only objective, denotative meanings, but also the subjective, connotative meanings.

_____ 2. I recognize that snarl and purr words describe the speaker's feelings and not objective reality.

_____ 3. I take special care to make spoken messages clear and unambiguous, especially when using terms for which people will have very different connotative meanings.

_____ 4. I recognize the gender and cultural differences in directness and can adjust my style of speaking and listening as appropriate.

_____ 5. I communicate with a clear recognition of the grammatical and cultural rules (and maxims, especially that of politeness) of the language.

_____ 6. I focus attention not only on words but also on the person communicating, recognizing that meanings are largely in the person.

_____ 7. I avoid disconfirmation and instead use responses that confirm the other person.

_____ 8. I avoid sexist, heterosexist, racist, and ageist language and, in general, language that puts down other groups.

_____ 9. I use the cultural identifiers that facilitate communication and avoid those that set up barriers to effective interaction.

_____ 10. I avoid responding intensionally to labels as if they are objects; instead, I respond extensionally and look first at the reality and secondarily at the words.

_____ 11. I end my statements with an implicit *etc.* in recognition that there is always more to be known or said.

_____ 12. I distinguish facts from inferences and respond to inferences with tentativeness.

_____ 13. I avoid indiscrimination by viewing the uniqueness in each person and situation.

_____ 14. I avoid polarization by using "middle ground" terms and qualifiers in describing the world, especially people.

_____ 15. I mentally date my statements and thus avoid static evaluation.

Key Word Quiz

Write T for those statements that are true and F for those that are false. In addition, for those that are false, replace the italicized term with the correct term.

_____ 1. The meaning of a word that you would find in a dictionary is the word's *connotative meaning*.

_____ 2. The emotional meaning that speakers and listeners give to a word is known as the word's *denotative meaning*.

_____ 3. The word *magazine* differs from *Time* magazine in *abstraction*.

_____ 4. A pattern of communication in which you ignore someone's presence as well as that person's communication is known as *confirmation*.

_____ 5. A pattern of communication in which you acknowledge the presence of the other person as well as your acceptance of that person is known as *disconfirmation*.

_____ 6. Language that puts down members of either sex is known as *sexist language*.

_____ 7. The tendency to look at the world in terms of opposites and to describe it in extremes—good or bad, positive or negative, young or old—is known as *static evaluation*.

_____ 8. The tendency to look first at the actual person, object, or event and only afterwards at its label or the way it is talked about is known as *intensional orientation*.

_____ 9. The failure to distinguish between similar but different people, objects, or events is known as *discrimination*.

_____ 10. A useful antidote to allness is the *index*.

Answers: TRUE: 3, 6; FALSE: 1 (*denotative meaning*), 2 (*connotative meaning*), 4 (*disconfirmation*), 5 (*confirmation*), 7 (*polarization*), 8 (*extensional orientation*), 9 (*indiscrimination*), 10 (*etc.*)

6 Nonverbal Messages

Chapter Concepts	**Chapter Skills**
This chapter introduces the functions and the channels of nonverbal messages and explores cultural and gender variations in nonverbal communication.	After completing this chapter, you should be able to:
The Functions of Nonverbal Communication	identify the functions that nonverbal messages serve and use nonverbal messages to communicate a variety of meanings.
The Channels of Nonverbal Communication	use the varied channels of nonverbal communication to express your meanings and to complement your verbal messages.
Culture and Nonverbal Communication	communicate nonverbally with an understanding of cultural and gender differences.

Nonverbal communication is communication without words. You communicate nonverbally when you gesture, smile or frown, widen your eyes, move your chair closer to someone, wear jewelry, touch someone, raise your vocal volume, or even say nothing. The crucial aspect is that the message you send is in some way received by one or more other people. If you gesture while you are alone in your room and no one is there to see you, then, most theorists would argue, communication has not taken place. The same is true of verbal messages, of course; if you recite a speech and no one hears it, then communication has not taken place.

The ability to use nonverbal communication effectively can yield two major benefits (Burgoon & Hoobler, 2002). First, the greater your ability to send and receive nonverbal signals, the higher your popularity and psychosocial well-being are likely to be. Second, the greater your nonverbal skills, the more successful you're likely to be at influencing (as well as deceiving) others. Skilled nonverbal communicators are highly persuasive. This persuasive power can be used to help or support another, or it can be used to deceive and fool.

Research shows that women are the better senders and receivers of nonverbal messages (Hall, 1998; Burgoon & Hoobler, 2002). Although this superiority does not hold in all contexts, it does apply in most. For example, in a review of 21 research studies, 71 percent found women to be superior senders of nonverbal signals. And in a review of 61 studies on decoding, 84 percent found women to be superior receivers (Hall, 1998).

As you begin your study of nonverbal communication, keep the following suggestions in mind.

- Analyze your own nonverbal communication patterns. Self-analysis is essential if you're to use this material in any meaningful way; for example, to change some of your behaviors.

- Observe. Observe. Observe. Observe the behaviors of those around you as well as your own. See in everyday behavior what you read about here and discuss in class. This will help you bring to a mindful state what may now be automatic and mindless.

- Resist the temptation to draw conclusions from nonverbal behaviors. Instead, develop hypotheses (educated guesses) about what is going on, and test the validity of your hypotheses on the basis of other evidence.

> **" Actions lie louder than words. "**
>
> —Carolyn Wells

- Connect and relate. Although textbooks (like this text) must present the areas of nonverbal communication separately, the various elements all work together in actual communication situations.
- Nonverbal messages may be used alone; may function as the primary channel of communication, with the verbal message in a secondary role; or may serve in a secondary role (Burgoon & Hoobler, 2002).

The Functions of Nonverbal Communication

Let's consider the functions of nonverbal communication by looking at (1) the ways in which nonverbal communication messages are integrated with verbal messages and (2) the functions that researchers have focused on most extensively.

Integrating Nonverbal and Verbal Messages

In face-to-face communication you blend verbal and nonverbal messages to best convey your meanings. While speaking, you also smile, frown, or gesture, for example. And it's this combination of verbal and nonverbal signals that communicates your meanings. Here are six ways in which nonverbal messages interact with verbal messages (Knapp & Hall, 2002).

- Nonverbal communication often serves to *accent* or emphasize some part of the verbal message. You might, for example, raise your voice to underscore a particular word or phrase, bang your fist on the desk to stress your commitment, or look longingly into someone's eyes when saying "I love you."
- Nonverbal communication may *complement* or add nuances of meaning not communicated by your verbal message. Thus, you might smile when telling a story (to suggest that you find it humorous) or frown and shake your head when recounting someone's deceit (to suggest your disapproval).
- You may deliberately *contradict* your verbal messages with nonverbal movements—for example, by crossing your fingers or winking to indicate that you're lying.
- Movements may serve to *regulate*—to control, or indicate your desire to control, the flow of verbal messages, as when you purse your lips, lean forward, or make hand gestures to indicate that you want to speak. You might also put up your hand or vocalize your pauses (for example, with "um" or "ah") to indicate that you have not finished and are not ready to relinquish the floor to the next speaker.
- You can nonverbally *repeat* or restate a verbal message. You can, for example, follow your verbal "Is that all right?" with raised eyebrows and a questioning look, or motion with your head or hand to repeat your verbal "Let's go."
- You may also use nonverbal communication to *substitute for* or take the place of verbal messages. For instance, you can signal "OK" with a hand gesture. You can nod your head to indicate yes or shake your head to indicate no.

Researching Nonverbal Communication Functions

Although nonverbal communication serves the same functions as verbal communication, researchers have singled out several specific functions in which nonverbal messages are especially significant (Burgoon, Buller, & Woodall, 1996; Burgoon & Hoobler, 2002; Burgoon & Bacue, 2003).

Forming and Managing Impressions It is largely through the nonverbal communications of others that you form impressions of them. Based on a person's body

Skill development experience

Integrating Verbal and Nonverbal Messages

Try reading each of the following aloud in two ways—first to communicate the statement's literal meaning, then to communicate a meaning opposite to the literal one. As you go along, try to identify the nonverbal differences between the literal and the opposite-meaning renditions. Look specifically at *(a)* your rate, pauses, and volume as you read the statements; *(b)* your facial and eye expressions; and *(c)* your gestures and body posture.

1. Yes, I have the relationship of a lifetime.
2. I can't wait to receive my test results.
3. Did you hear his last speech?
4. Did you see the way she designed the store?

size, skin color, and dress, as well as on the way the person smiles, maintains eye contact, and expresses himself or herself facially, you form impressions—you judge who the person is and what the person is like. One nonverbal researcher groups these impressions into four categories: credibility, or how competent and believable you find the person; likeability, or how much you like or dislike the person; attractiveness, or how attractive you find the person; and dominance, or how powerful the individual is (Leathers, 1997).

Of course, you reveal yourself to others largely through the same nonverbal signals you use to size up others. But not only do you communicate your true self nonverbally; you also manage the impression that you give to others. Impression management may, for example, mean appearing brave when you're really scared or happy when you're really sad.

Forming and Defining Relationships   Much of your relationship life is lived nonverbally. Largely through nonverbal signals, you communicate the nature of your relationship to another person; and you and that person communicate nonverbally with each other. Holding hands, looking longingly into each other's eyes, and even dressing alike are ways in which you communicate closeness in your interpersonal relationships.

You also use nonverbal signals to communicate your relationship dominance and status (Knapp & Hall, 2002). The large corner office with the huge desk communicates high status just as the basement cubicle communicates low status.

Structuring Conversation and Social Interaction   When you're in conversation, you give and receive cues—signals that you're ready to speak, to listen, to comment on what the speaker just said. These cues regulate and structure the interaction. These turn-taking cues may be verbal (as when you say, "What do you think?"), but most often they're nonverbal: A nod of the head in the direction of someone else, for example, signals that you're ready to give up your speaking turn and want this other person to say something.

You also show that you're listening and that you want the conversation to continue (or that you're not listening and want the conversation to end) largely through nonverbal signals.

Influence and Deception   You can influence others not only through what you say but also influence through your nonverbal signals. A focused glance that says you're committed; gestures that further explain what you're saying; appropriate dress that says, "I'll easily fit in with this organization"—these are a few examples of ways in which you can exert nonverbal influence.

www.researchnavigator.com

Read an Article: Read a scholarly or popular article on one of the types of nonverbal communication discussed in this chapter. On the basis of this article, what can you add to the discussion presented here?

And with the ability to influence, of course, comes the ability to deceive—to lie, to mislead another person into thinking something is true when it's false or that something is false when it's true. One common example of nonverbal deception is using your eyes and facial expressions to communicate a liking for other people when you're really interested only in gaining their support in some endeavor. Not surprisingly, you also use nonverbal signals to detect deception in others. For example, you may well suspect a person of lying if he or she avoids eye contact, fidgets, and conveys inconsistent verbal and nonverbal messages.

Emotional Expression   Although people often explain and reveal emotions verbally, nonverbal expressions communicate a great part of your emotional experience. For example, you reveal your level of happiness or sadness or confusion largely through facial expressions. Of course, you also reveal your feelings by posture (for example, whether tense or relaxed), gestures, eye movements, and even the dilation of your pupils.

Nonverbal messages often help people communicate unpleasant messages, messages they might feel uncomfortable putting into words (Infante, Rancer, & Womack, 2003). For example, you might avoid eye contact and maintain large distances between yourself and someone with whom you didn't want to interact or with whom you wanted to decrease the intensity of your relationship.

The Channels of Nonverbal Communication

You communicate nonverbally through a wide range of channels: the body, the face and eyes, space, artifacts, touch, paralanguage and silence, and time.

Body Messages

The body communicates with movements and gestures and just with its general appearance.

Body Movements   Nonverbal researchers identify five major types of body movements: emblems, illustrators, affect displays, regulators, and adaptors (Ekman & Friesen, 1969; Knapp & Hall, 1997).

Emblems are body gestures that directly translate into words or phrases—for example, the OK sign, the thumbs up for "good job," and the V for victory. You use these consciously and purposely to communicate the same meaning as the words. But emblems are culture specific, so be careful when using your culture's emblems in other cultures (see Figure 1.6 on page 15). For example, when President Richard Nixon visited Latin America and gestured with the OK sign, which he thought communicated something positive, he was quickly informed that this gesture was not universal. In Latin America the gesture has a far more negative meaning. Here are a few cultural differences in the emblems you may commonly use (Axtell, 1991):

- In the United States, you wave with your whole hand moving from side to side to say "hello"; but in a large part of Europe, that same signal means "no." In Greece such a signal would be considered insulting to the person to whom you were waving.
- The V for victory common throughout much of the world—if used with the palm toward your face—is as insulting in England as the raised middle finger is in the United States.
- In Texas the raised fist with raised little finger and index finger is a positive expression of support, because it represents the Texas longhorn steer. But in Italy it is an insult that means "cuckold." In parts of South America, it is a gesture used to ward off evil. In parts of Africa, it is a curse: "May you experience bad times."

- In the United States and much of Asia, hugs are rarely exchanged among acquaintances; but among Latin Americans and southern Europeans, hugging is a common greeting gesture, and failing to hug someone may communicate unfriendliness.

Illustrators enhance (literally "illustrate") the verbal messages they accompany. For example, when referring to something to the left, you might gesture toward the left. Most often, you illustrate with your hands, but you can also illustrate with head and general body movements. You might, for example, turn your head or your entire body toward the left. You might also use illustrators to communicate the shape or size of objects you're talking about. Recent research points to an interesting advantage of illustrators—namely, that they increase your ability to remember. In this research people who illustrated their verbal messages with gestures remembered some 20 percent more than those who didn't gesture (Goldin-Meadow, Nusbaum, Kelly, & Wagner, 2001).

Affect displays are movements of the face (smiling or frowning, for example) but also of the hands and general body (body tenseness or relaxed posture, for example) that communicate emotional meaning. You use affect displays to accompany and reinforce your verbal messages, but also as substitutes for words; for example, you might smile while saying how happy you are to see your friend, or you might simply smile. Affect displays, being primarily centered in the facial area, are covered in more detail in the next section.

Regulators are behaviors that monitor, control, coordinate, or maintain the speech of another individual. When you nod your head, for example, you tell the speaker to keep on speaking; when you lean forward and open your mouth, you tell the speaker that you would like to say something.

Adaptors are gestures that satisfy some personal need, such as scratching to relieve an itch or moving your hair out of your eyes. **Self-adaptors** are self-touching movements (for example, rubbing your nose). **Alter-adaptors** are movements directed at the person with whom you're speaking—for example, removing lint from a person's jacket or straightening his or her tie or folding your arms in front of you to keep others a comfortable distance from you. **Object-adaptors** are gestures focused on objects—for example, doodling on or shredding a Styrofoam coffee cup. Table 6.1 summarizes these five types of body movements.

TABLE 6.1   Five Body Movements

What other examples can you think of for these five movements?

	NAME AND FUNCTION	EXAMPLES
	EMBLEMS directly translate words or phrases; they are especially culture specific.	"OK" sign, "come here" wave, hitchhiker's sign
	ILLUSTRATORS accompany and literally "illustrate" verbal messages.	Circular hand movements when talking of a circle; hands far apart when talking of something large
	AFFECT DISPLAYS communicate emotional meaning.	Expressions of happiness, surprise, fear, anger, sadness, disgust/contempt
	REGULATORS monitor, maintain, or control the speech of another.	Facial expressions and hand gestures indicating "keep going," "slow down," or "what else happened?"
	ADAPTORS satisfy some need.	Scratching your head

Chapter 6 Nonverbal Messages   **109**

Body Appearance   Your general body appearance also communicates. Height, for example, has been shown to be significant in a wide variety of situations. Tall presidential candidates have a much better record of winning elections than do their shorter opponents. Tall people seem to be paid more and are favored by personnel interviewers over shorter job applicants (Keyes, 1980; DeVito & Hecht, 1990; Knapp & Hall, 1997).

Your body also reveals your race through skin color and tone and may even give clues as to your nationality. Your weight in proportion to your height will also communicate messages to others, as will the length, color, and style of your hair.

Your general **attractiveness,** which includes both visual appeal and pleasantness of personality, is also a part of body communication. Attractive people have the advantage in just about every activity you can name. They get better grades in school, are more valued as friends and lovers, and are preferred as coworkers (Burgoon, Buller, & Woodall, 1996). Although we normally think that attractiveness is culturally determined—and to some degree it is—some research seems to show that definitions of attractiveness are becoming universal (*New York Times,* March 21, 1994, p. A14). A person rated as attractive in one culture is likely to be rated as attractive in other cultures—even in cultures in which people are generally quite different in appearance from people in the first culture.

Facial and Eye Movements

The facial area, including the eyes, is probably the single most important source of nonverbal messages.

Facial Communication   Throughout your interpersonal interactions, your face communicates many things, especially your emotions. In fact, facial movements alone seem to communicate the degree of pleasantness, agreement, and sympathy felt; the rest of the body doesn't provide any additional information in those realms. But for other aspects—for example, the intensity with which an emotion is felt—both facial and bodily cues enter in (Graham, Bitti, & Argyle, 1975; Graham & Argyle, 1975). These cues are so important in communicating your full meaning that graphic representations are now commonly used in Internet communication. In some

VIEWPOINT

On a 10-point scale, with 1 indicating "extremely unimportant" and 10 indicating "extremely important," how important is body appearance to your own romantic interest in another person? Do the men and women you know conform to the stereotypes—that males are more concerned with the physical (supporting the belief that "men fall in love with their eyes") and females more concerned with personality (supporting the belief that "women fall in love with their ears")?

TABLE 6.2 Some Popular Emoticons

These are some of the emoticons used in computer communication. The first six are widely used in the United States; the last three are popular in Japan and illustrate how culture influences such symbols. Because Japanese culture considers it impolite for women to show their teeth when smiling, the emoticon for a woman's smile shows a dot signifying a closed mouth. Additional emoticons, acronyms, and abbreviations can be found at http://www.cafeshops.com/netlingo.

EMOTICON	MEANING
:-)	Smile: I'm kidding
:-(	Frown; I'm feeling down
;-)	Wink
*	Kiss
{ }	Hug
{*****}	Hugs and kisses
^ . ^	Woman's smile
^_^	Man's smile
^o^	Happy

Internet Relay Chat groups (those that use GUI, Graphic User Interface), buttons are available to help you encode your emotions graphically. Table 6.2 identifies some of the more common "emoticons," icons that communicate emotions.

Some nonverbal research claims that facial movements may communicate at least the following eight emotions: happiness, surprise, fear, anger, sadness, disgust, contempt, and interest (Ekman, Friesen, & Ellsworth, 1972). Try to communicate surprise using only facial movements. Do this in front of a mirror and try to describe in as much detail as possible the specific movements of the face that make up a look of surprise. If you signal surprise like most people, you probably use raised and curved eyebrows, long horizontal forehead wrinkles, wide-open eyes, a dropped-open mouth, and lips parted with no tension. Even if there were differences from one person to another—and clearly there would be—you could probably recognize the movements listed here as indicative of surprise.

Of course, some emotions are easier to communicate and to decode than others. For example, in one study, participants judged happiness with accuracy ranging from 55 to 100 percent, surprise with 38 to 86 percent accuracy, and sadness with 19 to 88 percent accuracy (Ekman, Friesen, & Ellsworth, 1972). Research finds that women and girls are more accurate judges of facial emotional expression than men and boys (Hall, 1984; Argyle, 1988).

Facial Management. As you grew up, you learned your culture's system of nonverbal communication. You also learned certain **facial management techniques** that enable you to express feelings so as to achieve certain desired effects—for example, to hide certain emotions and to emphasize others. Consider your own use of such facial management techniques. As you do so, think about the types of interpersonal situations in which you would use facial management techniques for each of the following purposes (Malandro, Barker, & Barker, 1989; Metts & Planalp, 2002). Would you

- *intensify?* For example, would you exaggerate your astonishment at a surprise party to make your friends feel better?
- *deintensify?* Would you cover up your own joy about good news in the presence of a friend who didn't receive any such news?

What do you say?

Smiling: Sally smiles almost all the time. Even when she criticizes or reprimands a subordinate, she ends with a smile, and this dilutes the strength of her message. As Sally's supervisor you need her to realize what she's doing and to change her nonverbals. *What do you say? Through what channel?*

- *neutralize?* Would you cover up your sadness so as not to depress others?
- *mask?* Would you express happiness in order to cover up your disappointment at not receiving a gift you expected?
- *simulate?* Would you express an emotion you didn't feel?

Facial management techniques help you display emotions in socially acceptable ways. For example, if someone gets bad news in which you secretly take pleasure, the social display rule dictates that you frown and otherwise nonverbally signal sorrow. If you place first in a race and your best friend barely finishes, the display rule requires that you minimize your expression of happiness—and certainly avoid any signs of gloating. If you violate these display rules, you'll appear insensitive. So, although facial management techniques may be deceptive, they're expected and even required by the rules for polite interaction.

"Look at me. Do I look worried?"

The Facial Feedback Hypothesis.

According to the **facial feedback hypothesis,** your facial expression influences your level of physiological arousal. People who exaggerate their facial expressions show higher physiological arousal than those who suppress these expressions. In research studies, those who neither exaggerated nor suppressed their expressions had arousal levels between these two extremes (Lanzetta, Cartwright-Smith, & Kleck, 1976; Zuckerman, Klorman, Larrance, & Spiegel, 1981). In one interesting study, subjects held a pen in their teeth in such a way as to simulate a sad expression. They were then asked to rate photographs. Results showed that mimicking sad expressions actually increased the degree of sadness the subjects reported feeling when viewing the photographs (Larsen, Kasimatis, & Frey, 1992). So not only does your facial expression influence the judgments and impressions others have of you; it also influences your own level of emotional arousal (Cappella, 1993).

Eye Communication

From Ben Jonson's poetic observation "Drink to me only with thine eyes, / And I will pledge with mine" to the scientific observations of contemporary researchers (Hess, 1975; Marshall, 1983), the eyes have long been regarded as the seat of the most important nonverbal message system.

The messages communicated by the eyes vary depending on the duration, direction, and quality of the eye behavior. For example, every culture has rather strict, though unstated, rules for the proper duration of eye contact. In one study conducted in England, the average length of gaze is 2.95 seconds. The average length of mutual gaze (two persons gazing at each other) is 1.18 seconds (Argyle & Ingham, 1972; Argyle, 1988). When eye contact falls short of this amount, members of some cultures may think the person is uninterested, shy, or preoccupied. When the appropriate amount of time is exceeded, they may perceive the person as showing unusually high interest or even hostility.

The direction of the gaze also communicates. In the United States it is considered appropriate to glance alternately at the other person's face, then away, then again at the face, and so on. The rule for public speakers is to scan the entire audience, not focusing for too long on or ignoring any one area of the audience. When you break these directional rules, you communicate different meanings—abnormally high or low interest, self-consciousness, nervousness over the interaction, and so on. How wide or narrow your eyes get during an interaction also communicates meaning, especially interest level and emotions such as surprise, fear, and disgust.

The Functions of Eye Movements.

You communicate a variety of messages through eye movements. For example, you can seek feedback: In talking with someone, you might look at her or him intently, as if to say, "Well, what do you think?"

You can also inform the other person that the channel of communication is open and that he or she should now speak. You see this in college classrooms when the instructor asks a question and then locks eyes with a student. Without saying anything, the instructor conveys the expectation that the student will answer the question, and the student gets the message.

Eye movements may also signal the nature of a relationship, whether positive (an attentive glance) or negative (avoidance). You can also signal your power through "visual dominance behavior" (Exline, Ellyson, & Long, 1975). The average speaker, for example, maintains a high level of eye contact while listening and a lower level while speaking. When people want to signal dominance, they may reverse this pattern—maintaining a high level of eye contact while talking but a lower level while listening. You'll see this pattern, if you visualize a manager criticizing a subordinate. You'll probably picture the manager maintaining direct eye contact with the subordinate while criticizing and with little eye contact when listening to excuses he or she considers inadequate.

Eye contact also can change the psychological distance between yourself and another person. When you catch someone's eye at a party, for example, you become psychologically close even though physically far apart. By avoiding eye contact—even when physically close, as in a crowded elevator—you increase the psychological distance between you and others.

When you avoid eye contact or avert your glance, you help others maintain their privacy. You may engage in this **civil inattention** when you see a couple arguing in public, for example (Goffman, 1967). You turn your eyes away (although your eyes may be wide open) as if to say, "I don't mean to intrude; I respect your privacy."

Eye avoidance also can signal lack of interest—in a person, a conversation, or some visual stimulus. At times you may hide your eyes to block off unpleasant stimuli or close your eyes to block out visual stimuli and thus heighten other senses. For example, you may listen to music with your eyes closed. Lovers often close their eyes while kissing, and many prefer to make love in a dark or dimly lit room.

Because eye-contact messages vary from one culture to another, you risk breaking important rules when you communicate with eye movements. Americans, for example, consider direct eye contact an expression of honesty and forthrightness, but the Japanese often view this as a lack of respect. A Japanese person will glance at the other person's face rarely, and then only for very short periods (Axtell, 1990).

Women make eye contact more and maintain it longer (both in speaking and in listening) than men. This holds true whether women are interacting with other women or with men. This difference in eye behavior may result from women's greater tendency to display their emotions (Wood, 1994).

> " An eye can threaten like a loaded and leveled gun, or it can insult like hissing or kicking; or, in its altered mood, by beams of kindness, it can make the heart dance for joy. "
>
> —Ralph Waldo Emerson

Spatial Messages

Space is an especially important factor in nonverbal interpersonal communication, although we seldom think about it. Edward T. Hall (1959, 1963, 1966), who pioneered the study of spatial communication, called this study **proxemics.** We can sample this broad area by looking at proxemic distances and territoriality.

Proxemic Distances   Hall (1959, 1966) distinguishes four distances that define types of relationships between people; each distance communicates specific kinds of messages.

At an **intimate distance,** ranging from actual touching to 18 inches, the presence of the other individual is unmistakable. Each person experiences the sound, smell, and feel of the other's breath. You use intimate distance for lovemaking and wrestling, for comforting and protecting. This distance is so short that most people do not consider it proper in public.

what do you say?

Proxemics: Like the close-talker in an episode of Seinfeld, one of your team members at work maintains an extremely close distance when talking. To compound the problem, this person is a heavy smoker and reeks of smoke. You need to say something. *What do you say? Through what channel?*

Personal distance constitutes the protective "bubble" that defines your personal space, which measures from 18 inches to 4 feet. This imaginary bubble keeps you protected and untouched by others. You can still hold or grasp another person at this distance—but only by extending your arms—allowing you to take certain individuals such as loved ones into your protective bubble. At the outer limit of personal distance, you can touch another person only if both of you extend your arms.

At **social distance,** ranging from 4 to 12 feet, you lose the visual detail you have at personal distance. You conduct impersonal business and interact at a social gathering at this social distance. The more distance you maintain in your interactions, the more formal they appear. Many people in executive and management positions place their desks so that they are assured of at least this distance from employees.

Public distance, measuring from 12 to 25 feet or more, protects you. At this distance you could take defensive action if threatened. On a public bus or train, for example, you might keep at least this distance from a drunk. Although you lose fine details of the face and eyes at this distance, you are still close enough to see what is happening. These four distances are summarized in Table 6.3.

The specific distances that you maintain between yourself and other individuals depend on a wide variety of factors (Burgoon, Buller, & Woodall, 1996). Among the most significant factors are *gender* (women in same-sex dyads sit and stand closer to each other than do men, and people approach women more closely than they approach men); *age* (people maintain closer distances with similarly aged others than they do with those much older or much younger); and *personality* (introverts and highly anxious people maintain greater distances than do extroverts). Not surprisingly, you'll tend to maintain shorter distances with people you're familiar with than with strangers, and with people you like than with those you don't like.

TABLE 6.3 **Relationships and Proxemic Distances**

Note that the four proxemic distances can be further divided into close and far phases and that the far phase of one level (say, personal) blends into the close phase of the next level (social). Do your relationships also blend into one another? Or are your personal relationships, totally separate from your social relationships?

RELATIONSHIP	DISTANCE	
Intimate Relationship	Intimate Distance 0 _____ 18 inches Close phase — Far phase	
Personal Relationship	Personal Distance 1½ _____ 4 feet Close phase — Far phase	
Social Relationship	Social Distance 4 _____ 12 feet Close phase — Far phase	
Public Relationship	Public Distance 12 _____ 25+ feet Close phase — Far phase	

Skill development experience

Selecting Seats at the Company Meeting

The graphic here represents a meeting table with 12 chairs, one of which is occupied by the boss. For each of the messages below, indicate *(a)* where you would sit to communicate each message and *(b)* any other possible messages that your choice of seat would likely communicate.

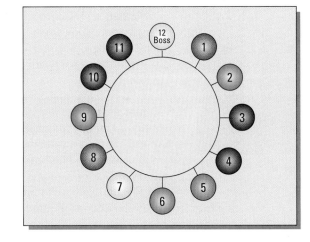

1. You want to ingratiate yourself with your boss.
2. You aren't prepared and want to be ignored.
3. You want to challenge a proposal by your boss that's scheduled to come up for a vote.
4. You want to get to know better the person seated at number 7.

Territoriality   Another type of communication having to do with space is **territoriality,** a possessive reaction to an area or to particular objects. You interact basically in three types of territories (Altman, 1975):

- **Primary territories** are areas that you might call your own; these areas are your exclusive preserve. Primary territories might include your room, your desk, or your office.

- **Secondary territories** are areas that don't belong to you but which you have occupied and with which you're associated. They might include your usual table in the cafeteria, your regular seat in the classroom, or your neighborhood turf.

- **Public territories** are areas that are open to all people; they may be owned by some person or organization, but they are used by everyone. They are places such as movie houses, restaurants, and shopping malls.

When you operate in your own primary territory, you have an interpersonal advantage, often called the **home field advantage.** In their own home or office, people take on a kind of leadership role: They initiate conversations, fill in silences, assume relaxed and comfortable postures, and maintain their positions with greater conviction. Because the territorial owner is dominant, you stand a better chance of getting your raise approved, your point accepted, or a contract resolved in your favor if you're in your own territory (your office, your home) rather than in someone else's (your supervisor's office, for example) (Marsh, 1988).

Like animals, humans mark both their primary and secondary territories to signal ownership. Humans use three types of **markers:** central, boundary, and earmarkers (Goffman, 1971). **Central markers** are items you place in a territory to reserve it for you—for example, a drink at the bar, books on your desk, or a sweater over a library chair.

Boundary markers serve to divide your territory from that of others. In the supermarket checkout line, the bar placed between your groceries and those of the person behind you is a boundary marker, as are fences, armrests that separate your chair from those on either side, and the contours of the molded plastic seats on a bus.

Earmarkers—a term taken from the practice of branding animals on their ears—are identifying marks that indicate your possession of a territory or object. Trademarks, nameplates, and initials on a shirt or attaché case are all examples of earmarkers.

Markers are also important in giving you a feeling of belonging. For example, one study found that students who marked their college dorm rooms by displaying personal items stayed in school longer than did those who didn't personalize their spaces (Marsh, 1988).

Again, like animals, humans use territory to signal their status. For example, the size and location of your territory (your home or office, say) indicates something about your status. Status is also signaled by the unwritten law governing the right of invasion. Higher-status individuals have a "right" to invade the territory of lower-status persons, but the reverse is not true. The boss of a large company, for example, can barge into the office of a junior executive, but the reverse would be unthinkable. Similarly, a teacher may invade a student's personal space by looking over her or his shoulder as the student writes, but the student cannot do the same to the teacher.

"We're moving you to a cubicle, Harrison."

© Charles Barsotti

Artifactual Communication

Artifactual messages are messages conveyed through objects or arrangements made by human hands. Color, the clothing or jewelry you wear, the way you decorate space, and even bodily scents communicate a wide variety of meanings.

Color Communication   When you're in debt, you speak of being "in the red"; when you make a profit, you're "in the black." When you're sad, you're "blue"; when you're healthy, you're "in the pink"; when you're covetous, you're "green with envy." To be a coward is to be "yellow" and to be inexperienced is to be "green." When you talk a great deal, you talk "a blue streak"; when you are angry, you "see red." As these clichés reveal, color symbolism abounds in language. Color symbolism varies greatly in different cultures, however, as we'll see in the final section of this chapter.

There is some evidence that colors affect us physiologically. For example, respiration rates increase in the presence of red light and decrease in the presence of blue light. Similarly, eye blinks increase in frequency when eyes are exposed to red light and decrease when exposed to blue. These findings seem consistent with our intuitive feelings that blue is more soothing and red more provocative. At one school, in fact, after the administration changed the classroom walls from orange and white to blue, the students' blood pressure levels decreased and their academic performance improved (Ketcham, 1958; Malandro, Barker, & Barker, 1989).

Colors surely influence our perceptions and behaviors (Kanner, 1989). People's acceptance of a product, for example, is strongly influenced by its package. For example, in one experiment consumers in the United States described the very same coffee taken from a yellow can as weak, from a dark brown can as too strong, from a red can as rich, and from a blue can as mild. Even our acceptance of a person may depend on the colors that person wears. Consider, for example, the comments of one color expert (Kanner, 1989, p. 23): "If you have to pick the wardrobe for your defense lawyer heading into court and choose anything but blue, you deserve to lose the case. . . ." Black is so powerful that it can work against the lawyer with the jury. Brown lacks sufficient authority. Green will probably elicit a negative response.

Clothing and Body Adornment   People make inferences about who you are partly on the basis of how you dress. Whether accurate or not, these inferences will affect what people think of you and how they react to you. Your social class, your seriousness, your attitudes (for example, whether you are conservative or liberal), your concern for convention, your sense of style, and perhaps even your creativity will all be judged—in part at least—by the way you dress. For instance, college students will perceive an instructor dressed informally as friendly, fair, enthusiastic, and flexible and the same instructor dressed formally as prepared, knowledgeable, and organized (Malandro, Barker, & Barker, 1989).

Your jewelry also communicates messages about you. Wedding and engagement rings are obvious examples that communicate specific messages. College rings and political buttons likewise communicate messages. If you wear a Rolex watch or large precious stones, others are likely to infer that you are rich. Men who wear earrings will be judged differently from men who don't.

The way you wear your hair says something about who you are—from a concern about being up to date, to a desire to shock, to perhaps a lack of interest in appearances. Men with long hair, to take just one example, will generally be judged as less conservative than those with shorter hair. And in a study of male baldness, participants rated a man with a full head of hair as younger and more dominant, masculine, and dynamic than the same man without hair (Butler, Pryor, & Grieder, 1998).

Body piercing and tattoos communicate too. Nose and nipple rings and tongue and belly-button jewelry send a variety of messages. Although people wearing such jewelry may wish to communicate positive meanings, those interpreting the messages of body piercings seem to infer that wearers are communicating an unwillingness to conform to social norms and a willingness to take greater risks than those without such piercings (Forbes, 2001). It's worth noting that in a study of employers' perceptions, employers rated and ranked job applicants with eyebrow piercings significantly lower than those without such piercings (Acor, 2001).

Tattoos—whether temporary or permanent—likewise communicate a variety of messages, often the name of a loved one or some symbol of allegiance or affiliation. Tattoos also communicate to the wearers themselves. For example, tattooed students see themselves (and perhaps others do as well) as more adventurous, creative, individualistic, and risk prone than those without tattoos (Drews, Allison, & Probst, 2000).

Space Decoration   The way you decorate your private spaces also tells a lot about you. The office with the mahogany desk and bookcase set and oriental rugs communicates your importance and status within the organization, just as the metal desk and bare floors indicate an entry-level employee much farther down in the company hierarchy.

Similarly, people will make inferences about you based on the way you decorate your home. The expensiveness of the furnishings may communicate your status and wealth; their coordination, your sense of style. The magazines on your coffee table may reflect your interests, and the arrangement of chairs around a television set may reveal how important watching television is to you. The contents of bookcases lining the walls reveal the importance of reading in your life. In fact, there is probably little in your home that would not send messages from which others would make inferences about you. Computers, wide-screen televisions, well-equipped kitchens, and oil paintings of great grandparents, for example, all say something about the people who live in a home.

Similarly, the lack of certain items will communicate something about you. Consider what messages you would get from a home where no television, phone, or books could be seen.

It's interesting to note that people also will make judgments about your personality on the basis of room decorations. For example, research finds that people will

What do you say?
Clothing Communication: One of your friends has been passed over for promotion several times, and you think you know the reason: Your friend dresses inappropriately. You want to help your friend. *What do you say? Through what channel?*

What do you say?
Artifactual Communication: One problem with a group of interns you're mentoring is that they've decorated their office spaces with items that communicate all the wrong messages. You need to address this seemingly minor but actually quite significant error. *What do you say?*

form opinions about your openness to new experiences (distinctive decorating usually communicates this, as would different types of books and magazines and travel souvenirs), conscientiousness, emotional stability, degree of extroversion, and agreeableness. And, not surprisingly, bedrooms prove more revealing than offices (Gosling, Ko, Mannarelli, & Morris, 2002).

Smell Communication   Smell communication, or olfactory communication, is extremely important in a wide variety of situations; indeed, the study known as **olfactics** is now "big business" (Kleinfeld, 1992). For example, there is some evidence (although clearly not very conclusive evidence) that the smell of lemon contributes to a perception of health. The smells of lavender and eucalyptus seem to increase alertness, and the smell of rose oil seems to reduce blood pressure. Research also finds that smells can influence your body's chemistry, which in turn influences your emotional state. For example, the smell of chocolate results in the reduction of theta brain waves, thus bringing a sense of relaxation and a reduced level of attention (Martin, 1998). Findings such as these have contributed to the growth of aromatherapy and to a new profession of aromatherapists (Furlow, 1996). Because humans possess "denser skin concentrations of scent glands than almost any other mammal," it has been argued that we need only to discover how we use scent to communicate a wide variety of messages (Furlow, 1996, p. 41). Two particularly important messages scent communicates are those of attraction and identification.

Attraction Messages.   In many animal species the female gives off a scent that draws males, often from far distances, and thus ensures the continuation of the species. Humans (perhaps similarly) use perfumes, colognes, aftershave lotions, powders, and the like in an effort to enhance attractiveness. Women, research finds, prefer the scent of men who bear a close genetic similarity to themselves—a finding that may account in part for people's tendency to be attracted to others much like themselves (Ober, Weitkamp, Cox, Dytch, Kostyu, & Elias, 1997; Wade, 2002). You also use scents to make yourself feel better; after all, you also smell yourself. When the smells are pleasant, you feel better about yourself; when the smells are unpleasant, you feel less good about yourself and probably shower and perhaps put on some cologne.

Identification Messages.   Smell is often used to create an image or an identity for a product. Advertisers and manufacturers spend millions of dollars each year creating scents for cleaning products and toothpastes, for example. These fragrances have nothing to do with products' cleaning power; instead, they function solely to create an image for the products. There is also evidence that we can identify specific significant others by smell. For example, young children were able to identify the T-shirts of their brothers and sisters solely on the basis of smell (Porter & Moore, 1981). And one researcher goes so far as to advise, "If your man's odor reminds you of Dad or your brother, you may want genetic tests before trying to conceive a child" (Furlow, 1996, p. 41).

Touch Communication

Touch communication, or tactile communication, is perhaps the most primitive form of nonverbal communication (Montagu, 1971). Touch develops before the other senses; a child is stimulated by touch even in the womb. Soon after birth, the child is fondled, caressed, patted, and stroked. In turn, the child explores its world through touch and quickly learns to communicate a variety of meanings through touch.

Touching varies greatly from one culture to another. For example, African Americans touch each other more than European Americans, and touching declines from kindergarten to the sixth grade for European Americans but not for African

" " For the sense of smell, almost more than any other, has the power to recall memories and it is a pity that you use it so little. **" "**

—Rachel Carson

American children (Burgoon, Buller, & Woodall, 1996). Japanese people touch each other much less than Anglo-Saxons, who in turn touch much less than southern Europeans (Morris, 1977; Burgoon, Buller, & Woodall, 1996).

Not surprisingly, touch also varies with your relationship stage. In the early stages of acquaintance, you touch little; in intermediate stages of relationship development (involvement and intimacy), you touch a great deal; and at stable or deteriorating stages of a relationship, you again touch little (Guerrero & Andersen, 1991).

The Meanings of Touch   Researchers in the field of **haptics,** or the study of touch communication, have identified the major meanings of touch (Jones & Yarbrough, 1985). Here are five of the most important.

- Touch may communicate *positive emotions* such as support, appreciation, inclusion, sexual interest or intent, and affection.

- Touch often communicates *playfulness,* either affectionately or aggressively.

- Touch may also *control* or direct the behaviors, attitudes, or feelings of another person. To get attention, for example, you may touch a person as if to say, "Look at me" or "Look over here."

- *Ritual* touching centers on greetings and departures, as in shaking hands to say hello or good-bye or hugging, kissing, or putting your arm around another's shoulder when greeting or saying farewell.

- *Task-related* touching occurs while you are performing some function—for example, removing a speck of dust from another person's face or helping someone out of a car.

Touch Avoidance   Much as we have a tendency to touch and be touched, we also have a tendency to avoid touch from certain people or in certain circumstances. Researchers in nonverbal communication have found some interesting relationships between **touch avoidance** and other significant communication variables (Andersen & Leibowitz, 1978).

> *"* 'There is a very simple rule about touching,' the manager continued. 'When you touch, don't take. Touch the people you manage only when you are giving them something—reassurance, support, encouragement, whatever.' *"*
>
> —Kenneth Blanchard and Spencer Johnson

Communicating with power

Signaling Power Nonverbally

If you want to signal your power nonverbally, try these suggestions (Lewis, 1989; Burgoon, Buller, & Woodall, 1996).

- Avoid self-manipulations (playing with your hair or touching your face, for example) and backward leaning; these signals communicate a lack of comfort and an ill-at-ease feeling and are likely to damage your persuasiveness.

- Walk slowly and deliberately. To appear hurried is to appear powerless, as if you were rushing to meet the expectations of those who have power over you.

- Use facial expressions and gestures as appropriate; these help you express your concern for the other person and for the interaction and help you communicate your comfort and control of the situation.

- Select chairs you can get in and out of easily; avoid deep plush chairs that you sink into and have trouble getting out of.

- To communicate dominance with your handshake, exert more pressure than usual and hold the grip a bit longer than normal.

- Use consistent packaging; in other words, be careful that your verbal and nonverbal messages do not contradict each other, a signal of uncertainty and a lack of conviction.

Enhancing Your Communication Power

What nonverbal signals do you regularly use that might communicate a lack of power? What might you do to eliminate these and enhance your communication power?

What do you say?

Touch Boundaries: A colleague at work continually touches you in passing—your arm, your shoulder, your waist. These touches are becoming more frequent and more intimate. You want the touching to stop. *What do you say? To whom? Through what channel?*

Touch avoidance is positively related to communication apprehension: Those who fear oral communication also score high on touch avoidance. Touch avoidance is also high in those who self-disclose little. Both touch and self-disclosure are intimate forms of communication; people who are reluctant to get close to another person by self-disclosing also seem reluctant to get close by touching.

Touch avoidance is also affected by age and gender (Guerrero & Andersen, 1994; Crawford, 1994). Older people have higher touch-avoidance scores for opposite-sex persons than do younger people. As we get older, we are touched less by members of the opposite sex, and this decreased frequency may lead us to further avoid touching. Males score higher on same-sex touch avoidance than do females, which matches our stereotypes (Martin & Anderson, 1993). That is, men avoid touching other men, but women may and do touch other women. On the other hand, women have higher touch-avoidance scores for opposite-sex touching than do men (Andersen, Andersen, & Lustig, 1987).

Paralanguage and Silence

Paralanguage is the vocal but nonverbal dimension of speech. It has to do with *how* you say something rather than what you say. As for silence: As we'll see, silence is the absence of sound but not of communication.

Paralanguage   An old exercise teachers used to increase students' ability to express different emotions, feelings, and attitudes was to have the students repeat a sentence while accenting or stressing different words each time. Placing the stress on different words easily communicates significant differences in meaning. Consider the following variations of the sentence "Is this the face that launched a thousand ships?"

1. *Is* this the face that launched a thousand ships?
2. Is *this* the face that launched a thousand ships?
3. Is this the *face* that launched a thousand ships?
4. Is this the face that *launched* a thousand ships?
5. Is this the face that launched *a thousand ships?*

Each sentence communicates something different—in fact, each asks a different question, even though the words are the same. All that varies the sentences is the stress on different words, one aspect of paralanguage.

In addition to stress, paralanguage includes such vocal characteristics as rate, volume, and rhythm. It also includes vocalizations you make in crying, whispering, moaning, belching, yawning, and yelling (Trager, 1958, 1961; Argyle, 1988). A variation in any of these vocal features communicates. When you speak quickly, for example, you communicate something different from when you speak slowly. Even though the words are the same, if the speed (or volume, rhythm, or pitch) differs, the meanings people receive will also differ.

Judgments about People.   Do you make judgments about people's personalities on the basis of their paralinguistic cues? For example, do you conclude that your colleague who speaks softly when presenting ideas at a meeting isn't sure of the ideas' usefulness and believes that no one really wants to listen to them? Do you assume that people who speak loudly have overinflated egos? Do those who speak with no variation, in a complete monotone, seem uninterested in what they are saying? Might you then assume that they have a lack of interest in life in general? All such judgments are based on little evidence, yet they persist in much popular talk.

Research has found that people can accurately judge the socioeconomic status (whether high, middle, or low) of speakers from 60-second voice samples (Davitz,

1964). Many listeners in this study made their judgments in less than 15 seconds. Participants also rated people whom they judged to be of high status as more credible than speakers judged middle and low.

Listeners also can accurately judge the emotional states of speakers from vocal expression alone. In these studies speakers recite the alphabet or numbers while expressing emotions. Some emotions are easier to identify than others; it is easy to distinguish between hate and sympathy but more difficult to distinguish between fear and anxiety. And, of course, listeners vary in their ability to decode, and speakers in their ability to encode, emotions (Scherer, 1986).

Judgments about Communication Effectiveness.   Speech rate is an important component of paralanguage. In one-way communication (when one person is doing all or most of the speaking and the other person is doing all or most of the listening), those who talk fast (about 50 percent faster than normal) are more persuasive. That is, people agree more with a fast speaker than with a slow speaker and find the fast speaker more intelligent and objective (MacLachlan, 1979).

There are cultural differences in this persuasiveness effect, however. For example, among Koreans, researchers found the opposite effect: Male speakers who spoke rapidly received unfavorable credibility ratings (Lee & Boster, 1992). Researchers have suggested that people in individualistic societies tend to see a rapid-rate speaker as more competent than a slow-rate speaker, whereas people in collectivist cultures judge a speaker who uses a slower rate to be more competent.

When we look at comprehension, rapid speech shows an interesting effect. When the speaking rate increases by 50 percent, the comprehension level drops by only 5 percent. When the rate doubles, the comprehension level drops only 10 percent. In terms of efficiency, then, these 5 and 10 percent comprehension losses are more than offset by the increased speed; faster speech rates are thus much more efficient in communicating information. If the speeds are more than twice that of normal speech, however, the comprehension level begins to fall dramatically.

Exercise caution in applying this research to all forms of communication (MacLachlan, 1979). While the speaker is speaking, the listener is generating, or framing, a reply. If the speaker talks too rapidly, the listener may not have enough time to compose a reply and may become resentful. Furthermore, the increased rate may seem so unnatural that the listener may focus on the speed rather than on the message being communicated.

Skill development experience

Expressing Praise and Criticism

To consider how nonverbal messages can communicate praise and criticism, read aloud each of the following statements, first to communicate praise and second to express criticism. In the second and third columns, record the nonverbal signals you used to help you communicate praise and criticism.

Message	Nonverbal Cues to Communicate Praise	Nonverbal Cues to Communicate Criticism
You lost weight. You look happy. You're an expert. Your parents are something else.		

Silence   "Speech," wrote Thomas Mann, "is civilization itself. The word, even the most contradictory word, preserves contact; it is silence which isolates." Philosopher Karl Jaspers, on the other hand, observed that 'the ultimate in thinking as in communication is silence," and philosopher Max Picard noted that "silence is nothing merely negative; it is not the mere absence of speech. It is a positive, a complete world in itself." The one thing on which these contradictory observations agree is that **silence** communicates. Your silence communicates just as intensely as anything you verbalize (see Jaworski, 1993).

Functions of Silence.   Silence allows the speaker and the listener *time to think,* time to formulate and organize the meaning of the message. For example, a lawyer may have many sophisticated points to make during closing arguments to the jury. A skilled lawyer will use silence not only to give herself or himself time to present these issues in an organized way, but also to give the jury time to digest the information presented. Before messages indicative of intense conflict, as well as those confessing undying love, there is often silence. Again, silence seems to prepare the receiver for the importance of these messages.

Some people use silence as a *weapon* to hurt others. We often speak of giving someone "the silent treatment." After a conflict, for example, one or both individuals may remain silent as a kind of punishment. Silence used to hurt others may also take the form of refusal to acknowledge the presence of another person, as in disconfirmation (see Chapter 5); in this case, silence is a dramatic demonstration of the total indifference one person feels toward the other.

People sometimes use silence because of *personal anxiety* or shyness, or in response to threats. You may feel anxious or shy among new people and prefer to remain silent. By remaining silent you preclude the chance of rejection. Only when you break your silence and attempt to communicate with another person do you risk rejection.

People may also use silence *to prevent communication* of certain messages. In conflict situations silence is sometimes used to prevent certain topics from surfacing and to prevent one or both parties from saying things they may later regret. In such situations silence often allows people time to cool off before expressing hatred, severe criticism, or personal attack—which, as we've seen, are irreversible.

Communicating ethically

Communication Silence

In the U.S. legal system, you have the right to remain silent and to refuse to incriminate yourself. But in general you don't have the right to refuse to reveal information about, for example, criminal activities of others that you may have witnessed. Rightly or wrongly (and this itself is an ethical issue), psychiatrists and lawyers are often exempt from this general rule. Similarly, a wife can't be forced to testify against her husband or a husband against his wife.

In most communication situations, however, there aren't any written rules—so it's not always clear if or when silence is ethical or unethical. For example, most people (though not all) would agree that you have the right to withhold information that has no bearing on the matter at hand. Thus, in job-related contents your previous relationship history, affectional orientation, or religion is usually irrelevant to your ability to function and so may be kept private in most work settings.

What Would You Do?

You witness a mother verbally abusing her three-year-old child. Your first impulse is to tell this woman that verbal abuse can have lasting effects on the child and often leads to physical abuse. At the same time, you don't want to interfere with a mother's rights. Nor do you want to aggravate a mother who may later take out her frustration on the child. What is your ethical obligation in this case? What would you do in this situation?

Like the eyes, face, or hands, silence can also be used to *communicate emotional responses* (Ehrenhaus, 1988). Sometimes silence communicates a determination to be uncooperative or defiant: By refusing to engage in verbal communication, you defy the authority or the legitimacy of the other person's position. Silence often communicates annoyance; in this case, it is usually accompanied by a pouting expression, arms crossed in front of the chest, and flared nostrils. Silence also may express affection or love, especially when coupled with long and longing gazes into another's eyes.

Of course, you also may use silence when you simply have *nothing to say,* when nothing occurs to you or when you do not want to say anything. James Russell Lowell expressed this well: "Blessed are they who have nothing to say and who cannot be persuaded to say it."

Time Communication

The study of **temporal communication,** known technically as **chronemics,** concerns the use of time—how you organize it, react to it, and communicate messages through it (Bruneau, 1985, 1990).

An especially important aspect of temporal communication is **psychological time:** the relative importance we place on the past, present, or future. With a *past* orientation, we have a particular reverence for the past. We relive old times and regard the old methods as the best. We see events as circular and recurring and find that the wisdom of yesterday is applicable also to today and tomorrow. With a *present* orientation, we live in the present—for now—without planning for tomorrow. With a *future* orientation, we look toward and live for the future. We save today, work hard in college, and deny ourselves luxuries because we are preparing for the future. Before reading about some of the consequences of the way we view time, take the following self-test, "What time do you have?" to assess your own psychological time orientation.

> Those who live to the future must always appear selfish to those who live to the present.
>
> —Ralph Waldo Emerson

Test Yourself

What Time Do You Have?

INSTRUCTIONS: For each statement, indicate whether the statement is true (T) or untrue (F) of your general attitude and behavior. A few statements are repeated; this is to facilitate interpreting your score.

_____ ❶ Meeting tomorrow's deadlines and doing other necessary work comes before tonight's partying.

_____ ❷ I meet my obligations to friends and authorities on time.

_____ ❸ I complete projects on time by making steady progress.

_____ ❹ I am able to resist temptations when I know there is work to be done.

_____ ❺ I keep working at a difficult, uninteresting task if it will help me get ahead.

_____ ❻ If things don't get done on time, I don't worry about it.

_____ ❼ I think that it's useless to plan too far ahead because things hardly ever come out the way you planned anyway.

_____ ❽ I try to live one day at a time.

_____ ❾ I live to make better what is rather than to be concerned about what will be.

_____ ❿ It seems to me that it doesn't make sense to worry about the future, since fate determines that whatever will be, will be.

_____ ⓫ I believe that getting together with friends to party is one of life's important pleasures.

_____ ⓬ I do things impulsively, making decisions on the spur of the moment.

_____ ⓭ I take risks to put excitement in my life.

_____ ⓮ I get drunk at parties.

_____ ⓯ It's fun to gamble.

_____ ⓰ Thinking about the future is pleasant to me.

_____ ⓱ When I want to achieve something, I set subgoals and consider specific means for reaching those goals.

_____ ⓲ It seems to me that my career path is pretty well laid out.

_____ ⓳ It upsets me to be late for appointments.

_____ ⓴ I meet my obligations to friends and authorities on time.

_____ ㉑ I get Irritated at people who keep me waiting when we've agreed to meet at a given time.

_____ ㉒ It makes sense to invest a substantial part of my income in insurance premiums.

_____ ㉓ I believe that "A stitch in time saves nine."

_____ ㉔ I believe that "A bird in the hand is worth two in the bush."

_____ ㉕ I believe it is important to save for a rainy day.

_____ ㉖ I believe a person's day should be planned each morning.

_____ ㉗ I make lists of things I must do.

_____ ㉘ When I want to achieve something, I set subgoals and consider specific means for reaching those goals.

_____ ㉙ I believe that "A stitch in time saves nine."

HOW DID YOU DO? This time test measures seven different factors. If you selected true (T) for all or most of the questions within any given factor, you are probably high on that factor. If you selected untrue (F) for all or most of the questions within any given factor, you are probably low on that factor.

The first factor, measured by questions 1 through 5, is a future, work motivation, perseverance orientation. People high in this factor have a strong work ethic and are committed to completing tasks despite difficulties and temptations. The second factor (questions 6 through 10) is a present, fatalistic, worry-free orientation. High scorers on this factor live one day at a time, not necessarily to enjoy the day but to avoid planning for the next day or anxiety about the future. The third factor (questions 11 through 15) is a present, pleasure-seeking, partying orientation. People high in this factor enjoy the present, take risks, and engage in a variety of impulsive actions. The fourth factor (questions 16 through 18) is a future, goal-seeking, and planning orientation. High scorers on this factor derive special pleasure from planning and achieving a variety of goals.

The fifth factor (questions 19 through 21) is a time-sensitivity orientation. People who score high are especially sensitive to time and its role in social obligations. The sixth factor (questions 22 through 25) is a future, practical action orientation. People high in this factor do what they have to do—take practical actions—to achieve the future they want. The seventh factor (questions 26 through 29) is a future, somewhat obsessive daily planning orientation. High scorers on this factor make daily "to do" lists and devote great attention to specific details.

www.researchnavigator.com

Investigate Key Terms: Investigate one of the key terms discussed in this chapter (for example, body gestures, facial management, facial feedback, eye contact, touch, paralanguage, silence, space, distance, territoriality, artifactual communication, scent, time communication, or silence). What additional insights can you provide?

WHAT WILL YOU DO? Now that you have some idea of how you treat the different types of time, consider how these attitudes and behaviors work for you. For example, will your time orientations help you achieve your social and professional goals? If not, what might you do about changing these attitudes and behaviors?

Source: Adapted from "Time In Perspective" by Alexander Gonzalez and Philip G. Zimbardo. Reprinted with permission from *Psychology Today* magazine. Copyright © 1985 (Sussex Publishers, Inc.).

> Know the true value of time; snatch, seize, and enjoy every moment of it. No idleness, no laziness, no procrastination; never put off till tomorrow what you can do today. **"**
>
> —Lord Chesterfield

Consider some of the findings on these time orientations (Gonzalez & Zimbardo, 1985). Future income is positively related to future orientation; the more future oriented you are, the greater your income is likely to be. Present orientation is strongest among lowest-income males and also among those with high emotional distress and hopelessness (Zaleski, Cycon, & Kurc, 2001).

The time orientation you develop depends on your socioeconomic class and your personal experiences. The researchers who developed the scale in the self-test and on whose research these findings are based observe, "A child with parents in unskilled and semiskilled occupations is usually socialized in a way that promotes a present-oriented fatalism and hedonism. A child of parents who are managers, teachers, or other professionals learns future-oriented values and strategies designed to promote achievement" (Gonzalez & Zimbardo, 1985). Similarly, the future-oriented person who works for tomorrow's goals will frequently look down on the present-oriented person as lazy and poorly motivated for enjoying today and not planning for tomorrow. In turn, the present-oriented person may see those with strong future orientations as obsessed with amassing wealth or rising in status.

Different time perspectives also account for much intercultural misunderstanding, because different cultures often teach their members drastically different time orientations. For example, members of some Latin cultures would rather be late for an appointment than end a conversation abruptly. The Latin person sees this behavior as politeness toward the person with whom he or she is conversing—but others may see this as impolite to the person with whom he or she had the appointment (Hall & Hall, 1987).

VIEWPOINT
What one principle or skill of nonverbal communication would you consider the most important for your career success? For your relationship success?

Listening with Nonverbals

Ineffective listening often involves mainly nonverbal behaviors. Let's look at some general types of listeners who, largely (though not exclusively) through their nonverbal messages, make conversation difficult—and at some recommended alternative strategies.

Listener Type	Ineffective Listening Behavior	Effective Alternatives
The static listener	Gives no feedback; remains relatively motionless and expressionless.	Get involved with the speaker; react so the speaker knows that you're listening.
The monotonous feedback giver	Seems responsive, but the responses never vary; regardless of what the speaker says, the response is the same.	Respond to the speaker with a broad repertoire of nonverbal feedback messages.
The overly expressive listener	Reacts to just about everything with extreme responses.	Consider moderation; keep the attention on the speaker and not on listener reactions.
The eye avoider	Looks all around the room and at others but never at the speaker.	Focus on the speaker visually and with a facing posture.
The preoccupied listener	Listens to other things at the same time, often with headphones or with the television on.	Really listen when you listen; give the speaker the same focused attention you'd like to receive.
The waiting listener	Listens for a chance to take over the speaking turn.	Listen fully; it's not always easy, but it is considerate.
The thought-completing listener	Listens a little and then finishes the speaker's thought.	Listen to the speaker, not to yourself speaking for the speaker.

Applying Listening Skills

What additional steps can you take to prevent yourself from falling into one of these ineffective listening patterns?

Culture and Nonverbal Communication

> **"** Culture is communication, and communication is culture. **"**
>
> —Edward T. Hall

Throughout this chapter we've occasionally noted cultural and gender differences in nonverbal communication. Some cultural variations in nonverbal communication, however, have become the focus of sustained research. Here we consider just a sampling of research on communication via the face, color, silence, touch, and time in different cultures.

Culture and Facial Expression

The wide variations in facial communication that we observe in different cultures seem to have to do more with which reactions are publicly permissible than with differences in the ways people show their emotions. For example, in one study Japanese and American students watched a film of an operation (Ekman, 1985). The experimenters videotaped the students both in an interview about the film and alone while watching the film. When alone, the students showed very similar reactions. In the interview, however, the American students displayed facial expressions indicating displeasure, whereas the Japanese students did not show any great emotion. Similarly, it's considered "forward" or inappropriate for Japanese women to reveal broad smiles, so women in Japan will hide their smiles, sometimes with their hands (cf. Ma, 1996). Women in the United States, on the other hand, have no such restrictions and are more likely to smile openly. Thus, many differences may reflect not the way different cultures express emotions but rather the cultural rules for displaying emotions in public (cf. Matsumoto, 1991).

Similarly, cultural differences exist in decoding the meaning of a facial expression. For example, researchers asked American and Japanese students to judge the meanings of smiling and neutral facial expressions. The Americans rated the smiling face as more attractive, more intelligent, and more sociable than the neutral face. The Japanese, however, rated the smiling face as more sociable but not as more attractive; and they rated the neutral face as more intelligent (Matsumoto & Kudoh, 1993). Another study found that participants rated people who smile as more likeable and more approachable than people who don't smile or who only pretend to smile (Gladstone & Parker, 2002).

Web Explorations

Several exercises and self-tests will help you better understand how nonverbal communication works and will give you opportunities to practice the skills of nonverbal communication (www.ablongman.com/devito): (1) Facial Expressions, (2) Eye Contact, (3) Interpersonal Interactions and Space, (4) Artifacts and Culture: The Case of Gifts, (5) Communicating Vocally but Nonverbally, (6) Communicating Emotions Nonverbally, (7) Recognizing Verbal and Nonverbal Message Functions, (8) Coloring Meanings, and (9) Do You Avoid Touch?

Culture and Colors

Colors vary greatly in their meanings from one culture to another. Table 6.4 presents some of these cultural differences—but before looking at the table, think about the meanings given to colors such as red, green, black, white, blue, yellow, and purple in your own culture(s).

TABLE 6.4	Some Cultural Meanings of Color

This table, constructed from research reported by Henry Dreyfuss (1971), Nancy Hoft (1995), and Norine Dresser (1996), summarizes some of the different meanings that colors may communicate and how colors are viewed in different cultures. As you read this table, consider the meanings you give to these colors and where your meanings came from.

COLOR	CULTURAL MEANINGS AND COMMENTS
Red	Red signifies prosperity and rebirth in China and is used for festive and joyous occasions. It signifies masculinity in France and the United Kingdom, blasphemy or death in many African countries, and anger and danger in Japan. Red ink is used by Korean Buddhists only to write a person's name at the time of death or on the anniversary of the person's death; it therefore creates problems when American teachers use red ink to mark Korean students' homework.
Green	Green signifies capitalism, "go ahead," and envy in the United States; patriotism in Ireland; femininity among some Native Americans; fertility and strength in Egypt; and youth and energy in Japan.
Black	Black signifies old age in Thailand, courage in parts of Malaysia, and death in much of Europe and North America
White	White signifies purity in Thailand, purity and peace in many Muslim and Hindu cultures, and death and mourning in Japan and other Asian countries.
Blue	Blue signifies something negative in Iran, virtue and truth in Egypt, joy in Ghana, and defeat among the Cherokee.
Yellow	Yellow signifies wealth and authority in China, caution and cowardice in the United States, happiness and prosperity in Egypt; and femininity in many countries throughout the world.
Purple	Purple signifies death in Latin America, royalty in Europe, virtue and faith in Egypt, grace and nobility in Japan, and barbarism in China.

Culture and Touch

The functions and examples of touching discussed earlier were based on studies in North America; in other cultures these functions are not served in the same way. In some cultures, for example, some task-related touching is viewed negatively and is to be avoided. Among Koreans it is considered disrespectful for a store owner to touch a customer in, say, handing back change; doing so is considered too intimate a gesture. Members of other cultures who are used to such touching may consider the Koreans' behavior cold and aloof. Muslim children are socialized to refrain from touching members of the opposite sex, a practice that can easily be interpreted as unfriendly by American children who are used to touching one another (Dresser, 1996).

One study on touch surveyed college students in Japan and in the United States (Barnlund, 1975). Students from the United States reported being touched twice as much as did the Japanese students. In Japan there is a strong taboo against strangers' touching, and the Japanese are therefore especially careful to maintain sufficient distance.

Some cultures, such as those of southern Europe and the Middle East, are contact cultures. Others, such as those of northern Europe and Japan, are noncontact cultures. Members of contact cultures maintain close distances, touch each other in conversation, face each other more directly, and maintain longer and more focused eye contact. Members of noncontact cultures maintain greater distance in their interactions, touch each other rarely if at all, avoid facing each other directly, and maintain much less direct eye contact. As a result, northern Europeans and Japanese may be perceived as cold, distant, and uninvolved by southern Europeans—who may in turn be perceived as pushy, aggressive, and inappropriately intimate.

Culture and Silence

Not all cultures view silence as functioning in the same way. In the United States, for example, silence often is interpreted negatively. At a business meeting or even in informal social groups, people may see a silent member as not listening, having nothing interesting to add, not understanding the issues, being insensitive, or being too self-absorbed to focus on the messages of others. Other cultures, however, view silence more positively. In many situations in Japan, for example, silence is considered a more appropriate response than speech (Haga, 1988).

The traditional Apache regard silence very differently than European Americans (Basso, 1972). Among the Apache, mutual friends do not feel the need to introduce strangers who may be working in the same area or on the same project. The strangers may remain silent for several days. This period enables the individuals to observe and evaluate one another. After this assessment period, the individuals talk. When courting, especially during the initial stages, the Apache remain silent for hours; if they do talk, they generally talk very little. Only after a couple has been dating for several months will they have lengthy conversations. The use of silence is explicitly taught to Apache women, who are especially discouraged from engaging in long discussions with their dates. Silence during courtship is a sign of modesty to many Apache.

Culture and Time

Culture influences time communication in a variety of ways. Here we look at three: formal and informal time, monochronism and polychronism, and the social clock.

Formal and Informal Time   In the United States and in most of the world, formal time divisions consist of units such as seconds, minutes, hours, days, weeks, months, and years. Some cultures, however, may use phases of the moon or changing seasons to delineate time periods. In the United States, if your college is on the semester system, your courses are divided into 50- or 75-minute periods that meet two or three times a week for 14-week periods. Eight semesters of 15 or 16 periods per week equal a college education. As these examples illustrate, formal time units are arbitrary. The culture establishes them for convenience.

Informal time terms denote approximate intervals—for example, "forever," "immediately," "soon," "right away," or "as soon as possible." Informal time expressions create the most communication problems, because the terms have different meanings for different people.

Attitudes toward time vary from one culture to another. For example, one study measured the accuracy of clocks in six cultures—Japan, Indonesia, Italy, England, Taiwan, and the United States. Japan had the most accurate and Indonesia the least accurate clocks. The researchers also measured the speed at which people in these six cultures walked; results showed that the Japanese walked the fastest, the Indonesians the slowest (LeVine & Bartlett, 1984).

Monochronism and Polychronism Another important cultural distinction exists between **monochronic** and **polychronic time orientations** (Hall, 1959, 1976; Hall & Hall, 1987). Monochronic peoples or cultures such as those of the United States, Germany, Scandinavia, and Switzerland schedule one thing at a time. These cultures compartmentalize time and set sequential times for different activities. Polychronic peoples or cultures such as those of Latin America, the Mediterranean, and the Arab world, on the other hand, schedule multiple things at the same time. Eating, conducting business with several different people, and taking care of family matters may all go on at once. No culture is entirely monochronic or polychronic; rather these are general or preponderant tendencies. Some cultures combine both time orientations; in Japan and in parts of American culture, for example, both orientations can be found. Table 6.5 identifies some of the distinctions between these two time orientations.

VIEWPOINT

Another type of time, biological time, has to do with the different ways your body functions at different times. According to theories of biorhythms, your intellectual, physical, and emotional lives are lived in cycles that influence your effectiveness. Detailed explanations and instructions for calculating your own cycles can be found in DeVito (1989). Or, even better, you can visit a website that will compute your biorhythms at www.kfu.com/~nsayer/compat.html.

TABLE 6.5   Monochronic and Polychronic Time

As you read down this table, based on Hall (1983) and Hall & Hall (1987), note the potential for miscommunication that might develop when M-time and P-time people interact. Have any of these differences ever created interpersonal misunderstandings for you?

THE MONOCHRONIC-TIME PERSON	THE POLYCHRONIC-TIME PERSON
Does one thing at a time	Does several things at once
Treats time schedules and plans very seriously; feels they may be broken only for the most serious of reasons	Treats time schedules and plans as useful (not sacred); feels they may be broken for a variety of purposes
Considers the job the most important part of a person's life, ahead of even family	Considers the family and interpersonal relationships more important than the job
Considers privacy extremely important; seldom borrows or lends to others; works independently	Is actively involved with others; works in the presence of and with lots of people at the same time

---

The Social Clock   An especially interesting aspect of cultural time is the "social clock" (Neugarten, 1979). Your culture, and your more specific society within that culture, maintain a schedule that dictates the right times to do a variety of important things; for example, the right times to start dating, to finish college, to buy your own home, to have a child. You also may feel that you should be making a certain salary and working at a particular level of management by a certain age. Most people learn about and internalize this clock as they grow up. On the basis of your social clock, you evaluate your own social and professional development. If you're on time relative to the rest of your peers—for example, if you all started dating at around the same age or you're all finishing college at around the same age—then you will feel well adjusted, competent, and a part of the group. If you're late, you will probably experience feelings of dissatisfaction and inadequacy.

Summary of Concepts and Skills

This chapter explored nonverbal communication—communication without words—and looked at the functions nonverbal messages serve, the channels of nonverbal communication, and some of the cultural influences on and differences in nonverbal communication.

1. Nonverbal messages may be integrated with verbal messages to *accent* or emphasize a part of the verbal message; to *complement* or add nuances of meaning; to *contradict* verbal messages (as when people cross their fingers or wink to indicate that they're lying); to *regulate,* control, or indicate a desire to control the flow of verbal messages; to *repeat* or restate a verbal message; and to *substitute* or take the place of verbal messages.

2. Important relationship functions of nonverbal communication include forming and managing impressions, forming and defining relationships, structuring conversation and social interaction, influence and deception, and emotional expression.

3. The body communicates a variety of meanings with different types of nonverbal behaviors: emblems (which rather directly translate words or phrases); illustrators (which accompany and literally "illustrate" the verbal messages); affect displays (which communicate emotional meaning); regulators (which coordinate, monitor, maintain, or control the speech of another individual); and adaptors (which occur without conscious awareness and usually serve some kind of need, as in scratching an itch).

4. Facial movements may communicate a wide variety of emotions. The most frequently studied are happiness, surprise, fear, anger, sadness, and disgust/contempt. Through facial management techniques you can control your facial expression of emotions. The facial feedback hypothesis claims that facial display of an emotion can lead to physiological and psychological changes.

5. Eye movements may seek feedback, cue others to speak, signal the nature of a relationship, and compensate for increased physical distance.

6. Proxemics is the study of the communicative function of space and spatial relationships. Four major proxemic distances are: intimate distance, ranging from actual touching to 18 inches; personal distance, ranging from 18 inches to 4 feet; social distance, ranging from 4 to 12 feet; and public distance, ranging from 12 to 25 feet or more.

7. Your treatment of space is influenced by such factors as status, culture, context, subject matter, sex, age, and positive or negative evaluation of the other person.

8. Territoriality is a possessive reaction to an area of space or to particular objects. Markers are devices that identify a territory as ours; these include central, boundary, and ear-markers.

9. Artifactual communication involves messages conveyed by human-made objects or arrangements, including the use of color, clothing and body adornment, smell, and space decoration.

10. Haptics is the study of touch communication. Touch may communicate a variety of meanings, the most important being positive affect, playfulness, control, ritual, and task-relatedness. Touch avoidance is the desire to avoid touching and being touched by others.

11. Paralanguage consists of the vocal but nonverbal dimension of speech. It includes stress, rate, pitch, volume, and rhythm as well as pauses and hesitations. On the basis of paralanguage we make judgments about people, conversational turns, and believability. Silence also serves important communication functions.

12. The study of time communication (chronemics) examines the messages communicated by our treatment of time. Psychological time focuses on time orientations, whether toward the past, present, or future.

13. Among important cultural differences in nonverbal communication are variations in facial expressions and displays, the meanings of color, the uses of silence, the appropriateness and uses of touch, and the treatment of time.

This chapter has covered a wide variety of nonverbal communication skills. Check your ability to apply these skills, using the following rating scale: 1 = almost always; 2 = often; 3 = sometimes; 4 = rarely; and 5 = hardly ever.

_____ 1. I recognize the varied functions that nonverbal messages (my own and those of others) serve; for example, to form and manage impressions, to define relationships, and to structure conversations.

_____ 2. I use body and gesture messages to help communicate my desired meanings, and I recognize these messages in others.

_____ 3. I use my eyes to seek feedback, to inform others to speak, to signal the nature of my relationship with others, and to compensate for physical distance.

_____ 4. I give others the space they need; for example, I give extra space to those who are angry or disturbed.

_____ 5. I am sensitive to the markers (central, boundary, and earmarkers) of others and use these markers to define my own territories.

_____ 6. I use artifacts thoughtfully to communicate desired messages.

_____ 7. I am sensitive to the touching behaviors of others and distinguish among touches that communicate positive emotion, playfulness, control, and ritual or task-related messages.

_____ 8. I recognize and respect each person's touch-avoidance tendency. I am especially sensitive to cultural and gender differences in touching preferences and in touch-avoidance tendencies.

_____ 9. I vary paralinguistic features (rate, emphasis, pauses, tempo, volume, etc.) to communicate my intended meanings.

_____ 10. I interpret time cues with an awareness of the cultural perspective of the person with whom I am interacting.

_____ 11. I balance my time orientation and don't ignore the past, present, or future.

Key Word Quiz

Write T for those statements that are true and F for those that are false. In addition, for those that are false, replace the italicized term with the correct term.

_____ 1. The nonverbal OK sign or the head nod that signals agreement are examples of *illustrators*.

_____ 2. Emotional expressions are called *affect displays*.

_____ 3. Facial and hand expressions that try to control the other person's speaking (for example, nonverbal movements that tell the speaker to speed up or clarify something) are known as *adaptors*.

_____ 4. The assumption that your facial expression influences your level of positive and negative physiological arousal is known as the *facial feedback hypothesis*.

_____ 5. Erving Goffman called the act of avoiding eye contact or averting your glance to help others maintain their privacy *civil inattention*.

_____ 6. The study of the way in which people use space in relating to each other and even to the layout of their towns and cities is known as *territoriality*.

_____ 7. Communication through messages of color, clothing, jewelry, and the decoration of space is known as *artificial communication*.

_____ 8. The study of communication through touch is known as *haptics*.

_____ 9. The vocal but nonverbal aspect of speech is called *paralanguage*.

_____ 10. Communication by the way in which you treat time is known as *chronemics*.

Answers: TRUE: 2, 4, 5, 8, 9, 10; **FALSE:** 1 (*emblems*), 3 (*regulators*), 6 (*proxemics*), 7 (*artifactual communication*).

7 Interpersonal Communication: Conversation and Conflict

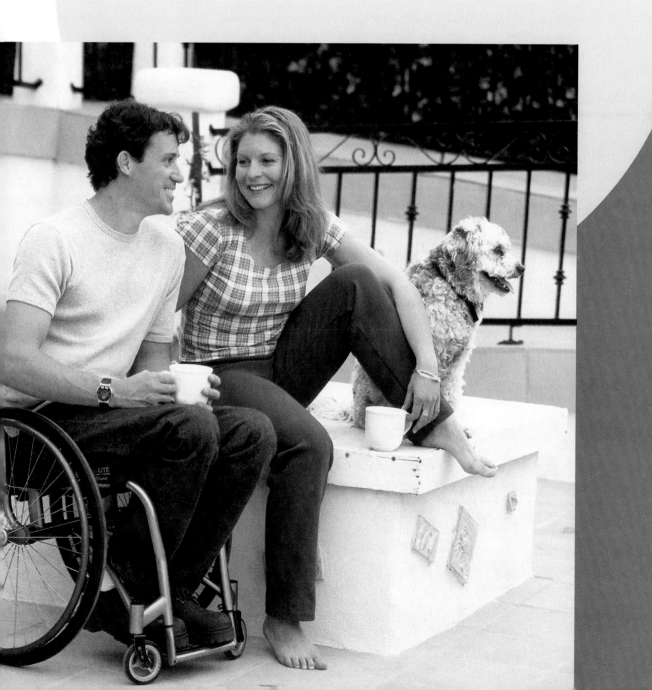

Chapter Concepts	Chapter Skills
This chapter covers conversation and conflict, two processes that are similar and yet also very different from each other.	After completing this chapter, you should be able to:
Conversation	effectively open, maintain, and close conversations.
Effective Conversation	use the qualities of effective conversation as appropriate to the specific situation.
Conflict	engage in interpersonal conflict with a realistic understanding of the myths about conflict and their potential effects.
Effective Conflict Management	manage conflict using fair-fight strategies.

❝ Conversation is the socializing instrument par excellence, and in its style one can see reflected the capacities of a race. **❞**

—José Ortega y Gasset

❝ Can we talk? **❞**

—Joan Rivers

Interpersonal communication is communication that occurs between two people who have a clearly defined relationship. It thus includes what takes place between a waiter and a customer, a son and his father, two people in an interview, and so on. This definition makes it almost impossible for communication between two people not to be considered interpersonal—inevitably, some relationship exists. Even a stranger asking directions from a local resident has established a clearly defined relationship as soon as the first message is sent. Sometimes this "relational" or "dyadic" definition is extended to include small groups of people, such as family members, groups of three or four friends, or work colleagues.

The first part of this chapter examines conversation, its stages, and the qualities that make it effective. The second part of the chapter explores interpersonal conflict, how it works, and how you can manage it for greater interpersonal effectiveness. A website devoted to interpersonal communication maintained by the publisher of this book provides additional insights into both conversation and conflict (see the home page on page 135).

Conversation

Conversation, whether face-to-face or online, takes place in five steps: opening, feedforward, business, feedback, and closing, as shown in Figure 7.1. Of course, there are variations in the process depending on whether your interaction is face-to-face or via some computer connection. For example, unlike face-to-face interaction, e-mail does not take place in real time. You may send your letter today, but the receiver may not read it for a week and may take another week to respond. In chat groups, in contrast, communication does take place in real time.

The major difference, of course, is that face-to-face messages are a combination of audio and visual signals. For most people today (though this is changing, as pointed out in Chapter 1), e-mail and chat messages are written signals. Also, e-mail and chat messages are like postcards (rather than private conversations or letters) in that they can be read by others along the route. As already noted in Chapter 1, electronic communication is virtually unerasable; and its text (though not audio or video components) can easily be forwarded or made public by anyone who has access to your files. Consequently, people may not be willing to write in e-mail what they would readily say in private or on the phone.

When reading about the process of conversation, therefore, keep in mind the wide range of forms in which conversation can take place—face-to-face as well as via the Internet—and the similarities and differences between them.

Similarly, realize that not everyone speaks with the fluency and ease that many textbooks often assume. Speech and language disorders, for example, can seriously disrupt the conversation process if some elementary guidelines aren't followed. Table 7.1 on page 136 offers suggestions for making such conversations run more smoothly.

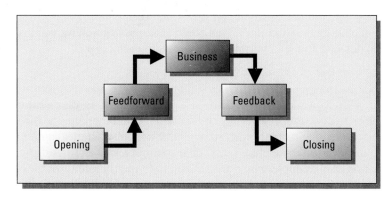

Figure **7.1**

The Conversation Process

This model of the stages of conversation is best seen as a way of talking about conversation, not as a map of unvarying stages that all conversations follow. Can you use this diagram to explain the structure of a recent conversation? How would you diagram a model of communication by e-mail?

TABLE 7.1 *Interpersonal Communication Tips*

BETWEEN PEOPLE WITH AND WITHOUT SPEECH AND LANGUAGE DISORDERS

Speech and language disorders vary widely—from fluency problems such as stuttering, to indistinct articulation, to aphasia, or difficulty in finding the right word. A few simple guidelines greatly facilitate communication between people with and without speech and language disorders.

If you're the person without a speech or language disorder:

1. Avoid finishing sentences for someone who stutters or has difficulty finding words. It may communicate the idea that you're impatient and don't want to spend the extra time necessary to interact effectively.

2. Avoid giving directions to the person with a speech disorder. Saying "slow down" or "relax" will often prove insulting and can make further communication more difficult.

3. Maintain eye contact and avoid showing signs of impatience or embarrassment.

4. If you don't understand what the person said, ask him or her to repeat it. Don't pretend that you understand when you don't.

5. Don't treat people who have language problems like children. A person with aphasia, say, may have difficulty with names or with nouns generally but is in no way childlike.

If you're the person with a speech or language disorder:

1. Let the other person know what your special needs are. For example, if you stutter, you might tell others that you have difficulty with certain sounds and so they need to be patient.

2. Demonstrate your comfort with and positive attitude toward the interpersonal situation. If you appear comfortable and positive, others will also.

Sources: These suggestions were drawn from a variety of sources: The National Stuttering Association, http://www.nsastutter.org; The National Aphasia Association, http://www.aphasia.org/NAAcommun.html; and Constance Dugan, MA/CCC-SLP, http://www.conniedugan.com/tips.html, all accessed April 5, 2002.

Opening

The first step in conversation is the opening, which usually involves some kind of greeting: "Hi." "How are you?" "Hello, this is Joe." In face-to-face conversation, greetings can be verbal or nonverbal but are usually both (Krivonos & Knapp, 1975; Knapp, 1984). In e-mail (and in most computer communication), the greetings are verbal with perhaps an emoticon or two thrown in. As video and sound are added to Internet connections, this difference from face-to-face conversation will diminish. Verbal greetings include, for example, verbal salutes ("Hi," "Hello"), initiation of the topic ("The reason I called . . ."), references to the other ("Hey, Joe, what's up?"), and personal inquiries ("What's new?" "How are you doing?"). Nonverbal greetings include waving, smiling, shaking hands, and winking (and their emoticon equivalents).

In your greeting you can accomplish several purposes (Krivonos & Knapp, 1975; Knapp & Vangelisti, 2000). For example, you can *signal a stage of access;* you can indicate that the channels of communication are open for more meaningful interaction. This is a good example of **phatic communication,** or "small talk" that opens the way for "big talk." Or you can *reveal important information about the relationship between the two of you.* For example, a big smile and a warm "Hi, it's been a long time" signals that your relationship is still a friendly one. With greetings you can also *help maintain the relationship.* You see this function served between colleagues who frequently pass by each other in the workplace. This greeting-in-passing assures you that even though you do not stop and talk, you still have access to each other.

Feedforward

In the second step of conversation, you usually give some kind of feedforward in which you might seek to accomplish a variety of functions. One function is to *open the channels of communication,* usually with some phatic message—a message that signals that communication will take place rather than communicates any significant denotative information. An example would be "Haven't we met before?" or "Nice day, isn't it?" In e-mail, this is done simply by sending the message—it tells the other person that you want to communicate.

> **❝** A good conversationalist is not one who remembers what was said, but says what someone wants to remember. **❞**
>
> —John Mason Brown

Another function of feedforward is to *preview future messages*, for example, "I'm afraid I have bad news for you" or "Listen to this before you make a move" or "I'll tell you all the gory details." In office memos and e-mail, this function is served—in part—with headers that indicate the subject of your message, the recipients, and those who'll receive courtesy copies.

Feedforward can also help to *altercast*. **Altercasting** is placing the receiver in a specific role and requesting that the receiver respond in terms of this assumed role (Weinstein & Deutschberger, 1963; McLaughlin, 1984)—as in "But you're my best friend; you have to help me" or "As an advertising executive, what do you think of advertising directed at children?"

You can also use feedforward to *disclaim*. A **disclaimer** is a statement used to persuade the listener to hear your message as you wish it to be heard (Hewitt & Stokes, 1975). Examples include "Don't get me wrong, I'm not sexist," "I didn't read the entire report, but . . . ," and "Don't say anything until you hear my side." In e-mail and other forms of computer communication, you can use emoticons to indicate that you're only joking and thereby disclaim any negative intent.

Business

The third step is the business, or the substance and focus, of the conversation. *Business* is a good term to use for this stage, because it emphasizes that most conversations are directed at achieving some goal. You converse to fulfill one or several of the general purposes of interpersonal communication: to learn, relate, influence, play, or help, as you saw in Chapter 1. In conversation you conduct this business through an exchange of speaker and listener roles—you talk about the new supervisor, what happened in class, or your vacation plans. This is obviously the longest part of the conversation; both the opening and the feedforward steps support and foreshadow this part of the conversation.

The Principle of Turn-Taking   The defining feature of face-to-face conversation is that the participants exchange the roles of speaker and listener frequently throughout the interaction. Usually, brief (rather than long) **conversational turns** characterize mutually satisfying conversations. This is where e-mail differs greatly from most face-to-face communication. In e-mail you send a message without any interruptions or feedback from the receiver. Then the receiver responds. Then you respond. E-mail communication thus better resembles the linear model of communication, in which either speaker or listener communicates, but never both at once. Face-to-face conversation better fits the transactional model (see Chapter 1), in which each person sends and receives messages simultaneously; this model is more closely represented in, for example, instant messaging systems. Here are just a few suggestions for sending and receiving messages in both face-to-face and computer-mediated communication.

- Ask questions of clarification and extension to show that you're listening and that you're interested. Ask for opinions and ideas to draw the person into the conversation and to initiate an exchange of thoughts. Paraphrase important ideas to make sure you understand what the sender is thinking and feeling, and give her or him an opportunity to correct or modify your paraphrase ("Does this mean you're going to quit your job?").

- Strive for a balance between sending and receiving, at least most of the time. Be sure to have good reasons if your speaking time or e-mail sending is greatly different from your listening time or your e-mail responses.

- Beware of detouring—taking a word or idea from a message and then going off on a tangent. Too many of these tangents can cause you to lose the opportunity to achieve any conversational depth. Keep the main subject of the conversation clearly in mind as you talk and as you listen.

❝ Their remarks and responses were like a Ping-Pong game with each volley clearing the net and flying back to the opposition. **❞**

—Maya Angelou

- In face-to-face situations, try to avoid interrupting. (Interruptions are only possible in face-to-face conversation; you can't interrupt someone's e-mail writing.) Generally, interruptions that take the speaking turn away from the speaker damage a conversation by preventing each person from saying what he or she wants to say.

- Do, however, use **backchanneling cues,** signals that you send back to the speaker that do not take away the speaker's turn (Burgoon, Buller, & Woodall, 1996; Kennedy & Camden, 1988; Pearson & Spitzberg, 1990). Backchanneling cues include, for example, indicating agreement or disagreement through smiles or frowns, gestures of approval or disapproval, or brief comments such as "right" or "never." They also include displaying *involvement* or *boredom* with the speaker through attentive or inattentive posture, forward or backward leaning, and focused or no eye contact. You can also give the speaker *pacing* cues, for example, indicating by raising your hand near your ear and leaning forward that he or she should slow down. And you can ask for *clarification* with a puzzled facial expression, perhaps coupled with a forward lean.

- Pay attention to turn-taking cues. In face-to-face conversation, look for verbal and nonverbal cues that the speaker wants to maintain or give up a turn as speaker or that a listener wants to say something (or simply remain a listener). Also, pay attention to **leave-taking cues,** signals that the other person wants to end the conversation or the e-mail relationship. See the discussion of ways of closing a conversation on page 140.

- When conversing electronically, be sure to clarify anything that might not be understood—because the absence of the nonverbal dimension in most current e-mail systems makes misunderstandings more likely. Use emoticons to show that you are being sarcastic or making a joke, for example. Also, don't be disturbed when the formalities customary in traditional letter writing are omitted in e-mail. E-mail is often viewed more like a memo, with the *to, from, subject, date,* and *courtesy copy recipients* in the preformatted heading. Still, it's important to remember that different organizations will have different standards for acceptable e-mail style. Generally, the more formal the organization, the more likely it is that e-mail style will be expected to resemble that of printed business correspondence. For example, emoticons would probably be avoided in a formal organization.

The Principle of Dialogue   Think about your own communication tendencies. Which of the following paired descriptions *generally* characterize your interpersonal interactions?

1. You frequently use negative criticism ("I didn't like that explanation") and negative personal judgments ("You're not a very good listener, are you?").

1. You avoid negative criticism and negative personal judgments; you practice using positive criticism ("I like those first two explanations best; they were really well reasoned").

2. You frequently use dysfunctional communication, such as expressing unwillingness to talk or introducing messages unrelated to the topic of discussion ("There's no sense discussing this; I can see you're not rational").

2. You keep the channels of communication open ("I really don't know what I did that offended you, but tell me. I don't want to hurt you again").

3. You rarely demonstrate by paraphrasing or summarizing that you understand the other person's meaning.

3. You frequently paraphrase or summarize what the other person has said to ensure accurate understanding.

❝ Most conversations are monologues delivered in the presence of witnesses. ❞
—Margaret Millar

4. You rarely request clarification of the other person's perspectives or ideas.

4. You request clarification as necessary, and you ask for the other person's point of view because of a genuine interest in the other person's perspective.

5. You frequently request personal positive statements or statements of approval ("How did you like the way I told that guy off? Clever, no?").

5. You avoid requesting personal positive statements or statements of approval.

The descriptions in the left column are examples of monologue; items on the right are examples of dialogue. **Monologue** is communication in which one person speaks and the other person listens; there's no real interaction between them. *Monologic communication,* by extension, is communication in which there is no genuine interaction, in which one person speaks without any real concern for the other person's feelings or attitudes. The monologic communicator is concerned only with his or her own goals and is interested in the other person only insofar as that person can serve to promote those goals. In monologic interaction you communicate what will advance your own goals, prove most persuasive, and benefit you.

Not surprisingly, effective communication is based not on monologue but on its opposite, **dialogue** (Buber, 1958; Brown & Keller, 1979; Thomlison, 1982; Yau-fair Ho, Chan, Peng, & Ng, 2001; McNamee & Gergen, 1999). In dialogue there is two-way interaction. Each person is both speaker and listener, sender and receiver. *Dialogic communication* involves real concern for the other person and for the relationship between the two people. The objective of dialogue is mutual understanding and empathy. There is respect for the other person, not because of what this person can do or give but simply because he or she is a human being and therefore deserves to be treated honestly and sincerely.

In a dialogic interaction you respect the other person enough to allow that person the right to make his or her own choices without coercion, without the threat of punishment, without fear or social pressure. A dialogic communicator implicitly or explicitly lets others know that whatever choices they make, they will still be respected as people.

> " There is no such thing as conversation. It is an illusion. There are intersecting monologues, that is all. "
>
> —Rebecca West

> " Two monologues do not make a dialogue. "
>
> —Jeff Daly

Feedback

The fourth step of conversation, feedback, is the reverse of the second. In feedback you reflect back on the conversation. You normally do this immediately in face-to-face conversation and in your response to a previous e-mail. You say, for example, "So, you may want to send Jack a get-well card," or, "Wasn't that the dullest meeting you ever went to?"

Feedback can be viewed in terms of five important dimensions: positive–negative, person focused–message focused, immediate–delayed, low monitoring–high monitoring, and critical–supportive. To give effective feedback, you need to make educated choices along each dimension.

Most obviously, perhaps, feedback may vary between *positive* and *negative.* **Positive feedback** (applause, smiles, head nods signifying approval, or a "thank you" e-mail) tells the speaker or e-mail sender that the message is well received and that he or she should continue communicating in the same general mode. **Negative feedback** (boos, puzzled looks, or verbal criticism) tells the sender that something is wrong and that some adjustment needs to be made to the communication.

Feedback may be *person focused* or *message focused;* that is, it may center on the person ("You're sweet," "You have a great smile") or on the message ("Can you repeat that phone number?" "Your argument is a good one"). In some situations (for example, giving criticism in a public speaking class), it's especially important to make clear that your feedback is message focused—that you are critical of the speech's organization and not of the speaker as a person.

Feedback may be *immediate* or *delayed*. In interpersonal situations you most often send feedback immediately after receiving a message. And when you applaud or ask questions of a public speaker or compliment the message in the previous e-mail, your feedback is relatively immediate. In other communication situations, however, feedback may be delayed. Instructor evaluation questionnaires completed at the end of a course provide feedback long after the class began. In interview situations the feedback may come weeks afterwards. In media situations some feedback comes immediately through, for example, Nielsen ratings; other feedback comes much later, when sponsors examine viewing and buying patterns.

Another dimension of feedback is the variation from the spontaneous and totally honest reaction (*low-monitored* feedback) to the carefully constructed response designed to serve a specific purpose (*high-monitored* feedback). In most interpersonal situations you probably give feedback spontaneously; you allow your responses to show without any monitoring. At other times, however, you may be more guarded, as when your boss asks you what you think of the new direction the company is taking or when someone sends you an e-mail message asking for a big favor.

Critical feedback is evaluative. When you give critical feedback, you judge another's performance—as when, for example, you evaluate a speech or coach someone learning a new skill. Feedback can also be *supportive,* as when you console someone, simply encourage someone to talk, or affirm someone's self-definition.

Closing

The fifth and last step of the conversation process, the opposite of the first step, is the closing, the good-bye (Knapp, Hart, Friedrich, & Shulman, 1973; Knapp & Vangelisti, 2000). Like the opening, the closing may be verbal or nonverbal but usually is a combination of both. Just as the opening signals access, the closing signals the intention to end access. The closing usually also signals some degree of supportiveness—for example, you express your pleasure in interacting ("Well, it was good talking with you"). The closing may also summarize the interaction to offer more of a conclusion to the conversation.

Closing a conversation in e-mail follows the same principles as closing a face-to-face conversation. But exactly when you end the e-mail exchange is often not clear, partly because the absence of nonverbal cues creates ambiguity. For example, if you ask someone a question and the other person answers, do you then e-mail again and say, "thanks"? If so, should the other person e-mail you back and say, "It was my pleasure"? And if so, should you then e-mail back again and say, "I appreciate your willingness to answer my questions"? And if so, should the other person then respond with something like "It was no problem"?

On the one hand, you don't want to prolong the interaction more than necessary. On the other hand, you don't want to appear impolite. So how do you signal (politely) that the e-mail exchanges should stop? Here are a few suggestions (Cohen, 2002):

- Include in your e-mail the notation NRN (no reply necessary).
- If you're replying with information the other person requested, end your message with something like "I hope this helps."
- Title or head your message FYI (for your information), indicating that your purpose is merely to keep someone in the loop.
- When you make a request for information, end your message with "thank you in advance."

> To listen closely and reply well is the highest perfection we are able to attain in the art of conversation.
> —François de La Rochefoucauld

Opening and Closing Conversations

How might you open a conversation with the persons described in each of these situations? What approaches would meet with favorable responses? What approaches would meet with unfavorable responses?

1. On the first day of class, you and another student are the first to come into the classroom and are seated in the room alone.
2. You've just started a new job in a large office where you're one of several computer operators. It seems as if most of the other people know one another.

How might you close each of the following conversations? What types of closings would be most effective? Which would be least effective?

1. You and a friend have been talking on the phone for the last hour, but at this point nothing new is being said. You have work to do and want to close the conversation.
2. After a long meeting, your colleague doesn't seem to know how to end the conversation and continues to go over what has already been said. You have to get back to your desk.

Reflections on the Model of Conversation

Not all conversations divide neatly into these five steps, of course. Often the opening and the feedforward are combined, as when you see someone on campus and say, "Hey, listen to this," or when someone in a work situation says, "Well, folks, let's get the meeting going." In a similar way, the feedback and the closing may be combined: "Look, I've got to think more about this commitment, okay?"

As already noted, the business is the longest part of the conversation. The opening and the closing are usually about the same length as the feedforward and feedback stages. When these relative lengths are severely distorted, you may feel that something is wrong. For example, when someone uses a long feedforward or too short an opening, you may suspect that what is to follow is extremely serious.

Different cultures, however, vary the basic steps of conversation. In some cultures the openings are especially short, and in others they are elaborate, lengthy, and in some cases highly ritualized. It is easy to violate another culture's conversational rules in intercultural communication situations. Being overly friendly, too formal, or too forward may hinder the remainder of the interchange. Such violations may have significant consequences—because, if you are not aware of cultural differences, you may interpret someone's "violations" as aggressiveness, stuffiness, or pushiness, take an immediate dislike to the person, and put a negative cast on future communications.

The five-stage model may help you to identify skill weaknesses and distinguish effective and satisfying conversations from those that are ineffective and unsatisfying. Consider, for example, the following violations and how they can damage an entire conversation:

- The use of openings that are insensitive, such as "Wow, you've gained a few pounds"
- The use of overly long feedforwards that make you wonder if the speaker will ever get to the business at hand
- The omission of feedforward before a truly shocking message (for example, the death or illness of a friend or relative), which can lead you to judge the other person as insensitive or uncaring
- Conducting business without the normally expected greeting, as when you go to a doctor who begins the conversation by saying, "Well, what's wrong?"

> " Conversation should be pleasant without scurrility, witty without affectation, free without indecency, learned without conceitedness, novel without falsehood. "
>
> —William Shakespeare

- The omission of feedback, which can lead you to wonder whether the speaker heard or read what you said
- The omission of an appropriate closing, which can make you wonder whether the other person is disturbed or angry with you

Effective Conversation

Skill in conversation depends on your ability to make adjustments along several dimensions. Recall from Chapter 4 that your listening effectiveness depends on your ability to make adjustments between, for example, empathic and objective listening. In a similar way, your effectiveness in conversation depends on your ability to make adjustments along the following specific skill dimensions: openness, empathy, positiveness, immediacy, interaction management, expressiveness, and other-orientation. We'll look at each of these, but first let's consider a few general skills that are fundamental to all effective conversation.

General Conversational Skills

Four general skills will prove crucial in helping you adjust and regulate the more specific skills: mindfulness, flexibility, cultural sensitivity, and metacommunication.

Mindfulness   **Mindfulness** is a state of awareness in which you're conscious of your reasons for thinking or behaving. Its opposite, **mindlessness,** is a lack of conscious awareness of what or how you're thinking (Langer, 1989). To apply interpersonal skills effectively, it's important to be mindful of the unique communication situation you're in, your available communication options, and the reasons why one option is likely to be better than the others (Langer, 1989; Elmes & Gemmill, 1990; Burgoon, Berger, & Waldron, 2000).

Increasing Mindfulness.   To increase mindfulness, try the following suggestions (Langer, 1989).

- *Create and recreate categories*. Learn to see objects, events, and people as belonging to a wide variety of categories. For example, try to see your prospective romantic partner in a variety of roles—child, parent, employee, neighbor, friend, financial contributor, and so on. Avoid storing in memory an image of a person with only one specific label; if you do, you'll find it difficult to recategorize the person later.

- *Be open to new information and points of view,* even when these contradict your most firmly held beliefs. New information forces you to reconsider what might be outmoded ways of thinking. New information can help you challenge long held but now inappropriate beliefs and attitudes. Be willing to see your own and others' behaviors from the viewpoints of people very different from yourself.

- *Beware of relying too heavily on first impressions* (Chanowitz & Langer, 1981; Langer, 1989). Treat first impressions as tentative—as hypotheses that need further investigation. Be prepared to accept, revise, or reject these initial impressions.

Flexibility   **Flexibility** is a quality of thinking and behaving in which you vary your messages on the basis of the unique situation. One test of flexibility asks you how true you believe certain statements are; for example, "People should be frank and spontaneous in conversation" or "When angry, a person should say nothing rather than say something he or she will be sorry for later." The "preferred" answer to all such questions is "sometimes true," underscoring the importance of flexibility in all interpersonal situations (Hart, Carlson, & Eadie, 1980).

Increasing Flexibility.   Here are a few ways to cultivate flexibility.

- *Realize that no two situations or people are exactly alike.* Ask yourself what is different about this situation or this person, and take these differences into consideration as you decide what to say and how to say it.

- *Realize that communication always takes place in a context* (Chapter 1); ask yourself what is unique about this specific context and how this uniqueness should influence your messages.

- *Realize that everything is in a state of flux.* If the way you communicated last month was effective, that doesn't necessarily mean it will be effective today or tomorrow. Realize, too, that sudden changes (the breakup of a relationship or a fatal illness) will influence what are and what are not appropriate messages with a given person.

- *Realize that every situation offers you different options* for communicating. Think about these options and try to predict the outcome of each approach.

Cultural Sensitivity

Cultural sensitivity is an attitude and way of behaving in which you're aware of and acknowledge cultural differences. Cultural sensitivity is crucial in global efforts such as campaigns for world peace and economic growth; it's also central in effective interpersonal communication as well as in general personal success (Franklin & Mizell, 1995). Without cultural sensitivity there can be no effective interpersonal communication between people who are different in gender or race or nationality or affectional orientation. So be mindful of the cultural differences between yourself and the other person. Remember that the techniques of interpersonal communication that work well with European Americans may not work well with Asian Americans; that what proves effective in Japan may not succeed in Mexico. The close physical distance that is normal in Arab cultures may prove too familiar or too intrusive in much of the United States and Northern Europe. The empathy that most Americans welcome may be uncomfortable for the average Korean (Yun, 1976).

Increasing Cultural Sensitivity.   Here are a few guidelines to follow for achieving greater cultural sensitivity.

- *Prepare yourself.* Read about and listen carefully for culturally influenced behaviors.

- *Recognize and face fears* of acting inappropriately in interactions with members of different cultures.

- *Recognize differences*—differences between yourself and culturally different groups, differences among members of those groups, and differences in meaning (words rarely mean the same thing to members of different cultures).

- *Become conscious of the cultural rules* and customs of others. Resist the temptation to assume that what works in your culture will necessarily work in others.

Metacommunication

Metacommunication is communication that refers to other communications; it's communication about communication. Both verbal and nonverbal messages can be metacommunicational. Verbally, for example, you can say, "Do you understand what I'm trying to say?" Nonverbally, for example, you can hug someone you're consoling.

Interpersonal effectiveness often hinges on the ability to metacommunicate. For example, in conflict situations it's often helpful to talk about the way you fight. In romantic relationships it's often helpful to talk about what each of you means by terms like "steady" or "really caring." On the job it's often necessary to talk about the way orders are delegated or the way criticism should be expressed.

Web Explorations

A variety of exercises on conversation will help clarify the nature of this important process (**www.ablongman.com/devito**): (1) Conversational Turns, (2) How Do You Talk? As a Woman? As a Man? (3) Gender and the Topics of Conversation, (4) The Qualities of Effectiveness, (5) Responding Effectively, (6) Communicating Your Emotions, (7) Expressing Negative Feelings, (8) Communicating Emotions Effectively, (9) Giving and Receiving Compliments, (10) Conversational Analysis: A Chance Meeting, and (11) Giving and Taking Directions. Self-tests on conversational issues include (12) How Polite Is Your Conversation (Long Form)? (13) How Satisfying Is Your Conversation? (14) How Apprehensive Are You in Conversations? (15) How Shy Are You? and (16) How Much Do You Self-Monitor?

Metacommunicating. Here are a few suggestions for increasing your meta-communicational effectiveness.

- *Explain the feelings that go with the thoughts.* Often people communicate only the thinking part of their message, with the result that listeners aren't able to appreciate the other parts of the meaning.

- *Give clear feedforward* to help the other person get a general picture of the messages that will follow.

- *Paraphrase your own complex messages* so as to make your meaning extra clear. Similarly, check on your understanding of another's message by paraphrasing what you think the other person means. Then ask if that's what the person meant.

- *Use metacommunication when you want to clarify* the communication patterns between yourself and another person. Say, for example, "I'd like to talk about the way you talk about me to our friends" or "I think we should talk about the way we talk about sex."

Specific Conversational Skills

The skills of conversational effectiveness we'll describe here are derived from a wide spectrum of ongoing research (Bochner & Kelly, 1974; Wiemann, 1977; Spitzberg & Hecht, 1984; Spitzberg & Cupach, 1984, 1989, 2002; Rubin, 1985; Rubin & Graham, 1988; Greene & Burleson, 2003). As you read about these concepts, keep in mind the four general skills discussed above.

Openness   **Openness** involves your willingness to self-disclose—to reveal information about yourself that you might normally keep hidden, provided that such disclosure is appropriate (as discussed in Chapter 2). Openness also has to do with your willingness to listen openly to and to react honestly to the messages of others.

Communicating Openness.   Consider these few ideas.

- *Self-disclose when appropriate.* Be mindful about your self-disclosures, remembering that there are both benefits and dangers to this form of intimate communication.

- *Respond to those with whom you're interacting with spontaneity* and with appropriate honesty (but also with an awareness of what you're saying and what the possible outcomes of your messages might be).

- *Own your own feelings and thoughts.* Take responsibility for what you say, using **I-messages** instead of **you-messages.** In other words, instead of saying, "You make me feel stupid when you don't ask my opinion," own your feelings and say, for example, "I feel stupid when you ask everyone else what they think but don't ask me." When you own your feelings and thoughts—when you use I-messages—you say, in effect, "This is how *I* feel," "This is how *I* see the situation," and "This is what *I* think." When you use I-messages, you make it explicit that your feelings result from the interaction between what is going on outside your skin (what others say, for example) and what is going on inside your skin (your preconceptions, attitudes, and prejudices, for example).

Empathy   **Empathy** is an ability to feel what another person feels from that person's point of view; to feel another's feelings in a somewhat similar way, although without losing your own identity. Empathy enables you to understand emotionally what another person is experiencing. (To sympathize, in contrast, is to feel *for* the person—to feel sorry or happy for the person, for example.)

What Do You Say?

Empathy: Your roommate just made the dean's list and as a reward received a new Lexus from a rich uncle. Your roommate is ecstatic and runs to you to share the news. You want to demonstrate empathy, but you're annoyed that some people just seem to get everything. *What do you say?*

Communicating Empathy.   Here are a few suggestions to help you communicate empathy effectively (Authier & Gustafson, 1982).

- *Avoid evaluating, judging, or criticizing* the other person's behaviors. Make it clear that you're not evaluating or judging but trying to understand.
- *Focus your concentration.* Maintain eye contact, an attentive posture, and physical closeness. Express your involvement through appropriate facial expressions and gestures.
- *Reflect back* to the speaker the feelings that you think are being expressed, both to check the accuracy of your perceptions and to show your commitment to understanding the speaker. In doing so, you may find it helpful to make tentative statements about what you think the person is feeling; for example, "You seem really angry with your father" or "I hear some doubt in your voice."
- *When appropriate, use your own self-disclosures* to communicate your understanding. Be careful, however, that you don't get so caught up in your own disclosures that you refocus the discussion on yourself.

Positiveness   **Positiveness** in interpersonal communication means using positive rather than negative messages. For example, instead of the negative "I wish you wouldn't ignore my opinions," consider the positive alternative: "I feel good when you ask my opinions." Instead of the negative "You look horrible in stripes," consider "I think you look great in solid colors."

Communicating Positiveness.   Here are a few suggestions for communicating positiveness. Implementing these ideas may be a bit easier for women than for men, because women generally are more apt to express positiveness in their evaluations in both face-to-face and computer-mediated communication (Adrianson, 2001).

- *Look for the positive* in the person or in the person's work and compliment it. Compliment specifics; overly general compliments ("Your project was interesting") are rarely as effective as those that are specific and concrete ("Your proposal will be a great financial saving").
- *Express satisfaction* when communicating with others by, for example, using friendly facial expressions, maintaining a reasonably close but appropriate distance, and focusing eye contact and avoiding glancing away from the other person for long periods of time.
- *Express positiveness with a recognition of cultural differences* (Dresser, 1996; Chen, 1992). For example, in the United States it's considered appropriate for a supervisor to compliment a worker for doing an exceptional job. But in some other cultures, particularly collectivist cultures, this would be considered inappropriate—because it singles out one individual and separates that person from the group.

Immediacy   **Immediacy** has to do with the joining of speaker and listener; it's the creation of a sense of togetherness, of oneness. When you communicate immediacy you convey a sense of interest and attention, a liking for and an attraction to the other person. People respond more favorably to communication that is immediate than to communication that is not. For example, students of instructors who communicated immediacy felt that the instruction was better and the courses more valuable than students of instructors who did not communicate immediacy (Moore, Masterson, Christophel, & Shea, 1996; Witt & Wheeless, 2001). Students and teachers liked each other largely on the basis of immediacy (Wilson & Taylor, 2001; Baringer & McCroskey, 2000).

"Clemson here. How may I disappoint you?"

What Do You Say?

Complimenting: A coworker you've worked with for years was recently named employee of the year for an extraordinary sales record and comes to you with the news. *What do you say?*

Communicating Immediacy.   Here are a few suggestions for communicating immediacy.

- *Express psychological closeness and openness* by, for example, maintaining physical closeness and arranging your body to exclude third parties. Maintain appropriate eye contact, limit looking around at others, smile, and express your interest in the other person.
- *Use the other person's name;* for example, say, "Joe, what do you think?" instead of "What do you think?"
- *Focus on the other person's remarks.* Make the speaker know that you heard and understood what was said, and give the speaker appropriate verbal and nonverbal feedback.
- *Express immediacy with cultural sensitivity.* In the United States people generally see immediacy behaviors as friendly and appropriate. Members of other cultures, however, may view the same immediacy behaviors as overly familiar—as presuming closeness when only acquaintanceship exists (Axtell, 1993).

Interaction Management   **Interaction management** consists of techniques and strategies by which you regulate and carry on an interpersonal interaction. Effective interaction management results in an interaction that's satisfying to both parties. Neither person feels ignored or on stage; each contributes to and benefits from the interpersonal exchange.

Managing Communication Interactions.   This entire text is devoted to the effective management of interpersonal interactions—but here are a few specific suggestions.

- *Maintain and exchange speaker and listener roles* through appropriate eye movements, vocal expressions, and body and facial gestures.
- *Keep the conversation fluent,* avoiding long or awkward pauses. For example, studies have found that patients are less satisfied with their interaction with their doctor when the silence between their comments and the doctor's response is overly long (Rowland-Morin & Carroll, 1990).
- *Make sure that verbal and nonverbal messages are consistent* and reinforce one another. Avoid sending contradictory signals—for example, a nonverbal message that contradicts the verbal message.

Expressiveness   **Expressiveness** in communication means communicating genuine involvement. It includes, for example, taking responsibility for your thoughts and feelings, encouraging expressiveness or openness in others, and providing appropriate feedback.

Communicating Expressiveness.   Here are a few suggestions for enhancing expressiveness in conversation.

- *Use appropriate variations in vocal qualities* such as rate, pitch, volume, and rhythm to convey involvement and interest. Use appropriate variations in verbal language, too; avoid clichés and trite expressions, which can signal a lack of originality and personal involvement.
- *Use appropriate gestures,* especially those that focus on the other person rather than yourself. For example, maintain eye contact and lean toward the person; at the same time, avoid self-touching gestures or directing your eyes to others in the room.
- *Communicate expressiveness with cultural awareness.* Some cultures (Italian and Greek, for example) encourage expressiveness and teach children to be

What Do You Say?

Expressing Thanks: Because of family problems you fell behind in your rent and were threatened with eviction. Your next-door neighbor and friend bailed you out by paying the overdue rent. You want to express your deep appreciation. *What do you say? Through what channel?*

expressive. Other cultures (Japanese and Thai, for example) encourage a more reserved response style (Matsumoto, 1996). Some cultures (Arab and many Asian cultures, for example) consider expressiveness by women in business settings to be generally inappropriate (Lustig & Koester, 2002; Axtell, 1993; Hall & Hall, 1987).

- *Give verbal and nonverbal feedback* to show that you're engaged. Such feedback—called "conversational pitchback" by one researcher—promotes relationship satisfaction (Ross, 1995).

Other-Orientation   **Other-Orientation** involves attentiveness and interest in the other person and in what the person says. Other-orientation in conversation gives you the ability to adapt your messages to the other person.

What do you think is the most important conversational skill? What conversational skill do you find most often violated?

Communicating Other-Orientation.   You'll recognize the following behaviors in those with whom you enjoy talking.

- *Show consideration and respect;* for example, ask if it's all right to dump your troubles on someone before doing so, or ask if your phone call comes at a good time before launching into conversation.

- *Acknowledge the other person's feelings as legitimate.* Comments such as "You're right" or "That's interesting" or "I can understand why you're so angry; I would be, too" help focus the interaction on the other person and assure the person that you're listening. At the same time, grant the other person permission either to express or not to express her or his feelings. A simple statement such as "I know how difficult it is to talk about feelings" opens up the topic of feelings and gives the person permission to pursue such a discussion—or to say nothing.

- *Acknowledge the presence and the importance of the other person.* Ask the other person for suggestions and opinions. Similarly, ask for clarification as appropriate. This will ensure that you understand what the other person is saying from his or her point of view.

- *Focus your messages on the other person.* Verbally, ask open-ended questions (as opposed to questions that merely call for a yes or no answer) to involve the other person in the interaction; make statements that directly address the person. Nonverbally, use focused eye contact and appropriate facial expressions; smile, nod, and lean toward the other person.

Research Navigator.c⊛m

www.researchnavigator.com

Investigate Key Terms: Investigate one of the key terms discussed in this chapter (for example, conversation, mindfulness, disclaimer, excuse, conversational turns, interpersonal conflict, aggressiveness, argumentativeness, or conflict avoidance). What additional insights can you provide?

Skill development experience

Formulating Excuses

Excuses are explanations that often can help lessen the negative effects of mishaps in interpersonal interactions. Formulate an appropriate excuse for one of the situations listed below, following these five steps (Slade, 1995; Coleman, 2002): (1) Demonstrate that you understand the problem and that your partner's feelings are justified. (2) Acknowledge responsibility. (3) Acknowledge your regret at what you did. (4) Request forgiveness; be specific. And (5) Make clear that this will never happen again.
    The situations:

1. Your boss (justifiably) accuses you of making lots of personal long-distance phone calls from work, a practice that's explicitly forbidden.
2. Your relationship partner catches you in a lie: You weren't at work but were with a former lover.

Conflict

Interpersonal conflicts develop over innumerable issues, but many of these issues fall into predictable patterns. For example, in a study on conflicts in gay, lesbian, and heterosexual couples, six major problem areas turned out to be virtually identical for all couples (Kurdek, 1994). Consider your own conflict behavior by asking yourself which, if any, of these issues you argue about in your relationships. The list below is arranged in order, with number 1 being the issue most often mentioned.

1. Intimacy issues such as affection or sex
2. Power issues such as excessive demands or possessiveness, lack of equality in the relationship, friends, or leisure time
3. Personal flaws issues such as drinking, smoking, grooming, or driving style
4. Distance issues such as frequent absences or school or job commitments
5. Social issues such as politics, parents, or personal values
6. Distrust issues such as previous lovers or lying

Interpersonal conflict can be further explained in terms of the content–relationship distinction introduced in Chapter 1. *Content conflict* centers on objects, events, and people that are usually, though not always, external to the parties involved in the conflict. Content conflicts include the millions of issues that we argue and fight about every day—the merits of a particular movie, what to watch on television, the fairness of the last exam or job promotion, or how to spend our savings.

Relationship conflicts are equally numerous and include situations such as those of a younger brother who does not obey his older brother, partners who each want an equal say in making vacation plans, and a mother and daughter who each want to have the final word concerning the daughter's lifestyle. Relationship conflicts arise not so much from an external object as from relationships between individuals. They tend to focus on issues such as who is in charge, how much equality exists in a primary relationship, and who has the right to establish rules of behavior.

As with many such concepts, content and relationship conflicts are easier to separate in a textbook than they are in real life; many real-life conflicts contain elements of both factors. But in understanding and effectively managing conflict, it helps if you can recognize which disagreements pertain primarily to content issues and which primarily to relationship matters.

Myths about Conflict

One of the problems in dealing with interpersonal conflict is that you may be operating with false assumptions about what conflict is and what it means. For example, do you think the following are true or false?

- If two people in a relationship fight, it means they have a bad relationship.
- Fighting hurts an interpersonal relationship.
- Fighting is bad because it reveals our negative selves—for example, our pettiness, our need to control, our unreasonable expectations.

As with most things, simple answers are usually wrong. Each of the three assumptions above may be true or may be false. It depends. In and of itself, conflict is neither good nor bad. Conflict is a part of every interpersonal relationship, whether between parents and children, between brothers and sisters, or between friends, lovers, or coworkers. If it isn't, the relationship is probably dull, irrelevant, or insignificant.

Conflict can have both negative and positive effects. Among the potential negative effects is that conflict may lead to increased negative feelings for your "opponent" (who may be your best friend or lover). It may cause a depletion of energy better spent on other areas, or it may lead you to close yourself off from the other person. When you hide your true self from an intimate, you prevent meaningful communication.

The major positive value of interpersonal conflict is that it forces you to closely examine a problem that you might otherwise avoid and to work toward a potential solution. If you both can use productive conflict strategies, a stronger, healthier, and more satisfying relationship may well emerge from the encounter. The very fact that you are trying to resolve a conflict means that you feel the relationship is worth the effort; otherwise, you would walk away from the problem. Through conflict you learn more about each other, and with that knowledge comes understanding.

The key point is that it is not so much conflict that creates problems as the way in which the individuals approach and deal with it. This is why the major portion of this chapter's discussion will focus on ways of managing conflict rather than on ways of avoiding it.

Cultural Context

Cultural context is important when we try to understand and effectively manage conflict. Culture influences not only the issues people fight about, but also what people consider appropriate and inappropriate when dealing with conflict (Tardiff, 2001). For example, cohabitating 18-year-olds are more likely to experience conflict with their parents about their living style if they live in the United States than if they live in Sweden, where cohabitation is much more accepted. Similarly, male infidelity is more likely to cause conflict among American couples than among southern European couples. Students from the United States are more likely to engage in conflict with another U.S. student than with someone from another culture. Chinese students, on the other hand, are more likely to engage in conflict with a non-Chinese student than with another Chinese student (Leung, 1988).

In another example of this cultural influence on conflict, researchers find that members of collectivist cultures tend to avoid conflict more than members of individualist cultures (Dsilva & Whyte, 1998; Haar & Krabe, 1999; Cai & Fink, 2002). Further, people in the United States and Japan differ in their views of the aim or purpose of conflict. Japanese people generally see conflicts and their resolution in terms of compromise; many Americans, on the other hand, see conflict in terms of winning (Gelfand, Nishii, Holcombe, Dyer, Ohbuchi, & Fukuno, 2001).

Similarly, when American and Chinese students were asked to analyze a conflict episode, say between a mother and her daughter, they saw it quite differently (Goode, 2000). The American students were more likely to decide in favor of the mother or the daughter—to see one side as right and one side as wrong. The Chinese students, however, were more likely to see the validity of both sides—to say that both mother and daughter were right, but both also were wrong. This finding is consistent with the Chinese preference for proverbs that contain a contradiction (for example, "too modest is half boastful") and the American view that these proverbs are "irritating" (Goode, 2000).

The ways in which members of different cultures express conflict also differ. In Japan, for example, it's especially important that you not embarrass the person with whom you are in conflict, especially if the conflict occurs in public. This **face-saving** principle prohibits the use of strategies such as personal rejection or verbal aggressiveness. In the United States, men and women, ideally at least, are both expected to express their desires and complaints openly and directly. Many Middle Eastern and Pacific Rim cultures, however, would discourage women from such expressions. Rather, members of these cultures would expect a more agreeable and permissive posture.

Even within a given general culture, more specific cultures differ from each other in their approaches to conflict management. African American men and women and

European American men and women, for example, engage in conflict in very different ways (Kochman, 1981). The issues that cause and aggravate conflict, the conflict strategies expected and accepted, and the entire attitude toward conflict vary between groups and between genders.

For example, one study found that African American men prefer to manage conflict with clear arguments and a focus on problem solving. African American women, however, deal with conflict by expressing assertiveness and respect (Collier, 1991). In another study, African American females were found to use more direct controlling strategies (for example, assuming control over the conflict and arguing persistently for their point of view) than European American females. European American females used more problem-solving conflict management styles than African American women. Interestingly, African American and European American men were very similar in their conflict management strategies: Both tended to avoid or withdraw from relationship conflict. They preferred to keep quiet about disagreements or downplay their significance (Ting-Toomey, 1986).

Among Mexican Americans, men preferred to achieve mutual understanding by discussing the reasons for the conflict, whereas women focused on being supportive of the relationship. Among Anglo Americans, men preferred direct and rational argument, whereas women preferred flexibility (Collier, 1991).

These, of course, are merely examples. The underlying principle is that techniques for dealing with interpersonal conflict will be viewed differently by different cultures.

Conflict on the Net

Even in cyberspace you can experience conflict. Conflict occurs there for the same reasons and deals with the same topics as in face-to-face interactions. So the suggestions for dealing with conflict remain essentially the same for computer-mediated and face-to-face encounters. There is, however, one category of conflict that is unique to cyberspace: the conflict created when the rules of netiquette, the rules for communicating politely over the Internet, are violated or ignored. You can avoid this source of conflict by following these rules of netiquette:

- Read the list of frequently asked questions (FAQs). Before asking questions about the system, go to the FAQ page and see if you can find an answer to your question. Chances are your question has probably been asked before. This way, you'll put less strain on the system and be less likely to annoy other users.

- Don't shout. WRITING IN ALL CAPS IS PERCEIVED AS SHOUTING. While it's acceptable to use caps occasionally to achieve emphasis, it's better to underline, _like this_, or to use asterisks *like this*.

- Lurk before speaking. Lurking is reading the posted notices and conversations without contributing. In computer communication, lurking is good, not bad. Lurking will educate you about the rules of a particular group and help you avoid saying things you'd like to take back.

- Be brief. Follow the "maxim of quantity" by communicating only the information that is needed; follow the "maxim of manner" by communicating clearly, briefly, and in an organized way (see Chapter 5 for maxims).

- Be especially kind when talking to newbies; remember that you were once a newbie yourself.

- Don't send commercial messages to those who didn't request them. Paper junk mail is easy to throw out, but on the Internet the receiver has to pay for the time it takes to read and delete these unwanted messages.

- Don't spam. Spamming is sending someone unsolicited mail; repeatedly sending the same mail; or posting the same message on lots of bulletin boards, mailing lists, or newsgroups, especially when the message is irrelevant to the group's focus. Like electronic junk mail, spamming costs people money, in addition to wasting time. Because you're paying to read your e-mail, for example, you're paying to read something you didn't want in the first place. Also, of course, spam clogs the system, slowing it down for everyone and wasting everyone's time.

- Don't flame. Flaming is personally attacking another user. Personal attacks are best avoided on the Internet, as they are in face-to-face conflicts. So avoid participating in flame wars.
- Don't troll. Trolling is posting information you know to be false just so you can watch other people try to correct you. It's a waste of others' time and of the system's resources.

Conflict Styles

Figure 7.2 illustrates an approach to conflict that identifies five basic styles or ways of engaging in conflict; this approach is especially relevant to an understanding of interpersonal and small group conflicts (Blake & Mouton, 1984). The five styles, plotted along the dimensions of "concern for oneself" and "concern for the other person," provide considerable insight into the ways people engage in conflict and indicate some of the advantages and disadvantages of each style. As you read through these styles, try to identify your own most frequent conflict style as well as the styles of those with whom you have close relationships.

- *Competing.* The competitive style reflects great concern for your own needs and desires and little for those of others. As long as your needs are met, the conflict has been dealt with successfully. In conflict motivated by competitiveness, you'd be likely to be verbally aggressive while blaming the other person. The competing style represents an *I win, you lose* philosophy.
- *Avoiding.* The avoider fails to address his or her own or the other side's needs or desires. This person avoids any real communication about the problem, changes the topic when the problem comes up, and generally withdraws from the scene both psychologically and physically. As you can appreciate, the avoiding style does little to resolve any conflicts and may be viewed as an *I lose, you lose* philosophy.
- *Accommodating.* In accommodating you sacrifice your own needs for the needs of the other person. Your major purpose is to maintain harmony and peace in the relationship or group. This style may help you achieve the immediate goal of maintaining peace and perhaps may satisfy the other person; but it does little to meet your own needs, which are unlikely to go away. The accommodating style represents an *I lose, you win* philosophy.
- *Collaborating.* In collaborating you focus concern on both your own and the other person's needs. This style, often considered the ideal, takes time, a willingness to communicate, and especially a readiness to listen to the perspectives and needs of the other person. Ideally, the collaborating style of conflict resolution results in each person's needs being satisfied, an *I win, you win* situation.
- *Compromising.* The compromising style is in the middle; there is some concern for your own needs and some concern for the other's needs. Compromising is the kind of strategy you might refer to as "meeting each other halfway," "horse trading," or "give and take." This strategy is likely to help you maintain peace but to involve some dissatisfaction over the inevitable loses that have to be endured. Compromising results in an *I win and lose and you win and lose* outcome.

Figure 7.2

Five Conflict Styles

This figure is adapted from Blake and Mouton's (1984) approach to managerial leadership and conflict. Try to locate your usual conflict style on this grid. How well does this style work for you?

www.researchnavigator.com

Find Answers: Try finding answers to one of the following questions, or design a research study to answer it: Are people who give lots of backchanneling cues perceived in the same way as people who give few or no backchanneling cues? Are men or women more likely to use avoidance (or blame, force, manipulation, ridicule, silencers, beltlining, gunnysacking, or personal rejection) as a conflict strategy in romantic relationships? What kinds of people are high argumentatives?

Before and After the Conflict

If you are to make interpersonal conflict truly productive, you will need to consider a few suggestions for preparing for the conflict and for using the conflict as a method for relational growth.

Before the Conflict   Try to arrange to fight in private (assuming there's no danger that violence will occur). The reason is that in front of others you may not be willing to be totally honest. You also run the risk of incurring resentment and hostility by embarrassing your partner in front of other people. If there is danger of violence resulting from the conflict, however, then it may be wise to air differences in front of trusted others.

Although conflicts typically arise at the most inopportune times, you can choose the time when you will try to resolve them. For example, the moment when your partner comes home after a hard day of work may not be the right time for a confrontation. Make sure you both are relatively free of other problems and ready to deal with the conflict at hand.

Fight about problems you can solve. Fighting about past behaviors or about family members or situations over which you have no control is usually counterproductive.

After the Conflict   Learn from the conflict and from the process you went through in trying to resolve it. For example, try to identify the fight strategies that aggravated the situation and those that were generally effective. Consider the usefulness of a cooling-off period and the need for extra space during conflict. Try to identify what causes minor issues to escalate into major arguments and how such issues might be confronted before erupting.

Keep the conflict in perspective; don't blow it out of proportion. Also, avoid the tendency to see any and all disagreements as inevitably leading to major fights.

Attack your negative feelings. Negative feelings frequently arise because people use unfair fight strategies. Resolve surely to avoid such unfair tactics in the future; but at the same time let go of guilt and of blame toward both yourself and your partner.

Increase the exchange of rewards and cherishing behaviors, to demonstrate your positive feelings and to show that you are over the conflict. It's a good way of saying you want the relationship to survive and flourish.

Listening to Conflict Starters

Usually, conflicts develop over a period of time; they begin with a word here and a disagreement there, and eventually a fully developed conflict blows up in your face. Recognizing the beginnings of conflict may help you defuse a problem issue or bring it into the open before it explodes. The skill, of course, is to be able to hear these beginnings in your own speech and in that of others. Here are a few types of potential conflict starters:

- I can't bear another weekend sitting home watching television. I'm not going to do it.
- You think I'm fat, don't you?
- Just leave me alone.
- You never think I contribute anything to these department meetings, do you?
- You should have been more available when he needed us. You were always at work.
- You shouldn't have said that. I hate when you do that.

Applying Listening Skills

What suggestions would you give to someone confronted with each of these statements? What suggestions would you give to the person making these statements?

Effective Conflict Management

Throughout the process of resolving a conflict, avoid the common but damaging strategies that can destroy a relationship. At the same time, consciously apply strategies that will help resolve the conflict and even improve the relationship; research finds that using productive conflict strategies can have lots of beneficial effects (Weitzman & Weitzman, 2000; Weitzman, 2001). Here we consider eight general strategies, each of which has a destructive and a productive dimension: win–lose and win–win strategies, avoidance and fair fighting, force and talk nonassertive and assertive strategies, gunnysacking and present focus, face-enhancing and face-detracting strategies, attack and acceptance, and verbal aggressiveness and argumentativeness.

> **❝** Honest disagreement is often a good sign of progress. **❞**
>
> —Gandhi

Win–Lose and Win–Win Strategies

In any interpersonal conflict, you have a choice. You can look for solutions in which one person wins—usually you—and the other person loses (win–lose solutions). Or you can look for solutions in which you and the other person both win (win–win solutions). Obviously, win–win solutions are more desirable, at least when the conflict is interpersonal. Too often, however, we fail even to consider the possibility of win–win solutions and to ask what they might be.

For example, let's say that I want to spend our money on a new car (my old one is unreliable), but you want to spend it on a vacation (you are exhausted and feel the need for a rest). In the best circumstances, we learn what each of us really wants through our conflict and its resolution. We may then be able to figure out a way for each of us to get what we want. For example, I might accept a good used car, and you might accept a less expensive vacation. This solution will satisfy both of us—it's a win–win solution.

> **❝** The aim of an argument or discussion should not be victory, but progress. **❞**
>
> —Joseph Joubert

Avoidance and Fighting Actively

Avoidance is physical or psychological withdrawal from the conflict situation. Sometimes it involves physical flight: You leave the scene of the conflict (walk out of the apartment or go to another part of the office or shop). Sometimes avoidance involves setting up a physical barrier, such as blasting the stereo to drown out all conversation. Sometimes it takes the form of emotional or intellectual withdrawal. In this case, you leave the conflict psychologically by not dealing with any of the arguments or problems raised. In all its forms, avoidance is unproductive as a conflict strategy.

Skill development experience

Generating Win–Win Solutions

For any one situation below, *(a)* generate as many win–lose solutions as you can—solutions in which one person wins and the other loses; *(b)* generate as many possible win–win solutions as you feel the individuals involved in the conflict could reasonably accept; and *(c)* explain in one sentence the difference between win–lose and win–win solutions.

1. Pat and Chris plan to take a two-week vacation. Pat wants to go to the shore and relax by the water. Chris wants to go to the mountains and go hiking and camping.
2. Pat recently got an unexpected $3,000 bonus and wants to buy a new computer and printer. Chris wants to take a much needed vacation.
3. Pat hangs around the house in underwear. Chris hates this, and they argue about it almost daily.

This does not mean that taking time out to cool off is never useful, however. Sometimes it is. In a conflict via e-mail, for example, delaying your response is an easy-to-use and often effective strategy. When you've had time to think things out more logically and calmly, you'll be better able to respond constructively, resolve the conflict, and get the relationship back on a less hostile plane.

In general, instead of avoiding the issues, take an active role in your interpersonal conflicts. Don't close your ears or mind. The point is that if you wish to resolve conflicts, you need to confront them actively.

Another part of active fighting involves taking responsibility for your thoughts and feelings. For example, when you disagree with your partner or find fault with her or his behavior, take responsibility for these feelings, using I-messages as described earlier in this chapter. Say, for example, "I disagree with . . ." or "I don't like it when you. . . ." Avoid statements that deny your responsibility—for example, "Everybody thinks you're wrong about . . ." or "Chris thinks you shouldn't. . . ."

Force and Talk

When confronted with conflict, many people prefer not to deal with the issues but rather to force their position on the other person. **Force** may be emotional or physical. In either case, however, the conflict fails to resolve the issues at hand, and the person who "wins" is the one who exerts the most force. This unproductive technique is common among warring nations, children, and even some normally sensible and mature adults. Force often seems to be the technique of those who are dissatisfied with the power they perceive themselves to have in a relationship (Ronfeldt, Kimerling, & Arias, 1998). This is surely one of the most serious problems confronting relationships today—although many approach it as if it were of only minor importance or even something humorous, as in the cartoon below.

More than 50 percent of both single and married couples in many studies report that they have experienced physical violence in their relationship. If we add symbolic violence (for example, threatening to hit the other person or throwing something), the percentages are above 60 percent for singles and above 70 percent for marrieds (Marshall & Rose, 1987). In another study, 47 percent of a sample of 410 college students reported some experience with violence in a dating relationship. In most cases the violence was reciprocal—each person in the relationship used violence. In cases in which only one person was violent, the research results are conflicting. For example, Deal and Wampler (1986) found that in cases in which one partner was violent, the aggressor was significantly more often the female partner. Earlier research found a similar sex difference (e.g., Cate, Henton, Koval, Christopher, & Lloyd, 1982). Other research, however, has found that the popular belief that men are more likely than women to use force is indeed valid (DeTurck, 1987): Men are more apt than women to use violent methods to achieve compliance.

One of the most puzzling findings is that many victims of violence interpret it as a sign of love. For some reason, they see being beaten, verbally abused, or raped as a sign that their partner is fully in love with them. Many victims, in fact, accept the blame for contributing to the violence instead of blaming their partners (Gelles & Cornell, 1985).

"What's amazing to me is that this late in the game we *still* have to settle our differences with rocks."

The only real alternative to force is talk. Instead of using force, we need to talk and listen. The qualities of openness, empathy, and positiveness discussed earlier, for example, are suitable starting points.

Nonassertive and Assertive Strategies

Nonassertiveness, another unproductive strategy, is a failure to express your thoughts and feelings in certain or all communication situations. Nonassertive people fail to assert their rights. In many instances these people too often do what others tell them to do—parents, employers, and the like—without questioning and without concern for what is best for them. They operate on the basis of a "you win, I lose" philosophy, giving others what they want without concern for themselves (Lloyd, 1995). Nonassertive people often ask permission from others to do what is their perfect right. They are often anxious in social situations, and their self-esteem is likely to be low.

Assertiveness is behavior that enables you to act in your own best interests *without* denying or infringing on the rights of others. Not surprisingly, assertiveness is especially helpful in interpersonal conflict situations (Fodor & Collier, 2001). Assertive people have an "I win, you win" philosophy; they assume that both parties can gain something in an interpersonal conflict. Assertive people speak their minds and welcome others' doing likewise. Assertive people also tend to be more positive and to score higher than others on measures of hopefulness (Velting, 1999).

There are wide cultural differences in assertiveness, however. For example, individualistic cultures are more likely to extol the values of assertiveness than collectivist cultures. Cultures that stress competition, individual success, and independence tend to value assertiveness more; cultures that stress cooperation, group success, and the interdependence of all members tend to value it less. American students, for example, are found to be significantly more assertive than Japanese or Korean students (Thompson, Klopf, & Ishii, 1991; Thompson & Klopf, 1991). Thus, in situations that call for assertiveness in one culture, assertiveness may create problems in another culture.

Here are a few suggestions to help you communicate more assertively:

- Describe the problem; don't evaluate or judge it: "We both want what's right for the kids, but we haven't gotten together to discuss the problems." Be sure to use I-messages and to avoid messages that accuse or blame the other person.

- State how the problem affects you: "I'm worrying about this during the day and it's affecting my job."

- Propose solutions that are workable and that allow both people to save face: "Let's make some time tomorrow to discuss how we want to handle things."

- Confirm your understanding: "Would that be okay? Say, about eight?"

Gunnysacking and Present Focus

A gunnysack is a large bag, usually made of burlap. As a conflict strategy, **gunnysacking** is the practice of storing up grievances for unloading at another time. The immediate occasion may be relatively simple (or so it might seem at first); for example, perhaps you come home late one night without calling. Instead of arguing about this, the gunnysacker unloads all past grievances: the birthday you forgot two years ago, the time you arrived late for dinner last month, the hotel reservations you forgot to make. But this strategy is unproductive. As you probably know from experience, gunnysacking begets gunnysacking. When one person gunnysacks, the other person often reciprocates. As a result, two people end up dumping stored-up grievances on one another. Frequently the original problem never gets addressed. Instead, resentment and hostility escalate.

❝ Get bored with your past; it's over. ❞

—Caroline Myss

Responding to Power Plays

People often use power unfairly in conversations, whether at home or in the workplace. Here are three examples of **power plays,** or consistent patterns of behavior designed to control another person (Steiner, 1981).

In *Nobody Upstairs* the player ignores socially and commonly accepted (but unspoken) rules, such as rules against opening other people's mail or going through their wallets. The power play takes the form of an expressed ignorance of the rules: "I didn't know you didn't want me to look in your wallet." In *You Owe Me* a person, often a friend or coworker, does something for you and then asks for something in return: "But I lent you money when you needed it." In *Thought Stoppers* someone literally stops you from thinking and from expressing your thoughts, often by interrupting, using profanity, or shouting.

What do you do when confronted by a power play (Steiner, 1981)? Instead of ignoring it or treating it as an isolated instance, try a more effective cooperative approach. The recommended strategy consists of three steps:

- Express your feelings; tell the person that you're angry or disturbed by this behavior: "I'm angry that you persist in opening my mail."

- Identify the behavior to which you object in language that describes rather than evaluates: "You've opened my mail four times this week."

- State a cooperative response, in a cooperative tone: "I want to open my mail. If there's anything in it that concerns you, I'll let you know."

Enhancing Your Communication Power

How would you respond to someone who engaged in still another type of power play—consistently making your contributions seem trivial and unworthy of consideration by saying, for example, "You've got to be kidding" or "You can't be serious"?

A present focus is far more constructive than gunnysacking. Focus your conflict on the here and now rather than on issues that occurred in the past. Similarly, focus your conflict on the person with whom you are fighting, not on the person's mother, child, or friends.

Face-Enhancing and Face-Detracting Strategies

Another dimension of conflict strategies is that of face orientation. Protecting your image, or face, particularly in the midst of conflict, is important to everyone; it's especially important to members of the collectivist cultures of Asia (Zane & Yeh, 2002). Face-detracting or face-attacking strategies involve treating the other person as incompetent or untrustworthy, as unable or bad (Donahue & Kolt, 1992). Such attacks can vary from mildly embarrassing the other person to severely damaging his or her ego or reputation. When such attacks become extreme, they may be similar to verbal aggressiveness—a tactic we'll examine shortly. So be especially careful to avoid "fighting words"—words that are sure to escalate the conflict rather than to help resolve it. Words like *stupid, liar,* and *bitch,* as well as words like *always* and *never* (as in "you always . . ." or "you never . . ."), invariably create additional problems.

One popular but destructive, face-detracting strategy is **beltlining** (Bach & Wyden, 1968). Much like fighters in a ring, each of us has a psychological or emotional "beltline." When you hit below it, you can inflict serious injury. When you hit above the belt, however, the person is able to absorb the blow. With most interpersonal relationships, especially those of long standing, you know where the beltline is. You know, for example, that to hit Pat with the inability to have children is to hit below the belt. You know that to hit Chris with the failure to get a permanent job is to

Web Explorations

To further explore interpersonal conflict, see one or more of the exercises and self-tests at www.ablongman.com/devito: (17) Power Plays, (18) Dealing with Conflict Starters, (19) Analyzing a Conflict Episode, (20) Confronting Intercultural Obstacles, (21) How Verbally Aggressive Are You? and (22) How Flexible Are You in Communication?

hit below the belt. This type of face-detracting strategy causes all persons involved added problems. Keep blows to areas your opponent can absorb and handle.

Face-enhancing techniques involve helping the other person maintain a positive image as someone who is competent and trustworthy, able and good. There is some evidence to show that even when you get what you want, say at bargaining, it is wise to help the other person retain positive face. This makes it less likely that future conflicts will arise (Donahue & Kolt, 1992). Not surprisingly, people are more likely to make a greater effort to support the listener's "face" if they like the listener than if they don't (Meyer, 1994). Confirming the other person's definition of self (Chapter 5), avoiding attack and **blame,** and using excuses and apologies as appropriate are some generally useful face-enhancing strategies.

“ In conflict, be fair and generous. **”**

—Tao Te Ching

Attack and Acceptance

An attack can come in many forms. In **personal rejection,** for example, one party to a conflict withholds love and affection. He or she seeks to win the argument by getting the other person to break down in the face of this withdrawal. In withdrawing affection, the individual hopes to make the other person question his or her own self-worth. Once the other is demoralized and feels less than worthy, it is relatively easy for the "rejector" to get his or her way. The "rejector," in other words, holds out the renewal of love and affection as a reward for resolving the conflict in his or her favor.

As you can readily understand, this kind of personal attack is never a productive conflict strategy if you want a relationship to survive. Instead, it's vital that you express positive feelings for the other person and for the relationship between the two of you. In fact, research shows that positiveness is a crucial factor in the survival of a relationship (Gottman, 1994). When a conflict involves rejection or other forms of attack, many harsh words will probably be exchanged and later regretted. As you saw in Chapter 1, communication is irreversible; the words cannot be unsaid or uncommunicated, but they can be partially offset by the expression of positive statements. If you are engaged in combat with someone you love, remember that you are fighting with a loved one and express that feeling: "I love you very much, but I still don't want your mother on vacation with us. I want to be alone with you."

Communicating ethically

Ethical Fighting

This chapter has placed strong emphasis on distinctions between effective and ineffective conflict strategies. But all communication strategies also have an ethical dimension, and we need to look not only at the usefulness but also at the ethical implications of different conflict resolution strategies. For example:

- Does conflict avoidance have an ethical dimension? For example, is it unethical for one relationship partner to refuse to discuss disagreements?
- Can the use of physical force to influence another person ever be ethical? Can you identify a situation in which it would be appropriate for someone with greater physical strength to overpower someone else so as to make the other person accept his or her point of view?
- Are face-detracting strategies inherently unethical, or might it be appropriate to use them in certain situations? Can you identify such situations?
- What are the ethical implications of verbal aggressiveness?

What Would You Do?

At your highly stressful job you sometimes use cocaine with your colleagues. This happens several times a month, and you don't use drugs of any kind at any other times. Your partner asks you if you take drugs. Because it's such a limited use and because you know that admitting this will cause a huge conflict in your already shaky relationship, you wonder if you can ethically lie about this. What would you do?

Verbal Aggressiveness and Argumentativeness

An especially interesting perspective on conflict has emerged from work on verbal aggressiveness and argumentativeness (Infante & Rancer, 1982; Infante, 1988; Infante & Wigley, 1986).

Verbal aggressiveness is an unproductive strategy in which one person tries to win an argument by inflicting psychological pain—by attacking the other person's self-concept. It is a type of disconfirmation in that it seeks to discredit the person's view of himself or herself. Aggressive talk often leads to physical force (Infante & Wigley, 1986; Infante, Sabourin, Rudd, & Shannon, 1990; Infante, Riddle, Horvath, & Tumlin, 1992). And, not surprisingly, if people see you as verbally aggressive, they will dislike you (Myers & Johnson, 2003).

Argumentativeness, on the other hand (and contrary to popular usage), can be a productive quality in conflict resolution. Argumentative people are willing to argue for a point of view, to speak their mind on significant issues. Argumentativeness is the preferred alternative to verbal aggressiveness for dealing with disagreements. Before reading about ways to increase your argumentativeness, take the self-test "How argumentative are you?"

VIEWPOINT

What is the single most important principle for engaging in productive interpersonal conflict with a work colleague? How can following this principle impact on your work relationship?

Test Yourself

How Argumentative Are You?

INSTRUCTIONS: This questionnaire contains statements about approaches to conflict. Indicate how often each statement is true for you personally, using the following scale: 1 = almost never true; 2 = rarely true; 3 = occasionally true; 4 = often true; and 5 = almost always true.

_2_ **❶** While in an argument, I worry that the person I am arguing with will form a negative impression of me.

_5_ **❷** Arguing over controversial issues improves my intelligence.

_3_ **❸** I enjoy avoiding arguments.

_4_ **❹** I am energetic and enthusiastic when I argue.

_2_ **❺** Once I finish an argument, I promise myself that I will not get into another.

_3_ **❻** Arguing with a person creates more problems for me than it solves.

_4_ **❼** I have a pleasant, good feeling when I win a point in an argument.

_1_ **❽** When I finish arguing with anyone, I feel nervous and upset.

_1_ **❾** I enjoy a good argument over a controversial issue.

_3_ **❿** I get an unpleasant feeling when I realize I am about to get into an argument.

_4_ **⓫** I enjoy defending my point of view on an issue.

_4_ **⓬** I am happy when I keep an argument from happening.

_4_ **⓭** I do not like to miss the opportunity to argue a controversial issue.

_3_ **⓮** I prefer being with people who rarely disagree with me.

_4_ **⓯** I consider an argument an exciting intellectual challenge.

_2_ **⓰** I find myself unable to think of effective points during an argument.

_5_ ⑰ I feel refreshed and satisfied after an argument on a controversial issue.

_4_ ⑱ I have the ability to do well in an argument.

_4_ ⑲ I try to avoid getting into arguments.

_2_ ⑳ I feel excitement when I expect that a conversation I am in is leading to an argument.

HOW DID YOU DO? To compute your argumentativeness score, follow these steps:

1. Add your scores on items 2, 4, 7, 9, 11, 13, 15, 17, 18, and 20.
2. Add 60 to the sum obtained in step 1.
3. Add your scores on items 1, 3, 5, 6, 8, 10, 12, 14, 16, 19.
4. To compute your argumentativeness score, subtract the total obtained in step 3 from the total obtained in step 2.

The following guidelines will help you interpret your score:

Scores between 73 and 100 indicate high argumentativeness.
Scores between 56 and 72 indicate moderate argumentativeness.
Scores between 20 and 55 indicate low argumentativeness.

Generally, those who score high in argumentativeness have a strong tendency to state their position on controversial issues and to argue against the positions of others. A high scorer sees arguing as exciting and intellectually challenging, and as an opportunity to win a kind of contest.

The person who scores low in argumentativeness tries to prevent arguments. This person experiences satisfaction not from arguing but from avoiding arguments. The low-argumentative person sees arguing as unpleasant and unsatisfying. Not surprisingly, this person has little confidence in his or her ability to argue effectively.

The moderately argumentative person possesses some of the qualities of the high-argumentative person and some of the qualities of the low-argumentative person.

WHAT WILL YOU DO? The researchers who developed this test note that both high and low argumentatives may experience communication difficulties. The high-argumentative person, for example, may argue needlessly, too often, and too forcefully. The low-argumentative person, on the other hand, may avoid taking a stand even when it seems necessary. People scoring somewhere in the middle are probably the more interpersonally skilled and adaptable, arguing when it is necessary but avoiding the many arguments that are needless and repetitive. Does your experience support this observation? What specific actions might you take to improve your argumentativeness?

Source: This scale was developed by Dominic Infante and Andrew Rancer and appears in Dominic Infante and Andrew Rancer, "A Conceptualization and Measure of Argumentativeness," *Journal of Personality Assessment, 46* (1982), 72–80. Reprinted by permission of Lawrence Erlbaum Associates and the author.

To cultivate argumentativeness and at the same time to prevent it from degenerating into aggressiveness, treat disagreements as objectively as possible. That is, avoid assuming that because someone takes issue with your position or your interpretation, they are attacking you as a person (Infante, 1988). Also, avoid attacking the other person (rather than the person's arguments); even if this gave you a temporary tactical advantage, it would probably backfire at some later time and make your relationship more difficult. Center your arguments on issues rather than people.

In arguing remember to affirm the other person's sense of competence; compliment the other person as appropriate. Allow the other person to save face; never humiliate the other person. Avoid interrupting; allow the other person to state her or his position fully before you respond. Stress equality and the similarities that you share;

What Do You Say?

Verbal Aggressiveness: Your partner persists in being verbally aggressive whenever you have an argument. Regardless of what the conflict is about, you find your self-concept under attack. You've had enough and you want to stop this kind of aggression. *What do you say? Through what channel?*

stress your areas of agreement before attacking the disagreements. Throughout the conflict episode, express interest in the other person's position, attitude, and point of view. And again, be especially careful to avoid disconfirmation (Chapter 5).

Summary of Concepts and Skills

In this chapter we looked at the nature of interpersonal communication, focusing specifically on the qualities that make for effectiveness in conversation and in interpersonal conflict.

1. The conversation process consists of at least five steps: opening, feedforward, business, feedback, and closing.
2. General conversational skills that support communication effectiveness are mindfulness, flexibility, cultural sensitivity, and metacommunication.
3. The qualities of interpersonal communication effectiveness are openness, empathy, positiveness, immediacy, interaction management, expressiveness, and other-orientation.
4. Interpersonal conflict (in face-to-face situations and in cyberspace) can be content or relationship oriented but is usually a combination of both, can have both negative and positive effects, always occurs within a cultural context, and may be pursued with a variety of conflict styles.
5. Useful guides to fair fighting are: Look for win–win strategies; fight actively; use talk instead of force; use assertive rather than nonassertive messages; focus on the present rather than gunnysacking; use face-enhancing instead of face-detracting strategies; express acceptance rather than attacking the other person; and use your skills in argumentation, not in verbal aggressiveness.

The skills covered in this chapter are vital to effective interpersonal interactions and relationships. Check your ability to apply these skills, using the following rating scale: 1 = almost always; 2 = often; 3 = sometimes; 4 = rarely; and 5 = hardly ever.

_____ 1. I open conversations with comfort and confidence.

_____ 2. I use feedforward that is appropriate to my message and purpose.

_____ 3. I exchange roles as speaker and listener to maintain mutual conversational satisfaction.

_____ 4. I vary my feedback as appropriate on the basis of positiveness, focus (person or message), immediacy, degree of monitoring, and supportiveness.

_____ 5. I close conversations at the appropriate time and with the appropriate parting signals.

_____ 6. I approach communication situations with an appropriate degree of mindfulness.

_____ 7. I am flexible in the way I communicate and adjust my communications on the basis of the unique situation.

_____ 8. I am sensitive to the cultural differences that influence the ways conversation and conflict are pursued.

_____ 9. I use metacommunication to clarify ambiguous meanings.

_____ 10. I practice an appropriate degree of openness.

_____ 11. I communicate empathy to others.

_____ 12. I express supportiveness.

_____ 13. I communicate positiveness in attitudes and through stroking others.

_____ 14. I express equality in my interpersonal interactions.

_____ 15. I communicate confidence in voice and bodily actions.

_____ 16. I express immediacy both verbally and nonverbally.

_____ 17. I manage interpersonal interactions to the satisfaction of both parties.

_____ 18. I self-monitor my verbal and nonverbal behaviors in order to communicate the desired impression.

_____ 19. I communicate expressiveness verbally and nonverbally.

_____ 20. I communicate other-orientation in my interactions.

_____ 21. I avoid using unproductive methods of conflict resolution.

_____ 22. I make active use of fair fighting guides.

Key Word Quiz

Write T for those statements that are true and F for those that are false. For those that are false, replace the italicized term with the correct term.

_____ 1. The small talk that paves the way for the big talk is known as *phatic communication*.

_____ 2. Positive–negative, person-focused–message-focused, immediate–delayed, low-monitoring–high-monitoring, and supportive–critical are dimensions of *feedforward*.

_____ 3. Creating and recreating categories, being open to new information and to different points of view, and not relying too heavily on first impressions are ways to achieve *flexibility*.

_____ 4. Communication about communication is called *metacommunication*.

_____ 5. The ability to feel as another person feels is known as *sympathy*.

_____ 6. The degree to which the speaker and the listener are connected or joined is known as *interaction management*.

_____ 7. The management of interpersonal interactions to the satisfaction of both parties is referred to as *expressiveness*.

_____ 8. The process of storing up grievances so that you can unload them at another time (usually during an interpersonal conflict) is known as *beltlining*.

_____ 9. Your willingness to defend a point of view, to speak your mind on significant issues, is called *argumentativeness*.

_____ 10. Nobody Upstairs, You Owe Me, and Thought Stoppers are examples of *attack strategies*.

Answers: TRUE: 1, 4, 9; FALSE: 2 (*feedback*), 3 (*mindfulness*), 5 (*empathy*), 6 (*immediacy*), 7 (*interaction management*), 8 (*gunnysacking*), 10 (*power plays*)

8 Interpersonal Relationships

Chapter Concepts	Chapter Skills	
This chapter examines the nature of relationships, the stages you go through in creating relationships, and the influence of culture and gender on your interpersonal relationships.	After completing this chapter, you should be able to:	
Characteristics of Interpersonal Relationships	identify the characteristics of interpersonal relationships and their advantages and disadvantages.	
Stages in Interpersonal Relationships	identify the major relationship stages and the types of communication occurring in each.	
Relationships in Contexts of Culture and Gender, Technology, and Work	explain the cultural, technological, and workplace influences on interpersonal relationships.	

Contact with other human beings is so important that when you're deprived of it for long periods, depression sets in, self-doubt surfaces, and you may find it difficult to manage even the basics of daily life. Research shows clearly that the most important contributor to happiness—outranking money, job, and sex—is a close relationship with one other person (Freedman, 1978; Laroche & deGrace, 1997). The desire for relationships is universal; they're important to men and to women, to homosexuals and to heterosexuals, to young and to old (Huston & Schwartz, 1995).

This chapter looks at this all-important topic. We'll explore the characteristics of interpersonal relationships; the stages relationships go through; and the influences of culture, gender, technology, and work on relationships. Throughout, we'll focus on ways to improve a wide variety of interpersonal relationships.

Characteristics of Interpersonal Relationships

Relationships exist on a continuum, from the impersonal at one end to highly personal (that is, interpersonal) at the other end. Interpersonal relationships are those that exist between people who are interdependent; that is, one person's behavior has a significant impact on the other person. We can distinguish interpersonal relationships from impersonal relationships on the basis of three main factors: psychological data, explanatory knowledge, and personally established rules.

> **"** Communication is to a relationship what breathing is to maintaining life. **"**
>
> —Virginia Satir

Psychological Data

In impersonal relationships people respond to each other chiefly as members of the class or group to which each belongs. For example, initially you respond to a particular college professor as you respond to college professors in general. Similarly, the college professor responds to you as he or she responds to students generally. As your relationship becomes more personal, however, both of you begin to respond to each other not as members of groups but as unique individuals. Put differently, in impersonal relationships the social or cultural role of the person governs your interaction; in personal or interpersonal relationships, the psychological uniqueness of the person tells you how to interact.

This progression from social to psychological data happens in the United States and in most European cultures. In many Asian and African cultures, however, the individual's group membership is always important; it never recedes into the background.

Thus, in these cultures a person's group membership (or social data) is always important, even in the closest intimate relationships—often more important than the person's individual or psychological characteristics (Moghaddam, Taylor, & Wright, 1993).

Explanatory Knowledge   In impersonal relationships you can do little more than *describe* a person or a person's way of communicating. As you get to know someone a bit better, you can *predict* his or her behavior. If you get to know the person even better, you'll become able to *explain* the behavior. The college professor, in an impersonal relationship, may be able to describe, say, your habitual lateness. Perhaps the professor also can predict that you'll be five minutes late to class each Friday. In an interpersonal situation, however, the professor can go beyond these levels to explain the behavior—in this case, to give reasons why you're late.

Personally Established Rules

In impersonal relationships social norms set the rules of interaction. For example, in such relationships students and professors behave toward one another according to the social norms established by their culture and society. However, as a relationship between a student and a professor becomes interpersonal, the social rules no longer totally regulate the interaction. Student and professor begin to establish rules of their own—largely because they begin to see each other as unique individuals rather than merely as members of the social categories "student" and "professor."

A good way to begin the study of interpersonal relationships is to examine your own relationships (past, present, or those you look forward to) by taking the self-test "What do your relationships do for you?" It highlights the advantages and the disadvantages that relationships serve.

Test Yourself

What Do Your Relationships Do for You?

INSTRUCTIONS: Focus on your own relationships in general (friendship, romantic, family, and work), or focus on one particular relationship (say, your life partner, your child, or your best friend), or focus on one type of relationship (say, friendships). Respond to the following by indicating the extent to which your relationship(s) serve each of these functions. Use a 10-point scale on which 1 indicates that your relationship(s) never serve this function, 10 indicates that your relationship(s) always serve this function, and the numbers in between indicate levels between these extremes.

_____ ❶ My relationships help to lessen my loneliness.

_____ ❷ My relationships put uncomfortable pressure on me to expose my vulnerabilities.

_____ ❸ My relationships help me to secure intellectual, physical, and emotional stimulation.

_____ ❹ My relationships increase my obligations.

_____ ❺ My relationships help me gain in self-knowledge and in self-esteem.

_____ ❻ My relationships prevent me from developing other relationships.

_____ ❼ My relationships help enhance my physical and emotional health.

_____ ❽ My relationships scare me because they may be difficult to dissolve.

_____ ❾ My relationships maximize my pleasures and minimize my pains.

_____ ❿ My relationships hurt me.

HOW DID YOU DO? The numbers from 1 to 10 that you used to respond to each statement should give you some idea of how strongly your relationships serve these func-

" Love is a fire. But whether it is going to warm your hearth or burn down your house, you can never tell. **"**

—Joan Crawford

tions. The odd-numbered statements (1, 3, 5, 7, and 9) express what most people would consider advantages of interpersonal relationships:

1. One of the major benefits of relationships is that they help to lessen loneliness (Rokach & Brock, 1995). They make you feel that someone cares, that someone likes you, that someone will protect you, that someone ultimately will love you.
3. As plants are *heliotropic* and orient themselves to light, humans are *stimulotropic* and orient themselves to sources of stimulation (Davis, 1973). Human contact is one of the best ways to secure this stimulation—intellectual, physical, and emotional.
5. Through contact with others you learn about yourself and see yourself from different perspectives and in different roles: as a child or parent, as a coworker, as a manager, as a best friend. Healthy interpersonal relationships help enhance self-esteem and self-worth. Simply having a friend or romantic partner helps you feel desirable and worthy, at least most of the time.
7. Research consistently shows that interpersonal relationships contribute significantly to physical and emotional health (Rosen, 1998; Goleman, 1995a; Rosengren et al., 1993; Pennebacker, 1991) and to personal happiness (Berscheid & Reis, 1998). Without close interpersonal relationships you're more likely to become depressed; this depression, in turn, can contribute significantly to physical illness. Isolation, in fact, contributes as much to mortality as high blood pressure, high cholesterol, obesity, smoking, or lack of physical exercise (Goleman, 1995a).
9. The most general function served by interpersonal relationships, and a benefit that encompasses all the others, is that of maximizing pleasure and minimizing pain. Your good friends, for example, will make you feel even better about your good fortune and less hurt when you're confronted with hardships.

The even-numbered statements (2, 4, 6, 8, and 10) express what most people consider disadvantages of interpersonal relationships:

2. Close relationships put pressure on you to reveal yourself and to expose your vulnerabilities. This is generally worthwhile in the context of a supporting and caring relationship, but it may backfire if the relationship deteriorates and these weaknesses are used against you.
4. Close relationships increase your obligations to other people, sometimes to a great extent. Your time is no longer entirely your own. And although you enter relationships to spend more time with these special people, you also incur time (and perhaps financial) obligations with which you may not be happy.
6. Close relationships can result in your abandoning other relationships. Sometimes this happens with someone you like but your partner can't stand. More often, however, it's simply a matter of time and energy; relationships take a lot of both, and you have less to give to other and less intimate relationships.
8. The closer your relationship, the more emotionally difficult it will be to dissolve, a reality that may be uncomfortable for some people. If the relationship deteriorates, you may feel distress or depression. In some cultures, for example, religious pressures may prevent married couples from separating. And if lots of money is involved, dissolving a relationship can often mean giving up assets you've spent your life accumulating.
10. And, of course, your partner may break your heart. Your partner may leave you—against all your pleading and promises. Your hurt will be in proportion to how much you care and need your partner. If you care a great deal, you're likely to experience great hurt; if you care less, the hurt will be less—it's one of life's little ironies.

WHAT WILL YOU DO? One way to use this self-test is to consider how you might lessen the disadvantages of your interpersonal relationships, at least those disadvantages that you indicate are always or almost always present in your relationships. Consider, for example, if your own behaviors are contributing to the problems. For example, do you bury yourself in one or two relationships and discourage the development of others? At the same time, consider how you can maximize the advantages that your relationships currently serve.

www.researchnavigator.com

Read an Article: Read a scholarly or popular article on interpersonal relationships; the stages that relationships go through; or the influence of culture, gender, technology, or work on relationships. On the basis of this article, what can you add to the discussion presented here?

Reward and Coercive Power

You have **reward power** over a person if you have the ability to give that person rewards—whether material (money, promotion, jewelry) or social rewards (love, friendship, respect). Conversely, you have **coercive power** if you have the ability to remove rewards from that person or to administer punishments. Usually, if you have reward power you also have coercive power. For example, as a boss you can shower an employee with praise for a job well done and offer a nice year-end bonus (reward power), but you also can criticize and deny that same employee a promotion (coercive power).

Reward power increases attractiveness; we like those who have the power to reward us and who do in fact give us rewards. Coercive power, on the other hand, decreases attractiveness; we dislike those who have the power to punish us and who threaten us with punishment, whether they actually follow through or not.

Enhancing Your Communication Power

How might you use these types of power as a parent? As a teacher? As a friend?

 VIEWPOINT

Most research and theory argue that you develop an attraction to those who are similar to you. But consider, instead, that you actually develop repulsion for those who are dissimilar to you (Rosenbaum, 1986). For example, you may be repulsed by people who disagreed with you and therefore exclude them from those with whom you might develop a relationship. You'd therefore be left with a pool of possible partners who had ideas similar to yours. What do you think of this "repulsion hypothesis"? Do you and your relationship history more closely follow the predictions of repulsion theory or of the theory that attraction is most heavily influenced by similarity?

Stages in Interpersonal Relationships

You and another person don't become intimate friends immediately upon meeting. Rather, you build an intimate relationship gradually, through a series of steps or stages. The same is true of most relationships. To be sure, the "love at first sight" phenomenon creates a problem for this stage model of relationships. But rather than argue that such love cannot occur (my own feeling is that it can and frequently does), it seems wiser to claim simply that the stage model characterizes most relationships for most people most of the time.

The six-stage model in Figure 8.1 describes the main stages in most relationships: contact, involvement, intimacy, deterioration, repair, and dissolution. Each stage has an early and a late phase. These stages describe relationships as they are; they don't evaluate or prescribe how relationships should be. For a particular relationship, you might wish to modify the basic model. But as a general description of the course of relationships, the stages seem fairly standard. Do realize, of course, that both partners may not perceive their relationship in the same way; one person, for example, may see the relationship as having reached the intimate stage, but the other may not.

Contact

At the initial phase of the **contact** stage, there is some kind of *perceptual contact*—you see, hear, and perhaps smell the person. From this you get a physical picture—gender, approximate age, height, and so on. After this perception there is usually *interactional contact*. Here the contact is superficial and relatively impersonal. This is the stage at which you exchange basic information that is preliminary to any more intense involvement ("Hello, my name is Joe"); you initiate interaction ("May I join you?") and engage in invitational communication ("May I buy you a drink?"). According to some researchers, it's at this stage—

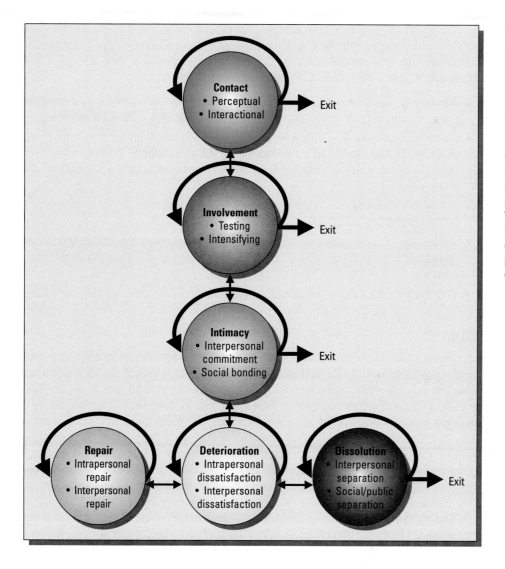

Figure **8.1**

A Six-Stage Model of Relationships
Because relationships differ so widely, it's best to think of this or any relationship model as a tool for talking about relationships rather than as a specific map that indicates how you move from one relationship position to another. Can you identify other steps or stages that would further explain what goes on in relationship development? What happens when the two people in a relationship experience the stages differently? Can you provide an example from literature or from your own experience?

within the first four minutes of initial interaction—that you decide whether you want to pursue the relationship (Zunin & Zunin, 1972).

At the contact stage, physical appearance is especially important because it's the most readily seen. Yet through verbal and nonverbal behaviors, qualities such as friendliness, warmth, openness, and dynamism are also revealed.

Involvement

At the **involvement** stage a sense of mutuality, of being connected, develops. Here you experiment and try to learn more about the other person. At the initial phase of involvement, a kind of *testing* goes on. You want to see whether your initial judgment proves reasonable. So you may ask questions: "Where do you work?" "What are you majoring in?" If you want to get to know the person even better, you might continue your involvement by intensifying your interaction and by beginning to reveal yourself, though in a preliminary way. In a dating relationship, you might, for example, use a variety of strategies to help you move to the next stage and perhaps to intimacy. For example, you might increase contact with your partner; give your partner tokens of affection such as gifts, cards, or flowers; increase your own personal attractiveness; do things that suggest intensifying the relationship, such as flirting or making your partner jealous; and become more physically intimate (Tolhuizen, 1989).

" True love comes quietly, without banners or flashing lights. If you hear bells, get your ears checked. "

—Erich Segal

What Do You Say?

Refusing a Date: A fellow student in one of your classes has asked you for a date for the last three weekends. You don't want to go, so each time you've made an excuse. But you realize that this can't go on; you want to end these embarrassing requests and refusals. *What do you say? Through what channel?*

Throughout the relationship process, but especially during the involvement and early intimacy stages, you test your partner; you try to find out how your partner feels about the relationship. Among the testing strategies you may use are these (Baxter & Wilmot, 1984; Bell & Buerkel-Rothfuss, 1990):

- *Directness*. You ask your partner directly how he or she feels, or you disclose your own feelings on the assumption that your partner also will self-disclose.
- *Indirect suggestion*. You may joke about a shared future together, touch more intimately, or hint that you're serious about the relationship. Similar responses from your partner will mean that he or she wishes to increase the intimacy of the relationship.
- *Public presentation*. You may try introducing your partner as your "boyfriend" or "girlfriend" to see how your partner responds.
- *Separation*. You separate yourself physically to see how the other person responds. If your partner calls, then you know he or she is interested in the relationship.
- *Third party*. You ask mutual friends about your partner's feelings and intentions.

Intimacy

The contact and involvement stages make up **relationship development**—a movement toward intimacy. At the **intimacy** stage you commit yourself still further to the other person and establish a relationship in which this individual becomes your best or closest friend, lover, or companion. You also come to share each other's social networks, a practice followed by members of widely different cultures (Gao & Gudykunst, 1995). Not surprisingly, your relationship satisfaction also increases with the move to this stage (Siavelis & Lamke, 1992). One research study defined intimacy as the feeling that you can be honest and open when talking about yourself and about thoughts and feelings that you don't reveal in other relationships (Mackey, Diemer, & O'Brien, 2000).

The intimacy stage usually divides itself into two phases. In the *interpersonal commitment* phase, the two people commit themselves to each other in a private way. In the *social bonding* phase, the commitment is made public—perhaps to family and friends, perhaps to the public at large. Here you and your partner become a unit, an identifiable pair.

When the intimacy stage involves a lifetime partnership, you face three main anxieties (Zimmer, 1986). *Security anxiety* involves the worry that your partner may leave you for someone else or that he or she will be sexually unfaithful. *Fulfillment anxiety* has to do with concerns that you may not be able to achieve a close, warm, and special rapport or that you won't be able to have an equal relationship. *Excitement anxiety* is concern that boredom and routine may set in or that you'll lose your freedom and become trapped.

Of course, not everyone strives for intimacy (Bartholomew, 1990; Thelen, Sherman, & Borst, 1998; Bumby & Hansen, 1997). Some people are so fearful of the consequences of intimacy that they actively avoid it. Others dismiss intimacy and defensively deny their need for more and deeper interpersonal contact. And still others, of course, are happy without an intimate relationship.

Intimacy and Risk   To some people relational intimacy seems extremely risky. To others, it involves only low risk.

Consider your own view of relationship risk by responding to the following questions.

1. Is it dangerous to get really close to people?
2. Are you afraid to get really close to someone because you might get hurt?

> ❝ True intimacy is a positive force only if it is a combining of strengths and energies with other mature persons for the continued growth of each. ❞
>
> —Leo F. Buscaglia

3. Do you find it difficult to trust other people?

4. Do you believe that the most important thing to consider in a relationship is whether you might get hurt?

People who answer yes to these and similar questions see intimacy as involving considerable risk (Pilkington & Richardson, 1988). Such people have fewer close friends, are less likely to have a romantic relationship, have less trust in others, have a lower level of dating assertiveness, have lower self-esteem, are more possessive and jealous in their love, and are generally less sociable and extroverted than those who see intimacy as involving little risk (Pilkington & Woods, 1999).

What Do You Say?

Relationship Stage: Your partner gives you a gift that's out of keeping with your perceived relationship stage. The gift is much too intimate and too expensive for the casual relationship you believe you are in. *What do you say? Through what channel?*

Intimacy and Social Penetration According to **social penetration theory,** as you progress from contact through involvement to intimacy, both the number of topics you talk about, or **breadth,** and the degree of "personalness" with which you pursue them, or **depth,** increase (Altman & Taylor, 1973; Hensley, 1996). Such increases are influenced greatly by attitude similarity; when you perceive attitude similarity between yourself and another person, you're more likely to increase social penetration than if you didn't see this similarity (Hammer, 1986). Visualize a relationship as a circle divided into various parts (to represent the topics of interpersonal communication or the breadth of the relationship) and into layers (to represent the degree of personalness with which you talk or the depth of the relationship). For illustration, see Figure 8.2 on page 170. Each circle in the figure contains eight topic areas to depict breadth (labeled A through H) and five levels of intimacy to depict depth (represented by the concentric circles). Note that in circle 1, only three topic areas are penetrated. Of these, two are penetrated only to the first level and one to the second. In this type of interaction, three topic areas are discussed, and only at rather superficial levels. This is the type of relationship you might have with an acquaintance. Circle 2 represents a more intense relationship with greater breadth and depth; more topics are discussed, and to deeper levels of penetration. This is the type of relationship you might have with a friend. Circle 3 represents a still more intense relationship. Here there is considerable breadth (seven of the eight areas are penetrated) and depth (most of the areas are penetrated to the deepest levels). This is the type of relationship you might have with a lover or a parent.

Skill development experience

Talking Cherishing

Cherishing behaviors are an especially insightful way to affirm another person and to increase favor exchange, a concept that comes from the work of William Lederer (1984). Cherishing behaviors are those small gestures you enjoy receiving from your partner (a smile, a wink, a squeeze, a kiss, a phone call).

Prepare a list of 10 cherishing behaviors that you would like to receive from your real or imagined relationship partner. Identify cherishing behaviors that are

• specific and positive—nothing overly general or negative

• focused on the present and future rather than on issues about which the partners have argued in the past

• capable of being performed daily

• easily executed—nothing for which you really have to go out of your way to accomplish

To implement a pattern of cherishing in a relationship, each partner would prepare such a list. Then the partners would exchange lists and, ideally, perform the hoped-for cherishing behaviors during their normal activities. In time these behaviors should become a normal part of their interaction.

Figure **8.2**

Models of Social Penetration
How accurately do the concepts of breadth and depth express your communication in relationships of different intensities? Can you identify other aspects of messages that change as you go from talking to an acquaintance, to a friend, or to an intimate?

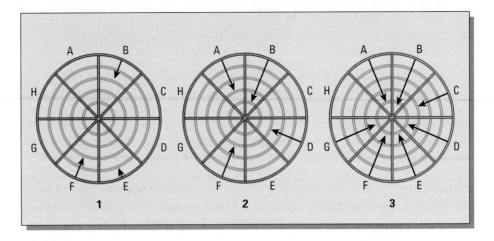

All relationships—friendships, loves, families—may be described in terms of breadth and depth. In its initial stage a relationship is normally characterized by narrow breadth (few topics are discussed) and shallow depth (the topics are discussed only superficially). As the relationship grows in intensity and intimacy, breadth and depth increase. Equally important, these increases are seen as comfortable, normal, and natural progressions. At the same time, your communication becomes more personalized, more synchronized, and easier (Gudykunst, Nishida, & Chua, 1987).

Intimacy and Love   Most people think of the intimacy stage as the stage of falling in love. This is the time when you "become lovers" and commit yourselves to being romantic partners. It's important to note, however, that the word *love* means very different things to different people. To illustrate this important concept and to give you an opportunity to explore your own love preferences, take the following self-test, "What kind of lover are you?"

Test Yourself

What Kind of Lover Are You?

INSTRUCTIONS: Respond to each of the following statements with T for "true" (if you believe the statement to be a generally accurate representation of your attitudes about love) or F for "false" (if you believe the statement does not adequately represent your attitudes about love).

_____ ❶ My lover and I have the right physical "chemistry" between us.

_____ ❷ I feel that my lover and I were meant for each other.

_____ ❸ My lover and I really understand each other.

_____ ❹ I believe that what my lover doesn't know about me won't hurt him/her.

_____ ❺ My lover would get upset if he/she knew of some of the things I've done with other people.

_____ ❻ When my lover gets too dependent on me, I want to back off a little.

_____ ❼ I expect to always be friends with my lover.

_____ ❽ Our love is really a deep friendship, not a mysterious, mystical emotion.

_____ ❾ Our love relationship is the most satisfying because it developed from a good friendship.

_____ ⑩ In choosing my lover, I believed it was best to love someone with a similar background.

_____ ⑪ An important factor in choosing a partner is whether or not he/she would be a good parent.

_____ ⑫ One consideration in choosing my lover was how he/she would reflect on my career.

_____ ⑬ Sometimes I get so excited about being in love with my lover that I can't sleep.

_____ ⑭ When my lover doesn't pay attention to me, I feel sick all over.

_____ ⑮ I cannot relax if I suspect that my lover is with someone else.

_____ ⑯ I would rather suffer myself than let my lover suffer.

_____ ⑰ When my lover gets angry with me, I still love him/her fully and unconditionally.

_____ ⑱ I would endure all things for the sake of my lover.

HOW DID YOU DO? This scale, from Hendrick and Hendrick (1990), is based on the work of Lee (1976), as is the discussion of the six types of love that follows. This scale is designed to enable you to identify your own beliefs about love. The statements refer to the six types of love that we'll soon examine: eros, ludus, storge, pragma, mania, and agape. Statements 1–3 are characteristic of the eros lover. If you answered "true" to these statements, you have a strong eros component to your love style. If you answered "false," you have a weak eros component. Statements 4–6 typify ludus love; 7–9, storge love; 10–12, pragma love; 13–15, manic love; and 16–18, agapic love.

WHAT WILL YOU DO? Are there things you can do to become more aware of the different love styles and to become a more well-rounded lover? Incorporating the qualities of effective interpersonal communication—for example, being more flexible, more polite, and more other-oriented—will go a long way toward making you a more responsive love partner.

Source: From "A Relationship-Specific Version of the Love Attitudes Scale" by C. Hendrick and S. Hendrick. Copyright © 1990 Select Press, _Journal of Social Behavior and Personality 5,_ 1990. Reprinted by permission.

The self-test identified six types of love: eros, ludus, storge, pragma, mania, and agape.

Eros love seeks beauty and sensuality and focuses on physical attractiveness, sometimes to the exclusion of qualities we might consider more important and more lasting. The erotic lover has an idealized image of beauty that is unattainable in reality. Consequently, the erotic lover often feels unfulfilled.

Ludic love seeks entertainment and excitement and sees love as fun, a game. To the ludic lover, love is not to be taken too seriously; emotions are to be held in check lest they get out of hand and make trouble. The ludic lover retains a partner only so long as the partner is interesting and amusing. When the partner is no longer interesting enough, it's time to change.

Storge love is a peaceful and tranquil love. Like ludus, storge lacks passion and intensity. Storgic lovers set out not to find a lover but to establish a companionable relationship with someone they know and with whom they can share interests and activities. Storgic love is a gradual process of unfolding thoughts and feelings and is sometimes difficult to separate from friendship.

Pragma love is practical and traditional and seeks compatibility and a relationship in which important needs and desires will be satisfied. The pragma lover is concerned with the social qualifications of a potential mate even more than with personal qualities; family and background are extremely important to the pragma lover, who relies not so much on feelings as on logic.

> ❝ If you have ever loved, been loved, or wanted to be in love, you have had to face a frustrating fact: different people can mean different things by that simple phrase 'I love you.' ❞
>
> —John Alan Lee

Manic love is an obsessive love that needs to give and receive constant attention and affection. When this is not given or received, or when an expression of increased commitment is not returned, reactions such as depression, jealousy, and self-doubt are often experienced and can lead to the extreme lows characteristic of the manic lover.

Agapic love is compassionate and selfless. The agapic lover loves both the stranger on the road and the annoying neighbor. Jesus, Buddha, and Gandhi practiced and preached this unqualified spiritual love—a love that is offered without concern for personal reward or gain and without any expectation that the love will be returned or reciprocated.

Each of these six varieties of love can combine with others to form new and different patterns (for example, manic and ludic or storge and pragma). The six styles illustrate the complexity of any love relationship; they should also make it clear that different people want different things, that each person seeks satisfaction in a unique way. The love that may seem lifeless or crazy or boring to you may be ideal for someone else. At the same time, another person may see these very same negative qualities in the love you're seeking.

Love changes. A relationship that began as pragma may develop into ludus or eros. A relationship that began as erotic may develop into mania or storge. One approach sees love as a developmental process having three major stages (Duck, 1986):

- First stage: Initial attraction: eros, mania, and ludus
- Second stage: Storge (as the relationship develops)
- Third stage: Pragma (as relationship bonds develop)

Deterioration

The relationship **deterioration** stage is characterized by a weakening of the bonds between the friends or lovers. The first phase of deterioration is usually *intrapersonal dissatisfaction:* You begin to experience personal dissatisfaction with everyday interactions and begin to view the future with your partner more negatively. If this dissatisfaction grows, you pass to the second phase, *interpersonal deterioration.* You withdraw and grow further and further apart. You share less of your free time. When you're together, there are awkward silences, fewer disclosures, less physical contact, and a lack of psychological closeness. Conflicts become more common and their resolution more difficult.

According to the *reversal hypothesis,* when a relationship begins to deteriorate, the breadth and depth (which increase as the relationship becomes more intimate) will often reverse themselves—a process of **depenetration.** For example, in the process of terminating a relationship, you might eliminate certain topics from your interpersonal interactions and at the same time discuss acceptable topics in less depth. You might reduce the level of your disclosure, revealing less and less of your inner feelings. This reversal does not always occur, however (Baxter, 1983). There is some evidence to show, for example, that, among friends, although depth decreases in the early stages of deterioration, it may later increase (Tolhuizen, 1986).

Relationship deterioration involves special communication patterns. These patterns are in part a response to the deterioration; you communicate the way you do because you feel that your relationship is in trouble. However, these patterns are also causative: The communication patterns you use largely determine the fate of your relationship. Here are a few communication patterns that characterize relationship deterioration.

VIEWPOINT

When researchers asked college students to identify the features that characterize romantic love, the five factors noted most frequently were trust, sexual attraction, acceptance and tolerance, spending time together, and sharing thoughts and secrets (Regan, Kocan, & Whitlock, 1998). How would you characterize love? Would men and women characterize love similarly? Would heterosexuals and homosexuals characterize love similarly?

- *Withdrawal*. Nonverbally, withdrawal is seen in the greater space the partners need and in the speed with which tempers and other signs of disturbance arise when that space is invaded. Other nonverbal signs of withdrawal include a decrease in eye contact and touching; less similarity in clothing; and fewer displays of items associated with the other person, such as bracelets, photographs, and rings (Miller & Parks, 1982; Knapp & Vangelisti, 2000). Verbally, withdrawal involves a decreased desire to talk and especially to listen. At times partners may use small talk not as a preliminary to serious conversation but as an alternative, perhaps to avoid confronting the serious issues.

- *Decline in self-disclosure*. Self-disclosing communications decline significantly. If the relationship is dying, you may think self-disclosure isn't worth the effort. Or you may limit your self-disclosures because you feel that the other person may not accept them or can no longer be trusted to be supportive and empathic.

- *Deception*. Deception increases as relationships break down. Sometimes this takes the form of clear-cut lies that people may use to avoid arguments over such things as staying out all night, not calling, or being seen in the wrong place with the wrong person. At other times, lies may be used because of a feeling of shame; you may not want the other person to think less of you. One of the problems with deception is that it has a way of escalating, eventually creating a climate of distrust and disbelief.

- *Positive and negative messages*. During deterioration there's an increase in negative and a decrease in positive messages. Once you praised the other's behaviors, but now you criticize them. Often the behaviors have not changed significantly; what has changed is your way of looking at them. What was once a cute habit now becomes annoying; what was once "different" now becomes inconsiderate. When a relationship is deteriorating, requests for pleasurable behaviors decrease ("Will you fix me my favorite dessert?") while requests to stop unpleasant or negative behaviors increase ("Will you stop monopolizing the phone?") (Lederer, 1984). Even the social niceties that accompany requests get lost as they deteriorate from "Would you please make me a cup of coffee, honey?" to "Get me some coffee, will you?" to "Where's my coffee?"

> **"** Falling out of love is very enlightening; for a short while you see the world with new eyes. **"**
>
> —Iris Murdoch

Repair

At the relationship **repair** stage, some relational partners may pause during deterioration and try to repair their relationship. Others, however, may progress—without stopping, without thinking—to dissolution.

At the first repair phase, *intrapersonal repair,* you analyze what went wrong and consider ways of solving your relational difficulties. You might at this stage consider changing your behaviors or perhaps changing your expectations of your partner. You might also evaluate the rewards of your relationship as it is now and the rewards to be gained if your relationship ended.

Should you decide that you want to repair your relationship, you might move to the *interpersonal repair* phase—you might discuss with your partner the problems in the relationship, the changes you want to see, and perhaps what you'd be willing to do and what you'd want your partner to do. This is the stage of negotiating new agreements and new behaviors. You and your partner might try to repair your relationship by yourselves, or you might seek the advice of friends or family, or perhaps go for professional counseling.

A wide variety of strategies can help you improve your relationship. Here are six that conveniently spell the word R-E-P-A-I-R. These same strategies may be viewed as ways to maintain your relationship even when it is not in danger of deteriorating or dissolving. Just as you take your car in for regular maintenance before it breaks down, you may want to devote time to **relationship maintenance**—to make sure your relationship functions the way you want it to and doesn't break down.

- *R*ecognize the problem. Specify what is wrong with your relationship and the changes you feel are needed to improve it (in concrete and specific terms). Exchange your perspectives empathically and with an open mind. Try to see the problem from your partner's point of view and to have your partner see the problem from yours. Try, too, to be descriptive when discussing grievances, being especially careful to avoid such troublesome terms as *always* and *never* or phrases that blame your partner.

- *E*ngage in productive conflict resolution. Look back at Chapter 7 for some of the tools for resolving conflict effectively.

- *P*ose possible solutions. After the problem is identified, discuss possible solutions—ways to lessen or eliminate the difficulty. Look for win–win solutions instead of win–lose solutions. With win–lose solutions, resentment and hostility are likely to fester.

- *A*ffirm each other. Increase supportiveness and positive evaluations. For example, communicate agreement, approval, and positive affect—qualities that characterize the communication of happy couples (Dindia & Fitzpatrick, 1985). Clearly, these behaviors result from the positive feelings these spouses have for each other. But it also can be argued that these expressions help to increase the positive regard that each person has for his or her partner.

- *I*ntegrate solutions into normal behavior. Often, conflict solutions that are reached after an argument are followed for only a very short time; the couple then goes back to their previous unproductive behavior patterns. Instead, make these solutions a part of your normal behavior.

- *R*isk. Risk being supportive—and support even without the certainty of reciprocity. Risk rejection—make the first move toward conciliation. Risk change—be willing to adapt and take on new responsibilities.

Skill development experience

Writing Your Relationship Résumé

This exercise is designed to encourage you to look at yourself as a relationship partner by constructing a *relationship résumé*. Much as you would write a résumé when looking for a job, you can identify your relationship experiences and relationship competencies in your relationship résumé. After you've completed your résumé, altercast a bit: Put yourself into the position of your own actual or potential friend or romantic partner and evaluate the résumé as objectively as you can. Ideally, you'll discover strengths to capitalize on and weaknesses to correct. Here are some guides for completing the résumé.

Interpersonal Relationship Résumé

Relationship Objectives: Identify (1) the kind of friend or romantic partner you're looking for (be specific, but not so specific that you limit your choices unrealistically) and (2) the type of relationship you're looking for (for example, a friend to hang out with, a lifetime romantic partner, or someone to have a good time with).

Relationship History: List your three most notable relationship experiences (friendships or romantic involvements), and identify what you gained as a relationship partner from each of them.

Relationship Competencies: List your abilities as a relationship partner. Examples could include listening abilities; ability to self-disclose and respond appropriately to the disclosures of your relationship partner; ability to empathize, be supportive, and be other-oriented; ability to deal positively with conflict; and, in fact, your ability to use any of the skills you have encountered throughout this course.

Relationship References: List three people who could recommend you as a suitable relationship partner. No relatives, please.

Dissolution

The **dissolution** stage, the last stage in the relationship model, involves cutting the bonds that tie you together. In the beginning it usually takes the form of *interpersonal separation:* You might move into your own apartments and begin to lead separate lives. If the separation works better than the original relationship, you enter the phase of *social* or *public separation.* Avoidance of each other and a return to a "single" status are among the primary characteristics of the dissolution of a relationship.

The reasons for the dissolution of relationships are many. Sometimes there is simply not enough to hold you together. Sometimes there are problems that cannot be resolved. Sometimes the costs are too high and the rewards too few, or the partners recognize the relationship as destructive and escape as the only alternative. Regardless of the specific reason, relationship breakups are difficult to deal with; they invariably cause stress (Simpson, 1987; Frazier & Cook, 1993).

Given both the inevitability that some relationships will break up and the significant effects such breakups will have on you, here are some steps you can take to ease the pain during this difficult time. These suggestions apply to the termination of any type of relationship—whether a friendship or a love affair, and whether through death, separation, or breakup.

- *Break the Loneliness–Depression Cycle.* The two most common feelings following the end of a relationship are loneliness and depression. These feelings are significant, so treat them seriously. Depression, for example, often leads to serious physical illness. In most cases, fortunately, loneliness and depression are temporary. Depression, for example, rarely lasts forever. When depression does last, is especially deep, or disturbs your normal functioning, it's time to seek professional help.

- *Take Time Out.* Resist the temptation to jump into a new relationship while you still have strong feelings about the old one and before a new one can be assessed with some objectivity. At the same time, resist swearing off all relationships. Neither extreme works well. Take time out for yourself. Renew your relationship with yourself.

- *Bolster Self-Esteem.* If your relationship fails, you may experience a decline in self-esteem (Collins & Clark, 1989). Your task now is to regain the positive self-image you need in order to function effectively. Recognize that having been in a relationship that failed—even if you view yourself as the main cause of the breakup—does not mean that *you* are a failure. Nor does it mean that you cannot succeed in a new and different relationship. It does mean that something went wrong with this particular relationship. And (ideally) you have now learned something important about yourself and about your relationship behavior.

- *Remove or Avoid Uncomfortable Symbols.* Remove the symbols of your relationship—the photographs, gifts, and letters, for example. Give them to a friend to hold or put them in a closet where you won't see them. Similarly, try to avoid places you frequented together. Research shows that the more vivid your memory of a broken love affair—a memory greatly aided by these relationship symbols—the greater your depression is likely to be; so try to avoid those things that will remind you of the relationship (Harvey, Flanary, & Morgan, 1986). After you have achieved some emotional distance, you can go back and enjoy the memorabilia as reminders of the good times you had with your former partner.

- *Seek Support.* Seeking the support of others is one of the best antidotes to the unhappiness caused when a relationship ends. Tell your friends and family of your situation—in only general terms, if you prefer—and make it clear that you want support. Seek out people who are positive and nurturing, and avoid those who will paint the world in even darker tones or blame you for what happened. Make the distinction between seeking support and seeking advice. If you feel you need advice, consult a professional.

> After all, my erstwhile dear,
> My no longer cherished,
> Need we say it was not love,
> Just because it perished?
>
> —Edna St. Vincent Millay

What Do You Say?

Relationship Dissolution:
You realize that your six-month relationship is going nowhere, and you want to break it off. It's just not exciting and not taking you where you want to go. *What do you say? Through what channel?*

- *Avoid Repeating Negative Patterns*. Use the knowledge gained from your failed relationship to avoid repeating the same patterns. At the same time, don't see vestiges of the old in every relationship. Treat a new relationship as the unique relationship it is without evaluating it through past experiences. Use past relationships and experiences as guides, not filters.

In addition, remember that the qualities of effective interpersonal communication covered in Chapter 7 (openness, empathy, positiveness, immediacy, interaction management, expressiveness, and other-orientation—performed mindfully, flexibly, and with metacommunication when necessary) and such skills as appropriate self-disclosure, active listening, and confirmation are also maintenance and repair strategies.

"We swam. We made sand castles. I'm sorry, Michael—I thought you understood that this was just a summer thing."

Reflections on the Model of Relationships

Before moving on to a discussion of relationship types, consider some of the implications of this six-stage model of relationships.

1. Because relationships differ so widely, it's best to think of any relationship model as a tool for talking about relationships rather than as a specific map that indicates how you move from one relationship position to another. The model presented here is certainly not the only way you can look at relationships.

2. Within each relationship and within each relationship stage, there are dynamic tensions between several opposites. The assumption made by **relationship dialectics theory** is that all relationships can be defined by a series of competing opposites. For example, some research has found three such pairs of opposites (Baxter, 1988, 1990; Baxter & Simon, 1993). The tension between *autonomy and connection* involves your desire to remain an individual but also to

Listen to this

Listening to Stage Talk

Listening carefully to messages that express a desire to move a relationship in a particular way or to maintain it at a particular stage will help you better understand and manage your interpersonal relationships. Over the next few days, listen carefully to all stage-talk messages. Listen to messages referring to your own relationships as well as to messages that friends or coworkers disclose to you about their relationships. Collect these messages and classify them into the following categories.

- *Contact messages* express a desire for contact: "Hi, my name is Joe."
- *Closeness messages* express a desire for increased closeness, involvement, or intimacy: "I'd like to see you more often."
- *Maintenance messages* express a desire to stabilize the relationship at one stage; "Let's stay friends for now. I'm afraid to get more involved at this point in my life."
- *Distancing messages* express a desire for more space in a relationship: "I think we should spend a few weeks apart."
- *Repair messages* express a desire to correct relationship problems: "Let's discuss this issue again, this time in a more constructive way. I didn't mean to hurt your feelings."
- *Dissolution messages* express a desire to break up the relationship: "Look, it's just not working out as we planned; let's each go our own way."

Applying Listening Skills

What suggestions would you offer a friend whose work colleague—with whom your friend wants to have a close working relationship but not a romantic relationship—has started sending closeness messages?

intimately connect to another person and to a relationship. This theme appears in women's magazines, which seem to teach readers to want both autonomy and connection (Prusank, Duran, & DeLillo, 1993). The tension between *novelty and predictability* centers on the dual desires for newness and adventure on the one hand and sameness and comfortableness on the other. The tension between *closedness and openness* relates to the desires to be both in an exclusive relationship and in a relationship that is open to different people. The closedness–openness tension is more in evidence during the early stages of relationship development. Autonomy–connection and novelty–predictability tend to become factors more as the relationship progresses.

3. A more obvious type of movement is depicted in Figure 8.1 by the different types of arrows. The exit arrows show that each stage offers the opportunity to exit the relationship; after saying "hello" you can say "good-bye." The vertical or movement arrows going to the next stage and back again represent the fact that you can move to another stage: either to a more intense stage (say, from involvement to intimacy) or to a stage that is less intense (say, from intimacy to deterioration). The self-reflexive arrows—the arrows that return to the beginning of the same level or stage—signify that any relationship may become stabilized at any point. You may, for example, continue to maintain a relationship at the intimate level without its deteriorating or going back to a less intense stage.

4. Movement through the various stages is usually a gradual process; you don't jump from contact to involvement to intimacy. Rather, you progress gradually, a few degrees at a time. Yet there are leaps that take place (Baxter & Bullis, 1986). For example, during the involvement stage of a romantic relationship, the first kiss or the first sexual encounter requires a leap. It requires a change in the kind of communication and in the kind of intimacy experienced by the two people. Before you take these leaps, you probably first test the waters. Before the first kiss, for example, you may hold each other, look longingly into each other's eyes, and perhaps caress each other's face.

Research Navigator.com

www.researchnavigator.com

Investigate Key Terms: Investigate one of the key terms discussed in this chapter (for example, interpersonal relationship, online relationship, relationship development, relationship maintenance, relationship deterioration, relationship repair, or intimacy). What additional insights can you provide?

Relationships in a Context of Culture and Gender, Technology, and Work

Interpersonal relationships vary widely depending on the culture, on the technological channels used, and on whether the relationships occur inside or outside the workplace. For a more complete understanding of interpersonal relationships today, we need to look at these three factors.

Relationships, Culture, and Gender

Cultural contexts and gender distinctions vary greatly around the world. This text's discussion of relationships up to this point has assumed that you voluntarily choose your relationship partners—that you consciously choose to pursue certain relationships and not others. In some cultures, however, your parents choose your romantic partner for you. In some cases your husband or wife is chosen to solidify two families or to bring some financial advantage to your family or village. An arrangement such as this may have been entered into by your parents when you were an infant or even before you were born. In most cultures, of course, even when arranged marriages are not the norm, there's pressure to marry "the right" person and to be friends with certain people and not others.

In the United States researchers study and textbook authors write about dissolving relationships and how to survive relationship breakups. It's assumed that you have the right to exit an undesirable relationship. But in some cultures you simply cannot dissolve a relationship once it's formed or once there are children. In the practice of Roman Catholicism, once people are validly married, they're always married and cannot dissolve that relationship. More important to such cultures may be issues such as "How do you maintain a relationship that has problems?" "What can you do to survive in this unpleasant relationship?" and "How can you repair a troubled relationship?" (Moghaddam, Taylor, & Wright, 1993).

Further, the culture will influence the difficulty that you go through when relationships break up. For example, married persons whose religion forbids divorce and remarriage will experience religious disapproval and condemnation as well as the same economic and social difficulties and emotional pain everyone else goes through. In the United States child custody almost invariably goes to the woman, and this presents an added emotional burden for the man. In Iran child custody goes to the man, which presents added emotional burdens for the woman. In India women experience greater difficulty than men in divorce because of their economic dependence on men, the cultural beliefs about women, and the patriarchal order of the family (Amato, 1994). And in Jordan it was only recently that a wife was granted a divorce. Prior to this, only men had been granted divorces (*New York Times*, May 15, 2002, p. A6).

In most of the United States, interpersonal friendships are drawn from a relatively large pool. Out of all the people you come into regular contact with, you choose relatively few of these as friends. With computer chat groups, the number of friends you can have has increased enormously, as has the range from which these friends can be chosen. In rural areas and in small villages throughout the world, however, you would have very few choices. The two or three other children your age would become your friends, because these would be the only possible friends you could make.

Most cultures assume that relationships should be permanent or at least long-lasting. Consequently, it's assumed that people want to keep relationships together and will expend considerable energy to maintain relationships. Because of this bias, little research has studied how to move effortlessly from one intimate relationship to another or suggests ways to do this more effectively and efficiently.

Culture influences heterosexual relationships by assigning different roles to men and women. In the United States men and women are supposed to be equal—at least that is the stated ideal. As a result, both men and women can initiate relationships and both can dissolve them. Both men and women are expected to derive satisfaction from their interpersonal relationships; and when that satisfaction isn't present, either may seek to exit the relationship. In Iran, on the other hand, only the man has the right to dissolve a marriage without giving reasons.

Gay and lesbian relationships are accepted in some cultures and condemned in others. In some areas of the United States, "domestic partnerships" may be registered; these partnerships grant gay men, lesbians, and (in some cases) unmarried heterosexuals rights that were formerly reserved only for married couples, such as health insurance benefits and the right to make decisions when one member is incapacitated. In Norway, Sweden, and Denmark, on the other hand, same-sex relationship partners have the same rights as married partners.

Not surprisingly, there are significant gender differences in interpersonal relationships. Perhaps the best-documented finding—already noted in the discussion of self-disclosure in Chapter 2—is that women self-disclose more than men. This difference holds throughout male and female friendships. Male friends self-disclose less often and with less intimate details than female friends do, and men generally do not view self-disclosure as a necessary aspect of their friendships (Hart, 1990). Women engage in significantly more affectional behaviors with their friends than do

What Do You Say?

Compliance Resisting: Your friend asks you for a loan of $150 to pay off some bills. But you've never been paid back by this friend when you've lent money in the past, and you don't want to do it again. Yet you don't want to lose this otherwise wonderful friend. *What do you say?*

Communicating ethically

Censoring Relationships

Throughout your life the messages you receive are censored. When you were young, your parents may have censored certain television programs, magazines, and movies—perhaps even tapes and CDs—that they thought inappropriate, usually because the materials were too sexually explicit or too violent. Moderators of computer mailing lists and chat groups also may censor messages; in fact, they may ban certain members from participating in the group if their messages are considered inappropriate or destructive to the group.

Relationships, too, are often censored. When you were young, your parents may have encouraged you to play with certain children and not to play with others. Sometimes these decisions were based on the character of the other children. Sometimes they may have had to do with the racial, religious, or national background of the would-be friends. Today, the most obvious instances of relationship censoring concern romantic relationships between interracial and homosexual couples. These prohibitions prevent certain people from interacting in the manner they choose. Interracial and gay and lesbian couples run into difficulty finding housing, employment, and, most significantly, acceptance into a community.

What Would You Do?

Your roommate has been intercepting and concealing calls from someone who wants to date you because of a belief that this relationship would be bad for you. If your roommate were in danger of entering a destructive relationship, would you hide such information? What would you do?

males, which may account for the greater difficulty men experience in initiating and maintaining close friendships (Hays, 1989). **Relational communication,** in all its forms and functions, seems a much more important dimension of women's friendships.

Men's friendships often are built around shared activities—attending a ball game, playing cards, working on a project at the office. Women's friendships, on the other hand, are built more around a sharing of feelings, support, and "personalism." In one study similarity (for example, in academic major, in status, in willingness to protect a friend in uncomfortable situations, and even in proficiency in playing Password) contributed greatly to relationship closeness between male–male friends but not between female–female or female–male friends (Griffin & Sparks, 1990). Perhaps, then, similarity is a criterion for male friendships but not for female or mixed-sex friendships.

There are also gender similarities and differences in love. Women and men seem to experience love to a similar degree (Rubin, 1973). However, women indicate greater love than men do for their same-sex friends. This may reflect a real difference between the sexes, or it may be a function of the greater social restrictions on men. A man is not supposed to admit his love for another man, but women are permitted to communicate their love for other women.

Men and women also differ in the types of love they prefer (Hendrick et al., 1984). For example, on a love self-test similar to the "What kind of lover are you?" test presented earlier, men scored higher on erotic and ludic love, whereas women scored higher on manic, pragmatic, and storgic love. No difference was found for agapic love.

Women report having their first romantic experiences earlier than men. The median age of first infatuation is 13 for women and 13.6 for men; the median age for first time in love is 17.1 for women and 17.6 for men (Kirkpatrick & Caplow, 1945; Hendrick et al., 1984).

Another gender difference frequently noted is that of romanticism. Research generally confirms that, contrary to popular depictions in the media, men are more romantic than women. For example, researchers have found that "men are more likely than women to believe in love at first sight, in love as the basis for marriage

and for overcoming obstacles, and to believe that their partner and relationship will be perfect" (Sprecher & Metts, 1989). This difference seems to increase as the romantic relationship develops: Men become more romantic and women less romantic (Fengler, 1974).

One further gender difference concerns differences between men and women in breaking up relationships (Blumstein & Schwartz, 1983; cf. Janus & Janus, 1993). In a survey asking about their reasons for breaking up, only 15 percent of the men indicated that it was their own interest in another partner, whereas 32 percent of the women stated this as a cause of the breakup. These findings are consistent with their partners' perceptions as well; 30 percent of the men but only 15 percent of the women reported that their partner's interest in another person was the reason for the breakup.

In their reactions to broken romantic affairs, women and men exhibit both similarities and differences. For example, the tendency to recall only pleasant memories and to revisit places with past associations was about equal among women and men. However, men engage in more dreaming about the lost partner and in more daydreaming as a reaction to the breakup than women do.

Relationships and Technology

Perhaps even more obvious than culture or gender is the influence of technology on interpersonal relationships. Clearly, online interpersonal relationships are on the increase. The number of Internet users is rapidly increasing, and commercial websites devoted to introducing people are proliferating, making it especially easy to develop online relationships. The afternoon television talk shows frequently focus on computer relationships, especially getting people together who have established a relationship online but who have never met. Clearly, many are turning to the Internet to find a friend or romantic partner. In MOOs (online role-playing games), 93.6 percent of the users formed ongoing friendship and romantic relationships (Parks & Roberts, 1998). Some are using the Internet as their only means of interaction; others are using it as a way of beginning a relationship and intend later to supplement computer talk with photographs, phone calls, and face-to-face meetings.

In one study almost two-thirds of newsgroup users had formed new acquaintances, friendships, or other personal relationships with someone they met on the Internet. Almost one-third said that they communicated with their partner at least three or four times a week; more than half communicated on a weekly basis (Parks & Floyd, 1996).

Women, it seems, are more likely to form relationships on the Internet than men. About 72 percent of women and 55 percent of men had formed personal relationships online (Parks & Floyd, 1996). Not surprisingly, those who communicated more frequently formed more relationships.

As relationships develop on the Internet, network convergence occurs; that is, as a relationship between two people develops, they begin to share their network of other communicators with each other (Parks, 1995; Parks & Floyd, 1996). This, of course, is similar to relationships formed through face-to-face contact. Online work groups are also on the increase and have been found to be more task oriented and more efficient than face-to-face groups (Lantz, 2001). Online groups also provide a sense of belonging that may once have been thought possible only through face-to-face interactions (Silverman, 2001).

There are lots of advantages to establishing relationships online. For example, online relationships let people avoid the potential for physical violence or sexually transmitted diseases. Unlike relationships established in face-to-face encounters, in which physical appearance tends to outweigh personality, Internet relationships allow your inner qualities to be communicated first. Rapport and mutual self-disclosure become more important than physical attractiveness in promoting intimacy (Cooper & Sportolari, 1997). And, contrary to some popular opinions, online relationships rely just as heavily on the ideals of trust, honesty, and commitment as do face-to-face relationships (Whitty & Gavin, 2001). Friendship and romantic interaction on the Internet are a natural boon for shut-ins and for extremely shy people, for whom traditional ways of meeting someone are often difficult. Computer talk is empowering for those with "physical disabilities or disfigurements," for whom face-to-face interactions are often superficial and often end with withdrawal (Lea & Spears, 1995; Bull & Rumsey, 1988). By eliminating the physical cues, computer talk equalizes the interaction and doesn't put a person with a disfigurement, for example, at an immediate disadvantage in a society where physical attractiveness is so highly valued. Online you're free to reveal as much or as little about your physical self as you wish, when you wish.

Another obvious advantage of online relationships is that the number of people you can reach is so vast that it's relatively easy to find someone who matches what you're looking for. The situation is comparable to your chances of finding a book that covers just what you need in a library of millions of volumes rather than in a collection of only a few thousand. Still another advantage for many is that the socioeconomic and educational status of people on the Net is significantly higher than you're likely to find in a bar or singles group.

Of course, there are also disadvantages. For one thing, you can't see the person. Unless you exchange photos or meet face-to-face, you won't know what the person looks like. Even if photos are exchanged, how certain can you be that the photos are of the person or that they were taken recently? In addition, you can't hear the person's voice, and this too hinders you in formulating a total picture. Of course, you can always add an occasional phone call to give you this information.

Online, people can present a false self with little chance of detection. For example, minors may present themselves as adults; and adults may present themselves as children for illicit and illegal sexual communications and, perhaps, meetings.

Web Explorations

A variety of exercises are available to help you work actively with the concepts discussed in this chapter (www.ablongman.com/devito): (1) I Prefer Someone Who . . . , (2) The Television Relationship, (3) Explaining Relationship Problems, (4) Relational Repair from Advice Columnists, (5) Male and Female, and (6) Interpersonal Relationships in Songs and Greeting Cards. In addition, several self-tests will help you further explore some of the concepts alluded to in this chapter: (7) How Confirming Are You? (8) How Committed Are You? (9) How Romantic Are You? (10) What Type of Relationship Do You Prefer? and (11) What Do You Believe about Relationships?

Repairing Relationships

What relationship repair advice would you give in each of these situations?

1. *Friends and colleagues*. Mike and Jim—friends for 20 years—had a falling out over the fact that Mike supported another person for promotion over Jim. Jim is resentful and feels that Mike should have given him his support; that support would have ensured Jim's getting the promotion and a raise, which he could surely use. Mike feels that his first obligation was to the company and that he endorsed the person he felt would be the best for the job. Assuming that both Mike and Jim want the friendship to continue (or will do so at some later time), what do you suggest that Mike do? What do you suggest that Jim do?
2. *Betraying a confidence*. Pat and Chris have been best friends since elementary school and even now, in their twenties, speak every day and rely on each other for emotional and sometimes financial support. Recently, however, Pat betrayed a confidence and told several mutual friends that Chris had been having emotional problems and had been considering suicide. Chris found out and no longer wants to maintain the friendship. Assuming that the friendship is more good than bad and that both parties will be sorry if they don't patch it up, what would you suggest that Pat do? What would you suggest that Chris do?

Similarly, people can present themselves as poor when they're rich, as mature when they're immature, as serious and committed when they're just enjoying the experience. Although you can also misrepresent yourself in face-to-face relationships, the fact that it's easier to do online probably accounts for greater misrepresentation in computer relationships (Cornwell & Lundgren, 2001).

Another potential disadvantage—though some might argue it is actually an advantage—is that computer interactions may become all consuming and may substitute for face-to-face interpersonal relationships.

Relationships and the Workplace

Workplace relationships, especially workplace romances, provide a unique perspective on the advantages and disadvantages of relationships. Real life is quite different from television depictions of workers, who are always best friends and who move in and out of interoffice romances with no difficulty—at least no difficulty that can't be resolved in 24 minutes.

Opinions vary widely concerning workplace romances. Some organizations, on the assumption that romantic relationships are basically detrimental to the success of the workplace, have explicit rules prohibiting dating among employees. In some organizations workers can even be fired for having such relationships.

On the positive side, the work environment seems a perfect place to meet a potential romantic partner. After all, by virtue of the fact that you're working in the same office, you're probably both interested in the same field, have similar training and ambitions, and spend considerable time together—all factors that foster the development of a successful interpersonal relationship.

Similarly, office romances can lead to greater work satisfaction. After all, if you're romantically attracted to another worker, it can make going to work, working together, and even working added hours more enjoyable and more satisfying. If the relationship is good and mutually satisfying, the individuals are likely to develop empathy for each other and to act in ways that are supportive, cooperative, and friendly; in short, the workers are more likely to act with all the characteristics of effective communication noted throughout this book.

However, even when the relationship is good for the two individuals, it may not necessarily be good for other workers. Seeing the loving couple every day in every

What Do You Say?

Relationship Résumé: Although you've been mostly honest in your two-month Internet relationship, you have padded your relationship résumé—lopped off a few years and pounds and made your temporary job seem like the executive fast track. You now want to come clean. *What do you say?*

Reducing Relationship Distance

Affinity-seeking strategies are ways of communicating that aim to make others like you, to draw people closer to you (Bell & Daly, 1984). As you read and think about each strategy below, try composing at least one message (verbal, nonverbal, or both) that would help you communicate these qualities and thereby to reduce relationship distance and move closer toward intimacy. Here are several useful affinity-seeking strategies.

- *Assuming equality:* Present yourself as socially equal to the other.
- *Comfortable self:* Present yourself as comfortable and relaxed with the other.
- *Conversational rule-keeping:* Follow the cultural rules for polite, cooperative conversation.
- *Dynamism:* Appear active, enthusiastic, and dynamic.
- *Self-concept confirmation:* Show respect for the other person and help the person feel positive about himself or herself.

way may generate destructive office gossip. Others may see the lovers as a team that must be confronted as a pair; they may feel that they can't criticize one without incurring the wrath of the other.

Similarly, such relationships may cause problems for management when, for example, a promotion is to be made or relocation decisions are necessary. Can you legitimately ask one lover to move to Boston and the other to move to San Francisco? Will it be difficult for management to promote one lover to a position in which he or she will become the supervisor of the other?

The workplace also puts pressure on the individuals. Most organizations, at least in the United States, are highly competitive environments in which one person's success often means another's failure. A romantic couple may find, for example, that the self-disclosures that regularly accompany increased intimacy (which often reveal weaknesses, doubts, and misgivings) may actually prove a liability in this kind of competitive context.

There's a popular belief that women enter office romances to achieve some kind of personal gain. For example, a survey of 218 male and female business school graduates found that people perceived women as entering office romances for personal advancement, despite a lack of any evidence (Anderson & Fisher, 1991). So the woman who does participate in an office romance may have to deal with both male and female colleagues' suspicions that she is in this relationship just to advance her career.

Of course, when the romance goes bad or when it's one-sided, there are even more disadvantages. One obvious problem is that it can be stressful for the former partners to see each other regularly and perhaps to work together. And other workers may feel they have to take sides, being supportive of one partner and critical of the other. This can easily cause friction throughout the organization. Another and perhaps more serious issue is the potential for charges of sexual harassment, especially if the romance is between a supervisor and a worker. Whether the charges are legitimate or result merely from an unhappy love affair that had nothing to do with the organization, management will find itself in the middle, facing lawsuits and time and money lost from investigating and ultimately acting on the charges.

The generally negative attitude of management toward workplace relationships and the problems inherent in dealing with the normal stresses of both work and romance seem to outweigh the positive benefits that may be derived from such relationships. All in all, workers are generally advised not to romance their colleagues. Friendships seem the much safer course.

www.researchnavigator.com

Find Answers: Try finding answers to one of the following questions, or design a research study to answer it: Do the perceived advantages and disadvantages of relationships change with age? How can relationship communication be improved? What are the common consequences of relationship dissolution?

Summary of Concepts and Skills

In this chapter we explored interpersonal relationships—their nature, development, deterioration, and repair. We also examined several theories that explain what happens in interpersonal relationships, and we considered the effects of culture, gender, technology, and the workplace on relationships.

1. Both face-to-face and online relationships have advantages (for example, they lessen loneliness and enhance your self-esteem) and disadvantages (for example, they involve increased obligations and may increase isolation).
2. Relationships typically have six stages: contact, involvement, intimacy, deterioration, repair, and dissolution. Each of these stages can be further broken down into an early and a later phase.
3. Love is perhaps the most important form of intimacy. Several types of love are eros, ludus, storge, pragma, mania, and agape.
4. Among the major causes of relationship deterioration are a lessening of the reasons for establishing the relationship, changes in the people involved, sexual difficulties, and work and financial problems.
5. Relationships of all kinds and in all their aspects are heavily influenced by culture, as are the theories that explain relationships and the topics research focuses on.
6. Gender differences in both friendship and love are often considerable and influence the ways in which these relationships are viewed and the communication that takes place within them.
7. All aspects of relationships—from development through maintenance, and sometimes to dissolution—are greatly influenced by the Internet and the opportunities it affords for communication.
8. Workplace relationships can create both opportunities and problems, both of which need to be assessed by anyone contemplating such relationships.

Check your competence in using the skills of effective relationship development, using the following rating scale: 1 = almost always; 2 = often; 3 = sometimes; 4 = rarely; and 5 = hardly ever.

_____ 1. I understand that relationships involve both advantages and disadvantages.

_____ 2. I adjust my communication patterns on the basis of the relationship's intimacy.

_____ 3. I can identify changes in communication patterns that may signal deterioration.

_____ 4. I can use the accepted repair strategies to heal an ailing relationship—for example, reversing negative communication patterns, using cherishing behaviors, and adopting a positive action program.

_____ 5. I can apply to my own relationships communication skills such as identifying relational messages, exchanging perspectives due to differences in punctuation, empathic and supportive understanding, and eliminating unfair fight strategies.

_____ 6. I can effectively manage physical proximity, reinforcement, and emphasizing similarities as ways to increase interpersonal attractiveness.

_____ 7. I can identify and to some extent control the rewards and costs of my relationships.

_____ 8. I can appreciate the other person's perception of relationship equity and can modify my own behavior to make the relationship more productive and satisfying.

_____ 9. I increase the breadth and depth of a relationship gradually.

_____ 10. I understand relationships as cultural institutions.

_____ 11. I take gender differences into consideration in trying to understand friendship and love.

Key Word Quiz

Write T for those statements that are true and F for those that are false. In addition, for those that are false, replace the italicized term with the correct term.

_____ 1. *Interactional contact* is the first phase of an interpersonal relationship.

_____ 2. *Social penetration theory* argues that relationships exist in dynamic tension between opposites such as autonomy and connection.

_____ 3. The lover who focuses most heavily on beauty and physical attractiveness is the *agapic lover*.

_____ 4. The love that is compassionate, egoless, and self-giving is *storge*.

_____ 5. The relationship stage of interpersonal commitment and social bonding is *involvement*.

_____ 6. The power base that is the opposite of reward power and that actually decreases interpersonal attractiveness is *coercive power*.

_____ 7. *Men's* friendships are usually based on shared activities.

_____ 8. The relationship stage of testing and intensifying is the *intimacy stage*.

_____ 9. *Relationship dialectics theory* describes relationships in terms of breadth and depth.

_____ 10. As your relationship becomes more intimate, you're more likely to interact on the basis of *personal rather than socially established rules*.

Answers: TRUE: 6, 7, and 10; FALSE: 1 (*perceptual contact*), 2 (*relationship dialectics theory*), 3 (*erotic lover*), 4 (*agape*), 5 (*intimacy*), 8 (*involvement stage*), 9 (*social penetration theory*).

9 Small Group Communication

Chapter Concepts	Chapter Skills
This chapter introduces small group communication, the major types of small groups, and ways to use small groups effectively.	After completing this chapter, you should be able to:
The Small Group	recognize the norms of the groups in which you function and take these into consideration when interacting.
The Brainstorming Group	brainstorm effectively.
Information-Sharing Groups	employ organizational structure in educational or learning groups.
Problem-Solving Groups	participate effectively in a wide variety of problem-solving groups.

Consider the number of groups to which you belong. Your family is the most obvious example, but you're probably also a member of a team, a class, a club, an organization, a sorority or fraternity, a collection of friends, or perhaps a band or theater group. Some of your most important and satisfying communications probably take place in small groups like these. In this chapter we look at the nature and characteristics of small groups and examine three types of small groups. A website devoted to small group communication maintained by the publisher of this book provides a wealth of additional insights (see the home page on page 188).

> " A group is best defined as a dynamic whole based on interdependence rather than on similarity. "
>
> —Kurt Lewin

The Small Group

A **small group** is a relatively small number of individuals who share a common purpose and follow similar organizing rules. It's a collection of individuals, few enough in number that all may communicate with relative ease as both senders and receivers. Generally, a small group consists of approximately 5 to 12 people; if the group is much larger than 12 people, communication becomes difficult. To constitute a group, members must share a common purpose. This does not mean that all members must have exactly the same purpose. But there must be some similarity in their reasons for interacting.

Groups operate by following certain organizing rules. Sometimes these rules are extremely rigid—as in groups operating under parliamentary procedure, in which comments must follow prescribed rules. At other times, the rules are more loosely defined, as in a social gathering. Even here, however, there are rules—for example, two people do not speak at the same time; a member's comments or questions are responded to, not ignored; and so on.

Relationship and Task Groups

You can think of groups as serving two broad and overlapping types of purposes: social or relationship purposes and work or task purposes. Social or relationship groups include, for example, your immediate family, your group of friends at school, your neighbors. Usually these groups serve your relationship needs for affiliation,

> **What Do You Say?**
>
> **Group Norms:** The first 20 minutes of just about every meeting at work invariably revolves around personal talk. You really don't enjoy this interaction; you want to participate in the work part of the meeting but not in the interpersonal part. *What do you say? To whom? Through what channel?*

affirmation, and affection. Some of these groups, like family, are extremely long lasting; some, like friends at college, may last only a year or two.

Task groups are groups formed to accomplish something. Some task groups are put together to solve a specific problem; for example, a committee of college professors might be assembled to hire a new faculty member, select a textbook, or serve as a graduate student's dissertation committee. Once the specific task is accomplished, the group is dissolved. Other task groups have more long range concerns—committees established to oversee diversity in the workplace, to monitor fairness in advertising, or to rate feature films may be ongoing, permanent groups.

Relationship and task functions often overlap. In fact, it would be difficult to find a group in which these two functions were not combined in some way at some times. The coworkers who bowl together or the two chemistry professors who begin dating are clear examples of how the functions often overlap. Not surprisingly, when groups normally devoted to one function start serving another function, they often encounter difficulties. For example, the much-in-love couple who are effective at home may find their relationship under stress when they open a business together.

Small Group Stages

Small group interaction develops in much the same way as a conversation. As in conversation (see Chapter 7), there are five stages: opening, feedforward, business, feedback, and closing. The *opening* period is usually a getting-acquainted time during which members introduce themselves and engage in small talk ("How was your weekend?" "Does anyone want coffee?"). After this preliminary get-together, there is usually some *feedforward,* some attempt to identify what needs to be done, who will do it, and so on. In a more formal group, the agenda (which is a perfect example of feedforward) may be reviewed and the tasks of the group identified. The *business* portion is the actual discussion of the tasks—the problem solving, the sharing of

Gaining Group Compliance

Although small group interactions are cooperative, persuasion still plays a part in most small groups. One way to persuade and exert power is to use **compliance-gaining strategies,** or behaviors that are directed toward gaining the agreement of others (Marwell & Schmitt, 1967; Miller & Parks, 1982):

- *Liking.* To get work colleagues in a good mood so that they'll comply with your request, be generous and friendly. For example, you might treat colleagues to lunch, then say, "I'd like to be elected to the personnel committee; I'm hoping I can count on your support."

- *Promise.* Promise to reward people if they comply with your request: "With me on the personnel committee, you'll have a great chance at promotion."

- *Positive self-feelings.* Show that people will feel better if they comply with your request or will feel worse (experience negative self-feelings) if they don't comply: "You'll feel a lot more comfortable with me on the committee" or, "You don't want someone who doesn't know you as I do."

- *Moral appeals.* Stress the moral and ethical reasons why your colleagues should comply: "It's only fair that you vote for me; I'm really the most qualified."

Enhancing Your Communication Power

How might you use these compliance-gaining strategies in a typical day at school, at home, or at work?

information, or whatever else the group needs to achieve. At the *feedback* stage, the group may reflect on what it has done and perhaps on what remains to be done. Some groups may even evaluate their performance at this stage. At the *closing* stage, the group members again return to their focus on individuals and will perhaps exchange closing comments ("Good seeing you again," "See you next time").

Note that the group focus shifts from people to task and then back again to people. A typical pattern would look like Figure 9.1. Different groups will naturally follow different patterns. For example, a work group that has gathered to solve a problem is likely to spend a great deal more time focused on the task—whereas an informal social group, say two or three couples who get together for dinner, will spend more time focused on people concerns. Similarly, the amount of time spent on the opening or business or closing, for example, will vary with the type and purposes of the group.

Small Group Formats

Small groups serve their functions in a variety of formats. Among the most popular are the roundtable, panel, symposium, and symposium–forum formats.

In the **roundtable,** group members arrange themselves in a circular or semicircular pattern. They share information or solve a problem without any set pattern of who speaks when. Group interaction is informal, and members contribute to the discussion as they see fit. A leader or moderator may be present and may, for example, try to keep the discussion focused on the topic or encourage more reticent members to contribute.

The **panel** format is similar to the roundtable; however, panel participants are "experts." As in the roundtable format, members' remarks are informal and there is no set pattern for who speaks when. Another difference is that the panel is observed

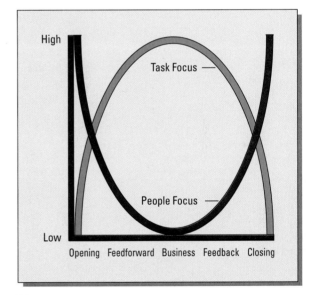

Figure 9.1

Small Group Stages and the Focus on Task and People

Do the groups to which you belong follow these five stages when interacting? How do these groups divide their focus between people and task?

Figure 9.2

Small Group Formats
With how many of these group formats have you had experience?

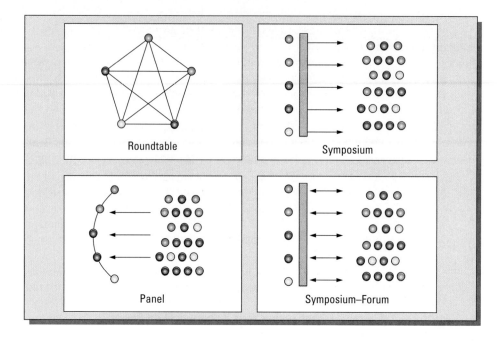

by an audience, whose members may interject comments or ask questions. Many television talk shows, such as *Ricki Lake* and *The Oprah Winfrey Show,* use this format. A variation is the two-panel format, which includes an expert panel and a lay panel. The lay panel discusses the topic but turns to the expert panel when in need of technical information, additional data, or direction.

The **symposium** consists of a series of prepared presentations much like public speeches. All speeches address different aspects of a single topic. The leader of a symposium introduces the speakers, provides transitions from one speaker to another, and may provide periodic summaries.

The *symposium–forum* consists of two parts: a symposium of prepared speeches and a **forum** consisting largely of questions and comments from the audience and responses from the symposium speakers. The symposium leader introduces the speakers and moderates the question-and-answer session.

These four formats, illustrated in Figure 9.2, are general patterns that describe a wide variety of groups. Within each type, there will naturally be considerable variation. For example, in the symposium–forum, there is no set pattern for how much time will be spent on the symposium part and how much on the forum part. Combinations may also be used. Thus, for example, group members may each present a position paper (basically a symposium) and then participate in a roundtable discussion.

Mailing Lists and Chat Groups

Small groups use a wide variety of channels. Often, of course, they take place face-to-face, and this is the type of group that probably comes to mind when you think of group interaction. But much small group interaction also takes place online. Online groups are proliferating and becoming a part of people's experience throughout the world. They are important personally and socially as well as professionally. Online work groups are also on the increase and have been found to be more task oriented and more efficient than face-to-face groups (Lantz, 2001). In addition, online groups provide a sense of belongingness that may once have been thought possible only through face-to-face interactions (Silverman, 2001).

"Honey, please don't talk to Daddy when he's in a chat room."

Two major types of online groups are mailing-list groups and chat groups. Mailing-list groups or listservs consist of groups of people interested in a particular topic who communicate with each other through e-mail. Generally, you subscribe to a list and communicate with all other members by addressing your mail to the group e-mail address. Perhaps the most popular source for listservs is Topica (http://www.topica.com/) which currently lists thousands of discussion groups and newsletters organized around such topics as art and design, music, personal finance, sports and recreation, women and family, and lots more. To locate a mailing list, or discussion group concerned with your speech topic, just use Topica's convenient search feature.

Chat groups allow members to communicate with one another in real time in discussion groups called channels. There are so many chat groups that your chance of finding a topic you're interested in is extremely high. Chat groups, like mailing lists, enable you to communicate with people you would never meet and interact with otherwise. Because such groups are international, they provide excellent exposure to other cultures, other ideas, and other ways of communicating. If you need help with chat group communication, take a look at the website for this text at www.ablongman.com/devito or Research Navigator at www.researchnavigator.com, or, for suggestions on participating in chat groups, visit http://www.irchelp.org.

Communication in a chat group resembles the conversation you would observe at a large party. The total number of guests divides into small groups—which may be as small as two people or include many people—and each group discusses its own topic or version of a general topic. For example, in a chat group about food, 10 people may be discussing food calories, 8 people may be discussing restaurant food preparation, and 2 people may be discussing the basic food groups. So, although you may be communicating in one primary group (say, a group dealing with restaurant food), you also have your eye trained to pick up something particularly interesting in another group (much as you do at a party).

VIEWPOINT

Research on chat groups finds that people are more likely to comment on a member's message when that message is negative than when it is positive (Rollman, Krug, & Parente, 2000). Why do you think this occurs? Do you find this occurs in face-to-face conversations as well?

Small Group Culture

Many small groups—especially long-standing groups—develop a distinctive culture, in some ways similar to that of a national, racial, or religious group. Especially significant in this culture are the **group norms,** the rules or standards identifying which behaviors are considered appropriate (such as willingness to take on added tasks or to direct conflict toward issues rather than toward people) and which are considered inappropriate (such as arriving late or not contributing actively). These rules for appropriate behavior are sometimes explicitly stated in a company contract or policy: "All members must attend department meetings." Sometimes they are unstated: "Group members should be well groomed." Regardless of whether or not norms are spelled out, they are powerful regulators of members' behaviors.

Norms may apply to individual members as well as to the group as a whole and, of course, will differ from one group to another (Axtell, 1990, 1993). For example, although Americans prefer to get right down to business, the Japanese prefer rather elaborate socializing before addressing the business at hand. In the United States, men and women in business are expected to interact when making business decisions as well as when socializing. In Muslim and Buddhist societies, however, religious restrictions prevent mixing the sexes. In some cultures (for example, those of the United States, Bangladesh, Australia, Germany, Finland, and Hong Kong), punc-

What Do You Say?

Group Pressure: All your colleagues at your new job pad their expense accounts. You don't want to go along with this; but if you don't, everyone else will be found out. You don't want to make waves, and yet you don't want to do something unethical. *What do you say? To whom? Through what channel?*

Telling Secrets

Close friends, family members, or members of standing workplace committees often exchange secrets with the unspoken assumption that these confidences will not be revealed to outsiders. For example, it would be considered unethical if you revealed a group member's financial status to people outside the group who had no right to know this information. But in some instances it's not so easy to tell when revealing a secret would be considered unethical.

Ethicist Sissela Bok (1983) argues that it's unethical to reveal secrets when it would invade the privacy that everyone has a right to; for example, when it concerns matters that are no one else's business. It also is unethical to reveal secrets that can hurt the individuals involved. Conversely, there are likely to be situations in which you may have an obligation to reveal a secret. For example, Bok (1983) argues that you have an obligation to reveal a secret when keeping the information hidden will do more harm than good. Here are a variety of situations that raise ethical dilemmas about revealing secrets.

What Would You Do?

- *An instructor who supervises your study group confides to you that she is a confirmed racist and proud of it.*
- *A 16-year-old member of your wilderness group confides that she's having unprotected sex with her married history teacher.*
- *A community religious leader confides to you that he is skimming a portion of the members' contributions to fund his retirement.*

tuality for business meetings is very important. But in others (for example, those of Morocco, Italy, Brazil, Zambia, Ireland, and Panama), punctuality is less important; being late is no great insult and in some situations is even expected. In the United States and in much of Asia and Europe, meetings are held between two parties. In many Gulf states, however, a business executive is likely to conduct meetings with several different groups—sometimes dealing with totally different issues—at the same time. In this situation you have to share what in the United States would be "your time" with these other groups. In the United States very little interpersonal touching goes on during business meetings; in Arab countries touching (for example, hand holding) is common and is a gesture of friendship.

You're more likely to accept the norms of your group's culture when you feel your group membership is important and you want to continue your membership in the group. You're also more likely to accept these norms when your group is cohesive: when you and the other members are closely connected, are attracted to one another, and depend on one another. Lastly, you're more apt to accept these norms if you'd be punished by negative reactions or exclusion from the group for violating them (Napier & Gershenfeld, 1989).

"I don't know how it started, either. All I know is that it's part of our corporate culture."

Small Group Apprehension

Just as you may have some apprehension in interpersonal conversations (Chapter 7), you probably experience apprehension to some degree in group discussions. Because small groups vary so widely, you're likely to experience different degrees of apprehension depending on the nature of the specific group. Work groups, for example, may cause greater apprehension than groups of friends. And interacting with superiors is likely to generate greater apprehension than meeting with peers or subordinates. Similarly, the degree of familiarity you have with the group members and the extent to which you see yourself as a part of the group (as opposed to an outsider) will also influence your apprehension. You may wish at this point to take the following self-test, "How apprehensive are you in group discussions?"

How Apprehensive Are You in Group Discussions?

INSTRUCTIONS: This brief test is designed to measure your apprehension in small group communication situations. The questionnaire consists of six statements concerning your feelings about communication in group discussions. Indicate the degree to which each statement applies to you by marking whether you (1) strongly agree, (2) agree, (3) are undecided, (4) disagree, or (5) strongly disagree. (Each of these answers then becomes the "score" for each item.) There are no right or wrong answers. Do not be concerned that some of the statements are similar. Work quickly; just record your first impression.

_4_ ❶ I dislike participating in group discussions.

_2_ ❷ Generally, I am comfortable while participating in group discussions.

_4_ ❸ I am tense and nervous while participating in group discussions.

_2_ ❹ I like to get involved in group discussions.

_3_ ❺ Engaging in a group discussion with new people makes me tense and nervous.

_3_ ❻ I am calm and relaxed while participating in group discussions.

HOW DID YOU DO? To obtain your apprehension for group discussions score, use the following formula:

Start with 18; add the scores for items 2, 4, and 6; then subtract the scores for items 1, 3, and 5.

A total above 18 shows some degree of apprehension.

25
11
____
14

WHAT WILL YOU DO? Think about the kinds of groups that generate the most apprehension for you. Can you identify the major characteristics of these high-apprehension groups? How do these differ from groups generating little apprehension? What other factors might influence your small group apprehension? As you read the suggestions for reducing apprehension given in Chapter 13, consider how you might use them in the various types of groups in which you participate.

Source: From James C. McCroskey, _An Introduction to Rhetorical Communication,_ 7th ed. Copyright © 1997 by Allyn and Bacon. Reprinted by permission.

The Brainstorming Group

Many small groups exist solely to generate ideas. **Brainstorming** is a process often used in generating ideas; it's a technique for analyzing a problem through a process of generating as many ideas as possible (Osborn, 1957; Beebe & Masterson, 2003). Although brainstorming also can be useful when you're trying to generate ideas by yourself—ideas for speeches or term papers, ideas for a fun vacation, or ways to make money—it is more typically seen in small group settings. Organizations have come to embrace brainstorming because it lessens group members' inhibitions and encourages all participants to exercise their creativity. It also fosters cooperative teamwork; members soon learn that their own ideas and creativity are sparked by the contributions of others. The technique builds member pride and ownership in the final solution or product or service, because all members contribute to it.

Brainstorming occurs in two phases. The first is the brainstorming period proper; the second is the evaluation period. The procedures are simple. First, a

> **"** The best way to have a good idea is to have a lot of ideas. **"**
>
> —Linus Pauling

What Do You Say?

Brainstorming: You're in charge of a brainstorming group whose task is to generate ideas for improving the company website. The problem that you anticipate on the basis of past experiences is that a few of the members will just sit there, afraid to offer any suggestions. *What do you say? To whom?*

problem is selected. The "problem" may be almost anything that is amenable to many possible solutions or ideas—for example, how to devise an effective advertising campaign, how to recruit new members to the organization, or how to market a new product. Before the actual session, group members are informed of the problem so they can think about the topic. When the group meets, each person contributes as many ideas as he or she can think of. Companies often use chalkboards or easels to record all the ideas. If ideas are to be recorded on tape, a tape recorder is set up (and tested) at the beginning of the session. During this idea-generating session, members follow four rules:

- No evaluation is permitted at this stage. All ideas are recorded for the group to see (or hear later). Any evaluation—whether verbal or nonverbal—is criticized by the leader or members. Prohibiting evaluation encourages group members to participate freely.
- Quantity of ideas is the goal. The more ideas generated, the more likely a useful solution will be found.
- Combinations and extensions of ideas are encouraged. Although members may not criticize a particular idea, they may extend or combine it. The value of a particular idea may well be in the way it stimulates another member.
- Freewheeling (developing as wild an idea as possible) is desirable. A wild idea can be tempered easily, but it's not so easy to elaborate on a simple or conservative idea.

After all the ideas are generated—a period that lasts about 15 or 20 minutes—the group evaluates the entire list. Unworkable ideas are crossed off the list; those showing promise are retained and evaluated. During this phase, criticism is allowed.

Information-Sharing Groups

The purpose of information-sharing groups is to acquire new information or skills by sharing knowledge. In most information-sharing groups, all members have something to teach and something to learn; a good example is a group of students sharing information to prepare for an exam. In others, the group interaction takes place because some members have information and some do not. An example is a discussion between patients and health care professionals.

Educational or Learning Groups

Members of educational or learning groups may follow a variety of discussion patterns. For example, a historical topic such as the development of free speech or equal

Listen to this

Listening in Small Groups

Listening in small groups is much the same as listening in conversation. Yet there are some listening suggestions that seem especially appropriate in small groups, whether social or business.

- Respond visibly but in moderation; an occasional nod of agreement or a facial expression that says "that's interesting" are usually sufficient. Too little response says you aren't listening, and too much response says you aren't listening critically. Use backchanneling cues—head nods and brief oral responses that say you're listening.

- Avoid adaptors such as playing with your hair or a pencil or drawing pictures on a Styrofoam cup; they signal your discomfort.

- Maintain an open posture. When seated around a table, resist covering your face, chest, or stomach with your hands; this may make you appear defensive.

- Avoid interrupting the speaker or completing the speaker's thoughts; these behaviors are generally perceived as indicating a lack of communication savvy and business etiquette.

Applying Listening Skills

Jennifer is a bright and diligent worker, but at company meetings she seems so uninvolved that other members ignore her; they don't ask her advice and don't even make eye contact with her. What listening advice would you offer to help Jennifer appear more involved and more a part of group interactions?

rights might be developed chronologically, with the discussion progressing from the past into the present and perhaps predicting the future. Issues in developmental psychology, such as a child's language development or physical maturity, might also be discussed chronologically. Other topics lend themselves to spatial development. For example, the development of the United States might take a spatial pattern—from east to west—or a chronological pattern—from 1776 to the present. Other suitable patterns, depending on the topic and the group's needs, might be cause and effect, problem and solution, or structure and function.

Perhaps the most popular discussion pattern is the topical pattern. A group might discuss the legal profession by itemizing and discussing each of the profession's major functions. Another might consider a corporation's structure in terms of its major divisions. Groups could further systematize each of these topics by, say, listing the legal profession's functions in order of importance or complexity, or ordering the corporation's major structures in terms of decision-making power.

> ❝ The wisest mind has something yet to learn. ❞
>
> —George Santayana

Focus Groups

A different type of learning group is the **focus group,** a kind of in-depth interview of a small group. The aim here is to discover what people think about an issue or product; for example, what do men between 18 and 25 think of the new aftershave lotion and its packaging? What do young executives earning more than $70,000 think of buying foreign luxury cars?

In the focus group the leader tries to discover the members' beliefs, attitudes, thoughts, and feelings so as to guide decisions on, for example, changing the scent or redesigning the packaging or constructing advertisements for luxury cars. It is the leader's task to prod members to analyze their thoughts and feelings on a deeper level and to use the thoughts of one member to stimulate the thoughts of others.

Generally, a focus group leader assembles approximately 12 people. The leader explains the process, the time limits, and the general goal of the group—let's say, for example, to discover why these 12 individuals requested information on the XYZ health plan but purchased a plan from another company. Here, of course, the 12 group members are standing in for or representing the general population. The

Research Navigator.com

www.researchnavigator.com

Investigate Key Terms: Investigate one of the key terms discussed in this chapter (for example, group norms, brainstorming, focus group, listserv, chat group, Delphi method, nominal group technique, quality circles, or problem-solving group. What additional insights can you provide?

Combating Idea Killers

Think about how you can be on guard against negative criticism and how you can respond to "idea killers" such as those listed below. As you read down the list of these commonly heard messages, formulate at least one response you might use if someone used one of these on you.

- We tried it before and it didn't work.
- No one would vote for it.
- It's too complex.
- It's too simple.
- It would take too long.

- It's too expensive.
- We don't have the facilities.
- What we have is good enough.
- It just doesn't fit us.
- It's impossible.

leader, who is usually a professional facilitator rather than a member of the organization itself, asks a variety of questions. In our example these might be questions such as How did you hear about the XYZ health plan? What other health plans did you consider before making your actual purchase? What influenced you to buy the plan you eventually bought? Were any other people influential in helping you make your decision? Through the exploration of these and similar questions, the facilitator and the relevant organizational members (who may be seated behind a one-way mirror, watching the discussion) may put together a more effective health plan or more effective advertising strategies.

Problem-Solving Groups

A **problem-solving group** meets to solve a particular problem or to reach a decision on some issue. In a sense, this is the most demanding kind of group. It requires not only a knowledge of small group communication techniques but also a thorough knowledge of the particular problem on the part of all group members. Also, for the most successful outcome, it usually demands faithful adherence to a set of procedural rules.

? VIEWPOINT

Groups frequently make more extreme decisions than do individuals—a tendency known as group polarization (Friedkin, 1999; Brauer, Judd, & Gliner, 1995). For example, groups tend to take greater risks if the members are already willing to take some risks, or to become even more cautious if the members are already cautious. Have you ever observed this group polarization tendency? What happened? What implications does this theory have for, say, teenagers who join a gang? For athletes who join a new team?

In companies or other organizations, problem-solving group members may all come from the same area or department; all may be sales representatives or all may be teachers, for example. At other times the group members make up what has come to be called an integrated work team, which consists of members from different areas of the organization who have related goals and who must work together to accomplish them (Hill, 1997). For example, a publishing company work team might consist of people from the editorial, design, advertising, production, and marketing departments.

The Problem-Solving Sequence

The **problem-solving sequence** discussed here identifies six steps and owes its formulation to philosopher John Dewey's insights into how people think (see Figure 9.3). These steps are designed to make problem solving more efficient and effective.

Define and Analyze the Problem In many instances the nature of the problem is clearly specified. For example, a work team might discuss how to package the new CD-ROMs for Valentine's Day. In other instances, however, the problem may be vague and it may be up to the group to define it. For example, the general problem may be poor campus communications, but such a vague and general topic is difficult to tackle in a problem-solving discussion. So, for purposes of discussion, a group might be more specific and focus on improving the college website.

Define the problem as an open-ended question ("How can we improve the college website?") rather than as a statement ("The website needs to be improved") or as a yes/no question ("Does the website need improvement?"). The open-ended question allows greater freedom of exploration.

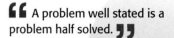

" A problem well stated is a problem half solved. "

—Charles F. Kettering

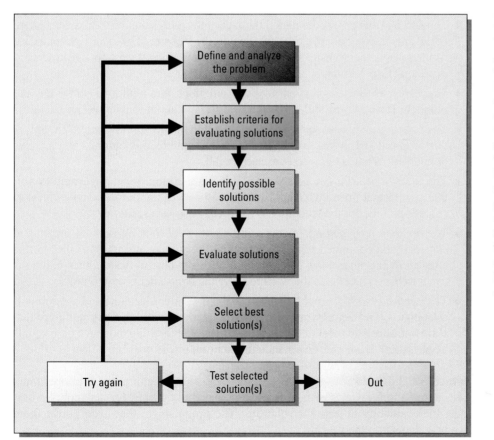

Figure **9.3**

The Problem-Solving Sequence

Although most small group theorists would advise you to follow the problem-solving pattern as presented here, others would alter it somewhat. For example, some would advise you to reverse steps 2 and 3: to identify possible solutions first and then consider the criteria for evaluating them (Brilhart & Galanes, 1992). The advantage of this approach is that you're likely to generate more creative solutions, because you will not be restricted by standards of evaluation. The disadvantage is that you may spend a great deal of time generating impractical solutions that will never meet the standards you will eventually propose.

Limit the problem to a manageable area for discussion. A question like "How can we improve communication at the college?" is too broad and general. Focus on one subdivision of the issue—such as, in this example, the student newspaper, student–faculty relationships, registration, examination scheduling, student advisory services, or the college website.

Establish Criteria for Evaluating Solutions

Decide how you'll evaluate the solutions before proposing any of them. Identify the standards or criteria you'll use in evaluating solutions or in preferring one solution over another. Generally, problem-solving groups consider two types of criteria: practical and value criteria. As an example of practical criteria, you might decide that the solutions must not increase the budget or that a solution must lead to a 10 percent increase in website visits.

The value criteria are more difficult to identify. For example, value criteria might state that the website information must not violate anyone's right to privacy or must provide a forum for all members of the college community.

Identify Possible Solutions

Identify as many solutions as possible. Focus on quantity rather than quality. Brainstorming may be particularly useful at this point. Solutions to the website improvement problem might include incorporating reviews of faculty publications, student evaluations of specific courses, reviews of restaurants in the campus area, outlines for new courses, and employment information.

Evaluate Solutions

After all solutions have been proposed, evaluate each. For example, does incorporating reviews of area restaurants meet the criteria? Would it increase the budget, for example? Would posting grades violate students' rights to privacy? Each potential solution should be matched against the evaluating criteria.

Critical thinking pioneer Edward deBono (1987) suggests we use six "thinking hats" to evaluate solutions. Wearing each "hat," you look at the problem and the proposed solutions from a different perspective.

- The *fact hat* focuses on the data—the facts and figures that bear on the problem. For example, what are the relevant data on the website? How can I get more information on the website's history? How much does it cost to construct and maintain? Can we include advertising?

- The *feeling hat* focuses on your feelings, emotions, and intuitions concerning the problem. How do you feel about the website and about making major changes?

- The *negative argument hat* asks you to become the devil's advocate. Why might this proposal fail? What are the problems with publishing outlines and reviews of courses? What is the worst-case scenario?

- The *positive benefits hat* asks you to look at the upside. What opportunities will this new format open up? What benefits will publishing outlines and reviews of courses provide for the students? What is the best-case scenario?

- The *creative new idea hat* focuses on new ways of looking at the problem and can easily be combined with brainstorming techniques discussed earlier in this chapter. What other ways can you look at this problem? What other functions can a website serve? Can the website serve the nonacademic community as well?

- The *control of thinking hat* helps you analyze what you've done and are doing. It asks that you reflect on your own thinking processes and synthesize the results. Have you adequately defined the problem? Are you focusing too much on insignificant issues? Have you given enough attention to the possible negative effects?

Select the Best Solution(s)

Select the best solution and put it into operation. Let's assume that reviews of faculty publications and outlines for new courses best meet the evaluating criteria for solutions. The group might then incorporate these two new items into the website.

Groups use different decision-making methods when deciding, for example, which solution to accept. The method to be used should, naturally, be stated at the outset of the group discussion. The three main decision-making methods are:

- *Decision by authority:* Group members voice their feelings and opinions, but the leader, boss, or chief executive makes the final decision. This method has the advantages of being efficient and of giving greater importance to the suggestions of more experienced members. The big disadvantage is that members may feel that their contributions have too little influence and therefore may not participate with real enthusiasm.

- *Majority rule:* The group agrees to abide by the majority decision and may vote on various issues as the group searches to solve its problem. Like decision by authority, this method is efficient. A disadvantage is that it may lead the group to limit discussion by calling for a vote once a majority has agreed. Also, members not voting with the majority may feel disenfranchised and left out.

- *Consensus:* In some situations, consensus means unanimous agreement; for example, a criminal jury must reach a unanimous decision to convict or acquit a defendant. In most business groups, consensus means that members agree that they can live with the solution; they agree that they can do whatever the solution requires (Kelly, 1994). Consensus is especially helpful when the group wants each member to be satisfied and committed to the decision and to the decision-making process as a whole (DeStephen & Hirokawa 1988; Beebe & Masterson, 2003). Consensus obviously takes the most time of any of the decision-making methods and can lead to a great deal of inefficiency, especially if members wish to prolong the discussion process needlessly or selfishly.

Note that these decision-making methods may be used at any point in the problem-solving sequence. For example, the vice-president may decide what problem to study (decision by authority) or the members may vote on what criteria the solution should meet (decision by majority vote).

Test Selected Solution(s)   After putting the solution(s) into operation, test their effectiveness. The group might, for example, poll the students or college employees about the new website. Or the group might analyze the number of visits to the website to see if the number of visits increased by the desired 10 percent. If the selected solutions prove ineffective, the group will need to return to a previous stage and repeat that part of the process. This often involves selecting other solutions to test. But it also may mean going even further back in the process—to a reanalysis of the problem, an identification of other solutions, or a restatement of criteria, for example.

> " Some problems are so complex that you have to be highly intelligent and well informed just to be undecided about them. "
>
> —Laurence J. Peter

Skill development experience

Solving Problems in Groups

Together with four, five, or six others, form a problem-solving group and discuss one of the following questions: *(a)* What should we do about the homeless? *(b)* What should we do to improve employee morale? *(c)* What should we do to better prepare ourselves for the job market? *(d)* How can we improve student–faculty communication? or *(e)* What should be the college's responsibility concerning students and faculty who are HIV positive?

Before beginning the discussion, prepare a discussion outline, answering the following questions:

1. What is the problem? What caused it? What are its effects?
2. What are some possible solutions?
3. What are the advantages and disadvantages of each of these solutions?
4. What solution seems best (in light of the advantages and disadvantages)?
5. How might you test this solution?

Problem Solving at Work

The problem-solving sequence discussed here is used widely in work settings in a variety of different types of groups. Three group interaction types that rely largely on the problem-solving sequence are popular in business: the nominal group technique, the Delphi method, and quality circles.

The Nominal Group Technique   The **nominal group** technique is a method of problem solving that uses limited discussion and confidential voting to obtain a group decision. It is extremely useful for increasing the number of ideas generated by group members (Roth, Schleifer, & Switzer, 1995). A nominal group is especially helpful when some members are reluctant to voice their opinions in a regular problem-solving group or when the issue is controversial or sensitive—for example, "what can be done about sexism, racism, or homophobia in the workplace," "office romantic relationships," or "ways to downsize." With this technique each member contributes equally and each contribution is treated equally. Another advantage of this technique is that it can be accomplished in a relatively short period of time. The nominal group procedure can be divided into seven steps (Kelly, 1994):

VIEW POINT

What one rule, norm, or principle of small group interaction do you find is violated most often? How would the groups you participate in be different if this rule were followed instead of violated?

1. The problem is defined and clarified for all members.

2. Each member writes down (without discussion or consultation with others) his or her ideas on or possible solutions to the problem.

3. Each member—in sequence—states one idea from his or her list, which is recorded on a board or flip chart so everyone can see it. This process is repeated until all suggestions are stated and recorded. Duplicates are then eliminated. Group agreement is secured before ideas are combined.

4. Each suggestion is clarified (without debate). Ideally, each suggestion should be given equal time.

5. Each member rank-orders the suggestions.

6. The rankings of the members are combined to get a group ranking, which is then written on the board.

7. Clarification, discussion, and possible reordering may follow.

The highest-ranking solution might then be selected to be tested, or several high-ranking solutions may be put into operation.

The Delphi Method   The **Delphi method,** utilizes a group of experts, but there is no interaction among them; instead, they communicate by repeatedly responding to questionnaires (Tersine & Riggs, 1980; Kelly, 1994). The method is especially useful when you want to involve people who are geographically distant from one another, when you want all members to act as part of the solution and to uphold it, and when you want to minimize the effects of dominant members or even of peer pressure. For example, the Delphi method might be used by a group of communication professors to write a statement of ethical guidelines for technological communication or by a group of health care professionals to identify the requirements for nurse practitioners. The method is best explained as a series of steps (Kelly, 1994):

1. The problem is defined (for example, "We need to improve intradepartmental communication"). What each member is expected to do is specified (for example, "Each member should contribute five ideas on this specific question").

2. Each member then anonymously contributes five ideas in writing. This stage used to be completed through questionnaires sent through traditional mail but

What Do You Say?

Illegal Groups: While surfing the Net you come upon a chat group devoted to terrorism, complete with plans for building bombs and for evading airport security systems. *What do you do?*

now is more frequently done through e-mail, which greatly increases the speed with which this entire process can be accomplished.

3. The ideas of all members are combined, written up, and distributed to all members, who may be asked to, say, select the three or four best ideas from this composite list.

4. Members then select the three or four best ideas and submit them.

5. From these responses another list is produced and distributed to all members, who may be asked to select the one or two best ideas.

6. Members then select the one or two best ideas and submit them.

7. From these responses another list is produced and distributed to all members. The process may be repeated any number of times, but usually three rounds are sufficient for achieving a fair degree of agreement.

8. The "final" solutions are identified and are communicated to all members.

Quality Circles   **Quality circles** are groups of workers (usually 6 to 12) whose task it is to investigate and make recommendations for improving the quality of some organizational function. The members are drawn from the workers whose area is being studied. Thus, for example, if the problem is to improve advertising on the Internet, the quality circle membership would consist of people from the advertising and computer departments. Generally, the motivation for establishing quality circles is economic; the company's aim is to improve quality and profitability. Another related goal is to improve worker morale; because quality circles involve workers in decision making, workers may feel empowered and more essential to the organization (Gorden & Nevins, 1993).

The basic idea is that people who work on similar tasks will be better able to improve their departments or jobs by pooling their insights and working through problems they share. The quality circle style of problem solving is often considered one of the major reasons for the success of Japanese businesses, where it's widely used. In the United States, hundreds of organizations use quality circles, but generally with less success than in Japan (Gorden & Nevins, 1993; Tang & Butler, 1997).

Quality circle members investigate problems using any method they feel might be helpful—for example, face-to-face problem-solving groups, nominal groups, or the Delphi method. The group then reports its findings and its suggestions to those who can do something about it. In some cases the quality circle members may implement their solutions without approval from upper management levels.

Summary of Concepts and Skills

This chapter provided an overview of the small group's nature, the ways in which some major types of small groups (brainstorming, information-sharing, and problem-solving) work, and the popular small group formats.

1. A small group is a collection of individuals, few enough for all members to communicate with relative ease as both senders and receivers. The members are related by some common purpose and have some degree of organization or structure.
2. Small groups may be looked at in terms of relationship and task. Relationship groups generally serve relationship needs for affiliation, affirmation, and affection and include family and friendship networks. Task groups are formed to accomplish something, often a work-related goal, and may then be disbanded.
3. Small groups generally follow the five stages of conversation: opening, feedforward, business, feedback, closing.
4. Four popular small group formats are the roundtable, the panel, the symposium, and the symposium–forum.
5. Small groups develop norms (rules or standards of behavior) that are heavily influenced by the larger culture of which the groups are a part.
6. Two popular Internet groups are the mailing-list group and the chat group. Both are changing the way we think about small group communication.
7. The brainstorming group attempts to generate as many ideas as possible by avoiding critical evaluation and encouraging quantity, combinations and extensions, and freewheeling.
8. Information-sharing groups (for example, the educational or learning group or the focus group) attempt to acquire new information or skill through a mutual sharing of knowledge or insight.
9. The problem-solving group attempts to solve a particular problem, or at least to reach a decision that may be a preface to solving the problem, and may do so through decision by authority, majority rule, or consensus.
10. The six steps in the problem-solving approach are: Define and analyze the problem, establish criteria for evaluating solutions, identify possible solutions, evaluate solutions, select best solution(s), and test solution(s).
11. A useful technique for analyzing problems is the six critical thinking hats technique, in which you approach a problem in terms of facts, feelings, negative arguments, positive benefits, creative ideas, and overall analysis.
12. Three problem-solving techniques popular in business today are the nominal group, the Delphi method, and quality circles.

The skills covered in this chapter focus on your ability to function effectively in a variety of small groups. Check your ability to apply these skills using the following scale: 1 = almost always; 2 = often; 3 = sometimes; 4 = rarely; and 5 = hardly ever.

_____ 1. I actively seek to discover the norms of the groups in which I function and take these norms into consideration when interacting in the group.

_____ 2. I can communicate in mailing-list and chat groups.

_____ 3. I follow the general rules when brainstorming: I avoid negative criticism, strive for quantity, combine and extend the contributions of others, and contribute as wild an idea as I can.

_____ 4. I appropriately restimulate a brainstorming group that has lost its steam.

_____ 5. I employ organizational structure in educational or learning groups.

_____ 6. I follow the six steps when in group problem-solving situations: Define and analyze the problem, establish the criteria for evaluating solutions, identify possible solutions, evaluate solutions, select the best solution(s), and test selected solution(s).

_____ 7. I use the six critical thinking hats technique and think about problems and solutions in terms of facts, feelings, negative arguments, positive benefits, creative ideas, and overall analysis.

_____ 8. I can make use of techniques such as the nominal group, the Delphi method, and quality circles.

Key Word Quiz

Write T for those statements that are true and F for those that are false. For those that are false, replace the italicized term with the correct term.

_____ 1. No evaluation, an emphasis on quantity, combinations and extensions, and freewheeling are desired characteristics of the *problem-solving group*.

_____ 2. An in-depth interview of a small group to discover what people think about an issue or product is known as a *learning group*.

_____ 3. Defining and analyzing the problem, establishing criteria for evaluating solutions, identifying possible solutions, evaluating solutions, selecting the best solutions, and testing the selected solutions are stages in the *consciousness-raising group*.

_____ 4. An Internet group that allows you to communicate in real time is the *mailing-list group*.

_____ 5. A number of people working on a problem together—although separated in space—who submit solutions in writing and don't talk directly with one another is known as a *focus group*.

_____ 6. Groups of workers whose task it is to improve working conditions or productivity are known as *quality circles*.

_____ 7. When a group reaches a decision that all members agree with or feel they can live with, the decision is said to be by *consensus*.

_____ 8. A general discussion, largely of questions and answers from the audience directed at group members, is known as a *symposium*.

_____ 9. Authority, majority rule, and consensus are types of *decision-making methods*.

_____ 10. The type of group in which a pool of experts interacts not interpersonally but by repeatedly responding to questionnaires is known as the *Delphi method*.

Answers: TRUE: 6, 7, 9, 10; **FALSE:** 1 (*brainstorming group*), 2 (*focus group*), 3 (*problem-solving group*), 4 (*chat group*), 5 (*nominal group*), 8 (*forum*).

10 Members and Leaders in Small Group Communication

Chapter Concepts	Chapter Skills
This chapter focuses on the roles of members and leaders and on the influence of culture in small group communication.	After completing this chapter, you should be able to:
Members in Small Group Communication	participate in small groups with a group orientation by performing group task, building, and maintenance roles and avoiding dysfunctional (individual) roles.
Leaders in Small Group Communication	adjust your leadership style to the task at hand and the needs of group members.
Membership, Leadership, and Culture	communicate in groups with cultural awareness and sensitivity.

As you saw in Chapter 9, you're a part of many different groups and serve a wide variety of roles and functions in these groups. This chapter focuses on both membership and leadership in small groups. By gaining insight into these roles and functions, you'll increase your own effectiveness as a group member and leader.

Members in Small Group Communication

Each of us serves many **roles,** patterns of behaviors that we customarily perform and that we're expected by others to perform. Javier, for example, is a part-time college student, father, bookkeeper, bowling team captain, and sometime poet. That is, he acts as a student—attends class, reads textbooks, takes exams, and does the things we expect of college students. He also performs those behaviors associated with fathers, bookkeepers, and so on. In a similar way, you develop ways of behaving when participating in small groups.

Member Roles

Kenneth Benne and Paul Sheats (1948) proposed a classification of members' roles in small group communication that still provides the best overview of this important topic (Lumsden & Lumsden, 1993; Beebe & Masterson, 2003). They divide members' roles into three general classes: group task roles, group building and maintenance roles, and individual roles. Leaders, of course, often perform these roles as well.

> **"** Do not wait for leaders; do it alone, person to person. **"**
>
> —Mother Teresa

Group Task Roles *Group task roles* help the group focus on achieving its goals. Effective group members serve several roles. Some people do lock into a few specific roles, but this single focus is usually counterproductive—it's better for the roles to be spread more evenly among the members and for the roles to be alternated frequently. Here are some examples of group task roles.

- *The information seeker or giver* and *the opinion seeker or giver* asks for or gives facts and opinions, seeks clarification of issues being discussed, and presents facts and opinions to group members.

- *The evaluator–critic* evaluates the group's decisions, questions the logic or practicality of the suggestions, and provides the group with both positive and negative feedback.
- *The procedural technician* or *recorder* takes care of various mechanical duties, such as distributing group materials and arranging the seating; writes down the group's activities, suggestions, and decisions; and/or serves as the group's memory.

Group Building and Maintenance Roles   No group can be task oriented at all times. Group members have varied interpersonal relationships, and these need to be nourished if the group is to function effectively. Group members need to be satisfied if they are to be productive. Group building and maintenance roles serve these relationship needs. Here are some examples of these roles.

- *The encourager* or *harmonizer* provides members with positive reinforcement through social approval or praise for their ideas and mediates the various differences between group members.
- *The compromiser* tries to resolve conflict between his or her ideas and those of others and offers compromises.
- *The follower* goes along with members, passively accepts the ideas of others, and functions more as an audience than as an active member.

Individual Roles   Group task roles and group building and maintenance roles are productive. They help the group achieve its goal and are group oriented. Individual roles, on the other hand, are counterproductive. They hinder the group from achieving its goal and are individual rather than group oriented. Such roles, often termed dysfunctional, hinder the group's effectiveness in terms of both productivity and personal satisfaction. Here are some examples of individual roles.

- *The aggressor* or *blocker* expresses negative evaluation of members and attacks the group, is generally disagreeable, and opposes other members or their suggestions regardless of their merit.
- *The recognition seeker* and *self-confessor* try to focus attention on themselves, boast about their accomplishments rather than the task at hand, and express their own feelings rather than focus on the group.
- *The dominator* tries to run the group or members by pulling rank, flattering members, or acting the role of boss.

A popular individual role born on the Internet is *trolling*, the practice of posting messages that you know are false or outrageous just so you can watch the group members correct you or get emotionally upset by your message. As in any group, this type of behavior wastes time and energy and diverts the group from its primary objective.

Member Participation

Here are several guidelines to help make your participation in small group communication more effective and enjoyable. These guidelines may look familiar, as they are in fact an elaboration and extension of the basic characteristics of effective interpersonal communication described in Chapter 7.

Be Group or Team Oriented   When participating in a small group, you serve as a member of a team. You share common goals with the other group members, and your participation is valuable to the extent that it advances this shared goal. So in a team situation, you need to pool your talents, knowledge, and insights to promote the

VIEWPOINT

What general type of role do you most often play in small groups: task, building and maintenance, or individual? Within this general category, what more specific roles do you regularly play? Do you find that these roles help you to achieve your purposes and goals?

best possible solution for the group. Although a group orientation calls for the participation and cooperation of all group members, this guideline does not suggest that you abandon your individuality, personal values, or beliefs for the group's sake. Individuality with a group orientation is *most* effective. And because the most effective and the most creative solutions often emerge from a combination of ideas, approach small group situations with flexibility; come to the group with ideas and information but without firmly formulated conclusions. The importance of a group orientation is also seen in one of the rules of netiquette, which holds that you should not protest the subject of, say, a mailing list or a chat group. If you don't wish to be group oriented and discuss what the group is discussing, you're expected to unsubscribe from the mailing list or withdraw from the group.

Skill development experience

Responding to Individual Roles

For each of the three individual roles (three others are described on page 206) identified in the left column, write a response or two that you might make as a leader in trying to deal with this dysfunctional role playing. Be careful that your responses don't alienate the individual or the group.

Individual, Dysfunctional Roles	Responding to Individual Roles
The aggressor expresses negative evaluation of the group and its members.	
The blocker is disagreeable, opposing other members and their ideas regardless of their merit.	
The self-confessor personalizes everything instead of focusing on the group.	

the well-being and effectiveness of the group. In fact even in leaderless groups, in which all members are equal, leadership functions must still be served.

Approaches to Leadership

Not surprisingly, **leadership** has been the focus of considerable research attention. Researchers have identified several views of leadership, which are termed *approaches*. Looking at a few of these approaches will give you a better idea of the varied ways in which leadership may be viewed and a better grasp of what leadership is and how it may be achieved.

The Traits Approach   The *traits approach* views the leader as the one who possesses those characteristics or skills (or traits) that contribute to leadership. This approach is valuable for stressing the characteristics that often (though not always) distinguish leaders from nonleaders. For example, some of the world's leading corporations seek technology project managers and leaders by looking for people who have "the right mix of technological savvy, teambuilding skills, communication know-how, and interpersonal management skills" (Crowley, 1999, p. 76). Research has found that traits more frequently associated with leadership than others include intelligence, self-confidence, determination, integrity, and sociability (Northouse, 1997). And Attila the Hun, who had much to say about leadership and particularly about the traits of effective leaders, noted that effective leaders demonstrate empathy, courage, accountability, dependability, credibility, stewardship, loyalty, desire, emotional stamina, physical stamina, decisiveness, anticipation, timing, competitiveness, self-confidence, responsibility, and tenacity (Roberts, 1987). If you demonstrate these qualities, the traits approach argues, you'll find yourself in leadership positions.

The problem with the traits approach is that these qualities often vary with the group situation, with the members, and with the culture in which the leader functions. Thus, for some groups (for example, a new computer game company), a youthful, energetic, humorous leader might be effective; for other groups (for example, a medical diagnosis team), an older, more experienced and serious leader might be effective.

The Functional Approach   The *functional approach* to leadership focuses on what the leader should do in a given situation. We've already encountered some of these functions in the discussion of group roles. Other functions associated with leadership are setting group goals, giving the group members direction, and summarizing the group's progress (Schultz, 1996). Additional functions are identified in the section entitled "Functions of Leadership" later in this chapter.

The Transformational Approach   The *transformational approach* describes a "transformational" (also called visionary or charismatic) leader who elevates the group's members, enabling them not only to accomplish the group task but also to emerge as more empowered individuals (Hersey, Blanchard, & Johnson, 2001). At the center of the transformational approach is the concept of charisma, that quality of an individual that makes us believe or want to follow him or her. Gandhi, Martin Luther King Jr., and John F. Kennedy are often cited as examples of transformational leaders. These leaders were role models, were seen as extremely competent and able, and articulated moral goals (Northouse, 1997). We'll return to this concept of charisma and to these qualities when we examine credibility in Chapter 14.

The Situational Approach   The *situational approach* holds that the effective leader adjusts his or her emphasis between task accomplishment (identifying and focusing on the specific problem that the group must solve) and member satisfaction

> 44 Reason and judgment are the qualities of a leader. 55
>
> —Tacitus

> 44 Leadership is action, not position. 55
>
> —Donald H. McGannon

> 44 Learn to lead in a nourishing manner. Learn to lead without being possessive. Learn to be helpful without taking the credit. Learn to lead without coercion. 55
>
> —John Heider

(providing for the psychological and interpersonal needs of the group members) on the basis of the specific group situation. This twofold function, you'll notice, rests on essentially the same distinction between relationship and task groups that we considered in Chapter 9. Some groups call for a high focus on task issues and need little people encouragement; this might be the case, for example, with a group of experienced scientists researching a cure for AIDS. In contrast, a group of recovering alcoholics might require leadership that stressed the members' emotional needs. The general idea of situational leadership is that there is no one style of leadership that fits all situations; each situation will call for a different combination of emphasis on task and member satisfaction (Fielder, 1967).

An interesting extension of this basic theory views leadership as consisting of four basic styles, illustrated in Figure 10.1 (Hersey, Blanchard, & Johnson, 2001). This theory claims that groups differ in their task and relationship maturity. In a group with task maturity, the members are knowledgeable about and experienced with the topic, task, and group process. Because of this maturity, the members are able to set realistic and attainable goals and are willing to take on responsibility for their decisions. In a group with relationship maturity, the members are motivated to accomplish the task and are confident in their abilities to accomplish it.

Effective leadership, then, depends on the leader's assessment of the group's task and relationship maturity. And, to complicate matters just a bit, the maturity of a group will change as the group develops—so the particular style of leadership will have to change in response. As shown in Figure 10.1, this theory identifies four leadership styles.

- The *telling style,* most appropriate for the group lacking both task and relationship maturity, is highly directive; the leader, who is significantly more knowledgeable or more powerful than the members, tells the group what has to be done and what they have to do to accomplish it. The experienced surgeon might

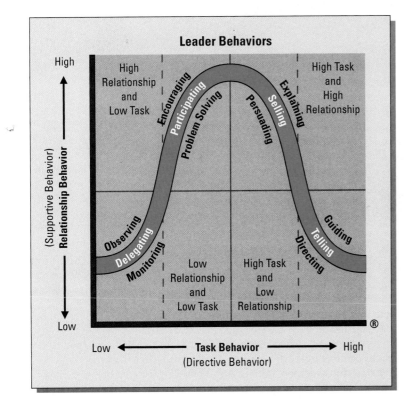

Leader Behaviors

High

(Supportive Behavior) Relationship Behavior

Low

High Relationship and Low Task

Encouraging
Participating
Problem Solving

Explaining
Selling
Persuading

High Task and High Relationship

Observing
Delegating
Monitoring

Low Relationship and Low Task

High Task and Low Relationship

Guiding
Telling
Directing

®

Low ← **Task Behavior** → High
(Directive Behavior)

Figure 10.1

A Model of Situational Leadership

This figure depicts four different styles of leadership that differ in the degree to which they are supportive or directive. Are there any leadership styles with which you're uncomfortable? What skills can you acquire to help you feel more comfortable and competent with these styles?

Source: "Model of Situational Leadership" by Paul Hersey and Kenneth Blanchard in *Management of Organizational Behavior,* p. 277. © Copyrighted material. Reprinted with permission of Center for Leadership Studies, Escondido, CA 92025. All Rights Reserved.

Chapter 10 Members and Leaders in Small Group Communication

What Do You Say?

Situational Leadership: You're serving on an advanced Internet design team whose leader uses a telling style, creating resentment among team members. You've been elected to clue the leader into appropriate and inappropriate styles. *What do you say? Through what channels?*

use this style in leading a group of young interns through the required surgical procedures.

- The *selling style* is both directive and supportive. The leader using this style, sometimes called *coaching,* tries to sell the members on the task to be accomplished, much as a coach would energize and motivate a team before a big game.

- The *participating style* is nondirective and highly supportive; the leader's focus is almost entirely on member satisfaction and member relationships. A leader supervising a group of volunteers working for a political candidate might use this style; the group would already be committed to the task but might need to be supported to continue their volunteering.

- The *delegating style,* often used with mature and knowledgeable groups, is low in both direction and support. This leader allows the group members to set their own goals, to define the problem as they see fit, and to progress through the problem-solving process with little leader interference.

As you can tell from these descriptions, the leader exerts more control with immature groups (telling and selling) and less control with mature groups (participating and delegating). As groups become more mature, members assume greater responsibility and control and leaders' control diminishes.

At this point you should find it interesting to analyze your own leadership qualities by taking the following self-test, "Are you leader material?" It will help personalize the preceding discussion on the four approaches to leadership.

 VIEWPOINT

Three general types of leadership are often distinguished (Shaw, 1981; Bennis & Nanus, 1985). The **laissez-faire leader** takes no (or very little) initiative in directing or suggesting courses of action; rather this leader allows the group to develop and progress on its own, even allowing it to make its own mistakes. The **democratic leader** provides direction but allows the group to develop and progress the way members wish, encouraging members to determine goals and procedures and stimulating members' self-direction and self-actualization. The **authoritarian leader** determines the group's policies, assigns tasks to members, and makes decisions without getting agreement from or even consulting with members. In what specific group situations would each of these leadership types be appropriate? In what specific situations would these types be inappropriate?

 **Test** Yourself

Are You Leader Material?

INSTRUCTIONS: This self-test will help you think about yourself in the role of leader. Respond to the following statements in terms of how you perceive yourself and how you think others perceive you, using a 10-point scale on which 10 = extremely true and 1 = extremely false.

What Do You Say?

Leadership Styles: The appointed leader of your work group is extremely authoritarian, and the entire group has asked you to confront the leader and ask for a more democratic approach. *What do you say? Through what channels?*

Others See Me As	I See Myself As	Perceptions
_____ ❶	_____ ❶	Popular with group members
_____ ❷	_____ ❷	Knowledgeable about the topics discussed
_____ ❸	_____ ❸	Dependable
_____ ❹	_____ ❹	Effective in establishing group goals
_____ ❺	_____ ❺	Competent in giving directions
_____ ❻	_____ ❻	Capable of energizing group members
_____ ❼	_____ ❼	Charismatic (dynamic, engaging, powerful)
_____ ❽	_____ ❽	Empowering of group members
_____ ❾	_____ ❾	Moral and honest
_____ ❿	_____ ❿	Skilled in satisfying both task and relationship needs
_____ ⓫	_____ ⓫	Flexible in adjusting leadership style on the basis of the situation
_____ ⓬	_____ ⓬	Able to delegate responsibility

HOW DID YOU DO? This test was designed to encourage you to look at yourself in terms of the four approaches to leadership discussed in the text. Perceptions 1–3 refer to the traits approach to leadership, which defines a leader as someone who possesses certain qualities. Perceptions 4–6 refer to the functional approach, which defines a leader as someone who performs certain functions. Perceptions 7–9 refer to the transformational approach, which defines a leader as someone who enables the group members to become the best they can be. Perceptions 10–12 refer to the situational approach, which defines a leader as someone who can adjust his or her style to balance the needs of the specific situation.

To compute your scores:

- Add your scores for items 1–3: _____. This will give you an idea of how you and others see you in terms of the leadership qualities identified by the trait approach.

- Add your scores for items 4–6: _____. This will give you an idea of how you and others see you in relation to the varied leadership functions considered in the functional approach.

- Add your scores for items 7–9: _____. This will give you an idea of how you and others see you as a transformational leader.

- Add your scores for items 10–12: _____. This will give you an idea of how you and others see you as a situational leader.

WHAT WILL YOU DO? As you read the remainder of this chapter and this book, try to identify specific skills and competencies you might learn that would enable you to

Be willing to make decisions. That's the most important quality in a good leader. Don't fall victim to what I call the 'ready-aim-aim-aim-aim syndrome.' You must be willing to fire.

—T. Boone Pickens

Functions of Leadership

Keeping the various views of leadership in mind, especially the situational theory with its concern for both task and people, we can look at some of the major functions leaders serve. These functions are not exclusively the leader's; they are often shared or served wholly by group members. But when there's a specific leader, she or he is expected to perform these functions.

Prepare Members and Start Interaction   Groups form gradually and often need to be eased into meaningful discussion. As the leader, you need to prepare members for the small group interaction as well as for the discussion of a specific issue or problem. Don't expect diverse members to work together cohesively to solve a problem without first becoming familiar with one another. Similarly, if members are to discuss a specific problem, a proper briefing may be necessary. If materials need to be distributed before the actual discussion, consider e-mailing them to members. Or perhaps members need to view a particular film or television show. Whatever the preparations, you need to organize and coordinate them. Once the group is assembled, you may need to stimulate the members to interact.

Maintain Effective Interaction   Even after the group has begun to interact, you'll need to monitor the members' effective interaction. When the discussion begins to drag, you may need to step in and motivate the group: "Do we have any additional comments on the proposal to eliminate required courses?" "What do you, as members of the college curriculum committee, think about the proposal?" You'll also want to ensure that all members have an opportunity to express themselves.

Guide Members through the Agreed-Upon Agenda   As the leader, you need to keep the discussion on track by asking relevant questions, summarizing the group

Communicating with power

Leadership and Empowering Others

Group leaders are in a particularly good position to empower others: to help group members (including relationship partners, coworkers, students, or siblings) gain increased power over themselves and their environment. This enhancing of their power will enable members to function more effectively in the small group and in a wide variety of other communication situations as well. In fact, giving people a sense of power may even reduce the stress and heart-related problems that are associated with feeling powerless and not being in control of life (Lynch, 2000). As an added bonus, the increased empowerment that you give to others will spill over and enhance your own growth and power as a leader.

- Raise the person's self-esteem by complimenting and being supportive. Resist faultfinding; it doesn't benefit anyone and in fact disempowers.
- Share skills and share decision-making power and authority.
- Be constructively critical. Be willing to offer your perspective; for example, to lend an ear to a first-try singing effort or to listen to a new poem.
- Encourage growth in all forms: academic, relational, and professional.

Enhancing Your Communication Power

How might you empower your best friend? Your romantic partner? Your work colleague? If you were a college instructor, how might you empower your students?

discussions periodically, or by offering a transition from one issue to the next. This involves following the tasks to be accomplished by the group as outlined in the meeting agenda and efficiently managing the amount of time allotted for each event.

Ensure Member Satisfaction   Members have different psychological needs and wants, and many people enter groups because of them. Even though a group may, for example, deal with political issues, members may have come together for psychological as well as for political reasons. If a group is to be effective, it must achieve the group goal (in this case, political) without denying the psychological purposes or goals that motivate many of the members to come together. One way to meet these needs is for you to allow digressions and personal comments, assuming they are not too frequent or overly long. Another way is to be supportive and reinforcing.

Encourage Ongoing Evaluation and Improvement   All groups encounter obstacles as they try to solve a problem, reach a decision, or generate ideas. No group is totally effective. All groups have room for improvement. To improve, the group must focus on itself. Along with trying to solve some external problem, it must try to solve its own internal problems—for example, personal conflicts, failure of members to meet on time, or members who come unprepared. When you notice some serious group failing, address it, perhaps posing this very issue (say, member lateness) as a problem to be solved.

Manage Conflict   As in interpersonal relationships, conflict is a part of small group interaction. And it's a leader's responsibility to deal with it effectively. Small group communication researchers distinguish between procedural and people conflicts and offer a wide variety of conflict management strategies (Patton, Giffin, & Patton, 1989; Folger, Poole, & Stutman, 1997; Kindler, 1996).

Farcus   by David Waisglass / Gordon Coulthart

"The kids want to know what's next on the agenda."

   Procedural and People Conflicts.   *Procedural conflicts* involve disagreements over who is in charge (who is the leader or who should be the leader), what the agenda or task of the group should be, and how the group should conduct its business. The best way to deal with procedural problems is to prevent them from occurring in the first place by establishing early in the group's interaction who is to serve as leader and what the agenda should be. If procedural problems arise after these agreements are reached, members or the leader can refer the conflicting participants to the group's earlier decisions. When members disagree or become dissatisfied with these early decisions, they may become negative or antagonistic and cease to participate in the discussion. When this happens (or if members want to change procedures), a brief discussion of the procedures may help. The important point to realize is that the procedural conflicts should be dealt with as procedural conflicts, and not allowed to escalate into something else.

   People conflicts can occur when one member dominates the group, when several members battle for control, or when some members refuse to participate. As the leader, try to secure the commitment of all members and to help all members realize that the progress of the group depends on everyone's contributions. At times it may be necessary to redirect the focus of the group and to concentrate on satisfying members' needs for group approval, periodic rewards, or encouragement.

   People conflicts are also created when people rather than ideas are attacked. Make a special effort to ensure that attacks and disagreements are clearly focused on ideas, not people. If a personal attack does get started, you may need to step in to refocus the difference in opinion onto the idea and away from the person.

What Do You Say?

Small Group Conflicts: You're leading a group of four students and four instructors who are charged with evaluating the core curriculum. The problem is that neither the teachers nor the students want to listen fairly to each other. *What do you say? To whom? Through what channel?*

Listening to Complaints

Complaints—whether in an interpersonal, small group, or organizational situation—are essential sources of feedback; they tell you that at least one person, is dissatisfied with the way things are going and that something may need changing. If you wish to keep this channel of vital information open, listen to complaints positively.

- Welcome complaints; let the person know that you view complaints as helpful sources of information and that you're listening.
- Express concern for both thoughts and feelings; for example, respond both to a worker's point about the inadequate copying facilities and to the frustration the worker feels in turning in work that looks sloppy.
- Respect confidentiality. Let the person know that you'll treat the complaint in confidence or that you'll reveal it only to those he or she wishes.
- Ask the person what he or she would like you to do about the complaint. Sometimes all a person wants is that someone hear the complaint and appreciate its legitimacy.
- Express thanks to the person for voicing the complaint, and state your intention to follow up on the complaint.

Applying Listening Skills

Suppose you are working as a manager at McDonalds, and a regular customer complains about the server: "I don't like the way she treated me and I'm not coming back here." What would you say to the customer? What would you say to the server?

Conflict Management Strategies for Small Groups. The conflict management strategies presented in Chapter 7 also are applicable to the small group situation. In addition, here are four further principles that have special relevance to small groups (Kindler, 1996):

- *Preserve the dignity and respect of all members.* Assume, for example, that each person's disagreement is legitimate and stems from a genuine concern for the good of the group. Therefore, treat disagreements kindly; even if someone attacks you personally, it's generally wise not to respond in kind but to redirect the criticism to the issues at hand.

- *Listen empathically.* See other members' perspectives; try to feel what they're feeling without making critical judgments. Try to ask yourself why they see the situation differently from the way you see it.

Skill development experience

Dealing with Small Group Complaints

You're the leader of a work team consisting of members from each of the major departments in your company. For each of the following complaints, explain (1) what you would say and (2) what objective your response is designed to achieve.

1. "Reducing costs is an impossible task; we're wasting our time here. Costs have gone up; there's no way we can reduce costs. Period. The end."
2. "You're calling these meetings much too often and much too early to suit us. We'd like fewer meetings scheduled for late in the day."
3. "That's not fair. Why do I always have to take the minutes of these meetings? Can't we have a real secretary in here?"
4. "There's a good reason why I don't contribute to the discussion. I don't contribute because no one listens to what I say."

- *Seek out and emphasize common ground.* Even in the midst of disagreement, there are areas of common interest, common beliefs, and common aims. Find these and build on them.
- *Value diversity and differences.* Creative solutions often emerge from conflicting perspectives. So don't gloss over differences; instead, explore them for the valuable information they can give you.

Mentoring

Another function of leadership that extends well beyond the small group situation is that of mentoring. A **mentoring** relationship occurs when an experienced individual helps to train a less experienced person. An accomplished teacher, for example, might mentor a younger teacher who is newly arrived or who has never taught before. The mentor guides the new person through the ropes, teaches the strategies and techniques for success, and otherwise communicates his or her accumulated knowledge and experience to the "mentee."

The mentoring relationship provides an ideal learning environment. It's usually a one-on-one relationship between expert and novice, a relationship that is supportive and trusting. There's a mutual and open sharing of information and thoughts about the job. The relationship enables the novice to try out new skills under the guidance of an expert, to ask questions, and to obtain the feedback so necessary to learning complex skills. It's a relationship that's perhaps best characterized as one in which the experienced and powerful mentor empowers the novice, giving the novice the tools and techniques needed for gaining the same power the mentor now holds.

One study found the mentoring relationship to be one of the three primary paths for career achievement among African American men and women (Bridges, 1996). And another study (of middle-level managers) demonstrated that those who had mentors and participated in mentoring relationships got more promotions and higher salaries than those who didn't have mentors (Scandura, 1992).

www.researchnavigator.com

Investigate Key Terms: Investigate one of the key terms discussed in this chapter (for example, role, leadership, transformational leader, leadership traits, authoritarian leadership, mentoring, individual and collective orientations, high- and low-power-distance cultures, or groupthink). What additional insights can you provide?

VIEWPOINT

Using the traits approach, the functional approach, the transformational approach, or the situational approach, how would you describe yourself as a leader? What do you think is the single most important principle for a group leader to follow?

Communicating ethically

Justifying the Ends

Do the ends justify the means? Is it ethical for a group to do things that would normally be considered unethical? For example, would it be ethical for an advertising team to write deliberately misleading advertising copy, if the end the team hoped to achieve were a worthy one such as keeping children from using drugs? Those taking an objective position (see the Communicating Ethically box in Chapter 2) would argue that the ends never justify the means; that a lie, for example, is always wrong regardless of the specific situation. Those taking a subjective position would argue that at times the end does justify the means and at times it doesn't; it depends on the specific means and ends in question. The following situations raise ethical dilemmas caused largely by conflicts between means and ends.

What Would You Do?

Would you

- *lie about your past to your romantic partner to preserve peace and stability in the relationship?*
- *misrepresent yourself on an Internet group to spice things up?*
- *make up statistics to support your point of view in a forum because you know that what you are advocating will benefit the audience?*

Web Explorations

Two useful self-tests are available at www.ablongman.com/devito to help you further explore the concepts of leadership and leader influence: (1) How Machiavellian Are You? and (2) What Kind of Leader Are You?

At the same time, the mentor benefits from clarifying his or her thoughts, from seeing the job from the perspective of a newcomer, and from considering and formulating answers to a variety of questions. Just as a teacher learns from teaching, a mentor learns from mentoring.

Membership, Leadership, and Culture

Most of the research (and so also the resulting theory) concerning small group communication, membership, and leadership has been conducted in universities in the United States and reflects American culture. So it's important that we look at both membership and leadership from the point of view of different cultures.

For example, each culture maintains its own belief system, which influences group members' behavior. Members of many Asian cultures, influenced by Confucian principles, believe that "the protruding nail gets pounded down" and are therefore not likely to voice disagreement with the majority of the group. Americans, on the other hand, influenced by the belief that "the squeaky wheel gets the grease," are more likely to voice disagreement or to act in ways different from other group members in order to get what they want (Hofstede, 1997).

Also, each culture has its own rules of preferred and expected leadership style. In the United States the general and expected style for a group leader is democratic. Our political leaders are elected by a democratic process; similarly, company directors are elected by the shareholders of their corporations. In other situations, of course, leaders are chosen by those in authority. The president of a company will normally decide who will supervise and who will be supervised. Even in this situation, however, the supervisor is expected to behave democratically—to listen to the ideas of the employees; to take their views into consideration when decisions are to be made; to keep them informed of corporate developments; and not to discriminate on the basis of sex, race, or affectional orientation. Also, we expect that organizational and other group leaders will be changed fairly regularly, much as we change political leaders on a regular basis. In some other cultures leaders get their positions by right of birth. They are not elected, nor are they expected to behave democratically. Similarly, their tenure as leaders is usually extremely long and may in fact last their entire lives. Their leadership roles are then passed on to their children. In other cases leaders may be chosen by a military dictator.

Individual and Collective Orientation

Small group cultures and cultures in general differ in the extent to which they promote individualistic values (for example, power, achievement, hedonism, and stimulation) versus collectivist values (for example, benevolence, tradition, and conformity).

One of the major differences between an **individual orientation** and a **collective orientation** is in the extent to which an individual's goals or the group's goals are given precedence. Individual and collective tendencies are, of course, not mutually exclusive; this is not an all-or-none orientation, but rather one of emphasis. You probably have both tendencies. Thus, you may, for example, compete with other members of your basketball team to make the most baskets or win the most valuable player award (and thus emphasize individual goals). At the same time, however, you will—in a game—act in a way that will benefit the entire team (and thus emphasize group goals). In actual practice, both individual and collective tendencies will help both you and your team achieve your goals. Still, most people and most cultures have a dominant orientation: They're more individually oriented (they see themselves as independent) or more collectively oriented (they see themselves as interdependent) in most situations, most of the time (cf. Singelis, 1994).

❝ If everyone is thinking alike, then somebody isn't thinking. ❞

—George S. Patton

In an **individualistic culture** you're responsible to your own conscience; responsibility is largely an individual matter. In a **collectivist culture** you're responsible to the rules of the social group; all members share responsibility for accomplishments as well as for failures. Individualistic cultures foster competition, whereas collectivist cultures promote cooperation.

In a small group situation in an individualistic culture, you might compete for leadership, and there would likely be a very clear distinction between leaders and members. In a collectivist culture, in contrast, group leadership would be shared and rotated; there would likely be little distinction between leader and members. These orientations will also influence the kinds of communication members consider appropriate in an organizational context. For example, individualistic members will favor clarity and directness, but collectivists will favor face-saving and the avoidance of hurting others or arousing negative evaluations (Kim & Sharkey, 1995).

One obvious consequence of this difference in orientation can be seen in how individualistic and collectivist groups treat members who commit serious errors. A group governed by individualistic norms is likely to single out, reprimand, and perhaps fire an errant member. Further the leader or supervisor is likely to distance himself or herself from this member for fear that the error will reflect negatively on his or her leadership. In a more collectivist culture, the error is more likely to be seen as a group mistake. The group is unlikely to single out the member—especially not in public—and the leader is likely to bear part of the blame. The same is true when one member comes up with a great idea. In individualistic cultures that person is likely to be singled out for praise and rewards, even though the effort was to benefit the group. In collectivist cultures the group is recognized and rewarded for the idea.

What Do You Say?

Leader Guidance: Members of your group are not participating equally. Of the eight members, three monopolize the discussion and five say as little as possible. *What do you say? To whom?*

High and Low Power Distances

In some cultures power is concentrated in the hands of a few, and there is a great difference between the power held by these people and that held by the ordinary citizen. These are called high-power-distance cultures; examples are Mexico, Brazil, India, and the Philippines (Hofstede, 1997). In low-power-distance cultures, power is more evenly distributed throughout the citizenry; examples include Denmark, New Zealand, Sweden, and to a lesser extent the United States. These differences affect interpersonal communication and relationships in a variety of ways.

The power distance between groups will influence both friendship and dating relationships (Andersen, 1991). For example, in India (high power distance) friendships and romantic relationships are expected to take place within your cultural class; in Sweden (low power distance) a person is expected to select friends and romantic partners on the basis not of class or culture but of individual factors such as personality, appearance, and the like.

In low-power-distance cultures, there is a general feeling of equality, which is consistent with acting assertively; so you're expected to confront a friend, partner, or supervisor assertively (Borden, 1991). In high-power-distance cultures, direct confrontation and assertiveness may be viewed negatively, especially if directed at a superior.

In high-power-distance cultures, you're taught to have great respect for authority; people in these cultures see authority as desirable and beneficial and generally do not welcome challenges to authority (Westwood, Tang, & Kirkbride, 1992; Bochner & Hesketh, 1994). In low-power-distance cultures, there's a certain distrust for authority; it's seen as a kind of necessary evil that should be limited as much as possible. This difference in attitudes toward authority can be seen right in the classroom. In high-power-distance cultures, there's a great power distance between students and teachers; students are expected to be modest, polite, and totally respectful. In low-power-distance cultures, students are expected to demonstrate their knowledge and command of the subject matter, participate in discussions with the teacher,

www.researchnavigator.com

Find Answers: Try finding answers to one of the following questions or design a research study to answer it: Are men and women equally effective as small group leaders? How do members of individualist and collectivist cultures view small group leadership? What personality traits are most important to someone becoming a group leader?

and even challenge the teacher—something many high-power-distance culture members wouldn't even think of doing.

High-power-distance cultures rely more on symbols of power. For example, titles (Dr., Professor, Chef, Inspector) are more important in high-power-distance cultures. Failure to include these honorifics in forms of address is a serious breach of etiquette. Low-power-distance cultures rely less on symbols of power, so there is less of a problem if you fail to use a respectful title (Victor, 1992)—although you may create problems if, for example, you call a medical doctor, police captain, military officer, or professor Ms. or Mr.

The groups in which you'll participate as a member or a leader will vary in power distance; some will be high-power-distance groups and others will be low. You need to recognize which is which, to follow the cultural rules generally, and to break the rules only after you've thought through the consequences.

Summary of Concepts and Skills

In this chapter we looked at membership and leadership in the small group. We examined the roles of members—some productive and some counterproductive—and considered leadership theories, leadership functions, and cultural factors in small groups.

1. A popular classification of small group member roles divides them into three types: group task roles, group building and maintenance roles, and individual roles.

2. Among the group task roles are those of information seeker or giver, opinion seeker or giver, evaluator–critic, and procedural technician or recorder. Among the group building and maintenance roles are encourager/harmonizer, compromiser, and follower. Among the individual (dysfunctional) roles are aggressor/blocker, recognition seeker/self-confessor, and dominator.

3. Group members should be group oriented, center conflict on issues, be critically open-minded, and ensure understanding.

4. Groupthink is an excessive concern with securing agreement that discourages critical thinking and the exploration of alternative ways of doing things.

5. Three theories of leadership are especially helpful in understanding the varied nature of leadership. The traits approach identifies characteristics, such as intelligence and self-confidence, that contribute to leadership. The transformational approach focuses on leaders as people who raise the performance of group members and empower them. The situational approach views leadership as varying its focus between accomplishing the task and serving the members' social and emotional needs, depending on the specific group and the unique situation.

6. An extension of the situational approach to leadership identifies four major leadership styles: the telling, selling, participating, and delegating styles. The appropriate style to use depends on the group's level of task and relationship maturity.

7. Three major leadership styles are laissez-faire, democratic, and authoritarian.

8. Among the leader's task functions are to prepare members and start the group interaction, maintain effective interaction, guide members through the agreed-upon agenda, ensure member satisfaction, encourage ongoing evaluation and improvement, prepare members for the discussion, and manage conflict.

9. Group membership and leadership attitudes and behaviors are likely to be heavily influenced by culture, especially by the individual–collective and power-distance orientations.

The skills identified in this discussion center on increasing your ability to function more effectively as a small group member and leader. Check your ability to apply these skills, using the following rating scale: 1 = almost always; 2 = often; 3 = sometimes; 4 = rarely; and 5 = hardly ever.

_____ 1. I avoid playing the popular but dysfunctional individual roles in a small group: aggressor, blocker, recognition seeker, self-confessor, or dominator.

_____ 2. When participating in a small group, I am group rather than individual oriented, center the conflict on issues rather than on personalities, am critically open-minded, and make sure that my meanings and the meanings of others are clearly understood.

_____ 3. I recognize the symptoms of groupthink and actively counter my own groupthink tendencies as well as those evidenced in the group.

_____ 4. I adjust my leadership style according to the task at hand and the needs of group members.

_____ 5. As a small group leader, I start group interaction, maintain effective interaction throughout the discussion, keep members on track, ensure member satisfaction, encourage ongoing evaluation and improvement, and prepare members for the discussion as necessary.

_____ 6. I recognize and appreciate the cultural differences that people have toward group membership and leadership.

Key Word Quiz

Write T for those statements that are true and F for those that are false. For those that are false, replace the italicized term with the correct term.

_____ 1. Information seeker, evaluator–critic, and procedural technician are examples of *group building and maintenance roles.*

_____ 2. Encourager, compromiser, and follower are examples of *group task roles.*

_____ 3. Aggressor/blocker, recognition seeker/self-confessor, and dominator are examples of *functional roles.*

_____ 4. The leader who elevates and empowers group members is a *transformational leader.*

_____ 5. The leadership style in which the leader takes no initiative in directing or suggesting courses of action is known as *democratic.*

_____ 6. The leadership style in which the leader determines the group's agenda and decisions is known as *laissez-faire.*

_____ 7. The group (rather than the individual) is likely to be given greater emphasis in *individualistic cultures.*

_____ 8. The way of thinking that group members engage in when agreement becomes all important and overrides logical and realistic analysis is known as *groupthink.*

_____ 9. The *traits* approach views the leader as the one who possesses specific characteristics and skills.

_____ 10. Group problems such as members competing for leadership positions, having a lack of clarity about their functions, or short-circuiting the process of analyzing the problem are examples of *personality conflicts.*

Answers: TRUE: 4, 8, 9; FALSE: 1 (*group task roles*), 2 (*group building and maintenance roles*), 3 (*dysfunctional roles*), 5 (*laissez-faire leader*), 6 (*authoritarian*), 7 (*collectivist cultures*), 10 (*procedural conflicts*)

11 Public Speaking Preparation (Steps 1–6)

Chapter Concepts	Chapter Skills
This chapter defines public speaking and covers the first six steps in preparing a speech.	After completing this chapter, you should be able to:
The Nature of Public Speaking	appreciate the benefits and skills of public speaking and effectively manage your communication apprehension.
Step 1. Select Your Topic and Purpose	select and limit appropriate topics and purposes for public speeches.
Step 2. Analyze Your Audience	analyze an audience to make predictions about audience members' knowledge, attitudes, and beliefs and make appropriate adaptations in your speech.
Step 3. Research Your Topic	research varied topics, using the most relevant, efficient, and reliable sources.
Step 4. Formulate Your Thesis and Identify Your Major Propositions	select appropriate theses (main assertions) and expand them by asking strategic questions to develop the main ideas.
Step 5. Support Your Propositions	support your propositions with appropriate amplifying materials and evidence.
Step 6. Organize Your Information	organize the main ideas into an appropriate pattern.

Before getting to the steps for preparing and presenting a public speech, let's define public speaking and consider the benefits that will reward your public speaking efforts. In addition, we'll address what is probably your number one problem; namely, the fear that so often accompanies giving speeches. As a preface to this chapter and the remaining discussions of public speaking in Chapters 12 through 14, become familiar with Allyn and Bacon's public speaking website (see www.abacon.com/pubspeak). The home page is shown in Figure 11.1 on page 224.

The Nature of Public Speaking

Public speaking is a form of communication in which a speaker addresses a relatively large audience with a relatively continuous discourse, usually in a face-to-face situation. A student delivering a report to a political science class, a teacher lecturing on the structure of DNA, a minister preaching a sermon, and a politician delivering a campaign speech are all examples of public speaking. Also, delivering a speech to a television camera to be broadcast to an entire nation or over the radio to be heard by a few thousand or a few million people is similar in many ways to what we traditionally think of as public speaking. It differs in that these mediated messages are not face-to-face, so the audience cannot respond immediately to the message and the speaker, in turn, cannot make adjustments on the basis of this feedback.

The closest electronic counterpart to public speaking is probably the newsgroup, a public forum for the exchange of ideas. One difference between newsgroups and

Figure 11.1

The Allyn & Bacon Public Speaking Website

Log on to this website. In what ways might this site help you in preparing and presenting your speeches?

face-to-face public speaking is that the messages in newsgroups are written. Another difference is that in electronic communication, as in television or radio, feedback from listeners is delayed rather than immediate, so the speaker cannot make on-the-spot adjustments. Voice and video enhancements are eliminating (or at least blurring) these differences. Even given these differences, the principles of public speaking discussed in this and the remaining chapters apply to these mediated and electronic communications as well as to face-to-face communication.

In addition to the speeches that you will give in this class and during your college career, you will also be called on to make formal and informal speeches throughout your life. For example, you may make a presentation about a new product at a sales meeting; present your company's rules and regulations to a group of new employees; explain the benefits of a new playground to members of your local PTA; or give a speech about your family genealogy at a family reunion. Regardless of the circumstances under which you give a speech, you will find the 10 steps to public speaking preparation discussed in this chapter and the next extremely practical.

Benefits and Skills of Public Speaking

Public speaking draws together a wide variety of social, academic, and career skills. Although these skills are central to public speaking, they also enrich other competencies. Among these are your ability to present yourself to others with confidence and self-assurance and your ability to conduct research efficiently and effectively. Public speaking skills will further help you to understand human motivation, to analyze and evaluate the validity of persuasive appeals, and to use persuasion effectively.

Public speaking will also develop and refine your general communication abilities by helping you

- explain complex concepts clearly
- organize a variety of messages for clarity and persuasiveness
- develop logical, emotional, and ethical appeals to support an argument
- communicate credibility
- improve listening and delivery skills

> " All the great speakers were bad speakers at first. "
>
> —Ralph Waldo Emerson

It's important to remember, however, that effective public speakers aren't born; they're made. Through instruction, exposure to different speeches, feedback, and individual learning experiences, you can become an effective speaker. Regardless of your present level of competence, you can improve your public speaking skills through proper training.

Dealing with Communication Apprehension

Now that you have a good idea of what public speaking is and what benefits you'll derive from studying it, consider what is probably your major concern: **communication apprehension,** or stage fright. People experience apprehension in all types of communication (as illustrated throughout this text), but it is in the public speaking situation that apprehension is most common and most severe (McCroskey, 1997; Richmond & McCroskey, 1998). Take the accompanying apprehension self-test to measure your own fear of speaking in public.

? VIEWPOINT
What is the single most important career benefit you can derive from your study of public speaking?

Test Yourself

How Apprehensive Are You about Public Speaking?

INSTRUCTIONS: This questionnaire consists of six statements concerning your feelings about public speaking. Indicate the degree to which each statement applies to you by marking whether you (1) strongly agree, (2) agree, (3) are undecided, (4) disagree, or (5) strongly disagree with each statement. There are no right or wrong answers. Don't be concerned that some of the statements are similar to others. Work quickly; just record your first impression.

_____ ❶ I have no fear of giving a speech.

_____ ❷ Certain parts of my body feel very tense and rigid when I am giving a speech.

_____ ❸ I feel relaxed while giving a speech.

_____ ❹ My thoughts become confused and jumbled when I am giving a speech.

_____ ❺ I face the prospect of giving a speech with confidence.

_____ ❻ While giving a speech, I get so nervous that I forget facts I really know.

HOW DID YOU DO? To obtain your public speaking apprehension score, use the following formula: Start with 18 points; add the scores for items 1, 3, and 5; then subtract the scores for items 2, 4, and 6.

A score above 18 shows some degree of apprehension. Most people score above 18, so if you scored relatively high, you're among the vast majority of people. You may find it interesting to compare your apprehension scores from this test and the test in Chapter 9. Most people would score higher on public speaking apprehension than on apprehension in group discussions.

WHAT WILL YOU DO? As you read the suggestions for reducing apprehension in the text, consider what you can do to incorporate these ideas into your own public speaking experiences. Consider too how these suggestions might be useful in reducing apprehension more generally—for example, in social situations and in small groups and meetings.

Source: Adapted from *An Introduction to Rhetorical Communication,* 7th ed., by James C. McCroskey. Copyright © 1997 by Allyn and Bacon. Reprinted by permission.

> ❝ The human brain starts working the moment you're born and never stops until you stand up to speak in public. ❞
>
> —George Jessel

What Do You Say?

Apprehension Management: This is your first experience with public speaking and you're very nervous. You're afraid you'll forget your speech or stumble somehow, so you're wondering if it would be a good idea to alert your audience to your nervousness. *What do you say?*

Reducing Your Apprehension   The following suggestions will help you reduce your public speaking apprehension as well as any communication apprehension in small group and interpersonal communication situations (Beatty, 1988; Richmond & McCroskey, 1998).

Gain Experience.   New and different situations such as public speaking are likely to make you anxious, so try to reduce their newness and differentness. The best way to do this is to get as much public speaking experience as you can. With experience your initial fears and anxieties will give way to feelings of control, comfort, and pleasure. Experience will show you that the feelings of accomplishment in public speaking are rewarding and will outweigh any initial anxiety. Try also to familiarize yourself with the public speaking context. For example, try to rehearse in the room in which you will give your speech.

Think Positively.   When you see yourself as inferior—when, for example, you feel that others are better speakers or that they know more than you do—anxiety increases. To gain greater confidence, think positive thoughts and be especially thorough in your preparation. At the same time, maintain realistic expectations for yourself. Fear increases when you feel that you can't meet your own or your audience's expectations (Ayres, 1986). Keep in mind that your second speech does not have to be better than that of the previous speaker, but that it should be better than your first speech.

See Public Speaking as Conversation.   When you're the center of attention, as you are in public speaking, you feel especially conspicuous; this often increases anxiety. It may help, therefore, to think of public speaking as another type of conversation (some theorists call it "enlarged conversation"). Or, if you're comfortable talking in small groups, visualizing your audience as an enlarged small group may dispel some anxiety.

Stress Similarity.   When you feel like (rather than different from) your audience, your anxiety should lessen. Therefore, try to emphasize the similarity between yourself and your audience, especially when your audience consists of people from cultures different from your own (Stephan & Stephan, 1992). With a culturally different audience, you're likely to feel less similarity with your listeners and thus to experience greater anxiety (Gudykunst & Nishida, 1984; Gudykunst, Yang, & Nishida, 1985). So with all audiences, but especially with multicultural gatherings, stress similarities in experiences, attitudes, and values; it will make you feel more at one with your listeners.

Prepare and Practice Thoroughly.   Much of the fear you experience is a fear of failure. Adequate and even extra preparation will lessen the possibility of failure and the accompanying apprehension. Because apprehension is greatest during the beginning of the speech, try memorizing the first few sentences of your talk. If there are complicated facts or figures, be sure to write these out and plan to read them; this will remove the worry of forgetting them from your mind.

> **If you're going to play the game properly, you'd better know every rule.**
>
> —Barbara Jordan

Move About and Breathe Deeply.   Physical activity—gross bodily movements as well as the small movements of the hands, face, and head—lessens apprehension. Using a visual aid, for example, will temporarily divert attention from you and will allow you to get rid of your excess energy. If you breathe deeply a few times before getting up to speak, you'll sense your body relax. This will help you overcome your initial fear of walking to the front of the room.

Avoid Chemicals as Tension Relievers. Unless prescribed by a physician, avoid any chemical means for reducing apprehension. Tranquilizers, marijuana, and artificial stimulants are likely to create problems rather than to reduce them. They're likely to impair your ability to remember the parts of your speech, to accurately read audience feedback, and to regulate the timing of your speech. And, of course, alcohol does nothing to reduce public speaking apprehension (Himle, Abelson, & Haghight-gou, 1999).

With the nature of public speaking and its benefits in mind, and with an understanding of communication apprehension and some techniques for managing it, we can look at the first six of the ten essential steps for preparing an effective public speech, as summarized in Figure 11.2. The final four steps will be covered in Chapter 12.

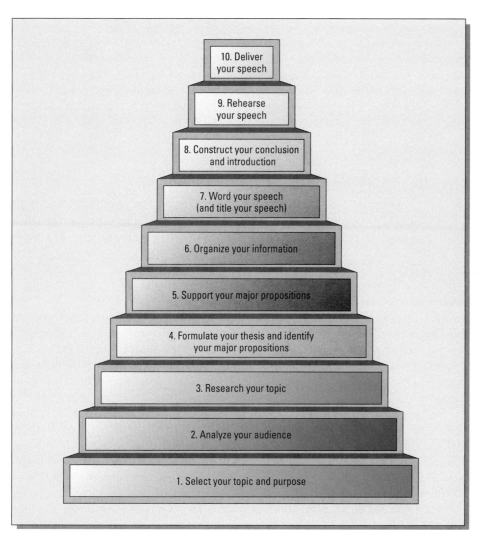

10. Deliver your speech

9. Rehearse your speech

8. Construct your conclusion and introduction

7. Word your speech (and title your speech)

6. Organize your information

5. Support your major propositions

4. Formulate your thesis and identify your major propositions

3. Research your topic

2. Analyze your audience

1. Select your topic and purpose

Figure 11.2

The Steps in Public Speaking Preparation and Delivery

Speakers differ in the order in which they follow these steps. Some speakers, for example, prefer to begin with audience analysis, asking themselves what the audience is interested in and then selecting the topic and purpose. Some speakers prefer to identify their major propositions before conducting extensive research; others prefer to allow the propositions to emerge from the research. The order presented here will prove useful to most speakers for most situations, but vary the order when it serves your purposes. As long as you cover all steps, you should be in good shape.

Listening to Help Reduce Apprehension

As a listener you can help speakers with their apprehension.

- *Positively reinforce the speaker*. An occasional nod or smile and an attentive appearance throughout the speech will help put the speaker at ease. Resist any temptation to pick up a newspaper or talk with a friend.

- *Ask questions in a supportive manner*. If there's a question period, ask information-seeking questions rather than firing off critical challenges. In other words, ask questions in a way that won't encourage defensiveness. Instead of saying, "Your criticism of heavy metal music is absurd," say, "Why do you find the lyrics of heavy metal harmful?"

- *Don't focus on errors*. If the speaker fumbles, don't put your head down, cover your eyes, or otherwise communicate your awareness of the fumble. Instead, continue listening to the content of the speech; let the speaker know that you're focused on what is being said.

Applying Listening Skills

You notice that the speaker approaching the front of the room to give a speech is visibly nervous. What specifically can you do as a listener to help the speaker manage this apprehension and get through the speech?

What Do You Say?

Topic Appropriateness: Stephen, a 20-year-old student, gave a speech on flower arranging—a topic so unexpected that members of the audience giggled and avoided eye contact with the speaker throughout the speech. You're called upon to offer a critique of the speech. *What do you say?*

> **❝** There is no such thing as an uninteresting subject; there are only uninteresting people. **❞**
>
> —G. K. Chesterton

Step 1: Select Your Topic and Purpose

The first step in preparing an effective public speech is to select the topic on which you'll speak and the general and specific purposes you hope to achieve.

Your Topic

Select a worthwhile topic that will prove interesting to the audience. If your first speech is an informative one, select a topic that your audience probably knows little about but that will make them curious to learn more. If your first speech is persuasive, you might select a topic about which you and the audience agree and aim to strengthen their attitudes. Or you might select a topic on which you and the audience disagree; your aim then would be to persuade them to change their attitudes in your direction.

Not surprisingly, the appropriateness of a speech topic will vary with the culture of the audience. For example, each culture has its own topics that will often cause conflict. Generally these are subjects that should be avoided, especially by visitors from other cultures. Table 11.1 gives several examples of **taboo** topics that Roger Axtell, in *Do's and Taboos Around the World* (1993), recommends that visitors from the United States avoid. These examples are not intended to be exhaustive, but rather to remind you that each culture defines what is and is not an appropriate topic for public speaking.

Finding Your Topic   Public speaking topics are all around you. Select a topic area that you're interested in and know something about. And, of course, select a topic that your audience will find interesting and worthwhile. You can find topics by examining lists of suitable topics, surveys, and news items or by brainstorming.

Topic Lists.   Most public speaking textbooks contain suggestions for topics suitable for public speeches as do books for writers (for example, Lamm & Lamm [1999]). This text's companion website (www.ablongman.com/devito, see "Dictionary of Topics" in Chapter 13) contains a list of hundreds of topics. Another source of

TABLE 11.1 Taboos around the World

Can you think of other topics that may cause difficulties in certain cultural contexts?

CULTURE	TABOOS
Belgium	Politics, language differences between French and Flemish, religion
Norway	Salaries, social status
Spain	Family, religion, jobs, negative comments on bullfighting
Egypt	Middle Eastern politics
Nigeria	Religion
Libya	Politics, religion
Japan	World War II
Pakistan	Politics
Philippines	Politics, religion, corruption, foreign aid
South Korea	Internal politics, criticism of the government, socialism, communism
Bolivia	Politics, religion
Colombia	Politics, criticism of bullfighting
Mexico	Mexican–American war, illegal aliens
Caribbean	Race, local politics, religion

topics is the list of best-selling nonfiction books printed in most newspaper book reviews or found in well-stocked bookstores. Or visit one of the online bookstores (www.amazon.com, www.barnesandnoble.com, or www.borders.com) and search the lists of their most popular books. The popularity of these books tells you that people are interested in these topics.

Surveys. An excellent way to determine what is worthwhile to your audience is to look at some of the national and regional polls concerning what issues people feel are most significant. Search for polling sites with your favorite search engine or start with one of the most widely used, the Gallup poll at www.gallup.com. Surveys of major concerns of people appear regularly in newspapers and magazines and are perhaps the most timely. Some search engines and websites list the topics that users ask for or visit most often; these, too, are useful for helping you discover what people are interested in and what they want to hear about more.

News Items. Still another useful starting point is a good daily newspaper. Here you'll find the important international, domestic, financial, and social issues all conveniently covered in one place. The editorial page and letters to the editor are also useful for learning what concerns people. News magazines such as *Time* and *Newsweek* and business-oriented magazines such as *Forbes, Money, Business Week,* and *Fortune* will provide a wealth of suggestions. News shows such as *20/20* and *60 Minutes* and the numerous talk shows often discuss the very issues that concern us all. And, of course, you can surf the Net and discover a host of topics that command people's interest and attention in health, education, politics, religion, science, technology, or just about any other area in which you're interested.

"My summer vacation: How I made money in a bear market."

Figure 11.3

Tree Diagram for Limiting Speech Topics
Construct a different tree diagram by selecting film, radio, or advertising and subdividing it until you reach a level that would be appropriate for 5- to 10-minute informative or persuasive speeches.

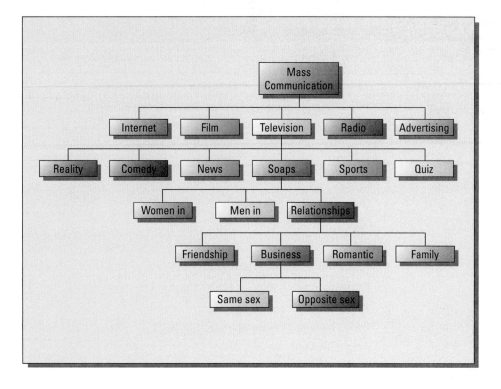

Limiting Your Topic Plan to cover a limited topic in depth rather than a broad topic superficially. The limiting process is simple: Repeatedly divide the topic into its significant parts. For example, divide your general topic into its component parts, then divide one of these parts into its component parts. Continue until the topic seems manageable, one that you can reasonably cover in some depth in the allotted time.

For example, take television programs as the first general topic area. Television programs, without some limitation, would take a lifetime to cover adequately. But you could divide this general subject into subtopics such as comedy, children's programs, educational programs, news, movies, soap operas, game shows, and sports. You might then take one of these topics, say comedy, and divide it into subtopics. You might consider comedy on a time basis and divide television comedy into its significant time periods: pre-1960, 1961–1989, 1990 to the present. Or you might focus on situation comedies. Here you might examine a topic such as "Women in Television Comedy," "Race Relations in Situation Comedy," or "Families in Television Comedies." At this stage the topic is beginning to look manageable. Figure 11.3 presents a tree diagram to further illustrate this process. The diagram begins with a topic even broader than television programs—mass communication. Notice how from the general "Mass Communication" you can get to the relatively specific "Same-Sex or Opposite-Sex Business Relationships in Television Soaps."

A more technologically sophisticated way of both selecting and limiting your topic is to let a search directory do some of the work for you. Using the search directory's nested list of topics, go from the general to the specific by selecting a topic, then a subdivision of that topic, then a subdivision of that topic, and so on. Eventually you'll be directed to relatively specific areas and websites that will suggest topics that may be suitable for a classroom public speech.

Your Purpose

In some cases you'll select your topic and purpose almost simultaneously. At other times you'll select your topic and later formulate your purpose. In preparing public speeches, you'll need to formulate both a general and a specific purpose.

Skill development experience

Using Cultural Beliefs as Assumptions

How effective would it be to use each of the following cultural beliefs as a basic assumption in presenting a speech to your public speaking class? Use the following scale: *A* = the audience would favorably accept this assumption and would welcome a speaker with this point of view; *B* = some members would listen receptively and others wouldn't; or *C* = the audience would reject this assumption and would not welcome a speaker with this point of view. On the basis of this analysis, what might you do—and what should you not do—in your next speech?

_____ 1. A return to religious values is the best hope for the world.

_____ 2. The welfare of the family must come first, even before your own individual needs.

_____ 3. Winning is all important; it's not how you play the game, it's whether or not you win that matters.

_____ 4. Keeping the United States militarily superior is the best way to preserve world peace.

Your General Purpose   The two major kinds of public speeches are informative and persuasive. The informative speech creates understanding; it clarifies, enlightens, corrects misunderstandings, demonstrates how something works, or explains how something is structured (see Chapter 13). The persuasive speech, on the other hand, influences attitudes or behaviors. It may strengthen existing attitudes or change the audience's beliefs. Or it may move the audience to act in a particular way (see Chapter 14).

Your Specific Purpose   Your specific purpose identifies the information you want to communicate (in an informative speech) or the attitude or behavior you want to change (in a persuasive speech). For example, your specific purpose in an informative speech might be

- to inform my audience of three ways to save time using the Internet for research
- to inform my audience about how the new interoffice e-mail system works
- to inform my audience of the benefits of integrated work teams

  Your specific purpose in a persuasive speech might be

- to persuade my audience that all cigarette advertising should be abolished
- to persuade my audience that the college should establish courses in AIDS and STDs prevention
- to persuade my audience to contribute time to working with students with disabilities

Whether you intend to inform or to persuade, limit your specific purpose so you'll be able to go into it in some depth. Your audience will benefit more from a speech that covers a small area in depth than from one that covers a broad topic superficially.

Avoid the common pitfall of trying to accomplish too much in too short a time. For example, "to inform my audience about the development of AIDS and the recent testing procedures for HIV infection" is actually two specific purposes. Select one of them and build your speech around it. Follow the same principle in developing your specific purpose for your persuasive speeches. Thus, for example, "to persuade my audience of the prevalence of AIDS in our community and to influence them to contribute money for AIDS services" contains two specific purposes. Select either one.

> ❝ Speech is power; speech is to persuade, to convert, to compel. ❞
>
> —Ralph Waldo Emerson

Negative Power

Sometimes, attempts to influence backfire; the possibility that *negative power* may operate always exists. Negative power creates results that are the reverse of what you intend. For example, you may warn a child to stay away from the hot stove under threat of punishment; but if negative power operates, the child will do exactly what you said not to do. In this example the threat of punishment may actually make the forbidden behavior seem exciting or challenging. In a public speaking situation, you may try to get your audience to, say, vote for a candidate by recalling her previous long-term political service or her educational background. But the possibility exists that the audience may see your candidate as too elitist or too entrenched in the political machine, say, and may support her opponent. So whenever you try to exert power and influence others, remember that there is always the potential for negative power to work against you. The best defense against this is thorough audience analysis. If you know your audience's attitudes and beliefs and use this information in constructing your appeals, you stand a much better chance of keeping negative power out of the equation.

Enhancing Your Communication Power

How might you use audience analysis to lessen the likelihood of negative power?

Step 2: Analyze Your Audience

If you are to inform or persuade an audience, you must know who they are. What do they already know? What would they want to know more about? What are their opinions, attitudes, and beliefs? Where do they stand on the issues you wish to address? Specifically, you will want to look at the sociological and psychological characteristics of your audience.

Analyze the Sociology of the Audience

In analyzing an audience, be careful not to assume that people covered by the same label are necessarily all alike. As soon as you begin to use a sociological characteristic with an expressed or implied "all," consider the possibility that you may be stereotyping. Don't assume that all women or all older people or all highly educated people think or believe the same things. They don't.

Nevertheless, there are characteristics that seem to be more common among one group than another, and it is these characteristics that you want to explore in analyzing your audience. Four of the most important factors are (1) cultural factors, (2) age, (3) gender, and (4) religion and religiousness.

Cultural Factors   Cultural factors such as nationality, race, and cultural identity are crucial in audience analysis. Largely because of different training and experiences, the interests, values, and goals of various cultural groups also will differ. Further, cultural factors will influence each of the remaining factors; for example, attitudes toward age and gender will differ greatly from one culture to another.

Perhaps the primary question to ask is "Are the cultural beliefs and values of the audience relevant to your topic and purpose?" In other words, might the cultural membership(s) of your audience members influence the way they see the topic? If so, find out what these beliefs and values are and take these into consideration as you build your speech.

Age   Different age groups have different attitudes and beliefs, largely because they have had different experiences in different contexts. Take these differences into consideration in preparing your speeches. For example, let's say that you're an

- -

Limiting Topics

Here are a few overly general topics. Using one of the methods discussed in this chapter (or any other method you're familiar with), limit one of these topics to one that would be reasonable for a 5- to 10-minute speech: (1) dangerous sports, (2) race relationships, (3) parole, (4) censorship on the Internet, (5) ecological problems, (6) problems faced by college students, (7) morality, (8) health and fitness, (9) ethical issues in politics, and (10) urban violence.

- -

investment counselor and you want to persuade your listeners to invest their money to increase their income. Your speech would have to be very different if you were addressing an audience of retired people (say, people in their 60s) than if the audience consisted of young executives (say, people in their 30s).

In considering the age of your audience, ask yourself if age groups differ in the goals, interests, and day-to-day concerns that may be related to your topic and purpose. Graduating from college, achieving corporate success, raising a family, and saving for retirement are concerns that differ greatly from one age group to another. Ask too if groups differ in their ability to absorb and process information. Will they differ in their responses to visual cues? With a young audience it may be best to keep up a steady, even swift pace. With older persons you may wish to maintain a more moderate pace.

Gender   Gender is one of the most difficult audience variables to analyze. The rapid social changes taking place today make it difficult to pin down the effects of gender. As you analyze your audience in terms of gender, ask yourself if men and women differ in the values that they consider important and that are related to your topic and purpose. Traditionally, men have been found to place greater importance on theoretical, economic, and political values. Traditionally, women have been found to place greater importance on aesthetic, social, and religious values. In framing appeals and in selecting examples, use the values your audience members consider most important.

Ask too if your topic will be seen as more interesting by one gender or the other. Will men and women have different attitudes toward the topic? Men and women do not, for example, respond in the same way to such topics as abortion, rape, and equal pay for equal work. Select your topics and supporting materials in light of the genders of your audience members. When your audience is mixed, make a special effort to give men ways to connect to "women's" topics and women ways to connect to "men's" topics.

Religion and Religiousness   The religion and religiousness of your hearers will often influence the audience's responses to your speech. Religion permeates all topics and all issues. On a most obvious level, we know that attitudes on such issues as birth control, abortion, and divorce are closely connected to religion. Similarly, views about premarital sex, marriage, child-rearing, money, cohabitation, responsibilities toward parents, and thousands of other issues are clearly influenced by religion. Religion is also important, however, in areas where its connection is not so obvious. For example, religion influences people's ideas concerning such topics as obedience to authority, responsibility to government, and the usefulness of qualities such as honesty, guilt, and happiness.

Ask yourself if your topic or purpose might be seen as an attack on the religious beliefs of any segment of your audience. If so, then you might want to make adjustments—not necessarily to abandon your purpose, but to rephrase your arguments or

What Do You Say?

Unpopular Thesis: You've decided to tackle the hypocrisy you see in your classmates, who publicly support the values of racial equality but privately express racist attitudes. You're afraid, however, that your audience will walk out on you as soon as you state your thesis. *What do you say?*

incorporate different evidence. When dealing with any religious beliefs, and particularly when disagreeing with them, recognize that you're going to meet stiff opposition. Proceed slowly and inductively. That is, present your evidence and argument before expressing your disagreement.

Analyze the Psychology of the Audience

Focus your psychological analysis of the audience on three questions: How willing is your audience? How favorable is your audience? And how knowledgeable is your audience?

How Willing Is Your Audience?   If you face an audience that is willing (even anxious) to hear your speech, you'll have an easy time relating your speech to them. If, however, your audience is listening unwillingly, consider the following suggestions:

- Secure their attention as early in your speech as possible—and maintain their interest throughout—with supporting materials that will speak to their motives, interests, and concerns.
- Reward the audience for their attendance and attention; compliment them for being there, and show respect for what they know and think.
- Relate your topic and supporting materials directly to your audience's needs and wants; show them how what you are saying will help them achieve what they want.
- Show the audience why they should listen to your speech by connecting your purpose to their purposes, their motives.
- Involve the audience directly in your speech by showing them that you understand their perspective, by asking rhetorical questions, and by referring to their experiences and interests.
- Focus on a few very strong issues or even on a single strong issue.

How Favorable Is Your Audience?   If you face an audience that has unfavorable attitudes toward your topic or your purpose, or even toward you, consider these suggestions:

- Build on commonalities; emphasize not the differences but the similarities between you and the audience.
- Build your speech from areas of agreement, through areas of slight disagreement, up to the major differences.
- Strive for small gains.

How Knowledgeable Is Your Audience?   Listeners differ greatly in the knowledge they have of your topic. If your audience knows little about your topic, consider these suggestions:

- Don't talk down to audience members.
- Don't confuse a lack of knowledge with a lack of intelligence.

If your audience knows a great deal about your topic, consider these suggestions:

- Let the audience know that you are aware of their knowledge and expertise and that your speech will not simply repeat what they already know but will go beyond that.
- Emphasize your credibility, especially your competence in this general subject area (see Chapter 14).

What Do You Say?

Unfavorable Audience: From the expressions on the faces of your audience, you immediately recognize that they are totally against your thesis and are ready to tune you out. *What do you say?*

Research Navigator.com

www.researchnavigator.com

Investigate Key Terms: Investigate one of the key terms discussed in this chapter (for example, public speaking, Internet, database, motivated sequence, or audience). What additional insights can you provide?

Analysis and Adaptation during the Speech

In your classroom speeches you'll face a known audience, an audience you've already analyzed and for which you've made appropriate adaptations. At other times, however, you may face an audience that you've not been able to analyze beforehand or that differs greatly from what you expected. In these cases you'll have to analyze and adapt as you speak. Here are a few suggestions.

Focus on Listeners as Message Senders   As you're speaking, look at your listeners. Remember that just as you're sending messages to your audience, they're also sending messages to you. Pay attention to these messages, and make necessary adjustments on the basis of what they tell you.

You can make a wide variety of adjustments to each type of audience response. For example, if your audience shows signs of boredom, increase your volume, move closer to them, or tell them that what you're going to say will be of value to them. If your audience shows signs of disagreement or hostility, stress a similarity you have with them. If your audience looks puzzled or confused, pause a moment and rephrase your ideas, provide necessary definitions, or insert an internal summary. If your audience seems impatient, say, for example, "my last argument" instead of your originally planned "my third argument."

Ask "What If" Questions   The more preparation you put into your speech, the better prepared you'll be to make on-the-spot adjustments and adaptations. For example, let's say you have been told that you're to explain the opportunities available to the nontraditional student at your college. You've been told that your audience will consist mainly of working women in their 30s and 40s who are just beginning college. As you prepare your speech with this audience in mind, ask yourself "what if" questions. Some examples:

- What if the audience has a large number of men?
- What if the audience consists of women much older than 40?
- What if the audience members come with their spouses or their children?

Keeping such questions in mind will force you to consider alternatives as you prepare your speech. This way, you'll have adaptations readily available if you face a new or different audience.

Address Audience Responses Directly   Another way of dealing with audience responses is to confront them directly. To those who are giving disagreement feedback, for example, you might say:

> You may disagree with this position, but all I ask is that you hear me out and see if this new way of doing things will not simplify your accounting procedures.

Or, to those who seem puzzled, you might say:

> I know this plan may seem confusing; but bear with me; it will become clear in a moment.

Or, to those who seem impatient, you might respond:

> I know this has been a long day, but give me just a few more minutes and you'll be able to save hours recording your accounts.

By responding to your listeners' reactions and feedback, you acknowledge your audience's needs. You let them know that you hear them, that you're with them, and that you're responding to their very real needs.

What Do You Say?

Correcting Errors: In your speech you say that more than 70 percent of students surveyed favored banning alcohol. Toward the end of the speech, you realize that you mixed up the figures: Only 30 percent favored banning alcohol. During the question-and-answer period no one asks about the figures. *What do you say?*

Step 3: Research Your Topic

Research is essential if your speech is to be worthwhile and if you and the audience are to profit from it. First, read some general source—an article in an encyclopedia or magazine. You might pursue some of the references in the article or seek books on the topic from the library catalog. You might also consult one or more of the guides to periodical literature for recent articles in journals, magazines, and newspapers. For some topics, you might want to consult individuals: professors, politicians, physicians, or others with specialized information. The following discussion focuses on databases and the Internet, which will help you to find the information you want quickly and easily.

> **"** False words are not only evil in themselves, but they infect the soul with evil. **"**
>
> —Plato

Databases

After you've read a general article, you'll want to assemble a list of references you plan to consult and begin your reading. For this, go to the available databases. A "database" is simply information contained in one place. A dictionary, an encyclopedia, and an index to magazines—whether in print or electronic form—are all examples of databases. Fortunately, many of the indexes and abstracts formerly available only in print are now available online and on CD-ROM. This makes finding information easy, enjoyable, and extremely fast.

Perhaps the best starting place is Research Navigator—a collection of easily accessed databases that comes with this text (www.researchnavigator.com). Your college also is likely to subscribe to a variety of databases, to which you'll have access at the college and probably from your home computer as well. As you'll see when you log on, regardless of the topic of your speech, there are several databases that are likely to contain information you'll find useful.

Personal Reference Works

The databases discussed above are available through libraries as well as through a variety of private vendors such as CompuServe and America Online (AOL). But there are other reference books and CD-ROMs that are more limited and that you can purchase for your own library. Dictionaries, thesauruses, books of quotations, atlases, encyclopedias, almanacs, *Time* magazines from the last 50 years, and the like are useful research tools to have at home. The computerized versions of these standard reference works are becoming less and less expensive and have the advantages of speed of access and ability to print citations and records. In addition, many of these contain photos, audio clips, and animations that clarify complex processes. The hypertext–hypermedia feature makes these as enjoyable to use as they are efficient.

The Internet

If you're looking for copies of state laws and Supreme Court decisions, news reports, book reviews, classic works of literature, weather reports, statistics, job listings, or simply ways to network with others who share your interests, the Internet may be your answer. The Internet is changing so rapidly that any book that tries to cover it will be out of date by the time it's published. Changing equally rapidly are the tools (the browsers and the search engines) that enable you to find the information you want. So complement this discussion with a recent publication on the Internet—these now make up a major section in the computer area of your bookstore. Here are just a few of the ways you can use the Internet to research your speech topic.

E-mail and mailing lists (see Chapters 7 and 9) enable you to write to individuals or corporations for copies of speeches, annual reports, or other information you

Plagiarizing (and How to Avoid It)

You commit plagiarism when you use material from another source without giving proper credit. The source can be oral or written or visual. Presenting as your own portions of someone else's speech, article, or diagram are all examples of plagiarism. It's plagiarism whether the material comes from a formal presentation (as in a lecture at your college or an article in an academic journal) or from an informal presentation (as in a discussion with your instructor after class or a letter to the editor in a local newspaper). The material may be well known, or it may be old and obscure—the date something was said or written is irrelevant. Here are some forms plagiarism can take and some ways you can avoid it.

- *Using the exact words of another person.* If you're going to use another person's exact words—whether a short catchphrase, a full sentence, or a paragraph—then cite the quotation exactly as it was written or spoken and credit the source. For example, in a speech on nonverbal communication in different cultures, you might say something like this:

  According to Roger Axtell, in his *Gestures: The Do's and Taboos of Body Language Around the World,* touching varies from one culture to another. Axtell says, for example, "In the Middle East, two Arab male friends may even be seen walking down the street hand-in-hand and all it signifies is friendship."

  In your speech outline, give the full bibliographic reference of any quoted material just as you would in a history or sociology paper. Be sure you use quotation marks for any citation in which you use the person's exact words, just as you would in a written essay. And make it clear to your listeners that you're using the person's exact words, as was done in the example above. You can do this by changing your inflection, stepping forward, or reading the specific words from your notes. Also, be sure that the audience knows when you're beginning to use material from another person and when you're stopping.

- *Using the ideas of another person.* If you're using the ideas, arguments, insights, or examples of someone else, even if you're not quoting directly, you still have to acknowledge your source. Weave the sources into your speech with subtlety and without disturbing the natural flow and rhythm of your speech. For example:

  A recent article in *Time* magazine noted that. . . .

  Professor Fox, in her lecture last week on Western Civilization, argued that. . . .

- *Using the organizational structure of another.* If you're using an organizational structure drawn from another source, acknowledge your indebtedness. In these cases you can say something like:

  I'm here following the arguments given by Professor Marishu in her lecture on culture and racism.

  This pattern for Web design comes from the work of Edward Almost in his book *Designing Your Own Web Site.*

To guard against unintentional plagiarism, take notes carefully. Indicate exactly and with quotation marks the words you're quoting directly from an article or speech or website. In addition, record all bibliographical information that you'll need to include in your list of references as well as the information that you'll include in your actual speech.

What Would You Do?

You're pressed to prepare a speech on a contemporary social issue and just don't have the time to research it. Fortunately, a friend wrote a term paper for her sociology course and got an A on it. You could easily adapt the paper to fulfill your assignment. You figure that this would be similar to using research you'd find in newspapers and magazines; besides, you're going to be writing the outline and delivering the speech. What would you do? Would you use your friend's paper? If so, how would you acknowledge your source?

might need for your speech. If your speech is on a timely topic, chances are that there are many others who have spoken or written on the topic who would be pleased to e-mail you copies of their materials. You might also subscribe to a mailing list devoted to your topic. Chat groups (see Chapter 9) are often useful for getting other perspectives and trying out your ideas on others.

Currently, there are thousands of *newsgroups* devoted to specific interests. Newsgroups are hierarchically organized, with a general topic at the top and more specific topics as you go down the hierarchy. Currently, there are eight major newsgroup hierarchies, dealing with computers and computing; Usenet and newsgroups; recreation; science and scientific issues; social issues; and the catch-all categories of alt., misc., and talk.

Newsgroups are useful to the public speaker for two main reasons. First, they are useful sources of information. Because there are so many newsgroups, you should have no problem finding several that deal with topics related to those you'll be speaking on. You'll find news items, letters, and papers on just about any topic you can think of. You can also save the news items you're particularly interested in to your own file. Through newsgroups, you can ask questions and get the opinions of scientists for, say, your next speech on "recent advances in cryonics." The second reason newsgroups are important in public speaking is that they provide an easily available and generally receptive audience to whom you can communicate your thoughts and feelings.

The World Wide Web is the most interesting and most valuable part of the Internet for research. It's a collection of documents—some containing graphic, audio, and video components. In searching the Web, keep the following in mind (Stewart, 1996):

- The Web is more useful for certain topics. Web documents are more extensive and more up-to-date on scientific subjects (especially computer-related information) than on, say, history or the humanities generally.

- When searching the Web, try using the meta–search engines first; these are the search programs that search several databases at the same time and will yield a lot more hits than will a single database. As I write this the best meta–search engines include Google (www.google.com), Ask Jeeves (www.ask.com), Dogpile (www.dogpile.com), and Vivisimo (www.vivisimo.com). As you pursue your research, you'll quickly find the search engines that work best for you and may wish to bookmark them.

- Learn the websites that are most appropriate for topics you're interested in. For example, if you were especially interested in health issues, you would want to become familiar with the National Institute of Health's website (http://www.nih.gov). Save the addresses of the sites you'll want to revisit.

- When in doubt, press the help key.

Critically Evaluate Research

Collecting research materials—whether from traditional print sources, listservs and the Web, or interviews with experts—is only part of the research process; the other part is critically evaluating the materials. Here are some questions to ask.

Is the Information Current? Generally, the more recent the material, the more useful it will be. With some topics (for example, unemployment statistics, developments in AIDS research, or tuition costs) the recency of the information is crucial to its usefulness. Check important figures in a recent almanac, newspaper, or frequently updated Internet source.

The date of a newspaper, the copyright date of a book, or the date of a cited article or e-mail will help you identify the recency of the information. Unfortunately, not all Internet documents are dated and so at times you won't be able to tell when a

What Do You Say?

Asking a Favor: You're preparing a speech on the architectural ideas for rebuilding Ground Zero, and you want to ask some of the famous architects a few questions so you can integrate their most recent thoughts (and interject a more personalized note) into your speech. *What do you say? Through what channel?*

document was written. You may be able to write to the author and ask, however; many Internet writers include their e-mail addresses.

Is the Information Fair and Unbiased? Bias is not easy to determine, but do try to examine any sources of potential bias. Obvious examples come quickly to mind: cigarette manufacturers' statements on the health risks from smoking; newspaper and network editorials on the fairness of news reporting; the National Rifle Association's arguments on gun control. Try checking the credibility of your sources in a biographical dictionary or in relevant newspaper articles. By reviewing the research in the area you'll be able to see how other experts view the author of a particular article. You'll also be able to see if the author's view of the situation takes into consideration all sides of the issue and if these sides are represented fairly and accurately. In some cases the author presents her or his credentials, and you can easily check these if you wish.

Recognize that anyone can "publish" on the Internet. Articles on the Internet can be written by world-renowned scientists or by elementary school students, by fair and objective reporters or by those who would spin the issues to serve political or religious or social purposes. And it's not always easy to tell which is which. Find out what the author's qualifications are. Look carefully at any statistics or figures. Are these drawn from reliable and recent sources? One useful technique used by many Web writers is to include in their documents Internet links to the sources from which they derived, say, their statistics or predictions or arguments. If you find these links, it's often worth checking them to see if the author did in fact fairly and accurately present the information.

Recognize also, however, that much information on the Internet is identical to the information you regularly read in print. Encyclopedias, newspapers and newsmagazines, and professional journals that appear on the Internet are often identical to the print copies, so there's no need to draw distinctions between print and Internet information when dealing with sites such as these.

Lots of additional assistance for evaluating Web materials is on the Web. Here are just a few sources recommended in the *Research Navigator Guide* (Doyle & Barr, 2004): Purdue University Library's www.lib.purdue.edu/InternetEval, Lehigh University's www.lehigh.edu/infodome/infotemp.html, the University of Illinois' http://lrs.ed.uiuc.edu/wp/credibility/page3.html, and UCLA's www.library.ucla.edu/libraries/college/help/critical/.

Is the Evidence Reliable and the Reasoning Logical? The most important questions in evaluating research must focus on the evidence and reasoning used in arriving at a conclusion. Ask yourself if the conclusions have been arrived at logically rather than emotionally. Does the author offer clear evidence and sound arguments to support conclusions rather than, say, anecdotes or testimonials from like-minded people?

Another way to estimate reliability is to look at the publisher. In particular, note whether the publisher is a special interest group with a specific corporate, religious, political, or social agenda. If it is, try to balance this perspective with information that represents the other sides of the issue.

Some Internet sources contain "about" files that will help you learn more about the author and perhaps the author's sources. Sometimes, as noted earlier, you'll be able to contact the author via e-mail.

Integrate Research into Your Speech

By integrating and acknowledging your sources of information in the speech, you'll give fair credit to those whose ideas and statements you're using; at the same time you'll help establish your own reputation as a responsible researcher. Here are a few suggestions for integrating your research into your speech.

> " The ultimate goal of all research is not objectivity, but truth. "
>
> —Helene Deutsch

Mention the sources in your speech by citing at least the author and, if helpful, the publication and the date. Say, quite simply, something like:

> These references were suggested by Terrence Doyle and Linda Barr in their book *Research Navigator Guide,* published in 2004.

> These statistics come from the January 1, 2004, issue of the *New York Times*.

Provide smooth transitions between your words and the words of the author you're citing. Instead of using such useless expressions as "I have a quote here" or "I want to quote an example," let the audience know that you're quoting in more subtle ways. For example, pause before the quote, take a step forward, or refer to your notes to read the extended quotation. Or use such lead-ins as "As Senator Hillary Clinton said. . . ." or "Jerry Springer put it perfectly when he said. . . ." If you feel it's crucial that the audience know you're quoting, and you want to state that this is a quotation, you might do it this way:

> Recently, Mary Kay Ash put this in perspective, and I quote: "A woman can no more duplicate the male style of leadership than an American businessman can exactly reproduce the Japanese style."

Here's an example of how you might orally cite your source and establish credibility at the same time.

> Don't expect an extremely effective drug to treat most cases of hepatitis C within the next two years. Dr. Howard J. Worman of New York Presbyterian Hospital, one of the leading scientists in the field of liver disease, the author of more than 70 medical and scientific papers and of *The Liver Disorders Sourcebook,* and the creator of the Diseases of the Liver website, expressed this opinion in his article *Hepatitis C: An Epidemic Ignored* published on the healthology.com website which I accessed this week.

Here's another example:

> My discussion of the symptoms of arrhythmia is based on the insights of Dr. Anthony R. Magnano (2001), a Clinical Fellow in Cardiology at Columbia University College of Physicians and Surgeons. Magnano is an active researcher on arrhythmia and has written widely on the topic. In an article on arrhythmias on the healthology.com website, which I last accessed on August 21, 2001, Magnano identifies three symptoms he sees most often in his patients: heart palpitations, lightheadedness, and fainting spells.

Skill development experience

Accessing Information

Select one of the following items of information and, in a brief two-minute speech, report back to the class both the answer and the reference work(s) you used to find the answer.

1. The literacy rate for China
2. The main languages of Cambodia
3. The prime interest rate for today
4. The author of the quotation "Though it be honest, it is never good to bring bad news"
5. The major religions and languages of Nigeria
6. The use and origin of the word *cyberspace*
7. The political configuration of Europe
8. The rules for playing chess
9. Transcripts of speeches of the President of the United States
10. The core principles and main beliefs of Islam

You would then, in the reference list following the speech, identify the author, title of article, URL address, and the speaker's date of visit. It would look like this:

Magnano, Anthony R. (2001). Arrhythmias: An introduction. http://earthlink2 .healthology.com/focus_article.asp?f=cardio&c=arrhythmias_intro (August 20, 2001).

Although it's possible to overdo the oral citation—giving more information than the listeners really need—there are even greater dangers with leaving out potentially useful information. Since your speeches in this course are learning experiences, it will be better to err on the side of being more rather than less complete.

Step 4: Formulate Your Thesis and Identify Your Major Propositions

In this step you choose your thesis and then use it to generate your major propositions or ideas.

Choose Your Thesis

The **thesis** is the main idea that you want to convey to the audience. The thesis of Lincoln's Second Inaugural Address was that northerners and southerners should work together for the good of the entire country. The thesis of many science fiction movies is that working together, people, often from very different cultures and different areas of life, can repel any force and achieve just about anything.

Let's say, for example, you're planning to deliver a persuasive speech in favor of Senator Winters. Your thesis statement might be "Winters is the best candidate." This is what you want your audience to believe, what you want your audience to remember even if they forget everything else. In an informative speech, on the other hand, the thesis statement focuses on what you want your audience to learn. For example, for a speech on jealousy, a suitable thesis might be "Two main theories of jealousy exist."

The thesis and the purpose of a speech are similar in that they both guide you in selecting and organizing your materials. In some ways, however, they are different:

- Thesis and purpose differ in their form of expression. The thesis is phrased as a complete declarative sentence. The purpose is phrased as an infinitive phrase ("to inform . . . ," "to persuade . . .").

- The thesis focuses on the message; the purpose focuses on the audience. The thesis succinctly identifies the central idea of your speech. The purpose identifies the change you hope to bring about in your audience—for example, to impart information, to change attitudes, to influence people to act in a certain way.

VIEWPOINT

George and Iris want to give their speeches on opposite sides of Megan's law—the law requiring that community residents be notified if a convicted sex offender is living in close proximity. George is against the law and Iris is for it. If George and Iris were giving their speeches to your class, what would you advise each of them to do concerning the statement of their theses?

Especially in the early stages of mastering public speaking, formulate both your thesis statement and your purpose. From there, you will be able to construct a more coherent and more understandable speech. Limit your thesis statement to one central idea. A statement such as "We should support Winters and the entire Democratic party" contains not one but two basic ideas.

Low-context cultures (the United States, Germany, and Sweden, for example) generally expect information to be communicated explicitly, so in such cultures most audiences wish to hear a direct statement of the speaker's position and an explicit statement of what he or she wants the audience to do. In contrast, **high-context cultures** (Japan, China, and Arabic countries, for example) prefer a less explicit statement and prefer to be led indirectly to the speaker's conclusion. An explicit statement ("Vote for Smith" or "Buy Viterall") may be interpreted as too direct and even insulting.

Generate Your Main Ideas

Use your thesis statement to generate your main ideas. Once you phrase the thesis statement, the main divisions of your speech will suggest themselves. Let's say you are giving a speech on the values of a college education to a group of people in their 30s and 40s who are considering returning to college. Your thesis is *"A college education is valuable."* You then ask yourself, "Why is it valuable?" From these answers you generate your major propositions. You might first brainstorm the question and identify as many answers as you can. Your list might look something like this:

A college education is valuable because

1. it helps you get a job.
2. it increases your potential to earn a good salary.
3. it gives you greater job mobility.
4. it helps you secure more creative work.
5. it helps you appreciate the arts more fully.
6. it helps you understand an increasingly complex world.
7. it helps you understand different cultures.
8. it helps you avoid taking a regular job for a few years.
9. it helps you meet lots of people and make friends.
10. it helps you increase personal effectiveness.

For purposes of illustration, let's stop at this point. You have 10 possible main points—too many to cover in a short speech. Further, not all are equally valuable or relevant to your audience. Look over the list to make it shorter and more relevant. Here are some suggestions:

Eliminate Points That Seem Least Important You might want to eliminate, say, number 8—because it's inconsistent with the positive values of college, the thesis of your speech. Further, your audience is unlikely to be able to stop working to go to college full time.

Combine Points That Have a Common Focus Notice, for example, that the first four points center on jobs. You might, therefore, consider grouping them under a general heading:

A college education will help you secure a better job.

This might be one of your major propositions, which you can develop by defining what you mean by "a better job." You might also use some of the ideas you generated in your brainstorming session. This main point and its elaboration might look like this:

I. A college education will help you secure a better job.

  A. College graduates earn higher salaries.

  B. College graduates enter more creative jobs.

  C. College graduates have greater job mobility.

Note that A, B, and C are all aspects or subdivisions of "a better job."

www.researchnavigator.com

Find Answers: Try finding answers to one of the following questions, or design a research study to answer it: Does organization help people understand a public speech? What are the most important issues college students are concerned with today? How does experience in public speaking relate to success in business?

Select Points That Are Most Relevant   Ask yourself what will interest your audience most. On this basis, you might drop number 5 on the assumption that your audience will be more interested in more practical outcomes. You might eliminate number 9 on the assumption that your audience is not looking to college to help them make friends; they probably have lots of friends and families that occupy most of their time. Further, you might conclude that this audience cares a lot about personal effectiveness, so you might make this your second major proposition:

> II. A college education will help you increase your personal effectiveness.

Much as you developed the subordinate points in your first proposition by defining what you meant by "a good job," you would define what you mean by "personal effectiveness":

> II. A college education will help you increase your personal effectiveness.
>> A. A college education will help you increase your ability to communicate.
>> B. A college education will help you acquire learning skills.
>> C. A college education will help you acquire coping skills.

You then follow the same procedure used to generate these subordinate points (A, B, and C) to develop the subheadings. For example, you might divide A into two major subheads:

> A. A college education will improve your ability to communicate.
>> 1. A college education teaches writing skills.
>> 2. A college education teaches speech skills.

Use Two, Three, or Four Main Points   Remember, your aim is not to cover every aspect of a topic but to emphasize selected parts. Further, you want to have enough time to amplify and support the points you present. With too many propositions, this becomes impossible. Also, you don't want to present too much information, because your audience will simply not be able to remember it.

Phrase Propositions in Parallel Style   To make it easier for listeners to follow and remember your speech, use similar structures in wording your major propositions.

NOT THIS:

Mass Media Functions

> I. The media entertain.
> II. The media function to inform their audiences.
> III. Creating ties of union is a major media function.
> IV. The conferral of status is a function of all media.

THIS:

Mass Media Functions

> I. The media entertain.
> II. The media inform.
> III. The media create ties of union.
> IV. The media confer status.

"Sorry, Pop, but your message is no longer relevant to the younger audience."

confronting home health aides: Industry lures away the most qualified graduates of the leading universities, many health aides leave the field after two or three years, and the occupation suffers from a low status in many undergraduates' minds. In the second part, you would consider the possible solutions to these problems: making health aides' salaries competitive with those in private industry, making benefits as attractive as those offered by industry, and raising the status of the health aide profession.

The speech, in outline form, would look like this:

I. Three major problems confront home health care.
   A. Industry lures away the most qualified graduates.
   B. Numerous excellent health aides leave the field after a few years.
   C. Home health care is currently a low-status occupation.
II. Three major solutions to these problems exist.
   A. Increase salaries for home health aides.
   B. Make benefits for health aides more attractive.
   C. Raise the status of the home health care profession.

Cause–Effect/Effect–Cause Pattern

Especially appropriate for persuasive speeches and similar to the problem–solution pattern of organization is the cause–effect or effect–cause pattern. Using this pattern, you divide the speech into two major sections—causes and effects. For example, a speech on the reasons for highway accidents might fit into a cause–effect pattern. In such a speech you might first consider the causes of highway accidents—unlicensed drivers, alcohol and drugs, the roles of anger and ill temper—and then some of the effects, such as accidents, deaths, and property damage. Similarly, illnesses or low self-esteem can be explained with a cause–effect pattern. An outline of the causes and effects of low self-esteem might look something like this:

I. Low self-esteem often has two main causes.
   A. A history of criticism can contribute to low self-esteem.
   B. Unrealistic goals can contribute to low self-esteem.
II. Low self-esteem often has two main effects.
   A. Depression is one frequent effect.
   B. An unwillingness to socialize with others is another frequent effect.

The Motivated Sequence

The **motivated sequence** is a pattern in which you arrange information to motivate your audience to respond positively to your purpose (McKerrow, Gronbeck, Ehninger, & Monroe, 2000). This pattern is useful for organizing both informative and persuasive speeches. It consists of five steps: (1) attention, (2) need, (3) satisfaction, (4) visualization, and (5) action. An extended discussion of the motivated sequence may be found at www.ablongman.com/devito.

1. Attention   Make the audience give you their undivided attention. If you execute this step effectively, your audience should be anxious to hear what you have to say. You can gain audience attention by, for example, asking a rhetorical question, referring to specific audience members, or using a dramatic or humorous story. These and other ways of gaining attention are discussed more fully in Chapter 12.

2. Need   Now you prove that a need exists. The audience should feel that they need to learn or do something. You can establish need by:

- stating the need or problem as it exists or will exist
- illustrating the need with specific examples, illustrations, statistics, testimony, and other forms of support
- pointing to how this need affects your specific listeners—for example, their financial status, career goals, or individual happiness

For example, in a speech to convince people in their 60s and 70s to purchase home computers, you might say in this step, "A survey of persons in their 60s and 70s reported that one of their greatest needs was easy and rapid access to medical information. If you are like those in this survey, then the home computer may be your answer."

3. Satisfaction   In the satisfaction step you present the "solution" that satisfies the need you demonstrated in step 2. This step should convince the audience that what you are informing them about or persuading them to do will satisfy the need. You answer the question "How will the need be satisfied by what I am asking the audience to learn, believe, or do?" This step usually contains two types of information:

- a clear statement (with examples and illustrations if necessary) of what you want the audience to learn, believe, or do
- a statement of how or why what you are asking them to learn, believe, or do will lead to satisfying the need identified in step 2

For example, you might say, "With a home computer, you'll be able to get information on thousands of potential drug interactions in seconds." You might then show your listeners how this would be done with, perhaps, an actual demonstration.

4. Visualization   Visualization intensifies the audience's feelings or beliefs. It takes the audience beyond the present place and time and helps them imagine the situation as it would be if the need were satisfied as suggested in step 3. You can accomplish this by (1) demonstrating the positive benefits to be derived if this advocated proposal is put into operation or (2) demonstrating the negative consequences that will occur if your plan is not followed.

Of course, you could combine the two methods and demonstrate both the positive benefits of your plan and the negative effects of the existing situation or of a competing proposal. For example, you might say, "With this simple CD-ROM and these few Web addresses, you'll be able to stay at home and get valuable medical information." You might then demonstrate with a specific example how they would find this information.

5. Action   In the action step you tell the audience what they should *do* to satisfy the need you have identified. Your goal is to move the audience in a particular direction. For example, you might want them to speak for Farrington or against Williamson, to attend the next student government meeting, or to work for a specific political candidate. Here are a few ways to accomplish this step.

- State exactly what audience members should do.
- Appeal to your listeners' emotions.
- Give the audience guidelines for future action.

For example, you might say, "Read this pamphlet, 'Life on the Computer after 60,' and take a walk to your neighborhood computer store and talk with the salespeople." Or you might suggest that they consider taking an appropriate adult education course at the local community college.

VIEWPOINT

You're to give a speech to your class on the need to establish a day care center at your college for parents who attend school but have no means to hire people to take care of their children. You want to use the motivated sequence. How would you gain attention? Establish the need? Satisfy the need? Visualize the problem solved? Ask for action?

Notice that an informative speech could have stopped after the satisfaction step. You accomplish the goal of informing the audience about some advantages of home computers for older people with the satisfaction step. In some cases, though, you may believe it helpful to progress through the action step to emphasize your point.

In a persuasive speech, on the other hand, you must go at least as far as visualization if you limit your purpose to strengthening or changing attitudes or beliefs. If you aim to get your listeners to behave in a certain way, you'll need to go all the way through the action step.

Additional Patterns

The six organizational patterns just considered are the most common and are useful for many public speeches. But there are other patterns that also may prove appropriate for some presentations.

Structure–Function   The structure–function pattern is useful in informative speeches in which you want to discuss how something is constructed—its structure—and what it does—its function. This pattern might be useful, for example, in a speech about what an organization is and what it does, about the parts of a university and how they operate, or about the sensory systems of the body and their functions. This pattern might also be useful in a discussion about the nature of a living organism: its anatomy (or structure) and its physiology (or function).

Comparison and Contrast   A comparison-and-contrast pattern can work well in informative speeches in which you want to analyze two different theories, proposals, departments, or products in terms of their similarities and differences. In this type of speech, you not only explain each theory or proposal, but also explain primarily how they are similar and how they are different.

Skill development experience

Evaluating a Poorly Constructed Informative Speech

The speech presented below illustrates some broad as well as some rather subtle errors that a beginning speaker might make in constructing an informative speech. First, read the entire speech without looking at any of the questions in the right-hand column. Then, after you've read the entire speech, reread each paragraph and respond to the critical thinking questions. What other questions might prove productive to ask?

THREE JOBS	
Well, I mean, hello. Er . . . I'm new at public speaking so I'm a little nervous. I've always been shy. So, don't watch my knees shake.	The title seems adequate, but it's not terribly exciting. After reading the speech, try to give it a more appealing title. Generally, don't use your title as your opening words.
Eum, let me see my notes here. [Mumbles to self while shuffling notes: One, two, three, four, five—oh, they're all here.] Okay, here goes.	This nervous reaction is understandable, but it is probably best not to share it with the listeners. After all, you don't want them to be uncomfortable for you.

Going through your notes makes the audience feel that you didn't prepare adequately and may just be wasting their time. |
| Three jobs. That's my title and I'm going to talk about three jobs. | |
| The Health Care Field. This is the fastest-growing job in the country, one | This is the speaker's orientation. Is this sufficient? What else might the speaker have done in the introduction? |

of the fastest, I guess I mean. I know that you're not interested in this topic and that you're all studying accounting. But there are a lot of new jobs in the health care field. The *Star* had an article on health care and said that health care will be needed more in the future than it is now. And now, you know, like they need a lot of health care people. In the hospital where I work—on the west side, uptown—they never have enough health aides and they always tell me to become a health aide, like, you know, to enter the health care field. To become a nurse. Or maybe a dental technician. But I hate going to the dentist. Maybe I will.

I don't know what's going to happen with the government's health plan, but whatever happens, it won't change the need for health aides. I mean, people will still get sick; so, it really doesn't matter what happens with health care.

The Robotics Field. This includes things like artificial intelligence. I don't really know what that is but it's like growing real fast. They use this in making automobiles and planes and I think in computers. Japan is a leading country in this field. A lot of people in India go into this field but I'm not sure why.

The Computer Graphics Field. This field has a lot to do with designing and making lots of different products, like CAD and CAM. This field also includes computer aided imagery—CAI. And in movies, I think. Like *Star Wars* and *Terminator 2*. I saw *Terminator 2* four times. I didn't see *Star Wars* but I'm gonna rent the video. I don't know if you have to know a lot about computers or if you can just like be a designer and someone else will tell the computer what to do.

I got my information from a book that Carol Kleiman wrote, *The 100 Best Jobs for the 1990s and Beyond*. It was summarized in last Sunday's *News*.

My conclusion. These are three of the fastest growing fields in the U.S. and in the world I think—not in third-world countries, I don't think. China and India and Africa. More like Europe and Germany. And the U.S.—the U.S. is the big one. I hope you enjoyed my speech. Thank you.

I wasn't as nervous as I thought I'd be. Are there any questions?

Here the speaker shows such uncertainty that we question his or her competence.
And we begin to wonder: Why is the speaker talking about this to us?

What the *Star* says may be entertaining, but it doesn't constitute evidence. What does this reference do to the credibility you ascribe to the speaker?

Everything in the speech must have a definite purpose. Asides such as comments about not liking to go to the dentist are probably best omitted.

Here the speaker had an opportunity to connect the topic with important current political events but failed to say anything that wasn't obvious.

Introducing the topics this way is clear but is probably not very interesting. How might the speaker have introduced each of the three main topics more effectively?

Notice how vague the speaker is—"includes things like," "and I think in computers," "I'm not sure why." Statements like this communicate very little information to listeners and leave them with little confidence that the speaker knows what he or she is talking about.

Again, there is little that is specific. CAD and CAM are not defined; CAI is explained as "computer aided imagery" but unless we already knew what this was, we would still not know even after hearing the speaker. Again, the speaker inserts personal notes (for example, seeing *Terminator 2* four times) that have no meaningful connection to the topic.

The speaker uses only one source and, to make matters worse, doesn't even go to the original source but relies on a summary in the local newspaper. Especially with a topic like this, listeners are likely to want a variety of viewpoints and additional reliable sources.
Note too that the speech lacked any statistics. This is a subject on which statistics are essential. Listeners will want to know how many jobs will be available in these fields, what these fields will look like in 5 or 10 years, how much these fields pay, and so on.

Using the word *conclusion* to signal that you're concluding isn't a bad idea, but work it into the text instead of using it like a heading in a book chapter.

Again, the speaker's lack of certainty makes us question his or her competence and preparation.
Again, personal comments are best left out.

Preparing a Two-Minute Speech

Prepare and present a two-minute speech in which you accomplish one of the following:

- explain (with lots of examples) what you think would be good and bad speech topics for your class
- discuss the sociology or psychology of your class as an audience
- identify and describe one valuable reference book or Internet site that would be especially appropriate for researching speech topics
- describe "the ethical speaker"
- analyze a print ad in terms of the motivated sequence

Pro and Con, Advantages and Disadvantages   The pro-and-con pattern, sometimes called the advantages–disadvantages pattern, is useful in informative speeches in which you want to explain objectively the advantages (the pros) and the disadvantages (the cons) of a plan, method, or product.

Claim and Proof   The claim-and-proof pattern is especially appropriate for a persuasive speech in which you want to prove the truth or usefulness of a particular proposition. It's the pattern that you see frequently in trials: The prosecution makes a claim that the defendant is guilty and presents proof in the form of varied evidence—for example, evidence that the defendant had a motive, had the opportunity, and had no alibi. This pattern divides your speech into two major parts. In the first part you explain your claim (for example, "Tuition must not be raised," "Library hours must be expanded," or "Courses in AIDS education must be instituted"). In the second part you offer your evidence or proof as to why, for example, tuition must not be raised.

Multiple Definition   The multiple-definition pattern serves well in informative speeches in which you want to explain the nature of a concept (What is a born-again Christian? What is a scholar? What is multiculturalism?). In this pattern each major heading consists of a different type of definition or way of looking at the concept. A variety of definition types are discussed in Chapter 13.

Who, What, Why, Where, When   The "who, what, why, where, when" pattern is the primary pattern in journalism and is useful in informative speeches in which you want to report or explain an event—for example, a robbery, political coup, war, or trial. You divide your speech into five major parts, each answering one of the five "W" questions.

Because your chosen organizational pattern will serve primarily to help your listeners follow your speech, you may want to tell your listeners (in your introduction or as a transition between the introduction and the body of your speech) what pattern you'll be following. Here are just a few examples:

- "In our discussion of language development, we'll follow the baby from the earliest sign of language through true communication."
- "In touring Central America, we'll travel from north to south."
- "I'll first explain the problems with raising tuition and then propose a workable solution."
- "First we'll examine the causes of hypertension and then we'll look at its effects."

Summary of Concepts and Skills

This chapter explained the nature of public speaking and began describing the steps to preparing an effective public speech.

1. In public speaking a speaker addresses a relatively large audience with a relatively continuous discourse, usually in a face-to-face situation.
2. Manage your apprehension by reversing the factors that contribute to apprehension, trying performance visualization, practicing systematic desensitization, and using the basic skills of public speaking.
3. The preparation of a public speech involves 10 steps: (1) select your topic and purpose, (2) analyze your audience, (3) research your topic, (4) formulate your thesis and identify your major propositions, (5) support your propositions, (6) organize your speech materials, (7) word your speech, (8) construct your conclusion and introduction, (9) rehearse your speech, and (10) deliver your speech. The first six of these were discussed in this chapter; the remaining four are discussed in Chapter 12.
4. Speech topics should deal with significant issues that interest the audience. Subjects and purposes should be limited in scope.
5. When analyzing the audience, consider audience members' age; sex; cultural factors; occupation, income, and status; and religion and religiousness. Also consider the occasion and the specific context.
6. Research your topic, beginning with general sources and gradually exploring more specific and specialized sources.
7. Formulate the thesis of your speech. Develop your major propositions by asking relevant questions about this thesis.
8. Support your propositions with a variety of materials that amplify and provide evidence.
9. Organize your speech materials into a clear, easily identifiable pattern. Suitable patterns include time, spatial,

topical, problem–solution, cause–effect/effect–cause, motivated sequence, structure–function, comparison and contrast, pro and con, claim and proof, multiple definition, and the five W's (who, what, why, where, when).

These first six steps in preparing a public speech entail a variety of specific skills. Check your ability to apply these skills using the following rating scale: 1 = almost always; 2 = often; 3 = sometimes; 4 = rarely; and 5 = hardly ever.

_____ 1. When preparing a public speech, I follow a logical progression of steps, such as the sequence outlined here.

_____ 2. I select appropriate topics and purposes and narrow them to manageable proportions.

_____ 3. I analyze my audience in terms of members' sociological and psychological characteristics, and I adapt the speech on the basis of these findings.

_____ 4. I research topics effectively and efficiently and critically evaluate the reliability of the research material.

_____ 5. After selecting my thesis (the main assertion), I expand it by asking strategic questions to develop my main ideas or propositions.

_____ 6. After generating my possible major propositions, I eliminate those points that seem least important to my thesis, combine those that have a common focus, and select those most relevant to my audience.

_____ 7. I support my propositions with amplifying materials such as examples, statistics, and visual aids and with logical, emotional, and ethical proofs.

_____ 8. When organizing the speech's main points, I select a pattern appropriate to the subject matter, purpose, and audience.

Key Word Quiz

Write T for those statements that are true and F for those that are false. For those that are false, replace the italicized term with the correct term.

_____ 1. Useful ways to find topics are *surveys, news items,* and *brainstorming.*

_____ 2. The general and specific purposes of a speech are usually stated as *complete sentences.*

_____ 3. A useful device for repeatedly dividing a topic into its significant parts is the *tree diagram.*

_____ 4. The main idea of your speech, the single thing that you want to communicate to your audience, is known as the *speech purpose.*

_____ 5. When you possess *referent power,* people respond to your persuasive attempts by doing the opposite of what you want.

_____ 6. A pattern of speech organization that consists of five steps (attention, need, satisfaction, visualization, and action) is known as the *problem–solution pattern.*

_____ 7. The first step in the motivated sequence is *establishing a need.*

_____ 8. The parts of the motivated sequence that are optional in informative speeches but essential in persuasive speeches are the *satisfaction and action steps.*

_____ 9. A speech on the layout of a nineteenth-century townhouse that explains the layout of the first floor, then the second, then the third, and so on is organized in a *topical pattern.*

_____ 10. A speech whose two main points are that (I) AIDS is increasing in our city and (II) two factors account for this increase is organized according to a *cause–effect pattern.*

Answers: TRUE: 1, 3; FALSE: 2 (*infinitives*), 4 (*thesis*), 5 (*negative power*), 6 (*motivated sequence*), 7 (*gaining attention*), 8 (*visualization and action steps*), 9 (*spatial pattern*), 10 (*effect–cause pattern*)

Clarity

Clarity in speaking style should be your primary goal. Here are some guidelines to help you make your speech clear.

Be Economical. Don't waste words. Notice the wasted words in expressions such as "at 9 a.m. *in the morning,*" "we *first* began the discussion," "I *myself personally,*" and "blue *in color.*" By withholding the italicized terms, you eliminate unnecessary words and move closer to a more economical and clearer style.

Use Specific Terms and Numbers. As we get more and more specific, we get a clearer and more detailed picture. Be specific. Don't say "dog" when you want your listeners to picture a St. Bernard. Don't say "car" when you want them to picture a limousine. The same is true of numbers. Don't say "earned a good salary" if you mean "earned $90,000 a year." Don't say "taxes will go up" when you mean "taxes will increase 7 percent."

Use Guide Phrases. Use guide phrases to help listeners see that you're moving from one idea to another. Use phrases such as "now that we have seen how . . . , let us consider how . . . ," and "my next argument. . . ." Terms such as *first, second, and also, although,* and *however* will help your audience follow your line of thinking.

Use Short, Familiar Terms. Generally, favor the short word over the long word. Favor the familiar over the unfamiliar word. Favor the more commonly used over the rarely used term.

Carefully Assess Idioms. Idioms are expressions that are unique to a specific language and whose meaning cannot be deduced from the individual words used. Expressions such as "to kick the bucket," and "doesn't have a leg to stand on" are idioms. Either you know the meaning of the expression or you don't; you can't figure it out from only a knowledge of the individual words. The positive side of idioms is that they give your speech a casual and informal style; they make your speech sound like a speech and not like a written essay. The negative side is that idioms create problems for audience members who are not native speakers of your language. Many such listeners will simply not understand the meaning of your idioms.

Vividness

Select words that make your ideas vivid, that make them come alive in the listeners' minds.

Use Active Verbs. Favor verbs that communicate activity. The verb *to be,* in all its forms—*is, are, was, were,* and *will be*—is relatively inactive. Try replacing such forms with action verbs. Instead of saying "Management will be here tomorrow," consider "Management descends on us [or jets in] tomorrow."

Use Figures of Speech. A figure of speech is a stylistic device in which words are used beyond their literal meaning. One of the best ways to achieve vividness is to use figures of speech. Table 12.1 on page 256 presents a few that you may find helpful.

Use Imagery. Another way to inject vividness into your speech is to appeal to the audience's senses, especially their visual, auditory, and tactile senses. Using imagery can make them see, hear, and feel what you're talking about.

Visual imagery enables you to describe people or objects in images the audience can see. When appropriate, describe visual qualities such as height, weight, color, size, shape, length, and contour. Let your audience see the sweat pouring down the

> If you have an important point to make, don't try to be subtle or clever. Use a pile-driver. Hit the point once. Then come back and hit it again. Then hit it a third time—a tremendous whack.
>
> —Winston Churchill

TABLE 12.1 Figures of Speech

These are just a few of the many figures of speech you can use in your speeches. Too many similes or too much hyperbole is likely to make your speech sound unnatural and overly formal, so use these sparingly. On the other hand, a good figure goes a long way toward making your speech memorable. Can you think of additional examples for each of the figures identified here?

FIGURE	DEFINITION	EXAMPLES
Alliteration	Repetition of the same initial consonant sound in two or more words close to one another	Fifty Famous Flavors March Madness
Hyperbole	Use of extreme exaggeration	I'm so hungry I could eat a horse.
Metaphor	Comparison of two unlike things	She's a lion when she wakes up. He's a real bulldozer.
Personification	Attribution of human characteristics to inanimate objects	This room cries out for activity. My car is tired and wants water.
Simile	Comparison of two unlike objects using the words *like* or *as*	This chairperson takes charge like a bull. The teacher is as gentle as a lamb.
Rhetorical Question	A question used to make a statement or produce some desired effect rather than to secure an answer, which is obvious	Do you want to be popular? Do you want to get promoted? Do you want to pass the next exam?

faces of coal miners and the short, overweight executive in a pin-striped suit smoking an enormous cigar. *Auditory imagery* helps you appeal to the audience's sense of hearing. Let listeners hear the car screeching, the wind whistling, the bells chiming, and the roar of the angry tenants. *Tactile imagery* enables you to make the audience feel the temperature or texture you're talking about. Let listeners feel the cool water running over their bodies, the fighter's punch, the sand beneath their feet, and a lover's soft caress.

Appropriateness

Appropriate language is consistent in tone with your topic, your audience, and your own self-image. It's language that does not offend anyone or make anyone feel uncomfortable. It's language that seems natural given the situation. Here are some guidelines to help you choose appropriate language.

Speak at the Appropriate Level of Formality. Although public speaking usually takes place in a relatively formal situation, relatively informal language seems to work best in most situations. One way to achieve a more informal style is to use contractions: *don't* instead of *do not, I'll* instead of *I shall,* and *wouldn't* instead of *would not.* Contractions give a public speech the sound and rhythm of conversation—a quality listeners generally like.

Avoid Written-Style Expressions. Avoid expressions that are more familiar in writing, such as "the former" or "the latter" as well as expressions such as "the argument presented above." These make listeners feel you're reading to them rather than talking with them.

VIEWPOINT
When images are too vivid, they may divert the audience from following a logically presented series of thoughts or arguments (Frey & Eagly, 1993). The listener's brain focuses on these extremely vivid images and loses track of the speaker's sequence of ideas. So if you suspect that your listeners may concentrate on the image rather than the idea, drop the image. In the same way that a speech can be too vivid, can your speech be too clear? Too appropriate? Too personal?

Avoid Slang, Vulgar, and Offensive Expressions.   Be careful not to offend your audience with language that embarrasses them or makes them think you have little respect for them. Although your listeners may use such expressions, they generally resent their use by public speakers. Above all, avoid terms that might be interpreted as sexist, heterosexist, or racist (see Chapter 5).

Personal Style

Audiences favor speakers who use a personal rather than an impersonal style—who speak *with* them rather than *at* them. A personal style makes the audience feel more involved with the speaker and with the speech topic.

Use Personal Pronouns.   Say "I," "me," "he," "she," and "you." Avoid expressions such as the impersonal *one* (as in, "One is led to believe that . . ."), *this speaker,* or *you, the listeners*. These expressions are overly formal and distance the audience, creating barriers rather than bridges.

Direct Questions to the Audience.   Involve the audience by asking them questions. With a small audience, you might even briefly take responses. With larger audiences, you might ask the question, pause to allow the audience time to consider their responses, and then move on. When you direct questions to your listeners, you make them feel a part of the experience.

Create Immediacy.   Immediacy is a connectedness, a relatedness, a oneness with your listeners. Create immediacy by referring directly to your listeners, using *you;* say "*you'll* enjoy reading . . ." instead of "everyone will enjoy reading. . . ." Refer to commonalities between you and the audience. Say, for example, "We're all children of immigrants," or, "We all want to see this agency run smoother and receive fewer complaints from clients." Refer also to shared experiences and goals. Say, for example, "We all need a more responsive PTA." Finally, recognize and refer to audience feedback. Say, for example, "I can see from your expressions that we're all here for the same reason."

Sentence Construction

Effective public speaking style also requires careful attention to the construction of sentences. Here are some guidelines that will help you achieve a clear, vivid, appropriate, and personal speaking style.

Favor Short over Long Sentences.   Short sentences are more forceful and economical. They are easier to understand and to remember. Listeners don't have the time or inclination to unravel long and complex sentences. Help them to listen more efficiently: Use short rather than long sentences.

Favor Direct over Indirect Sentences.   Direct sentences are easier to understand. They are also more forceful. Instead of saying, "I want to tell you the three main reasons why we should not adopt the Bennett Proposal," say, "We should not adopt the Bennett Proposal. Let me give you three good reasons."

Favor Active over Passive Sentences.   Active sentences are easier to understand. They also make your speech livelier and more vivid. Instead of saying, "The lower court's original decision was reversed by the Supreme Court," say, "The Supreme Court reversed the lower court's decision." Instead of saying, "The change was favored by management," say, "Management favored the change."

Favor Positive over Negative Sentences.   Positive sentences are easier to comprehend and to remember (DeVito, 1976; Clark, 1974). Notice how sentences A and C are easier to understand than B and D.

A. The committee rejected the proposal.
B. The committee did not accept the proposal.
C. This committee works outside the normal company hierarchy.
D. This committee does not work within the normal company hierarchy.

Vary the Type and Length of Sentences.   The advice to use short, direct, active, and positive sentences is valid most of the time. But too many sentences of the same type or length will make your speech boring. Use variety while generally following the guidelines given above.

Step 8: Construct Your Conclusion and Introduction

Your conclusion and introduction need special care because they will determine, in large part, the effectiveness of your speech. Construct your conclusion first and your introduction next.

The Conclusion

Devote special care to this brief but crucial part of your speech. In your conclusion, summarize your main points and close.

Summarize   You may summarize your speech in a variety of ways.

Restate Your Thesis.   Restate the essential thrust of your speech—your thesis or perhaps the purpose you hoped to achieve.

Restate the Importance of Your Thesis.   Tell the audience again why your topic or thesis is so important. Here is how Carrie Willis (Schnoor, 2000, p. 15), a student from Tallahassee Community College, in a speech on "drowsy driving," re-

> Begin low, speak low;
> Take fire, rise higher;
> When most impressed
> Be self-possessed;
> At the end wax warm,
> And sit down in a storm.
>
> —John Leifchild

stated the importance of her thesis and summarized the major propositions of her speech:

> While this problem is as old as cars, it's not disappearing. And it won't disappear until you choose to do something about it. Today, we have gained a better understanding of the problem of falling asleep at the wheel, and why it continues to exist, while finally suggesting several initiatives to help end this epidemic. Six innocent college students were killed, all because someone didn't take the precautionary steps to avoid the tragedy. So next time you're on the road and you find yourself dozing off, pull over and take a nap, because those 30 minutes could save your life.

Restate Your Major Propositions. Simply reiterate your two, three, or four major propositions. For example, in a speech on problems with volunteer fire departments, one student speaker restated his propositions like this: "By examining how volunteer firefighters are jeopardizing our safety, why our communities remain so dependent, and finally prescribing some solutions, we have set the stage for reform" (Schnoor, 1999, p. 46).

In a speech on hate crimes, the speaker restates the thesis and its importance and summarizes the major propositions all in one simple statement: "Today we've seen the reality of hate crimes against homosexuals, some of the reasons these crimes are committed, the limitations of our current legislation, and the need for the Hate Crimes Prevention Act of 1998" (Schnoor, 1999, p. 61).

Close The conclusion's second function is to provide closure—to give the speech a crisp and definite end. Don't leave your audience wondering whether you've finished.

Use a Quotation. A quotation that summarizes your thesis or provides an interesting perspective on your point of view often provides effective closure. Make sure that it's clearly and directly related to your speech purpose; otherwise, the audience will spend their time trying to figure out the connection.

Pose a Challenge or Question. You may wish to end your speech with a provocative question or challenge:

- "What do you intend to do about the company's refusal to increase wages?"
- "Go home and clean high-cholesterol foods out of your refrigerator."
- "Sign this petition; it will help put an experienced person in office."
- "What are you going to do to help end the AIDS crisis?"

Here's how one student, in a speech on the problems with our diet culture, challenged her audience: "There's a whole generation of kids out there who need our action. This is our wakeup call as a society. Don't diet—eat smart. For your sake, and for the sake of the children in your life" (Schnoor, 1999, p. 127).

Thank the Audience. Speakers frequently thank their audience. If you do this, do it a bit more elaborately than by simply saying "Thank you." You might relate the thanks to your thesis: "I really appreciate your attention and hope you'll join us in Sunday's protest." Or you might say, "Thank you for your attention and your active concern about this crisis," or "I want to thank you for listening and for your willingness to sign Williams's petition."

The Introduction

In your introduction, try to accomplish two goals: First, gain your audience's attention, and second, orient the audience—tell them a little bit about what you'll talk about.

> 'Where shall I begin, please your majesty?' she asked.
> 'Begin at the beginning,' the King said, very gravely, 'and go on till you come to the end: then stop.'
>
> —Lewis Carroll, *Alice in Wonderland*

Gain Attention   In your introduction, focus the audience's attention on your topic. Then work to maintain that attention throughout your speech.

Ask a Question.   Questions are effective because they are a change from normal statements and involve the audience. They tell the audience that you're talking directly to them and care about their responses.

Refer to Specific Audience Members.   Involving members directly makes them perk up and pay attention.

Refer to Recent Happenings.   Being familiar with recent news events, the audience will pay attention to your approach. For example, in a speech on colon cancer, one student used the familiar example of Katie Couric's campaign against this form of cancer, undertaken soon after her husband died from it (Schnoor, 1999, p. 29).

Use Illustrations or Dramatic or Humorous Stories.   We are all drawn to illustrations and stories about people—they make a speech vivid and concrete. Use them to secure audience attention in the introduction and to maintain it throughout.

Use Visual Aids.   These will engage attention because they are new and different. Chapter 13 provides lots of specific examples.

Orient the Audience   Previewing what you're going to say will help your listeners follow your thoughts more closely. You can orient the audience in several ways.

Give the Audience a General Idea of Your Subject.   One student, for example, in a speech on the problems of Internet education, oriented her audience not only to the topic but also to her problem–solution organizational pattern: "I am going to describe the problem of phony academic institutions on the Internet, focusing primarily on the misleading nature of their names as an advertising strategy. I will then provide some simple solutions to aid the general public in avoiding and exposing these disreputable organizations" (Schnoor, 1999, p. 10).

Give a Detailed Preview of Your Main Propositions.   Identify the propositions you will discuss—for example, "In this brief talk, I will cover four major attractions of New York City: the night life, the theater, restaurants, and museums."

Identify the Goal You Hope to Achieve.   A librarian addressing my public speaking class oriented the audience by stating goals in this way: "Pay attention for the next few minutes and you'll be able to locate anything we have in the library by using the new touch-screen computer access system."

"I'll tell you what this election is about. It's about homework, and pitiful allowances, and having to clean your room. It's also about candy, and ice cream, and staying up late."

Guidelines for Avoiding Some Common Faults

Don't Start Your Speech Immediately   Instead, survey your audience; make eye contact and engage their attention. Stand in front of the audience with a sense of control. Pause briefly, then begin speaking.

Don't Display Discomfort or Displeasure   When you walk to the speaker's stand, display enthusiasm and a desire to speak. People much prefer listening to a speaker who shows that she or he enjoys speaking to them.

Constructing Conclusions and Introductions

Prepare a conclusion and an introduction to a hypothetical speech on one of the topics listed below, making sure that in your conclusion you (1) review the speech's main points and (2) provide closure, and that in your introduction you (1) gain attention and (2) orient the audience.

1. Foreign language requirements should be abolished.
2. All killing of wild animals should be declared illegal.
3. Properties owned by religious institutions should be taxed.
4. Assisted suicide should be legalized.
5. Gambling should be declared illegal by all states.

Don't Apologize   A common fault is to apologize for something in your speech. Don't. Your inadequacies, whatever they may be, will be clear enough to any discerning listener. Don't point them out. In the United States, avoid expressions such as "I am not an expert on this topic," "I wanted to illustrate these ideas with a videotape, but I couldn't get my hands on a VCR," or "I didn't do as much reading on this topic as I should have." And never start a speech with "I'm not very good at giving public speeches." Be aware, however, that this rule does not hold in all cultures. For example, in Iran, a speaker would be expected to use self-deprecating terms to indicate his or her humility and modesty (Keshavarz, 1988). A similar modesty claim would be expected in many Asian cultures.

Don't Preface Your Introduction   Don't begin with such common but ineffective statements as "I'm really nervous, but here goes," "Before I begin my talk, I want to say . . . ," or "I hope I can remember everything I want to say."

Don't Introduce New Material in Your Conclusion   Once you reach your conclusion, it's too late to introduce new material. Instead, reinforce what you have already said, summarize your essential points, or give new expression to ideas already covered.

Don't Race Away from the Speaker's Stand   After your last statement, pause, maintain audience eye contact, and then walk (don't run) to your seat. Show no signs of relief; focus your attention on whatever activity is taking place. Glance over the audience and sit down. If a question period follows your speech and you're in charge of this, pause after completing your conclusion. Ask audience members in a direct matter if they have any questions. If there's a chairperson who will ask for questions, pause after your conclusion, then nonverbally signal to the chairperson that you're ready.

Transitions and Internal Summaries

Transitions (sometimes called "connectives") are words, phrases, or sentences that connect the various parts of your speech. Because your audience will hear your speech just once, they may not see the connections you want them to see. By using transitions, you can help your listeners see how one point leads to another or where one argument ends and another begins. Use transitions in at least the following places:

- between the introduction and the body of the speech
- between the body and the conclusion
- between the main points in the body of the speech

What Do You Say?

Audience Adaptation: You're one of four people running for the presidency of your building's tenant association. Each candidate must give a brief talk stating what he or she would do for the building. All of the tenants except you belong to the same race. You wonder if you should mention race in your talk? *What do you say?*

Here are the major transitional functions and some stylistic devices that you might use to serve these functions.

1. *To announce the start of a major proposition or piece of evidence:* "First . . . ," "A second argument . . . ," "A closely related problem . . . ," "If you want further evidence, look at . . . ," "My next point . . . ," or "An even more compelling argument. . . ."

2. *To signal that you're drawing a conclusion from previously given evidence and argument:* "Thus . . . ," "Therefore . . . ," "So, as you can see . . . ," or, "It follows, then, that. . . ."

3. *To alert the audience that you're introducing a qualification or exception:* "But . . . ," "However, also consider . . . ," or, "On the other hand. . . ."

4. *To remind listeners of what you've just said and to stress that it's connected with another issue you now want to consider:* "In contrast to . . . ," "Consider also . . . ," "Not only . . . , but also . . . ," or "In addition to . . . , we also need to look at. . . ."

5. *To signal the part of your speech that you're approaching:* "By way of introduction . . . ," "In conclusion . . . ," "Now, let's discuss why we are here today . . . ," or, "So, what's the solution? What should we do?"

You can enhance a transition nonverbally by pausing between the transition and the next part of your speech. This will help the audience see that you're beginning a new part of your speech. You might also take a step forward or to the side after saying your transition to echo the movement from one part of your speech to another.

Closely related to the transition is the internal summary, a statement that summarizes what you have already discussed. Usually it summarizes some major subdivision of your speech. Incorporate several internal summaries into your speech—perhaps working them into the transitions connecting, say, the major arguments or issues. An internal summary that is also a transition might look something like this:

The three arguments advanced here were (1) . . . , (2) . . . , (3) . . . . Now, what can we do about them? I think we can do two things. First, . . .

Another example:

Inadequate recreational facilities, poor schooling, and a lack of adequate role models seem to be the major problems facing our youngsters. Each of these, however, can be remedied and even eliminated. Here's what we can do.

Now that you have completed your speech, you need to put it all together in the form of an outline, something you have already been doing as you identified your major propositions and amplified them with illustrations and definitions, for example. Here we look at preparation, skeletal, and delivery outlines that will help you not only to organize your thoughts more coherently, but also to deliver your speech more effectively.

The Preparation Outline

Here is a relatively detailed outline similar to the one you might prepare when constructing your speech. The sidenotes should clarify both the content and the format of a preparation outline.

Title: HAVE YOU EVER BEEN CULTURE SHOCKED?

Thesis: Culture shock can be described in four stages.

Purpose: To inform my audience of the four phases of culture shock

Generally, the title, thesis, and purpose of the speech are prefaced to the outline. When the outline is an assignment that is to be handed in, additional information may be required.

INTRODUCTION

I. How many of you have experienced culture shock?

    A. Many people experience culture shock, a reaction to being in a culture very different from what they were used to.

    B. By understanding culture shock, you'll be in a better position to deal with it if and when it comes.

II. Culture shock occurs in four stages (Oberg, 1960).

    A. The Honeymoon occurs first.

    B. The Crisis occurs second.

    C. The Recovery occurs third.

    D. The Adjustment occurs fourth.

[Let's follow the order in which these four stages occur beginning with the first stage, the honeymoon.]

BODY

I. The Honeymoon occurs first.

    A. The honeymoon is the period of fascination with the new people and culture.

    B. You enjoy the people and the culture.

        1. You love the people.

            a. For example, the people in Zaire spend their time very differently from the way New Yorkers do.

            b. For example, my first 18 years living on a farm was very different from life in a college dorm.

        2. You love the culture.

            a. The great number of different religions in India fascinated me.

            b. Eating was an especially great experience.

[But, like many relationships, contact with a new culture is not all honeymoon; soon there comes a crisis.]

II. The Crisis occurs second.

    A. The crisis is the period when you begin to experience problems.

        1. One-third of American workers abroad fail because of culture shock (Samovar & Porter, 1991, p. 232).

        2. The personal difficulties are also great.

    B. Life becomes difficult in the new culture.

        1. Communication is difficult.

        2. It's easy to offend people without realizing it.

[As you gain control over the various crises, you begin to recover.]

Note the general format for the outline; the headings are clearly labeled and the indenting helps you clearly see the relationship between the items. For example, in introduction II, the outline format helps you to see that A, B, C, and D are explanations for II.

Note that the introduction, body, and conclusion are clearly labeled and separated visually.

Although the speaker assumes that the audience is familiar with culture shock, he or she still includes a brief definition in case some audience members don't know what it is and to refresh the memory of others.

Note that references are integrated throughout the outline, just as they would be in a term paper. In the actual speech, the speaker might say: "Anthropologist Kalervo Oberg, who coined the term *culture shock*, said it occurs in four stages."

The introduction serves two functions: It gains attention by involving the audience and by stressing the importance of the topic to the audience's desire to gain self-understanding, and it orients the audience to what is to follow. This particular orientation identifies both the number and the names of the stages. If this speech were much longer and more complex, this orientation might also have included brief definitions of each stage.

Another function often served by the introduction is to establish a relationship between yourself as the speaker, the topic, and the audience. In this particular speech, this function might have been served by your telling the audience how you experienced culture shock and how knowing the stages helped you cope with the difficulties. You might then tell the audience that the same would be true for them and thus connect all three major elements of the speech.

The transition at the end of the introduction tells the audience to expect a four-part presentation. Also, the numbers repeated throughout the outline will further aid the audience in keeping track of where you are in the speech. Most important, the transition tells the audience that the speech will follow a temporal thought pattern.

Notice the parallel structure throughout the outline. For example, note that I, II, III, and IV in the body are all phrased in exactly the same way. Although this may seem unnecessarily repetitive, it will help your audience follow your speech more closely and will also help you structure your thoughts logically.

Notice that there are lots of examples in this speech. These examples are identified only briefly in the outline and would naturally be elaborated on in the speech.

Notice, too, the internal organization of each major point. Each main assertion in the body contains a definition of the stage (IA, IIA, IIIA, and IVA) and examples (IB, IIB, IIIB, and IVB) to illustrate the stage.

When you cite a specific fact, some style manuals require that you include the page number in the source reference.

III. The Recovery occurs third.

    A. The recovery is the period when you learn how to cope.

    B. You begin to learn intercultural competence (Lustig & Koester, 2003).

        1. You learn how to communicate.

            a. Being able to go to the market and make my wants known was a great day for me.

            b. I was able to ask for a date.

        2. You learn the rules of the culture.

            a. The different religious ceremonies each have their own rules.

            b. Eating is a ritual experience in lots of places throughout Africa.

[Your recovery leads naturally into the next and final stage, the adjustment.]

IV. The Adjustment occurs fourth.

    A. The adjustment is the period when you come to enjoy the new culture.

    B. You come to appreciate the people and the culture.

[Let me summarize, then, the stages you go through in experiencing culture shock.]

CONCLUSION

  I. Culture shock can be described in four stages.

    A. The honeymoon is first.

    B. The crisis is second.

    C. The recovery is third.

    D. The adjustment is fourth.

  II. By knowing the four stages, you can better understand the culture shock you may now be experiencing on the job, at school, or in your private life.

References

Lustig, Myron W., & Koester, Jolene. (2003). *Intercultural competence: Interpersonal communication across cultures* (4th ed.). New York: HarperCollins.

Oberg, Kalervo. (1960). Culture shock: Adjustment to new cultural environments. *Practical Anthropology, 7,* 177–182.

Samovar, Larry A., & Porter, Richard E. (1991). *Communication between cultures.* Belmont, CA: Wadsworth.

Note that each statement in the outline is a complete sentence. You can easily convert this outline into a phrase or key word outline for use in delivery. The full sentences, however, will help you see relationships among items more clearly.

The transitions are inserted between all major parts of the speech. Although they may seem too numerous in this abbreviated outline, they will be appreciated by your audience because the transitions will help them follow your speech.

Notice that these four points correspond to IIA, B, C, and D of the introduction and to I, II, III, and IV of the body. Notice how the similar wording adds clarity.

This step provides closure; it makes it clear that the speech is finished. It also serves to encourage reflection on the part of the audience as to their own experiences of culture shock.

This reference list includes only those sources that appear in the completed speech.

The Skeletal Outline

The skeletal outline is a template for structuring a speech. This particular example of the skeletal outline would be appropriate for a speech using a time, spatial, or topical organization pattern. Note that in this outline there are three major propositions (I, II, and III in the body). These correspond to items IIA, B, C, and D in the introduction (where you would orient the audience) and to IA, B, C, and D in the conclusion (where you would summarize your major propositions). The transitions are signaled by square brackets. As you review this outline—the watermarks will remind you of the functions of each outline item—you will see how it can be adapted for use with other organization patterns, such as problem–solution, cause–effect, or the motivated sequence. Additional skeletal outlines for a variety of organizational patterns may be found at www.ablongman.com/devito.

SKELETAL OUTLINE

Thesis: _____ *your main assertion; the core of your speech* _____

Specific Purpose: _____ *what you hope to achieve from this speech* _____

Introduction

    I. _____ *gain attention* _____

    II. _____ *orient audience* _____

        A. _____ *first major proposition; same as I in body* _____

        B. _____ *second major proposition; same as II in body* _____

        C. _____ *third major proposition; same as III in body* _____

[Transition: _____ *connect the introduction to the body* _____]

Body

    I. _____ *first major proposition* _____

        A. _____ *support for I (the first major proposition)* _____

        B. _____ *further support for I* _____

[Transition: _____ *connect the first major proposition to the second* _____]

    II. _____ *second major proposition* _____

        A. _____ *support for II (the second major proposition)* _____

        B. _____ *further support for II* _____

[Transition: _____ *connect the second major proposition to the third* _____]

    III. _____ *third major proposition* _____

        A. _____ *support for III* _____

        B. _____ *further support for III* _____

[Transition: _____ *connect the third major proposition (or all major propositions) to the conclusion* _____]

Conclusion

    I. _____ *summary* _____

        A. _____ *first major proposition; same as I in body* _____

        B. _____ *second major proposition; same as II in body* _____

        C. _____ *third major proposition: same as III in body* _____

    II. _____ *closure* _____

The Delivery Outline

The delivery outline assists you in presenting the speech. Don't use your preparation outline: you may feel inclined to read from it, which is not an effective way to give a speech. So write a brief delivery outline such as that presented below, which was constructed from the preparation outline on culture shock. If you're using Power-Point—discussed in detail in the next chapter—then your delivery outline is going to be either the PowerPoint slides themselves or the speaker's notes that you generate along with your PowerPoint presentation (see pages 299–300 and 303). Here are some guidelines for delivery outlines.

- *Be brief.* Don't allow the outline to stand in the way of speaker–audience contact. Use key words to trigger in your mind the ideas you wish to discuss. Notice how brief the sample delivery outline is compared to the preparation outline. You'll be able to use this brief outline effectively without losing eye contact with the audience. It uses abbreviations (for example, CS for culture shock) and phrases rather than complete sentences. And yet it's detailed enough to include all essential parts of your speech, even transitions.

- *Be delivery-minded.* Include any delivery guides you might wish to remember while you're speaking—for example, notes to pause or to show the visual aid.

- *Rehearse your speech with this delivery outline.* Make your rehearsal as close to the real thing as possible.

DELIVERY OUTLINE

PAUSE!

LOOK OVER THE AUDIENCE!

    I. Many experience CS

        A. CS: the reaction to being in a culture very different from your own

        B. By understanding CS, you'll be better able to deal with it

PAUSE—SCAN AUDIENCE

    II. CS occurs in 4 stages (WRITE ON BOARD)

        A. Honeymoon

        B. Crisis

        C. Recovery

        D. Adjustment

[Let's examine these stages of CS]

PAUSE/STEP FORWARD

    I. Honeymoon

        A. fascination w/ people and culture

        B. enjoyment of people and culture

            1. Zaire example

            2. farm to college dorm

[But, life is not all honeymoon—the crisis]

    II. Crisis

        A. problems arise

            1. 1/3 Am workers fail abroad

            2. personal difficulties

        B. life becomes difficult

            1. communication

            2. offend others

[As you gain control over the crises, you learn how to cope]

PAUSE

    III. Recovery

        A. period of learning to cope

        B. you learn intercultural competence

            1. communication becomes easier

            2. you learn the culture's rules

[As you recover, you adjust]
    IV. Adjustment
        A. learn to enjoy (again) the new culture
        B. appreciate people and culture
[These then are the 4 stages; let me summarize]
PAUSE
CONCLUSION
      I. CS occurs in 4 stages: honeymoon, crisis, recovery, & adjustment
     II. By knowing the 4 stages, you can better understand the culture shock you may now be experiencing on the job, at school, or in your private life.
PAUSE
ASK FOR QUESTIONS

Step 9: Rehearse Your Speech

Let's start the discussion of rehearsal by identifying the general methods of delivery. Then we can look at some general suggestions for making your rehearsals efficient and effective.

Methods of Delivery

Speakers vary widely in delivery methods. Some speak off-the-cuff with no apparent preparation. Others read their speeches from manuscript. Others construct a detailed outline and compose the speech at the moment of delivery. These represent the three general methods of delivery: impromptu, manuscript, and extemporaneous.

The Impromptu Method An **impromptu speech** involves speaking without preparation. On some occasions, you can't avoid impromptu speaking. In a classroom, you may be asked to comment on the speaker and speech you just heard: in effect, you give an impromptu speech of evaluation. At meetings, people are often asked for impromptu comments on various issues. Or you may have to fill in for someone who has not shown up. You can greatly improve impromptu speaking by cultivating public speaking ability in general. The more proficient you are as a speaker, the better you will be impromptu.

The Manuscript Method If you give a **manuscript speech,** you write out the speech and read it. This is the safest method when exact timing and wording are required. It could be disastrous if a political leader did not speak from manuscript on sensitive issues. An ambiguous word, phrase, or sentence that proved insulting, belligerent, or conciliatory might cause serious problems. With a manuscript speech, you can control style, content, organization, and all other elements. A variation of the manuscript method is to write out the speech and then memorize it. You then recite the entire speech from memory, much as an actor recites a part in a play. The great disadvantages of the manuscript method are that the speech doesn't sound natural and there is no opportunity to adjust the speech on the basis of audience feedback.

The Extemporaneous Method The **extemporaneous speech** is useful when exact timing and wording are not required. Good lecturing by college teachers is extemporaneous. They have prepared thoroughly, know what they want to say, and have the lecture's organization clearly in mind. But they are not committed to exact wording. This method allows greater flexibility for feedback. Should a point need clarification, you can elaborate when it will be most effective. It's also easy to be

natural, because you're being yourself. And you may move about and interact with the audience.

The major disadvantage of this method is that you may stumble and grope for words. You can address this disadvantage by rehearsing the speech several times. Although you can't give the precise attention to style that you can in the manuscript and memorized methods, you can memorize certain key phrases.

I recommend the extemporaneous method for most situations. Overall, it offers the greatest advantages with the fewest disadvantages. However, consider the advantages of memorizing certain parts of your speech:

- Even in extemporaneous speaking, memorize your opening and closing lines—perhaps the first and last two or three sentences. This will help you focus your attention on the audience at the two most important moments of your speech.

- Memorize the major propositions and the order in which you will present them. After all, if you expect your audience to remember these points, they will expect you to remember them as well.

Rehearsing the Speech

Rehearsal should enable you to see how the speech will flow as a whole and to make any necessary changes and improvements. It will also allow you to time your speech so that you stay within the allotted time. The following procedures should help you use your rehearsal time most effectively.

- Rehearse the speech from beginning to end rather than in parts. Be sure to include all the examples and illustrations (and audiovisual aids if any) in your rehearsal.

- Time the speech during each rehearsal. Adjust your speech—both what you say and your delivery rate—on the basis of this timing.

- Rehearse the speech under conditions as close as possible to those under which you'll deliver it. If possible, rehearse in the room in which you'll present the speech and in front of a few supportive listeners. Get together with two or three other students or colleagues so you can each serve both as speaker and as listener/critic.

- Rehearse the speech in front of a full-length mirror to help you see how you'll appear to the audience. Practice your eye contact, your movements, and your gestures in front of the mirror.

- Don't interrupt your rehearsal to make notes or changes; do these between rehearsals. If possible, record your speech (ideally, on videotape) so you can hear and see exactly what your listeners will hear and see. This will also enable you to see whether you exhibit habits or tics that you may want to alter before you give the "real" speech.

- Rehearse at least three or four times, or as long as your rehearsals continue to result in improvements.

Step 10: Deliver Your Speech

Use your voice and body to complement and reinforce your verbal message.

Voice

Your voice is your major tool in delivering your message. Use your vocal volume and rate, articulation and pronunciation, and pauses to complement and reinforce your message.

By permission of John L. Hart FLP, and Creators Syndicate, Inc.

Volume   The **volume** of your voice is its relative loudness or softness. In an adequately controlled voice, volume varies according to factors such as the distance between you and your listeners, the competing noise, and the emphasis you want to give an idea. A voice that is too soft will require listeners to strain to hear, and they will soon tire of listening. A voice that is too loud will intrude on the listeners' psychological space. Vary your volume to best reflect your ideas—perhaps increasing volume for key words or phrases, lowering volume when talking about something extremely serious. Be especially careful not to fade away at the ends of sentences.

Rate   Your speech **rate** is the speed at which you speak. About 140 words per minute is average for speaking as well as for reading aloud. If you talk too fast, you deprive your listeners of the time they need to digest what you're saying. If your rate is too slow, your listeners' thoughts will wander. So speak at a pace that engages but doesn't bore and that allows listeners time for reflection. Vary your rate during the speech to call attention to certain points and to add variety.

Articulation and Pronunciation   **Articulation** results from movements of the speech organs as they modify and interrupt the air stream from the lungs. Different movements of the tongue, lips, teeth, palate, and vocal cords produce different sounds. **Pronunciation** consists of the production of syllables or words according to some accepted standard, such as that of a dictionary. Our concern here is to identify and correct some of the most common problems associated with faulty articulation and pronunciation.

Errors of Omission (Articulation).   Omitting sounds or even syllables is a common articulation problem that you can easily overcome with concentration and practice. Here are some examples:

Incorrect	Correct
gov-a-ment	gov-ern-ment
hi-stry	hi-sto-ry
wanna	want to
studyin	studying
a-lum-num	a-lum-i-num
comp-ny	comp-a-ny
vul-ner-bil-ity	vul-ner-a-bil-ity

Errors of Substitution (Articulation). Substituting an incorrect sound for the correct one is also easy to fix. Among the most common substitutions are [d] for [t] and [d] for [th]; for example, *wader* for the correct *waiter*, *dese* for the correct *these*, *bedder* for the correct *better*, and *ax* for the correct *ask*. Other prevalent substitution errors include *ekcetera* for the correct *etcetera*, *congradulations* for the correct *congratulations*, and *lenth* for the correct *length*.

Errors of Addition (Articulation). These errors involve adding sounds where they don't belong. Some examples include:

Incorrect	Correct
acrost	across
athalete	athlete
Americar	America
idear	idea
filim	film
lore	law

If you make any of these errors, you can correct them by following these steps:

1. Become conscious of your own articulation patterns and the specific errors you're making. Recording yourself on tape will help you become more aware of your own speech patterns and possible errors.

2. Listen carefully to the articulation of accomplished speakers—for example, broadcasters.

3. Practice the correct patterns until they become part of your normal speech behavior.

Errors of Accent (Pronunciation).   Each word has its own accepted **accent** or stress pattern. Examples of words that are often accented incorrectly include New Orleáns, ínsurance, compárable, and orátor for the correct New Órleans, insúrance, cómparable, and órator.

Errors of Adding Sounds (Pronunciation).   For some words, many people add sounds that are not part of the standard pronunciation. In the first three examples, the error involves pronouncing letters that are a part of the written word but should remain silent. In the last four examples, sounds are inserted where they don't belong.

Incorrect	Correct
homage	omage
Illinois	Illinoi
evening	evning
athalete	athlete
airaplane	airplane
burgalar	burglar
mischievious	mischievous

One way to correct pronunciation problems is to check a word's pronunciation in a dictionary. Learn to read your dictionary's pronunciation key. Another way is to listen to a dictionary on CD-ROM so you can hear the standard pronunciation.

Pauses   **Pauses** are interruptions in the flow of speech. *Filled pauses* are gaps that you fill with vocalizations such as *er, um,* and *ah*. Even expressions such as *well* and *you know,* when used merely to fill up silence, are filled pauses. These pauses are ineffective and detract from the strength of your message. They will make you appear hesitant, unprepared, and unsure.

Unfilled pauses, silences interjected into the stream of speech, can be especially effective if used correctly. Here are a few examples of places where unfilled pauses—silences of a few seconds—can enhance your speech.

- Pause at transitional points. This will signal that you're moving from one part of the speech or from one idea to another. It will help listeners separate the main issues you're discussing.
- Pause at the end of an important assertion. This allows the audience to think about its significance.
- Pause after asking a rhetorical question. This will give the audience time to think about how they would answer.
- Pause before an important idea. This will help signal that what comes next is especially significant.
- Pause before you begin your speech (to scan and assess the audience and gather your thoughts) and after you finish it (to allow your ideas to sink in and to dispel any idea that you're anxious to escape).

What Do You Say?

Audience Inactivity: You're giving a speech on the problems of teenage drug abuse and you notice that the back rows of your audience have totally tuned you out; they're reading, chatting, working on their laptops. *What do you say?*

Body Action

You speak with your body as well as with your mouth. The total effect of the speech depends not only on what you say but also on how you present it. The four aspects of body action that are especially important in public speaking are eye contact, facial expression, gestures and posture, and movement.

Eye Contact   The most important single aspect of bodily communication is eye contact. Keep in mind, however, that cultures differ widely on the amount and intensity of eye contact they consider appropriate. In some cultures, eye contact that is too intense may be considered offensive. In most of the United States, audiences want and expect to be looked at rather directly. Not surprisingly, then, the two major problems with eye contact are not enough eye contact and eye contact that does not cover the audience fairly. Speakers who do not maintain enough eye contact appear distant, unconcerned, and less trustworthy than speakers who look directly at their audience. And, of course, without eye contact, you will not be able to secure that all-important

Communicating with power

Power Cues

As a public speaker, do you think you'd get greater power and be more influential from emphasizing your competence and ability to do a task (task cues) or from threats (dominance cues)? Consider the results from one interesting study done in the context of small groups (Driskell, Olmstead, & Salas, 1993). In this study task cues included maintaining eye contact, sitting at the head of the table, using a relatively rapid speech rate, speaking fluently, and gesturing appropriately. Dominance cues, on the other hand, included speaking in a loud and angry voice, pointing fingers, maintaining rigid posture, using forceful gestures, and lowering the eyebrows. With which cues would you be more effective?

Results from this study showed that you'd be more influential if you used task cues. Listeners would also see you as more competent and more likable. If you used dominance cues, on the other hand, you'd be more likely to be perceived as less competent, less influential, less likable, and more self-oriented. The implication, from at least this one study, is that if you wish to gain influence and be liked, you should use task cues and avoid dominance cues.

Enhancing Your Communication Power

How might you use the results of this study to enhance your power in public speaking? For example, what kinds of cues might you use to enhance your power when you speak in public? What kinds of cues would you seek to avoid?

audience feedback. Maintain eye contact with the entire audience. Involve all listeners in the public speaking transaction. Communicate equally with the audience members on the left and on the right, in both the back and the front of the room.

Facial Expression   If you believe in your thesis, you'll probably display your meanings appropriately and effectively. Nervousness and anxiety, however, can prevent you from relaxing enough for your positive emotions to come through. But time and practice will allow you to relax, and your feelings will reveal themselves appropriately and automatically.

Gestures and Postures   Spontaneous and natural gestures will help illustrate your verbal messages. If you feel relaxed and comfortable with yourself and your audience, you'll generate natural body action without conscious or studied attention. When delivering your speech, stand straight but not stiff. Try to communicate a command of the situation rather than any nervousness you may feel. Avoid putting your hands in your pockets or leaning on the desk or chalkboard. With practice, you'll feel more at ease and will communicate this in the way you stand before the audience.

Movement   If you move too little, you may appear fearful or distant. If you move too much, you may lead the audience to concentrate on the movement itself, wondering where you'll wind up next. Use movement to emphasize transitions and to introduce important assertions. For example, when making a transition, you might step forward to signal that something new is coming. Similarly, use movement to signal an important assumption, bit of evidence, or closely reasoned argument.

Using Notes

Speakers who prepare their speeches around a series of slides such as you'd produce with one of the presentation software packages (such as PowerPoint or Corel Presentations) may use their slides as their notes. In most public speaking classes, your notes will consist of a delivery outline and your audiovisual aids. Effective delivery depends on the smooth use of notes—whether a series of slides or transparencies or an $8^{1}/_{2}$-by-11-inch piece of paper—during the speech. A few simple guidelines may help you avoid common errors (McCroskey, 1997; Kesselman-Turkel & Peterson, 1982).

 VIEWPOINT
What do you think is the single most important principle for preparing and delivering a public speech? What is the most frequently made mistake in public speaking?

- Use only your delivery outline when presenting your speech; never use the preparation outline. One 8½-by-11-inch page should be sufficient for most speeches. This aid will relieve anxiety over forgetting your speech but not be extensive enough to prevent meaningful speaker–audience interaction.

- Know your notes intimately. Rehearse at least twice with the same notes you will take to the speaker's stand.

- Use your notes with "open subtlety." Don't make your notes more obvious than necessary, but don't try to hide them. Don't gesture with them, but don't turn away from the audience to steal a glance at them, either. Watch the way television talk show personalities use notes; many of these media hosts provide useful models you might want to imitate.

Critically Evaluating Speeches

Part of your function in learning public speaking is learning to evaluate finished, delivered speeches and to express your evaluations in a clear and constructive way.

Speech Evaluation

The following questions, which come from topics covered in this chapter and Chapter 11, can serve as a beginning guide to speech evaluation. Use them to check your own speeches as well as to evaluate the speeches of others.

The subject and purpose

1. Is the subject worthwhile? Relevant? Interesting to the audience and speaker?
2. What is the speech's general purpose (to inform, to persuade)?
3. Is the topic narrow enough to be covered in some depth?
4. Is the specific purpose clear to the audience?

The audience

5. Has the speaker considered the culture, age, gender, occupation, income, status, and religion of the audience? How does the speaker take these factors into consideration?
6. Has the speaker considered and adapted to the willingness, favorableness, and knowledge of the audience?

The thesis and major propositions

7. Is the speech's thesis clear and limited to one main idea?
8. Are the speech's main propositions clearly related to the thesis?
9. Are there an appropriate number of major propositions in the speech (not too many, not too few)?

Research

10. Is the speech adequately researched? Are the sources reliable and up to date?
11. Does the speaker seem to understand the subject thoroughly?

Supporting materials

12. Is each major proposition adequately and appropriately supported?
13. Do the supporting materials amplify what they purport to amplify? Do they prove what they purport to prove?

Organization

14. How is the body of the speech organized? What is the organization pattern?
15. Is the organization pattern appropriate to the speech and to the audience?

Web Explorations

Several exercises and two self-tests will help personalize the material presented here (www.ablongman.com/devito): (1) Making Concepts Specific, (2) Rephrasing Clichés, (3) Organizing a Scrambled Outline, (4) Can You Distinguish Commonly Used Words? and (5) How Flexible Are You as a Public Speaker? In addition, there is an extended discussion of the (6) Motivated Sequence and a variety of (7) skeletal outlines to help you organize your speeches.

Listening to Criticism

Although it's a valuable part of public speaking and of life in general, listening to criticism is difficult. Here are some suggestions for making listening to criticism easier and more effective.

- *Listen with an open mind.* Because public speaking is so ego-involving, it's tempting to block out criticism. If you do, however, you'll lose out on potentially useful insights. So, to encourage the critic to share these insights, listen with an open mind, and demonstrate your willingness to listen: Nonverbally express appreciation for the critic's efforts. At the same time, recognize that when someone criticizes your speech, he or she is not criticizing your personality or worth as an individual. In other words, be open to criticism, but don't take it personally; view critical messages as dispassionately and as objectively as you can.

- *Accept the critic's viewpoint.* If the critic says the evidence wasn't convincing, it doesn't help to identify the 12 references that you used in your speech; this critic simply was not convinced. Instead, consider why your evidence was not convincing to your critic. Perhaps you didn't emphasize the credibility of the sources or didn't clarify their relevance to your proposition.

- *Seek clarification.* If you don't understand the criticism, ask for clarification. For example, if you're told that your specific purpose was too broad, but it's unclear to you how you might improve it, ask the critic how you might narrow the specific purpose.

Applying Listening Skills

You've just given a speech you thought was pretty good. Yet your audience looked bored, and during the criticism period one person says, "Your speech didn't hold my attention. I was bored. You really should have prepared more." In truth you put a great deal of time into this speech, and you know you incorporated just about every attention-gaining device imaginable. How do you respond?

Wording

16. Is the language clear, vivid, and appropriate?
17. Are the sentences short, direct, active, positive, and varied?

The conclusion, introduction, and transitions

18. Does the conclusion effectively summarize and close the speech?
19. Does the introduction gain the audience's attention and provide a clear orientation?
20. Are there adequate transitions?

Delivery

21. Does the speaker maintain eye contact with the audience?
22. Are the volume and rate appropriate to the audience, occasion, and topic?
23. Are the voice and body actions appropriate to the speaker, subject, and audience?

Expressing Your Evaluation

The major purpose of classroom evaluation is to improve class members' public speaking technique. Through constructive criticism, you, as a speaker and as a listener–critic, will more effectively learn the principles of public speaking. You will be shown what you do well and what you can improve.

For all the benefits of evaluation, however, many people resist this process. The main source of resistance seems to be that evaluations and suggestions for improvement are often perceived as personal attacks. Before reading the specific suggestions for expressing criticism, take the self-test, "What's wrong with these comments?" Then consider the suggestions for offering criticism more effectively that follow the self-test.

> ❝ Anyone can be accurate and even profound, but it is damned hard work to make criticism charming. ❞
>
> —H. L. Mencken

Test Yourself

What's Wrong with These Comments?

INSTRUCTIONS: Examine each of the following critical comments. For the purposes of this exercise, assume that each comment represents the critic's complete criticism. What's wrong with each?

____ ❶ I loved the speech. It was great. Really great.

____ ❷ The introduction didn't gain my attention.

____ ❸ You weren't interested in your own topic. How do you expect us to be interested?

____ ❹ Nobody was able to understand you.

____ ❺ The speech was weak.

____ ❻ The speech didn't do anything for me.

____ ❼ Your position was unfair to those of us on athletic scholarships; we earned those scholarships.

____ ❽ I found four things wrong with your speech. First, . . .

____ ❾ You needed better research.

____ ❿ I liked the speech; we need more police on campus.

HOW DID YOU DO? Before reading the following discussion, try to explain why each of these statements is ineffective.

WHAT WILL YOU DO? To help improve your criticism, try to restate the basic meaning of each of these comments in a more constructive manner.

Say Something Positive   Because most people suffer from apprehension and anxiety in public speaking, criticism is difficult to take. So emphasize the positive. First, positively comment on effective speech elements: "Your visual aids made the cost comparison so easy for me to see and really convinced me to change brands." Second, use positive comments as a preface to any negative ones. There are always positive characteristics, and it's more productive to mention these first. Thus, instead of saying—as in the self-test—"The speech didn't do anything for me," tell the speaker what you liked first and then bring up a weakness and suggest how it might be corrected: "Your introduction really made me realize that many colleges have problems with campus violence, but I wasn't convinced early on that we have one here at Andrews. I would have preferred to hear the examples that you gave near the end of the speech—which were excellent, by the way—in the introduction. Then I would have been convinced we had a problem and would have been more anxious to hear your solutions."

Be Specific   Criticism is most effective when it's specific. Statements such as "I thought your delivery was bad" or "I thought your examples were good" or, as in the self-test, "I loved the speech. . . . Really great" and "The speech was weak" are poorly expressed evaluations. These statements don't specify what the speaker might do to improve delivery or to capitalize on the examples used. When commenting on delivery, refer to specifics such as the evidence used, the language, the delivery, or whatever else is of consequence.

Criticizing Ethically

Just as the speaker and the listener have ethical obligations, so does the critic. Here are a few guidelines.

- First, the ethical critic separates personal feelings about the speaker from the evaluation of the speech. A liking for the speaker should not lead you to give positive evaluations to the speech, nor should disliking the speaker lead you to give negative evaluations.

- Second, the ethical critic separates personal feelings about the issues from an evaluation of the validity of the arguments. Recognize the validity of an argument even if it contradicts a deeply held belief; at the same time, recognize the fallaciousness of an argument even if it supports a deeply held belief.

- Third, the ethical critic is culturally sensitive and aware of his or her own ethnocentrism; the ethical critic doesn't negatively evaluate customs and forms of speech simply because they differ from her or his own. Conversely, the ethical critic does not positively evaluate a speech just because it supports her or his own cultural beliefs and values. The ethical critic does not discriminate against or favor speakers simply because they're of a particular sex, race, affectional orientation, nationality, religion, or age group.

What Would You Do?

You and your best friend are taking this course together. Your friend just gave a pretty terrible speech, and unfortunately, the instructor has asked you to offer a critique. The wrinkle here is that the grade the instructor gives will be heavily influenced by what the student critic says. So, in effect, your critique will largely determine your friend's grade. You'd like to give your friend a positive critique so he can earn a good grade—which he badly needs. Besides, you figure, you can always tell him the truth later and even help him to improve. What would you do?

Be Objective   When evaluating a speech, transcend your own biases as best you can. Avoid statements like the self-test example "Your position was unfair. . . . We earned those scholarships." Examine the speech from the point of view of the (detached) critic. Evaluate, for example, the validity of the arguments and their suitability to the audience, the language, the supporting materials. Analyze, in fact, all the ingredients that went into the preparation and presentation of the speech.

Limit Criticism   Cataloging a speaker's weak points, as in "I found four things wrong with your speech," will overwhelm, not help, the speaker. If you're one of many critics, chances are that others will bring up the same criticisms you noted and you can feel comfortable limiting your criticism to one or perhaps two points. If you're the sole critic, then you'll want to evaluate the entire speech.

Be Constructive   Give the speaker the insight that you feel will help him or her in future public speaking situations. For example, "The introduction didn't gain my attention" doesn't tell the speaker how he or she might have gained your attention. Instead, you might say, "The example about the computer crash would have more effectively gained my attention in the introduction."

Focus on Behavior   Focus criticism on what the speaker said and did during the actual speech. Try to avoid the very natural tendency to mind-read the speaker, to assume that you know why the speaker did one thing rather than another. Instead of saying, "You weren't interested in your topic" (a comment that attacks the speaker), say, "I would have liked to see greater variety in your delivery. It would have made me feel you were more interested." Instead of saying, "You didn't care about your audience," say, "I would have liked it if you looked more directly at us while speaking."

Analyzing a Poorly Constructed Persuasive Speech

The speech presented below illustrates some really broad as well as some rather subtle errors that a beginning speaker might make in constructing a persuasive speech. First, read the entire speech without looking at any of the questions in the right-hand column. Then, after you've read the entire speech, reread each paragraph and respond to the critical thinking questions. What other questions might prove productive to ask?

XXX HAS GOT TO GO

Speech

You probably didn't read the papers this weekend, but there's a XXX movie, I mean video, store that moved in on Broad and Fifth Streets. My parents, who are retired teachers, are protesting it, and so am I. My parents are organizing a protest for the next weekend.

There must be hundreds of XXX video stores in the country, and they all need to be closed down. I have a lot of reasons.

First, my parents think it should be closed down. My parents are retired teachers and have organized protests over the proposed new homeless shelter and to prevent the city from making that park on Elm Street. So they know what they're doing.

The XXX video place is un-Christian. No good Christian people would ever go there. Our minister is against it and is joining in the protest.

These stores bring crime into the neighborhood. I have proof of that. Morristown's crime increased after the XXX video store opened. And in Martinsville, where they got rid of the video store, crime did not increase. If we allow the video store in our own town, then we're going to be like Morristown and our crime is going to increase.

These stores make lots of garbage. The plastic wrappings from the videos will add to our already overextended and overutilized landfill. And a lot of them are going to wind up as litter on the streets.

The XXX Video House stays open seven days a week, 24 hours a day. People will be forced to work at all hours and on Sunday, and that's not fair. And the store will increase the noise level at night with the cars pulling up and all.

The XXX Video House—that's its name, by the way—doesn't carry regular videos that most people want. So why do we want them?

The XXX Video House got a lease from an owner who doesn't even live in the community, someone by the name of, well, it's an organization called

Critical Thinking Questions

What do you think of the title of the speech?

Visualizing yourself as a listener, how would the opening comment make you feel?

Does the speaker gain your attention?

What thesis do you think the speaker will support?

Does mentioning "my parents" help or hurt the speaker's credibility?

What is the speaker's thesis?

What impression are you beginning to get of the speaker?

How do the speaker's parents sound to you? Do they sound like credible leaders with a consistent cause? Or chronic protesters (with perhaps a negative agenda)?

What evidence is offered to support the assertion that you should believe the speaker's parents? Is this adequate? What would you need to know about these people before believing them?

What does this statement assume about the audience? How would your public speaking class respond to this statement? What are some reasons why the speaker might not have explained how XXX video stores are un-Christian? How will those in the audience who are not Christians react to this statement?

What do you think of the reasoning used here? Are there other factors that could have influenced Morristown's crime increase? Is there any evidence that getting rid of the video store resulted in the stable crime rate in Martinsville? What assumption about the audience does the speaker make in using Martinsville and Morristown as analogies?

Do you agree with this argument about the garbage? Is this argument in any way unique to the video store? Is it likely that people will open the wrappers and drop them on the street?

What validity do you give to each of these arguments? Given the 24-hour policy, how might you construct an argument against the video store? Are there advantages of a neighborhood store's 24-hour policy that the audience may be thinking of and thus countering the speaker's argument? If there are, how should the speaker deal with them?

Upon hearing this, would you be likely to extend this argument and start asking yourself, "Do we now close up all stores that most people don't want?"

Is there a connection between who the owner is and whether the video store should or should not be closed?

(continued)

XYZ Management. And their address is Carlson Place in Jeffersonville. So they don't even live here.

A neighboring store owner says he thinks the store is in violation of several fire laws. He says they have no sprinkler system and no metal doors to prevent the spread of a fire. So he thinks they should be closed down, too.

Last week on *Oprah,* three women were on and they were in the XXX movie business and they were all on drugs and had been in jail and they said it all started when they went into the porno business. One woman wanted to be a teacher, another wanted to be a nurse, and the other wanted to be a beautician. If there weren't any XXX video stores, then there wouldn't be a porn business and, you know, pornography is part of organized crime and so if you stop pornography you take a bite out of crime.

One of the reasons I think it should be closed is that the legitimate video stores—the ones that have only a small selection of XXX movies somewhere in the back—will lose business. And if they continue to lose business, they'll leave the neighborhood and we'll have no video stores.

That's a lot of reasons against XXX movie houses. I have a quote here: Reason is "a portion of the divine spirit set in a human body." Seneca.

In conclusion and to wrap it up and close my speech, I want to repeat and say again that the XXX Video stores should all be closed down. They corrupt minors. And they're offensive to men and women and especially women. I hope you'll all protest with the Marshalls—my mother and father—and there will be lots of others there, too. My minister, I think, is coming too.

Could the speaker have effectively used this information in support of the thesis to close the video store?

What credibility do you ascribe to the "neighboring store owner"? Do you begin to wonder whether the speaker would simply agree to have the store brought up to the fire code laws?

What is the cause and what is the effect that the speaker is asserting? How likely is it that the proposed cause actually produced the effect? Might there have been causes other than pornography that might have led these women into drugs?

What credibility do you give to people you see on talk shows? Does credibility vary with the specific talk show?

Do you accept the argument that there would be no pornography business without video stores? What would have to be proved to you before you accepted this connection?

How do you respond to the expression "take a bite out of crime"?

Is the speaker implying that this is the real reason against XXX video stores?

Do you start wondering whether the speaker is against XXX video—as seemed in the last argument—or just against stores that sell these exclusively? What effect does this impression have on your evaluation of the speaker's credibility and thesis?

How do you feel about the number of "reasons"? Would you have preferred fewer reasons more fully developed or more reasons?

What purpose does this quotation serve?

Might the speaker have introduced the conclusion differently?

Now what is the speaker's thesis?

What do you think of the argument that XXX video stores are offensive? What effect does this argument have coming here in the conclusion?

Do you think you'd go to the protest? Why?

Own Your Own Criticism   Take responsibility for your criticism. The best way to express this ownership is to use I-messages rather than you-messages. Instead of saying, "You needed better research," say, "I would have been more persuaded if you had used more recent research."

I-messages will also prevent you from using "should messages," a type of expression that almost invariably creates defensiveness and resentment. When you say, "You should have done this," or, "You shouldn't have done that," you assume a superior position and imply that what you're saying is correct and that what the speaker did was incorrect. When you own your evaluations and use I-messages, on the other hand, you're offering your perceptions. It's then up to the speaker to deal with them.

Be Culturally Sensitive   There are vast cultural differences in what is considered proper when it comes to criticism. In some cultures public criticism, even if it's designed to help teach important skills, is considered inappropriate. As noted in Chapter 7, some cultures place a heavy emphasis on face-saving, on allowing the other person always to remain in a positive light (James, 1995). In cultures in which face-saving is important, members may prefer not to say anything negative in public—and

❝ Within many cultures around the world, it is believed that the eyes are the windows to the soul. In public speaking, since we usually want to arouse both spirit and soul, the eyes becomes the most important physical equipment of all. ❞

—Roger E. Axtell

VIEWPOINT
What would you say to students in a public speaking class who may be reluctant to express public criticism?

may even be reluctant to say anything positive, for fear that the omissions may be construed as negatives. In cultures emphasizing face-saving (generally high-context cultures), criticism should take place only in private to enable the person to save face. Communication rules such as the following prevail in these cultures.

- Don't express negative evaluation in public; instead, compliment the person.
- Don't prove someone wrong, especially in public; express agreement even if you know the person is wrong.
- Don't correct someone's errors; don't even acknowledge them.
- Don't ask difficult questions lest the person not know the answer and lose face or be embarrassed; generally, avoid asking questions.

In some cultures, being kind to the person is more important than telling the truth, so members may say things that are complimentary but untrue in a logical sense.

In contrast, people in cultures that are highly individualistic and competitive (the United States, Germany, and Sweden are examples) may find public criticism a normal part of the learning process. Thus, people in these cultures may readily criticize others and are likely to expect the same "courtesy" from other listeners. After all, these people may reason, "If I'm going to criticize your skills to help you improve, I expect you to help me in the same way." People from cultures that are more collectivist and that emphasize the group rather than the individual (Japan, Mexico, and

What Do You Say?

Criticizing a Speech: A student has just given a speech on the glory of bullfighting, something you define as animal cruelty. To the speaker, however, bullfighting is an important part of a traditional culture. As you bristle inside, the instructor asks you to critique the speech. *What do you say?*

Skill development experience

Preparing a Two-Minute Speech

Prepare and present a two-minute speech in which you accomplish one of the following:

- describe the differences between individualistic and collectivist cultures
- explain how television commercials get your attention
- describe the introductions and conclusions used by television news shows
- compare the delivery styles of two announcers or sitcom stars
- evaluate a recently heard speech or lecture

Korea are examples) are likely to find giving and receiving public criticism uncomfortable, however. They may feel that it's more important to be polite and courteous than to help someone learn a skill. Cultural rules aimed at maintaining peaceful relations among the Japanese (Midooka, 1990) and politeness among many Asian cultures (Fraser, 1990) may conflict with the Western classroom cultural norm that supports voicing criticism.

The difficulties are compounded when you interpret unexpected behavior through your own cultural filters. For example, if a speaker who expects comments and criticism gets none, he or she may interpret the silence to mean that the audience didn't care or wasn't listening. But they may have been listening very intently. They may simply be operating according to a different cultural rule, a rule that says it's impolite to criticize or evaluate another person's work, especially in public.

Summary of Concepts and Skills

In this chapter we looked at the last four steps in the public speaking process: wording the speech, constructing the conclusion and the introduction, rehearsing, and delivering the speech.

1. Compared with written style, oral style contains shorter, simpler, and more familiar words; greater qualification; and more self-referential terms.
2. Effective public speaking style is clear (be economical and specific; use guide phrases and short, familiar, and commonly used terms); vivid (use active verbs, strong verbs, figures of speech, and imagery); appropriate to your audience (speak on a suitable level of formality; avoid written-style expressions; avoid slang, vulgar, and offensive terms); and personal (use personal pronouns, ask questions, and create immediacy).
3. When constructing sentences for public speeches, favor short, direct, active, and positively phrased sentences. Vary the type and length.
4. Conclusions should summarize and close the speech. Introductions should gain attention and orient the audience as to what is to follow.
5. Transitions and internal summaries help connect the parts of the speech so that they flow into one another and help the listeners better remember the speech.
6. There are three basic methods of delivering a public speech. The impromptu method involves speaking without any specific preparation. The manuscript method involves writing out the entire speech and reading it to the audience. The extemporaneous method involves thorough preparation and memorizing the main ideas and their order of appearance, but not a commitment to exact wording.
7. Use rehearsal to time and perfect your speech from beginning to end; rehearse under realistic conditions, and with listeners, if possible.
8. When you deliver your speech, regulate your voice for greatest effectiveness. Adjust your volume on the basis of the distance between you and your audience and the em-

phasis you wish to give certain ideas, for example. Adjust your rate on the basis of time constraints, the speech's content, and the listening conditions.
9. Avoid the major problems of articulation and pronunciation; errors of omission, substitution, addition, and accent.
10. Use unfilled pauses to signal a transition between the major parts of the speech, to allow the audience time to think, to allow the audience to ponder a rhetorical question, and to signal the approach of a particularly important idea. Avoid filled pauses; they weaken your message.
11. Effective body action involves maintaining eye contact with your entire audience, allowing your facial expressions to convey your feelings, using your posture to communicate command of the public speaking interaction, gesturing naturally, and moving around a bit.
12. When expressing critical evaluations, try to say something positive, be specific, be objective, limit your criticism, be constructive, focus on behavior, own your own criticism, and be culturally sensitive.

This chapter stressed several significant skills for style and delivery. Check your mastery of these skills, using the following scale: 1 = almost never; 2 = often; 3 = sometimes; 4 = rarely; and 5 = almost never.

_____ 1. I word my speech so it's clear, vivid, appropriate, and personal.

_____ 2. I construct sentences that are short, direct, active, and positive, and I vary the type and length of sentences.

_____ 3. I construct conclusions that summarize the major ideas of the speech and bring the speech to a crisp close.

_____ 4. I construct introductions that gain attention and preview what is to follow.

_____ 5. I use transitions and internal summaries to connect the parts of the speech and to help listeners remember what I say.

_____ 6. In general, I use the extemporaneous method of delivery.

_____ 7. I rehearse my speech often, perfect my delivery, rehearse the speech as a whole, time the speech at each rehearsal, approximate the specific speech situation as much as possible, see and think of myself as a public speaker, and incorporate any delivery notes that may be of value during the actual speech presentation.

_____ 8. I vary my vocal volume and rate to best reflect and reinforce my verbal messages and avoid the common problems with volume and rate.

_____ 9. I avoid the articulation and pronunciation errors of omission, substitution, addition, accent, and pronouncing sounds that should be silent.

_____ 10. I use pauses to signal transitions, to allow listeners time to think, and to signal the approach of a significant idea.

_____ 11. During the speech delivery I maintain eye contact with the entire audience, allow my facial expressions to convey my feelings, gesture naturally, and incorporate purposeful body movements.

_____ 12. When expressing critical evaluations of the speeches of others, I try to say something positive, be specific, be objective, be constructive, be culturally sensitive, and own my own responses.

Key Word Quiz

Write T for those statements that are true and F for those that are false. For those that are false, replace the italicized term with the correct term.

_____ 1. Being economical in your choice of words, using specific terms and numbers, and using short, familiar, and commonly used terms are recommended ways of achieving *clarity*.

_____ 2. A comparison of two unlike things (for example, "He's a regular Attila the Hun") is known as *personification*.

_____ 3. A question used to make a point rather than to secure an answer (which is always obvious) is known as a *rhetorical question*.

_____ 4. Face-saving is likely to be given greater importance in *individualistic cultures*.

_____ 5. Brief phrases and key words are sufficient and even recommended for use in the *delivery outline*.

_____ 6. Words, phrases, or sentences used to connect the various parts of your speech are called *transitions*.

_____ 7. Speaking without preparation is known as speaking *extemporaneously*.

_____ 8. The movements of the speech organs as they modify and interrupt the air stream sent from the lungs are called *pronunciation*.

_____ 9. The relative loudness of your voice as perceived by your listeners is your *pitch*.

_____ 10. The production of syllables or words according to an accepted standard (such as that set down in dictionaries) is known as *articulation*.

Answers: TRUE: 1, 3, 5, 6 [another appropriate term is connectives]; FALSE: 2 (*metaphor*), 4 (*collectivist cultures*), 7 (*impromptu*), 8 (*articulation*), 9 (*volume*), 10 (*pronunciation*)

13 The Informative Speech

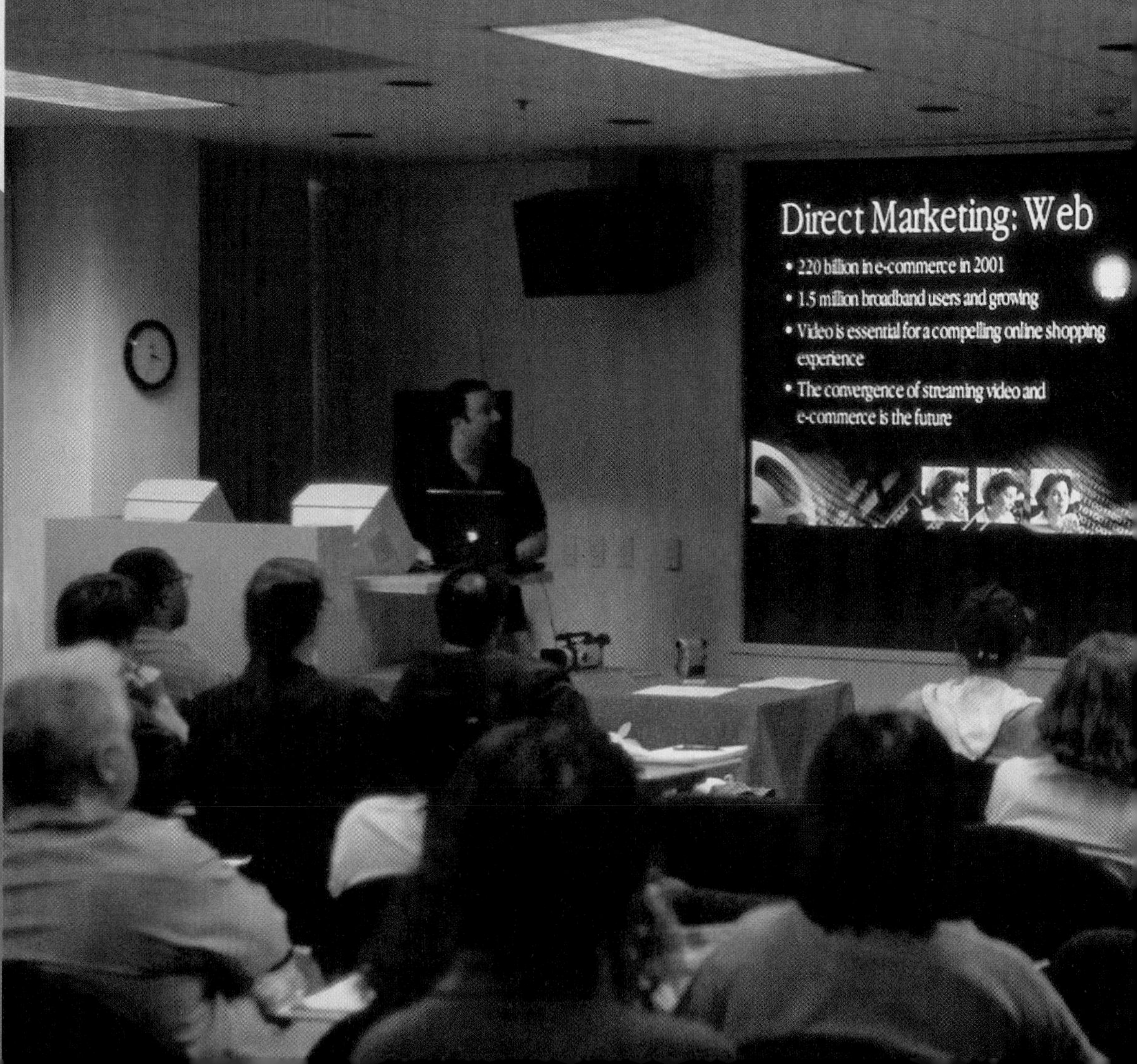

Chapter Concepts	Chapter Skills
This chapter looks at the informative speech, offers guidelines for different types of informative speeches, and identifies ways to amplify your ideas.	After completing this chapter, you should be able to:
Guidelines for Informative Speaking	use the principles of informative speaking to construct public speeches.
Types of Informative Speeches	develop effective informative speeches of description, definition, and demonstration.
Amplifying Materials	effectively use a variety of amplifying materials (examples, illustrations, testimony, definitions, statistics, and visual aids) in your speeches.

Whatever occupation you find yourself in, you will be asked to communicate information to others: to describe the new computer system, to demonstrate the new teaching approaches, or to define your company goals. The higher up you move in your organization's hierarchy, the more often you will be called on to inform others. This chapter covers speeches of information, through which you tell your listeners something they didn't already know; the next chapter covers speeches of persuasion, through which you change your listeners' attitudes or beliefs or get them to do something. (A thorough discussion of a third kind of speech, the "special occasion speech," may be found on the CD-ROM and at www.ablongman.com/devito.) Before beginning this journey into these two types of speeches—or after giving your next speech—you may want to examine your own satisfaction as a public speaker by taking the self-test "How satisfying is your public speaking?"

Test Yourself

How Satisfying Is Your Public Speaking?

INSTRUCTIONS: Respond to each of the following statements by recording the number best representing your feelings after a recent speech, using this scale: 1 = strongly agree; 2 = moderately agree; 3 = slightly agree; 4 = neutral; 5 = slightly disagree; 6 = moderately disagree; and 7 = strongly disagree.

_____ ❶ The audience let me know that I was speaking effectively.

_____ ❷ My speech accomplished nothing.

_____ ❸ I would like to give another speech like this one.

_____ ❹ The audience genuinely wanted to get to know me.

_____ ❺ I was very *dis*satisfied with my speech.

_____ ❻ I was very satisfied with the speech.

_____ ❼ The audience seemed very interested in what I had to say.

_____ ❽ I did *not* enjoy the public speaking experience.

_____ **❾** The audience did *not* seem supportive of what I was saying.

_____ **❿** The speech flowed smoothly.

HOW DID YOU DO? To compute your score, follow these steps:

1. Add the scores for items 1, 3, 4, 6, 7, and 10.
2. Reverse the scores for items 2, 5, 8, and 9 so that 7 becomes 1, 8 becomes 2, 5 becomes 3, 4 remains 4, 3 becomes 5, 2 becomes 6, and 1 becomes 7.
3. Add the reversed scores for items 2, 5, 8, and 9.
4. Add the totals from steps 1 and 3 to yield your communication satisfaction score.

You may interpret your score along the following scale:

10	20	30	40	50	60	70
Extremely Satisfying	Quite Satisfying	Fairly Satisfying	Average	Fairly Unsatisfying	Quite Unsatisfying	Extremely Unsatisfying

How accurately do you think this scale captures your public speaking satisfaction?

WHAT WILL YOU DO? As you become a more successful and effective public speaker, your satisfaction is likely to increase. What else can you do to increase your satisfaction?

Source: This test was adapted for public speaking on the basis of the conversational satisfaction test developed by Michael Hecht (1978), "The Conceptualization and Measurement of Interpersonal Communication Satisfaction," *Human Communication Research, 4,* 253–264, and is used by permission of the author and International Communication Association.

Guidelines for Informative Speaking

In informative speeches you tell your listeners something they didn't know before. Regardless of the type of information you're communicating, the following guidelines should help: stress usefulness, relate new information to old, present information through several senses, adjust the level of complexity, vary the levels of abstraction, limit the amount of information to avoid information overload, and recognize cultural variations.

Stress Usefulness

Listeners will best remember information they see as useful to their own needs or goals. If you want your audience to listen, relating your speech to your audience's needs, wants, or goals will capture their attention and make them eager to listen to the information you're presenting. There should be little doubt that you would have a most attentive and willing audience if you said, for example:

> We all want financial security. We all want to be able to buy those luxuries we read so much about in magazines and see every evening on television. Wouldn't it be nice to be able to buy a car without worrying about where to get the down payment or how to make the monthly payments? Actually, that is not an unrealistic goal, as I'll demonstrate in this speech. In fact, I will show you three ways you can invest your money to increase your income by at least 20 percent.

Relate New Information to Old

Listeners will learn information more easily and retain it longer when you relate it to what they already know. Information your audience already has can serve as a springboard for the new material you're about to present. Relate the new to the old, the unfamiliar to the familiar, the unseen to the seen. For example, a speaker might

VIEWPOINT

To keep usefulness in the forefront, assume—as you're preparing and refining your speech—that each person in the audience is going to be asking, "What's in this for me?" "How will this benefit me?" "Why should I be here listening to this speech?" How would you answer these audience questions in relation to your next speech topic?

begin a speech on personal information management (PIM) software with something like this:

> PIMs are similar to the schedule books that most of you carry around. They allow you to record what you have to do and to note important appointments. But they're also different. Let's look at PIMs and what they can do for you.

Present Information through Several Senses

Listeners best remember information they receive through several senses at once—through hearing, seeing, smelling, tasting, feeling. Try to reach your audience through as many senses as you can. If you're describing a football field's layout (presenting information through hearing), also show a picture of the field (presenting information through seeing as well). If you're giving a speech on stress and you're talking about muscular tension, make the audience feel their own muscle tension by asking them to tighten their leg or arm muscles.

Adjust the Level of Complexity

The level of complexity you use in communicating information should depend on the many factors we have considered throughout this text: the level of knowledge your audience has, the time you have available, the breadth of your purpose, the topic on which you're speaking, and so on. If you simplify a topic too much, you risk boring or, even worse, insulting your audience. If your talk is too complex, you risk confusing them and failing to communicate the desired information.

A common mistake beginning speakers make is to present information that is too complex without realizing that a 5- or 10-minute speech is not long enough to make an audience understand sophisticated concepts or a complicated process. Look at the topic from your audience's point of view; ask yourself how much they already know about your topic. Make sure the words you use are familiar to your audience; if they're not, explain and define them as you use them. Remember that jargon and technical vocabulary familiar to a computer programmer may not be familiar to the person who uses a computer only for word processing.

Vary the Levels of Abstraction

You can communicate information with varying levels of specificity. For example, in talking about freedom of the press, you can talk in high-level abstractions about the importance of getting information to the public by referring to the Bill of Rights and by relating a free press to the preservation of democracy. But you can also talk in low-level abstractions by, for example, citing how a local newspaper was prevented from running a story critical of the town council or about how Lucy Rinaldo was fired from the *Accord Sentinel* after she wrote a story critical of the mayor. Combining high- and low-level abstraction seems to work best.

Here is an example dealing with the homeless. Note that we have a relatively abstract description of homelessness in the first paragraph. The second paragraph, however, gets into specifics. In the last paragraph, the abstract and the concrete are connected.

> Homelessness is a serious problem for all metropolitan areas throughout the country. It is currently estimated that there are now more than 200,000 homeless people in New York City alone. But what is this really about? Let me tell you what it's about.
>
> It's about a young man. He must be about 25 or 30, although he looks a lot older. He lives in a cardboard box at the side of my apartment house. We call him Tom, although we really don't know his name. All his possessions are stored in a big refrigerator box. Actually, he doesn't have very much, and what he has easily fits in this box. There's a blanket my neighbor threw out, some plastic bottles he puts water in, and some Styrofoam containers he picked up from the garbage at Burger King. He uses these to store whatever food he finds.
>
> What is homelessness about? It's about Tom and 200,000 other "Toms" in New York and thousands of others throughout the rest of the country.

"Can you help me with my ethics homework, or would that be missing the point?"

Reprinted courtesy of Bunny Hoest and Parade Magazine.

Limit the Amount of Information

There's a limit to the amount of information that a listener can take in at one time. Resist the temptation to overload your listeners. Limit the breadth of information you communicate and instead, expand its depth. It's better to present two new items of information and to explain these in depth with examples, illustrations, and descriptions than to present five items without this needed amplification. The speaker who attempts to discuss the physiological, psychological, social, and linguistic differences between men and women, for example, is clearly trying to cover too much; the speech will have to cover these areas only superficially, and as a result little new information will be communicated. Even covering one of these areas is likely to prove too broad. Instead, select one subdivision of one area—say, language development or differences in language problems—and develop that in depth.

Recognize Cultural Variations

Linguists estimate that there are between 5,000 and 6,000 different languages spoken around the world. There are also numerous dialects spoken within many of these languages. Some dialects are *regional;* speakers from Arkansas, Wisconsin, and Massachusetts, for example, will speak differently but—perhaps with some small effort—are able to understand each other. *Social dialects,* on the other hand, are variations based on sociological factors such as social class, ethnic background, or occupation. A clear example of social dialects is heard in the language of teenagers. Depending on your age and the area of the country in which you live, you may or may not know the meaning of such terms as *fat pockets* (someone with lots of money), *kicks* (sneakers), *shoot the gift* (engage in conversation), *livin' large* (living

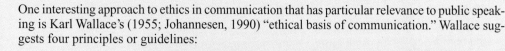

Speaking Ethically

One interesting approach to ethics in communication that has particular relevance to public speaking is Karl Wallace's (1955; Johannesen, 1990) "ethical basis of communication." Wallace suggests four principles or guidelines:

1. The speaker must have a thorough knowledge of the topic, an ability to answer relevant questions, and an awareness of the significant facts and opinions bearing on the issues discussed.
2. The speaker must present both facts and opinions fairly, without bending or spinning them to personal advantage. The speaker must allow the listener to make the final judgment.
3. The speaker must reveal the sources of these facts and opinions and must help the listeners evaluate any biases or prejudices in the sources.
4. The speaker must acknowledge and respect opposing arguments and evidence. The speaker must advocate a tolerance for diversity. Any attempt to hide valid opposing arguments from the audience is unethical.

What Would You Do?

You're giving a persuasive speech arguing for condom machines in rest rooms on campus. You know, however, that the money to install these machines will have to come from an increase in student fees. You wonder if you can ethically give the speech without mentioning that student fees will have to be increased. After all, you don't have time to include all the arguments and evidence, even those points that support your position. You also figure that it's the listeners' responsibility to ask where the money is coming from and not your job to tell them. What would you do?

in financial comfort), and *think it ain't* (I totally agree with you). But, for the most part and with such obvious exceptions, teenagers and older people can understand each other's language.

When addressing an audience from a culture different from your own, avoid trying to speak their dialect. Although the intention is often to appear to be one of the group, imitating others' dialects will probably backfire and mark you as an outsider trying to pretend to be someone you're not. It is also distracting for the audience and will muddy the information you're trying to convey. In a related vein, when using terms that are unique to your dialect, explain them. If at all possible, use terms that are common to both your own and your audience's dialect.

Types of Informative Speeches

Three major types of informative speeches are those of description, demonstration, and definition. (Another type of informative speech is the "speech of introduction," in which you introduce someone to an audience. For an annotated example of this type of speech, see www.ablongman.com/devito.) You might combine all three functions in one speech, or you might devote your entire speech to just one. Let's look at each type, the strategies appropriate to each, and the ways you can develop these speeches.

The Speech of Description

In a description speech, you explain an object or person or an event or process. For example, possible speech topics in the category describing "an object or person" might be the structure of the brain, the inventions of Thomas Edison, the parts of a telephone, the layout of Philadelphia, the college hierarchy, a computer, the skeletal structure of the body, a houseboat, the Internet, and a television station.

Research Navigator.com

www.researchnavigator.com

Read an Article: Read a scholarly or popular article on any of the topics discussed in this chapter. On the basis of this article, what can you add to the discussion presented here?

Listening to New Ideas

A useful technique in listening to new ideas—whether these are presented in informative speeches, in small group situations, or in conversation—is PIP'N, a technique that derives from the insights of Carl Rogers (1970) on paraphrase and from Edward deBono's (1976) PMI (plus, minus, interesting) approach. PIP'N involves four steps (DeVito, 1996a):

P = *Paraphrase.* Put into your own words what you think the speaker is saying. Paraphrasing will ensure that you and the speaker have the same general understanding and will give the speaker the opportunity to elaborate or clarify his or her ideas.

I = *Interesting.* Identify something interesting that you find in the idea. Think of why this idea might be interesting to you or to others.

P = *Positive.* Identify something positive about the idea. What's good about it? How might it solve a problem or make a situation better?

N = *Negative.* Identify any negatives that you think the idea might entail. Might it prove expensive? Will it be difficult to apply?

Applying Listening Skills

How might you use PIP'N? For practice, you may want to try PIP'N on the PIP'N technique itself: (1) paraphrase the PIP'N technique; (2) say why the technique is interesting; (3) say something positive about it; and (4) say something negative about it.

Examples of topics for a speech describing "an event or process" include the process of digestion, the events leading to World War II, organizing a body-building contest, posting an article to a newsgroup, printing money, tooth decay, buying stock, predicting the weather, writing a book, or the workings of an artificial heart.

Strategies for Describing   Here are some suggestions for describing objects and people, events and processes.

1. Consider using a spatial pattern, a topical pattern, or a "who, what, why, where, when" organization when describing objects and people (revisit Chapter 11 for a discussion of these organizational patterns). You might use a spatial pattern to describe a museum, starting from the first floor and working your way up to the top floor. To describe the inventions of Thomas Edison, you might select three or four major inventions and discuss each equally, using a topical pattern. Consider using a temporal pattern when describing events and processes. A temporal pattern would also be appropriate to describe how a hurricane develops, how a bodily process works, or how the Berlin Wall came to be torn down.

2. Use a variety of categories to describe the object or event. Use physical categories, and ask yourself questions such as: What color is it? How big is it? What is it shaped like? How much does it weigh? How long or short is it? What is its volume? How attractive or unattractive is it? Also ask, for example, Is it friendly? Unfriendly? Warm? Cold? Rich? Poor? Aggressive? Meek? Pleasant? Unpleasant? And, of course, is it anywhere between these extremes?

3. Use presentation aids. Show pictures of the brain, the inside of a telephone, the skeleton of the body. When describing an event or process, create a diagram or flowchart to illustrate stages: for example, to show the steps in buying stock, in publishing a newspaper, in putting a parade together.

Developing the Speech of Description   Here is an example of how you might go about constructing a speech of description. In this speech, the speaker describes the way in which fear works in intercultural communication.

Specific purpose: To describe the way fear works in intercultural communication

Thesis: Fear influences intercultural communication. (How does fear influence intercultural communication?)

    I. You fear disapproval.

   II. You fear embarrassing yourself.

  III. You fear being harmed.

In delivering such a speech, a speaker might begin by saying:

There are three major fears that interfere with intercultural communication. First, there's the fear of disapproval—from members of our own group as well as from members of the other person's group. Second, we fear embarrassing ourselves, even making fools of ourselves by saying the wrong thing or appearing insensitive. And third, we may fear being harmed—our stereotypes of the other group may lead us to see their members as dangerous or potentially harmful to us.

    Let's look at each of these fears in more detail so as to see how they influence our own intercultural communication behavior.

    Consider, first the fear of disapproval.

The Speech of Definition

What is leadership? What is a born-again Christian? What is the difference between sociology and psychology? What is safe sex? These are all suitable topics for informative speeches of definition. A definition is a statement of a concept's meaning. Use definitions to explain difficult or unfamiliar concepts or to make a concept more vivid or forceful.

In defining a term or giving an entire speech of definition, you may focus on a given term, system, or theory or on the similarities and differences between terms, systems, or theories. The subject may be new to the audience or may be a familiar topic presented in a new and different way. Here are some examples of terms that might make interesting speeches of definition: *applet, avatar, bull market, censorship, drug addiction, ESP, free speech, gay rights, glass ceiling, hypertext, netiquette, sexual harassment,* and *virtual reality.*

Suitable candidates for a speech defining a system, theory, or set of principles might include codependency, Confucianism, creative thinking, cultural imperialism, Freudian theory, legal issues in e-mail, Marxism, 12-step programs, the nature of "argumentativeness," Islam, Usenet, or the nature of socialism.

For speeches defining similar and dissimilar terms or systems, possible topics include communism and socialism, e-mail and snail mail, equities and bonds, football versus soccer, the Internet and intranets, Netscape and Internet Explorer, neurosis and psychosis, Oedipus and Electra complexes, and what Christians and Muslims have in common.

Strategies for Defining

1. Use a variety of definitions—definitions by etymology, authority, operations, or direct symbolization. See the discussion of definitions under "Amplifying Materials" on page 291.

2. Use credible sources. When you use an authority's definition of a term, make sure the person is in fact an authority on that topic. And be sure to tell the audience who the expert source is and why she or he is considered an authority. This recommendation is doubly important when you use Internet sources; remember, anyone can publish on the Internet.

3. Proceed from the known to the unknown. Start with what your audience knows and work up to what is new or unfamiliar. Let's say you wish to define phonemics (with which your audience is unfamiliar). The specific idea you wish to get

> " The beginning of wisdom is the definition of terms. "
>
> —Socrates

What Do You Say?

Defining: You want to give a speech defining the basic tenets of your religion. Some members of your audience have a fairly negative view of your religion; others hold positive views. You want to acknowledge your understanding of these attitudes. *What do you say?*

across is that each phoneme stands for a unique sound. You might begin your definition like this:

We all know that in the written language each letter of the alphabet stands for a unit of the written language. Each letter is different from every other letter. A *t* is different from a *g*, and a *g* is different from a *b*, and so on. Each letter is called a "grapheme." In English, we have 26 graphemes.

We can look at the spoken language in much the same way. Each sound is different from every other sound. A *t* sound is different from a *d* sound, and a *d* sound is different from a *k* sound, and so on. Each individual sound is called a "phoneme."

Developing the Speech of Definition   Here is an example of how you might go about constructing a speech of definition. The speaker selects three major types of lying and arranges them in a topical pattern. Here is the outline for the body of the speech:

Specific purpose: To define lying by explaining the major types
Thesis: There are three major kinds of lying. (What are the three major kinds of lying?)

   I. Concealment is hiding the truth.

  II. Falsification is presenting false information as if it were true.

 III. Misdirection is acknowledging a feeling but misidentifying its cause.

In delivering such a speech, the speaker might begin:

A lie is a lie is a lie. True? Well, not exactly. Actually, we lie in lots of ways. We can lie by concealing the truth. We can lie by falsification—by presenting false information as if it were true. And we can lie by misdirection—by acknowledging a feeling but misidentifying its cause. Let's look at the first type—the lie of concealment.

The Speech of Demonstration

In using demonstration in a speech, or in a speech devoted entirely to demonstration, you show your listeners how to do something or how something works. Topics for speeches in which you demonstrate how to do something might include, for example, balancing a checkbook, buying a stock, conducting an interview, designing a brochure with QuarkXpress, driving defensively, giving mouth-to-mouth resuscitation, complaining and getting results, criticizing without offending, piloting a plane, saving for retirement, and using Internet Explorer.

Suitable topics for speeches in which you demonstrate how something operates could include subjects like how a piano works, how dialysis maintains health, how modems work, how the body maintains homeostasis, how the Internet functions, or how the stock market operates.

Strategies for Demonstrating   For demonstrating how to do something or how something operates, consider the following guidelines:

1. In most cases, use a temporal organizational pattern. Explain each step in the sequence; don't skip steps, even if you think they are familiar to the audience. They may not be.

2. Connect the steps with appropriate transitions. For instance, in explaining the Heimlich maneuver, you might say, "Now that you have your arms around the choking victim's upper abdomen, your next step is to. . . ." Label the steps clearly by saying, for example, "the first step," "the second step," and so on.

3. Consider presenting first a broad general picture and then the detailed individual steps. For example, let's say you are talking about how to prepare a wall for painting. You might begin by giving your listeners a general idea of how you will demonstrate the process:

What Do You Say?

Unexpected Events: You're going to speak on the new version of Microsoft Windows, which you've used the last few weeks. Unfortunately, the speaker before you turns out to be a Microsoft program designer and gives a speech on exactly your topic. *What do you say?*

www.researchnavigator.com

Investigate Key Terms: Investigate one of the key terms discussed in this chapter (for example, information, example, illustration, narrative, testimony, definition, statistics, flowchart, organizational chart, graphs, authority, abstraction, information overload, dialects, presentation aids, or PowerPoint). What additional insights can you provide?

Legitimate and Information Power

Legitimate and information power will both prove useful to you as a public speaker; they are important means of influence. You have **legitimate power** over another individual when this person believes you have a right—by virtue of your position—to influence or control his or her behavior. Legitimate power usually comes from the roles people occupy. Teachers are often seen to have legitimate power, and this is doubly true for religious teachers. Employers, judges, managers, doctors, and police officers are others who may hold legitimate power.

Information power, also called persuasion power, is power that you get from being seen as someone who has extensive knowledge and who can communicate this information logically and persuasively. If your audience sees you as possessing information power, they will be more likely to believe and follow you. And, not surprisingly, this power also will follow you; when you give your next speech, you'll begin with this positive and powerful image.

Enhancing Your Communication Power

How does your audience perceive your level of legitimate and information power? What can you do to enhance your legitimate and information power?

In preparing the wall for painting, make sure the wall is smoothly sanded, free of dust, and dry. Sanding a wall is not like sanding a block of wood. So let's look at the proper way to sand a wall.

4. Use visual aids that show the steps in sequence. A good example is the familiar restaurant sign demonstrating the Heimlich maneuver. These signs demonstrate each step with pictures as well as words, making it easy to understand this important process.

What Do You Say?

Demonstrating: You want to demonstrate to your audience how e-mail works. Your audience is probably mixed in terms of their knowledge of technology generally—some know a great deal and others know very little. *What do you say?*

Developing the Speech of Demonstration   In this example of a speech of demonstration, the speaker's topic is how to listen actively. The three suggestions are arranged in a topical order—each is of generally equal importance—but they also follow a kind of temporal order. For example, you would generally paraphrase first, express understanding second, and ask questions third.

Specific purpose: To demonstrate three techniques of active listening

Thesis: We can learn active listening. (How can we learn active listening?)

   I. Paraphrase the speaker's meaning.

  II. Express understanding of the speaker's feelings.

 III. Ask questions.

In delivering the speech, you might begin:

Active listening is a special kind of listening. It's listening with total involvement, with a concern for the speaker. It's probably the most important type of listening you can engage in. Active listening involves three techniques: paraphrasing the speaker's meaning, expressing understanding of the speaker's feelings, and asking questions.

    Your first step in active listening is to paraphrase the speaker's meaning. What is a paraphrase? A paraphrase is a restatement in your own words of the speaker's meaning.

VIEWPOINT

What is the single most important principle of informative speaking? What one principle do you see violated most often?

Amplifying Materials

Once you have identified your specific purpose and your main assertions or propositions (the statements given Roman numerals in your speech outline), devote your

TABLE 13.1 **Additional Forms of Support**

Along with the forms of support covered in detail in the text, consider these additional forms; you'll find them useful for both informative and persuasive speeches.

FORM OF SUPPORT	SUGGESTIONS FOR USING
Quotations add spice and wit as well as authority to your speeches.	Quotations work best when they're short, easily comprehended, and directly related to the point you're making.
Comparisons and contrasts help to clarify two ideas or events or concepts.	Focus on major similarities and differences; avoid itemizing all possible ones. If necessary, supplement your oral discussion with a visual aid that presents the most crucial information.
Simple statements of facts or series of facts often help to illustrate or support a statement or position.	Make sure you clearly link the facts or series of facts to the propositions they support. State the connection when introducing the facts and perhaps again after you complete the list of facts.
Repetition (repeating ideas in the same words at strategic places) *and restatement* (repeating ideas in different words) add clarity and emphasis and will help compensate for the inevitable lapses in audience attention.	Avoid unnecessary repetition and restatement; be careful that you don't bore the audience by repeating what they already understand.

attention to amplifying these assertions—that is, making them more understandable, meaningful, and relevant. Your task is to develop your propositions so the audience will understand each more easily and fully. In this section we'll look at five ways to amplify your assertions: examples, illustrations, and narratives; testimony; definitions; statistics; and visual aids. In addition, Table 13.1 summarizes other forms of support that will enrich your presentation.

Examples, Illustrations, and Narratives

Examples, illustrations, and *narratives* are specific instances in varying degrees of detail that help to explain an idea. A relatively brief specific instance is an example. A longer, more detailed example is an illustration. A narrative is longer still and is a short story or anecdote that serves to illustrate a point. The parables in many religious works are good examples of narration used to illustrate a general principle.

Examples, illustrations, and narratives help make an idea vivid and memorable in the listeners' minds. To talk in general terms about starvation throughout the world might have some effect on listeners. But an example or illustration or a narrative of a six-year-old girl roaming the streets eating garbage would make the idea vivid and real.

Examples, illustrations, and narratives may be factual or imaginary. Thus, in explaining friendship, you might tell about an actual friend's behavior. Or you might formulate a composite ideal friend and describe how this person would act in a particular situation. Both approaches are useful and effective. Be sure to include only those details that are needed to help your audience understand the point you're making. Often it is the example, illustration, or narrative that listeners remember most clearly, so be sure to connect this very explicitly to the proposition in your speech. Here, for example, former New York mayor Rudolph Giuliani, in his address to the United Nations after the World Trade Center attack of September 11, 2001, gave relevant examples to support his proposition that we are a land of immigrants and must continue to be so (www.ci.nyc.ny.us/html/om/html/96/united.html):

> He or she is greatest who contributes the greatest original practical example.
>
> —Walt Whitman

New York City was built by immigrants, and it will remain the greatest city in the world as long as we continue to renew ourselves with and benefit from the energizing spirit from new people coming here to create a better future for themselves and their families. Come to Flushing, Queens, where immigrants from many lands have created a vibrant, vital commercial and residential community. Their children challenge and astonish us in our public school classrooms every day. Similarly, you can see growing and dynamic immigrant communities in every borough of our city: Russians in Brighton Beach, West Indians in Crown Heights, Dominicans in Washington Heights, the new wave of Irish in the Bronx, and Koreans in Willow Brook on Staten Island.

Testimony

Testimony may consist of experts' opinions or of witnesses' accounts. Testimony supports your ideas by adding a note of authority. You might, for example, want to cite an economist's predictions concerning the size of the deficit or the growth rate of the economy. Or you might discuss an art critic's evaluation of a painting or an art movement. Here, for example, in a speech on dishonesty in the funeral business, one student used testimony in this way (Schnoor, 1999, p. 76):

> I recently interviewed Lisa Carlson, the Executive Director of the Funeral and Memorial Societies of America, which serves as the most prominent watchdog of the funeral industry. She told me that the federal government must reopen the funeral rule for review because it sets the legal standard for the pricing tactics funeral homes may use. I took Carlson's advice and contacted my senator, John Ashcroft from Missouri, and he echoed Carlson's sentiments. Ashcroft said, "Families should have assurance that, in their time of greatest grief . . . they will not be preyed upon by unscrupulous funeral directors."

You might also consider using an eyewitness's testimony. You might, for example, cite the testimony of an eyewitness to an accident, the inmate who spent two years in a maximum-security prison, or the patient who underwent an operation.

You can also present testimony by quoting the person directly. And quotations, from either historical or contemporary figures, often allow you to explain an idea in a particularly clever or humorous way. Short, directly relevant, and clear quotations work best. If quotes are long, it is probably best to paraphrase them. Be sure to connect quotations to your own words as smoothly as possible. Always give credit to the source, whether you quote directly or paraphrase.

What Do You Say?

Testimony: You want to present testimony from a retired judge to explain the problems that probation causes. For your purposes, what would be the ideal qualifications of this judge? How might you weave these qualifications into your speech? *What do you say?*

Definitions

Definitions are almost always helpful in an informative speech. They can be overdone, however, as when speakers define terms that the audience already understands or give three or four definitions when one would suffice. Several types of definitions

Skill development experience

Critically Evaluating Testimony

If you were presenting expert testimony on one of these issues, how would you establish the person's qualifications so that your audience would accept what he or she had to say?

1. Nutritionist on the importance of a proper diet
2. Real estate agent advising people to buy real estate now
3. Nurse on the nature of bipolar disorder (manic depression)
4. Pet store owner on how to feed a pet
5. Teacher on how to write a book

may prove useful in clarifying concepts. One method is to define by *etymology,* to explain the term's origin. For example, to define the word *communication,* you might note that it comes from the Latin *communis,* meaning "common." By communicating, you seek to establish a commonness, a sameness, a similarity with another person.

Defining by *authority* involves citing some well-known authority's perspective on the meaning of the term. You might, for example, use the authority of satirist Ambrose Bierce and define *love* as nothing but "a temporary insanity curable by marriage" and *friendship* as "a ship big enough to carry two in fair weather, but only one in foul."

Defining by *operations* involves describing how you would construct the object. For example, in defining a chocolate cake, you would tell how to bake a cake.

Defining by *direct symbolization* involves showing your listeners the actual item or a model or picture of it. For example, to describe different clothing styles of past centuries, you might show actual samples or drawings and photographs of such clothing.

Statistics

Let's say you want to show that the salaries for home health aides should be raised, that suspects' affluence or poverty influences their likelihood of criminal conviction, or that significant numbers of people now get their news from the Internet. To support these types of propositions, you might use statistics—summary figures that help you communicate the important characteristic of a complex set of numbers. For most speeches and most audiences, simple statistics work best; for example, measures of central tendency, measures of correlation, and percentages.

Measures of central tendency describe the general pattern in a group of numbers. Two useful measures are the *mean* (the arithmetic average of a set of numbers) and the *median* (the middle score; 50 percent of cases fall above and 50 percent fall below it). When using such measures, make it clear why each figure is important. For example, if you want to show that home health aides should be paid more, you might compare the mean salaries of home health aides with those of other health care workers or with those of workers who have similar education and responsibilities. Once this statistical difference is clear to your audience, you can relate it to your thesis and demonstrate that this salary difference—this gap between the two means—is significant and needs to be redressed.

Measures of correlation describe how closely two or more things are related. For example, there's a high positive correlation between smoking and lung cancer; smokers have a much greater incidence of lung cancer than non-smokers. Correlations can also be negative. For example, there's a negative correlation between the amount of money you have and the likelihood that you'll be convicted of a crime; as your income level increases, your likelihood of criminal conviction decreases. When using correlations, make clear to your audience why the relationship between, say money and criminal conviction is important and how it relates to the proposition you want to support.

Percentages allow you to express a score as a number per 100. That is, if 78 percent of people favored coffee over tea, it would mean that 78 people out of every 100 favored coffee over tea. Percentages are useful if you want to show, say, the relative amount of a proposed tuition increase, the growth of cable television over the past 10 years, or the divorce rate in different parts of the world. In some cases you might want to compare percentages. For example, you might compare the percentage tuition increase at your school to the national average increase or to the average increase for schools similar to yours. To illustrate the growth of

VIEWPOINT

How would you use statistics to illustrate "the increase in school violence," "the federal deficit," "the cost of war," or "the rise in drug use in corporations"?

the Internet as a news medium, you might note that in 1995 only 4 percent of people in the United States got their news from the Internet but that by 2002 the percentage had grown to 40 percent.

In using statistics, consider these suggestions:

- Make sure the statistics are clear, remembering that your audience will hear the figures only once. Round off figures so they're easy to comprehend and retain. For example, instead of saying that the median income of workers in your city is "$49,347," consider saying "about $50,000."

- Make explicit the meaning of the statistics. For example, if you state that the average home health aide makes less than $30,000 a year, you need to compare this figure to the salaries of other workers and to your proposition that home health aide salaries need to be increased. Don't just rattle off statistics; use them to support a specific proposition.

- Reinforce your oral presentation of statistics with some type of presentation aid—perhaps a graph or a chart. Numbers presented without some kind of visual reinforcement are difficult to grasp and remember. When possible, then, let your audience both see *and* hear the numbers; the listeners will be better able to see the figures' relevance and remember them.

- Use statistics in moderation. Most listeners' capacity for numerical data presented in a speech is limited, so use all figures sparingly.

> **"** Averages and relationships and trends and graphs are not always what they seem. There may be more in them than meets the eye, and there may be a good deal less. **"**
>
> —Darrell Huff

Visual Aids

When you plan a speech, consider using visual aids—visual means of clarifying important ideas (Kemp & Dayton, 1985; Heinrich et al., 1983). At the start, ask yourself how you might use visual aids to enhance your speech. What type of visual aids would be most effective? Charts? Slides? Models? How should you go about creating the aids? What principles should you follow to make sure your aids help you achieve your public speaking purpose? How should you use the aids in the actual speech presentation?

Visual aids are integral parts of your speech and serve important functions. Perhaps the most important is that they help gain attention and maintain interest. Listeners perk up when the speaker says, "I want you to look at this chart showing the employment picture for the next five years."

Visual aids add clarity, something the designer in the cartoon at the right has not yet learned. Let's say you want to illustrate the growth of the cable television industry in the United States over the last 50 years. You could say, "In 1952 there were 14,000 subscribers. In 1955 there were 150,000 subscribers. . . ." But this gets pretty boring, and you still haven't

The 5th Wave   By Rich Tennant

"WELL, SHOOT! THIS EGGPLANT CHART IS JUST AS CONFUSING AS THE BUTTERNUT SQUASH CHART AND THE GOURD CHART. CAN'T YOU JUST MAKE A PIE CHART LIKE EVERYONE ELSE?"

© The 5th Wave, www.the5thwave.com

Skill development experience

Amplifying Statements

Select one of the following overly broad statements and amplify it, using at least three different methods of amplification. Because the purpose of this exercise is to provide greater insight into amplification forms and methods, you may, for this exercise, invent facts, figures, illustrations, examples, and the like.

1. Significant social contributions have been made by persons over 65.
2. The writer of this article is a real authority.
3. Attitudes toward women in the workplace have changed over the last 20 years.
4. Television advertising appeals to viewers emotionally rather than logically.

covered the 1960s, 1970s, 1980s, and 1990s. It would be a lot easier simply to use a bar graph, which would immediately drive your point home.

Visuals help listeners remember your speech. A great deal of the information we have in our minds is stored in visual form. For example, in answering the question "Where is Colorado in relation to California?" you probably picture the map of the United States. In a similar way, if you provide your audience with visual cues, they will be able to recall your speech more easily.

Visuals reinforce your message. A visual aid allows you to present the same information in two different ways—verbally and visually. This one-two punch helps the audience understand more clearly and remember more accurately what you have said.

Types of Visual Aids   If you decide that your speech can profit from the use of a visual aid, your next task is to decide the type of visual that will prove most effective. Let's take a look at some of the more popular visual aids.

The best visual aid generally is *the actual object;* integrate it into your speech if you can. If you're comparing two types of magazines, bring copies to show your audience. If you're talking about a new cellular phone, bring one to illustrate.

Replicas or *models* of the actual object are useful when explaining complex or very small structures, such as the vocal mechanism or the brain. Models clarify the relative size of structures, their position, and interface.

Word charts help highlight the key points that you cover in your speech in the order in which you cover them. Figure 13.1 provides an example of a simple word chart.

An *organizational chart* shows how an organization is structured, the hierarchy of the organization, and who supervises whom. Figure 13.2 provides an example of an organizational chart of a publishing company.

Figure 13.1

Word Charts
The relative value of this chart and, in fact, of any visual aid depends on the effect it has on the audience.

Figure 13.2

An Organizational Chart
This figure was constructed in Illustrator. But organizational charts can easily be constructed using the table function on most word processors and then enlarged for an entire audience to see.

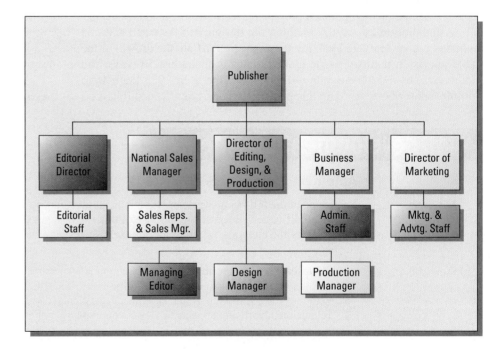

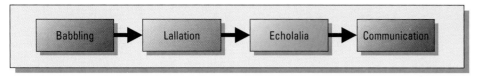

Figure **13.3**

A Flowchart

This chart identifies the stages a child goes through in learning language. Flowcharts are often useful to guide the audience through the entire speech—each section of the chart might represent a major proposition of your speech.

Flowcharts help clarify processes such as the steps involved in learning a skill or in performing a complex set of behaviors. Flowcharts are very much like word charts, except that they show the interaction of the various parts of the process. An example of a flowchart appears in Figure 13.3.

Bar, column, and *line graphs* are especially useful for comparing several items or for showing changes over time. For example, you might use a bar graph to illustrate the literacy rate in different countries; each bar or column would represent a different country. Or you might use such a graph to illustrate the relationship between divorce and religion; each bar or column would represent the number of divorces for each of the major religions. The bar and column graphs in Figure 13.4(a) and (b) on page 298 illustrate the time spent on each of the four communication activities.

Line graphs are also useful for showing changes over time. For example, you might use a line graph to show the increase in the growth of the stock market over the last 50 years. Or you might use a line graph to illustrate the changes in the divorce rate since the 1950s.

Pie charts are useful for showing how something is divided into parts. Figure 13.4(c) puts into pie chart form the same information concerning the time spent in communication activities as is shown in the bar and column charts in Figure 13.4(a) and (b). All parts of the pie must add up to 100 percent, so use this type of graphic only when you want to illustrate the parts of a whole.

Maps are useful for showing geographical elements and changes throughout history. Maps can illustrate factors such as population density, immigration patterns, economic conditions, and the location of resources.

Photos and *pictures* are useful for showing scenes you cannot easily describe. They help maintain attention, but only if easily seen. Don't pass pictures around the room; this procedure will draw your listeners' attention away from what you're saying.

Media of Visual Aids   Once you've decided on the type of visual aid you'll use, you need to decide on the medium you'll use to present it. The easiest to use, though not necessarily the most effective, is the *chalkboard*. It's readily available and may be used for recording key terms or important definitions. Because you don't want to lose eye contact with your audience, plan carefully beforehand exactly what you're going to write so you'll be able to write while only briefly turning away from the audience. Be careful, too, that you write legibly for all to see easily.

Chartboards are useful when you have just one or two relatively simple charts that you want to display during your speech. If you want to display charts for several minutes, be sure you have a way of holding them up; for example, bring tape if you intend to secure them to the chalkboard, or enlist the aid of an audience member to hold them up. Use a light-colored board—white works best. Write in black or red; it provides the best contrast and is the easiest for people to read.

Flip charts, large pads of paper mounted on a stand, can be used to record various types of information that you reveal by flipping the pages as you deliver your speech. You may find a flip chart useful if you have a large number of word charts

ff You can observe a lot just by watching. **JJ**

—Yogi Berra

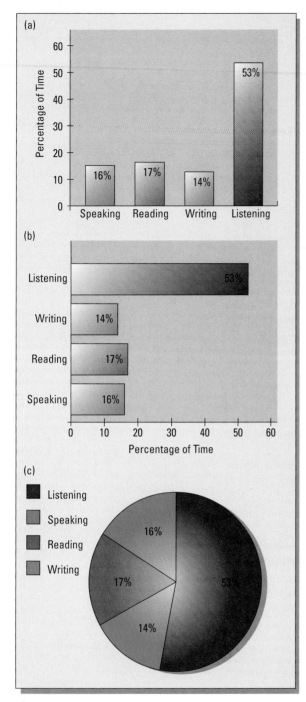

(a)

(b)

(c)

Listening
Speaking
Reading
Writing

Figure **13.4**
Three Graphs
These three graphs illustrate data from a study on the amounts of time people spend on the four communication activities (Barker, Edwards, Gaines, Gladney, & Holley, 1980). All three of these graphs are useful for illustrating comparisons. These are just three types of graphs that are easily constructed using the graphics software integrated with most word-processing packages or, of course, with the more sophisticated graphics programs.

that you want to have easy control over. Be sure that the chart is positioned so that everyone in the audience can see it clearly.

Slide and *transparency projectors* are helpful if you wish to show a series of visuals that may be of very different types—for example, photos, charts, or tables. The slides and transparencies can easily be created with many of the popular computer programs. Many printers will also enable you to use transparency paper to print out what you generate on your computer. Check to make sure that you have the proper equipment—for example, projector, table, nearby working outlet, control over the lighting in the room, and whatever else you'll need to enable the audience see the slides clearly.

Computers allow you to show a series of slides synchronized with your speech. You create the slides in one of the popular presentation software packages, such as PowerPoint or Corel Presentations.

Handouts, or printed material that can be of any type (word charts, statistical tables, interactive questions), are often helpful when you have a great deal of information to communicate that you want your audience to refer to after your speech. However, be aware that audiences tend to read anything handed out; they'll look at the handout rather than listen to the speaker. Be careful to distribute handouts only when you want your audience to refer to them.

Tips on Using Visual Aids   Use any visual aid only when it's relevant. Show it when you want the audience to concentrate on it, and then remove it. If you don't remove it, the audience's attention may remain focused on the visual when you want to continue with your speech.

Know your aids intimately. This is especially true when you're planning to use several. Be sure you know in what order they are to be used and what you will say when you introduce them. Know exactly what goes where and when. As already noted, do all your rehearsal with your visual aids. Test the aids before using them. Be certain they can be easily seen from all parts of the room.

Don't let a visual aid interfere with your contact with the audience. Don't talk to the aid; talk to your audience at all times. Know your aids so well that you can point to what you want without breaking eye contact with your audience. Or, at the most, break audience eye contact only very briefly.

Make sure your visual aids are easily interpreted by people from other cultures and that the aids are culturally sensitive. Just as what you say will be interpreted within a cultural framework, so, too, will the symbols and colors you use in your aid (revisit Table 6.4, Some Cultural Meanings of Color, page 127). For example, symbols that you may assume are universal may actually not be known by people new to a culture. When speaking to international audiences, you need to use universal symbols or to explain those that are not universal. Also, be careful that your icons don't reveal an ethnocentric bias. For example, using the American dollar sign to symbolize "wealth" may be quite logical in your public speaking class but might be interpreted as ethnocentric if used with an audience of international visitors.

Computer-Assisted Presentations   Computer-assisted presentations possess all of the advantages of aids already noted (for example, maintaining interest and attention, adding clarity, and reinforcing your message). In addition, however, they have advantages all their own—so many, in fact, that you'll want to seriously consider using this technology in your speeches. Because they're state of the art, they give your speech a professional, up-to-date look and thus add to your credibility. They show that you're prepared and that you care about your topic and audience.

There are a variety of presentation software packages available; PowerPoint, Corel Presentations, and Lotus Freelance are among the most popular and are very similar in what they do and how they do it. Figure 13.5 illustrates what a set of slides

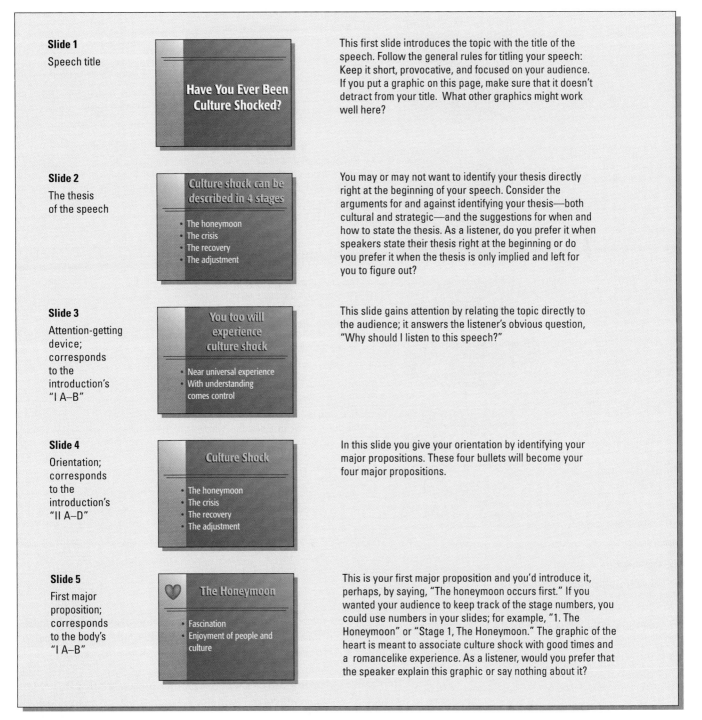

Slide 1
Speech title

Have You Ever Been Culture Shocked?

This first slide introduces the topic with the title of the speech. Follow the general rules for titling your speech: Keep it short, provocative, and focused on your audience. If you put a graphic on this page, make sure that it doesn't detract from your title. What other graphics might work well here?

Slide 2
The thesis of the speech

Culture shock can be described in 4 stages
- The honeymoon
- The crisis
- The recovery
- The adjustment

You may or may not want to identify your thesis directly right at the beginning of your speech. Consider the arguments for and against identifying your thesis—both cultural and strategic—and the suggestions for when and how to state the thesis. As a listener, do you prefer it when speakers state their thesis right at the beginning or do you prefer it when the thesis is only implied and left for you to figure out?

Slide 3
Attention-getting device; corresponds to the introduction's "I A–B"

You too will experience culture shock
- Near universal experience
- With understanding comes control

This slide gains attention by relating the topic directly to the audience; it answers the listener's obvious question, "Why should I listen to this speech?"

Slide 4
Orientation; corresponds to the introduction's "II A–D"

Culture Shock
- The honeymoon
- The crisis
- The recovery
- The adjustment

In this slide you give your orientation by identifying your major propositions. These four bullets will become your four major propositions.

Slide 5
First major proposition; corresponds to the body's "I A–B"

The Honeymoon
- Fascination
- Enjoyment of people and culture

This is your first major proposition and you'd introduce it, perhaps, by saying, "The honeymoon occurs first." If you wanted your audience to keep track of the stage numbers, you could use numbers in your slides; for example, "1. The Honeymoon" or "Stage 1, The Honeymoon." The graphic of the heart is meant to associate culture shock with good times and a romancelike experience. As a listener, would you prefer that the speaker explain this graphic or say nothing about it?

Figure 13.5
A Slide Show Speech

(continued)

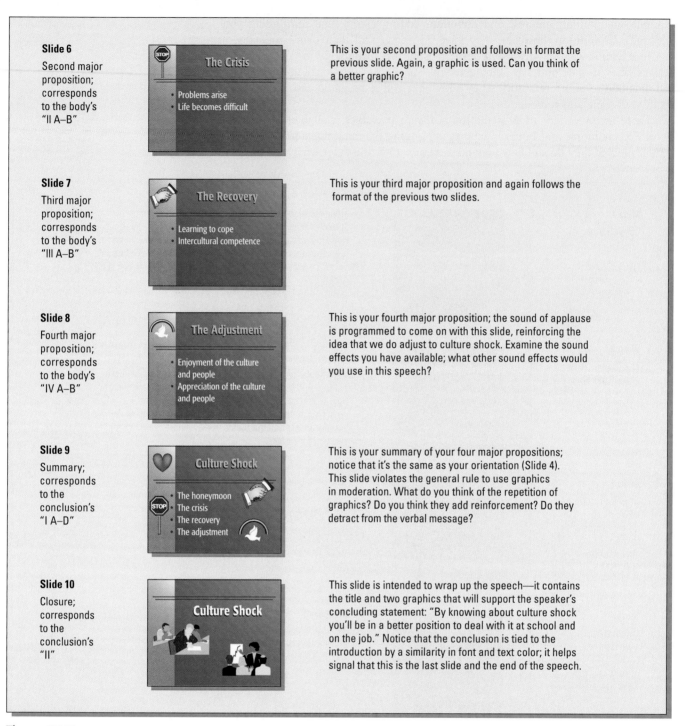

Slide 6

Second major proposition; corresponds to the body's "II A–B"

This is your second proposition and follows in format the previous slide. Again, a graphic is used. Can you think of a better graphic?

Slide 7

Third major proposition; corresponds to the body's "III A–B"

This is your third major proposition and again follows the format of the previous two slides.

Slide 8

Fourth major proposition; corresponds to the body's "IV A–B"

This is your fourth major proposition; the sound of applause is programmed to come on with this slide, reinforcing the idea that we do adjust to culture shock. Examine the sound effects you have available; what other sound effects would you use in this speech?

Slide 9

Summary; corresponds to the conclusion's "I A–D"

This is your summary of your four major propositions; notice that it's the same as your orientation (Slide 4). This slide violates the general rule to use graphics in moderation. What do you think of the repetition of graphics? Do you think they add reinforcement? Do they detract from the verbal message?

Slide 10

Closure; corresponds to the conclusion's "II"

This slide is intended to wrap up the speech—it contains the title and two graphics that will support the speaker's concluding statement: "By knowing about culture shock you'll be in a better position to deal with it at school and on the job." Notice that the conclusion is tied to the introduction by a similarity in font and text color; it helps signal that this is the last slide and the end of the speech.

Figure **13.5**

A Slide Show Speech (*continued*)

might look like; the slides are built around the speech outline discussed in Chapter 12 and were constructed in PowerPoint. As you review this figure, try to visualize how you'd use a slide show to present your next speech.

Ways of Using Presentation Software. Computer presentation software enables you to produce a variety of aids. For example, you can construct your slides on your computer and then have 35mm slides developed from disk. To do this you need a slide printer, or you can send them out (you can do this through your Internet connection) to a lab specializing in converting electronic files into 35mm slides. You may have access to a slide printer at your school, so check first. Similarly, your local office supply store or photocopy shop may have exactly the services you need.

Or you can create your slides and then show them on your computer screen. If you're speaking to a very small group, it may be possible to have your listeners gather around your computer as you speak. With larger audiences, however, you'll need a computer projector or LCD projection panel. Assuming you have a properly equipped computer in the classroom, you can copy your entire presentation to a floppy or any of the high-capacity disks available and bring it with you the day of the speech.

Computer presentation software also enables you to print out a variety of materials on paper. For example, you can print out your complete set of slides to distribute to your listeners. Or you can print out a selection of the slides or even slides that you didn't have time to cover in your speech but would like your audience to look at later.

The most popular options are to print out two, three, or up to six slides per page. The two-slide option provides for easy readability and is especially useful for slides of tables or graphs that you want to present to your listeners in an easy-to-read size. The three-slide option is probably the most widely used; it prints three slides down the left side of the page with space for listeners to write notes on the right. This option is useful if you want to interact with your audience and you want them to take notes as you're speaking. Naturally, you'd distribute this handout before you begin your speech, during your introduction, or perhaps at the point when you want your listeners to begin taking notes. Figure 13.6 on page 302 shows a sample printout. If you want to provide listeners with a complete set of slides, the six-slide option may be the most appropriate. You can, of course, also print out any selection of slides you wish—perhaps just those slides that contain graphs or perhaps just those slides that summarize your talk.

You can also print out your slides with your notes. With this option, you have your slides along with any notes you may find useful—examples you want to use, statistics that are difficult to memorize, quotations that you want to read to your audience, delivery notes, or anything that you care to record. The audience will see the slides but not the speaker's notes. It's generally best to record these notes in outline form, with key words rather than complete sentences. This will prevent you from falling into the trap of reading your speech. A sample printout appears in Figure 13.7 on page 303.

Another useful printout is the speech outline. Two outline options are available: the collapsed outline and the full outline. The collapsed outline contains only the slide titles and is useful if you want to give your audience a general outline of your talk. If you want your listeners to fill in the outline with the information you'll talk about, you can distribute this collapsed outline at the beginning of your speech. The

Web Explorations

Companion Website

An exercise and a self-test at www.ablongman.com/devito will help you work actively with presentation aids: (1) Analyzing Presentation Aids and (2) Can You Distinguish Universal from Culture-Specific Icons?

Skill development experience

Preparing an Informative Speech

Consult the online "Dictionary of Topics" (www.ablongman.com/devito) for suggestions for informative speech topics. Select a topic and:

a. formulate a thesis and a specific purpose suitable for an informative speech of approximately 10 minutes
b. analyze this class as your potential audience and identify ways that you can relate this topic to their interests and needs
c. generate at least two major propositions from your thesis
d. support these propositions with examples, illustrations, definitions, and so on
e. construct a conclusion that summarizes your main ideas and brings the speech to a definite close
f. construct an introduction that gains attention and orients your audience

Discuss these outlines in small groups or with the class as a whole. Try to secure feedback from other class members on how you can improve your outline.

Figure **13.6**

Slides with Space for Listeners' Notes

complete outline option (slide titles plus bullets) is useful for providing listeners with a relatively complete record of your speech; you may want to consider this if you cover lots of technical information that listeners will have to refer to later. The complete outline would be helpful, for example, if you were giving a speech on company health care or pension plans and you wanted to provide your listeners with detailed information on each option. It might also be helpful if you wanted to provide listeners with addresses and phone numbers that they might need. You usually distribute this type of complete outline after you've finished your speech, because such complete outlines may lead your audience to read rather than listen.

Overhead transparencies also can be created from your computer slides. You can make overheads on many printers and most copiers simply by substituting transparency paper for computer paper. Transparencies are certainly not state of the art. Nevertheless, they're often useful when all you have available is a transparency projector. If you create your slides with a computer presentation package, you'll produce professional-looking transparencies.

Rehearsal. Presentation packages are especially helpful for rehearsing your speech and timing it precisely. As you rehearse, the computer program records the time you spend on each slide and will display that time under each slide; it will also

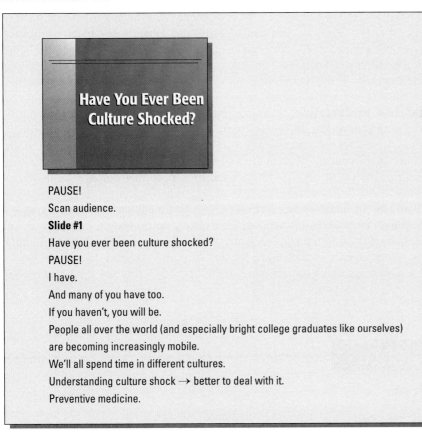

Figure **13.7**
Slide and Speaker's Notes

PAUSE!

Scan audience.

Slide #1

Have you ever been culture shocked?

PAUSE!

I have.

And many of you have too.

If you haven't, you will be.

People all over the world (and especially bright college graduates like ourselves) are becoming increasingly mobile.

We'll all spend time in different cultures.

Understanding culture shock → better to deal with it.

Preventive medicine.

record the presentation's total time. You can see these times at the bottoms of the slides in a variety of views, but they won't appear in the printed handout, such as that shown in Figure 13.6. You can use these times to program each slide so that the whole slide show runs automatically. Or you can use them to see whether you're devoting the proper amount of time to each of your ideas. If you find in your rehearsal that your speech is too long, these times can help you see the topics that you might be able to shorten.

Presentation software allows you to rehearse individually selected slides as many times as you want. But make sure that you go through the speech from beginning to end toward the end of your rehearsal period. Rehearse with this system as long as improvements result; when you find that rehearsal no longer serves any useful purpose, stop.

Another aspect of rehearsal involves checking out the equipment available in the room you'll speak in and its compatibility with the presentation software you're

What Do You Say?

Technical Problems: You've prepared a great slide show for your informative speech. Unfortunately, the necessary projector never arrives. But you have to give your speech, and you have to (or do you?) explain something of what happened. *What do you say?*

Skill development experience

Preparing a Two-Minute Speech

Prepare and present a two-minute speech in which you accomplish one of the following:

- describe "the ethical listener"
- define one of the following terms: audience, communication, interview, small group, sexual harassment
- explain how to perform a specific computer function that is relevant to preparing a public speech, such as accessing e-mail, visiting a particular website, using a search engine, creating a visual aid
- describe the use of visuals in a recent print advertisement

using. If possible, rehearse with the very equipment you'll have available on the day you're speaking. In this way, you can identify and remedy any incompatibilities or idiosyncrasies. Further, you'll discover how long it takes to warm up the slide projector or load PowerPoint and won't have to use up your speaking time for these preliminaries.

The Actual Presentation.   During your actual presentation, you can control your slides with your mouse, advancing to the next one or going back to a previously shown slide. If you set the slide show to run automatically, you won't be tied to the mouse. You can, of course, override the automatic programming simply by clicking your mouse either to advance or to go back to a slide that perhaps went by too quickly.

As with any presentation aid, make sure that you focus on your listeners; don't allow the computer or the slides to get in the way of your immediate contact with the audience. Consider using the pen—actually your mouse—to write on and highlight certain words or figures in the slides. It's not very easy to write with a mouse, so don't plan on writing much. Underlining or circling key terms and figures is probably the best use for the pen.

> " The skill to do comes from doing. "
>
> —Cicero

Skill development experience

Analyzing an Informative Speech

In contrast to the poorly constructed speeches you encountered in Skill Development Exercises in the previous chapters which were written specifically to illustrate common problems, this speech and the one in the next chapter are exceptionally well-crafted speeches and may well serve as models for your own speeches. In the following speech Steve Zammit of the University of Texas informs his listeners about the nature of the electric heart and claims that the device will significantly influence the treatment of heart problems. As you did with the poorly constructed speeches, read the entire speech without looking at the questions on the right. Then reread the speech paragraph by paragraph and respond to the critical thinking questions.

THE ELECTRIC HEART
STEVE ZAMMIT

On February 21, 2000, David Letterman returned to the *Late Show* after his quadruple bypass with a list of the "Top 10 Things You Don't Want to Hear When You Wake Up from Surgery." They include: Number 2—"Hello Mr. Letterman . . . or should I say Miss Letterman?" and Number 1—"We did what we could, Mr. Letterman, but this is Jiffy Lube." But after the gags, Dave brought his doctors on stage and choked up as he thanked them for "saving my life."

One year later, the *New York Times* of February 1, 2001, announced conditional FDA approval for a medical device that will bring similar results to millions of heart patients. But rather than bypass a clogged artery, this revolutionary device bypasses the heart itself, thus fulfilling the life vision of 55-year old scientist and heart surgeon, Dr. David Lederman. Dr. David Lederman is the inventor of the (VA) Electric Heart.

The Electric Heart is a safe, battery-operated, permanent replacement that is directly implanted into the body. The February 12, 2001, *Telegram and Gazette* predicts that within one generation, more than 10 million Americans will be living with terminal heart disease. For

How effective was the introduction? What purposes did it accomplish? Would you have sought to accomplish any other purpose(s)? If so, what would you have said?

Although you can't see the visual aids the speaker used, you can see where they were used and you can imagine what they were. If you had been listening to this speech, what would you have liked to see in these visuals?

them, and for the 100,000 transplant candidates who pray for a new heart when only 2,000 are annually available, hope has been fleeting . . . until now.

So to learn why UCLA transplant surgeon Dr. Steven Marelli calls it the "Holy Grail of Heart Surgery," let's first plug into the heart's development and see how it works. Next, flesh out its current status. So that finally we can see how the device's future impact will be heart-stopping.

In early 1982, Washington dentist Barney Clark's heart was stopping—literally. The world watched as Dr. Robert Jarvik implanted Clark with the first ever artificial heart. After 112 days marked by kidney failure, respiratory problems, and severe mental confusion, the heart stopped. It didn't take a rocket scientist to see that, as the *New York Times* of May 16, 1988, declared, artificial heart research was medical technology's version of Dracula. Basically, it sucked. Getting Dracula out of his coffin would require a little thinking outside the box. Enter Dr. David Lederman, who, in a happy coincidence, reported *Forbes* of April 17, 2000, is an actual rocket scientist. In fact, Lederman changed his career path in the early 1970s when he heard a lecture by a physicist who insisted artificial hearts would rise or fall based on fluid mechanics.

Lederman's design can be likened to space flight in that the concept is easy, but the tiniest problems can prevent a launch or cause an explosion. *What separates the Electric Heart from Jarvik's earlier model is the development and implementation of space-age technology.* In particular, the *Pittsburgh Post-Gazette* of January 28, 2001, explains that an artificial heart must simultaneously weigh two pounds, be flexible enough to expand and contract, and tough enough to absorb 40 million beats a year. The solution is a proprietary titanium compound called Angioflex, the first man-made material on earth that fits the mold.

A typical heart pumps blood through constant muscular contractions regulated by the nervous system. (VA) But Lederman's model propels blood using an internal motor regulated by a microprocessor imbedded inside the abdomen. A small external belt transmits energy through the skin to a copper coil, allowing the entire system to be continuously stimulated.

When he returned last February, David Letterman was stimulated by a hospital gown clad Robin Williams, who performed a zany strip tease. . . . I'll spare you the VA. But to see if Dr. Lederman is himself a tease, we must now evaluate his project's current status as well as the obstacles it faces.

The *Houston Chronicle* of January 31, 2001, reveals that FDA approval of the electric heart was based on its wild success when implanted in animals. More than 100 cows have been recipients of the heart, and in Dr. Lederman's words, three hours after surgery, "I have seen the animals standing in their stalls munching hay, with their original hearts in a jar nearby." Sometime in early June, surgical teams will swap an electric heart for the failing one in five critically ill human patients, for what Dr. Lederman calls "the most public clinical trials

What function does this section serve? Did you find it useful in understanding the speech?

What did you think of the way the speaker phrased the orientation to the major propositions of the speech? Did it add clarity? Did it add humor?

What functions did the Dracula example serve? Do you feel this was too "flippant" for a speech on such a serious topic? Do you feel it added the right note of levity?

Can you identify transitions the speaker used to connect the speech parts?

As you read the speech, did you feel that the speaker successfully involved you in the speech? If not, what might the speaker have done to make you feel he was talking about you to you?

(continued)

in history." For those skeptics who argue it's a little early to break out the bubbly, Dr. Lederman adamantly agrees. He told the February 5, 2001, *Glasgow Herald* "At first, you had the Wright brothers. Today, you can easily cross the Atlantic. Our heart is the equivalent of making the flight from Boston to New York." But the trip across the Atlantic is only a matter of time.

Despite the optimism, the beat will not go on until Dr. Lederman convincingly addresses two concerns about practicality. As the *British Medical Journal* of March 17, 2001, explains, organ transplant recipients must take expensive nauseating drugs to prevent clotting and rejection. Fortunately, Angioflex's producer, Abiomed, revealed in a 2000 Securities and Exchange Commission filing that the material is perfectly seamless and can withstand over 20 years of abuse without cracking. No cracks, no place for clots to form. And since the electric heart is made of inert materials, UCLA transplant surgeon Dr. Steven Marelli told the February 7, 2001, *University Wire*, the body will not reject it, an observation confirmed by animal trials. Essentially, Electric Heart recipients will come back without expensive drug therapy.

Speaking of comebacks, just as David Letterman's return culminated in an Emmy nomination, Dr. Lederman will soon be picking up some awards of his own, due to the Electric Heart's impact on individuals and society. As transplant pioneer Robert Jarvik once said, "the artificial heart must not only be dependable, but truly forgettable." But during periods of increased energy demand—including making love—Jarvik's model required a user to be tethered to a power unit in the wall. Lederman's model, in the words of the February 2001 *GQ*, is "The Love Machine." As *GQ* observes, the internal battery can allow "unassisted" exercise for 30 minutes—every man's dream. But the *Boston Globe* of February 1, 2001, reveals advances in battery technology eventually will allow a sleeping user to be charged for a full day—allowing recipients to emulate the Energizer Bunny in more ways than one.

But by normalizing life for individuals, the Electric Heart will be revolutionizing medicine in society. The March 26, 2001, *Los Angeles Times* notes that 400,000 Americans are diagnosed with heart failure each year. Add the number of other failing internal organs, as well as a glut of aging baby boomers, and we are a generation away from a crisis. To cope, some researchers have famously approached organ shortages by genetically engineering them to grow in a lab, a process that will still take years. But the Electric Heart is both more immediate, and carries none of the ethical entanglements of manipulating the human genome. As Dr. Ed Berger, vice president of Abiomed, explained in an April 2, 2001, telephone interview, Angioflex is so versatile, it could eventually be used to construct artificial kidneys and lungs.

Unfortunately, the *American Journal of Medicine* of February 1, 2001, reports that heart disease disproportionately strikes those in lower socioeconomic brackets, a group that often lacks access to advanced technology.

How effectively did the speaker integrate research into the speech?

Of all the research cited in the speech, which did you think was the most effective? Which was the least effective? Why?

What influence did the research and its integration into the speech have on your image of the speaker's credibility?

How effective do you think the speech title, "The Electric Heart," was? What other titles might have worked?

But the April 19, 2001, *Boston Herald* predicts the procedure will eventually retail for about $25,000, the same as a traditional heart bypass. Coupled with the cost savings on drug treatment, the procedure should be affordably covered by most insurance companies, including Medicare. So whether rich or poor, young or old, resting or energized, the Electric Heart will be an equal opportunity lifesaver.

Although you can never mend a broken heart, Dr. Lederman has done the next best thing. By reviewing the Electric Heart's unusual development and current testing, we have seen its future impact on viewers around the world. On the night of his comeback, David Letterman put a human face on heart disease. But for thousands who find themselves in the comedian's shoes, laughter—and everything else—are insufficient medicine. But soon, Dr. David Lederman will reach audiences with a message of hope. For them, the Electric Heart will not just make the Top 10 List. It will be number one.

Source: Stephen Zammit, Cornell University.

What one thing will you remember most from this speech? Why will you remember this? That is, what did the speaker say that made this one thing most memorable?

How effective was the speaker's conclusion? What functions did the conclusion serve? What other functions might it have served?

Now that you've finished reading the speech (don't look back), what were the major propositions of the speech? What did you learn from this speech?

Summary of Concepts and Skills

This chapter covered the nature of the informative speech and ways you can most effectively communicate information.

1. When preparing informative speeches, observe the guidelines for informative speaking: Stress the information's usefulness, relate new information to information the audience already knows, present information through several senses, adjust the level of complexity, vary the levels of abstraction, limit the amount of information, and recognize cultural variations.
2. Three general types of informative speeches are speeches of description, in which you explain an object, person, event, or process; speeches of definition, in which you define a term, system, theory, or set of principles; and speeches of demonstration, in which you explain how something works or how to do something.
3. To make your ideas clear to your audience, use amplifying materials such as examples, illustrations, and narratives; testimony; definitions; statistics; and visual aids.

Effective public speakers need to master a variety of informing skills. Check your own mastery of these skills, using the following rating scale: 1 = almost always; 2 = often; 3 = sometimes; 4 = rarely; and 5 = hardly ever.

_____ 1. In my informative speeches I follow the principles of informative speaking: I stress the information's usefulness, relate new information to information the audience already knows, present information through several senses, adjust the level of complexity, vary the levels of abstraction, limit the amount of information I present, and recognize cultural variations.

_____ 2. When developing a speech of information, I follow the suggestions for constructing speeches of description, definition, and demonstration.

_____ 3. For my informative speeches I select a variety of amplifying materials; examples, illustrations, and narratives; testimony; definitions; statistics; and visual aids.

Key Word Quiz

Write T for those statements that are true and F for those that are false. For those that are false, replace the italicized term with the correct term.

_____ 1. A speech in which you explain an object, person, event, or process is known as a *speech of description*.

_____ 2. A speech in which you show listeners how to do something or how something works is known as a *speech of definition*.

_____ 3. The power that you get from being seen as someone who can communicate logically, effectively, and convincingly is known as persuasion power or *information power*.

_____ 4. A longer, more detailed example is known as an *illustration*.

_____ 5. When you define a term by explaining its origin, you're defining by *authority*.

_____ 6. Variations in a language that are mutually intelligible to different groups of speakers of the language are known as *dialects*.

_____ 7. The variations in speech that you hear when people from Alabama, Texas, and New York speak are known as *social dialects*.

_____ 8. The statistical measures that tell you how closely two or more things are related are known as *percentiles*.

_____ 9. Examples and illustrations, testimony, definitions, statistics, and visual aids are means of *amplification*.

_____ 10. The parables used to illustrate general principles that are popular in many religious works are examples of *testimony*.

Answers: TRUE: 1, 3, 4, 6, 9; FALSE: 2 (*speech of demonstration*), 5 (*etymology*), 7 (*regional dialects*), 8 (*measures of correlation*), 10 (*narration*)

14 The Persuasive Speech

Chapter Concepts	Chapter Skills
This chapter covers the persuasive speech. It offers guidelines for preparing the different types of persuasive speeches and discusses the principles of persuasion.	After completing this chapter, you should be able to:
Guidelines for Persuasive Speaking	appropriately apply the principles of persuasion in speeches.
Types of Persuasive Speeches	develop persuasive speeches that seek to strengthen or change existing attitudes or to move listeners to action.
Logical Appeals	develop arguments and adapt them to your audience; detect reasoning fallacies and avoid them in your own speeches.
Motivational Appeals	develop motivational appeals and adapt them to your audience.
Credibility Appeals	establish your competence, character, and charisma.

You'll no doubt find yourself in a wide variety of situations in which you'll have to persuade others—to accept or reject a union proposal, to redesign a company's website, to negotiate business deals, or to donate blood or money or time, to give just a few examples. As with having to provide information, the higher up you go in your organization's hierarchy, the more you'll find yourself having to persuade others.

In this chapter we examine the speech of **persuasion,** the process of influencing attitudes and behavior. In a persuasive speech you try to change your listeners' attitudes or beliefs or try to get them to do something. The speeches of politicians, advertisers, and religious leaders are perhaps the clearest examples of persuasive speeches. In many of your own speeches, too, your goal will be persuasion.

> **❝** If all my possessions were taken from me with one exception, I would choose to keep the power of speech, for by it I would soon regain all the rest. **❞**
>
> —Daniel Webster

Guidelines for Persuasive Speaking

Your success in strengthening or changing attitudes or beliefs and in moving your listeners to action will depend on your use of the principles of persuasion (Woodward & Denton, 1996; Jamieson & Campbell, 2001). Let's look at four major principles: selective exposure, audience participation, identification, and amounts of change.

Selective Exposure

Audiences generally follow the "law of selective exposure," which has two parts:

1. Listeners actively seek information that supports their opinions, beliefs, values, decisions, and behaviors.

2. Listeners actively avoid information that contradicts their existing opinions, beliefs, attitudes, values, and behaviors.

The law of selective exposure has an important implication. If you are going to try to persuade an audience that holds attitudes different from your own, you can expect the selective exposure effect to be in force. Therefore, proceed inductively: Hold back on your thesis until you present your evidence and argument. Only then relate this evidence and argument to your thesis.

Let's say you're giving a speech on the need to divide the university athletic budget evenly between men's and women's athletic programs. If your audience agrees with you and wants to evenly divide athletic spending, you can lead with your thesis. If, however, your audience strongly favors the existing system (with the bulk of the money going to the men's programs), lead with your evidence and hold off on stating your thesis until the end of your speech. For example, before mentioning your thesis, you might mention that there are more women attending this university than men, or that all college funds have always been distributed in proportion to the student body population. Once your listeners realize facts such as these, they'll probably look at your thesis more positively than they would have if you hadn't presented such information.

Audience Participation

Persuasion is most effective when the audience participates actively, as in paraphrasing or summarizing. Demagogues who arouse huge crowds often have their audiences chant slogans, repeat catch phrases, and otherwise participate actively. The implication is simple: Persuasion is a transactional process. It involves both speaker and listeners. You will be more effective if you can get the audience to participate actively. So consider asking the audience questions and asking them to respond. Consider, too, asking the audience to do something—to look at their watches, to write something down, or to examine the contents of their briefcases. Naturally, such active participation must be integrally related to your speech topic and purpose.

Identification

The principle of identification states that if you can get your audience to identify with you—if you can show your listeners that you and they share important attitudes, beliefs, and values—you'll clearly advance your persuasive goal. Other similarities are also important. For example, in some cases similarity of cultural, educational, or social background may help you identify yourself with your audience. Be aware, however, that insincere or dishonest identification is likely to backfire and create problems. So avoid even implying similarities between yourself and your audience that don't exist.

Amounts of Change

The principle of amounts of change states that the greater and more important the change you want to produce in your audience, the more difficult your task will be. The reason is simple: People normally demand a greater number of reasons and lots more evidence before they make important decisions such as, say, changing careers, moving to another state, or investing in stocks. On the other hand, people may be more easily persuaded (and demand less evidence) on relatively minor issues—whether to take a course in "Small Group Communication" rather than "Persuasion," or whether to give to the United Heart Fund instead of the American Heart Fund.

Generally people change gradually, in small degrees over a long period of time. Persuasion, therefore, is most effective when it strives for small changes and works over a period of time. For example, a persuasive speech stands a better chance when it tries to get an alcoholic to attend just one AA meeting rather than to give up alcohol for life. If you try to convince your listeners to change their attitudes too radically or to do something to which they're strongly opposed, they may tune you out, closing their ears to even the best and most logical arguments.

When you have the opportunity to persuade your audience on several occasions (rather than simply delivering one speech), two strategies will prove helpful: the foot-in-the-door and door-in-the-face techniques.

Foot-in-the-Door Technique As its name implies, the foot-in-the-door approach involves figuratively getting your foot in the door by requesting something small, something that your audience will easily agree to. Once your listeners agree to this small request, you then make your real request (Freedman & Fraser, 1966; Dejong, 1979; Cialdini, 1984; Pratkanis & Aronson, 1991). People are more apt to comply with a large request after they've complied with a similar but much smaller request. For example, in one study the objective was to get people to permit installation of a "Drive Carefully" sign on their lawn (a large request). When this (large) request was made first, only about 17 percent of participants were willing to agree. However, when this request was preceded by a much smaller request (to sign a petition), between 50 and 76 percent granted permission to install the sign. Agreement with the smaller request seemed to pave the way for the larger request and put the audience into an agreement mode.

Door-in-the-Face Technique With the door-in-the-face technique, the opposite of the foot in the door, you first make a large request that you know will be refused and then follow it with a more moderate request. For example, your large request might be "We're asking people to donate $100 for new school computers." When your listeners refused, you would make a more moderate request—the request you really wanted your listeners to comply with, such as "Might you be willing to contribute $10?" In changing from the large to the more moderate request, you demonstrate your willingness to compromise and your sensitivity to your listeners. The general idea here is that your listeners will feel that because you've made concessions, they also should make concessions and at least contribute something. Listeners also will probably feel that $10 is actually quite little, considering the initial request; this will make them more likely to comply (Cialdini & Ascani, 1976; Cialdini, 1984).

What Do You Say?

Persuasive Strategy: To get listeners to contribute three hours per week to the college's program of helping high school students prepare for college, you decide to use the door-in-the-face strategy. *What do you say?*

VIEWPOINT
 What is the single most important principle of persuasion? What is the mistake most often committed by persuasive speakers?

Types of Persuasive Speeches

www.researchnavigator.com

Read an Article: Read a scholarly or popular article on any aspect of persuasion that interests you. On the basis of this article, what can you add to the discussion presented here?

In giving a persuasive speech, you try to achieve one of two goals. First, you may wish to strengthen or change your listeners' attitudes and beliefs. Or second, you may wish to motivate them to do something.

Speeches to Strengthen or Change Attitudes or Beliefs

Many speeches seek to strengthen existing attitudes or beliefs. In these cases the audience is favorably inclined to the speaker's message and therefore willing to listen. For example, people who listen to religious speeches are usually already believers, so these speeches aim to strengthen their hearers' attitudes and beliefs. This is usually much easier than getting audiences to change attitudes or beliefs. Most people resist change. When you try to change beliefs or attitudes, you're fighting more of an uphill battle.

Depending on the audience's initial position, you can view topics such as the following examples as candidates for speeches to strengthen or change attitudes and beliefs: legalize marijuana; rate tapes, CDs, and TV shows for excessive sex and violence; make Puerto Rico the 51st state; don't censor the Internet.

Strategies for Strengthening or Changing Attitudes, Beliefs, and Values

When you attempt to strengthen or change your listeners' attitudes, beliefs, and values, consider the following strategic guidelines, which are closely based on the principles just discussed.

Estimate Listeners' Attitudes, Beliefs, and Values. Carefully estimate—as best you can—the current state of your listeners' attitudes, beliefs, and values. If your goal is to strengthen these, then you can state your thesis and your objectives as early in your speech as you wish. Because your listeners are in basic agreement with you, your statement of your thesis will enable you to create a bond of agreement between you. You might say, for example:

> Like you, I am deeply committed to the fight against abortion. Tonight I'd like to explain some new evidence that has recently come to light that we must know if we are to be effective in our fight against legalized abortion.

If, however, you're in basic disagreement and you wish to change your listeners' attitudes, then reserve your statement of your thesis until you've detailed your evidence and argument. Get listeners on your side first by stressing as many similarities between you and your audience members as you can. Only after this should you try to change their attitudes and beliefs. Continuing with the abortion example (but this time with an audience that is opposed to your antiabortion stance), you might say:

> We're all concerned with protecting the rights of the individual. No one wants to infringe on the rights of anyone. And it is from this point of view—from the point of view of the inalienable rights of the individual—that I want to examine the abortion issue.

In this way, you stress your similarity with the audience before you state your antiabortion position to this pro-abortion rights audience.

Seek Small Changes. When you are addressing an audience that is opposed to your position and your goal is to change your listeners' attitudes and beliefs, seek change in small increments. Let's say, for example, that your ultimate goal is to get an antiabortion group to favor abortion on demand. Obviously, this amount of change is too great to achieve in one speech. Therefore, strive for small changes. Here, for example, is an excerpt in which the speaker attempts to get an antiabortion audience to agree that some abortions should be legalized. The speaker begins as follows:

One of the great lessons I learned in college was that most extreme positions are wrong. Most of the important truths lie somewhere between the extreme opposites. And today I want to talk with you about one of these truths. I want to talk with you about rape and the problems faced by the mother carrying a child conceived in this most violent of all the violent crimes we can imagine.

Notice that the speaker does not state a totally pro-abortion rights position but instead focuses on one area of the abortion debate and attempts to get the audience to agree that in some cases abortion should be legalized.

Demonstrate Your Credibility. Show the audience that you're knowledgeable about the topic (demonstrating your competence), that you have their best interests at heart (demonstrating your good character), and that you're willing and ready to speak out in favor of these important concerns (demonstrating your dynamism and charisma).

Developing the Speech to Strengthen or Change Attitudes and Beliefs

The following speech focuses on attitudes and beliefs. In this example, the speaker uses a problem–solution organizational pattern, presenting first the problems created by cigarette smoking and then the solution.

Specific purpose: To persuade my audience that cigarette advertising should be banned from all media

Thesis: Cigarette advertising should be abolished. (Why should cigarette advertising be abolished?)

    I. Cigarette smoking is a national problem.

        A. Cigarette smoking causes lung cancer.

        B. Cigarette smoking pollutes the air.

        C. Cigarette smoking raises the cost of health care.

    II. Cigarette smoking will be lessened if advertisements are prohibited.

        A. Fewer people would start to smoke.

        B. Smokers would smoke less.

You might begin such a speech like this:

I think we all realize that cigarette smoking is a national problem that affects each and every one of us. No one escapes the problems caused by cigarette smoking—not the smoker and not the nonsmoker. Cigarette smoking causes lung cancer. Cigarette smoking pollutes the air. And cigarette smoking raises the cost of health care for everyone.

    Let's look first at the most publicized of all smoking problems: lung cancer. There can be no doubt—the scientific evidence is overwhelming—that cigarette smoking is a direct cause of lung cancer.

Speeches to Move to Action

The persuasive speech designed to motivate a specific behavior may focus on just about any behavior. For example, such a speech might try to get an audience to eat in a way that would make them healthier, stop smoking, contribute blood, donate money to AMFAR, join an organization or club, buy a recreational vehicle, vote for Smith, major in economics, or buy American.

Strategies for Moving Listeners to Action   When designing a speech to get listeners to do something, keep the following guidelines in mind.

Be Realistic.   Set reasonable goals for what you want the audience to do. Remember that you have only 10 or 15 minutes; in that amount of time you cannot

❝ The audience is not the least important actor in the play and if it will not do its allotted share the play falls to pieces. The dramatist then is in the position of a tennis player who is left on the court with nobody to play with. **❞**

—W. Somerset Maugham

move the proverbial mountain. So ask for small, easily performed behaviors—behaviors such as signing a petition, voting in the next election, or donating a small amount of money.

Demonstrate Your Own Compliance. As a general rule, never ask the audience to do what you have not done yourself. So demonstrate your own willingness to do what you want the audience to do. If you don't, the audience will rightfully ask, "Why haven't you done it?" In addition to telling what you have done, show the audience that you're pleased to have done it. Express the satisfaction you've derived from donating blood or from reading to blind students.

Stress Specific Advantages. Stress the specific advantages of the sought-for behaviors to your specific audience. Don't ask your audience to engage in behaviors solely for abstract reasons. Give them concrete, specific reasons why they will benefit from the actions you want them to engage in. For example, instead of telling your listeners that they should devote time to reading to blind students because it's the right thing to do, show them how much they will enjoy the experience and how much they will personally benefit from it.

Developing the Speech to Move to Action Here is an example of a speech to move to action in which the speaker tries to persuade the audience to volunteer to work in a soup kitchen.

Specific purpose: To persuade my audience to volunteer to work in a soup kitchen.

Thesis: Working in a soup kitchen is rewarding. (Why is work in a soup kitchen rewarding? or What are the rewards of this work?)

    I. You'll gain personal satisfaction.

    II. You'll learn useful skills.

    III. You'll meet interesting people.

In such a speech, you might say:

Have you ever had nothing to do and so just stared at the television watching another mindless rerun of *Friends* or *Murder, She Wrote*? Well, you could have spent a really rewarding evening—gaining personal satisfaction and really feeling good about yourself, learning useful skills, and meeting some very interesting people. Let me tell you how you can trade watching Jessica Fletcher solve another murder for these rewarding experiences.

What Do You Say?

Changing Behavior: You're supervising a work team of 20 people. Your problem is that computer parts are being stolen by one or more of the workers, and you've been assigned the task of stopping the shrinkage. You decide to tackle this issue in your weekly meeting with the workers. *What do you say?*

www.researchnavigator.com

Investigate Key Terms: Investigate one of the key terms discussed in this chapter (for example, persuasion, selective exposure, reasoning, motivational appeals, or credibility). What additional insights can you provide?

Skill development experience

Constructing Proofs

Select one of the thesis statements below and construct two or three reasons you might use to influence your audience to accept the thesis. After completing this chapter, you may want to return to this exercise and rework your reasons along the lines of specific logical, motivation, and credibility appeals.

1. Condoms should be distributed to students in junior and senior high school.
2. Sports involving cruelty to animals, such as bullfighting, cockfighting, and foxhunting, should be universally condemned and declared illegal.
3. The United States should follow the lead of Belgium and the Netherlands in recognizing gay and lesbian marriage.
4. Affirmative action is morally warranted.

Logical Appeals

An **argument** consists of evidence (for example, facts) and a conclusion. Reasoning is the process of forming conclusions on the basis of evidence. For example, you might reason that because college graduates earn more money than nongraduates (evidence), Jack and Jill should go to college if they wish to earn more money (conclusion).

Note, however, that these ways of reasoning and the importance placed on evidence and argument are not universal throughout all cultures. Whereas in the United States we teach students to demand logical and reliable evidence before believing something, other cultures teach students to believe the leader (for example, the religious or political leader) simply because this person is the leader.

Further, some audiences favor a deductive pattern of reasoning; that is, they expect to hear the general principle first and the evidence, examples, and argument second. Other audiences favor a more inductive pattern (Asian audiences are often cited as examples); they prefer the examples and illustrations to be given first and the general principle or conclusion given second (Lustig & Koester, 2003; Dodd, 1995).

Throughout this discussion, we'll approach the forms of reasoning from the point of view of the speaker who is using them in a speech. But you should realize that these forms of reasoning are equally valuable for the listener. The forms of reasoning considered here are reasoning from specific instances to generalizations, analogy, causes and effects, and sign.

Reasoning from Specific Instances to Generalizations

In reasoning from **specific instances,** you examine several specific items and then make a conclusion about the whole. This form of reasoning is useful when you want to develop a general principle or conclusion but cannot examine every single instance. For example, perhaps you sample a few communication courses and conclude something about communication courses in general. Or you visit several Scandinavian cities and conclude something about all of Scandinavia.

Critically analyze reasoning from specific instances by applying these tests.

1. Were enough specific instances examined? Two general guidelines will help determine how much is enough. First, the larger the group you wish to cover by your conclusion, the greater the number of specific instances you should examine. For example, if you want to draw a conclusion about your college's entire student body, you will need to examine a much larger sample than if you limit your conclusion to members of your human communication class. Second, the greater the differences among items or people in the group you want to draw a conclusion about, the more specific instances you will have to examine. For example, if you want to draw conclusions about students throughout the world, your sample will have to be much larger and more varied than if you limit your conclusion to students in the United States.

2. Were the specific instances representative? If you want to draw conclusions about your school's entire student body, you cannot simply survey physics or art majors. Instead, you'll need to examine a representative sample.

3. Are there significant exceptions? When you examine specific instances and draw a conclusion about the whole, consider the exceptions. Thus, if you examined a sample of students and discovered that 40 percent came from families having incomes in the top 10 percent of the nation, you might conclude that the student body as a whole was rich. But what about those far below this top 10 percent? What about those in the bottom 10 percent? You would have to take these significant exceptions into consideration.

> " The best argument is that which seems merely an explanation. "
>
> —Dale Carnegie

> " How dangerous it always is to reason from insufficient data. "
>
> —Sherlock Holmes

Listening Critically

To be an effective consumer of persuasive messages, you need to listen critically. One useful technique for critical listening is to identify fallacies that you encounter as a listener (and also as a speaker). The following table presents seven such fallacies (Lee & Lee, 1972, 1995; Albrecht, 1980; Ruggiero, 1990; Pratkanis & Aronson, 1991; Goleman, 1992).

Fallacy	Examples	Critical Listening
Name calling labels an idea, a group of people, or an ideology with a name that the audience evaluates negatively.	"The proposal is antilabor." "He's an atheist, what do you expect?" "It's just another example of tax and spend."	Avoid condemning an idea or person without evidence; don't let negative labels prevent critical analysis.
Transfer associates an idea with something you respect to gain approval or with something you dislike to gain rejection.	"The proposal is in the best tradition of equality and democracy." "This is just another form of apartheid."	Not all language aims to describe or present facts objectively; much language is emotive and appeals to your emotions, not your reason.
Testimonial involves using the authority of some positively evaluated person to gain approval or of some negatively evaluated person to gain rejection.	Endorsements by soap opera stars for automobiles and by athletes for underwear. Glamorous models who sell everything from cereal to shampoo.	People selling products usually are no more authorities on the products than you are; they're simply getting paid millions to endorse the items.
Plain folks identifies the speaker and the proposal with the audience.	"We're all middle class and we need a break." "As parents—and I'm a parent just like you—we know. . . ."	The speaker's membership in the same groups as the audience does not necessarily have anything to do with the validity of what's said.
Card stacking involves selecting only the evidence that supports the case and ignores contrary evidence.	Almost any political campaign speech.	Most issues have many sides; if an issue is presented in terms of only one side, it may mean that the other side is being hidden.
Bandwagon involves persuading an audience to accept or reject an idea because "everybody" or "the right people" accept or reject it.	"Economists agree that. . . ." "The entire faculty agrees that. . . ."	Agreement is not proof; most of the world once thought the earth was flat or that women were too emotional to vote.
Attack involves accusing another person of some wrongdoing so that the issue under discussion never gets examined.	How can we support a candidate who has been unfaithful and has lied?	Don't allow messages about individuals' personal reputations or past behavior to distract you from the real issues.

Applying Listening Skills

How would you respond to a speaker who used each of these devices?

Reasoning from Analogy

In reasoning from **analogy,** you compare similar things and conclude that because they are alike in so many respects, they also must be alike in some other respect. Analogies may be literal or figurative. In a literal analogy, the items compared are from the same class—foods, cars, people, countries, cities, or whatever.

In a figurative analogy, the items compared are from different classes. These analogies are useful for amplification, but they are not logical proof. A figurative analogy might compare, for example, children with birds. You might note that as birds are free to roam all over the world, children need to be free to roam all over their new and unexplored universe.

When critically analyzing the adequacy of an analogy—here, of literal analogies—ask yourself two general questions:

1. Are the two cases alike in essential respects? A difference in significant respects will weaken an analogy.

2. Do the differences make a difference? In any analogy, regardless of how literal, compared items will be different; no two things are exactly the same. But in reasoning with analogies, ask yourself whether the differences make a difference. Obviously, not all do.

Reasoning from Causes and Effects

In reasoning from **causes and effects,** you can go in either of two directions. First, you can reason from a cause to an effect: You can draw the conclusion that a specific cause is producing a specific effect. Or second, you can reason from effect to cause: You can draw the conclusion that a specific effect was in fact produced by a specific cause.

Causal reasoning goes like this:

X results from Y.

X is undesirable.

Therefore, Y should be eliminated.

In an actual speech, the reasoning might be presented like this:

All the available evidence shows unmistakably that cancer [X] results from smoking [Y]. Cancer is a painful, costly, and deadly disease [X]; we have no choice but to do everything we can to eliminate smoking entirely [Y].

Alternatively, of course, you might argue that X results from Y; that X is desirable; and that therefore, Y should be encouraged. In a speech, you might say:

We know that general self-confidence [X] results from positively reinforcing experiences [Y]. Therefore, if you want to encourage the development of self-confidence in your children [X], give them positively reinforcing experiences [Y].

When critically analyzing reasoning from cause to effect or from effect to cause, ask yourself these questions.

1. Might other causes be producing the observed effect? If you observe a particular effect (say, high crime), ask yourself whether factors other than the cause you're postulating might be producing it. Thus, you might assume that poverty leads to crime, but other factors might actually be causing the high crime rate. Or poverty might be one cause but not the most important.

2. Is the causation in the predicted direction? If two things occur together, it is often difficult to determine which is the cause and which the effect. For example, let's say you notice that a lack of interpersonal intimacy and low self-confidence often occur together; the person who lacks self-confidence seldom has intimate relationships. But which is the cause and which the effect? The lack of intimate relationships might cause low self-confidence. However, low self-confidence might also cause a lack of intimacy. Or maybe some other cause (a history of negative criticism, for example) is producing both.

3. Is there, in fact, evidence for a causal rather than merely a time-sequence relationship? Although two things occur in sequence, they may not be related by cause and effect. Divorce frequently follows repeated infidelities, but infidelity itself may not be the cause. Rather, some other factor (for example, boredom or the desire for change) may be leading to both infidelity and divorce.

www.researchnavigator.com

Find Answers: Try finding answers to one of the following questions, or design a research study to answer it: What types of logical appeals would be especially effective with members of your class? Do men and women respond differently to motivational appeals? What occupations are the most credible? The least credible?

Reasoning from Sign

Reasoning from **sign** consists of drawing a conclusion on the basis of the presence of signs because the particular signs all frequently occur together. Medical diagnosis is a good example. The general procedure is simple. If a sign and a condition are frequently paired, doctors take the sign's presence as proof of the condition. Thus, tiredness, extreme thirst, and overeating are diagnostic signs of hyperthyroidism, because they frequently accompany the condition. When these signs (or symptoms) disappear after treatment, doctors conclude that the thyroid disease is under control.

Critically analyze reasoning from sign by asking these questions.

1. Do the signs necessitate the conclusion? Given the extreme thirst, overeating, and the like, how certain can you be of the hyperthyroidism conclusion? With most medical and legal matters, you can never be absolutely certain. You can be certain only beyond a reasonable doubt.

2. Are there other signs that point to the same conclusion? In the thyroid example, other factors could have caused the extreme thirst and the overeating. Yet taken together, these signs pointed to only one reasonable diagnosis. Generally, the more signs point toward the conclusion, the more confidence you can have that it is valid or correct.

3. Are there contradictory signs? For example, if blood tests or thyroid scans showed a normally functioning thyroid, you would have to look for other reasons for the thirst, overeating, and tiredness.

"In the interest of streamlining the judicial process, we'll skip the evidence and go directly to sentencing."

© The New Yorker Collection 1995 J.B. Handelsman from cartoonbank.com. All Rights Reserved.

Motivational Appeals

Motivational appeals—appeals to human needs, desires, and wants—are the most powerful means of persuasion you possess. When you use motivational appeals, you appeal to your listeners' needs and desires. You appeal to motives—to those forces that energize or move a person to strengthen, develop, or change particular attitudes or behaviors. For example, one motive might be the desire to obtain status. This motive might lead an individual to develop certain attitudes about what occupation to enter, the importance of saving and investing money, and so on.

One of the most useful analyses of human motives is Abraham Maslow's (1970) hierarchy of needs, a fivefold classification reproduced in Figure 14.1 on page 320. One of Maslow's assumptions is that people will seek to fulfill needs at the lowest level first and that only when those needs are satisfied do people progress to needs at the next higher level. Thus, according to Maslow, you would not concern yourself with the need for security or for freedom from fear if you were starving (that is, if your need for food had not been fulfilled). Similarly, you would not be concerned with friendship if your need for protection and security had not been fulfilled. The implication for the persuasive speaker is clear: You must determine which of your audience's needs have been satisfied so you can identify the needs that will motivate them.

Here are several useful types of motivational appeals organized around Maslow's classification. As you review these, try to visualize how you would use each category of appeal in your next speech.

Physiological Needs

In many parts of the world, and even in parts of the United States, the physiological needs of the people are not fully met and, as you can appreciate, are powerful motivating forces. Lech Walesa, former leader of the Solidarity party in Poland, recognized this when he wrote, "He who gives food to the people will win." In many of the

Figure 14.1

Maslow's Hierarchy of Needs
Which of these motives would be most effective in moving your class members to, say, believe that campus violence is a real problem? Which might move them to donate their used books to students who can't afford them?

Source: From Abraham Maslow, *Motivation and Personality*. Copyright © 1970. Reprinted by permission of Prentice-Hall, Inc., Upper Saddle River, NJ.

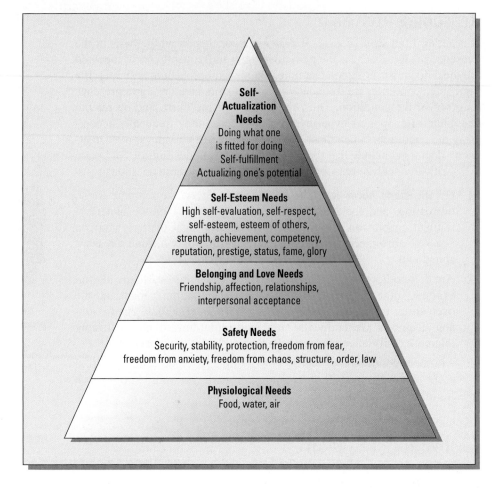

Self-Actualization Needs
Doing what one is fitted for doing
Self-fulfillment
Actualizing one's potential

Self-Esteem Needs
High self-evaluation, self-respect, self-esteem, esteem of others, strength, achievement, competency, reputation, prestige, status, fame, glory

Belonging and Love Needs
Friendship, affection, relationships, interpersonal acceptance

Safety Needs
Security, stability, protection, freedom from fear, freedom from anxiety, freedom from chaos, structure, order, law

Physiological Needs
Food, water, air

poorest countries of the world, the speaker who promises to meet basic physiological needs is the person the people will follow. Most college students in the United States, however, have their physiological needs for food, water, and air well satisfied; so these needs will not prove helpful in motivating and persuading them. In other words, if students already have sufficient food, they won't need it and won't be motivated to get it.

Safety Needs

Those who do not have their basic safety and freedom-from-fear needs met will be motivated by desires for security, protection, and freedom from physical harm and from psychological distress. You see appeals to this need in advertisements for burglar protection devices for home and car, in political speeches promising greater police protection on the streets and in schools, and in the speeches of motivational gurus who promise psychological comfort and freedom from anxiety.

Freedom from anxiety also seems to be the motive used in the advertisements of many psychic services, which promise to tell you what is really going on (with, say, your romantic partner) as well as what will happen in the future. With this information, these ads imply, you'll be free of the anxiety caused by lack of knowledge. You'll also learn what you should do—break off your relationship, move to the west coast, or take that new job. The fact that this "information" is totally without any basis in reality seems not to deter people from spending millions of dollars on psychics.

Sometimes the safety motive lies behind individuals' desires for order, structure, and organization—motives clearly appealed to in advertisements for personal data

Appealing to Emotions

Emotional appeals are all around. Persons who want to censor the Internet often appeal to parents' fears about their children's accessing pornographic materials; those who want to restrict media portrayals of violence may appeal to audiences' fear of increased violence in their communities. The real estate broker who appeals to your desire for status, the friend who wants a favor and appeals to your desire for social approval, and the salesperson who appeals to your desire for sexual rewards are familiar examples. Here are some examples of situations in which emotional appeals may or may not be ethical in attempts at persuasion.

What Would You Do?

You're a parent of two young teenagers, and you want to dissuade them from engaging in sexual relationships. Would it be ethical for you to use emotional appeals—to scare them, for example—to get them to avoid sexual relationships? Similarly, would it be ethical to use fear appeals to help prevent sexually transmitted diseases? Would it be ethical to use fear appeals if your motive was to sell SUVs?

assistants like the Palm Pilot, cell phones, and information management software. Many people fear what is unknown, and order and structure can help make things predictable and, hence, safe.

Belonging and Love Needs

Belonging and love needs are extremely powerful and comprise a variety of specific motives. For example, most people are motivated to love and be loved. For most persons, love and its pursuit occupy a considerable amount of time and energy. If you can teach an audience how to be loved and how to love, your audience will be not only attentive but also grateful.

We also want affiliation—friendship and companionship. Despite our equally potent desire for independence and individuality, we want to be a part of a group. Notice how advertisements for singles clubs and cruises and dating services emphasize appeals to this need for affiliation. On this basis alone they successfully gain the attention, interest, and participation of thousands. Again, such affiliation seems to assure us that we are in fact worthy creatures. If we have friends and companions, surely we are people of some merit.

> **❝** We are afraid of truth, afraid of fortune, afraid of death, and afraid of each other. **❞**
>
> —Ralph Waldo Emerson

Self-Esteem Needs

We all have a need for a positive self-image, a need to see ourselves in the best possible light. We want to see ourselves as self-confident, worthy, and contributing human beings. Inspirational speeches, speeches of the "you're the greatest" type, never seem to lack receptive and suggestible audiences.

Self-esteem is gained, at least in part, from the approval of others (something that is important in all cultures but especially in collectivist cultures). Most people are concerned with peer approval but also want approval from family, teachers, elders, and even children. The approval of others not only contributes to positive self-feelings but also ensures the attainment of related goals. For example, if people have peer approval, they probably also have influence. If they have approval, they're likely to have status. Be cautious with this motive, however: In relating your propositions to your audience's desire for approval, avoid being too obvious. Few people want to be told that they need or desire approval.

People also want power, control, and influence. First, they want power over themselves—control of their own destiny, responsibility for their own successes. As

What Do You Say?

Persuasive Appeals: You want to give a speech urging your listeners to vote in favor of establishing a hate speech code at the college. You want to use both logical and emotional appeals. *What do you say?*

Ralph Waldo Emerson put it, "Can anything be so elegant as to have few wants, and to serve them one's self?"

Also, many people want control or influence over other persons. Similarly, they may want to increase control over the environment and over events and things in the world. Because of this you'll motivate your listeners when you make them see that they can increase their power, control, and influence if they learn what you have to say or do as you suggest.

People want to achieve in whatever they do. Students want to be successful students; they also want to achieve as friends, as parents, as lovers. This is why books and speeches that purport to reveal how to be better achievers are so successful. At the same time, of course, people also want others to recognize their achievements as real and valuable. In using the achievement motive, be explicit in stating how your ideas will contribute to the listeners' achievements. At the same time, recognize that different cultures will view achievement very differently. Some cultural groups may define achievement primarily in financial terms, others in terms of group popularity, and still others in terms of security. Show your listeners how your message will help them achieve their specific goals, and you'll likely have an active and receptive audience.

Although this is often denied, most people are motivated to some extent by the desire for financial gain—for what money can buy, for what money can do. Concerns for lower taxes, for higher salaries, and for fringe benefits are all related to the money motive. Show the listeners that what you're saying or advocating will make them money, and they'll listen with considerable interest, much as they read the get-rich-quick books that flood the bookstores.

Self-Actualization Needs

The self-actualization motive, according to Maslow (1970), influences attitudes and behaviors only after all other needs are satisfied. And because people's other, lower-level needs are very rarely all satisfied, it might seem that public speaking time spent appealing to the self-actualization motive might better be spent on other motives. And yet it seems that regardless of how satisfied or unsatisfied people's other desires are, they have a desire to self-actualize, to become what they feel they're best fit for. If a woman sees herself as a poet, she must write poetry. If a man sees himself as a teacher, he must teach. Even if people don't pursue these ideal roles as occupations, they nevertheless have a desire to write poetry or to teach. Appeals to self-actualization—"to be the best you can be"—encourage listeners to strive for their highest ideals and are often welcomed.

Credibility Appeals

How believable are you as a speaker—apart from any evidence or argument you might advance? What is there about you as a person that makes others believe or not believe you? We call this believability quality speaker **credibility** (McCroskey, 1997; Riggio, 1987). Credibility is important to the politician, because it influences how people vote. It's important to the teacher, because it influences his or her impact on a class. Credibility is important to the business manager, because it has a bearing on the manager's effectiveness in the corporation.

Preparing a Persuasive Speech

Consult the online "Dictionary of Topics" (available with Chapter 13 materials at www.ablongman .com/devito) for suggestions for persuasive speech topics. Select a topic and:

a. formulate a thesis and a specific purpose suitable for a persuasive speech of approximately 10 to 15 minutes
b. analyze this class as your potential audience and identify ways that you can relate this topic to their interests and needs
c. generate at least two major propositions from your thesis
d. support these propositions with examples, illustrations, definitions, and so on
e. construct a conclusion that summarizes your main ideas and brings the speech to a definite close
f. construct an introduction that gains attention and orients your audience

Discuss these outlines in small groups or with the class as a whole. Try to secure feedback from other class members on how you can improve your outline.

Credibility is important in all cultures, but in some it may be more important than in others. In some cultures, for example, the religious leader is given absolute credibility; if this leader says something, it's taken as true and therefore believed. In other cultures, people assess religious leaders' credibility individually— not all religious leaders are perceived as equally believable. In still other cultures, religious leaders' credibility may actually be assessed negatively. Also, the Quran, the Old Testament, and the New Testament will all be perceived to have very different levels of credibility depending on the religious beliefs of the audience. And this will be true even when all three religious books say essentially the same thing.

Similarly, members of different cultures may perceive the credibility of the various media very differently. For example, members of a repressive society in which the government controls television news may come to attribute little credibility to such broadcasts. After all, a person in such a society may reason, television news is simply what the government wants you to know. This may be hard to understand or even recognize for someone raised in the United States, for example, where the media are free of such political control.

Before reading further about credibility, you may wish to take the self-test "How credible are you?"

"I've never actually stormed a castle, but I've taken a bunch of siege-management courses."

© The New Yorker Collection 2002 Danny Shanahan from cartoonbank.com. All Rights Reserved.

Test Yourself

HOW CREDIBLE ARE YOU?

INSTRUCTIONS: Score each of the following phrases to indicate how you think members of this class see you when you deliver a speech. Use the following scale: 7 = very true; 6 = quite true; 5 = fairly true; 4 = neither true nor untrue; 3 = fairly untrue; 2 = quite untrue; and 1 = very untrue.

_____ ❶ Knowledgeable and informed about the subject matter

_____ ❷ Experienced

> **❝** Some judge of authors' names, not works, and then
> Nor praise nor blame the writings, but the men. **❞**
>
> —Alexander Pope

Communicating with power

Credibility as Power

Credibility gives you power to influence others. Here are a few general guidelines for increasing your credibility to add to the text's specific suggestions for establishing your competence, character, and charisma.

- It will be easier to demonstrate competence, character, and charisma if you actually possess them; so work on developing the personal qualities you want to project, whether in public speaking or in any form of communication.
- Communicate all three qualities of credibility rather than relying on only one.
- Although it's important to demonstrate the qualities of credibility throughout your speech, make a special attempt to have your audience see you as competent, of high moral character, and charismatic at an early point.
- Demonstrate your possession of the qualities of credibility clearly but also in moderation. For example, don't emphasize your competence so much that the audience concludes that you therefore must be incompetent. "Doubt the man," advises Louise Colet, "who swears to his devotion."

Enhancing Your Communication Power

How would you describe your own credibility? Has your level of credibility helped or hindered your recent persuasive attempts? What can you do to enhance your credibility?

_____ ❸ Confident

_____ ❹ Fair in the presentation of material (evidence and argument)

_____ ❺ Concerned with the audience's needs

_____ ❻ Consistent over time on the issues addressed in the speech

_____ ❼ Positive rather than negative

_____ ❽ Assertive in personal style and enthusiastic about the topic

_____ ❾ Active rather than passive

HOW DID YOU DO? This test focuses on the three main components of credibility—competence, character, and charisma—and is based on a large body of research (e.g., McCroskey, 1997; Riggio, 1987). Items 1 through 3 refer to your perceived competence: How competent or capable does the audience consider you when you give a public speech? Items 4 through 6 refer to your perceived character: Does the audience see you as a person of good and moral character? Items 7 through 9 refer to your perceived charisma: Does the audience see you as dynamic and active rather than as static and passive?

WHAT WILL YOU DO? How might you go about increasing your credibility? What specific steps can you take to change any audience perception with which you may be unhappy?

 Web Explorations

A wide variety of exercises are available at www.ablongman.com/devito to help you further your study and understanding of persuasion and persuasive speaking: (1) Developing the Impromptu Speech, (2) Developing the Speech of Introduction, (3) Developing the Speech of Presentation/Acceptance, (4) Developing the Speech to Secure Goodwill, (5) Developing the Speech of Tribute, (6) Thinking Critically about Persuasive Speaking, (7) Points of View: Cultural Issues and Persuasion, (8) Evaluating the Adequacy of Reasoning, (9) Analyzing Arguments: The Toulmin Model, (10) Comparative Credibility Judgments, (11) Gender, Credibility, and the Topics of Public Speaking, and (12) When Is Persuasion Unethical? An extended discussion of (13) the persuasive speech on questions of fact, value, and policy may also be found on this website.

We can identify three major dimensions of credibility: (1) competence, or the knowledge and expertise the audience *perceives* the speaker to have; (2) character, or the speaker's intentions and concern for the audience; and (3) charisma, or the speaker's personality and dynamism.

Preparing a Two-Minute Speech

Prepare and present a two-minute speech in which you accomplish one of the following:

- describe the logical appeals used in this or another of your texts
- describe how one or more of the common persuasive fallacies appear in television commercials
- describe the credibility appeal of any media personality or politician
- explain how credibility operates in *(a)* dating, *(b)* meeting your partner's family, *(c)* teaching, *(d)* interviewing for a job, or *(e)* sales

Competence

The more knowledge and expertise your listeners perceive you to have, the more likely they are to believe you. For example, students believe a teacher to the extent that they think he or she is knowledgeable on the subject at hand. You can demonstrate your **competence** to your audience in several ways.

Tell the audience of any special experience or training that qualifies you to speak on this specific topic. For example, if you've successfully started your own business, you might tell an audience of budding entrepreneurs the story of starting up in your garage. At the same time, don't call attention to your inadequacies or to any gaps in your knowledge. Avoid such self-effecting statements as "I know I'm not an expert, but. . . ."

This first principle provides a good example of the need for cultural adjustment. This recommendation is generally a good one for most audiences you'll encounter in the United States. In many Asian cultures, however, an emphasis on your own competence or that of your corporation may be taken as a suggestion that your audience members are inferior or that their corporations are not as good as yours. In other cultures, if you don't stress your competence, your listeners may assume it's because you don't have any.

Cite a variety of research sources that you used in preparing the speech; this clearly shows that you have thoroughly researched the topic. Mention books you've read, people you've interviewed, articles you've consulted. Weave these references throughout your speech.

Stress particular competencies of your sources if your audience is not aware of them. Instead of saying, "Senator Smith thinks . . . ," establish the senator's credibility early by saying something like "Senator Smith, who headed the finance committee for three years and was formerly a professor of economics at MIT, thinks. . . ." For example, in a speech on sleep problems, one speaker noted that a source was a leading expert and had written a book by saying simply, "Dr. James Maas, the nation's leading sleep expert, reports in his book *Power Sleep* that the national sleep debt causes more than 100,000 accidents . . ." (Schnoor, 1999, p. 136).

 VIEWPOINT

Thom is planning to give a speech in support of gay marriage and wonders if revealing to the audience that he's gay would help or hinder his credibility. Consider your public speaking class as the target audience. If you would suggest that Thom reveal this information, when and how would you suggest he do so?

Character

A speaker's **character** consists of his or her honesty and basic nature. We want to know if we can trust the speaker. We believe a speaker we trust. As a speaker, demonstrate qualities of character that will increase your credibility. Here are some suggestions.

First, stress your fairness. When delivering a persuasive speech, stress that you have examined both sides of the issue and that your presentation is accurate and fair.

Also, stress your concern for enduring values. Make it clear to the audience that your position—your thesis—is related to higher-order values. Show them exactly how this is true. Notice how former President George H. W. Bush (1988) stressed his concern for enduring values such as family, religion, tradition, and individual power in his speech accepting the Republican presidential nomination:

> At the bright center is the individual. And radiating out from him or her is the family, the essential unit of closeness and of love. For it is the family that communicates to our children—to the 21st century—our culture, our religious faith, our traditions and history.
> From the individual to the family to the community, and so out to the town, to the church and school and, still echoing out, to the country, the state, the nation—each doing only what it does well, and no more. And I believe that power must always be kept close to the individual, close to the hands that raise the family and run the home.

Additionally, stress your similarity with the audience—particularly in your beliefs, attitudes, values, and goals. Once again, the more similar you are to your listeners, the more likely they are to perceive you as credible. At the same time, make it clear that the audience's interests are foremost in your mind. Here is how James Joseph (1997), U.S. ambassador to South Africa, expressed similarity:

> Like me, many of you grew up committed to two great movements, a civil rights movement in the United States and a liberation movement in Southern Africa. Our heroes were not only Frederick Douglass and Martin Luther King, but Albert Luthuli, Oliver Tambo, and Nelson Mandela as well. We shared the pride of the first wave of African independence with Kwame Nkrumah, Jomo Kenyatta, and Julius Nyerere. We felt the frustration of the second wave with military coups, failed states, and dysfunctional leaders, and we now share the enthusiasm of the third wave with Africa's new leaders who point to clear signs of an African renaissance.

Charisma

A speaker's **charisma** involves qualities of dynamism, assertiveness, and forcefulness. Here are some suggestions for communicating your charisma to your public speaking audience.

Demonstrate a positive attitude toward the entire speech encounter. Show your liking of the audience and your enjoyment of the experience of addressing them. People like those who like them, and that includes public speakers. Stress the positive rather than the negative, hope rather than despair, happiness rather than sadness.

Demonstrate assertiveness. Show the audience that you're a person who will stand up for your rights. Show them that you will not back off simply because the odds may be against you.

Demonstrate enthusiasm. The lethargic speaker who plods through the speech is the very opposite of the charismatic speaker. View a film of Martin Luther King Jr., or Billy Graham speaking. They are totally absorbed with the speech and the audience. They are excellent examples of the enthusiasm that adds to charisma.

Skill development experience

Analyzing a Persuasive Speech

Here is another excellent speech for analysis and modeling delivered by a college student, Upendri Gunasekera. As with the informative speech in Chapter 13, this speech is accompanied by a series of questions designed to give structure to your critical analysis. Read the speech as a whole first, then reread it paragraph by paragraph as you respond to the questions on the right.

THE PERILS OF PHILANTHROPY
UPENDRI GUNASEKERA

"Save the Children has touched the lives of millions of children and their families around the world with the help of caring people like you! You can help stop the suffering and give deserving children in need a better life today and hope for the future. Sponsor a child like this girl, Korotoumou Kone, a nine-year-old Malian, for $20 a month, just 67 cents a day, to provide for some of her basic needs."

But what if I were to tell you that only three months after your sponsorship began, the girl died. In fact, *The Chronicle of Philanthropy,* March 26, 1998, reported that the *Chicago Tribune* journalist who sponsored this child through Save the Children went to Mali to check up on the girl and found she had died nearly two years earlier. Save the Children never bothered to inform the reporter that the intended recipient of her generosity was dead. Oops.

The Chronicle of Philanthropy goes on to state that as of January 14, 1999, 400,000 Americans were child supporters, donating $400 million each year through these programs. Was the money they sent to those charities received by the hunger stricken children we see on TV? All too often, the answer is a resounding NO. The truth is that in the last year alone, the *Chicago Tribune* found 24 other children sponsored by Save the Children who died a year before their sponsor ever learned the devastating truth. In most cases, the money becomes a part of the bureaucracy or is given to the oppressive government. In order to fight the fraud, but still help the needy, the American public needs to realize the extent of international charity fraud and be made aware of the few trustworthy international relief charities that do exist.

To do this, we must first understand how the media skews our perspective of the situation through news reports and advertisements. Second, we will focus on international relief charities, and on who is really benefiting from your money. And finally, we will see how the situation can really be ameliorated with your help. First, let's do a little investigative journalism of our own.

Journalists and human rights investigators realize that human rights reporting is made more effective by graphic visual images, according to Frederic A. Moritz in *U.S. Human Rights Report,* September, 1998. "The concentration of refugees in camps supervised by international bodies such as the United Nations High Commission for Refugees provides relatively easy access for journalists who need to interview and photograph victims of war and repression. . . ." People send money because that's what the media feeds them.

George Alagiah of BBC Television was quoted in Alex de Waal's 1997 book, *Famine Crimes.* "Relief agencies depend upon us for publicity and we need them to tell us where the stories are. We try not to ask the questions too bluntly: 'Where will we find the most starving babies?' And they never answer explicitly. We get the pictures just the same." Even James Gibson, the director of the Childreach program in Haiti, quite frankly stated in 1998, "The American public is more inclined to respond to emotional rather than intellectual appeals." But Michael Maren in his

What do you think of the opening "attention getter"? Did it gain your attention? Did it make you want to hear or read more?

How effective is the speaker's orientation? Does the orientation make it clear what the major parts of the speech will be?

Do you agree that the American public is persuaded more by emotional than by intellectual appeals? Are you?

The visual aids the speaker used were not included in the published speech text, so we can't evaluate them. But if you were giving the speech, what types of visuals would you have shown at this point?

(continued)

1997 book, *The Road to Hell,* states, "There is perhaps nothing more wretched than the exploitation of children for fund raising, yet nothing more common." Exploitation like this picture. And this picture. And even this picture.

These children and communities need our assistance, but the exploitative journalism that captures our attention and calls us to action is causing us to throw money at a flawed system. Unfortunately, the good-hearted Americans who sent their money to this child would be grieved to know that their money actually went into this man's pocket. Mobutu Sese Seko, the recently fallen dictator of Zaire, is here pictured in his villa on the French Riviera, where the architecture and menu look nothing like the relief camps of his people.

The media squeezes out our every last teardrop, while the charity organizations get to cash in. This money is harming those we intend to help the most. The harm is delivered in the form of international relief charities like Save the Children, AmeriCares, the UN, and various religious agencies.

A November 10, 1998, *Fortune* magazine report found that this $50-billion-a-year industry was providing for six-figure salaries and first-class plane tickets. Kerby Anderson, in a 1998 *Probe Ministries International* report, also found that most of the money benefits political leaders and businessmen. And if it's not being pocketed, organizations like AmeriCares are using it to ship 10,000 cases of Gatorade to Zaire, for AmeriCares believed that the supposed energy nourishment one receives from Gatorade would be sufficient to protect an individual from the life threatening disease, cholera. However, Dr. Michael Toole from the Centers for Disease Control states, "While Gatorade might be good for athletes, it is not good for cholera victims." But, let's not forget the biggest charity organization of them all, the UN.

The *New Republic,* December, 1994, reveals that many third world countries see the United Nations, the world-renowned foreign aid organization, as inherently corrupt, "and UN bureaucrats are in Somalia only to enrich themselves." In fact, that same year, $4 million in cash disappeared from a UN compound. It could have been stolen, given to high-ranking government officials, pocketed by some locals, or carried off by fire ants—they just don't know. Even Sergio de Mello, the UN's Under Secretary General for Humanitarian Affairs and Emergency Relief, states in *London Mail Guardian,* April 8, 1998, that the UN has made mistakes and needs to be "more aware of the consequences." More aware of a $4 million loss? Here's a tip: when you put $4 million in a room, write down the room number. But unfortunately, the UN didn't take my advice, as was indicated in their recent charitable mission to Kosovo. *The Chronicle of Philanthropy,* April 22, 1998, reported that the disorganization of the UN High Commission for Refugees actually hindered relief efforts, resulting in the loss of medical supplies worth $500,000.

Or what about the March 15, 1998, *Chicago Tribune* report of how Children International raised $25,000 in sponsorships to provide a Filipino village with a number of doctors and 20 to 30 toilets. From the $25,000, the children only received one sporadic doctor and one toilet. Now, un-

Another unseen visual, of Seko's villa, would seem to provide an extremely vivid contrast to the pictures of starving children. Why do you think this technique of vivid contrast is generally so effective?

Here the speaker moves from the first major issue (the way the media appeals to our emotions) to the second issue (the relief charities). Is this transition clear? What other ways might the speaker have moved from the first to the second issue?

How effective are the sources cited here? Do they help to convince you of the speaker's position?

How effective are these examples in making you realize that much of the money given to help the children is wasted?

Does the speaker convince you that relief organizations have misused the money given to them? If so, what specifically convinced you? If not, what additional proof would you want?

less they contracted NASA to build one of those high-tech toilets, I don't think it could have cost $25,000. What happened to all the money? Your guess is as good as mine. And all those letters you receive from your child? Well, they're fabricated. At least that's what the Director of Christian Children's Fund said in the *Chicago Tribune,* March 22, 1998.

All of this paints a very bad picture for those people who need help. When donors don't know where their money is going, and then find out it is being squandered, they're not likely to give additional money to charities. Legitimate charities are hurt by exploitative nonlegitimate charities, unless you know who the legitimate international relief charities are.

There are two international relief charities, Oxfam and the French group, Doctors Without Borders, who have topped the list of charities that are morally and financially smart and effective in their originally intended purpose. The same cholera victims AmeriCares tried to help with Gatorade, Doctors Without Borders treated effectively and efficiently. In fact, in 1997, the National Charities Information Bureau found that 80 percent of the revenues generated for Doctors Without Borders was used for emergency and medical purposes. *The Chronicle of Philanthropy* also compiles an annual Philanthropy 400 list of the top charities based upon financial statements, annual reports, and a questionnaire response. The top five international relief charities issued November 25, 1998, are the American Red Cross, Gifts in Kind International, World Vision, Goodwill Industries International, and Campus Crusade International.

There are other international relief organizations worthy of your money, but it would be wise to follow the *Chronicle's* tips for safe giving so as not to fall prey to con artists. Beware of high emotion, no-substance ads and phone solicitations, and never pay by cash or credit card—always pay by check, payable to the full name of the charity, so only the specified charity may cash in on your money, thus insuring yourself as well as the charity.

Next time you see those ads on TV of starving children waiting for you to send them money, remember that they are suffering at the hands of those very charities. Today, we have seen how exploitative the media has become and how nonlegitimate charities have misused our money, and have identified the truly legitimate charities, those worthy of your donations. The sponsorship agent in charge of Korotoumou Kone told the sponsoring journalist that Korotoumou was healthy and continuing in her studies, but it had been exactly two years after her death. We cannot allow our ignorance to act as a partner in the exploitation of these people. As the journalist then responded, "She's dead. She did not live beyond her 12th birthday."

Source: Adapted from Gunasekera, U. (1999). The perils of philanthropy. In L. G. Schnoor (Ed.), *Winning Orations of the Interstate Oratorical Association* (pp. 98–100). Reprinted with permission from Interstate Oratorical Association, Mankato, MN, Larry Schnoor, Executive Secretary.

Here is the second transition, moving from the second major issue (the relief charities and how they waste the money given to them) to the third issue (what we can do to help the children and yet not contribute to those organizations that waste the money). Is this transition effective? In what other ways might you move from the second issue to the third?

Are you convinced that the charities named by the speaker are the best ones to contribute to? If not, what additional information would you want?

What do you think of the suggestions for ensuring that your money goes where you want it to go? What, if any, additional information might the speaker have included?

How effective is the summary statement of the three major issues covered in the speech?

What do you think of the speaker's technique of tying the conclusion back to the introduction (with the story of Korotoumou)?

Summary of Concepts and Skills

This chapter covered the nature of the persuasive speech and ways you can most effectively change attitudes and behaviors.

1. The major types of persuasive speeches are (1) those that aim to strengthen or change attitudes or beliefs and (2) those that aim to move listeners to action.
2. When preparing your persuasive speeches, consider the principles of selective exposure, audience participation, identification, and amounts of change (including the foot-in-the-door and door-in-the-face techniques).
3. *Argument* consists of a reason or a series of reasons that lead to or support a conclusion. Evidence plus the conclusion it supports equal an argument.
4. When critically analyzing reasoning fallacies, be alert to such techniques as name calling, transfer, testimonial, plain folks, card stacking, bandwagon, and attack.
5. When reasoning from specific instances to a generalization, we examine several specific instances and then conclude something about the whole.
6. When reasoning from analogy, we compare like things and conclude that because they are alike in so many respects, they are also alike in some unknown or unexamined respect. Analogies may be literal or figurative.
7. When reasoning from causes and effects, we may go in either of two directions: We can reason from known or observed cause to some unobserved effect, or from observed or known effect to some unobserved cause.
8. When reasoning from sign, we deduce that if a sign and an object, event, or condition are repeatedly or frequently paired, the sign's presence is taken as evidence or proof that the object, event, or condition is present.
9. Motivational appeals are directed at an individual's needs and desires and may address motives such as fear; power, control, and influence; self-esteem and approval; safety; achievement; and financial gain.
10. *Credibility* is a quality of persuasiveness that depends on the audience's perception of the speaker's character. Three dimensions of credibility are competence, character, and charisma.

To be an effective public speaker, you need to master a variety of persuading skills. Check your own ability to apply these skills, using the following rating scale: 1 = almost always; 2 = often; 3 = sometimes; 4 = rarely; and 5 = hardly ever.

_____ 1. In my persuasive speeches I apply (where relevant) the principles of persuasion: selective exposure, audience participation, identification, and amounts of change.

_____ 2. In my persuasive speeches I critically analyze reasoning from specific instances to generalizations, as well as reasoning from analogy, causes and effects, and sign.

_____ 3. When listening to persuasive attempts, I detect fallacies such as name calling, transfer, testimonial, plain folks, card stacking, bandwagon, and attack.

_____ 4. To motivate my audience I use motivational appeals—for example, appeals to desires for power, control, and influence; self-esteem and approval; safety; achievement; and financial gain.

_____ 5. In my speeches I seek to establish my credibility by displaying competence, high moral character, and dynamism or charisma.

Key Word Quiz

Write T for those statements that are true and F for those that are false. For those that are false, replace the italicized term with the correct term.

_____ 1. The assumptions that listeners actively seek information that supports their beliefs and avoid information that contradicts them are part of the law of *selective exposure*.

_____ 2. Beginning with a small request, gaining compliance, and then following with your larger desired request is a technique known as *door-in-the-face*.

_____ 3. When you examine several items and then conclude something about the whole, you're reasoning from *analogy*.

_____ 4. When you compare like things and conclude that because they are alike in so many respects they are also alike in some other respect, you're reasoning from *sign*.

_____ 5. The highest level of needs, according to Maslow, consists of *self-esteem needs*.

_____ 6. Appeals to desires for power, control, and influence; self-esteem and approval; achievement; and financial gain are examples of *motivational appeals*.

_____ 7. Competence, character, and charisma are dimensions of *credibility*.

_____ 8. If an audience believes you because of who you are rather than because of anything you say, you are said to be *low in credibility*.

_____ 9. Evidence (for example, facts, statistics, testimony) and a conclusion equal an *argument*.

_____ 10. When a speaker uses the authority or image of some positively evaluated person to gain your approval or of some negatively evaluated person to gain your rejection, the speaker is said to be using the *bandwagon technique*.

Answers: TRUE: 1, 6, 7, 9; FALSE: 2 (*foot-in-the-door*), 3 (*specific instances to a generalization*), 4 (*analogy*), 5 (*self-actualization needs*), 8 (*high in credibility*), 10 (*testimonial*)

Glossary of Human Communication Skills

---

abstractions. Use both abstract and specific terms when describing or explaining.

accommodation. Accommodate to the speaking style of your listener in moderation. Too much mirroring of the other person's manner of communicating may appear too obvious and even manipulative.

active and inactive listening. If you wish to listen actively, paraphrase the speaker's meaning, express understanding of the speaker's feelings, and ask questions when you need something clarified.

active interpersonal conflict. Engage in interpersonal conflict actively; generally, don't rely on silence as a way of avoiding the issues.

advantages and disadvantages of relationships. In evaluating your own relationship choices, consider both the advantages and the disadvantages of relationships generally and of your specific relationships.

allness. Avoid allness statements (for example, statements containing such words as *all, never,* or *always*); they invariably misstate the reality and will often offend the other person.

amplifying informative speeches. Select a variety of amplifying materials: examples, illustrations, and narratives; testimony; definitions; statistics; and visual aids.

amplifying materials. Support major propositions with amplifying materials such as examples, statistics, and visual aids and with logical, emotional, and ethical proofs.

analyze your perceptions. Increase accuracy in interpersonal perception by (1) identifying the influence of your physical and emotional state; (2) making sure that you're not drawing conclusions from too little information; and (3) identifying any perceptions that may be the result of mind reading.

anger management. To manage your anger, calm down as best you can, reflect on the fact that communication is irreversible, and review your available communication options and the relevant communication skills.

appreciating cultural differences. Look at cultural differences not as deviations from the norm or as deficiencies but simply as the differences they are. Remember, however, that recognizing differences and considering them as you communicate does not necessarily mean that you accept or adopt them.

appropriateness of self-disclosure. Consider the legitimacy of your motives for disclosing, the appropriateness of the disclosure, the listener's responses (is the dyadic effect operating?), and the potential burdens self-disclosures might impose.

argumentativeness. In conflict, avoid attacking the other person's self-concept. Instead, focus logically on the issues, emphasize finding solutions, and work to ensure that what is said will result in positive self-feelings for both individuals.

articulation and pronunciation. Avoid the articulation and pronunciation errors of omission, substitution, addition, accent, and pronouncing sounds that should be silent.

artifactual communication. Use artifacts (for example, color, clothing, body adornment, space decoration) to communicate your desired messages. But check to find out whether others are in fact receiving the messages you think you are communicating.

audience analysis. Analyze the audience in terms of its sociological and psychological characteristics and adapt your speech based on these findings.

before and after the conflict. Prepare for a conflict by arranging to fight in private, knowing what you're fighting about, and fighting about problems that can be solved. After the conflict, profit from it by learning what worked and what didn't, by keeping the conflict in perspective, and by increasing the exchange of rewards.

body movements. Use your body and hand gestures to reinforce your communication purposes.

brainstorming. Follow these general rules: Avoid negative criticism, strive for quantity, combine and extend the contributions of others, and contribute as wild ideas as possible.

channel. Assess your channel options (for example, speaking face-to-face, sending e-mail, or leaving a voicemail message when you know the person won't be home) before communicating important messages.

checking perceptions. Increase accuracy in perception by (1) describing what you see or hear and the meaning you assign to it and (2) asking the other person if your perceptions and meanings are accurate.

communicating assertively. Describe the problem, say how the problem affects you, propose solutions, confirm your understanding, and reflect on your own assertiveness.

communicating power. Communicate power by avoiding such powerless message forms as hesitations, too many intensifiers, disqualifiers, tag questions, one-word answers, self-critical statements, overly polite statements, and vulgar and slang expressions.

communicating with the grief-stricken. Use confirming messages, give the person permission to grieve, avoid directing the person, encourage the expression of feelings, and communicate empathy and support.

communication apprehension management. Acquire communication skills and experiences, focus on your prior successes, reduce unpredictability, and put apprehension in perspective.

communication options. Assess your communication options before communicating, especially in light of the fact that communication is inevitable, irreversible, and unrepeatable.

conclusions. Construct conclusions that summarize the major ideas of the speech and bring the speech to a crisp close.

confirmation. When you wish to be confirming, acknowledge (verbally and/or nonverbally) others in your group and their contributions.

conflict, culture, and gender. Approach conflict with an understanding of the cultural and gender differences in ideas about what constitutes conflict and how it should be pursued.

conflict styles. Adjust your conflict style to the specific conflict in which you find yourself.

connotative meanings. As a speaker, clarify your connotative meanings if you have any doubts that your listeners might misunderstand you; as a listener, ask questions if you have doubts about the speaker's connotations.

content and relationship. Listen to both the content and the relationship aspects of messages, distinguish between them, and respond to both.

content and relationship conflicts. Analyze conflict messages in terms of content and relationship dimensions and respond to each accordingly.

context adjustment. Adjust your messages to the unique communication context, taking into consideration its physical, cultural, social–psychological, and temporal aspects.

conversational maxims. Follow (generally) the basic maxims of conversation, such as the maxims of quantity, quality, relations, manner, and politeness.

conversational rules. Observe the general rules for conversation (for example, using relatively short speaking turns and avoiding interruptions), but break them when there seems logical reason to do so.

conversational turns. Maintain relatively short conversational turns and then pass the speaker's turn to another person nonverbally or verbally.

credibility appeals. Seek to establish credibility by displaying competence, high moral character, and dynamism or charisma.

critical analysis. Critically analyze reasoning from specific instances to generalizations and reasoning from analogy, causes and effects, and sign.

critical thinking. Using the critical thinking hats technique evaluate problems in terms of facts, feelings, negative arguments, positive benefits, creative ideas, and overall analysis.

cultural differences in listening. When listening in multicultural settings, realize that people from different cultures give very different listening cues and may operate with different rules for listening.

cultural identifiers. Use cultural identifiers that are sensitive to the desires of others; when appropriate, make clear the cultural identifiers you prefer.

cultural influences. Communicate with an understanding that culture influences communication in all its forms.

cultural sensitivity. Increase your cultural sensitivity by learning about different cultures, recognizing and facing your own fears of intercultural interaction, recognizing differences between yourself and others, and becoming conscious of the cultural rules and customs of other cultures.

culture and groups. Recognize and appreciate cultural differences in ideas about group membership and leadership.

culture and perception. Increase accuracy in perception by learning as much as you can about the cultures of those with whom you interact.

dating statements. Mentally date your statements to avoid thinking and communicating that the world is static and unchanging. In your messages, reflect the inevitability of change.

deciding to self-disclose. In deciding to self-disclose, consider the potential benefits (for example, self-knowledge) as well as the potential personal, relationship, and professional risks.

delivery method. In general, use the extemporaneous method of delivery.

delivery. During the speech presentation, maintain eye contact with the entire audience, allow facial expressions to convey feelings, gesture naturally, and incorporate purposeful body movements.

Delphi method. Use the Delphi method to solve problems when group members are separated geographically.

dialogic conversation. Treat conversation as a dialogue rather than a monologue; show concern for the other person, and for the relationship between you, with other-orientation.

disclaimers. Preface your comments with disclaimers if you feel you might be misunderstood. But avoid disclaimers when they aren't necessary; too many disclaimers can make you appear unprepared or unwilling to state an opinion.

disconfirming language. Avoid sexist, heterosexist, racist, and ageist language; such language is disconfirming and insulting and invariably contributes to communication barriers.

emotional communication. To communicate emotions effectively, (1) describe feelings, (2) identify the reasons for the feelings, (3) anchor feelings to the present, and (4) own your feelings and messages.

emotional display. Express your emotions and interpret the emotions of others in light of the cultural rules dictating what is and what isn't "appropriate" emotional expression.

emotionality in interpersonal communication. Include the inevitable emotionality in your thoughts and feelings in your interpersonal communication, both verbally and nonverbally.

emotional understanding. Be able to identify and describe emotions (both positive and negative) clearly and specifically. Learn the vocabulary of emotional expression.

empathic and objective listening. To listen empathically, punctuate the interaction from the speaker's point of view, engage in dialogue, and understand the speaker's thoughts and feelings. In listening objectively be careful that you don't hear what you want to hear.

empathic conflict. Engage in interpersonal conflict with empathy rather than blame. Also, express this empathy, as in "I can understand how you must have felt."

empathy. Communicate empathy when appropriate: Resist evaluating the person's behaviors, focus concentration on the person, express active involvement through facial expressions and gestures, reflect back the feelings you think are being expressed, self-disclose, and address any mixed messages.

ethnocentric thinking. Recognize your own ethnocentric thinking and how it influences your verbal and nonverbal messages.

evaluating. In evaluating messages, try first to understand fully what the speaker means. In addition, try to identify any biases or self-interests that might lead the speaker to give an unfair presentation of the material.

expressiveness. Communicate active involvement in the interaction: Use active listening, address mixed messages, use I-messages, and use appropriate variations in paralanguage and gestures.

eye movements. Use eye movements to seek feedback, exchange conversational turns, signal the nature of your relationship with others, and compensate for increased physical distance. At the same time, look for such meanings in the eye movements of others.

face-saving strategies. In conflict use strategies that allow your opponent to save face; avoid beltlining, or hitting your opponent with attacks that he or she will have difficulty absorbing and will resent.

facial messages. Use facial expressions to communicate that you're involved in the interaction. As a listener, look to the emotional facial expressions of others as additional cues to their meaning.

facts and inferences. Distinguish facts (verifiably true past events) from inferences (guesses, hypotheses, hunches), and act on inferences with tentativeness.

fallacy identification. Detect such fallacies as name calling, transfer, testimonial, plain folks, card stacking, bandwagon, and attack.

feedback. Listen to both verbal and nonverbal feedback—from yourself and from others—and use these cues to help you adjust your messages for greatest effectiveness.

feedforward. Preface your messages with some kind of feedforward when you feel your listener needs some background or when you want to ease into a particular topic, such as bad news.

flexibility. Because no two communication situations are identical, because everything is in a state of flux, and because everyone is different, cultivate flexibility and adjust your communication to the unique situation.

friendships. Establish friendships to help serve such needs as utility, ego support, stimulation, and security. At the same time, seek to serve similar needs that your friends have.

fundamental attribution error. Avoid the fundamental attribution error (whereby you attribute someone's behavior solely to internal factors) by focusing on the possible influence of situational forces.

gaining perspective on problems and solutions. View problems and solutions from the perspective of facts, feelings, negative arguments, positive benefits, creative new ideas, and control of thinking.

gender differences in listening. Speak to men and women with an understanding that women give more cues that they're listening and appear more supportive in their listening than men.

giving space. Give others the space they need, which varies on the basis of culture, gender, and emotional state. Look to the other person for any signs of spatial discomfort.

group norms. Actively seek to discover the norms of a group, and take these norms into consideration when interacting in the group.

group participation. Be group oriented rather than individually oriented, center debates on issues rather than on personalities, be critically open-minded, and make sure that meanings are clearly understood.

groupthink. Recognize and actively counter any groupthink tendencies evidenced in a group.

High- and low-context cultures. Adjust your messages and your listening in light of the differences between high- and low-context cultures.

I-messages. Use I-messages when communicating your feelings; take responsibility for your own feelings (as in "I get angry when you . . .") rather than attributing them to others (as in "you make me angry").

immediacy. Maintain nonverbal immediacy through close physical distances, eye contact, and smiling; maintain verbal im-

mediacy by using the other person's name and focusing on the other's remarks.

implicit personality theory. In order to subject your perceptions and conclusions about people to logical analysis, bring to your mindful state your implicit personality theory.

increasing assertiveness. Increase your own assertiveness by analyzing the assertive messages of others, rehearsing assertive messages, and communicating assertively.

indirect messages. Make judicious use of indirect messages when a more direct style might prove insulting or offensive. But be aware that indirect messages can create communication problems, because they are easier to misunderstand than direct messages.

indiscrimination. Avoid indiscrimination; treat each situation and each person as unique (when possible) even when they're covered by the same label or name. Index your key concepts.

individualistic and collectivist cultures. Adjust your messages and your listening on the basis of differences between individualistic and collectivist cultures.

individual roles. In a group avoid playing the popular but dysfunctional individual roles—those of the aggressor, blocker, recognition seeker, self-confessor, or dominator.

informative speaking. Follow the principles of informative speaking: Stress the information's usefulness, relate new information to information the audience already knows, present information through several senses, adjust the level of complexity, vary the levels of abstraction, avoid information overload, and recognize cultural variations.

initial impressions. Guard against drawing impressions too quickly or on the basis of too little information; be aware that initial impressions can function as filters that prevent you from forming more accurate perceptions on the basis of more information.

intensional orientation. Avoid intensional orientation. Respond to things first and to labels second; for example, the way a person is talked about is not the best measure of who that person really is.

interaction management. Speak in relatively short conversational turns, avoid long and frequent pauses, and use verbal and nonverbal messages that are consistent.

intercultural communication. When communicating interculturally, become mindful of (1) the differences between yourself and culturally different individuals, (2) the differences within the other cultural group, (3) cultural differences in meanings for both verbal and nonverbal signals, and (4) different cultural rules and customs. Communicate interculturally with appropriate openness, empathy, positiveness, immediacy, interaction management, expressiveness, and other-orientation.

introductions. Construct introductions that gain attention and preview what is to follow.

leadership style. Adjust leadership style to the task at hand and to the needs of group members.

leading a group. Start group interaction, maintain effective interaction throughout the discussion, keep members on track, ensure member satisfaction, encourage ongoing evaluation and improvement, and prepare members for the discussion as necessary.

listening to the feelings of others. In listening to the feelings of others, avoid the tendency to try to solve their problems; instead, listen, empathize, focus on the other person, and encourage the person to explore his or her feelings.

making excuses. Repair conversational problems by offering excuses that (1) demonstrate that you understand the problem, (2) acknowledge your responsibility, (3) acknowledge your regret for what you did, (4) request forgiveness, and (5) make it clear that this will never happen again.

managing relationship deterioration. To cope with the ending of a relationship, break the loneliness–depression cycle, take time out, bolster your self-esteem, seek the support of nourishing others, and avoid repeating negative patterns.

markers. Become sensitive to the markers (central, boundary, and ear) of others, and learn to use these markers to define your own territories and to communicate the desired impression.

masculine and feminine cultures. Adjust your messages and your listening to differences in cultural masculinity and femininity.

meanings depend on context. When deciphering messages, look at the context for cues as to how you should interpret the meanings.

meanings in people. When deciphering meaning, the best source is the person; meanings are in people. So when in doubt, find out—from the source.

message overload. Combat message overload by using and disposing of messages as they come to you, organizing your messages, getting rid of extra copies, and distinguishing between messages you should save and messages you should throw away.

metacommunication. Metacommunicate when you want to clarify the way you're talking or what you're talking about; for example, give clear feedforward and paraphrase your own complex messages.

mindfulness. Increase your mindfulness by creating and recreating categories, being open to new information and points of view, and avoiding excessive reliance on first impressions.

mixed messages. Avoid emitting mixed messages by focusing clearly on your purposes when communicating and by increasing conscious control over your verbal and nonverbal behaviors.

motivational appeals. Use motivational appeals (appeals to motives such as fear; power, control, and influence; safety; achievement; or financial gain) as appropriate to the speech and audience.

negatives and positives of conflict. Approach conflict to minimize the negative and maximize the positive benefits of conflict and its resolution.

networking. Establish a network of relationships to provide insights into issues relevant to your personal and professional life, and be willing to lend your expertise to the networks of others.

noise management. Reduce the influence of physical, physiological, psychological, and semantic noise to the extent that you can; use repetition and restatement and, when in doubt, ask if you're being clear.

nominal group. Use the nominal group technique to solve problems when anonymity in suggesting ideas may be desirable.

nonjudgmental and critical listening. When listening nonjudgmentally, keep an open mind, avoid filtering out difficult messages, and recognize your own biases. When listening to evaluate, listen extra carefully, ask questions when in doubt, and check your perceptions before offering criticism.

nonverbal communication and culture. Interpret the nonverbal cues of others not in light of the meanings assigned by your culture but (insofar as you can) in light of the meanings assigned by the speaker's culture.

online conflicts. Avoid the common causes of online conflicts—such as sending out unsolicited commercial messages, spamming, and flaming.

open expression in conflict. Try to facilitate open expression of your combatant.

openness. When appropriate, increase openness by self-disclosing, responding to those with whom you're interacting spontaneously and honestly, and owning your own feelings and thoughts.

organizing a speech. To organize the major propositions of a speech, select a thought pattern appropriate to the subject matter, purpose, and audience.

organizing learning discussions. Use an organizational structure in educational or learning groups—a chronological or spatial structure, for example—to give order to the discussion.

other-orientation. Acknowledge the importance of the other person; use focused eye contact and appropriate facial expressions; smile, nod, and lean toward the other person; express agreement when appropriate.

overattribution. Avoid overattribution; rarely is any one factor an accurate explanation of complex human behavior.

packaging. Make your verbal and nonverbal messages consistent; inconsistencies between, say, spoken words and body language, often create uncertainty and misunderstanding.

paralanguage. Vary paralinguistic features such as rate, pausing, pitch, and volume to communicate your meanings and to add interest and color to your messages.

pausing. Use pauses to signal transitions, to allow listeners time to think, and to signal the approach of a significant idea.

perceptual shortcuts. Be mindful of your perceptual shortcuts (for example, rules, schemata, and scripts) so that they don't mislead you and result in inaccurate perceptions.

persuasive speaking. Apply (where relevant) the principles of persuasion: selective exposure, audience participation, identification, and amounts of change.

polarization. Avoid thinking and talking in extremes by using middle terms and qualifiers. At the same time, remember that too many qualifiers may make you appear unsure of yourself.

positiveness. Communicate positiveness: Express your own satisfaction with the interaction, and compliment others by expressing your positive thoughts and feelings about and to the other person.

power communication. Communicate power through forceful speech; avoidance of weak modifiers and excessive body movement; and demonstration of your knowledge, preparation, and organization in the matters at hand.

power distance. Adjust your messages and listening based on the power distance orientation of the culture in which you find yourself.

power plays. Use cooperative strategies to deal with power plays: (1) Express your feelings, (2) describe the behavior to which you object, and (3) state a cooperative response.

present-focus conflict. Focus your conflict resolution messages on the present; avoid dredging up old grievances and unloading these on the other person (gunnysacking).

problem solving. Follow six steps when in group problem-solving situations: Define and analyze the problem, establish the criteria for evaluating solutions, identify possible solutions, evaluate solutions, select the best solution(s), and test selected solution(s).

problem-solving in conflicts. Deal with interpersonal conflicts systematically. For example, (1) define the problem, (2) examine possible solutions, (3) test the solution, (4) evaluate the solution, and (5) accept or reject the solution.

quality circles. Use the quality circle technique to improve organizational functions.

receiving. In receiving messages, focus attention on both verbal and the nonverbal signals, because both communicate meaning.

reducing uncertainty. Increase accuracy in perception by reducing your uncertainty, using passive, active, and interactive strategies.

rehearsal. Rehearse your speech often, perfect your delivery, rehearse the speech as a whole, time the speech at each rehearsal, approximate the specific speech situation as much as possible, see and think of yourself as a public speaker, and incorporate any delivery notes that may be of value during the actual speech presentation.

relationship messages. Formulate messages that are appropriate to the stage of the relationship. And listen to messages from relationship partners that may reveal differences in perception about your relationship stage.

relationship repair. Recognize the problem, engage in productive conflict resolution, pose possible solutions, affirm each other, integrate solutions into normal behavior, and take risks as appropriate.

relationship rules. Follow the rules for maintaining relationships when you do in fact wish to maintain and even strengthen them.

remembering. In remembering messages, identify the central ideas, summarize the message in an easy-to-retain form, and repeat (aloud or to yourself) key terms and names.

research. Research topics effectively and efficiently, and critically evaluate the reliability of the research material.

responding. In responding to messages, express support for the speaker using I-messages ("I didn't understand the point about . . .") instead of you-messages ("You didn't clarify what you meant about . . .").

responding to others' disclosures. Respond appropriately to the disclosures of another person by listening actively, supporting the discloser, and keeping the disclosures confidential.

restimulating brainstorming. Appropriately restimulate a brainstorming group that has lost its steam by asking for additional contributions or for further extensions of previously contributed ideas.

romantic workplace relationships. Establish romantic relationships at work only with a clear understanding of the potential problems.

selecting major propositions. After generating the possible major propositions for a speech, eliminate those that seem least important to the thesis, combine those that have a common focus, and select those most relevant to the purpose of the speech and the audience.

self-awareness. Increase self-awareness: Listen to others, increase your open self as appropriate, and seek out information (discreetly) to reduce any blind spots.

self-concept. Learn who you are: See yourself through the eyes of others; compare yourself to similar (and admired) others; examine the influences of culture; and observe, interpret, and evaluate your own message behaviors.

self-esteem. Raise your self-esteem: Challenge self-destructive beliefs, seek out nourishing people with whom to interact, work on projects that will result in success, and engage in self-affirmation.

self-fulfilling prophecy. Take a second look at your perceptions when they correspond very closely to your initial expectations; the self-fulfilling prophecy may be at work.

self-serving bias. Become mindful of any self-serving bias; that is, of giving too much weight to internal factors (when explaining your positives) and too little weight to external factors (when explaining your negatives).

sentence style. Construct sentences that are short, direct, active, and positive, and vary the type and length of sentences.

silence. Silence can communicate lots of different meanings (e.g., your anger or your need for time to think), so examine silence for meanings just as you would eye movements or body gestures.

spatial distance. Use spatial distance to signal the type of relationship you are in: intimate, personal, social, or public. Let your spatial relationships reflect your interpersonal relationships. Maintain spatial distances that are comfortable (neither too close nor too far apart) and that are appropriate to the situation and to your relationship with the other person.

speech of definition. Consider using a variety of definitions, citing credible sources, and proceeding from the known to the unknown.

speech of demonstration. Consider using a temporal pattern, employing transitions to connect the steps, presenting a broad overview and then the specific steps, and providing visual aids.

speech of description. Consider using a spatial, topic, or "5 W" organizational pattern; a variety of descriptive categories; and visual aids.

speech rate. Use variations in rate to increase communication efficiency and persuasiveness as appropriate.

stereotypes. Be careful of thinking and talking in stereotypes; recognize that members of all groups are different, and focus on the individual rather than on the individual's membership in one group or another.

supportive conflict. Engage in conflict in ways that will encourage supportiveness rather than defensiveness—avoid messages that evaluate or control, that are strategic or neutral, or that express superiority or certainty.

surface and depth listening. To listen in depth, focus on both verbal and nonverbal messages and on both content and relationship messages, and make special note of statements that refer back to the speaker. At the same time, do not avoid the surface or literal meaning.

talk, not force. Talk about your problems rather than trying to use physical or emotional force.

thesis and main ideas. Expand the thesis or main assertion of a speech by asking strategic questions to develop the main ideas or propositions.

time cues. Interpret time cues from the perspective of the other person with whom you're interacting. Be especially sensitive to leave-taking cues; for example, notice if the person comments that "It's getting late" or glances at his or her watch.

topic and purpose. Select speech topics and purposes that are appropriate to speaker, audience, and occasion, and narrow them to manageable proportions.

touch and touch avoidance. Respect the touch-avoidance tendencies of others; pay special attention to cultural and gender differences in touch preferences and in touch avoidance.

transitions. Use transitions and internal summaries to connect the parts of a speech and to help listeners remember the speech.

turn-taking cues. Respond to both the verbal and the nonverbal conversational turn-taking cues given you by others, and make your own cues clear to others.

understanding. To understand messages, relate new information to what you already know, ask questions, and paraphrase what you think the speaker said to make sure you understand.

vocal variation. Vary vocal volume and rate to best convey verbal messages; avoid a volume that is difficult to understand or a rate that is monotonous, too slow, or too fast.

win–win solutions. In interpersonal conflict, focus on win–win solutions rather than solutions in which one person wins and the other loses.

word style. Word a speech so it's clear, vivid, appropriate, and personal.

Bibliography

Acor, A. A. (2001). Employers' perceptions of persons with body art and an experimental test regarding eyebrow piercing. *Dissertation Abstracts International: Section B. The Sciences and Engineering, 61,* 3885.

Adrianson, L. (2001). Gender and computer-mediated communication: Group processes in problem solving. *Computers in Human Behavior, 17,* 71–94.

Akinnaso, F. N. (1982). On the differences between spoken and written language. *Language and Speech, 25 (Part 2),* 97–125.

Albert, R., & Nelson, G. L. (1993). Hispanic/Anglo American differences in attributions to paralinguistic behavior. *International Journal of Intercultural Relations, 17,* 19–40.

Albrecht, K. (1980). *Brain power: Learn to improve your thinking skills.* Englewood Cliffs, NJ: Prentice-Hall.

Alessandra, T. (1986). How to listen effectively. *Speaking of success* [Videotape Series]. San Diego, CA: Levitz Sommer Productions.

Altman, I. (1975). *The environment and social behavior.* Monterey, CA: Brooks/Cole.

Altman, I., & Taylor, D. (1973). *Social penetration: The development of interpersonal relationships.* New York: Holt, Rinehart & Winston.

Amato, P. R. (1994). The impact of divorce on men and women in India and the United States. *Journal of Comparative Family Studies, 25,* 207–221.

Andersen, J. F., Andersen, P. A., & Lustig, M. W. (1987, Summer). Opposite sex touch avoidance: A national replication sand extension. *Journal of Nonverbal Behavior, 11,* 89–109.

Andersen, P. A. (1991). Explaining intercultural differences in nonverbal communication. In Larry A. Samovar & Richard E. Porter (Eds.), *Intercultural communication: A reader* (6th ed., pp. 286–296). Belmont, CA: Wadsworth.

Andersen, P. A., & Leibowitz, K. (1978). The development and nature of the construct of touch avoidance. *Environmental Psychology and Nonverbal Behavior, 3,* 89–106.

Anderson, C. J. & Fisher, C. (1991, August). Male-female relationships in the workplace: Perceived motivations in office romance. *Sex Roles 25,* 163–180.

Angier, N. (1995, May 9). Scientists mull role of empathy in man and beast. *The New York Times,* pp. C1, C6.

Argyle, M. (1988). *Bodily communication* (2nd ed.). New York: Methuen.

Argyle, M., & Henderson, M. (1985). *The anatomy of relationships: And the rules and skills needed to manage them successfully.* London: Heinemann.

Argyle, M., & Ingham, R. (1972). Gaze, mutual gaze and distance. *Semiotica, 1,* 32–49.

Aronson, E., Wilson, T. D., & Akert, R. M. (2002). *Social psychology: The heart and the mind* (4th ed.). New York: Longman.

Aronson, J., Cohen, J., & Nail, P. (1998). Self-affirmation theory: An update and appraisal. In E. Harmon-Jones & J. S. Mills (Eds.), *Cognitive dissonance theory: Revival with revisions and controversies* (pp. 127–147). Washington, DC: American Psychological Association.

Asch, Solomon. (1946). Forming impressions of personality. *Journal of Abnormal and Social Psychology, 41,* 258–290.

Aune, R. Kelly, & Kikuchi, Toshiyuki. (1993). Effects of language intensity similarity on perceptions of credibility, relational attributions, and persuasion. *Journal of Language and Social Psychology, 12,* 224–238.

Authier, J. & Gustafson, K. (1982). Microtraining: Focusing on specific skills. In Eldon K. Marshall, P. David Kurtz, & Associates, *Interpersonal helping skills: A guide to training methods, programs, and resources,* (pp. 93–130). San Francisco: Jossey-Bass.

Axtell, Roger E. (1990). *Do's and taboos of hosting international visitors.* New York: Wiley.

Axtell, Roger E. (1991). *Do's and taboos of public speaking: How to get those butterflies flying in formation.* New York: Wiley.

Axtell, Roger. (1993). *Do's and taboos around the world* (3rd ed.). New York: Wiley.

Ayres, J. (1986). Perceptions of speaking ability: An explanation for stage fright. *Communication Education, 35,* 275–287.

Ayres, Joe, & Hopf, Tim. (1993). *Coping with speech anxiety.* Norwood, NJ: Ablex.

Ayres, J., & Hopf, T. (1995). An assessment of the role of communication apprehension in communicating with the terminally ill. *Communication Research Reports, 12,* 227–234.

Bach, G. R., & Wyden, P. (1968). *The intimate enemy.* New York: Avon.

Baringer, D. K., & McCroskey, J. C. (2000). Immediacy in the classroom: Student immediacy. *Communication Education, 49,* 178–186.

Barker, L. L. (1990). *Communication* (5th ed.). Englewood Cliffs, NJ: Prentice-Hall.

Barker, L., Edwards, R., Gaines, C., Gladney, K., & Holley, F. (1980). An investigation of proportional time spent in various communication activities by college students. *Journal of Applied Communication Research, 8,* 101–109.

Barna, L. M. (1988). Stumbling blocks in intercultural communication. In L. A. Samovar & R. E. Porter (Eds.), *Intercultural communication: A reader* (5th ed., pp. 322–330). Belmont, CA: Wadsworth.

Barnlund, D. C. (1970). A transactional model of communication. In J. Akin, A. Goldberg, G. Myers, & J. Stewart (Eds.), *Language behavior: A book of readings in communication.* The Hague: Mouton.

Barnlund, Dean C. (1975). Communicative styles in two cultures: Japan and the United States. In A. Kendon, R. M. Harris, & M. R. Key (Eds.), *Organization of behavior in face-to-face interaction.* The Hague: Mouton.

Barnlund, D. C. (1989). *Communicative styles of Japanese and Americans: Images and realities.* Belmont, CA: Wadsworth.

Barrett, L., & Godfrey, T. (1988, November). Listening. *Person Centered Review, 3,* 410–425.

Bartholomew, K. (1990). Avoidance of intimacy: An attachment perspective. *Journal of Social and Personal Relationships, 7,* 147–178.

Basso, K. H. (1972). To give up on words: Silence in Apache culture. In Pier Paolo Giglioli (Ed.), *Language and social context.* New York: Penguin.

Baumeister, R. F., Bushman, B. J., & Campbell, W. K. (2000). Self-esteem, narcissism, and aggression: Does violence result from low self-esteem or from threatened egotism? *Current Directions in Psychological Science, 9,* Issue 1.

Bavelas, J. B. (1990). Can one not communicate? Behaving and communicating: A reply to Motley. *Western Journal of Speech Communication, 54,* 593–602.

Baxter, L. A. (1983). Relationship disengagement: An examination of the reversal hypothesis. *Western Journal of Speech Communication, 47,* 85–98.

Baxter, L. A. (1984). An investigation of compliance-gaining as politeness. *Human Communication Research, 10,* 427–456.

Baxter, L. A. (1988). A dialectical perspective on communication strategies in relationship development. In S. W. Duck (Ed.), *Handbook of Personal Relationships.* New York: Wiley.

Baxter, L. A. (1990). Dialectical contradictions in relationship development. *Journal of Social and Personal Relationships, 7,* 69–88.

Baxter, L. A., & Bullis, C. (1986). Turning points in developing romantic relationships. *Human Communication Research, 12,* 469–493.

Baxter, L. A., & Simon, E. P. (1993). Relationship maintenance strategies and dialectical contradictions in personal relationships. *Journal of Social and Personal Relationships, 10,* 225–242.

Baxter, L. A., & Wilmot, W. W. (1984). "Secret tests": Social strategies for acquiring information about the state of the relationship. *Human Communication Research, 11,* 171–201.

Beatty, M. J. (1988). Situational and predispositional correlates of public speaking anxiety. *Communication Education, 37,* 28–39.

Beck, A. T. (1988). *Love is never enough.* New York: Harper & Row.

Beebe, S. A., & Masterson, J. T. (2000). *Communicating in small groups: Principles and practices* (6th ed.). Glenview, IL: Scott, Foresman.

Beier, E. (1974). How we send emotional messages. *Psychology Today, 8,* 53–56.

Bell, R. A., & Buerkel-Rothfuss, Nancy L. (1990). S(he) loves me, s(he) loves me not: Predictors of relational information-seeking in courtship and beyond. *Communication Quarterly, 38,* 64–82.

Bell, R. A., & Daly, J. A. (1984). The affinity-seeking function of communication. *Communication Monographs, 51,* 91–115.

Benne, K. D., & Sheats, P. (1948). Functional roles of group members. *Journal of Social Issues, 4,* 41–49.

Bennis, W., & Nanus, B. (1985). *Leaders: The strategies for taking charge.* New York: Harper & Row.

Berg, J. H., & Archer, R. L. (1983). The disclosure–liking relationship. *Human Communication Research, 10,* 269–281.

Berger, C. R., & Bradac, J. J. (1982). *Language and social knowledge: Uncertainty in interpersonal relations.* London: Edward Arnold.

Berger, C. R., & Calabrese, R. J. (1975). Some explorations in initial interaction and beyond: Toward a theory of interpersonal communication. *Human Communication Research, 1,* 99–112.

Berman, J. J., Murphy-Berman, V., & Singh, P. (1985). Cross-cultural similarities and differences in perceptions of fairness. *Journal of Cross-Cultural Psychology, 16,* 55–67.

Bernstein, W. M., Stephan, W. G., & Davis, M. H. (1979). Explaining attributions for achievement: A path analytic approach. *Journal of Personality and Social Psychology, 37,* 1810–1821.

Berscheid, E., & Hatfield, W. E. (1978). *Interpersonal attraction* (2nd ed.). Reading, MA: Addison-Wesley.

Berscheid, E., & Reis, H. T. (1998). Attraction and close relationships. In D. Gilbert, S. Fiske, & G. Lindzey (Eds.), *The Handbook of Social Psychology,* 4th ed. (Vol. 2, pp. 193–281).

Blake, R. R., & Mouton, J. S. (1984). *The managerial grid III* (3rd ed.) Houston, TX: Gulf Publishing.

Blieszner, R., & Adams, R. G. (1992). *Adult friendship.* Newbury Park, CA: Sage.

Blumstein, P., & Schwartz, P. (1983). *American couples: Money, work, sex.* New York: Morrow.

Bochner, A. (1984). The functions of human communication in interpersonal bonding. In C. C. Arnold & J. W. Bowers (Eds.), *Handbook of rhetorical and communication theory.* Boston: Allyn & Bacon.

Bochner, A., & Kelly, C. (1974). Interpersonal competence: Rationale, philosophy, and implementation of a conceptual framework. *Communication Education, 23,* 279–301.

Bochner, S., & Hesketh, B. (1994). Power distance, individualism/collectivism, and job-related attitudes in a culturally diverse work group. *Journal of Cross-Cultural Psychology, 25,* 233–257.

Bok, S. (1978). *Lying: Moral choice in public and private life.* New York: Pantheon.

Bok, S. (1983). *Secrets.* New York: Vintage.

Borden, G. A. (1991). *Cultural orientation: An approach to understanding intercultural communication.* Englewood Cliffs, NJ: Prentice-Hall.

Bourland, D. D., Jr. (1965–66). A linguistic note: Writing in E-prime. *General Semantics Bulletin, 32–33,* 111–114.

Bourland, D. D., Jr., & Johnston, P. D. (Eds.). (1998). *E-prime III! A third anthology.* Concord, CA: International Society for General Semantics.

Bower, B. (2001). Self-illusions come back to bite students. *Science News, 159,* 148.

Bransford, J. D., & Stein, B. S. (1993). *The ideal problem solver* (2nd ed.). New York: W. H. Freeman.

Brant, C. C. (1990). Native ethics and rules of behavior. *Canadian Journal of Psychiatry, 35,* 534–539.

Brauer, M., Judd, C. M, & Gliner, M. D. (1995, June). The effects of repeated expressions on attitude polarization during group discussions. *Journal of Personality and Social Psychology, 68,* 1014–1029.

Bravo, E., & Cassedy, E. (1992). *The 9 to 5 guide to combating sexual harassment.* New York: Wiley.

Brennan, M. (1991). Mismanagement and quality circles: How middle managers influence direct participation. *Employee Relations, 13,* 22–32.

Bridges, C. R. (1996). The characteristics of career achievement perceived by African American college administrators. *Journal of Black Studies, 26,* 748–767.

Brilhart, J., & Galanes, G. (1992). *Effective group discussion* (7th ed.). Dubuque, IA: Brown & Benchmark.

Brody, J. E. (1991, April 28). How to foster self-esteem. *The New York Times Magazine, 15,* 26–27.

Brody, J. E. (1994, March 21). Notions of beauty transcend culture, new study suggests. *The New York Times,* p. A14.

Brody, J. E. (2000, April 25). Memories of things that never were. *The New York Times,* p. F8.

Brown, C. T., & Keller, P. W. (1979). *Monologue to dialogue: An exploration of interpersonal communication* (2nd ed.). Englewood Cliffs, NJ: Prentice-Hall.

Brown, P. (1980). How and why are women more polite: Some evidence from a Mayan community. In S. McConnell-Ginet, R. Borker, & M. Furman (Eds.), *Women and language in literature and society* (pp. 111–136). New York: Praeger.

Brown, P., & Levinson, S. C. (1987). *Politeness: Some universals of language usage.* Cambridge, England: Cambridge University Press.

Brownell, J. (1987). Listening: The toughest management skill. *Cornell Hotel and Restaurant Administration Quarterly, 27,* 64–71.

Brownell, J. (2002). *Listening: Attitudes, principles, and skills* (2nd ed.). Boston: Allyn & Bacon.

Bruneau, T. (1985). The time dimension in intercultural communication. In L. A. Samovar & R. E. Porter (Eds.), *Intercultural communication: A reader* (4th ed., pp. 280–289). Belmont, CA: Wadsworth.

Bruneau, T. (1990). Chronemics: The study of time in human interaction. In J. A. DeVito & M. L. Hecht (Eds.), *The nonverbal communication reader* (pp. 301–311). Prospect Heights, IL: Waveland Press.

Buber, M. (1958). *I and thou* (2nd ed.). New York: Scribners.

Buchholz, E. (1998). The call of solitude. *Psychology Today, 31,* 50–54, 80, 82.

Bull, R., & Rumsey, N. (1988). *The social psychology of facial appearance.* New York: Springer.

Buller, D. B., & Aune, R. K. (1992). The effects of speech rate similarity on compliance: Application of communication accommodation theory. *Western Journal of Communication, 56,* 37–53.

Buller, D. B., LePoire, B. A., Aune, K., & Eloy, S. (1992). Social perceptions as mediators of the effect of speech rate similarity on compliance. *Human Communication Research, 19,* 286–311.

Bumby, K. M., & Hansen, D. J. (1997). Intimacy deficits, fear of intimacy, and loneliness among sexual offenders. *Criminal Justice and Behavior, 24,* 315–331.

Burgoon, J. K., & Bacue, A. E. (2003). Nonverbal communication skills. In J. O. Greene & B. R. Burleson (Eds.), *Handbook of communication and social interaction skills* (pp. 179–220). Mahwah, NJ: Erlbaum.

Burgoon, J. K., Berger, C. R., & Waldron, V. R. (2000). Mindfulness and interpersonal communication. *Journal of Social Issues, 56,* 105–127.

Burgoon, J. K., Buller, D. B., & Woodall, W. G. (1996). *Nonverbal communication: The unspoken dialogue* (2nd ed.). New York: McGraw-Hill.

Burgoon, J. K., & Hale, J. L. (1988). Nonverbal expectancy violations: Model elaboration and application to immediacy behaviors. *Communication Monographs, 55,* 58–79.

Burgoon, J. K., & Hoobler, G. D. (2002). Nonverbal signals. In M. L. Knapp & J. A. Daly (Eds.), *Handbook of interpersonal communication* (3rd ed., pp. 240–299). Thousand Oaks, CA: Sage.

Bush, George. (1988, October 15). Acceptance speech. *Vital Speeches of the Day,* 55.

Bushman, B. J., & Baumeister, R. F. (1998). Threatened egotism, narcissism, self-esteem, and direct and displaced aggression: Does self-love or self-hate lead to violence? *Journal of Personality and Social Psychology, 75,* 219–229.

Butler, P. E. (1981). *Talking to yourself: Learning the language of self-support.* New York: Harper & Row.

Butler, J., Pryor, B., & Grieder, M. (1998, February). Impression formation as a function of male baldness. *Perceptual and Motor Skills, 86,* 347–350.

Byers, E. S., & Demmons, S. (1999). Sexual satisfaction and sexual self-disclosure within dating relationships. *Journal of Sex Research, 36,* 180–189.

Cai, D. A., & Fink, E. L. (2002, March). Conflict style differences between individualists and collectivists. *Communication Monographs, 69,* 67–87.

Cappella, J. N. (1993). The facial feedback hypothesis in human interaction: Review and speculation. *Journal of Language and Social Psychology, 12,* 13–29.

Castleberry, S. B., & Shepherd, C. D. (1993). Effective interpersonal listening and personal selling. *Journal of Personal Selling and Sales Management, 13,* 35–49.

Cate, R. J., Henton, J., Koval, R., Christopher, & Lloyd, S. (1982). Premarital abuse: A social psychological perspective. *Journal of Family Issues, 3,* 79–90.

Cathcart, D., & Cathcart, R. (1985). Japanese social experience and concept of groups. In L. A. Samovar & R. E. Porter (Eds.), *Intercultural communication: A reader* (4th ed., pp. 190–197). Belmont, CA: Wadsworth.

Cawthon, S. W. (2001). Teaching strategies in inclusive classrooms with deaf students. *Journal of Deaf Studies and Deaf Education, 6,* 212–225.

Chang, H., & Holt, G. R. (1996). The changing Chinese interpersonal world: Popular themes in interpersonal communication books in modern Taiwan. *Communication Quarterly, 44,* 85–106.

Chanowitz, B., & Langer, E. (1981). Premature cognitive commitment. *Journal of Personality and Social Psychology, 41,* 1051–1063.

Chen, G. M. (1992). *Differences in self-disclosure patterns among Americans versus Chinese: A comparative study.* Paper presented at the annual meeting of the Eastern Communication Association, Portland, ME.

Chung, L. C., & Ting-Toomey, S. (1999, Spring). Ethnic identity and relational expectations among Asian Americans. *Communication Research Reports, 16,* 157–166.

Cialdini, R. T. (1984). *Influence: How and why people agree to things.* New York: Morrow.

Cialdini, R. T., & Ascani, K. (1976). Test of a concession procedure for inducing verbal, behavioral, and further compliance with a request to give blood. *Journal of Applied Psychology, 61,* 295–300.

Clark, Herbert. (1974). The power of positive speaking. *Psychology Today, 8,* 102, 108–111.

Cline, M. G. (1956). The influence of social context on the perception of faces. *Journal of Personality, 2,* 142–185.

Coates, J., & Cameron, D. (1989). *Women, men, and language: Studies in language and linguistics.* London: Longman.

Cohen, J. (2002, May 9). An e-mail affliction: The long goodbye. *The New York Times,* p. G6.

Coleman, P. (2002). *How to say it for couples: Communicating with tenderness, openness, and honesty.* Paramus, NJ: Prentice-Hall.

Collier, M. J. (1991). Conflict competence within African, Mexican, and Anglo American friendships. In Stella Ting-Toomey & Felipe Korzenny (Eds.), *Cross-cultural interpersonal communication* (pp. 132–154). Newbury Park, CA: Sage.

Collins, J. E., & Clark, L. F. (1989). Responsibility and rumination: The trouble with understanding the dissolution of a relationship. *Social Cognition, 7,* 152–173.

Comadena, M. E. (1984). Brainstorming groups: Ambiguity tolerance, communication apprehension, task attraction, and individual productivity. *Small Group Behavior, 15,* 251–254.

Comer, L. B., & Drollinger, T. (1999). Active emphatic listening and selling success: A conceptual framework. *Journal of Personal Selling and Sales Management, 19,* 15–29.

Cook, M. (1971). *Interpersonal perception.* Baltimore: Penguin.

Cooley, C. Horton. (1922). *Human nature and the social order* (Rev. ed.). New York: Scribners.

Coombes, A. (2003, June 30). E-termination: Employees are getting fired for e-mail infractions. Retrieved July 14, 2003, from CBS.MarketWatch.com.

Cooper, A., & Sportolari, L. (1997). Romance in cyberspace: Understanding online attraction. *Journal of Sex Education and Therapy, 22,* 7–14.

Coover, G. E., & Murphy, S. T. (2000). The communicated self: Exploring the interaction between self and social context. *Human Communication Research, 26,* 125–147.

Cornwell, B., & Lundgren, D. C. (2001). Love on the Internet: Involvement and misrepresentation in romantic relationships in cyberspace vs. realspace. *Computers in Human Behavior, 17,* 197–211.

Cragan, J. F., & Wright, D. W. (1990). Small group communication research of the 1980s: A synthesis and critique. *Communication Studies, 41,* 212–236.

Crawford, M. (1994, October). Rethinking the romance: Teaching the content and function of gender stereotypes in the Psychology of Women course. *Teaching of Psychology, 21,* 151–153.

Crohn, J. (1995). *Mixed matches.* New York: Fawcett.

Crowley, A. (1999, August 30). Project leaders wanted. *PC Week,* 76.

Davis, M. S. (1973). *Intimate relations.* New York: Free Press.

Davison, W. P. (1983). The third-person effects and the differential impact in negative political advertising. *Journalism Quarterly, 68,* 680–688.

Davitz, J. R. (Ed.). (1964). *The communication of emotional meaning.* New York: McGraw-Hill.

Deal, J. E., & Smith Wampler, K. (1986). Dating violence: The primacy of previous experience. *Journal of Social and Personal Relationships, 3,* 457–471.

deBono, E. (1976). *Teaching thinking.* New York: Penguin.

deBono, E. (1987). *The six thinking hats.* New York: Penguin.

DeJong, W. (1979). An examination of self perception mediation of the foot-in-the door effect. *Journal of Personality and Social Psychology, 37,* 2221–2239.

Derlega, V. J., Winstead, B. A., & Wong, P. T. P., & Greenspan, M. (1987). Self-disclosure and relationship development: An attributional analysis. In M. E. Roloff & G. R. Miller (Eds.), *Interpersonal Processes: New Directions in Communication Research* (pp. 172–187). Thousand Oaks, CA: Sage.

Derlega, V. J., Winstead, B., Wong, P. T. P., & Hunter, S. (1985). Gender effects in an initial encounter: A case where men exceed women in disclosure. *Journal of Social and Personal Relationships, 2,* 25–44.

DeStephen, R., & Hirokawa, R. (1988). Small group consensus: Stability of group support of the decision, task process, and group relationships. *Small Group Behavior, 19,* 227–239.

DeTurck, M. A. (1987). When communication fails: Physical aggression as a compliance-gaining strategy. *Communication Monographs, 54,* 106–112.

DeVito, J. A. (1965). Comprehension factors in oral and written discourse of skilled communicators. *Communication Monographs, 32,* 124–128.

DeVito, J. A. (1976). Relative ease in comprehending yes/no questions. In J. Blankenship & H. G. Stelzner (Eds.), *Rhetoric and communication* (pp. 143–154). Urbana: University of Illinois Press.

DeVito, J. A. (1981). *The psychology of speech and language: An introduction to psycholinguistics.* Washington, DC: University Press of America.

DeVito, J. A. (1989). *The nonverbal communication workbook.* Prospect Heights, IL: Waveland Press.

DeVito, J. A. (1996a). *Brainstorms: How to think more creatively about communication (or about anything else).* New York: Longman.

DeVito, J. A. (1996b). *Messages: Building interpersonal communication skills* (3rd ed.). New York: Longman.

DeVito, J. A., & Hecht, M. L. (Eds.). (1990). *The nonverbal communication reader.* Prospect Heights, IL: Waveland Press.

Diener, E., & Walbom, M. (1976). Effects of self-awareness on antinormative behavior. *Journal of Research in Personality, 10,* 107–111.

Dindia, K., & Fitzpatrick, M. A. (1985). Marital communication: Three approaches compared. In S. Duck & D. Perlman (Eds.), *Understanding personal relationships: An interdisciplinary approach* (pp. 137–158). Newbury Park, CA: Sage.

Dion, K., Berscheid, E., & Walster, E. (1972). What is beautiful is good. *Journal of Personality and Social Psychology, 24,* 285–290.

Dodd, C. H. (1995). *Dynamics of intercultural communication.* Dubuque, IA: William C. Brown.

Dolgin, K. G., Meyer, L., & Schwartz, J. (1991). Effects of gender, target's gender, topic, and self-esteem on disclosure to best and middling friends. *Sex Roles, 25,* 311–329.

Donahue, W. A., with Kolt, R. (1992). *Managing interpersonal conflict.* Thousand Oaks, CA: Sage.

Dosey, M., & Meisels, M. (1969). Personal space and self-protection. *Journal of Personality and Social Psychology, 38,* 959–965.

Dovidio, J. F., Gaertner, S. E., Kawakami, K., & Hodson, G. (2002). Why can't we just get along? Interpersonal biases and interracial distrust. *Cultural Diversity and Ethnic Minority Psychology, 8,* 88–102.

Doyle, T., & Barr, L. R. (2004). *Research Navigator Guide.* Boston: Allyn & Bacon.

Dresser, N. (1996). *Multicultural manners: New rules of etiquette for a changing society.* New York: Wiley.

Drews, D. R., Allison, C. K., & Probst, J. R. (2000). Behavioral and self-concept differences in tattooed and nontattooed college students. *Psychological Reports, 86,* 475–481.

Dreyfuss, H. (1971). *Symbol sourcebook.* New York: McGraw-Hill.

Driskell, J., Olmstead, B., & Salas, E. (1993). Task cues, dominance cues, and influence in task groups. *Journal of Applied Psychology, 78,* 51–60.

Dsilva, M., & Whyte, L. O. (1998). Cultural differences in conflict styles: Vietnamese refugees and established residents. *The Howard Journal of Communication, 9,* 57–68.

Duck, S. (1986). *Human relationships.* Thousand Oaks, CA: Sage.

Eden, D. (1992). Leadership and expectations: Pygmalion effects and other self-fulfilling prophecies in organizations. *Leadership Quarterly, 3,* 271–305.

Ehrenhaus, P. (1988). Silence and symbolic expression. *Communication Monographs, 55,* 41–57.

Einstein, E. (1995). Success or sabotage: Which self-fulfilling prophecy will the stepfamily create? In D. K. Huntley (Ed.), *Understanding stepfamilies: Implications for assessment and treatment.* Alexandria, VA: American Counseling Association.

Ekman, P. (1965). Communication through nonverbal behavior: A source of information about an interpersonal relationship. In S. S. Tomkins & C. E. Izard (Eds.), *Affect, cognition and personality.* New York: Springer.

Ekman, P. (1985). *Telling lies: Clues to deceit in the marketplace, politics, and marriage.* New York: Norton.

Ekman, P., & Friesen, W. V. (1969). The repertoire of nonverbal behavior: Categories, origins, usage, and coding. *Semiotica, 1,* 49–98.

Ekman, P., Friesen, W. V., & Ellsworth, P. (1972). *Emotion in the human face: Guidelines for research and an integration of findings.* New York: Pergamon Press.

Elfenbein, H. A., & Ambady, N. (2002). Is there an in-group advantage in emotion recognition? *Psychological Bulletin, 128,* 243–249.

Ellis, A. (1988). *How to stubbornly refuse to make yourself miserable about anything, yes anything.* Secaucus, NJ: Lyle Stuart.

Ellis, A., & Harper, R. A. (1975). *A new guide to rational living.* Hollywood, CA: Wilshire Books.

Elmes, M. B., & Gemmill, G. (1990). The psychodynamics of mindlessness and dissent in small groups. *Small Group Research, 21,* 28–44.

Esten, G., & Willmott, L. (1993). Double-bind messages: The effects of attitude towards disability on therapy. *Women and Therapy, 14,* 29–41.

Exline, R. V., Ellyson, S. L., & Long, B. (1975). Visual behavior as an aspect of power role relationships. In P. Pliner, L. Krames, & T. Alloway (Eds.), *Nonverbal communication of aggression.* New York: Plenum Press.

Fengler, A. P. (1974). Romantic love in courtship: Divergent paths of male and female students. *Journal of Comparative Family Studies,* 134–139.

Feraco, F. J. (1997). *Vital Speeches of the Day, 64,* 157–160.

Festinger, L. (1954). A theory of social comparison processes. *Human Relations, 7,* 117–140.

Field, R. H. G. (1989). The self-fulfilling prophecy leader: Achieving the metharme effect. *Journal of Management Studies, 26,* 151–175.

Fielder, F. E. (1967). *A theory of leadership effectiveness.* New York: McGraw-Hill.

Fischer, C. S., & Oliker, S. J. (1983). A research note on friendship, gender, and the life cycle. *Social Forces, 62,* 124–133.

Fodor, I. G., & Collier, J. C. (2001). Assertiveness and conflict resolution: An integrated Gestalt/cognitive behavioral model for working with urban adolescents. In M. McConville & G. Wheeler (Eds.), *The heart of development: Vol. II. Adolescence: Gestalt approaches to working with children, adolescents and their worlds* (pp. 214–252). Cambridge, ME: Analytic Press.

Folger, J. P., Poole, M. S., & Stutman, R. K. (1997). *Working through conflict: A communication perspective* (3rd ed.). New York: Longman.

Forbes, G. B. (2001). College students with tattoos and piercings: Motives, family experiences, personality factors, and perception by others. *Psychological Reports, 89,* 774–786.

Franklin, C. W., & Mizell, C. A. (1995). Some factors influencing success among African-American men: A preliminary study. *Journal of Men's Studies, 3,* 191–204.

Fraser, B. (1990). Perspectives on politeness. *Journal of Pragmatics, 14,* 219–236.

Frazier, P. A., & Cook, S. W. (1993). Correlates of distress following heterosexual relationship dissolution. *Journal of Social and Personal Relationships, 10,* 55–67.

Freedman, J. (1978). *Happy people: What happiness is, who has it, and why.* New York: Ballantine.

Freedman, J., & Fraser, S. (1966). Compliance without pressure: The foot-in-the door technique. *Journal of Personality and Social Psychology, 4,* 195–202.

Frey, K. J., & Eagly, A. H. (1993, July). Vividness can undermine the persuasiveness of messages. *Journal of Personality and Social Psychology, 65,* 32–44.

Friedkin, N. E. (1999, December). Choice shift and group polarization. *American Sociological Review, 64,* 856–875.

Furlow, F. B. (1996). The smell of love. *Psychology Today,* 38–45.

Furnham, A., & Bitar, N. (1993). The stereotyped portrayal of men and women in British television advertisements. *Sex Roles, 29,* 297–310.

Galvin, K., Bylund, C., & Brommel, B. J. (2004). *Family communication: Cohesion and change* (6th ed.). New York: Longman.

Gamble, T. K., & Gamble, M. W. (2003). *The gender communication connection.* Boston: Houghton Mifflin.

Gao, G., & Gudykunst, W. B. (1995). Attributional confidence, perceived similarity, and network involvement in Chinese and American romantic relationships. *Communication Quarterly, 43,* 431–445.

Gelfand, M. J., Nishii, L. H., Holcombe, K. M., Dyer, N., Ohbuchi, K., & Fukuno, M. (2001). Cultural influences on cognitive representations of conflict: Interpretations of conflict episodes in the United States and Japan. *Journal of Applied Psychology, 86,* 1059–1074.

Gelles, R., & Cornell, C. (1985). *Intimate violence in families.* Newbury Park, CA: Sage.

Giles, H., Mulac, A., Bradac, J. J., & Johnson, P. (1987). Speech accommodation theory: The first decade and beyond. In Margaret L. McLaughlin (Ed.), *Communication yearbook 10* (pp. 13–48). Thousand Oaks, CA: Sage.

Gladstone, G. L., & Parker, G. B. (2002, June). When you're smiling, does the whole world smile for you? *Australasian Psychiatry, 10,* 144–146.

Glucksberg, S., & Danks, J. H. (1975). *Experimental psycholinguistics: An introduction.* Hillsdale, NJ: Erlbaum.

Goffman, E. (1967). *Interaction ritual: Essays on face-to-face behavior.* New York: Pantheon.

Goffman, E. (1971). *Relations in public: Microstudies of the public order.* New York: HarperCollins.

Goldin-Meadow, S., Nusbaum, H., Kelly, S. D., & Wagner, S. (2001). Gesture—psychological aspects. *Psychological Science, 12,* 516–522.

Goldsmith, D. J., & Fulf, P. A. (1999). "You just don't have the evidence": An analysis of claims and evidence. In M. E. Roloff (Ed.), *Communication yearbook 22* (pp. 1–49). Thousand Oaks, CA: Sage.

Goleman, D. (1992, Oct. 27). Voters assailed by unfair persuasion. *The New York Times,* pp. C1, C8.

Goleman, D. (1995a). *Emotional intelligence.* New York: Bantam.

Goleman, D. (1995b). For man and beast, language of love shares many traits. *The New York Times,* pp. C1, C9.

Gonzalez, A., & Zimbardo, P. G. (1985). Time in perspective. *Psychology Today, 19,* 20–26.

Goode, E. (2000, August 8). "How Culture Molds Habits of Thought," *The New York Times,* F1, F8.

Goodwin, R., & Lee, I. (1994). Taboo topics among Chinese and English friends: A cross-cultural comparison. *Journal of Cross-Cultural Psychology, 25,* 325–338.

Gorden, W. I., & Nevins, R. J. (1993). *We mean business: Building communication competence in business and professions.* New York: HarperCollins.

Gordon, T. (1975). *P.E.T.: Parent effectiveness training.* New York: New American Library.

Gosling, S. D., Ko, S. J., Mannarelli, T., & Morris, M. E. (2002, March). A room with a cue: Personality judgments based on offices and bedrooms. *Journal of Personality and Social Psychology, 82,* 379–398.

Goss, B., Thompson, M., & Olds, S. (1978). Behavioral support for systematic desensitization for communication apprehension. *Human Communication Research, 4,* 158–163.

Gottman, J. (1994). What makes marriage work? *Psychology Today, 27,* 38–43, 68.

Graham, E. E. (1994). Interpersonal communication motives scale. In R. B. Rubin, P. Palmgreen, & H. E. Sypher (Eds.), *Communication research measures: A sourcebook* (pp. 211–216). New York, Guilford.

Graham, E. E. (1997). Turning points and commitment in post-divorce relationships. *Communication Monographs, 64,* 350–368.

Graham, E. E., Barbato, C. A., & Perse, E. M. (1993). The interpersonal communication motives model. *Communication Quarterly, 41,* 172–186.

Graham, J. A., & Argyle, M. (1975). The effects of different patterns of gaze combined with different facial expressions on impression formation. *Journal of Movement Studies, 1,* 178–182.

Graham, J. A., Bitti, P. R., & Argyle, M. (1975). A cross-cultural study of the communication of emotion by facial and gestural cues. *Journal of Human Movement Studies, 1,* 68–77.

Greene, J. O., & Burleson, B. R. (Eds.). (2003). *Handbook of communication and social interaction skills.* Mahwah, NJ: Erlbaum.

Griffin, E., & Sparks, G. G. (1990). Friends forever: A longitudinal exploration of intimacy in same-sex friends and platonic pairs. *Journal of Social and Personal Relationships, 7,* 29–46.

Gross, L. (1991). The contested closet: The ethics and politics of outing. *Critical Studies in Mass Communication, 8,* 352–388.

Gu, Y. (1997). Polite phenomena in modern Chinese. *Journal of Pragmatics, 14,* 237–257.

Gudykunst, W. B. (1994). *Bridging differences: Effective intergroup communication* (2nd ed.). Newbury Park, CA: Sage.

Gudykunst, W. B. (Ed.). (1983). *Intercultural communication theory: Current perspectives.* Newbury Park, CA: Sage.

Gudykunst, W. B., & Kim, Y. Y. (1984). *Communicating with strangers: An approach to intercultural communication.* New York: Random House.

Gudykunst, W. B., & Kim, Y. Y. (Eds.). (1992). *Readings on communication with strangers: An approach to intercultural communication.* New York: McGraw-Hill.

Gudykunst, W. B., & Nishida, T. (1984). Individual and cultural influence on uncertainty reduction. *Communication Monographs, 51,* 23–36.

Gudykunst, W. B., Nishida, T., & Chua, E. (1987). Perceptions of social penetration in Japanese-North American dyads. *International Journal of Intercultural Relations, 11,* 171–189.

Gudykunst, W. B., Yang, S., & Nishida, T. (1985). A cross-cultural test of uncertainty reduction theory: Comparisons of acquaintance, friend, and dating relationships in Japan, Korea, and the United States. *Human Communication Research, 11,* 407–454.

Guerrero, L. K., & Andersen, P. A. (1991). The waxing and waning of relational intimacy: Touch as a function of relational stage, gender and touch avoidance. *Journal of Social and Personal Relationships, 8,* 147–165.

Gupta, U., & Singh, P. (1982). Exploratory studies in love and liking and types of marriages. *Indian Journal of Applied Psychology, 19,* 92–97.

Haar, B. F., & Krabe, B. (1999). Strategies for resolving interpersonal conflicts in adolescence: A German–Indonesian comparison. *Journal of Cross-Cultural Psychology, 30,* 667–683.

Haga, Y. (1988). Traits de langage et caractère Japonais. *Cahiers de Sociologie Economique et Culturelle, 9,* 105–109.

Hall, E. T. (1959). *The silent language.* Garden City, NY: Doubleday.

Hall, E. T. (1963). A system for the notation of proxemic behavior. *American Anthropologist, 65,* 1003–1026.

Hall, E. T. (1966). *The hidden dimension.* Garden City, NY: Doubleday.

Hall, E. T. (1976). *Beyond culture.* Garden City, NY: Doubleday.

Hall, E. T., & Hall, M. R. (1987). *Hidden differences: Doing business with the Japanese.* Garden City, NY: Doubleday.

Hall, J. A. (1984). *Nonverbal sex differences.* Baltimore: Johns Hopkins University Press.

Hall, J. A. (1998). How big are nonverbal sex differences? The case of smiling and sensitivity to nonverbal cues. In D. J. Canary & K. Dindia (Eds.), *Sex differences and similarities in communication: Critical essays and empirical investigations of sex and gender in interaction* (pp. 155–178). Mahwah, NJ: Erlbaum.

Hall, J. K. (1993). Tengo una bomba: The paralinguistic and linguistic conventions of the oral practice Chismeando. *Research on Language and Social Interaction, 26,* 55–83.

Hambrick, R. S. (1991). *The management skills builder: Self-directed learning strategies for career development.* New York: Praeger.

Hammer, M. R. (1986). The influence of ethnic and attitude similarity on initial social penetration. In Kim, Y. Y. (Ed.), *Interethnic communication: Current research. International and intercultural communication annual, 10,* 225–237.

Han, G., & Park, B. (1995). Children's choice in conflict: Application of the theory of individualism–collectivism. *Journal of Cross-Cultural Psychology, 26,* 298–313.

Haney, W. (1973). *Communication and organizational behavior: Text and cases* (3rd ed.). Homewood, IL: Irwin.

Hart, F. (1990). The construction of masculinity in men's friendships: Misogyny, heterosexuality, and homophobia. *Resources for Feminist Research, 19,* 60–67.

Hart, R. P., Carlson, R. E., & Eadie, W. F. (1980). Attitudes toward communication and the assessment of rhetorical sensitivity. *Communication Monographs, 47,* 1–22.

Harvey, J. H., Flanary, R., & Morgan, M. (1986). Vivid memories of vivid loves gone by. *Journal of Social and Personal Relationships, 3,* 359–373.

Hatfield, E., & Rapson, R. L. (1992). Similarity and attraction in close relationships. *Communication Monographs, 59,* 209–212.

Hatfield, E., & Rapson, R. L. (1996). *Love and sex: Cross-cultural perspectives.* Boston: Allyn & Bacon.

Hatfield, E., & Traupman, J. (1981). Intimate relationships: A perspective from equity theory. In S. Duck & R. Gilmour (Eds.), *Personal relationships: Vol. 1. Studying personal relationships* (pp. 165–178). New York: Academic Press.

Hayakawa, S. I., & Hayakaws, A. R. (1989). *Language in thought and action* (5th ed.). New York: Harcourt Brace Jovanovich.

Hays, R. B. (1989). The day-to-day functioning of close versus casual friendships. *Journal of Social and Personal Relationships, 6,* 21–37.

Hecht, M. L. (1978). The conceptualization and measurement of interpersonal communication satisfaction. *Human Communication Research, 4,* 253–264.

Hecht, M. L., Collier, M. J., & Ribeau, S. (1993). *African American communication: Ethnic identity and cultural interpretation.* Thousand Oaks, CA: Sage.

Heenehan, M. (1997). *Networking.* New York: Random House.

Heinrich, R., et al. (1983). *Instructional media: The new technologies of instruction.* New York: Wiley.

Hendrick, C., & Hendrick, S. (1990). A relationship-specific version of the love attitudes scale. In J. W. Heulip (Ed.), Handbook of replication research in the behavioral and social sciences [Special issue]. *Journal of Social Behavior and Personality, 5,* 239–254.

Hendrick, C., Hendrick, S., Foote, Franklin H., & Slapion-Foote, Michelle J. (1984). Do men and women love differently? *Journal of Social and Personal Relationships, 1,* 177–195.

Henley, N. M. (1977). *Body politics: Power, sex, and nonverbal communication.* Englewood Cliffs, NJ: Prentice-Hall.

Hensley, W. E. (1996). A theory of the valenced other: The intersection of the looking-glass-self and social penetration. *Social Behavior and Personality, 24,* 293–308.

Hersey, P., Blanchard, K. H., & Johnson, D. E. (2001). *Management of organizational behavior: Leading human resources* (8th ed.). Upper Saddle River, NJ: Prentice-Hall.

Hess, E. H. (1975). *The tell-tale eye.* New York: Van Nostrand Reinhold.

Hess, U., Kappas, A., McHugo, G. J., Lanzetta, J. T. (1992, May). The facilitative effect of facial expression of the self-generation of emotion. *International Journal of Psychophysiology, 12,* 251–265.

Hewitt, J. P. (1998). *The myth of self-esteem: Finding happiness and solving problems in America.* New York: St. Martin's Press.

Hewitt, J., & Stokes, Randall. (1975). Disclaimers. *American Sociological Review, 40,* 1–11.

Hickson, M. L., & Stacks, D. W. (1989). *NVC: Nonverbal communication: Studies and applications* (2nd ed.). Dubuque, IA: William C. Brown.

Hill, S. E. K. (1997). Team leadership theory. In P. G. Northouse (Ed.), *Leadership: Theory and practice* (pp. 159–183). Thousand Oaks, CA: Sage.

Himle, J. A., Abelson, J. L., & Haghightgou, H. (1999, August). Effect of alcohol on social phobic anxiety. *American Journal of Psychiatry, 156,* 1237–1243.

Hocker, J. L., & Wilmot, W. W. (1985). *Interpersonal conflict* (2nd ed.). Dubuque, IA: William C. Brown.

Hoffner, C., et al. (2001, June). The third-person effect in perceptions of the influence of television violence. *Journal of Communication, 51,* 283–299.

Hofstede, G. (1997). *Cultures and organizations: Software of the mind.* New York: McGraw-Hill.

Hoft, N. L. (1995). *International technical communication: How to export information about high technology.* New York: Wiley.

Holmes, J. (1986). Compliments and compliment responses in New Zealand English. *Anthropological Linguistics, 28,* 485–508.

Holmes, J. (1995). *Women, men and politeness.* New York: Longman.

Honeycutt, J. (1986). A model of marital functioning based on an attraction paradigm and social penetration dimensions. *Journal of Marriage and the Family, 48,* 51–59.

Huston, M., & Schwartz, P. (1995). The relationships of lesbians and gay men. In J. T. Wood & S. Duck (Eds.), *Under-studied relationships: Off the beaten track* (pp. 89–121). Thousand Oaks, CA: Sage.

Infante, D. A. (1988). *Arguing constructively.* Prospect Heights, IL: Waveland Press.

Infante, D. A., & Rancer, A. (1982). A conceptualization and measure of argumentativeness. *Journal of Personality Assessment, 46,* 72–80.

Infante, D. A., Rancer, A.S., & Womack, D. F. (2002) *Building communication theory* (4th ed.). Prospect Heights, IL: Waveland Press.

Infante, D. A., Riddle, B. L., Horvath, C. L., & Tumlin, S. A. (1992). Verbal aggressiveness: Messages and reasons. *Communication Quarterly, 40,* 116–126.

Infante, D. A., Sabourin, T. C., Rudd, J. E., & Shannon, E. A. (1990). Verbal aggression in violent and nonviolent marital disputes. *Communication Quarterly, 38,* 361–371.

Infante, D. A., & Wigley, C. J. (1986). Verbal aggressiveness: An interpersonal model and measure. *Communication Monographs, 53,* 61–69.

Insel, P. M., & Jacobson, L. F. (Eds.). (1975). *What do you expect? An inquiry into self-fulfilling prophecies.* Menlo Park, CA: Cummings.

Jablin, F. M. (1981). Cultivating imagination: Factors that enhance and inhibit creativity in brainstorming groups. *Human Communication Research, 7,* 245–258.

Jacobson, D. (1999). Impression formation in cyberspace: Online expectations and offline experiences in text-based virtual communities. *Journal of Computer Mediated Communication, 5.*

Jaksa, J. A., & Pritchard, M. S. (1994). *Communication ethics: Methods of analysis* (2nd ed.). Belmont, CA: Wadsworth.

James, D. L. (1995). *The executive guide to Asia-Pacific communications.* New York: Kodansha International.

Jamieson, K. H., & Campbell, K. K. (2001). *The interplay of influence* (5th ed.). Belmont, CA: Wadsworth.

Jamieson, K. H., & Kohrs, C. K. (1996). *The interplay of influence* (4th ed.). Belmont, CA: Wadsworth.

Jandt, F. E. (1995). *Intercultural communication.* Thousand Oaks, CA: Sage.

Janis, I. (1983). *Victims of group thinking: A psychological study of foreign policy decisions and fiascoes* (2nd Rev. ed.). Boston: Houghton Mifflin.

Janus, S. S., & Janus, C. L. (1993). *The Janus report on sexual behavior.* New York: Wiley.

Jaworski, A. (1993). *The power of silence: Social and pragmatic perspectives.* Newbury Park, CA: Sage.

Jessmer, S. L., & Anderson, D. (2001). The effect of politeness and grammar on user perceptions of electronic mail. *North American Journal of Psychology, 3,* 331–346.

Johannesen, R. L. (1990). *Ethics in human communication* (3rd ed.). Prospect Heights, IL: Waveland Press.

Johansson, W., & Percy, W. A. (1994). *Outing, Shattering the conspiracy of silence.* New York: Harrington Park Press.

Johnson, C. E. (1987). An introduction to powerful and powerless talk in the classroom. *Communication Education, 36,* 167–172.

Johnson, G. B. (1991). *Vital Speeches of the Day, 57,* 393–398.

Johnson, G. M. (1992). Subordinate perceptions of superior's communication competence and task attraction related to superior's use of compliance-gaining tactics. *Western Journal of Communication, 56,* 54–67.

Johnson, M. P. (1991). Commitment to personal relationships. In W. H. Jones & D. Perlman (Eds.), *Advances in personal relationships* (Vol. 3, pp. 117–143). London: Jessica Kingsley.

Johnson, S. D., & Bechler, C. (1998). Examining the relationship between listening effectiveness and leadership emergence: Perceptions, behaviors, and recall. *Small Group Research, 29,* 452–471.

Joinson, A. N. (2001). Self-disclosure in computer-mediated communication: The role of self-awareness and visual anonymity. *European Journal of Social Psychology, 31,* 177–192.

Jones, E. E. (1990). *Interpersonal perception.* New York: W. H. Freeman.

Jones, E. E., & Pittman, T. S. (1982). Toward a general theory of strategic self-presentation. In J. Suls (Ed.), *Psychological perspectives on the self* (Vol. 1, pp. 231–262). Hillsdale, NJ: Erlbaum.

Jones, S., & Yarbrough, A. E. (1985). A naturalistic study of the meanings of touch. *Communication Monographs, 52,* 19–56.

Joseph, J. A. (1997). *Vital Speeches of the Day, 64,* 133–135.

Jourard, S. M. (1968). *Disclosing man to himself.* New York: Van Nostrand Reinhold.

Jourard, S. M. (1971a). *Self-disclosure.* New York: Wiley.

Jourard, S. M. (1971b). *The transparent self* (Rev. ed.). New York: Van Nostrand Reinhold.

Kanner, B. (1989, April 3). Color schemes. *New York Magazine,* pp. 22–23.

Kelley, H. H., & Thibaut, J. W. (1978). *Interpersonal relations: A theory of interdependence.* New York: Wiley/Interscience.

Kelly, P. K. (1994). *Team decision-making techniques.* Irvine, CA: Richard Chang Associates.

Kemp, J. E., & Dayton, D. K. (1985). *Planning and producing instructional media* (5th ed.). New York: Harper & Row.

Kennedy, C. W., & Camden, C. T. (1988). A new look at interruptions. *Western Journal of Speech Communication, 47,* 45–58.

Keshavarz, M. H. (1988). Forms of address in post-revolutionary Iranian Persian: A sociolinguistic analysis. *Language in Society, 17,* 565–575.

Kesselman-Turkel, J., & Peterson, F. (1982). *Note-taking made easy.* Chicago: Contemporary Books.

Ketcham, H. (1958). *Color planning for business and industry.* New York: Harper.

Keyes, R. (1980). *The height of your life.* New York: Warner.

Kim, H. J. (1991). Influence of language and similarity on initial intercultural attraction. In S. Ting-Toomey & F. Korzenny (Eds.), *Cross-cultural interpersonal communication* (pp. 213–229). Newbury Park, CA: Sage.

Kim, M., & Sharkey, W. F. (1995). Independent and interdependent construals of self: Explaining cultural patterns of interpersonal communication in multi-cultural organizational settings. *Communication Quarterly, 43,* 20–38.

Kindler, H. S. (1996). Managing disagreement constructively (Rev. ed.). Menlo Park, CA: Crisp Publications.

Kirkpatrick, C., & Caplow, T. (1945). Courtship in a group of Minnesota students. *American Journal of Sociology, 51,* 114–125.

Kleinfeld, N. R. (1992, October 25). The smell of money. *The New York Times,* Section 9, pp. 1, 8.

Kleinke, C. L. (1986). *Meeting and understanding people.* New York: W. H. Freeman.

Knapp, M. L. (1984). *Interpersonal communication and human relationships.* Boston: Allyn & Bacon.

Knapp, M., & Hall, J. (1997). *Nonverbal behavior in human interaction* (4th ed.). New York: Holt, Rinehart and Winston.

Knapp, M. L., & Hall, J. (2002). *Nonverbal communication in human interaction* (5th ed.). Fort Worth, TX: Harcourt Brace Jovanovich.

Knapp, M. L., & Taylor, E. H. (1994). Commitment and its communication in romantic relationships. In Ann L. Weber & J. H. Harvey (Eds.), *Perspectives on close relationships* (pp. 153–175). Boston: Allyn & Bacon.

Knapp, M. L., & Vangelisti, A. (2000). *Interpersonal communication and human relationships* (4th ed.). Boston: Allyn & Bacon.

Knapp, M. L., Hart, R. P., Friedrich, G. W., & Shulman, G. M. (1973). The rhetoric of goodbye: Verbal and nonverbal correlates of human leave-taking. *Communication Monographs, 40,* 182–198.

Knobloch, L. K., & Solomon, D. H. (1999, Winter). Measuring the sources and content of relational uncertainty. *Communication Studies, 50,* 261–278.

Kochman, T. (1981). *Black and white: Styles in conflict.* Chicago: University of Chicago Press.

Komarovsky, M. (1964). *Blue collar marriage.* New York: Random House.

Korda, M. (1975). *Power! How to get it, how to use it.* New York: Ballantine.

Korzybski, A. (1933). *Science and sanity.* Lakeville, CT: International Non-Aristotelian Library.

Kramarae, C. (1974a). Folklinguistics. *Psychology Today, 8,* 82–85.

Kramarae, C. (1974b). Stereotypes of women's speech: The word from cartoons. *Journal of Popular Culture, 8,* 624–630.

Kramarae, C. (1977). Perceptions of female and male speech. *Language and Speech, 20,* 151–161.

Kramarae, C. (1981). *Women and men speaking.* Rowley, MA: Newbury House.

Kramer, R. (1997). Leading by listening: An empirical test of Carl Rogers's theory of human relationship using interpersonal assessments of leaders by followers. *Dissertation Abstracts International: Section A. Humanities and Social Sciences, 58,* 514.

Krivonos, P. D., & Knapp, M. L. (1975). Initiating communication: What do you say when you say hello? *Central States Speech Journal, 26,* 115–125.

Kurdek, L. A. (1994). Areas of conflict for gay, lesbian, and heterosexual couples: What couples argue about influences relationship satisfaction. *Journal of Marriage and the Family, 56,* 923–934.

Kurdek, L. A. (1995). Developmental changes in relationship quality in gay and lesbian cohabiting couples. *Developmental Psychology, 31,* 86–93.

Kushner, R. (1996). Some ways of looking at conflict. *NASSP Bulletin, 80,* 104–108.

Laing, M. (1993). Gossip: Does it play a role in the socialization of nurses. *Journal of Nursing Scholarship, 25,* 37–43.

Laing, R. D., Phillipson, H., & Lee, A. R. (1966). *Interpersonal perception.* New York: Springer.

Lamm, K. (1993). *10,000 ideas for term papers, projects, reports and speeches* (3rd ed.). New York: Prentice-Hall.

Lamm, K., & Lamm, K. (1999). *10,000 ideas for term papers, projects, reports, and speeches* (5th ed.). New York: Arco.

Langer, E. J. (1989). *Mindfulness.* Reading, MA: Addison-Wesley.

Lantz, A. (2001). Meetings in a distributed group of experts: Comparing face-to-face, chat and collaborative virtual environments. *Behaviour and Information Technology, 20,* 111–117.

Lanzetta, J. T., Cartwright-Smith, J., & Kleck, R. E. (1976). Effects of nonverbal dissimulations on emotional experience and autonomic arousal. *Journal of Personality and Social Psychology, 33,* 354–370.

Laroche, C., & deGrace, G. R. (1997). Factors of satisfaction associated with happiness in adults. *Canadian Journal of Counselling, 31,* 275–286.

Larsen, R. J., Kasimatis, M., & Frey, K. (1992). Facilitating the furrowed brow: An unobtrusive test of the facial feedback hypothesis applied to unpleasant affect. *Cognition and Emotion, 6,* 321–338.

Lea, M., & Russell, S. (1995). Love at first byte? Building personal relationships over computer networks. In J. T. Wood & S. Duck (Eds.), *Under-studied relationships: Off the beaten track* (pp. 197–233). Thousand Oaks, CA: Sage.

Lea, M., & Spears, R. (1995). Love at first byte? Building personal relationships over computer networks. In Julia T. Wood & S. Duck (Eds.), *Under-studied relationships: Off the beaten track* (pp. 197–233). Thousand Oaks, CA: Sage.

Leathers, D. G. (1997). *Successful nonverbal communication: Principles and applications* (3rd ed.). Boston, MA: Allyn & Bacon.

Lederer, W. J. (1984). *Creating a good relationship.* New York: Norton.

Lederman, L. (1990). Assessing educational effectiveness: The focus group interview as a technique for data collection. *Communication Education, 39,* 117–127.

Lee, A. M., & Lee, E. B. (1972). *The fine art of propaganda.* San Francisco: International Society for General Semantics.

Lee, A. M., & Lee, E. B. (1995). The iconography of propaganda analysis. *Etc.: A Review of General Semantics, 52,* 13–17.

Lee, C. M., & Gudykunst, W. B. (2001). Attraction in initial interethnic interactions. *Journal of Intercultural Relations, 25,* 373–387.

Lee, F. (1993). Being polite and keeping MUM: How bad news is communicated in organizational hierarchies. *Journal of Applied Social Psychology, 23,* 1124–1149.

Lee, H. O., & Boster, F. J. (1992). Collectivism–individualism in perceptions of speech rate: A cross-cultural comparison. *Journal of Cross-Cultural Psychology, 23,* 377–388.

Lee, J. A. (1976). *The colors of love.* New York: Bantam.

Lee, K. (2000, November 1). Information overload threatens employee productivity. *Employee Benefit News,* Securities Data Publishing, p. 1.

Leung, K. (1988, March). Some determinants of conflict avoidance. *Journal of Cross-Cultural Psychology, 19,* 125–136.

Leung, S. A. (2001). Editor's Introduction. *Asian Journal of Counseling, 8,* 107–109.

Lever, J. (1995). The 1995 Advocate survey of sexuality and relationships: The women, lesbian sex survey. *The Advocate, 687/688,* 22–30.

Levine, D. (2000). Virtual attraction: What rocks your boat. *CyberPsychology and Behavior, 3,* 565–573.

Levine, R. (1997). *A geography of time: The temporal misadventures of a social psychologist.* New York: Basic Books.

LeVine, R., & Bartlett, K. (1984). Pace of Life, Punctuality, and Coronary Heart Disease in Six Countries. *Journal of Cross-Cultural Psychology, 15,* 233–255.

Lewis, D. (1989). *The secret language of success.* New York: Carroll & Graf.

Lin, Y. W., & Rusbult, C. E. (1995). Commitment to dating relationships and cross-sex friendships in America and China. *Journal of Social and Personal Relationships, 12,* 7–26.

Littlejohn, S. W. (1996). *Theories of human communication* (5th ed.). Belmont, CA: Wadsworth.

Lloyd, S. R. (1995). *Developing positive assertiveness* (Rev. ed.). Menlo Park, CA: Crisp Publications.

Lu, L., & Shih, J. B. (1997). Sources of happiness: A qualitative approach. *Journal of Social Psychology, 137,* 181–188.

Luft, J. (1984). *Group process: An introduction of group dynamics* (3rd ed.). Palo Alto, CA: Mayfield.

Lujansky, H., & Mikula, G. (1983). Can equity theory explain the quality and stability of romantic relationships? *British Journal of Social Psychology, 22,* 101–112.

Lukens, J. (1978). Ethnocentric speech. *Ethnic Groups, 2,* 35–53.

Lumsden, G., & Lumsden, D. (1993). *Communicating in groups and teams.* Belmont, CA: Wadsworth.

Lustig, M. W., & Koester, J. (2003). *Intercultural competence: Interpersonal communication across cultures* (4th ed.). New York: HarperCollins.

Lynch, L. (2000, April 6). Feeling powerless can be health hazard. *Healthscout,* http://www.healthscout.com/cgi-bin/WebObjects/Af?ap=43&id=93729.

Ma, K. (1996). *The modern Madame Butterfly: Fantasy and reality in Japanese cross-cultural relationships.* Rutland, VT: Charles E. Tuttle.

Ma, R. (1992). The role of unofficial intermediaries in interpersonal conflicts in the Chinese culture. *Communication Quarterly, 40,* 269–278.

Mackey, R. A., Diemer, M. A., & O'Brien, B. A. (2000). Psychological intimacy in the lasting relationships of heterosexual and same-gender couples. *Sex Roles, 43,* 201–227

MacLachlan, J. (1979). What people really think of fast talkers. *Psychology Today, 13,* 113–117.

Malandro, L. A., Barker, L., & Barker, D. A. (1989). *Nonverbal communication* (2nd ed.). New York: Random House.

Manes, J., & Wolfson, N. (1981). The compliment formula. In F. Coulmas (Ed.), *Conversational routine* (pp. 115–132). The Hague: Mouton.

Mao, L. R. (1994). Beyond politeness theory: "Face" revisited and renewed. *Journal of Pragmatics, 21,* 451–486.

Marsh, P. (1988). *Eye to eye: How people interact.* Topside, MA: Salem House.

Marshall, Evan. (1983). *Eye language: Understanding the eloquent eye.* New York: New Trend.

Marshall, Linda L., & Rose, P. (1987). Gender, stress and violence in the adult relationships of a sample of college students. *Journal of Social and Personal Relationships, 4,* 299–316.

Martin, G. N. (1998). Human electroencephalographic (EEG) response to olfactory stimulation: Two experiments using the aroma of food. *International Journal of Psychophysiology, 30,* 287–302.

Martin, M. M., & Anderson, C. M. (1993, December). Psychological and biological differences in touch avoidance. *Communication Research Reports, 10,* 141–147.

Martin, M. M., & Anderson, C. M. (1995). Roommate similarity: Are roommates who are similar in their communication traits more satisfied? *Communication Research Reports, 12,* 46–52.

Marwell, G., & Schmitt, D. R. (1967). Dimensions of compliance-gaining behavior: An empirical analysis. *Sociometry, 39,* 350–364.

Masheter, C., & Harris, L. M. (1986). From divorce to friendship: A study of dialectic relationship development. *Journal of Social and Personal Relationships, 3,* 177–189.

Maslow, A. (1970). *Motivation and personality.* New York: HarperCollins.

Matsumoto, D. (1991). Cultural influences on facial expressions of emotion. *Southern Communication Journal, 56,* 128–137.

Matsumoto, D. (1994). *People: Psychology from a cultural perspective.* Pacific Grove, CA: Brooks/Cole.

Matsumoto, D. (1996). *Culture and psychology.* Pacific Grove, CA: Brooks/Cole.

Matsumoto, D., & Kudoh, T. (1993). American–Japanese cultural differences in attributions of personality based on smiles. *Journal of Nonverbal Behavior, 17,* 231–243.

Maynard, H. E. (1963). How to become a better premise detective. *Public Relations Journal, 19,* 20–22.

McCroskey, J. C. (1997). *An introduction to rhetorical communication* (7th ed.). Englewood Cliffs, NJ: Prentice-Hall.

McCroskey, J. C., & Wheeless, L. (1976). *Introduction to human communication.* Boston: Allyn & Bacon.

McGill, M. E. (1985). *The McGill report on male intimacy.* New York: Harper & Row.

McKerrow, Raymie E., Gronbeck, Bruce E., Ehninger, Douglas, & Monroe, Alan H. (2000). *Principles and Types of Speech Communication* (14th ed.). Boston: Allyn & Bacon.

McLaughlin, M. L. (1984). *Conversation: How talk is organized.* Newbury Park, CA: Sage.

McLoyd, V., & Wilson, L. (1992). Telling them like it is: The role of economic and environmental factors in single mothers' discussions with their children. *American Journal of Community Psychology, 20,* 419–444.

McNamee, S., & Gergen, K. J. (Eds.). (1999). *Relational responsibility: Resources for sustainable dialogue.* Thousand Oaks, CA: Sage.

McNatt, D. B. (2001). Ancient Pygmalion joins contemporary management: A meta-analysis of the result. *Journal of Applied Psychology, 85,* 314–322.

Merton, R. K. (1957). *Social theory and social structure.* New York: Free Press.

Metts, S., & Planalp, S. (2002). Emotional communication. In M. L. Knapp & J. A. Daly (Eds.), *Handbook of Interpersonal Communication* (3rd ed., pp. 339–373). Thousand Oaks, CA: Sage.

Meyer, J. R. (1994). Effect of situational features on the likelihood of addressing face needs in requests. *Southern Communication Journal, 59,* 240–254.

Midooka, K. (1990). Characteristics of Japanese style communication. *Media Culture and Society, 12,* 47–49.

Miller, J. G. (1984). Culture and the Development of Everyday Social Explanation. *Journal of Personality and Social Psychology, 46,* 961–978.

Miller, G. R., & Parks, M. R. (1982). Communication in dissolving relationships. In S. Duck (Ed.), *Personal relationships: Vol. 4. Dissolving personal relationships.* New York: Academic Press.

Mir, M. (1993). *Direct requests can also be polite.* Paper presented at the annual meeting of the International Conference on Pragmatics and Language Learning, Champaign, IL.

Moghaddam, F. M., Taylor, D. M., & Wright, S. C. (1993). *Social psychology in cross-cultural perspective.* New York: W. H. Freeman.

Molloy, J. (1981). *Molloy's live for success.* New York: Bantam.

Montagu, Ashley. (1971). *Touching: The human significance of the skin.* New York: Harper & Row.

Moon, D. G. (1966). Concepts of "culture": Implications for intercultural communication research. *Communication Quarterly, 44,* 70–84.

Moore, A., Masterson, J. T., Christophel, D. M., & Shea, K. A. (1996). College teacher immediacy and student ratings of instruction. *Communication Education, 45,* 29–39.

Morris, D. (1977). *Manwatching: A field guide to human behavior.* New York: Abrams.

Motley, M. T. (1990a). On whether one can(not) not communicate: An examination via traditional communication postulates. *Western Journal of Speech Communication, 54,* 1–20.

Motley, M. T. (1990b). Communication as interaction: A reply to Beach and Bavelas. *Western Journal of Speech Communication, 54,* 613–623.

Mullen, B., Salas, E., & Driskell, J. (1989). Salience, motivation, and artifact as contributions to the relation between participation rate and leadership. *Journal of Experimental Social Psychology, 25,* 545–559.

Mullen, B., Tara, A., Salas, E., & Driskell, J. E. (1994). Group cohesiveness and quality of decision making: An interaction of tests of the groupthink hypothesis. *Small Group Research, 25,* 189–204.

Myers, S. A., & Johnson, A. D. (2003). Verbal aggression and liking in interpersonal relationships. *Communication Research Reports, 20,* 90–96.

Naifeh, S., & Smith, G. W. (1984). *Why can't men open up? Overcoming men's fear of intimacy.* New York: Clarkson N. Potter.

Napier, R. W., & Gershenfeld, M. K. (1989). *Groups: Theory and experience* (4th ed.). Boston: Houghton Mifflin.

Neimeyer, R. A., & Mitchell, K. A. (1988). Similarity and attraction: A longitudinal study. *Journal of Social and Personal Relationships, 5,* 131–148.

Nelson, P., & Pearson, J. (1996). *Confidence in public speaking* (6th ed.). Dubuque, IA: Brown & Benchmark.

Neugarten, B. (1979). Time, age, and the life cycle. *American Journal of Psychiatry, 136,* 887–894.

Neuliep, J. W., & Grohskopf, E. L. (2000). Uncertainty reduction and communication satisfaction during initial interaction: An initial test and replication of a new axiom. *Communication Reports, 13,* 67–77.

Ng, S. H., & Bradac, J. J. (1993). *Power in language: Verbal communication and social influence.* Newbury Park, CA: Sage.

Noble, B. P. (1994, August 14). The gender wars: Talking peace. *The New York Times,* p. 21.

Noller, P. (1993). Gender and emotional communication in marriage: Different cultures or differential social power? [Special issue: Emotional Communication, Culture, and Power.] *Journal of Language and Social Psychology, 12,* 132–152.

Northouse, P. G. (1997). *Leadership: Theory and practice.* Thousand Oaks, CA: Sage.

O'Hair, H. D., Cody, M. J., & McLaughlin, M. L. (1981). Prepared lies, spontaneous lies, Machiavellianism, and nonverbal communication. *Human Communication Research, 7,* 325–339.

O'Hair, M. J., Cody, M. J., & O'Hair, D. (1991). The impact of situational dimensions on compliance-resisting strategies: A comparison of methods. *Communication Quarterly, 39,* 226–240.

Ober, C., Weitkamp, L. R., Cox, N., Dytch, H., Kostyu, D., & Elias, S. (1997). *American Journal of Human Genetics, 61,* 494–496.

Oberg, K. (1960). Cultural shock: Adjustment to new cultural Environments. *Practical Anthropology, 7,* 177–182.

Osborn, A. (1957). *Applied imagination* (Rev. ed.). New York: Scribners.

Osborn, M., & Osborn, S. (1997). *Speaking in public* (4th ed.). Boston: Houghton Mifflin.

Park, W. W. (1990). A review of research on groupthink. *Journal of Behavioral Decision Making, 3,* 229–245.

Parks, M. R. (1995). Webs of influence in interpersonal relationships. In C. R. Berger & M. E. Burgoon (Eds.), *Communication and social influence processes* (pp. 155–178). East Lansing: Michigan State University Press.

Parks, M. R., & Floyd, K. (1996). Making friends in cyberspace. *Journal of Communication, 46,* 80–97.

Parks, M. R., & Roberts, L. D. (1998). "Making MOOsic": The development of personal relationships on line and a comparison to their off-line counterparts. *Journal of Social and Personal Relationships, 15,* 517–537.

Patton, B. R., Giffin, K., & Patton, E. N. (1989). *Decision-making group interaction* (3rd ed.). New York: HarperCollins.

Paul, A. M. (2001). Self-help: Shattering the myths. *Psychology Today, 34,* 60ff.

Pearson, J. C. (1980). Sex roles and self-disclosure. *Psychological Reports, 47,* 640.

Pearson, J. C. (1993). *Communication in the family* (2nd ed.). New York: Harper & Row.

Pearson, J. C., & Spitzberg, B. H. (1990). *Interpersonal communication: Concepts, components, and contexts* (2nd ed.). Dubuque, IA: William C. Brown.

Pearson, J. C., West, R., & Turner, L. H. (1995). *Gender and communication* (3rd ed.). Dubuque, IA: William C. Brown.

Penfield, J. (Ed.). (1987). *Women and language in transition.* Albany, NY: State University of New York Press.

Pennebaker, J. W. (1991). *Opening up: The healing power of confiding in others.* New York: Morrow.

Petrocelli, W., & Repa, B. (1992). *Sexual harassment on the job.* Berkeley, CA: Nolo Press.

Pilkington, C. J., & Richardson, D. R. (1988). Perceptions of risk in intimacy. *Journal of Social and Personal Relationships, 5,* 503–508.

Pilkington, C., & Woods, S. P. (1999). Risk in intimacy as a chronically accessible schema. *Journal of Social and Personal Relationships, 16,* 249–263.

Piot, C. D. (1993). Secrecy, ambiguity, and the everyday in Kabre culture. *American Anthropologist, 95,* 353–370.

Pittenger, R. E., Hockett, C. F., & Danehy, J. J. (1960). *The first five minutes.* Ithaca, NY: Paul Martineau.

Porter, R. H., & Moore, J. D. (1981). Human kin recognition by olfactory cues. *Physiology and Behavior, 27,* 493–495.

Porter, S., Birt, A. R., Yuille, J. C., & Lehman, D. R. (2000, November). Negotiating false memories: Interviewer and rememberer characteristics relate to memory distortion. *Psychological Science, 11,* 507–510.

Pratkanis, A., & Aronson, E. (1991). *Age of propaganda: The everyday use and abuse of persuasion.* New York: W. H. Freeman.

Preidt, R. (2000). Are you listening, employers? http://www.healthscout.com/cgi-bin/WebObjects/Af?ap=43&id=95274.

Prusank, D. T., Duran, R. L., & DeLillo, D. A. (1993). Interpersonal relationships in women's magazines: Dating and relating in the 1970s and 1980s. *Journal of Social and Personal Relationships, 10,* 307–320.

Ramsey, S. J. (1981). The kinesics of femininity in Japanese women. *Language Sciences, 3,* 104–123.

Rankin, P. (1929). *Listening ability.* Proceedings of the Ohio State Educational Conference's Ninth Annual Session.

Regan, P. C., Kocan, E. R., & Whitlock, T. (1998). Ain't love grand! A prototype analysis of the concept of romantic love. *Journal of Social and Personal Relationships, 15,* 411–420.

Rich, A. L. (1974). *Interracial communication.* New York: Harper & Row.

Richards, I. A. (1951). Communication between men: The meaning of language. In Heinz von Foerster (Ed.), *Cybernetics: Transactions of the Eighth Conference.*

Richmond, V. P., & McCroskey, J. C. (1998). *Communication: Apprehension, avoidance, and effectiveness* (5th ed.). Needham Heights, MA: Allyn & Bacon.

Ridge, R. D., & Reber, J. S. (2002). "I think she's attracted to me": The effect of men's beliefs on women's behavior in a job interview scenario. *Basic and Applied Social Psychology, 24,* 1–14.

Riggio, R. E. (1987). *The charisma quotient.* New York: Dodd, Mead.

Roberts, W. (1987). *Leadership secrets of Attila the Hun.* New York: Warner.

Rogers, C. (1970). *Carl Rogers on encounter groups.* New York: Harrow Books.

Rogers, C., & Farson, R. (1981). Active listening. In J. DeVito (Ed.), *Communication: Concepts and processes* (3rd ed., pp. 137–147). Upper Saddle River, NJ: Prentice-Hall.

Rokach, A. (1998). The relation of cultural background to the causes of loneliness. *Journal of Social and Clinical Psychology, 17,* 75–88.

Rokach, A., & Brock, H. (1995). The effects of gender, marital status, and the chronicity and immediacy of loneliness. *Journal of Social Behavior and Personality, 19,* 833–848.

Rollman, J. B., Krug, K., & Parente, F. (2000). The chat room phenomenon: Reciprocal communication in cyberspace. *CyberPsychology and Behavior, 3,* 161–166.

Ronfeldt, H. M., Kimerling, R., & Arias, I. (1998, February). Satisfaction with relationship power and the perpetration of dating violence. *Journal of Marriage & Family, 60,* 70–78.

Rosen, E. (1998, October). Think like a shrink. *Psychology Today,* 54–69.

Rosenbaum, M. E. (1986). The repulsion hypothesis: On the non-development of relationships. *Journal of Personality and Social Psychology, 51,* 1156–1166.

Rosenfeld, L. (1979). Self-disclosure avoidance: Why I am afraid to tell you who I am. *Communication Monographs, 46,* 63–74.

Rosengren, A., et al. (1993). Stressful life events, social support, and mortality in men born in 1933. *British Medical Journal.*

Rosenthal, R., & Jacobson, L. (1968). *Pygmalion in the classroom.* New York: Holt, Rinehart & Winston.

Ross, J. L. (1995). Conversational pitchbacks: Helping couples bat 1000 in the game of communications. *Journal of Family Psychotherapy, 6,* 83–86.

Roth, P. L., Schleifer, L. L. F., & Switzer, F. S. (1995, May). Nominal group technique—an aid in implementing TQM. *The CPA Journal, 65,* 68–69.

Rothwell, J. D. (1982). *Telling it like it isn't: Language misuse and malpractice/what we can do about it.* Englewood Cliffs, NJ: Prentice-Hall.

Rowland-Morin, P. A., & Carroll, J. G. (1990). Verbal communication skills and patient satisfaction: A study of doctor-patient interviews. *Evaluation and the Health Professions, 13,* 168–185.

Ruben, B. D. (1985). Human communication and cross-cultural effectiveness. In L. A. Samovar & R. E. Porter (Eds.), *Intercultural communication: A reader* (4th ed., pp. 338–346). Belmont, CA: Wadsworth.

Ruben, B. D. (1988). *Communication and human behavior* (2nd ed.). New York: Macmillan.

Rubenstein, C. (1993, June 10). Fighting sexual harassment in schools. *The New York Times,* p. C8.

Rubin, R. B. (1985). The validity of the communication competency assessment instrument. *Communication Monographs, 52,* 173–185.

Rubin, R. B., Fernandez-Collado, C., & Hernandez-Sampieri, R. (1992). A cross-cultural examination of interpersonal communication motives in Mexico and the United States. *International Journal of Intercultural Relations, 16,* 145–157.

Rubin, R. B., & Martin, M. M. (1994). Development of a measure of interpersonal communication competence. *Communication Research Reports, 11,* 33–44.

Rubin, R. B., & Martin, M. M. (1998). Interpersonal communication motives. In J. C. McCroskey, J. A. Daly, M. M. Martin, & M. J. Beatty (Eds.), *Communication and Personality: Trait Perspectives* (pp. 287–307). Cresskill, NJ: Hampton Press.

Rubin, R. B., Pearse, E. M., & Barbato, C. A. (1988). Conceptualization and measurement of interpersonal communication motives. *Human Communication Research, 14,* 602–628.

Rubin, R. B., & Rubin, A. M. (1992). Antecedents of interpersonal communication motivation. *Communication Quarterly, 40,* 315–317.

Rubin, R. B., & Graham, E. E. (1988). Communication correlates of college success: An exploratory investigation. *Communication Education, 37,* 14–27.

Rubin, R., & McHugh, M. (1987). Development of parasocial interaction relationships. *Journal of Broadcasting and Electronic Media, 31,* 279–292.

Rubin, R. (1982). Assessing speaking and listening competence at the college level: The communication competency assessment instrument. *Communication Education, 31,* 19–32.

Rubin, Z., & McNeil, E. B. (1985). *Psychology: Being human* (4th ed.). New York: Harper & Row.

Rubin, Z. (1973). *Liking and loving: An invitation to social psychology.* New York: Holt, Rinehart & Winston.

Ruggiero, V. R. (1990). *The art of thinking: A guide to critical and creative thought* (3rd ed.). New York: HarperCollins.

Rundquist, S. (1992). Indirectness: A gender study of Fluting Grice's Maxims. *Journal of Pragmatics, 18,* 431–449.

Samovar, L. A., & Porter, R. E. (Eds.). (1991). *Communication between cultures.* Belmont, CA: Wadsworth.

Sapadin, L. A. (1988). Friendship and gender: Perspectives of professional men and women. *Journal of Social and Personal Relationships, 5,* 387–403.

Scandura, T. (1992). Mentorship and career mobility: An empirical investigation. *Journal of Organizational Behavior, 13,* 169–174.

Schafer, M., & Crichlow, S. (1996, September). Antecedents of groupthink. *Journal of Conflict Resolution, 40,* 415–435.

Schafer, R. B., & Keith, P. M. (1980). Equity and depression among married couples. *Social Psychology Quarterly, 43,* 430–435.

Scherer, K. R. (1986). Vocal affect expression. *Psychological Bulletin, 99,* 143–165.

Schnoor, L. G. (Ed.). (1999). *Winning orations of the interstate oratorical association.* Mankato, MN: Interstate Oratorical Association.

Schnoor, L. G. (Ed.). (2000). *Winning orations of the interstate oratorical association.* Mankato, MN: Interstate Oratorical Association.

Schoenberger, N. E., Kirsch, I., Gearan, P., Montgomery, G., et al. (1997). Hypnotic enhancement of a cognitive behavioral treatment for public speaking anxiety. *Behavior Therapy, 28,* 127–140.

Schultz, B. G. (1996). *Communicating in the small group: Theory and practice* (2nd ed.). New York: HarperCollins.

Schwartz, M., and the Task Force on Bias-Free Language of the Association of American University Presses. (1995). *Guidelines for bias-free writing.* Bloomington: Indiana University Press.

Sethna, B., Barnes, C. C., Brust, M., & Kay, L. (1999, July–August). E-mail communications in colleges and universities: Are they private? *Journal of Education for Business, 74,* 347–350.

Shannon, J. (1987). Don't smile when you say that. *Executive Female, 10,* 33, 43.

Shapiro, D., & Bies, R. J. (1994). Threats, bluffs, and disclaimers in negotiations. *Organizational Behavior and Human Decision Processes, 60,* 14–35.

Sharkey, W. F., & Stafford, L. (1990). Turn-taking resources employed by congenitally blind conversers. *Communication Studies, 41,* 161–182.

Shaw, M. (1981). *Group dynamics: The psychology of small group behaviors* (3rd ed.). New York: McGraw-Hill.

Shuter, R. (1990). The centrality of culture. *Southern Communication Journal, 55,* 237–249.

Siavelis, R. L., & Lamke, L. K. (1992). Instrumentalness and expressiveness: Predictors of heterosexual relationship satisfaction. *Sex Roles, 26,* 149–159.

Siegert, J. R., & Stamp, G. H. (1994). "Our First Big Fight" as a milestone in the development of close relationships. *Communication Monographs, 61,* 345–360.

Signorile, M. (1993). *Queer in America: Sex, the media, and the closets of power.* New York: Random House.

Silverman, T. (2001). Expanding community: The Internet and relational theory. *Community, Work and Family, 4,* 231–237.

Simpson, J. A. (1987). The dissolution of romantic relationships: Factors involved in relationship stability and emotional distress. *Journal of Personality and Social Psychology, 53,* 683–692.

Singelis, T. M. (1994). The measurement of independent and interdependent self-construals. *Personality and Social Psychology Bulletin, 20,* 580–591.

Slade, M. (1995, February 19). We forgot to write a headline. But it's not our fault. *The New York Times,* p. 5.

Smoreda, Z., & Licoppe, C. (2000). Gender-specific use of the domestic telephone. *Social Psychology Quarterly, 63,* 238–252.

Snyder, M. (1992, February). A gender-informed model of couple and family therapy: Relationship enhancement therapy. *Contemporary Family Therapy: An International Journal, 14,* 15–31.

Solomon, G. B., Striegel, D. A., Eliot, J. F., Heon, S. N., et al. (1996). The self-fulfilling prophecy in college basketball: Implications for effective coaching. *Journal of Applied Sport Psychology, 8,* 44–59.

Spitzberg, B. H. (1991). Intercultural communication competence. In Larry A. Samovar & R. E. Porter (Eds.), *Intercultural communication: A reader* (pp. 353–365). Belmont, CA: Wadsworth.

Spitzberg, B. H., & Cupach, W. R. (1984). *Interpersonal communication competence.* Beverly Hills, CA: Sage.

Spitzberg, B. H., & Cupach, W. R. (1989). *Handbook of interpersonal competence research.* New York: Springer.

Spitzberg, B. H., & Cupach, W. R. (2002). Interpersonal skills. In M. L. Knapp & J. A. Daly (Eds.), *Handbook of interpersonal communication* (3rd ed., pp. 564–611). Thousand Oaks, CA: Sage.

Spitzberg, B. H., & Hecht, M. L. (1984). A component model of relational competence. *Human Communication Research, 10,* 575–599.

Sprecher, S., & Metts, S. (1989). Development of the "romantic beliefs scale" and examination of the effects of gender and gender-role orientation. *Journal of Social and Personal Relationships, 6,* 387–411.

Sprecher, S. (1987). The effects of self-disclosure given and received on affection for an intimate partner and stability of the relationship. *Journal of Social and Personal Relationships, 4,* 115–127.

Starkey, J. A. (1996). *Multicultural communication strategies.* Chicago, IL: JAMS Publishing.

Strecker, I. (1993). Cultural variations in the concept of "face." *Multilingua, 12,* 119–141.

Steil, L. K., Barker, L. L., & Watson, K. W. (1983). *Effective listening: Key to your success.* Reading, MA: Addison-Wesley.

Steiner, C. (1981). *The other side of power.* New York: Grove.

Stephan, W. G., & Stephan, C. W. (1985). Intergroup anxiety. *Journal of Social Issues, 41,* 157–176.

Stephan, W. G., & Stephan, C. W. (1996). *Intergroup relations.* Dubuque, IA: Brown & Benchmark.

Sternberg, R. J. (1987). Questions and answers about the nature and teaching of thinking skills. In Joan Boykoff Baron & R. J. Sternberg (Eds.), *Teaching thinking skills: Theory and practice* (pp. 251–259). New York: W. H. Freeman.

Stewart, S. (1996). Stop searching and start finding. *The Net, 2,* 34–40.

Stewart, L. P., Cooper, P. J., Stewart, A. D., with Friedley, S. A. (2003). *Communication and gender* (4th ed.). Boston: Allyn & Bacon.

Szapocznik, J. (1995). Research on disclosure of HIV status: Cultural evolution finds an ally in science. *Health Psychology, 14,* 4–5.

Tang, T. L., & Butler, E. A. (1997, Summer). Attributions of quality circles' problem-solving failure: Differences among management, supporting staff, and quality circle members. *Public Personnel Management, 26,* 203–225.

Tannen, D. (1990). *You just don't understand: Women and men in conversation.* New York: Morrow.

Tannen, D. (1994a). *Gender and discourse.* New York: Oxford University Press.

Tannen, D. (1994b). *Talking from 9 to 5: How women's and men's conversational styles affect who gets heard, who gets credit, and what gets done at work.* New York: Morrow.

Tardiff, T. (2001). Learning to say "no" in Chinese. *Early Education and Development, 12,* 303–323.

Tersine, R. J., & Riggs, W. E. (1980). The Delphi technique: A long-range planning tool. In S. Ferguson & S. D. Ferguson (Eds.), *Intercom: Readings in organizational communication* (pp. 366–373). Rochelle Park, NJ: Hayden Book.

Thelen, M. H., Sherman, M. D., & Borst, T. S. (1998). Fear of intimacy and attachment among rape survivors. *Behavior Modification, 22,* 108–116.

Thibaut, J. W., & Kelley, H. H. (1959). *The social psychology of groups.* New York: Wiley.

Thomlison, D. (1982). *Toward interpersonal dialogue.* New York: Longman.

Thompson, C. A., & Klopf, D. W. (1991). An analysis of social style among disparate cultures. *Communication Research Reports, 8,* 65–72.

Thompson, C. A., Klopf, D. W., & Ishii, S. (1991). A comparison of social style between Japanese and Americans. *Communication Research Reports, 8,* 165–172.

Thorne, B., Kramarae, C., & Henley, N. (Eds.). (1983). *Language, gender and society.* Rowley, MA: Newbury House.

Ting-Toomey, S. (1981). Ethnic identity and close friendship in Chinese-American college students. *International Journal of Intercultural Relations, 5,* 383–406.

Ting-Toomey, S. (1985). Toward a theory of conflict and culture. *International and Intercultural Communication Annual, 9,* 71–86.

Ting-Toomey, S. (1986). Conflict communication styles in black and white subjective cultures. In Y. K. Young (Ed.), *Interethnic communication: Current research* (pp. 75–88). Thousand Oaks, CA: Sage.

Tolhuizen, J. H. (1986). Perceiving communication indicators of evolutionary changes in friendship. *Southern Speech Communication Journal, 52,* 69–91.

Tolhuizen, J. H. (1989). Communication strategies for intensifying dating relationships: Identification, use, and structure. *Journal of Social and Personal Relationships, 6,* 413–434.

Trager, G. L. (1958). Paralanguage: A first approximation. *Studies in Linguistics, 13,* 1–12.

Trager, G. L. (1961). The typology of paralanguage. *Anthropological Linguistics, 3,* 17–21.

Traxler, A. J. (1980). *Let's get gerontologized: Developing a sensitivity to aging.* Springfield, IL: Illinois Department of Aging.

U.S. Bureau of the Census. (2001). *Population by race and Hispanic or Latin origin for the United States.* Washington, D.C.: Author.

Uris, A. (1986). *101 of the greatest ideas in management.* NY: Wiley.

Veenendall, T. L., & Feinstein, M. C. (1995). *Let's talk about relationships: Cases in study* (2nd ed.). Prospect Heights, IL: Waveland Press.

Velting, D. M. (1999). Personality and negative expectations: Trait structure of the Beck Hopelessness Scale. *Personality and Individual Differences, 26,* 913–921.

Ventura, M. (1998). Taboo: Don't even think about it. *Psychology Today, 31,* 32–38, 66, 68.

Vernon, J. A., Williams, J. A., Phillips, T., & Wilson, J. (1990). Media stereotyping: A comparison of the way elderly women and men are portrayed on prime-time television. *Journal of Women and Aging, 4,* 55–68.

Victor, D. (1992). *International business communication.* New York: HarperCollins.

Wade, N. (2002, January 22). Scent of a man is linked to a woman's selection. *The New York Times,* p. F2.

Wallace, K. (1955). An ethical basis of communication. *Communication Education, 4,* 1–9.

Wardhaugh, R. (1998). *An introduction to sociolinguistics* (3rd ed.). Malden, MA: Blackwell.

Watson, A. K., & Dodd, C. H. (1984). Alleviating communication apprehension through rational emotive therapy: A comparative evaluation. *Communication Education, 33,* 257–266.

Watzlawick, P. (1977). *How real is real? Confusion, disinformation, communication: An anecdotal introduction to communications theory.* New York: Vintage.

Watzlawick, P. (1978). *The language of change: Elements of therapeutic communication.* New York: Basic Books.

Watzlawick, P., Helmick Beavin, J., & Jackson, D. D. (1967). *Pragmatics of human communication: A study of interactional patterns, pathologies, and paradoxes.* New York: Norton.

Weathers, M. D., Frank, E. M., & Spell, L. A. (2002). Differences in the communication of affect: Members of the same race versus members of a different race. *Journal of Black Psychology, 28,* 66–77.

Weinberg, H. L. (1959). *Levels of knowing and existence.* New York: Harper & Row.

Weinstein, E. A., & Deutschberger, P. (1963). Some dimensions of altercasting. *Sociometry, 26,* 454–466.

Weitzman, P. F. (2001). Young adult women resolving interpersonal conflicts. *Journal of Adult Development, 8,* 61–67.

Weitzman, P. F., & Weitzman, E. A. (2000). Interpersonal negotiation strategies in a sample of older women. *Journal of Clinical Geropsychology, 6,* 41–51.

Westwood, R. I., Tang, F. F., & Kirkbride, P. S. (1992). Chinese conflict behavior: Cultural antecedents and behavioral consequences. *Organizational Development Journal, 10,* 13–19.

Wetzel, P. J. (1988). Are "powerless" communication strategies the Japanese norm? *Language in Society, 17,* 555–564.

Wheeless, L. R., & Grotz, J. (1977). The measurement of trust and its relationship to self-disclosure. *Human Communication Research, 3,* 250–257.

Whitty, M., & Gavin, J. (2001). Age/sex/location: Uncovering the social cues in the development of online relationships. *CyberPsychology and Behavior, 4,* 623–630.

Wiemann, J. M. (1977). Explication and test of a model of communicative competence. *Human Communication Research, 3,* 195–213.

Wiemann, J. M., & Backlund, P. (1980). Current theory and research in communicative competence. *Review of Educational Research, 50,* 185–199.

Wilmot, W. W. (1995). *Relational communication.* New York: McGraw-Hill.

Wilson, A. P., & Bishard, T. G. (1994). Here's the dirt on gossip. *American School Board Journal, 181,* 27–29.

Wilson, J. H., & Taylor, K. W. (2001). Professor immediacy as behaviors associated with liking students. *Teaching of Psychology, 28,* 136–138.

Wilson, R. A. (1989). Toward understanding E-prime. *Etc.: A Review of General Semantics, 46,* 316–319.

Winquist, L. A., Mohr, C. D., & Kenny, D. A. (1998). The female positivity effect in the perception of others. *Journal of Research in Personality, 32,* 370–388.

Witt, P. L., & Wheeless, L. R. (2001). An experimental study of teachers' verbal and nonverbal immediacy and students' affective and cognitive learning. *Communication Education, 50,* 327–342.

Wolfson, N. (1988). The bulge: A theory of speech behaviour and social distance. In J. Fine (Ed.), *Second language discourse: A textbook of current research* (pp. 21–38). Norwood, NJ: Ablex.

Wolpe, J. (1957). *Psychotherapy by reciprocal inhibition.* Stanford, CA: Stanford University Press.

Won-Doornink, M. (1991). Self-disclosure and reciprocity in South Korean and U.S. male dyads. In Stella Ting-Toomey & Felipe Korzenny (Eds.), *Cross-cultural interpersonal communication* (pp. 116–131). Newbury Park, CA: Sage.

Won-Doornink, M. (1985). Self-disclosure and reciprocity in conversation: A cross-national study. *Social Psychology Quarterly, 48,* 97–107.

Wood, J. T. (1982). Communication and relational culture: Bases for the study of human relationships. *Communication Quarterly, 30,* 75–83.

Wood, J. T. (1994). *Gendered lives: Communication, gender, and culture.* Belmont, CA: Wadsworth.

Woodward, G. C., & Denton, R. E. (1996). *Persuasion and influence in American life* (3rd ed.). Prospect Heights, IL: Waveland Press.

Wrench, J. S., & McCroskey, J. C. (2003). A communibiological examination of ethnocentrism and homophobia. *Communication Research Reports, 20,* 24–33.

Yau-fair Ho, D., Chan, S. F., Peng, S., & Ng, A. K. (2001). The dialogical self: Converging East–West constructions. *Culture and Psychology, 7,* 393–408.

Yun, H. (1976). The Korean personality and treatment considerations. *Social Casework, 57,* 173–178.

Zaleski, Z., Cycon, A., & Kurc, A. (2001). Future time perspective and subjective well-being in adolescent samples. In P. Schmuck & K. M. Sheldon (Eds.), *Life goals and well-being: Towards a positive psychology of human striving* (pp. 58–67). Cambridge, MA: Hogrefe & Huber.

Zane, N., & Yeh, M. (2002). The use of culturally-based variables in assessment: Studies on loss of face. In K. S. Kurasaki (Ed.), *Asian American mental health: Assessment theories and methods* (pp. 123–138). New York: Kluwer.

Zimmer, T. A. (1986). Premarital anxieties. *Journal of Social and Personal Relationships, 3,* 149–159.

Zuckerman, M., Klorman, R., Larrance, D. T., & Spiegel, N. H. (1981). Facial, autonomic, and subjective components of emotion: The facial feedback hypothesis versus the externalizer–internalizer distinction. *Journal of Personality and Social Psychology, 41,* 929–944.

Zunin, L. M., & Zunin, N. B. (1972). *Contact: The first four minutes.* Los Angeles, CA: Nash.

Index

Communication (*continued*)
facial, 109, 110–113, 272
feedback messages as, 7, 8
feedforward messages as, 7–8
gender and, 18
inevitability of, 18–19
information overload in, 8–9
intercultural (*See* Intercultural communication)
interpersonal (*See* Interpersonal communication)
interviewing as, 2–3
intrapersonal, 2
irreversibility of, 19–20
mediated, 3
message form in, 7–9
message overload in, 8–9
metamessages as, 7
models of, 5, 5*f*, 6*f*
noise in, 9–10, 11*t*
nonverbal (*See* Nonverbal communication)
phatic, 136
principles of, 14–21, 15*f*, 19*f*
public (*See* Public speaking; Speeches)
punctuation of, 18
purpose of, 18, 19*f*
relational, 179
relationship dimension of, 16–17
small group (*See* Small groups)
spatial, 113–116, 114*t*
time, 123–125, 128–130, 129*t*
touch, 118–120, 128
unrepeatability of, 20
Communication accommodation theory, 15
Communication ambiguity, 16
Comparison and contrast pattern of organization, 248
Competence, 11–14, 12*f*
culture and, 12, 12*f*
ethics and, 11, 12*f*, 13
listening and, 12*f*, 13–14
persuasive speech and, 325
power and, 12*f*, 13
self-disclosure and, 35
thinking critically and, 12–13, 12*f*
Competition, 151, 151*f*
Complaints, 216
Compliance gaining, 189
Compromise
conflict and, 151, 151*f*
in small groups, 206
Computer-assisted presentations, 298–304, 299*f*, 300*f*, 302*f*, 303*f*
Corel, 299
Lotus Freelance, 299
PowerPoint, 299, 299*f*, 300*f*, 302*f*, 303*f*
printouts, 301–302, 302*f*, 303*f*
rehearsing, 302–304
using, 300–302
Computer communication, 4
conflict and, 150–151
dialogue *vs.* monologue, 138–139
e-mail overload in, 8–9
emoticons in, 111*t*, 138
information overload and, 8–9
informative speech using, 298–304, 299*f*, 300*f*, 302*f*, 303*f*
interpersonal relationships and, 180–182
irreversibility of, 20
maxim of quantity and, 85–86
message overload and, 8–9
netiquette, 87, 150–151
for public speaking research, 236, 238
style of, 138, 140
through chat groups, 190–191
through mailing lists, 190–191
Conclusion of speech, 258–259, 261
Confirmation, 89–91, 90*t*
Conflict, 148–160, 151*f*
acceptance during, 157
active, 153–154

argumentativeness and, 158–160
assertiveness in, 155
attack during, 157
avoidance of, 153–154
beginnings of, 152
beltlining and, 156–157
blame during, 157
content, 148
cultural context of, 149–150
effective management of, 153–160
face-detracting strategy in, 156–157
face-enhancing strategy in, 156–157
force in, 154–155
gunnysacking and, 155–156
listening during, 152
myths about, 148–149
nonassertiveness in, 155
online, 150–151
personal rejection and, 157
relationship, 148
in small groups, 208, 215–217
styles of, 151, 151*f*
verbal aggressiveness and, 158
win–lose strategy in, 153
win–win strategy in, 153
Connotation, 82–83
Constructing proofs for persuasive speech, 315
Contact stage of interpersonal relationships, 166–167, 167*f*
Content dimension of communication, 16–17
Content messages, 74
Context of communication, 5–6, 6*f*
Contrast rule of organization, 47
Conversation, 134–142, 135*f*, 136*t*. *See also* Conflict; Language; Listening; Verbal messages
altercasting in, 137
business stage of, 135*f*, 137–139
closing stage of, 135*f*, 140, 141
cultural sensitivity and, 143
disclaimer in, 137
effective, 142–147
empathy in, 144–145
expressiveness in, 146–147
feedback stage of, 135*f*, 139–140
feedforward stage of, 135*f*, 136–137
flexibility and, 142–143
immediacy in, 145–146
interaction management in, 146
interruptions in, 138
metacommunicational ability and, 143–144
mindfulness/mindlessness and, 142
model of, 134–142, 135*f*, 136*t*
negativeness in, 145, 147
opening stage of, 135*f*, 136, 141
openness in, 144
other-orientation in, 147
positiveness in, 145
power plays in, 156
speech disorders and, 136*t*
turn-taking in, 137–138
Cooperation, 85–86
Credibility
in persuasive speech, 322–326
power and, 324
Critical listening, 73
Criticism
culture and, 278–280
ethics of, 276
listening to, 274
of public speaking, 273–280
Cues
backchanneling, 70, 138
to emotion, 120–121
leave-taking, 138
pacing, 138
turn-taking, 137–138
Culture. *See* Intercultural communication

Dangers of self-disclosure, 40
Databases, for public speaking research, 236
Deafness, 68*t*, 94–95
Deception, 90
    nonverbal messages and, 107–108
    in relationships, 173
Decoding, 6–7, 6*f*
Decreasing power, 13
Definition speech, 289–290
Definitions in informative speech, 293–294
Delegating style of leadership, 211*f*, 212
Delivery of speeches, 268–273
    methods for, 267–268
    outline for, 265–267
Delphi method, 200–201
Demographic changes in United States, 21–22, 22*f*
Demonstration speech, 290–291
Denotation, 82–83
Depenetration, 172
Depth listening, 73–74
Descriptive speech, 287–289
Deterioration stage of interpersonal relationships, 167*f*,
    172–173
Dialogue
    with self, 34
    vs. monologue, 138–139
Directness, 83–85
Disclaimer, 137
Disclosure. *See* Self-disclosure
Disconfirmation, 89–91, 90*t*
Display rules, 77
Dissolution stage of interpersonal relationships, 167*f*, 175–176
Distance, spatial, 113–116, 114*t*
Diversity, 21–22, 22*f*
Dominator, in small groups, 206
Door-in-the-face technique, 312
Dress, 117
Dyadic effect, 37
Dysfunctional roles in small groups, 207

E-prime, 101
Earmarkers, 115–116
Economic interdependence, 22–23
Educational groups, 194–195
Effect–cause pattern of organization, 246
Effective listening, 71–76
Effects of communication, 10–11
Electronic communication. *See* Computer communication
Emblems, 108–109, 109*t*
Emoticons, 111*t*, 138
Emotions
    appeals to, 321
    emoticons, 111*t*, 138
    listening to, 71
    nonverbal messages and, 109
    paralinguistic cues to, 120–121
Empathy
    in conversation, 144–145
    in listening, 72
    perception and, 54
Empowerment, 214. *See also* Power
Encoding–decoding, 6–7, 6*f*
Encourager, in small groups, 206
Eros love, 171
Ethics, 10–11, 56
    of appeals to emotion, 321
    approaches to, 11
    of censored relationships, 179
    choice and, 56
    communication competence and, 11, 12*f*, 13
    of criticism, 276
    fighting and, 157
    of listening, 70
    of lying, 90
    of means and ends, 217

    objective view of, 11
    of outing, 35
    in persuasive speech, 321
    of plagiarism, 237
    in public speaking, 287
    of secret sharing, 192
    of silence, 122
    subjective view of, 11
Ethnic identity, 24–26
Ethnocentrism, 24–26
Evaluation
    listening and, 66*f*, 69–70
    in perception, 48
    in problem-solving, 197*f*, 198
    of public speaking, 273–280
    self-concept and, 31–32
    static, 101
Evaluator–critic, in small groups, 206
Examples in informative speech, 292–293
Excuses, 147
Exemplification, 52
Expectancy hearing, 72
Expert power, 66
Exposure. *See* Selective exposure
Expressiveness, 146–147
Extemporaneous speeches, 267–268
Extensional orientation, 97–98
Eye communication, 112–113
    in public speaking, 271–272

Face-detracting strategy, 156–157
Face-enhancing strategy, 156–157
Face-saving, 86
Facial communication, 109, 110–113
    culture and, 126–127
    feedback hypothesis of, 112
    management of, 111–112
    in public speaking, 272
Facial feedback hypothesis, 112
Fact *vs.* inference, 98–99
Feedback, 7, 8
    culture and, 77–78
    facial feedback hypothesis, 112
    as stage of conversation, 135*f*, 139–140
Feedforward, 7–8
    as stage of conversation, 135*f*, 136–137
Fighting ethically, 157
Figures of speech, 255, 256*t*
Five "W" questions pattern of organization, 250
Flaming, 151
Flexibility, 142–143
Flip charts, 297–298
Flowcharts, 297, 297*f*
Focus groups, 195–196
Follower, in small groups, 206
Foot-in-the-door technique, 312
Force, in conflict, 154–155
Formal time, 128–129
Forum, 190, 190*f*
Friendship. *See* Interpersonal relationships
Functional approach to leadership, 210
Fundamental attribution error, 57–58

"Galileo and the Ghosts" technique, 48
Gaze, 112
Gender, 21. *See also* Homosexuality
    computer communication and, 181
    directness and, 84
    eye communication and, 113
    interpersonal relationships and, 177–180, 181, 183
    listening and, 78–79
    politeness and, 88
    purposes of communication and, 18
    romanticism and, 179–180

Opening stage of conversation, 135*f,* 136, 141
Openness
    in conversation, 144
    intercultural, 30
Opinion seeker, in small groups, 205
Organization
    charts for, 296, 296*f*
    of perception, 47, 49–50
    of speeches, 244–250
Other-orientation, 147
Outing, 35
Outlines for speeches, 262–267
Overattribution, 56–57
Overload, information, 8–9

Pacing cues, 138
Panel, 189–190, 190*f*
Paralanguage, 120–121
Paraphrasing, 75
Participating style of leadership, 211*f,* 212
Pauses, in public speaking, 270–271
Peaceful relations, 86
People conflict in small groups, 215
Perception, 46–63
    analysis of, 58–59
    attribution and, 55–58
    checking of, 59, 60
    contrast rule of organization and, 47
    culture and, 50, 59–60, 61
    empathy and, 54
    evaluation of, 48
    fundamental attribution error and, 57–58
    implicit personality theory and, 51–52
    increasing accuracy of, 58–61
    interpersonal, defined, 46
    interpretation of, 48
    listening to others', 48
    memory in, 48–49, 50
    mind reading and, 59
    organization of, 47, 49–50
    overattribution and, 56–57
    primacy–recency and, 53–54
    processes of, 50–58
    proximity rule of organization and, 47
    recall of, 49
    reducing uncertainty of, 59–61
    schemata organization and, 47, 49–50
    script organization and, 47, 49–50
    self-fulfilling prophecy and, 53
    self-serving bias and, 56
    similarity rule of organization and, 47
    stages of, 46–50
    stereotyping and, 54–55
    stimulation of, 46–47
Perceptual contact, 166
Personal distance, 114, 114*t*
Personal rejection, 157
Personality, implicit, 51–52
Personification, 256*t*
Perspective, listening, 78
Persuasive speeches, 310–331
    for action, 314–315
    analogy in, 317–318
    audience participation in, 311
    cause and effect reasoning in, 318
    change and, 311–314
    character and, 325–326
    charisma and, 326
    competence and, 325
    constructing proofs for, 315
    credibility appeals in, 322–326
    door-in-the-face technique in, 312
    ethics in, 321
    foot-in-the-door technique in, 312
    guidelines for, 310–312

    identification in, 311
    listening critically to, 317
    logical appeals in, 316–319
    motivational appeals in, 319–322, 320*f*
    preparing, 323
    selective exposure and, 310–311
    signs in, 319
    from specific to general in, 316
    for strengthening or changing attitudes and beliefs, 311–314
    types of, 313–315
Phatic communication, 136
Photos in informative speech, 297
Physical context of communication, 6
Physical noise, 11*t*
Physiological needs, 319–320, 320*f*
Physiological noise, 11*t*
Pictures in informative speech, 297
Pie charts, 297, 298*f*
Piercings, 117
PIP'N technique, 288
Plagiarizing, 237
Polarization, 100–101
Politeness
    culture and, 88
    gender and, 88
    netiquette, 87, 150–151
    verbal messages and, 87–88, 88*f*
Polychronism, 129, 129*t*
Positiveness
    in conversation, 145
    in relationships, 173
Posture, in public speaking, 272
Power, 214
    coercive, 166
    communication competence and, 12*f,* 13
    compliance gaining and, 189
    conversational, 156
    credibility and, 324
    cultural differences in, 219–220
    decreasing, 13
    expert, 66
    in group compliance, 189
    increasing, 13
    information, 291
    of language, 86
    legitimate, 291
    negative, 232
    nonverbal signals of, 119
    public speaking, 271
    referent, 66
    reward, 166
    self-presentation and, 52
    through affirmation, 31
Power distance, 219–220
Pragma love, 171
Preparation outline for speeches, 262–264
Presentation software
    Corel presentstions, 299
    Lotus Freelance, 299
    PowerPoint, 298–304
Primacy effect, 53–54
Primary territories, 115
Principles of communication, 14–21, 15*f,* 19*f*–22
Pro and con pattern of organization, 250
Problem–solution pattern of organization, 245–246
Problem-solving
    in business, 200–201
    Delphi method for, 200–201
    nominal group technique for, 200
    problem definition in, 197–198, 197*f*
    quality circles for, 201
    in small groups, 196–201, 197*f*
    solution evaluation in, 197*f,* 198
    solution selection in, 197*f,* 198–199
    steps of, 197–199, 197*f*
Procedural conflict in small groups, 215

Procedural technician, in small groups, 206
Pronunciation, 269–271
Proofs for persuasive speech, 315
Prophecy, self-fulfilling, 53
Proxemics, 113–114, 114*t*
Proximity rule of organization, 47
Psychological data on interpersonal relationships, 163–164
Psychological noise, 11*t*
Psychological time, 123–125
Public communication, 3
Public distance, 114, 114*t*
Public speaking, 3, 223–281. *See also* Informative speeches; Persuasive speeches; Speeches
    criticism of, 273–280
    culture and, 229*t*, 231, 232
    notes in, 272–273
    preparation for, 226–227, 227*f*
Public territories, 115
Punctuation of communication, 18
Purpose
    of communication, 18, 19*f*
    of speeches, 230–232
Purr words, 82–83
Pygmalion effect, 53

Quality circles, for problem-solving, 201
Quality of verbal messages, 85
Quantity of verbal messages, 85–86
Questions, rhetorical, 256*t*, 257

Racism, 93, 95
Rate of speech, 121
Reasoning, 316–319
Recall of perception, 49
Receiver. *See* Source–receivers
Receiving stage of listening, 66*f*, 67
Recency effect, 53–54
Recognition seeker, in small groups, 206
Referent power, 66
Regulators, 109, 109*t*
Rehearsal of speeches, 267–268
Rejection
    personal, 157
    vs. disconfirmation, 89, 90, 91
Relation of verbal messages, 85
Relational communication, 179
Relational messages, 74
Relationship dialectics theory, 176–177
Relationship dimension of communication, 16–17
Relationship messages, 17
Relationships. *See* Interpersonal relationships
Religion
    identifiers of, 97
    speeches and, 233–234
Remembering stage of listening, 66*f*, 68–69
Repair stage of interpersonal relationships, 167*f*, 173–174, 192
Replicas in informative speech, 296
Research, for public speaking, 236–241
Responding stage of listening, 66*f*, 70
Reversal hypothesis, 172
Reverse halo effect, 52
Reward power, 166
Rewards of self-disclosure, 38–40
Rhetorical questions, 256*t*, 257
Risk, 168–169
Romanticism, 179–180
Roundtable, 189

Safety needs, 320–321, 320*f*
Saving face, 86
Schemata organization, 47, 49–50
Script organization, 47, 49–50
Secondary territories, 115
Secrets, 192

Security anxiety, 168
Selective exposure, 46
    persuasive speeches and, 310–311
Self
    blind, 32–33, 32*f*
    dialogue with, 34
    hidden, 32*f*, 33
    looking-glass, 29
    open, 32, 32*f*, 34
    unknown, 32*f*, 33
Self-actualization needs, 320*f*, 322
Self-adaptors, 109
Self-awareness, 32–34, 32*f*
    growth in, 33–34
    Johari window model of, 32–33, 32*f*
Self-concept, 29–32, 30*f*
Self-confessor, in small groups, 207
Self-confidence, self-disclosure and, 35
Self-denigration, 86
Self-destructive statements, 34
Self-disclosure, 34–43
    dangers of, 40
    guidelines for, 40–43
    listening and, 42
    motivations for, 40–41
    in relationships, 39, 173
    rewards of, 38–40
    topics and, 43
Self-esteem needs, 320*f*, 321–322
Self-fulfilling prophecy, 53
Self in communication, 29–44, 30*f*, 32*f*
Self-presentation, 52
Self-promotion, 52
Self-serving bias, 56
Selling style of leadership, 211*f*, 212
Semantic noise, 11*t*
Sentence construction, 258
Sex. *See* Gender
Sex-role stereotyping, 92
Sexism, 91–92, 95
Sexist language, 91–92
Sharpening, in listening, 73
Signal-to-noise ratio, 10
Significant others, 29, 30*f*
Signs, reasoning from, 319
Silence, 122–123
    culture and, 128
    ethics of, 122
Similarity rule of organization, 47
Simile, 256*t*
Situational approach to leadership, 210–211, 211*f*
Skeletal outline for speeches, 264–265
Slide show speech, 298–304
Slides in informative speech, 298, 299*f*, 300*f*, 302*f*, 303*f*
Small groups, 3, 187–203, 205–221
    apprehension in, 192–193
    brainstorming in, 193–194
    chat groups for, 190–191
    complaints in, 216
    compliance in, 189
    conflict in, 208, 215–217
    culture and, 191–192, 218–220
    defined, 187
    dysfunctional roles in, 207
    formats for, 189–190, 189*f*, 190*f*
    forum format for, 190, 190*f*
    group orientation in, 206–207
    groupthink in, 208–209
    idea-killers and, 196
    individual roles in, 205–206, 207
    information-sharing, 194–196
    leaders of, 209–218
    listening in, 195
    mailing lists for, 190–191
    maintenance roles in, 206
    member participation in, 206–208

member roles in, 205–206
members in, 205–209
mentoring in, 217–218
norms of, 191–192
open-mindedness in, 208
organizing rules of, 187
panel format for, 189–190, 190*f*
people conflict in, 215
power distances and, 219–220
problem-solving, 196–201, 197*f*
procedural conflict in, 215
relationship purposes of, 187–188
roundtable format for, 189, 190*f*
self-disclosure and, 37
stages of, 188–189, 189*f*
symposium format for, 190, 190*f*
task purposes of, 187–188
task roles in, 205–206
understanding in, 208
Small talk, 136
Smell communication, 118
Snarl words, 82–83
Social bonding, 168
Social clock, 130
Social comparison, 29, 30*f*
Social distance, 114, 114*t*
Social penetration theory, 169–170, 170*f*
Social–psychological context of communication, 6
Source–receivers, 6–7, 6*f*
Space decoration, 117–118
Spamming, 150–151
Spatial communication, 113–116, 114*t*
Spatial pattern of organization, 245
Speaking. *See* Public speaking; Source–receivers; Speech; Speeches
Specific to general reasoning, 316
Specificity, 255
Speech
   culture and, 77
   disorders of, 136*t*
   rate of, 121
Speeches, 3, 223–281. *See also* Public speaking
   adapting during, 235
   advantages–disadvantages pattern of organization, 250
   age and, 232–233
   apprehension about, 225–228
   appropriate language in, 256–257
   articulation in, 269–271
   audience analysis and, 232–235
   benefits of, 224–225
   body action in, 271–272
   breathing and, 226
   cause–effect pattern of organization in, 246
   claim and proof pattern of organization in, 250
   clarity in, 255
   common faults in, 260–261
   comparison and contrast pattern of organization in, 248
   conclusion in, 258–259, 261
   culture and, 229*t*, 231, 232, 242
   defined, 223–224
   delivery methods for, 267–268
   delivery of, 268–273
   delivery outline for, 265–267
   effect–cause pattern of organization in, 246
   effectiveness of, 283–284
   ethics of, 287
   evaluation of, 273–280
   experience in, 226
   extemporaneous, 267–268
   eye contact in, 271–272
   facial expression in, 272
   figures of speech in, 255, 256*t*
   five "W" questions pattern of organization in, 250
   formal language in, 256
   gender and, 233
   gesture in, 272
   guide phrases in, 255

idioms in, 255
imagery in, 255–256
immediacy in, 257
impromptu, 267
informal language in, 256
informative (*See* Informative speeches)
integrating research into, 239–241
internal summary in, 262
introduction in, 259–260, 261
listeners and, 228
main ideas for, 242–244
manuscript, 267
motivated sequence pattern of organization in, 246–248
movement in, 271–272
multiple definition pattern of organization in, 250
notes in, 272–273
offensive language in, 257
organization of, 244–250
outlines for, 262–267
pauses in, 270–271
personal pronouns in, 257
personal style in, 257
persuasive (*See* Persuasive speeches)
posture in, 272
power in, 271
practice for, 226
preparation for, 226–227, 227*f*
preparation outline for, 262–264
pro and con pattern of organization in, 250
problem–solution pattern of organization in, 245–246
pronunciation in, 269–271
questions in, 256*t*, 257
rehearsal of, 267–268
religion and, 233–234
sentence construction in, 258
skeletal outline for, 264–265
skills of, 224–225
spatial pattern of organization in, 245
specificity in, 255
speech rate in, 269
structure–function pattern of organization in, 248
summary in, 258–259, 261, 262
supporting propositions of, 244
thesis formulation for, 241–242
time pattern of organization in, 245
topic and purpose of, 228–232, 229*t*, 230*f*
topic research of, 236–241
topical pattern of organization in, 245
transitions in, 261–262
two-minute, 250, 279, 325
verbs in, 255
vividness in, 255–256, 256*t*
voice in, 268–271
word choice for, 254–258, 256*t*
Stage-talk messages, 176
Stages of perception, 46–50
Static evaluation, 101
Statistics, in informative speech, 294–295
Stereotyping, 54–55, 100
   sex-role, 92
Stimulation of perception, 46–47
Storge love, 171
Structure–function pattern of organization, 248
Study of communication, approach to, 3–4
Subjective view of ethics, 11
Summary, in public speaking, 258–259, 261, 262
Supplication, 52
Surface listening, 73–74
Surveys, for public speaking topic selection, 229
Symposium, 190, 190*f*

Taboos, 229*t*
Task groups, 187–188
Task roles, in small groups, 205–206
Tattoos, 117